W9-BJN-077

Inventory of Longitudinal Studies in the Social Sciences

Inventory of Longitudinal Studies in the Social Sciences

Copeland H. Young
Kristen L. Savola
Erin Phelps

SAGE PUBLICATIONS
The International Professional Publishers
Newbury Park   London   New Delhi

Based on original research sponsored by the Committee on Life Course Perspectives on Human Development of the Social Science Research Council.

For information address:

SAGE Publications, Inc.
2455 Teller Road
Newbury Park, California 91320

SAGE Publications Ltd.
6 Bonhill Street
London EC2A 4PU
United Kingdom

SAGE Publications India Pvt. Ltd.
M-32 Market
Greater Kailash I
New Delhi 110 048 India

Printed in the United States of America

Library of Congress Cataloging-in-Publication Data

Young, Copeland H.
  Inventory of longitudinal studies in the social sciences /
  Copeland H. Young, Kristen L. Savola, Erin Phelps.
      p.   cm.
  Includes bibliographical references and index.
  ISBN 0-8039-4315-6
  1. Social sciences—Research—Longitudinal studies. I. Savola,
Kristen L. II. Phelps, Erin. III. Title.
H62.Y667   1991
300—dc20   91-11195
                                                                CIP

FIRST PRINTING, 1991

Sage Production Editor: Michelle R. Starika

Contents

Acknowledgments

Many individuals contributed in crucial ways to the publication of this volume, and we are very grateful to each of them. This work was funded as part of a grant from the National Institute of Mental Health to Radcliffe College to develop and publicize an archive of longitudinal mental health data. The work of this grant, including the creation of the inventory, was guided by a distinguished advisory committee, whose members are: Paul Baltes, J. Brooks-Gunn, Glen Elder, Anne Petersen, Lee Robins, Jon Rolf, Michael Rutter, and George Vaillant. All of our work has been greatly enriched by their suggestions and insights.

The Social Science Research Council published the original edition of this inventory in two volumes. The first, the *Inventory of Longitudinal Studies of Middle and Old Age*, by Susan Migdal, Ronald P. Abeles, and Lonnie R. Sherrod, appeared in 1981. This was followed in 1984 by the publication of a companion volume, *Inventory of Longitudinal Research on Childhood and Adolescence*, compiled by Frederick Verdonik and Lonnie R. Sherrod. The Social Science Research Council gave us all of the materials that had been collected through 1985, and this served as the foundation for the current edition.

The researchers whose work is documented in this volume have spent collectively a great amount of time helping to assure the accuracy of the descriptions of their studies. Often this meant digging through boxes, looking for documentation of sample sizes and the like. We appreciate these efforts very much—there is no way we could have compiled the information without their help.

Anne Colby, the director of the Murray Center, advised in all aspects of this work, prodding and questioning every step of the way. She both obtained funding for and supervised the project, pushing us to meet contractual and publication deadlines. Without her sustained efforts, this inventory would not now exist.

Finally, there are staff whose efforts have been invaluable. In earlier stages of this work, Heather Knutson provided valuable assistance in developing a computerized database of all of the studies in the original SSRC volumes. Karl Staven assisted in the initial coding of many of the studies listed in the childhood and adolescence volume. Martha Morelock was very helpful with library research for locating information about suggested studies for inclusion. In the later stages of this work, Julie Shapiro offered much assistance in recoding sample and methodology characteristics for each study in the database. Sonya Walters and Leslie Nitabach provided valuable assistance through generating important information about sample sizes in several studies by running computer frequencies on data housed at the Murray Research Center. Special mention and gratitude must go to Fran Kaplan, who provided critical assistance in her extensive library research to help find important information for most of the studies included here, and to Janet Gibeau, whose endless perseverance in repeatedly entering and printing numerous drafts of every entry has been central to the successful completion of this volume.

Finally, Copeland Young would like to express deep appreciation to Roxanne Wilson for her enduring love and support, and also to express his love and indebtedness to his father and mother, Copeland and Arnet, who taught the lesson of perseverance by their own example. And Erin Phelps wants to acknowledge her gratitude to three professors—Albert Goss, Mary Goss, and Aimée Dorr—who through their personal and professional examples have had a permanent impact on her own personal and professional life and goals.

Copeland H. Young
Kristen L. Savola
Erin Phelps

Introduction

In 1981 the Committee on Life-Course Perspectives on Human Development of the Social Science Research Council published the *Inventory of Longitudinal Studies of Middle and Old Age* (Migdal, Abeles, & Sherrod). This was followed in 1984 by the publication of a companion volume, *Inventory of Longitudinal Research on Childhood and Adolescence* (Verdonik & Sherrod). Together they represented a comprehensive inventory of longitudinal studies, recognized as a tremendously valuable reference work for anyone interested in longitudinal research. Their purpose was to promote awareness of opportunities for:

a. secondary analyses of existing data;
b. additional follow-up assessments of currently accessible samples;
c. collaborative research;
d. comparisons of findings from different samples on which comparable measures have been taken;
e. the design of additional longitudinal studies. (Verdonik & Sherrod, 1984, p. 1)

In 1986 the Henry A. Murray Research Center of Radcliffe College was asked by the Social Science Research Council to continue the development of the inventories, since the committee had finished its work and was disbanding. The current volume is a revision, with additions and several modifications. Funding for this effort was provided by a grant from the National Institute of Mental Health to Radcliffe College.

IMPORTANCE OF LONGITUDINAL DATA AND SECONDARY ANALYSIS

Sharing of research data is an important part of the scientific method because it reinforces open scientific inquiry; allows for verification, refutation, and refinement of original findings; and ensures more efficient use of financial and other research resources. Although open access to all kinds of social and behavioral science data is important, sharing data from *longitudinal* studies is especially valuable. Because carrying out long-term longitudinal research requires such a major investment of time and money, only a few such studies are conducted. And yet, longitudinal data are necessary for addressing many research questions. The special value of longitudinal data is generally recognized as deriving from their unique

1

ability to preserve information about the nature of individual development. Sequences of events and patterns of change that occur within the individual, the family, or some other unit can be studied most effectively through the use of longitudinal data. Alternative methods, such as retrospective or cross-sectional studies, are subject to serious error that can be reduced by using longitudinal designs. Clearly, research questions about lifelong and intergenerational causal relationships are best answered by following respondents in real time, rather than retrospectively. (See Colby & Phelps, 1990.)

Long-term longitudinal data of substantial duration are difficult for researchers to collect during their own lifetimes, however. Few individual investigators are able to make the kind of time investment that is required and still meet their career goals. Consequently, there are only a relatively small number of investigators who are collecting longitudinal data at any given time. By making the data available and accessible to others, the process of data sharing allows individuals to conduct longitudinal studies in a few years that would otherwise require a prohibitive time commitment.

There are several reasons why a researcher may want to analyze someone else's data. One is a desire to check on the accuracy of another's results, either by directly replicating the analyses or by using somewhat different analytic techniques that may, for example, statistically control for a confounding variable not accounted for in the original analyses. Sharing data for this kind of reanalysis is required by scientific conventions that promote objectivity in research.

Another reason for using existing data is to address original research questions without collecting new data. Often this involves analyzing data that were collected but never analyzed by the original investigators. The economics of doing research are improved in this case, both for the original investigator, because information is not wasted, and for the secondary analyst, because the costs of data collection are decreased or avoided.

Finally, and perhaps most important, a researcher may have questions that are very difficult to answer adequately without using existing data. These questions include the effects of social change or historical events on the lives of the people who experience them, the relationships between very early development and outcomes in middle and late adulthood, and the early causal factors that explain the development of relatively rare outcomes, such as alcoholism or extraordinary achievement in adulthood.

This inventory provides a resource for researchers who wish to use existing data for any of these reasons. The studies are described in detail to facilitate a search for relevant data. At the same time, the inventory should serve as an incentive to encourage more and better use of existing data.

THE HENRY A. MURRAY RESEARCH CENTER

The Henry A. Murray Research Center of Radcliffe College was established in 1976 as a national repository for data from the fields of psychology, psychiatry, sociology, anthropology, economics, political science, and education. Unlike most other data banks, the Murray Center archives original subject records as well as coded, machine-readable data. These original records often include transcripts of in-depth interviews, behavioral observations, responses to projective tests, or other information that can be used profitably for secondary analysis. This makes possible a restructuring of the subject records and mitigates the degree to which one is locked in to the theoretical assumptions under which the data were collected.

In spite of the clear advantages of making raw data available, most data banks offer only coded computer data. Some major longitudinal studies, for example the *New York Longitudinal Study* (Thomas & Chess, 1977), are archived in a manner that allows access to the records by outside investigators, but in general each of these studies is housed separately. To our knowledge, the Murray Research Center is the only repository that is designed to offer a wide range of longitudinal data sets, many of which include raw data.

Data sets may be reanalyzed to explore questions other than those addressed by the original investigators. Reanalysis may involve recoding of the raw data. Data from studies that employ comparable designs and instruments may be combined to provide a larger, more varied sample than would be possible otherwise. In addition to reanalysis, these studies can be used as baseline data for replication studies to assess the effects of social change. In many cases, samples can be recontacted for further longitudinal follow-up. The availability of samples that can be followed up encourages the collection of longitudinal data that would otherwise be too costly or difficult to obtain. Furthermore, the data collected early in this century can be used to address questions of interest to social historians. Reviews of existing data can facilitate exploratory research by allowing a researcher to refine research questions, to assess the best means for addressing those questions, and to develop new research instruments or coding schemes. In addition to using the Murray Center's data sets in the ways mentioned above, faculty and students use these data in courses to illustrate how the data are collected and analyzed. A set of machine-readable files designed specifically for teaching statistics and methods courses is also available.

The resources of the Murray Center are open to students, faculty from any college or university, and other researchers worldwide. Staff members conduct several introductory workshops each semester and are available weekdays to provide individual consultation on using the Center's resources. Users are not charged for access to the data, only for special services they require (such as duplicating) and for the cost of computer time. Our *Guide to the Data Resources of the Henry A. Murray Research Center* provides information about not only the more than 190 data sets that are completely processed but also those that are still in the process of acquisition. In addition, an *Index to the Guide* is available and includes a detailed listing of the methods of data collection, content areas, and an index of the data sets according to these characteristics.

In addition to archiving data, the Murray Research Center sponsors workshops designed to draw attention to its data resources and provide training in the skills needed to carry out effective secondary analyses. Recent workshop topics have included methods for life course research focused on the data analysis techniques of event history analysis and causal modeling; methods for coding open-ended archival material for several important personality constructs; and secondary analysis of major longitudinal data sets, using case studies for the study of individual lives.

To facilitate the use of the data, the center has a program of research grants. The Radcliffe Research Support Program offers small grants to post-doctoral researchers who wish to use data housed at the center. In addition, there are two dissertation support programs in the areas of sex differences or female development, and personality or "the study of lives."

CHANGES IN THIS EDITION

Several changes have been made to the original inventories for this second edition. The *Inventory of Longitudinal Studies of Middle and Old Age* and the *Inventory of Longitudinal Research on Childhood and Adolescence* were merged into a single volume, with consistent descriptions and formats. European studies were deleted, leaving studies done on U.S. and Canadian samples. With funding from the European Science Foundation, Wolfgang Schneider (Max Planck Institute, Munich) and Wolfgang Edelstein (Max Planck Institute, Berlin) are compiling a more comprehensive European inventory, which will serve as a companion volume.

Additional U.S. studies have been included. Many of these had been identified by the authors of the original inventories, but were not included because they had received insufficient information by their publication deadline. Others were found through literature searches and from suggestions by other researchers, including studies that did not fit into the original inventories because they did not include either "middle and old age" or "childhood and adolescence" samples. Additionally, information was inserted for each study about waves completed since 1981/1984, sample characteristics of race/ethnicity and social class, and where data can be obtained for further analyses. To update the information and assure accuracy, investigators for all studies were contacted for this information and asked for final approval of the entry describing their study. Every effort was made to obtain a final confirmation for each and every study included in this edition.

Finally, all of the information was entered as a computerized database to facilitate searching for particular kinds of data sets. Each study is indexed by a series of categories describing the sample and methodology used (see Appendix). Keyword searching permits the location of studies that use particular constructs and/or measures. Thus, users can request searches by intersecting categories. In addition, the information in each entry was reorganized somewhat.

CRITERIA FOR INCLUSION

The criteria for determining which studies to include are essentially the same as those defined in the original *Inventory of Longitudinal Research in Childhood and Adolescence* (Verdonik & Sherrod, 1984, p. 1). These were defined to ensure that the studies were truly longitudinal and of sufficiently high quality that they could be used profitably by others. Studies included in the current edition meet the following criteria:

1. They are prospectively longitudinal in the sense that the investigators collected information during at least two time points, and preferably three, across a span of at least one year.
2. They have an attrition rate for the original sample that is low enough to maintain the longitudinal quality of the study.
3. They have extensive information on the sample, involving multiple measures, preferably across more than one domain of behavior.
4. They are currently active or, if inactive, either have plans for reactivation or have data available (or that could be made available) for secondary analyses by other investigators.

In addition, a decision was made *not* to add any studies of language acquisition in this edition, because there are hundreds of valuable studies and we did not feel expert enough nor have sufficient time to track them down and evaluate them. Fortunately, there is a forthcoming book describing the Child Language Data Exchange System that includes a catalog describing the studies included in the CHILDES data base (MacWhinney, in press).

INFORMATION ON DATABASE SEARCHES AND ADDING STUDIES

Future editions of this inventory may be issued as new longitudinal studies are conducted and existing studies are extended. If you are aware of research that fits the criteria enumerated above but is not included in the current volume, please get in touch with us. Please include as much information about the study as possible. Documents such as research proposals, publications, and measures are helpful in evaluating potential studies for inclusion.

To expedite use of the information contained in this inventory, computerized searches of studies that have specific characteristics can be done by members of the Murray Research Center staff. Studies can be identified according to sample and methodology characteristics described in the Appendix, as well as keyword searches of measures and constructs of interest. The primary benefit of a computerized search is that intersections of categories and keywords can be specified and generated very easily. Please call the Murray Center if you are interested in conducting such a search.

NOTE

1. An earlier inventory of longitudinal studies was published in 1959 by Stone and Onqué. Its purpose was to "provide a perspective of the overall contribution made by longitudinal research to psychological knowledge" (p. xiii) and it was focused on emotional and social behavior in infants and children. It serves as a historical counterpart to our current efforts.

REFERENCES

Colby, A., & Phelps, E. (1990). Archiving longitudinal data. In D. Magnussen & L. R. Bergman (Eds.), *Data quality in longitudinal research*. New York: Cambridge University Press.

MacWhinney, B. (In press). *CHILDES project: Computational tools for analyzing talk*. Hillsdale, NJ: Lawrence Erlbaum.

Migdal, S., Abeles, R. P., & Sherrod, L. R. (1981). *An inventory of longitudinal studies of middle and old age*. New York: Social Science Research Council.

Stone, A. A., & Onqué, G. C. (1959). *Longitudinal studies of child personality* Cambridge, MA: Harvard University Press.

Verdonik, F., & Sherrod, L. R. (1984). *An inventory of longitudinal research on childhood and adolescence*. New York: Social Science Research Council.

Sample and Methodology Characteristics for Studies for Database Searching

I. Data Collection

    A. Research Design (Laboratory Experiment, Field Experiment, Intervention Study, Field Study, Surveys, Case Studies, Institutional Records, Cross-sequential, Replication, Follow Back, Hereditary)

    B. Measurement (Opened-ended Questionnaire, Closed-ended Questionnaire, Open-ended Interview, Closed-ended Interview, Projective Measures, Other Personality Measures, Attitude Measures, Cognitive Measures, Achievement/Aptitude Measures, Behavioral Observations, Ratings, Physical Examination, Medical/Psychophysiological Tests, Institutional Records, Diaries/Logs/Life Events Reports, Psychiatric Evaluation, Clinical Case Notes/Treatment Sessions)

    C. Time of Data Collections (Eighteenth Century, Nineteenth Century, 1900-1939, 1940s, 1950s, 1960s, 1970s, 1980s, 1990s)

    D. Length of Data Collection (Two Years or Less, 3-5 Years, 6-10 Years, 11-20 Years, 21-50 Years, 51+ Years)

II. Sample

    A. Sample Size (Initial number of Ss in the sample)

    B. Sample Gender (Female, Male)

    C. Age of Sample

    D. Socioeconomic Status

    E. Number of Generations

    F. Race/Ethnicity (African-American, White, Hispanic, Asian-American, American Indian/Eskimo, Pacific Islander, Multiracial, Other, Mixed [if a nationally representative sample])

Vermont Infant Studies Project, 1980

Achenbach, Thomas M.; and Howell, Catherine T.

Contact Person: Thomas M. Achenbach
Address: Department of Psychiatry
               University of Vermont
               One South Prospect Street
               Burlington, VT 05401
Telephone No.: (802) 656-4563

SUBSTANTIVE TOPICS COVERED:

This study tested the outcome of an experimental intervention for low birthweight infants in terms of infant social, emotional, and behavioral problems; infant cognitive development; and maternal attitudes, self-confidence, anxiety, perception of infant, and satisfaction with mothering role.

CHARACTERISTICS OF THE ORIGINAL SAMPLE:

Year the study began: 1980
Subject selection process: The subjects selected were all organically intact low birthweight infants, born at the Medical Center Hospital of Vermont in 1980-1981, whose parents consented. Normal birthweight infants born concurrent with the low birthweight subjects were also included.
Total number of subjects at Time 1: N = 119
Ages at Time 1: Birth
Sex distribution: Approximately equal numbers of females and males throughout
Socioeconomic status: Approximately 50% working class, 50% middle/upper middle class
Race/ethnicity: 98% white, 2% biracial

Years of Completed Waves:

Years	N=	Age ranges
(Cohort 1: LBWex)[b]		
1980-1981[a]	38	Neonatal
1981-1982	*	1 yr.
1982-1983	27	2 yrs.
1983-1984	27	3 yrs.

Years of Completed Waves, Continued:

Years	N=	Age ranges
1984-1985	25	4 yrs.
1987-1988	24	7 yrs.
1989-1990	In progress	9 yrs.
(Cohort 2: LBWcon)[c]		
1980-1981[a]	40	Neonatal
1981-1982	*	1 yrs.
1982-1983	28	2 yrs.
1983-1984	28	3 yrs.
1984-1985	28	4 yrs.
1987-1988	32	7 yrs.
1989-1990	In progress	9 yrs.
(Cohort 3: NBW)[d]		
1980-1981	41	Neonatal
1981-1982	*	1 yr.
1982-1983	32	2 yrs.
1983-1984	32	3 yrs.
1984-1985	28	4 yrs.
1987-1988	37	7 yrs.
1989-1990	In progress	9 yrs.

Comments:
a. Ss were also followed at 4 mos. and 6 mos. in 1980-1981.
b. Cohort 1: Low Birthweight Experimental Group
c. Cohort 2: Low Birthweight Control Group
d. Cohort 3: Normal Birthweight Control Group

INFORMATION ON SAMPLE ATTRITION:

During the 10-year period of study, 26 of 119 Ss (21.8%) were not retrieved for further study. The core sample consists of approximately 93 Ss. Attrition is primarily due to subjects' refusal to participate, handicaps, and death.

CONSTRUCTS MEASURED: INSTRUMENTS USED

Maternal Response to Intervention

Quality of mothering, degree of receptivity to the program: Nurse ratings

Maternal Outcome

Mothers' attitudes: Semistructured interviews, home questionnaires
Maternal self-confidence: Seashore Self-Confidence Rating Paired Comparison
    Questionnaire
Maternal anxiety: Taylor Manifest Anxiety Scale
Maternal perceptions of infant temperament: Carey Infant Temperament Question-
    naire

Satisfaction with the mothering role: Semistructured home interview (The Satisfaction Scale)

Infant Outcome

Infant cognitive development: Bayley Scales of Infant Development, McCarthy Scales of Children's Abilities, Kaufman ABC
Behavioral/emotional problems: Child Behavior Checklist, Teacher's Report Form
Behavioral development: Minnesota Child Development Inventory
Parental views of child: Parent interview and self-reports
Vocabulary: Peabody Picture Vocabulary Test

REPRESENTATIVE REFERENCES:

Achenbach, T. M., Edelbrock. C., & Howell, C. T. (1987). Empirically based assessment of the behavioral/emotional problems of two- and three-year-old children. *Journal of Abnormal Child Psychology, 15,* 629-650.
Achenbach, T. M., Phares, V., Howell, C. T., Rauh, V. A., & Nurcombe, B. (in press). Seven-year outcome of the Vermont Intervention Program for low birthweight infants. *Child Development.*
Rauh, V. A., Achenbach, T. M., Nurcombe, B., Howell, C. T., & Teti, D. M. (1988). Minimizing adverse effects of low birthweight: Four-year results of an early interventional program. *Child Development, 59,* 544-553.

CURRENT STATUS OF THE STUDY:

a. Further waves of data collection are planned.
b. Most data are in machine-readable format.
c. Data are available for secondary analysis from the study contact person.

■ The National Survey of Children and Youth, 1986

Achenbach, Thomas M.; Conners, C. Keith; Howell, Catherine T.; McConaughy, Stephanie H.; and Quay, Herbert C.

Contact Person: Thomas M. Achenbach
Address: Department of Psychiatry
                University of Vermont
                One South Prospect Street
                Burlington, VT 05401
Telephone No.: (802) 656-4563

SUBSTANTIVE TOPICS COVERED:

This study assessed changes in behavioral and emotional problems of a national sample of children and youth.

CHARACTERISTICS OF THE ORIGINAL SAMPLE:

Year the study began: 1986
Subject selection process: Subjects were selected through a stratified random sampling procedure from 100 primary sampling sites. The sample was selected to be representative of the 48 contiguous United States.
Total number of subjects at Time 1: N = 2,765
Ages at Time 1: 4-16 yrs.
Sex distribution: Approximately equal numbers of females and males throughout
Socioeconomic status: Distribution is representative of United States.
Race/ethnicity: 76.2% white, 16.1% African-American, 4.3% Hispanic, 3.4% other

Years of Completed Waves:

Years	N=	Age ranges
1986	2,765	4-16 yrs.
1989	2,488[a]	7-19 yrs.

Comments:
a. This figure is approximate.

INFORMATION ON SAMPLE ATTRITION:

During the 3-year period of study, approximately 276 of 2,765 Ss (10%) were not retrieved for further study. Attrition was due to subjects' death, refusal to continue participation, or inability to locate subject. The core sample consists of approximately 2,488 Ss.

CONSTRUCTS MEASURED: INSTRUMENTS USED

Behavioral/emotional problems and competencies: ACQ Behavior Checklist, Child
  Behavior Checklist, Youth Self-Report, Teachers's Report Form
Family constellation, mental health contacts, stress: Parent interview

REPRESENTATIVE REFERENCES:

Achenbach, T. M., Conners, C. K., Quay, H. C., Verhulst, F. C., & Howell, C. T. (1989). Replica-
    tion of empirically derived syndromes as a basis for taxonomy of child/adolescent psycho-
    pathology. *Journal of Abnormal Child Psychology, 17,* 299-323.
Achenbach, T. M., Howell, C. T., Quay, H. C., & Conners, C. K. (in process). *Problems and com-
    petencies reported by parents for national normative and clinical sample of 4- to 16-year-
    olds.* Manuscript submitted.

CURRENT STATUS OF THE STUDY:

  a. Further waves of data collection are planned, beginning in 1992.
  b. Most data are in machine-readable format.
  c. Data are available for secondary analysis from the study contact person.

■ Baltimore Longitudinal Study of Attachment, 1963

Ainsworth, Mary

Contact Person: Mary Ainsworth
Address: Department of Psychology
                 University of Virginia
                 Gilmer Hall
                 Charlottesville, VA 22901
Telephone No.:   (804) 924-3374

SUBSTANTIVE TOPICS COVERED:

   This study examines infant-mother attachment during the first year of life, the
responsiveness of infant and mother to each other during interactions, and infants'
exploratory behavior in the home setting.

CHARACTERISTICS OF THE ORIGINAL SAMPLE:

Year the study began: 1963
Subject selection process: Ss were family-reared infants from families in Balti-
    more, Maryland. Families were contacted through pediatricians in private

practice, usually before the baby's birth. Six of the boys were firstborns and none of the girls were firstborns.

Total number of subjects at Time 1: N = 26

Ages at Time 1: Birth.

Sex distribution: Approximately equal numbers of females and males in Cohort 1; 73% males, 27% females in Cohort 2

Socioeconomic status: 100% middle/upper middle class

Race/ethnicity: 100% white

Years of Completed Waves:

Years[a]	N=	Age ranges
1963-1964	15	Birth (Cohort 1)
1966-1967	11	Birth (Cohort 2)

Comments:

a. Ss were studied over the course of a 54-week period on a continuous visiting schedule. The first 15 Ss were visited at home on a 3-week interval, 3 weeks to 54 weeks (4-hour visits). The second 11 Ss were visited at weeks 1, 2, 3, and 4 (2-hour visits) and at 6 weeks and every 3rd week until the 54th week (4-hour visits). Over the course of the study, visits averaged 16 hours for every 3 months for both groups of Ss. Because the two groups of subjects were combined for all analyses, the study cannot appropriately be described in terms of data waves.

INFORMATION ON SAMPLE ATTRITION:

During the 54-week period of study, all Ss were retrieved for further study (100.0%); however, three subjects were excluded from the laboratory strange situation, so all findings for the strange situation are based on 23 Ss. The core sample consists of 26 Ss.

CONSTRUCTS MEASURED: INSTRUMENTS USED

Derived from the detailed accounts of infant's behavior and relevant mother activities, three types of measures were devised:

1. maternal care behavior: 22 rating scales relevant to the first quarter and 4 relevant to the fourth quarter—sensitivity/insensitivity, acceptance/rejection, cooperation/interference, and accessibility/ignoring
2. infant and maternal behavior (generated from coding data): measures of infant crying and maternal responsiveness, behavior in face-to-face situations, behavior relevant to close bodily contact; responses to little everyday separations and reunions, infant compliance to maternal commands
3. classification of maternal feeding practices; and a classificatory system used by coders which assesses the balance between attachment behavior and exploratory behavior (naturalistic observations of the mother and child at home)

Material has not been fully analyzed yet, but has been utilized in some ratings (e.g., acceptance/rejection): Open-ended interview with mothers in the home

Intelligence (assessed every 9 weeks): Griffiths Scale of Mental Development (used for some Ss)

The shift from exploratory behavior to attachment behavior: Laboratory strange situation (eight episodes intended to increase mild stress and thus activate attachment behavior at increasingly higher intensity)

REPRESENTATIVE REFERENCES:

Ainsworth, M. D. S. (1979). Attachment as related to mother-infant interaction. In J. S. Rosenblatt, R. A. Hinde, C. Beer, & M. Busnel (Eds.), *Advances in the study of behavior* (Vol. 9). New York: Academic Press.

Ainsworth, M. D. S., Blehar, M. C., Waters, E., & Wall, S. (1978). *Patterns of attachment: A psychological study of the strange situation.* Hillsdale, NJ: Lawrence Erlbaum.

Bell, J. M., & Ainsworth, M. D. S. (1972). Infant crying and maternal responsiveness. *Child Development, 43,* 1171-1190.

Stayton, D. J., Ainsworth, M. D. S., & Main, M. (1973). The development of separation behavior in the first year of life: Protest, following, and greeting. *Developmental Psychology, 9,* 213-225.

CURRENT STATUS OF THE STUDY:

a. No further waves of data collection are planned.
b. Most data are not in machine-readable format.
c. Data are available for secondary analysis from the Henry A. Murray Research Center, Radcliffe College, 10 Garden Street, Cambridge, MA 02138.

■ Bennington Studies of Persistence and Change in Attitudes and Values, 1935

Alwin, Duane F.; Cohen, Ronald L.; and Newcomb, Theodore (deceased)

Contact Person: Duane F. Alwin
Address: 3048 Institute of Social Research
                  Ann Arbor, MI 48106-1248
Telephone No.:   (313) 764-6595

SUBSTANTIVE TOPICS COVERED:

The studies examine the formation and change of attitudes of students toward a variety of public issues in a period of rapid change in the United States (1935-1939) and the persistence of these attitudes during adulthood (1961-1963).

CHARACTERISTICS OF THE ORIGINAL SAMPLE:

Year the study began: 1935

Subject selection process: Classes entering Bennington College from 1932 through 1938 in attendance during the Fall 1935, Fall 1936, Fall 1937, Spring 1938, and Spring 1939 terms were given an opportunity to participate in the study. Participation was voluntary. All participants were female since Bennington was then an all-women's college.

Total number of subjects at Time 1: N = 527

Ages at Time 1: 17-21 yrs.

Sex distribution: 100% female

Socioeconomic status: 100% middle/upper middle class

Race/ethnicity: 99% white, 1% other

Years of Completed Waves:

Years	N=	Age ranges
1935-1939	527	17-21 yrs.
1960-1961	345	37-49 yrs.
1984	335	61-72 yrs.

INFORMATION ON SAMPLE ATTRITION:

During the 49-year period of study, 192 of 527 Ss (36.4%) were not retrieved for further study. The core sample consists of 266 Ss.

CONSTRUCTS MEASURED: INSTRUMENTS USED

Political views: Political and Economic Progressive Scale, Semistructured interview schedule, Alumnae Interview Schedule

Temperament: Omnibus Personality Inventory

Sociopolitical orientations (specifically attitudes toward public relief, the role of labor unions, and the legitimacy of private and corporate wealth): Political and Economic Progressive Score (1930s, 1960s, and 1984)

Respondents recollection of item-by-item responses given in the 1930s (1960s and 1984) and given in the 1960s (1984)

Presidential candidate preferences: Reports of candidate preferences for all Presidential elections since 1940

Political attitudes: Responses to a number of Likert-type attitude questions, combined into an index measuring liberal-conservative stance

Liberalism-Conservatism: Liberal-Conservative Self-Rating Scale

Respondent's recollection of her political viewpoint when she entered Bennington College, when she left Bennington College, and in the years 1960, 1972, and 1984: Recalled Scores on Liberal-Conservative Self-Rating Scale

Interest in public affairs and self-assessed changes in political interest: Responses to questions tapping the extent to which the respondent follows government and public affairs, interest in Presidential campaigns, and changes in levels of interest

Political involvement: Responses to questions concerning involvement in political activities and organizations, and activities and/or organizations whose purpose was a change in the status of women

Media involvement: Responses to questions concerning attention to television and other media-based political news

Rankings of six "important areas of interests in life" (theoretical, economic, aesthetic, social, political, and religious): Allport-Vernon Scale of Values

Political orientation of spouse, friends, and children (1960 and 1984): Respondent reports of political orientations of spouse, friends, and children on a variety of different measures

Sex-role attitudes: Responses to questions concerning the relationship of family and work

REPRESENTATIVE REFERENCES:

Alwin, D., Cohen, R., & Newcomb, T. (in press). *Aging, personality, and social change: Attitude persistence and change over the life-span.* Madison: University of Wisconsin Press.

Newcomb, T. (1943). *Personality and social change.* New York: Dryden.

Newcomb, T. (1953, 1957). *Personality and social change: Attitude formation in a student community.* New York: Dryden.

Newcomb, T. (1967). *Persistence and change: Bennington College and its students after 25 years.* New York: John Wiley.

CURRENT STATUS OF THE STUDY:

a. Further waves of data collection are planned for 1992.

b. Most data are in machine-readable format.

c. Data are not available for secondary analysis.

■ Minnesota Child to Adult Study, 1925

Anderson, John E. (deceased); Harris, Dale B.; and Deno, Evelyn

Contact Person: Evelyn Deno
Address: 740 River Drive
                Apartment 7E
                St. Paul, MN 55116
Telephone No.:   (612) 698-1811

SUBSTANTIVE TOPICS COVERED:

The study examines experience and behavior in early childhood and predicts adult adjustment from data acquired in early childhood.

CHARACTERISTICS OF THE ORIGINAL SAMPLE:

Year the study began: 1925
Subject selection process: Subjects were nursery school children.
Total number of subjects at Time 1: N = 1,101
Ages at Time 1: 2-5 yrs.
Sex distribution: Equal numbers of females and males throughout
Socioeconomic status: 52% working class, 48% middle/upper middle class
Race/ethnicity: 100% white

Years of Completed Waves[a]

Years	N=	Age ranges
1925-1933	1,101	2-5 yrs.
1957-1958[b]	789	30-34 yrs.

Comments:
a. During the years 1950-1955, The Parent-Child Resemblance Study was undertaken to compare the childhood intelligence scores of Ss with those of their children at the same age in a subsample of 60 Ss.
b. In 1958 The Environmental Stress Study focused upon the relationship between personality and adjustment to environmental stressors in a subsample of 85 Ss.

INFORMATION ON SAMPLE ATTRITION:

During the 33-year period of study, 312 of 1,101 Ss (28.3%) were not retrieved for further study. The core sample consists of 789 Ss.

CONSTRUCTS MEASURED: INSTRUMENTS USED

Child

Parents' occupation, age, education: Application for Entrance to the Nursery School

Child's intellectual social, emotional, and motor behavior, interests, special abilities, and disabilities: Nursery School Adjustment Report

General conduct of child, interests and occupations of members of household: General Record of the Nursery School Child at Home

Eating and sleeping patterns of child: Eating and Sleeping Record

Physical health: Preliminary Physical and Medical Examination

Physical health and history: Periodical Examination and Medical History

Physical activity, laughter, sociality, leadership, motor behavior, play and interests: Cross-sectional Behavior and Social Observations

Child Intelligence: Minnesota Preschool Tests (Form A and B); Kuhlman-Binet Intelligence Test; 1916 Stanford-Binet Intelligence Test; 1937 Stanford-Binet Intelligence Test; Merrill-Palmer Preschool Scale; and Arthur Performance Test (Form I)

Extroversion-Introversion: Marston Extroversion-Introversion Scales

Adjustment: Adult Adjustment Scores

Adult

Education, occupation, health, family, standard of living, social status indices, organization memberships, community activities, food likes and dislikes, interests, hobbies; account of important factors to own adult adjustment: Biographical Record Questionnaire (BR)

Satisfaction felt and attitudes toward education, work, co-workers, friends, family, standard of living, and self: Personal Satisfaction Scale (PSS)

Feelings about living conditions; taxes, education; domestic and foreign political situations, mass media, and other people: General Satisfaction Scale (GSS)

Morale: Morale questionnaire (MSO) (Sletto)

Attitudes of parents toward practices in child training; and parents' goals for their children: Minnesota Scale of Parents Opinions (MPOS)

Encouraging verbalization; fostering dependency, seclusion of the mother, breaking the will, marital conflict, strictness; irritability, excluding outside influences; suppression of aggression; egalitarianism; approval of activity; avoidance of communication; suppression of sex; comradeship and sharing; and deification of parent: Parent Attitude Research Instrument (PARI) (Schaefer & Bell)

Subject's memories of his own rearing; parents' practices; encouraging verbalization; seclusion of mother; breaking the will, marital conflict; strictness, irritability; excluding outside influences; suppression of aggression; egalitarianism; avoidance of communication; inconsiderateness of husband, inconsiderateness of wife; suppression of sex; ascendancy of mother; comradeship and sharing; deification of child; martyrdom, rejection of homemaking role; acceleration of development; fear of harming baby; ignoring the baby; fostering resignation; coordination of household

Adult

Identification with mother; identification with father, emotionality; clarity of policy; ineffectual discipline; criticism; guilt; sociability in family; deification of parents; consistency; autonomy; and avoidance of tenderness: Retrospective Report on Family Experience (RRFE)

Poise, ascendancy, and self-assurance (dominance, capacity for status, security, sociality, social presence, self-acceptance, and sense of well-being); socialization, maturity, and responsibility (responsibility, socialization, self-control, tolerance, good impression, and communality); achievement potential and intellectual efficiency (achievement via conformance, achievement via independence, and intellectual efficiency); and intellectual and interests modes (psychological mindedness, flexibility, and femininity): The California Personality Inventory (CPI) (Gough)

Evaluation of personality and adjustment; subject's life history; personal characteristics; interests; and attitudes towards education, occupation, leisure, family background, current family, sociality (friends); sociality (community); and personality adjustment: Semistructured Interview (by psychologist)

Adult intelligence: Wechsler Adult Intelligence Scale (WAIS)

REPRESENTATIVE REFERENCES:

Anderson, John E. (1963). *Experience and behavior in early childhood and the adjustment of the same persons as adults.* Minneapolis: Institute of Child Development.

CURRENT STATUS OF THE STUDY:

a. No further waves of data collection are planned.
b. Data are not in machine-readable format.
c. Data are available for secondary analysis at the Institute of Child Development, University of Minnesota, 51 East River Road, Minneapolis, MN 55455.

■ Role Outlook Survey, 1964

Angrist, Shirley S.; and Almquist, Elizabeth

Contact person: Elizabeth Almquist
Address: Department of Sociology
                North Texas State University
                Denton, TX 76203
Telephone No.: (817) 565-2295

SUBSTANTIVE TOPICS COVERED:

The study investigates the influence of college on the development or inhibition of young women's career aspirations and the degree to which familial, educational, and personal experiences contribute to an enhanced and expanded outlook on career options. The study also followed the impact of college on the process of role development in undergraduate women.

CHARACTERISTICS OF THE ORIGINAL SAMPLE:

Year the study began: 1964
Subject selection process: The sample consisted of first-year students from a women's college of a larger coeducational university that emphasized professional and technological orientations. Eligible students attended college full-time.
Total number of subjects at Time 1: N = 87
Ages at Time 1: 18 yrs.
Sex distribution: 100% female
Socioeconomic status: Predominantly middle/upper middle class
Race/ethnicity: Predominantly white

Years of Completed Waves:

Years	N=	Age ranges
1964-1965	87	18 yrs.
1965-1966	87	19 yrs.
1966-1967	87	20 yrs.
1967-1968	87	21 yrs.
1975	64	28 yrs.

INFORMATION ON SAMPLE ATTRITION:

During the 11-year period of study, 23 of 87 Ss (26.4%) were not retrieved for further study. The core sample consists of 64 Ss. The principal investigators indicated that some subjects were not followed up in 1975 because current addresses could not be obtained.

CONSTRUCTS MEASURED: INSTRUMENTS USED

Impressions of college; courses, major field, social and campus life, difficulties/satisfactions, role aspirations, family background, and high school experiences: Freshman year questionnaire

Impressions of college: Sophomore year questionnaire, junior year questionnaire

Occupational choice and future plans: Senior year questionnaire

Educational and work status: Follow-up questionnaire

REPRESENTATIVE REFERENCES:

Almquist, E. (1974). Sex stereotypes in occupational choice: The case for college women. *Journal of Vocational Behavior, 5,* 13-21.

Almquist, E., & Angrist, S. (1969). *Career salience and atypicality of occupational choice among college women.* Pittsburgh: Carnegie-Mellon University.

Angrist, S. (1970). Personality maladjustment and career aspirations of college women. *Sociological Symposium, 5,* 1-8.

Angrist, S., & Almquist, E. (1975). *Careers and contingencies.* New York: Dunellen.

CURRENT STATUS OF THE STUDY:

   a. Further waves of data collection are planned.
   b. The data are in machine-readable format.
   c. The data are archived and available for secondary analysis at the Henry A. Murray Research Center, Radcliffe College, 10 Garden Street, Cambridge, MA 02138.

■ St. Louis Risk Research Project, 1967

Anthony, E. James; and Worland, Julien

Contact Person: E. James Anthony
Address: Chestnut Lodge Hospital
                  500 West Montgomery
                  Rockville, MD 20850
Telephone No.:   (301) 424-8300

SUBSTANTIVE TOPICS COVERED:

   The study examines the impact of psychosis in a parent on the subsequent emotional, social, and cognitive development of the child. More specifically, the study investigates the extent to which children from families with a psychotic parent developed clearly defined psychopathology. The study also focused on identifying any protective factors, within the family or the child, which buttressed against the onset of maladjustment or psychiatric impairment in the child.

CHARACTERISTICS OF THE ORIGINAL SAMPLE:

Year the study began: 1967

Subject selection process: Subjects were located through psychiatric hospitals. All subjects were married, had at least one child age 6-12 years, and had a continuous marital relationship (except for period of hospitalization). Subjects had to be diagnosed as psychotic as well, without contaminating factors like physical disability or organic brain syndrome being present.

Total number of subjects at Time 1: N = 368

Ages at Time 1: 7-11 yrs.

Sex distribution: Approximately equal numbers of females and males throughout

Socioeconomic status: 34% middle class, 33% working class, 33% poverty class

Race/ethnicity: 65% white, 35% African-American (Cohort 1); 65% white, 35% African-American (Cohort 2); 59% African-American, 41% white (Cohort 3); and 63.1% white, 36.9% African-American (Cohort 4)

Years of Completed Waves:

Years	N=	Age ranges
(Cohort 1: Schizophrenic Families)		
1967-1972	100	7-11 yrs.
1975-1979	73	15-18 yrs.
1979-1982	62	19-21 yrs.
(Cohort 2: Manic Depressive)		
1967-1972	60	7-11 yrs.
1975-1979	46	15-18 yrs.
1979-1982	35	19-21 yrs.
(Cohort 3: Physically Ill Families)		
1967-1972	78	7-11 yrs.
1975-1979	59	15-18 yrs.
1979-1982	44	19-21 yrs.
(Cohort 4: Normal Control Families)		
1967-1972	130	7-11 yrs.
1975-1979	107	15-18 yrs.
1979-1982	80	19-21 yrs.

INFORMATION ON SAMPLE ATTRITION:

During the 15-year period of study, 147 of 368 Ss (39.9%), across four cohorts, were not retrieved for further study: 38 of 100 Ss (38%) in Cohort 1; 25 of 60 Ss

(41.7%) in Cohort 2; 34 of 78 Ss (43.6%) in Cohort 3; and 50 of 130 Ss (38.5%) in Cohort 4. The core sample consists of 221 Ss: 62 Ss (Cohort 1); 35 Ss (Cohort 2); 44 Ss (Cohort 3); and 80 Ss (Cohort 4).

CONSTRUCTS MEASURED: INSTRUMENTS USED

Intelligence: Wechsler Preschool and Primary Scale of Intelligence (WPPSI), Wechsler Intelligence Scale for Children (WISC)
Visual-motor coordination: Beery-Buktenica Developmental Form Sequence
Integration level: Rorschach Ink Blot Test
Time-span, affect, coping, and interaction: Thematic Apperception Test, figure drawing
Rating of child's disturbance: Clinical ratings
Ability to disembed figures—cognitive ability: Children's Embedded Figure Test
Analytical ability: Picture completion, object assembly, rod and frame tests
Egocentricity: Three Mountains Test, Broken Bridge Test
Impulsivity: Draw-a-Line, Draw-a-Circle
Psychosocial evaluation (home visit): Family life, home atmosphere, sharing of parents
Psychophysiological testing: Skin potential, vasomotor activity, responses to stimulus onset and offset, anticipatory responses
Child's academic achievement in word cognition, mathematics, and spelling: Wide Range Achievement Test
Personality: Minnesota Multiphasic Personality Inventory (MMPI)
Life patterns: General information questionnaire
Family environment: Family Environment Scale (Moos)
Feelings about family members and perceptions of other family members and perceptions of those family members' feelings toward subject: Bene-Anthony Family Relations Test
School behavior and achievement, friendship and peer interactions, family interactions, sexual behavior: Rochester Adaptive Behavior Inventory
School achievement: Pupil Rating Form, Devereux Elementary School Behavior Rating Scale, Hahnemann High School Behavior Rating Scale
Evaluation of child; strengths and weaknesses, behavior, parent's behavior as good or bad influence: Speech sample (audiotaped speech by parent)
Psychiatric diagnosis: Diagnostic interview schedule

REPRESENTATIVE REFERENCES:

Anthony, E. J., & Koupernik, C. (Eds.). (1974). *The child in his family: Children at psychiatric risk* (Vol. 3). New York: John Wiley.
Worland, J., Janes, C. L., Anthony, E. J., McGinnis, M., & Cass, L. (1984). St. Louis Risk Research Project: Comprehensive progress report of experimental studies. In N. F. Watt, E. J. Anthony, L. C. Wynne, & J. E. Rolf (Eds.), *Children at risk for schizophrenia: A longitudinal perspective* (pp. 105-147). New York: Cambridge University Press.

Worland, J., Lander, H., & Hesselbrock, V. (1979). Psychological evaluation of clinical disturbance in children at risk for psychopathology. *Journal of Abnormal Psychology, 88*(1), 13-
26.

Worland, J., Weeks, D., Weiner, S., & Schectman, J. (1982). Longitudinal prospective evaluation
of intelligence in children at risk. *Schizophrenia Bulletin, 8*(1), 135-141.

CURRENT STATUS OF THE STUDY:

a. No further waves of data collection are planned.

b. Data are in machine-readable format.

c. Data are available for secondary analysis through the study contact person.

■ The Cooperative Institutional Research Program (CIRP), 1966

Astin, A. W.

Contact Person: A. W. Astin
Address: Director of Higher Education Research Institute
                 University of California at Los Angeles
                 Los Angeles, CA 90024
Telephone No.:   (213) 825-1925

SUBSTANTIVE TOPICS COVERED:

The study examines college student development in American higher education and involves an annual freshman survey at some 600 institutions, with periodic longitudinal follow-ups.

CHARACTERISTICS OF THE ORIGINAL SAMPLE:

Year the study began: 1966

Subject selection process: All entering freshmen from a representative national sample of 600 institutions

Total number of subjects at Time 1: N = 300,000[a]

Ages at Time 1: 17-18 yrs.

Sex distribution: Equal numbers of females and males throughout

Socioeconomic status: Students

Race/ethnicity: 84% white, 8% African-American, 2% Hispanic, 2% Asian-American, 1% Native American, 3% other

Comments:

a. In each of the 25 years of the project, some 200 items of information have been collected from each of more than 7 million students. Four different faculty surveys involving 200,000 faculty have also been conducted.

Years of Completed Waves:

Years[ab]	N=	Age ranges
1966	19,422	17-18 yrs.
1969-1970	*	20-21 yrs.
1966	25,399	17-18 yrs.
1970	*	21-22 yrs.
1967	5,351	17-18 yrs.
1968	*	18-19 yrs.
1967	20,958	17-18 yrs.
1969-1970	*	19-20 yrs.
1967	34,346	17-18 yrs.
1971	*	21-22 yrs.
1968	21,458	17-18 yrs.
1969-1970	*	18-19 yrs.
1981	192,248 (surveyed)	17-18 yrs.
1985	11,862 (sampled)	21-22 yrs.
1985	3,820 (responded)	21-22 yrs.
1983	190,368 (surveyed)	17-18 yrs.
1985	12,090 (sampled)	19-20 yrs.
1985	4,207 (responded)	19-20 yrs.
1983	190,368 (surveyed)	17-18 yrs.
1987	16,095 (sampled)	21-22 yrs.
1987	3,897 (responded)	21-22 yrs.
1984	182,370 (surveyed)	17-18 yrs.
1988	24,454 (sampled)	21-22 yrs.
1988	6,389 (responded)	21-22 yrs.
1985	192,453 (surveyed)	17-18 yrs.
1987	14,534 (sampled)	19-20 yrs.
1987	3,756 (responded)	19-20 yrs.
1985	192,453 (surveyed)	17-18 yrs.
1989	20,317 (sampled)	21-22 yrs.
1989	4,580 (responded)	21-22 yrs.
1986	209,627 (surveyed)	17-18 yrs.
1988	26,411 (sampled)	19-20 yrs.
1988	7,316 (responded)	19-20 yrs.
1987	208,627 (surveyed)	17-18 yrs.
1989	20,100 (sampled)	19-20 yrs.
1989	4,382 (responded)	19-20 yrs.

Comments:
a. Since 1966, the study has surveyed 24 freshman cohorts, each involving roughly 300 students from each institution and 300,000 students total. Longitudinal follow-ups are usually done on smaller subsamples due to cost limitations. The study has included approximately 40 different longitudinal follow-ups at periods ranging from 3 months to 9 years, with sample sizes ranging from 5,000 to 50,000; 14 of these are displayed above. All years since 1982 have been followed up after 2 and 4 years. Except for 1986, these follow-ups have been completed by about 10,000-12,000 students per cohort.
b. During the years 1966-1981, follow-ups were conducted on a sporadic basis determined by available funding. Starting in 1982, 2-year and 4-year follow-ups were conducted on an annual basis, in which a stratified random sample of Ss was selected from a larger pool of Ss surveyed during a given year, 2 or 4 years prior. Number of Ss

for a given follow-up sample was defined by the number of Ss from the stratified random sample who responded to a follow-up survey. Subjects followed-up at 2 and 4 years were not identical. Along with a survey of students was also a survey of registrars, concerning surveyed students in terms of student's number of completed years, enrollment status, and/or whether student had received a degree.

INFORMATION ON SAMPLE ATTRITION:

Response rates to questionnaire follow-ups have varied from 30% to 60%. However, more recent follow-ups have produced lower percentages.

CONSTRUCTS MEASURED: INSTRUMENTS USED

Demographic information, high school activities and achievements, scholastic aptitude; career and academic aspirations, and personal objectives and opinions: The Freshmen Survey, follow-up survey

REPRESENTATIVE REFERENCES:

Astin, A. W. (1978). *Four critical years*. San Francisco: Jossey-Bass.
Astin, A. W. (1984). Using longitudinal data to study college impact. In Mednick, S. A., Harway, M., & Finello, K. M. (Eds.), *Handbook of longitudinal research* (Vol. 2). New York: Praeger.
Astin, A. W. (1987). *The American freshman: Twenty year trends*. Los Angeles: Higher Education Research Institute.
Astin, A. W., et al. (1989). *The American college freshman: National norms for fall 1988*. Los Angeles: Higher Education Research Institute.

CURRENT STATUS OF THE STUDY:

a. Further waves of data collection are planned.
b. Data are in machine-readable format.
c. Raw data are available for secondary analysis only by persons associated with the Institute, or through requests made by outsiders for analyses to be performed by the Institute at cost.

■ Impact of Retirement on Adjustment to Aging, 1975

Atchley, Robert

Contact person: Robert Atchley
Address: Scripps Foundation Gerontology Center
                 Miami University
                 Oxford, OH 45056
Telephone No.:   (513) 529-2916

SUBSTANTIVE TOPICS COVERED:

The study examines morale, self-concept, personal goals, retirement status, marital status, age, sex, income, health, activities, occupation, attitude toward work and retirement, living arrangements, disability, anxiety, transportation, pensions, retirement plans, marital satisfaction, and family structure.

CHARACTERISTICS OF THE ORIGINAL SAMPLE:

Year the study began: 1975

Subject selection process: The sample represents a fairly even distribution of occupational and educational levels, age, sex, marital status, and household living arrangements of a small township within a major metropolitan region in southwestern Ohio.

Total number of subjects at Time 1: N = 1,106

Age ranges at Time 1: 50-94 yrs.

Sex distribution: Approximately equal numbers of females and males throughout

Socioeconomic status: 33.3% middle/upper middle class, 33.3% working class, 33.3% poverty class

Race/ethnicity: 96% white, 4% African-American

Years of Completed Waves:[a]

Years	N=	Age ranges
1975	1,106	50-94 yrs.
1977	855	52-96 yrs.
1979	700[a]	54-98 yrs.
1981	675	56-93

Comments:
a. In addition, a subsample of 115 of the 700 respondents in 1979 who planned to retire between 1980 and 1985 were administered a preretirement questionnaire.

INFORMATION ON SAMPLE ATTRITION:

During the 6-year period of study, 431 of 1,106 Ss (38.9%) were not retrieved for further study. The core sample size consists of 675 Ss. Attrition was due to deaths and to Ss moving away.

CONSTRUCTS MEASURED: INSTRUMENTS USED

Marital status and history; education; employment status; rating of overall health; physical abilities; sleeping patterns, eating patterns and/or changes; level of rigidity/flexibility; perceived trend of health; level of loneliness; expectation versus reality of aging; level of satisfaction; morale, personal goals; activities; retirement status and plans; attitude toward work and retirement; skills and experience; income; self-concept; living arrangements; anxiety; disabilities; religion: Questionnaire

Retirement plans and expectations: Preretirement questionnaire (subsample = 112 Ss)

REPRESENTATIVE REFERENCES:

Atchley, R. C. (1982). The process of retirement: Comparing women and men. In M. Szinovacz (Ed.), *Women's retirement.* Beverly Hills, CA: Sage.

Atchley, R. C., & Miller, S. J. (1983). Types of elderly couples. In T. H. Brubaker (Ed.), *Family relationships in later life* Beverly Hills, CA: Sage.

Atchley, R. C., & Robinson, J. L. (1982). Attitudes towards retirement and distance from the event. *Research on Aging, 4,* 299-313.

Palmore, E., Burchett, B., Fillenbaum, G., George, L., & Wallman, L. (1985). *Retirement: Causes and consequences.* New York: Springer.

CURRENT STATUS OF THE STUDY:

a. Further waves of data collection are tentatively planned for 1991.

b. Most data are in machine-readable format.

c. Data are available for secondary analysis through the Henry A. Murray Research Center, Radcliffe College, 10 Garden Street, Cambridge, MA 02138.

■ Family Influences on School Readiness and Achievement in Japan and the United States, 1973

Azuma, Hiroshi; and Hess, Robert D. (retired)

Contact Person: Theresa McDevitt
Address: College of Education
                  University of Northern Colorado
                  Greeley, CO 80643
Telephone No.:   (303) 351-1890

SUBSTANTIVE TOPICS COVERED:

The study examines the usefulness of maternal variables for predicting school readiness at ages 4, 5, and 6, and academic performance at age 11 (from Japan) and age 12 (from the United States); identifies aspects of maternal behavior and the home that are associated with school achievement; identifies the degree to which family influences are operative during preschool years and carry over into achievement in later school years; compares the effectiveness of maternal measures with more general indicators such as socioeconomic status.

CHARACTERISTICS OF THE ORIGINAL SAMPLE:

Year the study began: 1973
Subject selection process: Subjects were firstborns recruited through day-care centers and nursery schools.
Total number of subjects at Time 1: N = 125: Japan (58)/U.S. (67)
Ages at Time 1: 3 yrs., 8 mos.
Sex distribution: Approximately equal numbers of females and males throughout (both cohorts)
Socioeconomic status: 60% working class, 40% middle/upper middle class
Race/ethnicity: 53.6% white, 46.4% Asian

Years of Completed Waves:

Year	N=	Age ranges
(Cohort 1: Japanese Ss)		
1973	58	3 yrs., 8 mos.
1974	58	4 yrs.
1975	58	5 yrs.
1976	58	6 yrs.
1981	44	11 yrs.
(Cohort 2: American Ss)		
1973	67	3 yrs., 8 mos.
1974	67	4 yrs.
1975	67	5 yrs.
1976	67	6 yrs.
1982	47	12 yrs.

INFORMATION ON SAMPLE ATTRITION:

During the 9-year period of study, 34 of 125 Ss across both cohorts were not retrieved for further study: Japanese sample, 14 of 58 Ss (24.1%); American sample, 20 of 67 Ss (29.9%). The core sample consists of 91 Ss: 44 Ss (Japanese sample), and 47 Ss (American sample).

CONSTRUCTS MEASURED: INSTRUMENTS USED

Intelligence: Revised Wechsler Intelligence Scale for Children
School performance in reading and mathematics: Teacher ratings of performance in school
Attribution of child's success: Teacher questionnaire
Mother's verbal ability: Verbal intelligence test
Verbal ability: Vocabulary test
Mother-child interactions: Mother-child interaction tasks (unstructured task, block sorting task, referential communication task)
Child's school performance in mathematics and mother's explanation(s): Mother interview
Verbal and mathematics abilities: Vocabulary and mathematics test

REPRESENTATIVE REFERENCES:

Hess, R. D., Azuma, H., Holloway, S., Wenegrat, A., & Kashiwagi, K. (1987). Cultural variations in the socialization of school achievement: Contrasts between Japan and the United States. *Journal of Applied Developmental Psychology, 8,* 421-440.

Hess, R., Azuma, H., Kashiwagi, K., Dickson, W., Nagano, S., Holloway, S., Miyake, N., & Price, G. (1984). Family influences on school readiness and achievement in Japan and the United States: An overview of a longitudinal survey. In H. Stevenson, H. Azuma, & K. Hakuta (Eds.), *Child development and education in Japan.* New York: Freeman.

Hess, R. D., Holloway, S. D., Dickson, W. P., & Price, G. G. (1984). Maternal variables as predictors of children's school readiness and later achievement in vocabulary and mathematics in sixth grade. *Child Development, 5,* 1902-1912.

Hess, R. D., & McDevitt, T. M. (1984). Some cognitive consequences of maternal intervention techniques: A longitudinal study. *Child Development, 55,* 2017-2030.

CURRENT STATUS OF THE STUDY:

a. No further waves of data collection are planned.
b. Most data are in machine-readable format.
c. The data are not available for secondary analysis.

B

Youth in Transition, 1966

Bachman, Jerald G.

Contact Person:	Jerald G. Bachman
Address:	University of Michigan
	Institute for Social Research
	P. O. Box 1248
	Ann Arbor, MI 48106
Telephone No:	(313) 763-5043

SUBSTANTIVE TOPICS COVERED:

The study examines occupational aspirations; job status and satisfaction; self-esteem; affective states; attitudes and views about government, military service, and race; delinquent behavior and drug use during adolescence, in relation to family background, academic ability, educational and occupational attainments, and marriage and parenthood experiences.

CHARACTERISTICS OF THE ORIGINAL SAMPLE:

Year the study began: 1966
Subject selection process: Ss were selected by a national representative sampling of 10th-grade males from 87 high schools. The sample is representative of the ages of 10th-grade males in 1966. Of the 2,277 Ss contacted, 92.2% participated in the study.
Total number of subjects at Time 1: N = 2,213
Ages at Time 1: 14-18 yrs.
Sex distribution: 100% male
Socioeconomic status: National representative sample
Race/ethnicity: 87% white, 12% African-American, 1% other

Years of Completed Waves:

Years	N=	Age ranges
1966	2,213	14-18 yrs.
1968	1,886	16-20 yrs.
1969	1,799	17-21 yrs.
1970	1,620	18-22 yrs.
1974	1,628	22-26 yrs.

INFORMATION ON SAMPLE ATTRITION:

During the 8-year period of study, 585 of 2,213 Ss (26.4%) were not retrieved for further study. The core sample consists of approximately 1,420 Ss. Attrition bias was calculated by the principal investigator; high school dropouts and absentees were disproportionately lost from the sample.

CONSTRUCTS MEASURED: INSTRUMENTS USED

Family background, race, urbanism, educational plans for college, educational attitudes and attainment, occupational attainment, environment/experiences, military service, marital/parental status, self-concepts associated with school ability, motives, test anxiety, need for self-development, need for self-utilization, affective states, social values and attitudes, occupational attitudes and aspirations, delinquent behaviors, drug use: Questionnaires

Ability: Composite ability, Quick Ability test, General Aptitude Test Battery-Part J (GATB-J), Gates Reading Test

College status ranking: College performance, College Mean American College Test (ACT) Score

High school academic performance: Mean Quick Test, Mean General Aptitude Test Battery-Part J (GATB-J), Mean Gates Reading Test

REPRESENTATIVE REFERENCES:

Bachman, J. G. (1970). *Youth in transition: Vol. II. The impact of family background and intelligence on tenth grade boys.* Ann Arbor, MI: Institute for Social Research.

Bachman, J., Kahn, R., Mednick, M., Davidson, T., & Johnston, L. (1967). *Youth in transition: Vol. I. Blueprint for a longitudinal study of adolescent boys.* Ann Arbor, MI: The Institute for Social Research.

Bachman, J., & O'Malley, P. M. (1984). The youth in transition project. In S. A. Mednick, M. Harway, & K. M. Finello (Eds.), *Handbook of longitudinal research, Vol. 2: Teenage and adult cohorts* (pp. 121-140). New York: Praeger.

Bachman, J., O'Malley, P., & Johnston, J. (1978). *Youth in transition: Vol. VI. Adolescence to adulthood—A study of change and stability in the lives of young men.* Ann Arbor, MI: The Institute for Social Research.

CURRENT STATUS OF THE STUDY:

    a. No further waves of data collection are planned.

    b. The data are in machine-readable format.

    c. The data are available for secondary analysis through the Inter-University Consortium for Political and Social Research (ICPSR) Institute for Social Research, University of Michigan, P.O. Box 1248, Ann Arbor, MI 48106.

■ Concentration Choice Study, 1978

Bailey, Susan; Burrell, Barbara; and Ware, Norma

Contact Person: Susan Bailey
Address: Director, Center for Research on Women
                  Wellesley College
                  Wellesley, MA 02181
Telephone No.:   (617) 431-1453

SUBSTANTIVE TOPICS COVERED:

This study investigates the reasons why undergraduate women intending to major in science change their plans before declaring a major.

CHARACTERISTICS OF THE ORIGINAL SAMPLE:

Year the study began: 1978

Subject selection process: Subjects selected were from the class of 1982 of a highly selective college and had scored 700 or above on their SAT scores for math. The Ss from the class of 1983 were chosen by their tentative intention to major in science or math.

Total number of subjects at Time 1: N = 247, Cohort 1; N = 234, Cohort 2

Ages at Time 1: 17-19 yrs.

Sex distribution: Approximately equal numbers of females and males throughout

Socioeconomic status: 100% student; more specific information in terms of percent distribution of socioeconomic classes was not available.

Race/ethnicity: Predominantly white

Years of Completed Waves:

Years	N=	Age ranges
(Cohort 1: Class of 1982)[a]		
1978-1979	247	17-19 yrs.
1979-1980	*	18-20 yrs.
1980-1981	*	19-21 yrs.
1981-1982	191	20-22 yrs.
(Cohort 2: Class of 1983)[a]		
1979-1980	234	17-19 yrs.
1980-1981	222	18-20 yrs.
1981-1982	211	19-21 yrs.
1982-1983	168	20-22 yrs.

Comments:

a. A subsample of 40 subjects from both classes (M = 16, F = 24) were interviewed each year, 32 of which completed interviews all 4 years.

* Information was not available about the number of Ss followed up during the years 1979-1980 and 1980-1981.

INFORMATION ON SAMPLE ATTRITION:

During the 5-year period of study, 122 of 481 Ss (25.4%) across two cohorts were not retrieved for further study. The core sample consists of 359 Ss: 191 for Cohort 1; and 168 for Cohort 2.

CONSTRUCTS MEASURED: INSTRUMENTS USED

Personal background, college experience, choice of concentration, plans for the future: Questionnaire

Understanding of academic experience, plans for career and family, perceptions of university programs, factors influencing choice of major: Interview (yearly subsample N = 40 Ss)

Need for achievement, motivation to avoid success, affiliation, power: Thematic Apperception Test (N = 217 Ss)

Ego development: Washington University Sentence Completion Test (Loevinger)

REPRESENTATIVE REFERENCES:

Bailey, S., & Burrell, B. (1980). *First report on the concentration choice study*. Cambridge, MA: Radcliffe College, Office of Institutional Policy Research on Women's Education at Harvard and Radcliffe.

Bailey, S., & Burrell, B. (1981). *Second report on the concentration choice study*. Cambridge, MA: Radcliffe College, Office of Institutional Policy Research on Women's Education at Harvard and Radcliffe.

Ware, N. C., Leserman, J., & Steckler, N. (1983). *Aspects of academic experience among prospective science concentrators*. Cambridge, MA: Radcliffe College, Special Projects.

Ware, N. C., & Steckler, N. A. (1983). Choosing a science major: The experience of men and women. *Women's Studies Quarterly, 11*(2), 12-15.

CURRENT STATUS OF THE STUDY:

a. No further waves of data collection are planned.

b. Data are in machine-readable format.

c. Data are available for secondary analysis from the Henry A. Murray Research Center, Radcliffe College, 10 Garden Street, Cambridge, MA 02138.

■ Longitudinal Study of the Occupational Stress and Health of Women Licensed Practical Nurses and Licensed Social Workers, 1985

Barnett, Rosalind; Baruch, Grace (deceased); and Marshall, Nancy L.

Contact Person: Rosalind Barnett
Address: Center for Research on Women
Wellesley College
Wellesley, MA 02181
Telephone No.: (617) 431-1453

SUBSTANTIVE TOPICS COVERED:

This study examines the relationship between the quality of experience in work and family roles and mental and physical health among women employed as social workers and licensed practical nurses.

CHARACTERISTICS OF THE ORIGINAL SAMPLE:

Year the study began: 1985
Subject selection process: Subjects were randomly selected from registries of professional women in metropolitan Boston and were disproportionately stratified by race, parenthood status, and partnership status (married or partnered versus single).
Total number of subjects at Time 1: N = 403
Ages at Time 1: 25-55 yrs.
Sex distribution: 100% female
Socioeconomic status: 64% middle/upper middle class, 36% working class
Race/ethnicity: 85% white, 15% African-American

Years of Completed Waves:

Years	N=	Age ranges
1985	403	25-55 yrs.
1986	377	26-56 yrs.
1987	377	27-57 yrs.

INFORMATION ON SAMPLE ATTRITION:

During the 3-year period of study, 26 of 403 Ss (6.5%) were not retrieved for further study. The core sample consists of 377 Ss. Attrition was due to either subjects' moving or refusing further participation.

CONSTRUCTS MEASURED: INSTRUMENTS USED

Quality of experience at job, as a parent, and in a partner relationship: Job Quality Scale (developed for study), Parent Quality Scale (developed for study), and Partner Quality Scale (developed for study)

Depression and anxiety: Symptom Check List (SCL-90: Depression Anxiety Subscales)

Psychological well-being, positive affect: Subjective well-being scale (modified Rand Well-Being Scale)

Physical health: Physical Symptom Checklist

Blood pressure: Sphygmomanometer

REPRESENTATIVE REFERENCES:

Barnett, R. C. (1988). On the relationship of adult daughters to their mothers. *Journal of Geriatric Psychiatry, 21,* 37-50.

Barnett, R. C., & Baruch, G. K. (1987). Social roles, gender and psychological distress. In R. C. Barnett, L. Biener, & G. K. Baruch (Eds.), *Gender and stress.* New York: Free Press.

Barnett, R. C., & Marshall, N. L. (1989). *Multiple roles, spillover effects and psychological distress* (Working Paper No. 200). Wellesley, MA: Wellesley College, Center for Research on Women.

Barnett, R. C., Marshall, N. L., & Davidson, H. (1989). *Occupational stress and health of women LPNs and LSWs: Final project report* (Working Paper No. 202). Wellesley, MA: Wellesley College, Center for Research on Women.

CURRENT STATUS OF THE STUDY:

a. No further waves of data collection are planned.

b. Most of the data are in machine-readable format.

c. Data are available for secondary analysis from study contact person.

■ Symbolic Development, 1978

Bates, Elizabeth; and Bretherton, Inge

Contact Person: Elizabeth Bates
Address: University of California at San Diego
Department of Psychology
La Jolla, CA 92038
Telephone No.: (619) 534-3007

SUBSTANTIVE TOPICS COVERED:

The study examines the development of symbolic functions during early childhood, with particular focus on the acquisition of a first language and the relation and transition of nonverbal to verbal symbols.

CHARACTERISTICS OF THE ORIGINAL SAMPLE:

Year the study began: 1978
Subject selection process: Subjects were solicited by letter and telephone calls on the basis of birth announcements made in newspapers.
Total number of subjects at Time 1: N = 32
Ages at Time 1: 10 mos.
Sex distribution: Equal numbers of males and females throughout
Socioeconomic status: 100% middle/upper middle class
Race/ethnicity: 96% white, 4% African-American

Years of Completed Waves:

Years	N=	Age ranges
1978	32	10 mos.
1978-1979	32	13 mos.
1979-1980	30	20 mos.
1980	30	28 mos.

INFORMATION ON SAMPLE ATTRITION:

During the 2-year period of study, 2 of 32 Ss (6.3%) were not retrieved for further study. The core sample consists of 30 Ss.

CONSTRUCTS MEASURED: INSTRUMENTS USED

Language use and development: Language observations

Child's vocabulary, word use, and context of use: Language interviews with mothers

Child's use of combinatorial and symbolic play schemes: Symbolic play observations and interviews, combinatorial play observations and interviews

Style of mother-child interaction as related to symbolic development of the child: Observations of mother-child interaction

Child's vocabulary development: Peabody Picture Vocabulary Test

Affective terms: Emotion Label Recognition Test

Grammar development: Grammatical Morphemes Test, Word Order Test

REPRESENTATIVE REFERENCES:

Bates, E., Bretherton, I., & Snyder, L. (1988). *From first words to grammar.* New York: Cambridge University Press.

Bretherton, I., Bates, E., McNew, S., Shore, C., Williamson, C., & Beeghley-Smith, M. (1981). Comprehension and production of symbols in infancy: An experimental study. *Developmental Psychology, 17*(6), 728-736.

Bretherton, I., McNew, S., & Bates, E. (1983). Individual differences at 20 months: Analytic and holistic strategies in language acquisition. *Journal of Child Language, 10*(2), 293-320.

Shore, C., O'Connell, B., & Bates, E. (1984). First sentences in language and symbolic play. *Developmental Psychology, 20*(5), 872-880.

CURRENT STATUS OF THE STUDY:

a. No further waves of data collection are planned.

b. Most data are in machine-readable format.

c. The data are available for secondary analysis from the Child Language Data Exchange, Carnegie-Mellon University.

■ Family Socialization and Developmental Competence Project, 1968

Baumrind, Diana

Contact Person: Diana Baumrind
Address: University of California
                Institute of Human Development
                1203 Edward Chace Tolman Hall
                Berkeley, CA 94720
Telephone No.: (415) 642-3603

SUBSTANTIVE TOPICS COVERED:

The study examines the influence of contrasting patterns of parental authority on the development of instrumental competence and dysfunction throughout childhood and adolescence; child status and family functioning throughout childhood, adolescence, and in early adulthood; dimensions of children's instrumental competence (social assertiveness, social responsibility, and cognitive competence) and dimensions of child rearing (demandingness and responsiveness); maturity demands, disciplinary practices, intellectual stimulation, and conformity and nurturance of parents.

CHARACTERISTICS OF THE ORIGINAL SAMPLE:

Year the study began: 1968
Subject selection process: Subjects were selected from 13 nursery schools in Berkeley, Oakland, Kensington, and El Cerrito, California. A supplementary sample was added at the second data point, drawn from primary schools in the same area. The supplementary sample is somewhat less well educated but otherwise the same.
Total number of subjects at Time 1: N = 134
Ages at Time 1: 4 yrs.
Sex distribution: Approximately equal numbers of females and males throughout
Socioeconomic status: 100% middle/upper middle class
Race/ethnicity: 100% white

Years of Completed Waves:

Years	N=	Age ranges
(Cohort 1)		
1968-1969	134	4 yrs.
1972-1973	104	9 yrs.
1978-1980	89	14 yrs.
(Cohort 2)		
1972-1973	60	9 yrs.
1978-1980	50	14 yrs.

INFORMATION ON SAMPLE ATTRITION:

During the 12-year period of study, 55 of 194 Ss (28.4%) across two cohorts were not retrieved for further study. By cohort, 45 of 134 (33.6%) Ss were not followed in Cohort 1, and 10 of 60 (16.7%) Ss were not followed in Cohort 2. Sample attrition was mainly due to subjects moving out of state and to insufficient funds to have Ss visit Berkeley for further interviewing and testing. The core sample consists of 139 Ss: 89 Ss from Cohort 1, and 50 Ss from Cohort 2.

CONSTRUCTS MEASURED: INSTRUMENTS USED

Creativity: Observation, Wallach & Kogan Pattern Meanings and Attentive Uses, Torrance Circles and Just Suppose

Cognitive style, field dependence: Observation, Witkin Rod & Frame, Crandall Intellectual Achievement Responsibility, Nowicki-Strickland Locus of Control

Sex role: Choice of toys in play session, Bem Sex Role Inventory

Traditional versus liberal beliefs; religiosity, religion as a source of morals, proscriptions: Jessor Traditional Beliefs

Social alienation: Observation, alienation scale

Social cognitive levels and attitudes: Social cognition interview (similar to Kohlberg), Kohlberg Moral Judgment Interview, Bull Value of Life

Aspiration: Observation, Hales Level of Aspiration Task

Self-esteem: Observation, Coopersmith Self-Esteem Inventory, Ideal-actual Q-sort Correlation

Social desirability: Crandall Social Desirability, Bem Social Desirability

Academic and social competence: Identity interview, adolescent interest interview, observation, academic transcripts

Health: Observation, health interview

Physical maturation level: Developmental questionnaire, Tanner Ratings

Nutritional status: 3-day Diet Record, dietary habits interview, activity interview

Physical fitness: Observation, Canadian 12-minute work test, cardiovascular pulmonary measures, strength, Parnells' technique of body typing

Parent-child relationship: Family card sort, family discussion questionnaire, extensive observation in home and laboratory

Parental psychological functioning: Observation, California Psychological Inventory

Cognition: Stanford-Binet Intelligence Scale (Form LM), Revised Wechsler Intelligence Scale for Children (WISCR); Raven's Advanced Progressive Matrices; Wechsler Adult Intelligence Scale (parents)

Parents' child-rearing attitudes: Parent attitude inventory, parent socialization interview, family life self-report questionnaire, parent socialization and health interview

Parents' child-rearing behavior: Home visit observations, family interaction discussion, family ethical discussion, parent teaches and plays, wrap-up session

Personal and family health: Child's physical problems observed and/or listed by parent, adolescent medical history booklet; health, fitness and substance use portion of parent socialization interview, adolescence substance use interview

Family demographic data: Section of parent attitude inventory, section of adolescent medical history booklet, background information sheet

Stressors: Family Stressor Index (modified version of Holmes and Rahe Social Readjustment Rating Questionnaire)

Internalizing and Externalizing Problem Behavior: Achenbach and Edelbrock's Child Behavior Checklist; ratings of parent problem behavior; ratings of adolescent and parent alcohol and substance use

Socioeconomic status: Stevens and Cho Socioeconomic Indexes and New 1980 Census Occupation Classification Scheme

REPRESENTATIVE REFERENCES:

Baumrind, D. (1987). A developmental perspective on adolescent risk-taking in contemporary America. In W. Damon (Ed.), *New directions for child development*. San Francisco: Jossey-Bass.

Baumrind, D. (in press). Parenting styles and adolescent development. In J. Brooks-Gunn, R. Lerner, & A. C. Petersen (Eds.), *Encyclopedia on adolescence*. New York: Garland.

Baumrind, D. (in press). Effective parenting during the early adolescent transition. In P. Cowan & E. M. Hetherington (Eds.), *Advances in family research*. New York: Lawrence Erlbaum.

Baumrind, D. (in press). The influence of parenting style on adolescent competence and problem behavior. *Journal of Early Adolescence*.

CURRENT STATUS OF THE STUDY:

a. Further waves of data collection are planned, pending availability of funding.

b. Most of the data are in machine-readable format.

c. The data are conditionally available for secondary analysis from the study contact person.

■ Bethesda Longitudinal Study of Early Child and Family Development, 1964

Bell, Richard Q.; Ryder, Robert G.; and Halverson, Charles F., Jr.

Contact Person: Richard Q. Bell
Address: Department of Psychology
                  University of Virginia
                  Charlottesville, VA 22903-2477
Telephone No.:   (804) 924-0665 or (404) 542-4926 (Halverson)

SUBSTANTIVE TOPICS COVERED:

The study examines the sequence of events from early marriage by which social, emotional, and cognitive behaviors develop in the young child. Husband and wife characteristics were studied prior to the birth of the first child, and the infants' characteristics prior to sustained interaction with their parents.

CHARACTERISTICS OF THE ORIGINAL SAMPLE:

Year the study began: 1964

Subject selection process: Spouses between 18 and 27 years of age who had been married either a few months or more than 2 years were located through records of marriage license applications in the Washington, D.C., area. Pregnancies up to the fall of 1969 then became the primary source sample for developmental studies of the newborns, 3- and 11-month-olds, and preschoolers.

Total number of subjects at Time 1: N = 875

Ages at Time 1: 18-27 yrs.

Sex distribution: Approximately equal numbers of females and males throughout

Socioeconomic status: Predominately middle class/upper middle class

Race/ethnicity: 85% white, 15% African-American

Years of Completed Waves:

Years	N=	Age ranges
(Cohort 1: Parents)		
1964-1968	875	18-27 yrs.
(Cohort 2: Children)		
1964-1969	135	Prenatal
1964-1969	125	3-11 mos.
1969-1973	132	2-3 yrs.

INFORMATION ON SAMPLE ATTRITION:

During the 9-year period of study, 3 of 135 Ss (2.2%) were not retrieved for further study. The core sample consists of 117 Ss.

CONSTRUCTS MEASURED: INSTRUMENTS USED

Marital satisfaction, closeness to family of orientation, role orientation, affect: Questionnaires, objective tests, interactive situations, interviews

Responsiveness to infant, conditioning to social context: Interviews, interaction situations

Reactivity, irritability, maturity, reflexive and discriminative sucking: Observations and physiological measurement of newborns

Tonicity, activity, sociability, and clarity of behavior: Home and laboratory observations (at 3 and 11 months)

Attentional, social and cognitive behavior, vigor and assertiveness in settings and experiments: Preschool observations and measurement

REPRESENTATIVE REFERENCES:

Bell, R. Q. (1975). The Bethesda Longitudinal Study: The overall study and some specific findings. In R. D. Wirt, G. Winoker, & M. Roff, (Eds.), *Life history research in psychopathology*. Minneapolis: University of Minnesota Press.

Ryder, R. Q., Kafka, J. S., & Olson, D. H. (1971). Separating and joining influences in courtship and early marriage. *American Journal of Orthopsychiatry, 41*, 450-464.

Yang, R. K., & Moss, H. (1978). Neonatal precursors of infant behavior. *Developmental Psychology, 14*, 607-613.

Waldrop, M. F., Bell, R. Q., McLaughlin, B., & Halverson, C. F. (1978). Newborn minor physical anomalies predict short attention span, peer aggression, and impulsivity at age 3 (sic). *Science, 199*, 563-564.

CURRENT STATUS OF THE STUDY:

a. No further waves of data collection are planned.

b. Most of the data are in machine-readable format.

c. Data are available for secondary analysis.

■ Longitudinal Study of Three-Generation Families, 1971

Bengtson, Vern L.; and Gatz, Margaret

Contact person: Vern L. Bengtson
Address: Andrus Research Institute
                Andrus Gerontology Center
                University of Southern California
                University Park, MC-0191
                Los Angeles, CA 90089-0191
Telephone No.: (213) 740-8242

SUBSTANTIVE TOPICS COVERED:

This study examines changes and continuity in family relationships, especially intergenerational social support, and their consequences for individual mental health, across the life course in a sample of three- and four-generation families followed over a period of 20 years.

CHARACTERISTICS OF THE ORIGINAL SAMPLE:

Year the study began: 1971

Subject selection process: Subjects were selected from families with living members representing three generations; they were recruited through the grandfathers (G1), who were members of a large metropolitan Health Maintenance Organization. The study was originally intended to be cross-sectional.

Total number of subjects at Time 1: N = 516 grandparents (Generation/Cohort 1); N = 701 parents (Generation/Cohort 2); N = 827 grandchildren (Generation/Cohort 3)

Ages at Time 1:[a] 67 yrs. (Cohort 1); 44 yrs. (Cohort 2); 19 yrs. (Cohort 3)

Sex distribution: Predominantly equal numbers of females and males throughout

Socioeconomic status: 100% middle/upper middle class

Race/ethnicity: 92% white, 2% African-American, 2% Hispanic, and 4% other

Years of Completed Waves:

Years	N=	Age ranges[a]
(Generation/Cohort 1: Grandparents)		
1971-1972	516	67 yrs.
1985-1986	223	78 yrs.
1988-1989	175	80 yrs.
(Generation/Cohort 2: Parents)		
1971-1972	701	44 yrs.
1985-1986	554	57 yrs.
1988-1989	565	60 yrs.

Years of Completed Waves, Continued:

Years	N=	Age ranges[a]
(Generation/Cohort 3: Grandchildren)		
1971-1972	827	19 yrs.
1985-1986	554	33 yrs.
1988-1989	741	36 yrs.

Comments:
a. Based on average ages.

INFORMATION ON SAMPLE ATTRITION:

The final number of Ss at waves 2 and 3 consist of longitudinal respondents as well as some formerly eligible persons who did not respond to an earlier wave *and* new participants who were added to the sample (i.e., spouses of the youngest generation respondents.) The core sample consists of 931 Ss: Generation/Cohort 1, 135; Generation/Cohort 2, 407; and Generation/Cohort 3, 389. Reasons for sample attrition included death of eldest Ss from Generation/Cohort 1, inability to participate due to developing mental or physical impairments, and Ss who could not be relocated.

CONSTRUCTS MEASURED: INSTRUMENTS USED

Family solidarity, sociodemographic status, occupational demands/rewards, health, family/individual transitions, family/individual response to transitions, alternative sources of cohesion: Questionnaire

Mental health: Psychological well-being (Bradburn ABS), avowed happiness; self-esteem (Rosenberg), depression (CES-D), locus of control (Rotter, with Gurin modifications), other psychiatric symptoms (BSI); personality traits (Wave 3); marital satisfaction

Family solidarity in response to health-related dependency: Semistructured qualitative interview (subsample)

REPRESENTATIVE REFERENCES:

Bengtson, V. L. (1986). Sociological perspectives on aging, families and the future. In M. Bergener (Ed.), *Perspectives on aging: The 1986 Sandoz lectures in gerontology* (pp. 237-261). New York/London: Academic Press.

Bengtson, V. L., Mangen, D. J., & Landry, P. H., Jr. (1984). The multi-generation family: Concepts and findings. In V. Garms-Homolova, E. M. Hoerning, & D. Schaeffer (Eds.), *Intergenerational relationships*. New York: C. J. Hogrefe.

Gatz, M., & Hurwicz, M. (1990). Are old people more depressed? Cross-sectional data on CES-D factors. *Psychology and Aging, 5,* 284-290.

Glass, J., Bengtson, V. L., & Dunham, C. C. (1986). Attitude similarity in three-generation families: Socialization, status inheritance, or reciprocal influence. *American Sociological Review, 51*(5), 685-698.

CURRENT STATUS OF THE STUDY:

a. Further waves of data collection are planned for 1991, 1994, and 1997.

b. Most data are in machine-readable format.

c. Data are available for secondary analysis from the Henry A. Murray Research Center, Radcliffe College, 10 Garden Street, Cambridge, MA 02138.

■ High School to College Transition Study, 1970

Berger, Alan S.; and Gagnon, John H.

Contact Person: Alan S. Berger
Address: Loyola University School of Social Work
Water Tower Campus
820 North Michigan Avenue
Chicago, IL 60601
Telephone No.: (312) 643-7280

SUBSTANTIVE TOPICS COVERED:

The purpose of this study was to determine the effects of the college experience on subjects' expectations and behavior.

CHARACTERISTICS OF THE ORIGINAL SAMPLE:

Year the study began: 1970

Subject selection process: Subjects were college freshmen who responded to mailed questionnaires.

Total number of subjects at Time 1: N = 1,425

Ages at Time 1: 17-19 yrs.

Sex distribution: Approximately equal numbers of females and males throughout

Socioeconomic status: Information was gathered, but not available in terms of percent distribution by socioeconomic class.

Race/ethnicity: Information was gathered, but not available in terms of percent distribution by race.

Years of Completed Waves:

Years	N=	Age ranges
1970 (Summer)	1,425	17-19 yrs.
1970 (Fall)	1,026	17-19 yrs.
1971 (Spring)	871	18-20 yrs.

INFORMATION ON SAMPLE ATTRITION:

During the one-year period of study, 554 of 1,425 Ss (38.9%) were not retrieved for further study. The core sample consists of 871 Ss. Attrition was mainly due to dropouts.

CONSTRUCTS MEASURED: INSTRUMENTS USED

Family background, high school experience, daily activities, academic interests, career plans, self-perceptions, college life plans, social and political attitudes: Questionnaire

Family background, high school experience, daily activities, academic interests, career plans, self-perceptions, college life plans, social and political attitudes, attitude toward sex: Follow-up questionnaire

REPRESENTATIVE REFERENCES:

No publications available.

CURRENT STATUS OF THE STUDY:

a. No further waves of data collection are planned.
b. Most of the data are in machine-readable format.
c. Data are available for secondary analysis through the Henry A. Murray Research Center, Radcliffe College, 10 Garden Street, Cambridge, MA 02138.

■ A Longitudinal Study of Ego and Cognitive Development, 1968

Block, Jack; and Block, Jeanne H. (deceased)

Contact Person: Jack Block
Address: Department of Psychology
                  University of California, Berkeley
                  Berkeley, CA 94720
Telephone No.:   (415) 642-0405

SUBSTANTIVE TOPICS COVERED:

The study examines personality (social-emotional) development; ego control and ego resiliency from early childhood to early adulthood; factors related to the development of gender differences; parental child-rearing attitudes and values during childhood and adolescence; the self-concept over time; among other topics. Emphasis is given to continuity and personality-context issues in development.

CHARACTERISTICS OF THE ORIGINAL SAMPLE:

Year the study began: 1968
Subject selection process: The sample was recruited from two cohorts of two nursery schools in Berkeley, California. All children were invited to participate; 95% responded.
Total number of subjects at Time 1: N = 128
Ages at Time 1: 3 yrs.
Sex distribution: Approximately equal numbers of females and males throughout
Socioeconomic status: Heterogeneous as measured by Duncan and Warner indices
Race/ethnicity: 68% white, 24% African-American, 8% Asian-American

Years of Completed Waves:

Years	*N=*	*Age ranges*
1969-1970	128	3 yrs.
1970-1971	128[a]	4 yrs.
1971-1972	118	5 yrs.
1973-1974	102	7 yrs.
1977-1978	105	11 yrs.
1980-1981	106	14 yrs.
1984-1985	106	18 yrs.
1989-1990	102	23 yrs.

Comments:
a. Twelve subjects were added to the original sample.

INFORMATION ON SAMPLE ATTRITION:

During the 20-year period of study, 26 of 128 Ss (20.3%) were not retrieved for further study. A core sample of 75 Ss participated completely in all eight data waves.

CONSTRUCTS MEASURED: INSTRUMENTS USED

Constructs

Ego development; Ego control; Ego resiliency; Delay of gratification; Distractibility; Vigilance of attention; Susceptibility to priming; Exploratory behavior; Ease of boredom; Planfulness strategies; Instrumental behaviors at barriers; Level of aspiration; Utilization of feedback; Cognitive differentiation; Cognitive development; Conservation ability; Creativity; Categorization behavior Reflection-impulsivity; Egocentrism; Focal attention; Generation of hypothe-

ses; Short- and long-term memory; Moral development; Social resourcefulness; Observer evaluations of personality; Self-perceptions of personality by
subject, mother, father; Development of sex role concepts; Quality of the environment; Affective Differentiation; Child-rearing attitudes of parents;
Parents' teaching strategies; Family interaction styles

Instruments

Ego Development Interview (videotaped); Decision confidence test; Autokinetic
phenomenon procedure; "Beeper" experience sampling method; Actometer;
Candy Train; Gift Opening; Accumulation of Rewards; Delay of gratification
payment schedule; Hardyck Speed-Accuracy Tradeoff Procedure;
Santostefano Number Distractibility; Signal Detection Task; Banta Curiosity
Box; Incidental Curiosity I, Incidental Curiosity II, Incidental Curiosity III;
Block Curiosity Box; Maccoby's Motor Inhibition Tasks; Competing Set;
Simon Says; Block Tower; Barrier Door; Barrier Drawer I; Barrier Block Box;
Barrier Puzzle; Dual Focus Test; Percept Formation Test; Gough's Perceptual
Illusions; Risk-taking; Sarason's Puzzle Choice; Sichel-Chandler version of
Stroop Test; Semantic Retrieval (Eysenck); Satiation/Cosatiation Tasks
(Block and Martin); Wechsler Preschool and Primary Scales of Intelligence
(Mazes); Peabody Picture Vocabulary Test; Raven's Progressive Matrices;
Wechsler Preschool and Primary Scales of Intelligence (Full Scale), Wechsler
Intelligence Scale for Children (Full Scale); Color/Form Test (Gaines); ETS
Thing Test; ETS Gestalt Completion Test; ETS Maze Tracing; Design prefer-
ence task, Form III; Day secret language; Persuasions Test (after Flavell);
Confidence in general information; Chapman Word Association Test; Eckblad
Assimilation Resistance Task; Strong Vocabulary Interest Blank; Illusion of
control experiment; Eysenck's semantic retrieval; WAIS-R Information,
WAIS-R Vocabulary Subtest, WAIS-R Digit Symbol Subtest, WAIS-R Object
Assembly Subtest, WAIS-R Similarities Subtest, WAIS-R Picture Completion
Subtest, WAIS-R Arithmetic Subtest, WAIS-R Comprehension Subtest,
WAIS-R Picture Arrangement Subtest, WAIS-R Block Design Subtest; Spon-
taneous Correspondence (Chittendon); Conservation of Number (Tuddenham),
Conservation of Mass (Tuddenham); Lowenfeld Mosaic Test; Instances (Wal-
lach & Kogan), Unusual Uses (Wallach & Kogan); Parallel Lines Test (Tor-
rance), Circles Test (Torrance); Word Association Forms I and II; Associative
drift; Metaphor Test, Similes Test (Schaefer); Sigel Object Sorting Test; Un-
structured Object Sorting (Gardner); McReynolds Concept Evaluation Test;
Classification of Poggles Task (Wallach & Caron); Classification of blues;
Tinkertoy classification task; Sex-role typing task; Pettigrew Category Width
Test; Matching Familiar Figures Test (Kagan); Rod and Frame Test (Witkin);
Preschool Embedded Figures Test (Coates), Children's Embedded Figures
Test (Karp & Konstaat), FASP Embedded Figures Test; Stanford Internal-Ex-
ternal Locus of Control Test; Vandenberg Mental Rotation Test; Book Orien-
tation Test I, Book Orientation Test II; Role-taking Cube (Flavell),
Role-taking Card (Flavell); Spatial Egocentrism (Piaget); Incidental Learning

(Banta), Incidental Learning I, II, and III; Incidental recall; Formulation of alternative hypotheses; Barriers extrapolation of consequences task; Narrative stories task; Landauer Short-term Memory Test; ETS Building Memory Test; Conceptions of badness test Resistance to Temptation Test (Ward); Distribution of rewards; Moral Judgment Test (Selman), Moral behavior situational tests; Defining Issues Test (Rest); Washington University Sentence Completion Test (Loevinger); Interpersonal Problem Solving Task (Spivack & Shure); Standardized Free Play Situation (After Murphy's World Test); Kelly Rep Test; Q-Sort of subjects by subject-nominated peers and adults; Self and Ideal Self Q-Sort; Spence Personal Attributes Questionnaires; School Records; Microcomputer-administered personality inventory (flexible placement); Adjective Q-Sort by subject of ideal love object; Core-conflict themes interview (videotaped); Preferred play activities (as observed by nursery school teachers); Sex-role-stereotyping toys; Self-reported free-time activities interview (checklist); Self-reported occupational interests interview; Maternal reports of child's free-time activities; Q-derived indices of agency, communion, and nonstereotyped characteristics; Environmental Q-Sort (Block & Block) completed by interviewer after home visit; ETS Alternative Uses Tasks, Guilford Alternate Uses (Form A); Stanford Internal-External Locus of Control; Interpersonal Problem Solving (Spivack and Shure); Affective responsiveness procedure (Galvanic Skin Conductance); Videotaping of expressive behaviors by subject; Adult Attachment interview (videotaped); Phenomenology of Emotion (Block); Physiognomic Perception (Ehrman); Family Interaction Situations (Mother-child, Father-child, Mother-Father-child); Personality Inventory (Mothers and Fathers); Block and Block Environmental Q-Sort by subject; Retrospective CRPR Q-Sort by subject of father during high school years; Adjective Q-sort completed by interviewer after home visit; Environmental Q-Sort by subject; Retrospective CRPR Q-Sort by subject of father of during high school years; Retrospective SRPR Q-Sort by subject of mother during high school years; Adjective Q-Sort by subject of mother; Adjective Q-Sort by subject of father; Questions regarding family context; CRPR Q-Sort by subject of "How I would ideally raise my own children"

REPRESENTATIVE REFERENCES:

Block, J., Block, J. H., & Keyes, S. (1988). Longitudinally foretelling drug usage in adolescence: Early childhood personality and environmental precursors. *Child Development, 59*, 336-355.

Block, J., Gjerde, P. S., & Block, J. H. (in press). Personality antecedents of depressive tendencies at age 18: A prospective study. *Journal of Abnormal and Social Psychology.*

Block, J. H., & Block, J. (1980). The role of ego-control and ego-resiliency in the organization of behavior. In W. A. Collines (Ed.), *The Minnesota symposia on child psychology: Vol. 13.* Hillsdale, NJ: Lawrence Erlbaum.

Block, J. H., Block, J., & Gjerde, P. S. (1986). The personality of children prior to divorce: A prospective study. *Child Development, 57,* 827-840.

CURRENT STATUS OF THE STUDY:

a. A further wave of data collection is planned for 1996.
b. Most data are in machine-readable format.
c. The data are available for restricted secondary analysis from the study contact person.

■ The Veterans Administration Normative Aging Study (NAS), 1963

Bossé, Raymond; Vokonas, Pantel; and Aldwin, Carolyn M.

Contact Person: Raymond Bossé
Address: Veterans Administration Medical Center
200 Springs Road
Building 70
Bedford, MA 01730
Telephone No.: (617) 275-7500, ext. 740

SUBSTANTIVE TOPICS COVERED:

The study examines the relationship between normal aging and the natural history of chronic diseases, changes that occur over time and their descriptions, correlations among large numbers of variables, and the delineation of true age change.

CHARACTERISTICS OF THE ORIGINAL SAMPLE

Year the study began: 1963
Subject selection process: A panel study was done of veteran males ages 25-75. The subjects incorporated a broad socioeconomic status spectrum and were not geographically mobile. The sample was prescreened for the following high levels of health: absence of chronic physical and mental disease, and blood pressure $\leq 140/90$; and geographic stability.
Total number of subjects at Time 1: N = 2,280
Ages at Time 1: 25-80 yrs.
Sex distribution: 100% male
Socioeconomic status: 60% middle/upper middle class, 40% working class (approximately)
Race/ethnicity: 92% white, 6% Hispanic, 2% African-American

Years of Completed Waves:[a]

Years	N=	Age ranges
1963-1968	2,280	21-80 yrs. (Cycle 1)[b]
1969-1990	1,800	27-92 yrs. (Cycles 2-9)

Comments:
a. Other waves were completed in 1968, 1973 and 1978.
b. Data collection is best described as continuous, with data being collected in cycles as opposed to waves. Cycle intervals for data collected varied in accordance with type of data being collected. Biomedical data collection occurred at 3-year intervals; intervals for psychosocial data collection varied according to type of data being collected and time period of the study as a whole (e.g., retired Ss receive a Work and Retirement Survey; Ss aged 52 years and younger are retested at 5-year intervals, whereas Ss older than 52 years are retested at 3-year intervals.)

INFORMATION ON SAMPLE ATTRITION:

During the 27-year period of study, approximately 480 of 2,280 Ss (21.1%) were not retrieved for further study. Sample attrition occurred at the rate of roughly 1% per year. Main reasons for sample attrition included deaths (350 as of 1990), moving away, and dropouts. The core sample consists of approximately 1,800 Ss.

CONSTRUCTS MEASURED: INSTRUMENTS USED[1]

Biomedical Measures

Clinical examination: Standardized medical history and review of systems, physical examination (clinical findings by organ system; height and weight, blood pressure: both arms, sitting, supine, standing, heart rate), biochemical studies (blood count, creatinine, uric acid, calcium, phosphorus, bilirubin, cholesterol, triglycerides, total protein, albumin, globulin, glucose tolerance), electrocardiogram, and medication history

Morbidity and mortality: Diseases (medical diagnoses coded according to ICDA-8), operations (surgical procedures coded according to ICDA-8), and mortality (date and causes(s) of death as per death certificate and corroborating medical information, coded according to ICDA-8)

Symptom reports: Cornell Medical Index (self-report physical and psychological symptoms) (Brodman et al.) (Mailed to Ss one month before examination)

Anthropometric examination and pulmonary function testing: Physical anthropometry (30 lengths and breadths; 10 circumferences; triceps and subscapular skinfolds, grip strength), and pulmonary function (forced vital capacity, forced expiratory volume in 1 sec., ATS respiratory questionnaire, chest X ray)

Special senses: Ophthalmology/optometry (retinal field, visual acuity, depth perception, pupil reaction, muscle action, fundus exam, glaucoma test), audiology (pure tone audiometry, speech reception and discrimination thresholds, air and bone conduction thresholds)

Psychosocial Measures

Phase I: 1961-1968

Social Screening Inventory (1961-1968): Social characteristics and networks, military experience, educational, occupational, residence, and family history

Psychological Assessment (1965-1967): Group administration of 16PF (Catell et al.) (Forms A & B) and General Aptitude Test Battery (GATB B-1002), Allport-Vernon-Lindzey Study of Values, and the Strong Vocational Interest Blank (Form T or M)

Phase II: 1973-1980

Personality: 16PF (Form A), Eysenck Personality Inventory (EPI-Q) (Short Form)

Work and retirement (1975, 1978, 1981, 1984, 1987): Employment and retirement circumstances and attitudes, leisure activities, social characteristics, financial circumstances, self-reported health, life satisfaction, subjective well-being

Smoking and personality (1976): These measures were given in four surveys at quarterly intervals; the number of respondents varies from the baseline of 1,100

Survey 1 (79%): Experience inventory (Coan), Personal Opinion Survey (Coan et al.), and Well-being scale (Bradburn)

Survey 2 (82%): Life events questionnaire (Holmes-Rahe), Social desirability scale (Crowne-Marlowe), EASI-III temperament scales (Buss & Plomin), and Well-being scale (Bradburn)

Survey 3 (73%): 16PF (5 scales from the 1962 Form A), Hopelessness scale (Beck et al.), and Well-being scale (Bradburn)

Survey 4 (54%): Washington University Sentence Completion Test (Form 11-68) (Loevinger & Wessler), Traditional family ideology (Levinson & Huffman), Personal security (Knutson), Eysenck Personality Inventory Form A (Eysenck & Eysenck), Mid-life crisis scale (Costa & McCrae), Well-being scale (Bradburn), Mood scale (Nowlis), and Life satisfaction measure (Farberow)

Life concerns (1977): Questionnaire (concerns in life, the Bradburn Well-being scale, and several open-ended items regarding goals, concerns, interests, life changes over the past 10 years, and the mid-life crisis) (Gould)

Phase III: 1985-present

Personality: Minnesota Multiphasic Personality Inventory-2, of the Eysenck Personality Inventory (EPI-Q) (Short form)

Social support (1985, 1988): Social networks, quantitative and qualitative support, received social support, life stress (ELSI; Aldwin), hassles, mental health (SCL-90-R; Derogatis), self-rated health, activities of daily living, and Optimism scale (Scheier & Carver)

Military and life experience (1990): Timing and duration of military service, effects on subsequent life, combat exposure (Keane et al.), Mississippi Post Traumatic Stress Disorder (Keane et al.), psychopathy (Levenson), CES-D

(Radloff), and Family Environment Scale (Short Form) (for both family of origin and of procreation)

Phase IV: 1988-present

Health and social behavior (1988-present): Brief Symptom Inventory, marital quality, quantitative and qualitative social support, coping (DeLongis), self-rated health, activities of daily living, employment or retirement circumstances and satisfaction, and financial status

Stress and coping (1988-present): Perceived Stress Scale (Cohen et al.), Stress and coping interview (multiple assessment of stress) (DeLongis et al.), and coping (DeLongis, 1988)

Health Behavior (smoking; drinking): Standardized interview (amount and type of tobacco smoked, age started, consumption of cigarettes, cigars, and pipes); Questionnaire (frequency and type of alcohol consumed, social context of drinking, problems)

Type A Behavior Pattern (1984): Jenkins Activity Survey (Form N)

Comments:

1. Biomedical Domain: Participants report every 3 years (age 52 or older) or 5 years (younger than age 52) for a comprehensive biomedical exam, including a medical history and a physical exam, administered by a board-certified internist. In addition, blood and urine samples are collected, ophthalmological and aural testing is conducted, and men are asked about medicine usage, and about surgical procedures or hospitalizations they have undergone. This exam defines their "cycle"; as of 1990, 77% of the men are in their 5th to 7th cycles. Visits are conducted on an outpatient basis. Biomedical areas of study include clinical medicine, special senses, dental health, anthropometry, and causes of morbidity and mortality.

Originally the anthropometric sequence was conducted as a separate data collection routine, with men reporting every 5 years regardless of age. Since 1985, this exam is conducted at the same time as the biomedical exam. In this exam, height, weight, and more than 30 body lengths, breadths, and circumferences are obtained.

Psychosocial Domain: Psychosocial data collection can be divided into four phases. In Phase I (1961-1968), initial data were collected. The Social Screening Survey was used to screen men for admission to the study, and to obtain basic demographic information (e.g., marital status, education, occupation), as well as information on their family life and geographic stability. Between 1965 and 1967, about half the men (N = 1,189) received the General Aptitude Test Battery (GATB: U.S. Department of Labor, 1967) and the 16PF questionnaire (Cattell et al., 1970; 1962 version Forms A & B) in small groups. These men were also given the Allport-Vernon-Lindzey Study of Values and the Strong Vocational Interest Blank to complete at home and return by mail.

In Phase II (1973-1980), psychosocial data were collected by mail surveys. With a sample of about 1,100 men, an array of data was obtained, via mail surveys, to examine relations between personality and smoking. During this phase, studies of work and retirement also were initiated.

In Phase III (1985-present), some studies begun during Phase II have continued and new ones have been initiated. Work and retirement data are gathered via mail surveys sent to Ss age 45 and older, or to those who have been retired for fewer than 7 years. These surveys were administered triennially between 1975 and 1987; since that date, information has been obtained via a survey the men are sent the month before their scheduled medical exam. Information on both qualitative and quantitative aspects of social support was obtained in two mail surveys in 1985 and 1988. In 1986 the NAS participated in the Minnesota Multiphasic Personality Inventory (MMPI) Restandardization project. Men were administered Form AX, which includes items from both the MMPI and the MMPI-2. During 1990 a survey on military experiences was administered to obtain additional data on the effects of military service, combat exposure, and the subsequent life course.

In Phase IV (1988-present), data are collected on mental health, stress and coping via questionnaire sent to Ss in the month prior to their scheduled biomedical examination. In addition, at the time of their medical exam, they also complete questionnaire measure of hassles, and are administered a semistructured interview on stress and coping.

Health Behavior Domain: Since the 1970s studies of smoking and drinking behavior have been conducted, both by mail and by structured interview at the time of the biomedical examination. In 1984 the Jenkins Activity Survey (an assessment of Type A behavior pattern) was administered by mail.

REPRESENTATIVE REFERENCES:

Aldwin, C., Spiro, A. III, Levenson, M. R., & Bossé, R. (1989). Longitudinal findings from the normative aging study. I: Does mental health change with age? *Psychology and Aging, 4*(3), 295-306.

Bell, R., Rose, C. L., & Damon, A. (1972). The Normative Aging Study: An interdisciplinary and longitudinal study of health and aging. *Aging and Human Development, 3,* 5-17.

Bossé, R., Ekerdt, D., & Silbert J. (1984). The Veterans Administration Normative Aging Study. In S. A. Mednick, M. Harway, & K. M. Finello (Eds.), *Handbook of longitudinal research: Vol. 2. Teenage and adult cohorts.* New York: Praeger.

Sparrow, D., Weiss, S. T., Vokonas, P. S., Cupples, L. A., Ekerdt, D. J., & Colton, T. (1988). Forced vital capacity and the risk of hypertension: The normative aging study. *American Journal of Epidemiology, 127,* 734-741.

CURRENT STATUS OF THE STUDY:

a. Further waves of data collection are planned.

b. Data are in machine-readable format.

c. Data are available for secondary analysis in collaboration with the principal investigators.

■ Personality Changes in Aging: A Longitudinal Study of Community Residents, 1955

Britton, Joseph H.; and Britton, Jean O.

Contact Person: Joseph H. Britton
Address: 500 East Marylyn Avenue
                          Apartment 124
                          State College, PA 16801
Telephone No.:   (814) 238-4239

SUBSTANTIVE TOPICS COVERED:

This study examines the factors related to consistency or change in personality and adjustment of older adults over time; social-psychological correlates of survival and differences between survivors; and how a small community regards its aged members, by investigating the social norms and expectations for the behavior of older persons.

CHARACTERISTICS OF THE ORIGINAL SAMPLE:

Year the study began: 1955
Subject selection process: A rural community in Pennsylvania provided the population pool from which a sample of older residents (age 64 or older) was followed. Community selection was based on stability of residents; similarity to other small communities; independence from large cities or institutions (e.g., industries or universities); and not having been previously researched. Criteria also required that the community's population needed to be both large enough to provide and maintain an adequate sample of older residents and small enough to enable following all of such residents.
Total number of subjects at Time 1: N = 205
Ages at Time 1: 64-84 yrs.
Sex distribution: 62.4% female, 37.6% male
Socioeconomic status: 75% middle/upper middle class, 25% working class
Race/ethnicity: 100% white

Years of Completed Waves:[a]

Years	N=	Age ranges
1955	205	64-84 yrs.
1956	146	65-85 yrs.
1962	81	71-91 yrs.
1965	53	74-94 yrs.

Comments:
a. The investigators updated a list of their subjects in 1967, 1969, and 1971 to monitor rates of survival.

INFORMATION ON SAMPLE ATTRITION:

During the 10-year period of study, 152 of 205 Ss (74.1%) were not retrieved for further study. Sample attrition was due to subjects' moving away and deaths. The core sample consists of 53 Ss.

CONSTRUCTS MEASURED: INSTRUMENTS USED

Subject's reports of participation in everyday activities of living: Chicago Activity Inventory
Attitude: Chicago Attitude Inventory
Attitudes toward human relations and traits of social participation: Personal Relations and Sociability Scale
Degree of consensus with community views: Opinion Conformity Scale
Personality and Adjustment: Thematic Apperception Test
Overall personal adjustment: Judge's Interview Rating, Cavan Adjustment Rating Scale
Interviewer's observations and impressions: Interviewer's Rating
Subject's reputation: Reputation Rating (from Community-wide survey)
Intellectual Functioning: WAIS Similarities Scale
Demographic and psychosocial information: 1955 Information Sheet, 1955 Interview Schedule, 1956 Interview Schedule

REPRESENTATIVE REFERENCES:

Britton, J. H. (1963). Dimensions of adjustment of older adults. *Journal of Gerontology, 18,* 60-65.
Britton, J. H., & Britton, J. O. (1962). Expectations for older persons in a rural community: Solving personal problems. *Geriatrics, 17,* 602-608.
Britton, J. H., & Britton, J. O. (1967). The middle-aged and older rural person and his family. In E. G. Youmans (Ed.), *Older rural Americans: A sociological perspective* (pp. 44-74). Lexington: University of Kentucky Press.
Britton, J. H., & Britton, J. O. (1972). *Personality changes in aging: A longitudinal study of community residents.* New York: Springer.

CURRENT STATUS OF THE STUDY:

a. No further waves of data collection are planned.
b. Most of the data were in machine-readable format.
c. Data are not available for secondary analysis.

■ The Collaborative Perinatal Project (NCPP), 1959

Broman, Sarah

Contact person: Sarah Broman
Address: Office 8CO6
                 Federal Building
                 7550 Wisconsin Avenue
                 NINDS/National Institute of Health
                 Bethesda, MD 20892
Telephone No.:   (301) 496-5821

SUBSTANTIVE TOPICS COVERED:

The study examines "the developmental consequences of complications in pregnancy and the perinatal period" originating in "relationships between conditions affecting parents and the occurrence and course of abnormalities in their offspring." Salient among conditions affecting parents investigated are "normal and abnormal conditions of pregnancy, labor and delivery; and environmental factors (e.g., social, economic, and biological)." Among offspring, the study follows the onset of such abnormalities of the nervous system as "cerebral palsy, mental retardation, behavior disorders; and neurological or sensory defects" as they occur at "delivery, during infancy, or in early childhood." The study also examines factors contributing to "fetal loss (early and late); prematurity, and mortality in infancy and early childhood; the relationship of physical and mental development in early childhood to genetic, biological and environmental factors; the identification of events in the postnatal environment related to the later development of disturbances of structure and function in the nervous system"; and attempts to provide more "precise definitions of the reproductive process and its outcome." Data were gathered from 12 medical research sites in the United States (Broman, 1984).

CHARACTERISTICS OF THE TOTAL ORIGINAL SAMPLE:

Year the study began: 1959
Subject selection process: See information by specific site.
Total number of subjects at Time 1: N = 53,043
Ages at Time 1: Birth
Sex distribution: Approximately equal numbers of females and males
Socioeconomic status:[a] 46.6 (mean SEI score); 56.6 (white Ss)–38.2 (African-American Ss). See information by site.
Race/ethnicity: 47.2% African-American, 45.1% white, 6.8% Puerto Rican, 1% other

Comments:
a. Socioeconomic status was defined by a socioeconomic index (SEI) score. This index was adapted from the United States Bureau of the Census. The index consists of a composite of scores on the education (0-90) and occupation of the head of the household (0-90) and the family income (0-100). The three subscores were "derived from cumulative percentages in the total sample." The socioeconomic index (SEI) averages the three scores

(education, family income, and occupation) when available, or is based on two scores otherwise. The SEI index ranges in scores from 0 to 95, with 95 representing the highest socioeconomic status. Socioeconomic status is presented in terms of the average SEI score for the sample in question, along with the range of average SEI scores by race.

Years of Completed Waves

Years[a]	N=	Age ranges
1959-1960	53,043	Birth
1966-1967	38,624	7 yrs.

Comments:
a. Ss were followed at 4 and 8 months, and at 1, 3, and 4 years of age at every collaborating institution.

INFORMATION ON SAMPLE ATTRITION:

During the 7-year period of study, 14,419 of 53,043 Ss (27.1%) were not retrieved for further study.

SITE: BOSTON LYING-IN HOSPITAL

CHARACTERISTICS OF THE ORIGINAL SAMPLE:

Year the study began: 1959
Subject selection process: All clinic patients were selected for the study.
Total number of subjects at Time 1: N = 12,193
Ages at Time 1: Birth.
Sex distribution: Approximately equal numbers of females and males
Socioeconomic status: 61.4 (mean SEI score); 61.4 (white Ss)–54.3 (Puerto Rican Ss)
Race/ethnicity: 89% white, 9.6% African-American, 1.1% Asian-American, 0.1% Hispanic, 0.2% other

Years of Completed Waves:

Years	N=	Age ranges
1959	12,193	Birth
1966	8,645	7 yrs.

INFORMATION ON SAMPLE ATTRITION:

During the 7-year period of study, 3,548 of 12,193 Ss (29.1%) were not retrieved for further study. The core sample consists of 8,645.

SITE: PROVIDENCE LYING-IN HOSPITAL:

For further information, see Lipsitt, Lewis P.; Tsuang, Ming T.; and Buka, Stephen L.

SITE: CHILDREN'S HOSPITAL, BUFFALO

CHARACTERISTICS OF THE ORIGINAL SAMPLE:

Year the study began: 1960
Subject selection process: Private patients seen by participating obstetricians were randomly selected per participating obstetrician. Walk-in patients, women who did not intend to deliver at Children's Hospital, and women who planned to move out of the area were excluded from the sample.
Total number of subjects and Time 1: N = 2,469
Ages at Time 1: Birth
Sex distribution: Approximately equal numbers of females and males
Socioeconomic status: 78.1 (mean SEI score); 78.6% (white Ss)–62.8 (African-American Ss)
Race/ethnicity: 96.4% white, 2.5% African-American, 0.5% Hispanic, 0.3% Asian-American, 3% other

Years of Completed Waves:

Years	N=	Age ranges
1960	2,469	Birth
1967	2,115	7 yrs.

INFORMATION ON SAMPLE ATTRITION:

During the 7-year period of study, 354 of 2,469 Ss (14.3%) were not retrieved for further study. The core sample consists of 2,115 Ss.

SITE: COLUMBIA-PRESBYTERIAN MEDICAL CENTER

CHARACTERISTICS OF THE ORIGINAL SAMPLE:

Year the study began: 1959
Subject selection process: Subjects selected were all admitted clinic patients.
Total number of subjects at Time 1: N = 2,138
Ages at Time 1: Birth
Sex distribution: Approximately equal numbers of females and males

Socioeconomic status: 51.3 (mean SEI score); 53.4 (African-American Ss)–45.7 (Puerto Rican Ss)
Race/ethnicity: 40.6% African-American, 28.8% white, 0.4% Hispanic, 2.4% other

Years of Completed Waves:

Years	N=	Age ranges
1959	2,138	Birth
1966	1,707	7 yrs.

INFORMATION ON SAMPLE ATTRITION:

During the 15-year period of study, 431 of 2,138 Ss (20.2%) were not retrieved for further study. The core sample consists of 1,707 Ss.

SITE: NEW YORK MEDICAL COLLEGE

CHARACTERISTICS OF THE ORIGINAL SAMPLE:

Year the study began: 1959
Subject selection process: Subject selected were all admitted clinic patients.
Total number of subjects at Time 1: N = 4,474
Ages at Time 1: Birth
Sex distribution: Approximately equal numbers of females and males
Socioeconomic status: 39.3 (mean SEI score); 42.9 (white Ss)–37.3 (Puerto Rican Ss)
Race/ethnicity: 59.2% Hispanic, 34.1% African-American, 6.3% white, 0.1% Asian-American, 0.2% other

Years of Completed Waves:

Years	N=	Age ranges
1959	4,474	Birth
1966	1,228[a]	7 yrs.

Comments:
a. Number of Ss followed is spuriously low due to closing this site in the midst of data collection for the 7-year follow-up.

INFORMATION ON SAMPLE ATTRITION:

During the 7-year period of study, 3,246 of 4,474 Ss (72.6%) were not retrieved for further study. The core sample consists of 1,228 Ss.

SITE: PENNSYLVANIA HOSPITAL

CHARACTERISTICS OF THE ORIGINAL SAMPLE:

Year the study began: 1959

Subject selection process: Subjects included comprised of all admitted clinic pa-
    tients. The study excluded clients having unregistered emergency deliveries;
    clients intending to have delivery elsewhere; and walk-ins.

Total number of subjects at Time 1: N = 9,792

Ages at Time 1: Birth

Sex distribution: Approximately equal numbers of females and males

Socioeconomic status: 38.8 (mean SEI score); 40.4 (white Ss)–31.2 (Puerto Rican
    Ss)

Race/ethnicity: 87.3% African-American, 9.4% white, 3.2% Hispanic, 0.1% Asian-
    American, 0.1% other

Years of Completed Waves:

Years	N=	Age ranges
1959	9,792	Birth
1966	7,461	7 yrs.

INFORMATION ON SAMPLE ATTRITION

During the 7-year period of study, 2,331 of 9,792 Ss (23.8%) were not retrieved
for further study. The core sample consists of 7,461 Ss.

SITE: JOHNS HOPKINS HOSPITAL

CHARACTERISTICS OF THE ORIGINAL SAMPLE:

Year the study began: 1959

Subject selection process: Subjects selected were clinic patients living within a 25-
    mile radius of metropolitan Baltimore. The study excluded transient clients,
    those referred to county clinics for obstetrical care, and walk-ins.

Total number of subjects at Time 1: N = 3,549

Ages at Time 1: Birth

Sex distribution: Approximately equal numbers of females and males

Socioeconomic status: 40.6 (mean SEI score); 41.2% (white Ss)–40.5 (African-
    American Ss)

Race/ethnicity: 76.4% African-American, 23.4% white, 0.2% other

Years of Completed Waves:

Years	N=	Age ranges
1959	3,549	Birth
1966	2,903	7 yrs.

INFORMATION ON SAMPLE ATTRITION:

During the 7-year period of study, 646 of 3,549 Ss (18.2%) were not retrieved for further study. The core sample consists of 2,903 Ss.

SITE: MEDICAL COLLEGE OF VIRGINIA

CHARACTERISTICS OF THE ORIGINAL SAMPLE:

Year the study began: 1959
Subject selection process: Clinic patients residing within a 50-mile radius of Richmond, Virginia. The study excluded clients who planned to place their child up for adoption; white welfare cases; and wards of the state residing in correctional institutions.
Total number of subjects at Time 1: N = 3,204
Ages at Time 1: Birth
Sex distribution: Approximately equal numbers of females and males.
Socioeconomic status: 33.3 (mean SEI score); 39.2 (white Ss)–31.3 (African-American Ss)
Race/ethnicity: 73.7% African-American, 25.1% white, 0.2% other

Years of Completed Waves:

Years	N=	Age ranges
1959	3,204	Birth
1966	2,669	7 yrs.

INFORMATION ON SAMPLE ATTRITION:

During the 7-year period of study, 535 of 3,204 Ss (16.7%) were not retrieved for further study. The core sample consists of 2,669 Ss.

SITE: UNIVERSITY OF TENNESSEE COLLEGE OF MEDICINE

CHARACTERISTICS OF THE ORIGINAL SAMPLE:

Year the study began: 1959
Subject selection process: Subjects were all admitted clinic patients residing within the city limits of Memphis, Tennessee.
Total number of subjects at Time 1: N = 3,523
Ages at Time 1: Birth
Sex distribution: Approximately equal numbers of females and males
Socioeconomic status: 32.3 (mean SEI score); 35.9 (white Ss)–32.3 (African-American Ss)
Race/ethnicity: 99.3% African-American, 0.7% white, 0.2% Asian-American

Years of Completed Waves:

Years	N=	Age ranges
1959	3,523	Birth
1966	2,800	7 yrs.

INFORMATION ON SAMPLE ATTRITION:

During the 7-year period of study, 723 of 3,523 Ss (20.5%) were not retrieved for further study. The core sample consists of 2,800 Ss.

SITE: CHARITY HOSPITAL, NEW ORLEANS

CHARACTERISTICS OF THE ORIGINAL SAMPLE:

Year the study began: 1959
Subject selection process: All African-American patients residing in Orleans Parish and assigned to Charity Hospital Services of Tulane or Louisiana State University. Sampling method was 10% systematic and based on all Outpatient Department numbers ending in zero. Some walk-in subjects were excluded.
Total number of subjects at Time 1: N = 2,582
Ages at Time 1: Birth
Sex distribution: Approximately equal numbers of females and males
Socioeconomic status: 30.1 (African-American Ss)
Race/ethnicity: 100% African-American

Years of Completed Waves:

Years	N=	Age ranges
1959	2,582	Birth
1966	2,119	7 yrs.

INFORMATION ON SAMPLE ATTRITION:

During the 7-year period of study, 463 of 2,582 Ss (17.9%) were not retrieved for further study. The core sample consists of 2,119 Ss.

SITE: UNIVERSITY OF MINNESOTA HOSPITAL

CHARACTERISTICS OF THE ORIGINAL SAMPLE:

Year the study began: 1959

Subject selection process: Subjects selected were all admitted clinic patients. Excluded women were those who never married; those divorced, widowed, or separated before the start of the current pregnancy; and those registered for the first time after 246 days of pregnancy.

Total number of subjects at Time 1: N = 3,147

Ages at Time 1: Birth

Sex distribution: Approximately equal numbers of females and males

Socioeconomic status: 60.1 (mean SEI score); 61.6% (African-American)-60.2 (white Ss)

Race/ethnicity: 94.1% white, 2% Asian-American, 0.7% African-American, 0.1% Hispanic, 3.1% other

Years of Completed Waves:

Years	N=	Age ranges
1959	3,147	Birth
1966	2,398	7 yrs.

INFORMATION ON SAMPLE ATTRITION:

During the 7-year period of study, 479 of 3,147 Ss (23.8%) were not retrieved for further study. The core sample consists of 2,398 Ss.

SITE: UNIVERSITY OF OREGON MEDICAL SCHOOL

CHARACTERISTICS OF THE ORIGINAL SAMPLE:

Year the study began: 1959

Subject selection process: Subjects selected were all admitted clinic patients residing within the Portland, Oregon, mailing area. The study excluded clients of private adoption agencies; medical students' wives; walk-ins; juvenile detention home and jail patients.

Total number of subjects at Time 1: N = 3,150

Ages at Time 1: Birth

Sex distribution: Approximately equal numbers of females and males

Socioeconomic status: 38.2 (mean SEI score); 39.7 (white Ss)–34.8 (African-American Ss)

Race/ethnicity: 71.1% white, 26.7% African-American, 0.2% Asian-American, and 2% other

Years of Completed Waves:

Years	N=	Age ranges
1959	3,150	Birth
1966	2,416	7 yrs.

INFORMATION ON SAMPLE ATTRITION:

During the 7-year period of study, 734 of 3,150 Ss (23.3%) were not retrieved for further study. The core sample consists of 2,416 Ss.

CONSTRUCTS MEASURED: INSTRUMENTS USED [ALL SITES]

Prenatal:

Physical history, health: Obstetric administrative record

Reproductive and gynecological history; medical history; socioeconomic status: Interview

Family history: Summary of antepartum hospitalization; interview

Labor and Delivery:

Repeat of prenatal and admissions history: Prenatal examination

Admission exam: Examination

Medical status: Laboratory record
Labor process: Labor room record
Delivery room events: Delivery room observation; delivery report
Medical history: Obstetric summary; anesthetic agents; summary of puerperium; placental exams (gross and microscopic)
Obstetric impressions: Obstetric diagnostic summary

Newborn:

Medical status: Neonatal examination
Nursery history: Nursery records; results of tests and procedures
Neurological status: Neurological examination
Medical history: Newborn Diagnostic Examination

4 Months:

Medical status: Pediatric examination
Medical history: Interval medical history

8 Months:

Motor and mental development: Bayley Scales of Mental and Motor Development
Infant behavior: Infant Behavior Profile; maternal behavior ratings

12 Months:

Neurological status: Neurological examination
Medical history: Interval medical history; diagnostic summary of one year

18 and 24 Months:

Medical history: Interval medical history

3 Years:

Language reception, auditory memory and discrimination, speech mechanism and production: Speech, language, and hearing examination
Medical history: Interval medical history

4 Years:

Intelligence: Stanford-Binet Intelligence Scale; Graham-Ernhart Block Sort Test
Motor coordination: Gross and fine motor tasks
Child's behavior: Behavior profile
Mother's intelligence: Science Research Associates non-verbal intelligence test

5 Years:

Medical history: Interval medical history

7 Years

Intelligence: Weschler Intelligence Scale; Goodenough-Harris Draw-A-Person Test; Bender Gestalt Test

Psycholinguistic abilities: Auditory-Vocal Association Test; Tactile Finger Recognition Test; Wide Range Achievement test

Child's behavior: Behavior profile

Family health and socioeconomic status: Family health history and socioeconomic status interview with mother

Neurological status: Pediatric neurological examination; visual screening and ophthalmology report

Medical history: Interval medical history; diagnostic summary for 1-7 years

8 Years:

Language comprehension and expression, auditory discrimination, speech mechanism and production: Speech, language, and hearing examination

REPRESENTATIVE REFERENCES:

Broman, S. (1984). The collaborative perinatal project: An overview. In Mednick, S. A., Harway, M., & Finello, K. M. (Eds.), *Handbook of longitudinal research: Vol. I* (pp. 185-215). New York: Praeger.

Broman, S., Nichols, P. L., Shaughnessy, P., & Kennedy, W. (1987). *Retardation in young children: A developmental study of cognitive deficit.* Hillsdale, NJ: Lawrence Erlbaum.

Hardy, J. B., Drage, J. S., & Jackson, E. C. (1979). *The first year of life: The collaborative perinatal project of the National Institute of Neurological and Communicative Disorders and Stroke.* Baltimore: The Johns Hopkins University Press.

Nichols, P. L., & Chen, T. (1981). *Minimal brain dysfunction: A prospective study.* Hillsdale, NJ: Lawrence Erlbaum.

CURRENT STATUS OF THE STUDY:

a. No further waves of data collection are planned.
b. Most of the data are in machine-readable format.
c. Data are available for secondary analysis through Dr. Bruce Amvacher or Dr. Margaret Adams at National Archives and Records Administration Reference and Reproduction Services, Machine-Readable Records Branch, Washington, DC 20409.

■ The Inteflex Longitudinal Study of Medical Students, 1972

Brown, Donald R.

Contact Person: Donald R. Brown
Address: The Center for Research on Learning and Teaching
                 University of Michigan
                 109 East Madison
                 Ann Arbor, MI 48104-2993
Telephone No.:   (313) 763-0161

SUBSTANTIVE TOPICS COVERED:

Initially, the study served to evaluate an experimental medical-educational program. A central focus of the study has been to examine the socialization of medical students into the medical profession. An evolving goal of the study has been to examine gender differences in terms of personality development, achievement, ethical orientation, values, and ideology in regard to social issues and health care delivery.

CHARACTERISTICS OF THE ORIGINAL SAMPLE:

Year the study began: 1972
Subject selection process: All students were enrolled in the Inteflex program at the University of Michigan between 1972 and 1989. In addition, matched controls were included.
Total number of subjects at Time 1: N = 350[a]
Ages at Time 1: 18 yrs.
Sex distribution: Approximately equal numbers of females and males at time of entrance for the Inteflex sample, and the undergraduate control sample (Control 1) for the first 10 years; 76% males, and 24% females for the Standard Medical School Program Ss (Control 2)
Socioeconomic status: Information was not available.
Race/ethnicity: 59% white, 30% Asian-American, 10% African-American, 1% Hispanic
Comments:
a. Each year a new cohort of 50 Ss is added. Follow-up of subjects continues for 10 years post-MD degrees.

Years of Completed Waves:

Years[a]	N=[b]	Age ranges[c]
Inteflex Program		
1972-1990	14	17-34 yrs.
1973-1990	80	17-33 yrs.
1974-1990	40	17-32 yrs.

Years of Completed Waves, Continued:

Years[a]	N=[b]	Age ranges[c]
1975-1990	31	17-31 yrs.
1976-1990	23	17-30 yrs.
1977-1990	35	17-29 yrs.
1978-1990	32	17-28 yrs.
1979-1990	23	17-27 yrs.
1980-1990	83	17-26 yrs.
1981-1990	30	17-25 yrs.
1982-1990	26	17-24 yrs.
1983-1990	35	17-23 yrs.
1984-1990	36	17-22 yrs.
1985-1990	43	17-21 yrs.
1986-1990	39	17-20 yrs.
Undergraduate: (Control Group 1)		
1972-1990	320	17-22 yrs.
Standard Medical School Program (Control Group 2)		
1972-1986	110	21-35 yrs.
1973-1987	94	21-35 yrs.
1974-1988	95	21-35 yrs.
1975-1989	110	21-35 yrs.
1976-1990	114	21-35 yrs.
1977-1990	121	21-34 yrs.
1978-1990	118	21-33 yrs.
1979-1990	102	21-32 yrs.
1980-1990	106	21-31 yrs.
1981-1990	106	21-30 yrs.
1982-1990	87	21-29 yrs.
1983-1990	83	21-28 yrs.
1984-1990	84	21-27 yrs.
1985-1990	82	21-26 yrs.
1986-1990	90	21-25 yrs.

Comments:

a. Years listed represent an estimate of the earliest year during which data for that cohort were collected and either the approximate year when data collection was concluded for a cohort or the latest year during which data were collected.

b. The number of Ss listed on each line represent distinct cohorts based on differing years of entry into the various programs.

c. Beginning Inteflex students were 17-18 years old when they entered the sample. They were then followed through to their postgraduate 10 age, which is about 30 to 34 years of age. Control Group 1 subjects were only interviewed into their senior year, so they began at 17-18 years old and ended at 21-22 years, unless they entered the University of Michigan Medical School. In that case, they were followed through the medical school years as Control Group 2 subjects and out into their 10th postgraduate year. Standard medical school subjects thus began at 21-22 years of age and were followed through their early thirties. Age ranges listed represent the youngest age of Ss entering a program, and the likely oldest age of Ss at the conclusion of their participation in the study.

INFORMATION ON SAMPLE ATTRITION:

Excluding the first year of data collection (1972), when the attrition rate was un-usually high (71%), attrition rates ranged from 10% to 54% for Inteflex students over an 18-year period, with a cumulative sample of 352 subjects. Comparable but less intensive data collection was undertaken in their freshman and senior years for Control Group 1 subjects (those who had applied to Inteflex but were not accepted and went to the University of Michigan as undergraduates). They numbered about 320 at initial testing and experienced a 10-15% attrition rate. Data collection for Control Group 2 students (those who were enrolled in the Standard Medical School Program) began with the entering class of 1976 and continued through their 10th postgraduate year. Their attrition rates ranged from 31% to 47%, and their cumulative number is about 1,350 subjects. It should be noted that during the academic phase of the data collection, attrition ranged only from 5% to 10% for most samples. Also of relevance is that the size of the initial Inteflex samples for the first 10 years was 50; since then it has dropped to 44. Similarly, for 10 years the Medical School accepted 220 students, but since then has downsized its entering class to 160—all of which has affected the beginning sample size over the years.

CONSTRUCTS MEASURED: INSTRUMENTS USED

Competence: National Medical Board Examination (NBME) Scores Parts I and II; academic performance; clinical ratings; postgraduate appointments (residency, and so forth); long-term follow-up of performance in the field

Liberal education: Comparison of Inteflex student electives and required curriculum transcripts with standard students and control premedical students for breadth and depth in non-preprofessional courses; assessment by interview and questionnaires of student's interests and course evaluations each term; assessment by standard instruments rated for cultural sophistication, breadth of interests, and other relevant dimensions of student development

Professional outlook: Student Development and Personality Measures; student and faculty interviews; ratings of clinical performances; choices of electives and major; post-graduate area choices and performance

Educational experimentation: Faculty interviews; student course evaluations; student census information; spin-off to the curricula of the two colleges; curriculum change

Student development: Assessment by interview and questionnaires of student's attitudes and development; assessment by interview of faculty impressions regarding Inteflex student attitudes and development; assessment by interview of students attitudes towards and use of counseling services; analysis of counseling services in terms of staff, numbers of students seen, timing and effectiveness of intervention; analysis of records and experiences of students who left the program, took leaves, or went on irregular programs; analysis of students course evaluations; assessment of effectiveness of student activities, self-governance, and interaction by interview and questionnaires

Vocational interest: Strong Vocational Interest Blank (SVIB)

Demographic information, college choice, concentration plans, value and attitudinal plans: ETS College Student Questionnaire (Parts 1 and 2) (CSQ)

Personality: Omnibus Personality Interview (OPI), Personality Research Form (PRF) (Jackson)

Perception of program (satisfactions and dissatisfactions), ideology, values concerning health care delivery, family and ethical issues: Fourth Year Interview (4th YRINT), Fourth Year Research Questionnaire (4YRQ)

Perceptions of training, career update, values, perceptions of medical profession, and personal life: Post Graduate Year Questionnaire (PGY)

Education satisfaction/dissatisfaction; social, medical, ethical issues; family and professional demands: Initial Research Questionnaire (IRQ), Medical School Questionnaire

REPRESENTATIVE REFERENCES:

Brown, D. R. (1976). A longitudinal program of evaluation of socialization and achievement in medical, legal and liberal arts programs. In Gruitjr, VanderKamp, & Crombag (Eds.), *Prospects in psychological and educational measurement*. New York: John Wiley.

Grant, L., Genero, N., Nurius, P., Moore, W. E., & Brown, D. R. (1986). Gender and time variations in medical student's value development. *Sex Roles, 15,* 95-108.

Grant, L., Ward, K. B., Brown, D., & Moore, W. (1987). The development of work and family commitments among women and men medical students. *Journal of Family Issues, 8*(2), 176-198.

Sloan, T. S., & Brown, D. R. (1978). The Clark-Trow Student Typology and applicants to a six-year A.B.-M.D. program. *Journal of College Student Personnel, 19,* 6-10.

CURRENT STATUS OF THE STUDY:

a. Further waves of data collection are planned.
b. Most of the data are in machine-readable format.
c. Data are available for secondary analysis from the study contact person on a limited basis.

■ Vassar Longitudinal Study, 1954

Brown, Donald R.; Sanford, Nevitt; and Freedman, Mervin

Contact Person: Donald R. Brown
Address: The Center for Research on Learning and Teaching
                109 East Madison
                University of Michigan
                Ann Arbor, MI 48109
Telephone No.: (313) 763-0161

SUBSTANTIVE TOPICS COVERED:

This study examines the total life history of Vassar College graduates with emphasis on educational development (1954), and personality, academic performance, and women's roles (1957-1958).

CHARACTERISTICS OF THE ORIGINAL SAMPLE:

Year the study began: 1954

Subject selection process: Subjects who volunteered for the 1954 wave were graduates of the Vassar classes of 1925 to 1935. In a second wave, the 1957-1958
college freshmen at Vassar were examined through their senior year, with
1962 and 1978 follow-ups.

Total number of subjects at Time 1: N = 50

Ages at Time 1: 50-60 yrs. (approximately)

Sex distribution: 100% female

Socioeconomic status: 100% middle/upper middle class

Race/ethnicity: 95% white, 3% Native American, 2% African-American

Years of Completed Waves:

Years	N=	Age ranges
(Cohort 1: Graduates, Classes of 1929 to 1935)[a]		
1954	50	50-60 yrs.
1960	48	56-66 yrs.
(Cohort 2: College Freshmen, Classes of 1957 and 1958)[b]		
1957-1958	300	17-18 yrs.
1963	200	22-23 yrs.
1979	100	38-39 yrs.

Comments:
a. Data collected from Ss in Cohort 1 were part of the Alumnae Assessment Study.
b. Data collected from Ss in Cohort 2 were part of the Ideal Student Study.

INFORMATION ON SAMPLE ATTRITION:

During the 24-year period of study, 2 of 50 Ss (4%) from the Alumni Assessment Study were not retrieved for further study. Approximately 200 of 300 Ss
(66%) from the Ideal Student Study were not retrieved for further study.

CONSTRUCTS MEASURED: INSTRUMENTS USED

Intellectual functioning and achievement: Scholastic Aptitude Test scores, College
Entrance Examination Board scores

Authoritarianism and its opposites, masculinity/femininity, attitudes and personality traits: Mellon Test Battery

Personality: Drawing completion test, Figure preference tests

Demographic information: Biographical data sheet

Educational history and response to college as an educational institution; leisure,
social, recreation activities and interests; general values; and family history:
Student interviews (Assessment Study)

Attitudes, authoritarianism, political values: Vassar Attitudinal Inventory

Integrative intelligence: Terman-Concept Mastery Test

REPRESENTATIVE REFERENCES:

Brown, D. R. (1956). Some educational patterns. In N. Sanford (Ed.), Personality development
    during the college years. *The Journal of Social Issues, 12,* 44-60.
Brown, D. R. (1960). Non-intellective qualities and the perception of the ideal student by college
    faculty. *The Journal of Educational Sociology, 33,* 269-278.
Brown, D. R. (1962). Personality, college environment, and academic productivity. In N. Sanford
    (Ed.), *The American college: A psychological and social interpretation of the higher learn-
    ing.* New York: John Wiley.
Brown, D. R. (1964). Academic excellence: The crucial effects of environment and personality. In
    College and character. New York: John Wiley.

CURRENT STATUS OF THE STUDY:

   a. Further waves of data collection are planned.
   b. Most of the data are in machine-readable format.
   c. Data are available for secondary analysis from the study contact person.

■ A First Language, 1962

Brown, Roger; Bellugi, Ursula; and Fraser, Colin

Contact Person: Roger Brown
Address: Department of Psychology
                  Harvard University
                  William James Hall
                  Cambridge, MA 02138
Telephone No.:   (617) 495-3873

SUBSTANTIVE TOPICS COVERED:

   The study examines the development of English as a first language in preschool
children and investigates the stages of language development in children.

CHARACTERISTICS OF THE ORIGINAL SAMPLE:

Year the study began: 1962
Subject selection process: Three children were chosen from a pool of approxi-
    mately 30 children, based on the following criteria: (a) were beginning to
    speak multiword sentences, (b) had highly intelligible speech, and (c) were
    highly voluble. All children were firstborns.
Total number of subjects at Time 1: N = 3
Ages at Time 1: 18-27 mos.
Sex distribution: 66.7% female, 33.3% male

Socioeconomic status: 67% middle class, 33% working class
Race/ethnicity: 67% white, 33% African-American

Years of Completed Waves:[a]

Years	N=	Age ranges
1962	3	18-27 mos.
1963	2	39 mos.
1972	2	12 yrs., 3 mos.

Comments:
a. Data collection occurred on a continuous testing schedule and cannot be appropriately described in terms of data waves. A major effort of data collection was undertaken during the first year of the study. However, the above information about the years of the data collection should not be regarded as the full range of time points in which data were collected.

INFORMATION ON SAMPLE ATTRITION:

During the 12-year period of study, 1 of 3 Ss (33.3%) was not retrieved for further study. The core sample consists of 2 Ss.

CONSTRUCTS MEASURED: INSTRUMENTS USED

Speech acts, Mean Length of Utterance (MLU), phonetic and paralinguistic aspects of speech, grammar: Audio tapes of spontaneous speech of the children alone, with their mothers and with others (Conversations were taped in the home)

REPRESENTATIVE REFERENCES:

Brown, R. (1968). The development of Wh-questions in child speech. *Journal of Verbal Learning and Verbal Behavior, 7,* 279-280.
Brown, R. (1973). *A first language: The early stages.* Cambridge, MA: Harvard University Press.
Brown, R., Cazden, C., & Bellugi-Klima, U. (1969). The child's grammar from 1 to 3. In J. P. Hill (Ed.), *Minnesota symposium on child psychology: Vol. 2* (pp. 28-73). Minneapolis: University of Minnesota Press.
Brown, R., & Hanlon, C. (1970). Derivational complexity and order of acquisition in child speech. In J. R. Hayes (Ed.), *Cognition and the development of language* (pp. 11-53). New York: John Wiley.

CURRENT STATUS OF THE STUDY:

a. No further waves of data collection are planned.
b. The data are in machine-readable format.
c. The data set is available for secondary analysis through Dr. Brian MacWhinney, Director of The Child Language Data Exchange System at Carnegie-Mellon University.

■ The Harlem Longitudinal Study of Black Youth, 1968

Brunswick, Ann F.

Contact person: Ann F. Brunswick
Address: School of Public Health
                  Columbia University
                  Youth and Adult Health Project
                  60 Haven Avenue
                  Box 394
                  New York, NY 10032
Telephone No.:   (212) 923-2269

SUBSTANTIVE TOPICS COVERED:

This study examines the biopsychosocial aspects of health among a representative sample of African-American adolescents living in Harlem, New York City.

CHARACTERISTICS OF THE ORIGINAL SAMPLE:

Year the study began: 1968
Subject selection process: Subjects were non-Hispanic African-American youths between the ages of 12 and 18 years, selected from a probability sample of households in central Harlem, over 2 years, using a sampling ratio of 4% households each year.
Total number of subjects at Time 1: N = 668
Ages at Time 1: 12-17 yrs.
Sex distribution: Approximately equal numbers of females and males throughout
Socioeconomic status: 50% welfare recipients, 50% working class
Race/ethnicity: 100% African-American

Years of Completed Waves:

Years	N=	Age ranges
1968-1970	668	12-17 yrs.
1975-1976	536	18-25 yrs.
1983-1984	426	26-31 yrs.
1989-1990[a]	*	32-37 yrs.

Comments:
a. Data collection is underway of which roughly 200 subjects have been recontacted thus far.

INFORMATION ON SAMPLE ATTRITION:

During the 16-year period of study, 242 of 668 Ss (36.2%) were not retrieved for further study. The core sample consists of 426 Ss. Sample attrition was attributed to Ss moving out of the area (12%), death (6%), and inability to locate current address (13%).

CONSTRUCTS MEASURED: INSTRUMENTS USED

Physical health, emotional health, social health, personality characteristics, school achievement and satisfaction, social networks, peer-parent influences, self-esteem, sense of self-efficacy, alienation: Structured interview (Wave 1)

School achievement, problems: School record abstracts

Physical health: Comprehensive medical examination

Current life conditions, drug use, work and educational aspirations, interpersonal relationships, personal characteristics: Structured interview (Wave 3)

REPRESENTATIVE REFERENCES:

Brunswick, A. F. (1980). Health stability and change: A study of urban black youth. *The American Journal of Public Health, 70*, 504-513.

Brunswick, A. F. (1984). Health consequences of drug use: A longitudinal study of urban black youth. In S. A. Mednick, M. Harway, & K. M. Finello (Eds.), *Handbook of longitudinal research: Vol. 2. Teenage and adult cohorts* (pp. 290-314). New York: Praeger.

Brunswick, A. F., & Josephson, E. (1972). Adolescent health in Harlem. *The American Journal of Public Health* (Supplement).

Brunswick, A. F., Merzel, C. R., & Messeri, P. A. (1985). Drug use initiation among urban black youth. *Youth and Society, 17*(2), 189-216.

CURRENT STATUS OF THE STUDY:

a. The fourth wave of data is currently being collected.

b. Most data are in machine-readable format.

c. Data from the first wave are available for secondary analysis from the Henry A. Murray Research Center, Radcliffe College, 10 Garden Street, Cambridge, MA 02138.

■ Duke Adaptation Study (Duke Second Longitudinal Study), 1968

Busse, Ewald W.; Siegler, Ilene C.; George, Linda; Palmore, Erdman; Maddox, George L.; and Nowlin, John B.

Contact Person: Ilene C. Siegler
Address: Duke University Medical Center
Box 2969
Durham, NC 27710
Telephone No.: (919) 684-6352

SUBSTANTIVE TOPICS COVERED:

The purpose of this study was to examine and understand the process of normal aging. (See also Maddox, G. L., *Duke Longitudinal Study of Aging (Duke First Longitudinal Study)*.)

CHARACTERISTICS OF THE ORIGINAL SAMPLE:

Year the study began: 1968
Subject selection process: An age-by-sex stratified random sample was taken from the membership list of a major health insurance association in Durham, North Carolina. The sample was supplemented at the upper age of ranges by the inclusion of subjects from Duke University Hospital.
Total number of subjects at Time 1: N = 502
Ages at Time 1: 45-69 yrs.
Sex distribution: Approximately equal numbers of females and males throughout
Socioeconomic status: 100% middle/upper middle class
Race/ethnicity: 100% white

Years of Completed Waves:

Years	N=	Age ranges
1968-1970	502	45-69 yrs.
1970-1972	438	47-71 yrs.
1972-1974	383	49-73 yrs.
1974-1976	375	51-75 yrs.
1978-1980	100[a]	53-77 yrs.
1984-1986	200[b]	64-88 yrs.

Comments:
a. A stratified random sample of the remaining 375 Ss was followed in 1978-1980; the data generated from these Ss comprised "The Coping Study."
b. This was a mail survey.

INFORMATION ON SAMPLE ATTRITION:

During 18-year period of study, 302 of 502 Ss (60.2%) were not retrieved for further study. Attrition was due to deaths and subjects dropping out of the study.

CONSTRUCTS MEASURED: INSTRUMENTS USED

Physiological functioning, physical health, psychomotor and perceptual functioning: Physical and laboratory examinations

Activities and satisfactions, marital and family relations, sexual behavior, health and illness behaviors, lifestyle, work status and history: Personal interview

Intelligence: Wechsler Adult Intelligence Scale (WAIS)

Stressors: The Schedule of Recent Events (SRE), Continuous Performance Task (CPT), Heart rate (HR), Nowalis Mood Adjective Checklist (MACL)

Cognitive or mental functioning: Wechsler Adult Intelligence Scale

Vision: Schellen Eye chart, reading card

Audition: Pure-tone audiometry, spondee words

Simple and choice reaction time and CPT: Reaction time

Sexual enjoyment, sexual feeling, frequency of sexual relations: Medical history questionnaire

Drug and medicine use, alcohol and tobacco use: Medical history section of physical examination

Drug-use personality factors: Social history questionnaire

Locus of Control: Internal-External Scale (Rotter)

Presence or absence of arteriosclerosis: Electrocardiogram

Hypertension: Self-report

Vibratory threshold: Biothesiometer

Personality: Cattell 16 PF (Personality Factor) Questionnaire

Driving habits, propensity toward drowsiness while driving: Questionnaire

Self-concept: Semantic differential scale (7-item) (involvement, evaluation/optimism, and freedom), Who-Are-You Test (Kuhn & McPartland)

REPRESENTATIVE REFERENCES:

Palmore, E. (Ed.) (1970). *Normal aging: Reports from the Duke Longitudinal Study, 1955-1969.* Durham, NC: Duke University Press.

Palmore, E. (Ed.) (1974). *Normal aging II: Reports from the Duke Longitudinal Study, 1970-1973.* Durham, NC: Duke University Press.

Siegler, I. C. (1983). Psychological aspects of the Duke Longitudinal Studies. In K. W. Schaie (Ed.), *Longitudinal studies of adult psychological development.* New York: Guilford Press.

Siegler, I. C., George, L. K., & Okun, M. A. (1979). Cross-sequential analysis of adult personality. *Developmental Psychology, 15,* 350-351.

CURRENT STATUS OF THE STUDY:

a. No further waves of data collection are planned.

b. Data are in machine-readable format.

c. Data are available for secondary analysis from Linda George, Data Archive and Adult Development and Aging, Box 3003, Duke University Medical Center, Durham, NC 27710, (919) 684-3204.

■ Riverside Community Research Project, 1963

Butler, Edgar W.; and Schuster, Tonya L.

Contact Person: Edgar W. Butler
Address: Department of Sociology
University of California, Riverside
Riverside, CA 92521
Telephone No.: (714) 787-5444

SUBSTANTIVE TOPICS COVERED:

This study examines the effects of family, individual, and environmental characteristics on health and well-being over time (1963-1984). Currently, the project is focusing on the elderly and their social networks, social support, mental and physical health, and the import of positive and negative life events.

CHARACTERISTICS OF THE ORIGINAL SAMPLE:

Year the study began: 1963

Subject selection process: Subjects were a stratified random sample of 10.5% of the population in Riverside, California.

Total number of subjects at Time 1: N = 8,750

Ages at Time 1: 0-66 yrs.

Sex distribution: 60% female, 40% male (approximately)

Socioeconomic status: 57% working class, 30% poverty class, 13% middle/upper class

Race/ethnicity: 86.7% white, 7% Hispanic, 5.2% African-American, 0.4% Asian-American, 0.7% other

Years of Completed Waves:

Years	N=	Age ranges
(Cohort 1: 0-5 yrs. in 1963)		
1963	*	0-5 yrs.
1975	1,117	12-17 yrs.
(Cohort 2: 6-15 yrs. in 1963)		
1963	*	6-15 yrs.
1974	986[a]	20-26 yrs.
(Cohort 3: 16-35 yrs. in 1963)		
1963	*	16-35 yrs.
1975	1,052[a]	28-47 yrs.
(Cohort 4: 36-65 yrs. in 1963)[b]		
1963	*	16-35 yrs.
1977	872[a]	48-77 yrs.
(Cohort 5: 66[a] yrs. in 1963)		
1963	*	66[a] yrs.
1977	666[a]	78[a] yrs.

Comments:
a. Samples were further subdivided into impaired and nonimpaired subsamples.
b. A subsample of 513 Ss aged 65 years or older were followed-up in 1984.

INFORMATION ON SAMPLE ATTRITION:

During the 21-year period of study, 4,057 of 8,750 Ss (46.4%), across five co-horts, were not retrieved for further study. Attrition was due to deaths, and deliberate sampling of impaired and non-impaired subjects and/or by age. The core sample consists of approximately 4,693 Ss.

CONSTRUCTS MEASURED: INSTRUMENTS USED

Developmental impairment: Vineland Social Maturity Scale, Gesell Developmental Scales
Physical impairment: Medical history of damage to central nervous system, assessment of present physical functioning
Emotional impairment: Items focusing on disturbing situations
Personal and demographic data, physical health condition, medical, educational, and behavioral history, and family background of each member of the household: Household Survey

REPRESENTATIVE REFERENCES:

Butler, E. W., & Friedman, S. S. (1984). Longitudinal studies of impaired competence in the community: A description of the Riverside Community Research Project (1963-1979). In S. A. Mednick, M. Harway, & K. M. Finello (Eds.), Handbook of longitudinal research (pp. 182-196). New York: Praeger.

Butler, E. W., Lei, T., & McAllister, R. J. (1978). Childhood impairments and subsequent social adjustment. *American Journal of Mental Deficiency, 83,* 223-232.

Schuster, T. L., & Butler, E. W. (1986). Labeling, mild mental retardation, and long-range social adjustment. *Sociological Perspectives, 29,* 461-483.

Schuster, T. L., & Butler E. W. (1989). Bereavement, social networks, social support, and mental health. In D. A. Lund (Ed.), *Older bereaved spouses* (pp. 55-68). New York: Hemisphere Press.

CURRENT STATUS OF THE STUDY:

a. Further waves of data collection are planned.

b. Most data are in machine-readable format.

c. Selected data are available for secondary analysis from the study contact person.

Framingham Heart Study, 1949

Castelli, William P.; and Feinleib, Manning

Contact Person: William P. Castelli
Address: The Framingham Heart Study
118 Lincoln Street
Framingham, MA 01701
Telephone No.: (508) 872-4386

SUBSTANTIVE TOPICS COVERED:

The Framingham Heart Study is a prospective community study of the incidence and precursors of cardiovascular disease. Primary emphasis is given to biomedical topics and risk factors for heart disease. Significant information is available regarding social, demographic, and behavioral variables. These have been analyzed mainly as risk factors for coronary heart disease.

CHARACTERISTICS OF THE ORIGINAL SAMPLE:

Year the study began: 1949
Subject selection process: A 66% probability sample of Framingham, Massachusetts, adults was used for the study. Between 1971 and 1975, 5,135 adult children of the original respondents were added.
Total number of subjects at Time 1: N = 5,209 (including 1,256 spouse pairs)
Ages at Time 1: 30-59 yrs.
Sex distribution: Equal numbers of females and males throughout
Socioeconomic status: 65% working class, 35% middle/upper-middle class
Race/ethnicity: 92% white, 8% African-American (approximately)

Years of Completed Waves:[a]

Years	N=	Age ranges
(Cohort 1: Parents)		
1948-1949	5,209	30-59 yrs.
1951	4,792	32-61 yrs.
1953	4,416	34-63 yrs.
1955	4,541	36-65 yrs.
1957	4,421	38-67 yrs.
1959	4,259	40-69 yrs.

Years of Completed Waves, Continued:[a]

Years	N=	Age ranges
1961	4,191	42-71 yrs.
1963	4,030	44-72 yrs.
1965-1975[b]	*	46-85 yrs.
1977	2,828	56-89 yrs.
1979	*	58-91 yrs.
1981	*	60-93 yrs.
1983-1985	2,500[a]	62-95 yrs.
1987	2,000[a]	66-97 yrs.
1989	1,500[a]	72-99 yrs.
(Cohort 2: Adult children)		
1970-1975	5,135	14-70 yrs.
1979-1983	4,000	23-78 yrs.
1983-1987	3,800	27-82 yrs.
1990[c]	*	34-90 yrs.

Comments:
a. Approximate sample size.
b. Data were also collected every other year between 1965 and 1975.
c. Data collection is currently in progress.

INFORMATION ON SAMPLE ATTRITION:

During the 30-year period of study, approximately 1,409 of 5,209 Ss (36.9%) were not retrieved for further study. Attrition was due to subjects moving away from Framingham, death, illness, or refusal to participate.

CONSTRUCTS MEASURED: INSTRUMENTS USED

Physical health with focus on cardiovascular system: Physical examination, laboratory tests

Medical history, medical care since last examination, alcohol use, coffee use, education, family information, physical activity, physiological anxiety, smoking history, work history: Interview

Behavior types, reactions to anger, situational stress, somatic strains, sociocultural mobility: Psychosocial interview

REPRESENTATIVE REFERENCES:

Eaker, E. D., Haynes, S. G., & Feinleib, M. (1983). Spouse behavior and coronary heart disease: Prospective results from the Framingham Heart Study. XVI International Congress of Internal Medicine: Psychophysiology testing in preventive cardiology. *Activitas Nervosa Superior, 25*(2), 81-90.

Haynes, S. G., & Feinleib, M. (1980). Women, work and coronary heart disease: Prospective findings from the Framingham Heart Study. *American Journal of Public Health, 70*(2), 133-141.

Haynes, S. G., Feinleib, M., & Kannel, W. B. (1980). The relationship of psychosocial factors to coronary heart disease in the Framingham study: III, Eight-year incidence of coronary heart disease. *American Journal of Epidemiology, 111*(1), 37-58.

Haynes, S. G., Levine, S., Scotch, N., Feinleib, M., & Kannel, W. B. (1978). The relationship of psychosocial factors to coronary heart disease in the Framingham Study: I, Methods and risk factors. *American Journal of Epidemiology, 107*(5), 362-383.

CURRENT STATUS OF THE STUDY:

a. Further waves of data collection are planned.
b. Data are in machine-readable format.
c. Data are available for secondary analysis through Dr. Robert Garrison, NHLDI, 7550 Wisconsin Avenue, Room 3A08, Bethesda, MD 20892.

■ Coping with Early Parenthood, 1979

Chester, Nia L.

Contact Person: Nia L. Chester
Address: Pine Manor College
                400 Heath Street
                Chestnut Hill, MA 02167
Telephone No.: (617) 731-7073

SUBSTANTIVE TOPICS COVERED:

The study examines the adjustment to new parenthood and investigates the particular stresses common to new parents.

CHARACTERISTICS OF THE ORIGINAL SAMPLE:

Year the study began: 1979
Subject selection process: A cohort of subjects who recently became parents were recontacted from Dr. Abigail Stewart's study, *Experience-Induced Affective Development in Children and Adults,* which examined the adjustment to major life transitions.
Total number of subjects at Time 1: N = 55 (24 couples; 7 additional mothers)
Ages at Time 1: 27-33 yrs. (approximately)
Sex distribution: Approximately equal numbers of females and males
Socioeconomic status: 100% middle/upper middle class
Race/ethnicity: 100% white

Years of Completed Waves:

Years	N=	Age ranges
1979-1980[a]	55	27-33 yrs.
1984	27	31-37 yrs.

Comments:
a. Follow-up of subsample began in 1979, although four waves of data collection had already occurred in 1976, 1977, 1977, 1979, and 1984 through Dr. Stewart's earlier study.

INFORMATION ON SAMPLE ATTRITION:

During the 5-year period of study, 28 of 55 Ss (50.9%) were not retrieved for further study. The core sample consists of 27 Ss. Attrition was due to refusal to participate primarily because of time and geographic constraints.

CONSTRUCTS MEASURED: INSTRUMENTS USED

New parent experience (satisfaction, expectations, difficulties, and so on): Open-ended interview
Occupational patterns and satisfaction of working women with preschool children; personality variables, motivation, self-definition: Mailed questionnaire

REPRESENTATIVE REFERENCES:

Chester, N. (1981). *Coping with the stresses of new parenthood: A longitudinal study.* Doctoral dissertation. Boston University. Dissertation Abstracts International, *42(6B)*, p. 2499.
Chester, N. (1990). Achievement motivation and employment decisions: Portraits of women with young children. In H. Grossman & N. Chester (Eds.), *The experience and meaning of work in women's lives.* Hillsdale, NJ: Lawrence Erlbaum.

CURRENT STATUS OF THE STUDY:

a. No further waves of data collection are planned.
b. Most of the data are in machine-readable format.
c. Data are available for secondary analysis from the Henry A. Murray Research Center, Radcliffe College, 10 Garden Street, Cambridge, MA 02138.

■ Harvard Child Maltreatment Project, 1979

Cicchetti, Dante; and Rizley, Ross

Contact Person: Dante Cicchetti
Address: Mt. Hope Family Center
                187 Edinburgh Street
                Department of Psychology
                University of Rochester
                Rochester, NY 14608
Telephone No.: (716) 275-3384

SUBSTANTIVE TOPICS COVERED:

This study examines the etiology, intergenerational transmission, and developmental sequelae of child maltreatment. A broad-based empirical approach was used to assess a variety of potential manifestations in multiple contexts and multiple domains of functioning.

CHARACTERISTICS OF THE ORIGINAL SAMPLE:

Year the study began: 1979
Subject selection process: Maltreating families were referred through the Department of Social Services. These families either had been reported to the State or had voluntarily requested services for maltreatment issues. Comparison families were low-income families matched on demographic variables. They were recruited through advertisements in local welfare offices, neighborhoods, and door-to-door recruitment.
Total number of subjects at Time 1: N = 400
Ages at Time 1: 1-8 yrs.
Sex distribution: Approximately equal numbers of females and males throughout
Socioeconomic status: 83% poverty class, 17% middle/upper middle class
Race/ethnicity: 86% white, 14% African-American or Hispanic

Years of Completed Waves:

Year	$N=$[a]	Age ranges
(Cohort 1: 1-4 yrs. old Ss)		
1980-1983	200	1-4 yrs.
1984	175	4-8 yrs.
1985	150	5-9 yrs.
(Cohort 2: 4-8 yrs. old Ss)		
1980-1983	200	4-8 yrs.
1984	175	8-12 yrs.
1985	150	9-13 yrs.

Comments:
a. N values are approximations.

INFORMATION ON SAMPLE ATTRITION:

During the 6-year period of study, 100 of 400 Ss (25%), across both cohorts, were not retrieved for further study. The core sample consists of 300 Ss: 150 Ss (Cohort 1), and 150 Ss (Cohort 2).

CONSTRUCTS MEASURED: INSTRUMENTS USED

Measure of child ego-control, ego-resiliency, and self-esteem: California Child Q-Sort

Parent report of child behavior problems and social competence: Child Social Competence & Behavior Problem Checklist (Achenbach & Edelbrock)

General intellectual functioning: Wechsler Adult Intelligence Scale Revised Subscales

Child-rearing practices: California Child-rearing Practices Q-Sort

Parent social-cognitive reasoning about child-rearing and the parenting process: Parent Child Relations Interview

Information on childhood history of parents: Parent History Interview

Moral reasoning: Kohlberg Moral Judgment Interview

Friendship: Selman's "Friends Dilemma"

Perceived availability of support in four areas of life including tangible, belonging, self-esteem, and appraisal: Interpersonal Support Evaluation List

Stressful events and their impact on parent functioning: Life Experience Survey

Coping mechanisms: Ways of Coping

Parent Psychiatric Disorder(s) according to DSM-III-R: Diagnostic Interview Schedule Version III-A

Classifies quality of child's current attachment relationships between 12 and 48 months: Strange Situation

Visual Self-Recognition: Mirror and Rouge Paradigm

Autonomy, independent exploration, and ability to cope with frustration: Tool Use/Problem-Solving Paradigm

Peer Interaction: Free Play with Peers

Yields constructs that denote adaptive (ego-resiliency and moderate control) and maladaptive ego-brittleness and either under- or over-control personality functioning: Ego Resiliency/Ego Control

Cognitive organization, including focal attention, field articulation, and leveling-sharpening: Cognitive Control Battery

Receptive vocabulary: Peabody Picture Vocabulary Test-Revised

General intellectual functioning: Revised Wechsler Intelligence Scale for Children

Friendship and peer relations, play/association, prosocial behavior, intimacy, loyalty, attachment and self-esteem enhancement, conflicts

Reasoning about the self, intrapsychic awareness, personality, and personality change: Puppy Story (Conceptions of Individuals)

Several aspects of play, (e.g., symbolic play and thematic play) can be coded from these interactions, moreover, syntactic, functional, and discourse aspects of language can be obtained; quality of maternal involvement, affect, and verbal input, among other variables: Mother-child semistructured and unstructured free play

REPRESENTATIVE REFERENCES:

Cicchetti, D. (1989). How research on child maltreatment has informed the study of child devel-
    opment: Perspectives from developmental psychopathology. In D. Cicchetti and V. Carlson
    (Eds.), *Child maltreatment: Theory and research on the causes and consequences of child
    abuse and neglect.* New York: Cambridge University Press.
Cicchetti, D., Carlson, V., Braunwald, K., & Aber, J. L. (1987). The Harvard Child Maltreatment
    Project: A context for research on the sequelae of child maltreatment. In R. Gelles and J.
    Lancaster (Eds.), *Research in child abuse: Biosocial perspectives* (pp. 277-298). New York:
    Plenum.
Cicchetti, D., & Rizley, R. (1981). Developmental perspectives of the etiology, intergenerational
    transmission and sequelae of child maltreatment. *New Directions for Child Development,
    11,* 32-59.
Rizley, R., & Cicchetti, D. (Eds.). (1981). *Developmental perspectives on child maltreatment.* San
    Francisco: Jossey-Bass.

CURRENT STATUS OF THE STUDY:

a. Further waves of data collection are planned.
b. Data are in machine-readable format.
c. Data are not available for secondary analysis.

■ Chicago Study of Child Care and Development, 1976

Clarke-Stewart, Alison

Contact Person: Alison Clarke-Stewart
Address: Program in Social Ecology
                 University of California
                 Irvine, CA 92717
Telephone No.:   (714) 856-7191

SUBSTANTIVE TOPICS COVERED:

The study examines the effects of different kinds of day-care arrangements (centers, homes, babysitters, and parents) on children's social, emotional, and intellectual development.

CHARACTERISTICS OF THE ORIGINAL SAMPLE:

Year the study began: 1976
Subject selection process: Ss were selected from mailing lists, referral lists, and
    churches, contacted by letters and with follow-up calls.
Total number of subjects at Time 1: N = 150
Ages at Time 1: 2-3 yrs.

Sex distribution: Approximately equal numbers of females and males throughout
Socioeconomic status: 80% middle/upper middle class, 20% working class
Race/ethnicity: 91% white, 5% African-American, 2% Hispanic, 2% Asian-American

Years of Completed Waves:

Years	N=	Age ranges
1976	150	2-3 yrs.
1978	130	3-5 yrs.

INFORMATION ON SAMPLE ATTRITION:

During the 2-year period of study, 20 of 150 Ss (13.3%) were not retrieved for
further study. The core sample consists of 128 Ss.

CONSTRUCTS MEASURED: INSTRUMENTS USED

Child's intellectual development, especially language; social competence with
    peers, social competence with an adult stranger, relationship with mother:
    Standard assessments of children in a playroom setting
Spontaneous, unstructured social interactions: Naturalistic observations at home
    and in daycare
Parents' attitudes, family demographics: Parents' interviews

REPRESENTATIVE REFERENCES:

Clarke-Stewart, A. (1977). *Child care in the family: A review of research and some propositions for policy.* New York: Academic Press.
Clarke-Stewart, A. (1982). *Daycare.* Cambridge, MA: Harvard University Press.
Clarke-Stewart, A. (1983). *Children: Development through adolescence.* New York: John Wiley.
Clarke-Stewart, A. (1984). Daycare: A new context for research and development. In M. Perlmutter (Ed.), *The Minnesota symposium on child psychology: Vol. 17.* Hillsdale, NJ: Lawrence Erlbaum.

CURRENT STATUS OF THE STUDY:

a. No further waves of data collection are planned.
b. Most data are in machine-readable format.
c. The data are available for secondary analysis.

■ Oakland Growth Study (O), 1931

Clausen, John A.; Jones, Harold E. (deceased); Jones, Mary C.
(deceased); and Stolz, Herbert

Contact Person: Intergenerational Studies Archivist
Address: University of California
                 Institute of Human Development
                 1203 Tolman Hall
                 Berkeley, CA 94720
Telephone No.:   (415) 642-2022

SUBSTANTIVE TOPICS COVERED:

The study examines physical, physiological, and personal-social (particularly peer group interaction) development during adolescence; adult assessments emphasizing social relationships within familial, employment, and community settings; satisfactions, dissatisfactions, competencies, and liabilities in these settings; social mobility; personality characteristics; and physical and emotional health. (See also Eichorn, D. H., *Berkeley Growth Study*; and Huffine, C., *Guidance Study*)

CHARACTERISTICS OF THE ORIGINAL SAMPLE:

Year the study began: 1931
Subject selection process: Participants were selected from five elementary schools in Oakland, California, and were in the fifth and sixth grades at the time of selection. The study includes data on offspring of the original sample collected during the second adult follow-up, when the children were between early childhood and young adulthood, and on spouses.
Total number of subjects at Time 1: N = 212
Ages at Time 1: 11-12 yrs.
Sex distribution: Approximately equal numbers of females and males throughout
Socioeconomic status: 60% middle class, 40% working class (approximately)
Race/ethnicity: 100% white

Years of Completed Waves:

Years	N=	Age ranges
1931	212	11-12 yrs.
1935-1936	160	18 yrs.
1959	117	38 yrs.
1970-1971	110	50 yrs.
1981-1982	92	62 yrs.

Comments:
Data were collected continuously from the start of the study through the late adolescence of the study members. By age 18, more than 160 study members were still being seen. Three full adult follow-ups have been conducted,

one in 1953-1959, one in 1970, and one in 1982. More than 90 study members took part in some or all of the 1982 data collection procedures.

INFORMATION ON SAMPLE ATTRITION:

After 50 years of study, 91 of 212 Ss (42.9%) were not retrieved for a follow-up. As of November 1, 1990, 38 study members were known to be deceased.

CONSTRUCTS MEASURED: INSTRUMENTS USED

Prenatal and early history: Retrospective Interview

Physical development and health information: Physical examination & health history, anthropometrics, skeletal X rays, Body Build Pictures, Physical Rating Scale, menstrual record, diet record, optometric examination, health record

Physiological development: Basal Data (pulse, blood pressure, metabolism), Exercise Tolerance (pulse, blood pressure), Urinalysis, Skin Conductance

Fine and gross motor coordination: Physical Abilities Tests, Reaction Time, Eye-hand Coordination Tests

Mental development and achievement: Stanford-Binet Intelligence Test, Terman Group, CAVD; Kuhlman-Anderson; Stanford Achievement Test, Iowa Reading; Learning & Verbal Tests, Maze

Personality development: Self-Reports (U.C. Adjustment Inventories, Interests, Annoyances, Preferences, Attitudes and Opinions, Activity Record, Judgment of Motivation, Strong Vocational) Ratings—Descriptive Notes, Observed Behavior (Same Sex, Mixed Groups, Class, Laboratory, Teacher and Sociometric); Counselor's Report, Creative Products, Projective Test, Word Association, Interview (Parental Subjects), Newsletter, Surveys, Mail

School behaviors: Attendance Record, grades, teachers' ratings, activity schedule

Home behaviors: Parental Interview, Tests—Burdick Apperception Test; Heilman Sims Test; Ratings of characteristics of mother

REPRESENTATIVE REFERENCES:

Eichorn, D. H., Clausen, J. A., Haan, N. Honzik, M. P. & Mussen, P. H. (Eds.). (1981). *Present and past in middle life*. New York: Academic Press.

Haan, M., & Day, D. (1974). A longitudinal study of change and sameness in personality development: Adolescence to later adulthood. *International Journal of Aging and Human Development, 5*(1), 11-39.

Jones, H. E., & Bailey, N. (1941). The Berkeley Growth Study. *Child Development, 12*(2), 167-173.

Jones, M. C., Bayley, N., Macfarlane, J. W., & Honzik, M. P. (Eds.). (1971). *The course of human development*. New York: John Wiley.

CURRENT STATUS OF THE STUDY:

   a. Further waves of data collection are planned.

   b. Data are in machine-readable format.

   c. Data are available for secondary analysis through the study contact person.

■ Personality Development in Monozygotic Twins: A Longitudinal Study, 1967

Cohen, Donald J.; and Dibble, Eleanor D.

Contact Person: Donald J. Cohen, Director
Address: Yale Child Study Center
                  230 South Frontage Road
                  P. O. Box 3333
                  New Haven, CT 06510
Telephone No.:   (203) 785-5759

SUBSTANTIVE TOPICS COVERED:

The study examines individual, interpersonal, intrafamilial, social, and health experiences; internal and external life; relations with family; behavioral and emotional difficulty; interests; competence; fantasies; sexual thoughts; personal ambitions.

CHARACTERISTICS OF THE ORIGINAL SAMPLE:

Year the study began: 1967
Subject selection process: Obstetricians referred parents for participation in the
    study when a multiple pregnancy was diagnosed.
Total number of subjects at Time 1: N = 16
Ages at Time 1: Newborn
Sex distribution: 75% male, 25% female
Socioeconomic status: 100% middle/upper middle class
Race/ethnicity: 90% white, 10% African-American

Years of Completed Waves:

Years	N=	Age ranges
1967-1969	16	Newborns
1970-1972	16	3 yrs.-3.5 yrs.
1977-1979	16	10-12 yrs.
1981-1983	16	14-16 yrs.

INFORMATION ON SAMPLE ATTRITION:

During the 16-year period of study, all 16 Ss (100%) were retrieved at all data points for further study. The core sample consists of 16 Ss.

CONSTRUCTS MEASURED: INSTRUMENTS USED

Health, physiological adaptation, calmness, vigor, attention, and neurology: First-week evaluation scale, interview, observations of parents and their children (every 2-3 months for the first 2 years)

Intelligence: Stanford-Binet Intelligence Test

Social adjustment: Rorschach Adaptation, nursery school observation of structured play, 10-Cohen-Frank Preadolescent Inventory of Social Adjustment

Health and behavior: Teachers' and pediatricians' reports based on semistructured interview with parent and child

REPRESENTATIVE REFERENCES:

Cohen, D., Allen, M., et al. (1972). Personality development in twins: Competence in the newborn and preschool periods. *Journal of the American Academy of Child Psychiatry, 11*(4), 625-644.

Cohen, D. J., Dibble, E., & Grawe, J. M. (1977). Fathers' and mothers' perceptions of children's personality. *Archives of General Psychiatry, 34*(4), 480-487.

Dibble, E., & Cohen, D. (1980). The interplay of biological endowment, early experience, and psychological influence during the first year of life. In E. J. Anthony & C. Chiland (Eds.), *The child in his family* (pp. 85-103). New York: Wiley-Interscience.

Dibble, E. D., & Cohen, D. (1981). Personality development in identical twins: The first decade of life. *Psychoanalytic Study of the Child, 34*(4), 480-487.

CURRENT STATUS OF THE STUDY:

a. Further waves of data collection are tentatively planned.

b. Most of the data are not in machine-readable format.

c. Data are not available for secondary analysis.

■ Early Identification of Later Developmental Problems, 1971

Cohen, Sarale E.; Sigman, Marian; Beckwith, Leila; and Parmelee, Arthur H.

Contact Person: Sarale E. Cohen
Address: Department of Pediatrics, Division of Child Development
University of California School of Medicine
10833 LaConte Avenue
Los Angeles, CA 90024
Telephone No.: (213) 206-8085

SUBSTANTIVE TOPICS COVERED:

This study includes child measures from birth, caregiver-infant and caregiver-child interactions at several age levels as well as other social indices. Processes of cognitive and behavioral development are examined, focusing on the context of bi-osocial interaction and the development of the social competence and school performance of preterm children and delineates the interaction of acculturation and biological problems in the children's behavioral development.

CHARACTERISTICS OF THE ORIGINAL SAMPLE:

Year the study began: 1971

Subject selection process: Preterm infants born at the UCLA nursery during 1972-1974, free of obvious congenital anomalies, were selected to participate in the study. Included were some Spanish-speaking families who were treated as a subgroup in these analyses.

Total number of subjects at Time 1: N = 126

Ages at Time 1: 9 mos.

Sex distribution: Approximately equal numbers of females and males throughout

Socioeconomic Status: 44% working class, 37% middle/upper middle class, and 19% poverty class

Race/ethnicity: 46% white, 31% Hispanic, 12% African-American, 6% Asian-American, and 5% biracial

Years of Completed Waves:

Years	N=	Age ranges
1973-1975	126	9 mos.
1975-1977	126	2 yrs.
1978-1980	100	5 yrs.
1981-1983	94	8 yrs.
1984-1986	104	12 yrs.

INFORMATION ON SAMPLE ATTRITION:

During the 9-year period of study, 22 of 126 Ss (17.5%) were not retrieved for further study. The core sample consists of 90 Ss.

CONSTRUCTS MEASURED: INSTRUMENTS USED

Cognitive development: Revised Wechsler Intelligence Scale for Children (WISC-R), Gesell Developmental Scale, Bayley Mental Scale, exploratory behavior, Stanford-Binet Intelligence Test, Formal Operations, Verbal analogies

School perfromance: Wide Range Achievement Test

Perceptual motor development: Bender-Gestalt

Language development: Language tests (Token, ITPA Subtest), receptive language

Social-emotional development: Roberts projective Test, Caregiver-infant interaction, Conner Child Behavior Rating (tester parent), Child Behavior Checklist, Perceived Competence (Harter, parent report)

School behavior: Teacher rating (Rutter and Conner)

Medical status: Medical examination, Obstetric Complications Scale, Postnatal Complications Scale, newborn neurological exams

Patterns of sleep: Sleep polygraph

Perceptual development: Visual attention, hand precision and sensorimotor schemata

Attention: Continuous Performance Task (CPT), Span of Apprehension, Trails, Reyes Tangled Lines

Parent personality: California Psychological Inventory

Family Environment: Family Environment Scale (Moos)

Child perception of self: Perceived Competence Scale for Children (Harter), Self-Image Questionnaire (Offer)

Social cognition: The Interpersonal Understanding Interview (Selman)

REPRESENTATIVE REFERENCES:

Beckwith, L., & Cohen, S. E. (1984). Home environment and cognitive competence in preterm children in the first five years. In A. W. Gottfried (Ed.), *Home environment and early mental development*. New York: Academic Press.

Cohen, S. E., & Parmelee, A. H. (1983). Prediction of five year Stanford-Binet scores in preterm infants. *Child Development, 54*, 1242-1253.

Cohen, S. E., Parmelee, A. H., Beckwith, L., & Sigman, M. (1986). Cognitive development in preterm infants. *Journal of Developmental Behavioral pediatrics, 7*, 102-110.

Sigman, M., Beckwith, L., Cohen, S. E., & Parmelee, A. H. (1989). Stability in the biosocial development of the child born preterm. In M. H. Bornstein & N. A. Krasnegor (Eds.), *Stability and continuity in mental development*. Hillsdale, NJ: Lawrence Erlbaum.

CURRENT STATUS OF THE STUDY:

a. A further wave of data collection is planned at 18 years.

b. Most of the data are in machine-readable format.

c. The data are available for secondary analysis from the study contact person.

■ Longitudinal Study of Social Status in Elementary School Children, 1975

Coie, John D.; and Dodge, Kenneth A.

Contact Person: John D. Coie
Address: Department of Psychology
                 Duke University
                 Durham, NC 27706
Telephone No.:   (919) 684-2581

SUBSTANTIVE TOPICS COVERED:

This study examines the year-to-year changes and continuities of social status and social preferences among a sample of third and fifth graders over a 5-year period.

CHARACTERISTICS OF THE ORIGINAL SAMPLE:

Year the study began: 1975

Subject selection process: Subjects were all of the children at the elementary school in Durham, North Carolina, who were in the third and fifth grades during the 1975-1976 academic year.

Total number of subjects at Time 1: N = 96

Ages at Time 1: 7-9 yrs.

Sex distribution: Approximately equal numbers of females and males throughout

Socioeconomic status: 100% working class

Race/ethnicity: 74% white, 26% African-American (Cohort 1); 71.4% white, 28.6% African-American (Cohort 2)

Years of Completed Waves:

Years	N=	Age ranges
(Cohort 1: Third Graders)		
1975-1976	96	7-9 yrs.
1976-1977	79	8-10 yrs.
1977-1978	73	9-11 yrs.
1978-1979	62	10-12 yrs.
1979-1980	76	11-13 yrs.
(Cohort 2: Fifth Graders)		
1975-1976	112	10-12 yrs.
1976-1977	106	11-13 yrs.
1977-1978	105	12-14 yrs.
1978-1979	54	13-15 yrs.
1979-1980	89	14-16 yrs.

INFORMATION ON SAMPLE ATTRITION:

During the 5-year period of study, 43 of 208 Ss (20.7%), were not retrieved for further study: 20 of 96 Ss (20.8%) in Cohort 1; and 23 of 112 Ss (20.5%) in Cohort 2. The core sample consists of 165 Ss: 76 Ss (Cohort 1) and 89 Ss (Cohort 2).

CONSTRUCTS MEASURED: INSTRUMENTS USED

Social preferences, ratings of schoolmates, social status of school mates: Sociometric interview
Perspective-taking: Chandler's Perspective-taking

REPRESENTATIVE REFERENCES:

Coie, J. D., & Dodge, K. A. (1983). Continuities and changes in children's social status: A five-year longitudinal study. *Merrill-Palmer Quarterly, 29*(3), 261-282.

Coie, J. D., Dodge, K. A., & Coppotelli, H. (1982). Dimensions and types of social status: A cross-age perspective. *Developmental Psychology, 18,* 557-570.

Dodge, K. A., Coie, J. D., and Brakke, N. P. (1982). Behavior patterns of socially rejected and neglected preadolescents. *Journal of Abnormal Child Psychology, 10,* 389-409.

Kupersmidt, J. B., and Coie, J. D. (in press). Preadolescent peer status, aggression, and school adjustment as predictors of externalizing problems in adolescence. *Child Development, 61.*

CURRENT STATUS OF THE STUDY:

a. No further waves of data collection are planned.

b. Most of the data are in machine-readable format.

c. Data are available for secondary analysis through the study contact person.

■ Longitudinal Study of Moral Development, 1955

Colby, Anne; Kohlberg, Lawrence (deceased); Gibbs, John; and
Lieberman, Marcus

Contact Person: Anne Colby
Address: Henry A. Murray Research Center
                 Radcliffe College
                 10 Garden Street
                 Cambridge, MA 02138
Telephone No.:   (617) 495-8140

SUBSTANTIVE TOPICS COVERED:

The study examines moral, social, and ego development from late childhood
through early adulthood; investigates the basic assumptions of Kohlberg's cognitive developmental account of moral judgment.

CHARACTERISTICS OF THE ORIGINAL SAMPLE:

Year the study began: 1955-1956
Subject selection process: Subjects were drawn from two suburban Chicago areas,
    one upper-middle class (UMC) and one lower and lower-middle class
    (LC/LMC); also, 12 delinquent boys were contacted through a detention
    home.
Total number of subjects at Time 1: N = 90
Ages at Time 1: 10-16 yrs.
Sex distribution: 100% male
Socioeconomic status: 50% middle/upper middle class, 50% working class (ap-
    proximately)
Race/ethnicity: 100% white

Years of Completed Waves:

Years	N=	Age ranges[a]
1955-1956[a]	90	10-16 yrs.
1960[b]	67	14-21 yrs.
1964	30	18-25 yrs.
1969	53	23-30 yrs.
1972-1973	46	26-33 yrs.
1976-1977	37	30-37 yrs.

Comments:
a. A comparison group of 12 delinquent boys was included at Time 1.
b. A group of 27 mothers and 27 fathers of the Ss were included at Time 2.

INFORMATION ON SAMPLE ATTRITION:

During the 22-year period of study, 53 of 90 Ss (58.9%) were not retrieved for further study. Fifty-eight subjects were tested at least twice. Thirteen subjects were tested at all six time points.

CONSTRUCTS MEASURED: INSTRUMENTS USED

Child's moral development, parent's moral development: Moral Judgment Interview (Kohlberg)
Motives, other personality variables: Thematic Apperception Test (Morgan and Murray)
Ego development: Washington University Sentence Completion Test (Loevinger)
Occupational role ratings: Social Respect Sort
Child's personal and occupational roles, parent's personal and occupational role: "Be Like" Sort
Interpersonal understanding: Interpersonal role-taking tasks (Selman)
Child's dependability, leadership, honesty: Teachers' ratings
Attitudes toward sex: 5-point scale
Ideas about morality and ethics: Meta-ethical questions
Cognitive development: Pendulum task (Piaget), Isolation of variables (Kuhn)
Intelligence: School records, Thurstone Primary Mental Abilities, Otis-Lennon Mental Ability Test
Type of work, moral aspects of job, work satisfaction/dissatisfaction, values associated with parenthood, aspirations for children, ideas about citizenship: Job and family description questionnaire
Subject ranking of various occupational roles based on their perceived importance and value: Occupational ratings
Sociometric status: Peer nominations
Father's personal opinions: Opinion Questionnaire
Additional information (Father): Questions from the Yale Decision Study
Additional information (Mother): Questions about parenting

REPRESENTATIVE REFERENCES:

Colby, A. (1978). Evolution of a moral developmental theory. In W. Damon (Ed.), *New directions in child development: Vol. 1, No. 2: Moral development.* San Francisco: Jossey-Bass.

Colby, A., Kohlberg, L., Gibbs, J., & Lieberman, M. (1983). A longitudinal study of moral judgment. *Monographs of the Society for Research in Child Development, 48*(6, 1-2). Chicago: The University of Chicago Press.

Colby, A., Kohlberg, L., et al. (1987). *The measurement of moral judgment.* New York: Cambridge University Press.

Kohlberg, L. (1969). Stage and sequence: The cognitive-developmental approach to socialization. In D. Goslin (Ed.), *Handbook of socialization theory and research.* Chicago: Rand-Mc-Nally.

CURRENT STATUS OF THE STUDY:

a. No further waves of data collection are planned.
b. Most of the data are in machine-readable format.
c. The data are available for secondary analysis through the Henry A. Murray Research Center, Radcliffe College, 10 Garden Street, Cambridge, MA 02318.

■ Kelly Longitudinal Study, 1935

Connolly, James J.; and Kelly, E. Lowell (deceased)[1]

Contact Person: James J. Connolly
Address: 75 Westmont Drive
                Middletown, CT 06457
Telephone No.: (203) 347-6337
Comments:
1. Professor E. Lowell Kelly was the principal investigator from 1933 to 1978 at the University of Michigan.

SUBSTANTIVE TOPICS COVERED:

The study examines assortative mating and subsequent marital adjustment; personality changes during marriage and with age; and fertility. The 1978-1980 wave examines marital adjustment in mature marriages as well as physical and mental health of the subjects and their social and recreational activities in retirement.

CHARACTERISTICS OF THE ORIGINAL SAMPLE:

Year the study began: 1935
Subject selection process: Subjects were from Connecticut, Massachusetts, and Rhode Island, and were above-average in intelligence and educational attainment. All participants were engaged.
Total number of subjects at Time 1: N = 600 (300 couples)
Ages at Time 1: 18-35 yrs.
Sex distribution: Equal numbers of females and males throughout
Socioeconomic status: 80% middle class, 20% working class (approximately)
Race/ethnicity: 100% white

Years of Completed Waves:

Years	N=	Age ranges
1935-1938	600	18-35 yrs.
1954-1955	446	37-52 yrs.
1979-1981	388	62-78 yrs.

INFORMATION ON SAMPLE ATTRITION:

During the 46-year period of study, 212 of 600 Ss (35.3%) were not retrieved for further study. At the end of the third wave of data collection 121 Ss were known to be deceased. The core sample consists of 388 Ss.

CONSTRUCTS MEASURED: INSTRUMENTS USED

Personality ratings of self, partner, and acquaintances: Personality Rating Scale
Mental ability: Otis Self-Administering Test of Mental Ability
Personality ratings of self: Bernreuter Personality Inventory, standardized self-report instruments
Retirement, activities, physical and emotional health, marital satisfaction: Questionnaire
Physical health: Cornell Medical Index

REPRESENTATIVE REFERENCES:

Conley, J. J. (1984). Longitudinal consistency of adult personality: Self-reported psychological characteristics across 45 years. *Journal of Personality and Social Psychology, 47*, 1325-1333.
Conley, J. J. (1985). Longitudinal stability of personality traits: A multitrait-multimethod-multioccasion analysis. *Journal of Personality and Social Psychology, 49*, 1266-1282.
Kelly, E. L. (1955). Consistency of the adult personality. *American Psychologist, 10*, 659-681.
Kelly, E. L., & Conley, J. J. (1987). Personality and compatibility: A prospective analysis of marital stability and marital satisfaction. *Journal of Personality and Social Psychology, 47*, 1325-1333.

CURRENT STATUS OF THE STUDY:

a. No further waves of data collection are planned.
b. Most of the data are in machine-readable format.
c. Data are available for secondary analysis through the Henry A. Murray Research Center, 10 Garden Street, Cambridge, MA 02138.

■ Fels Longitudinal Study of Human Growth and Development, 1929

Crandall, Virginia C.; and Roche, Alexander F.

Contact Person: Virginia C. Crandall (Re: psychological-social data)
Address: Wright State University School of Medicine
                 Division of Developmental Psychology
                 Sontag-Fels Hall
                 800 Livermore Street
                 Yellow Springs, OH 45387-1609
Telephone No.:   (513) 767-7254

Contact Person: Alexander F. Roche (Re: Physical data)
Address: Wright State University School of Medicine
                 Division of Human Biology
                 1005 Xenia Avenue
                 Yellow Springs, OH 45387
Telephone No.:   (513) 767-7327

SUBSTANTIVE TOPICS COVERED:

From 1929 through 1975, the study examined a wide variety of dimensions of psychological, social, and physical development. Subsequent to 1975, it has been focused exclusively on physical development.

CHARACTERISTICS OF THE ORIGINAL SAMPLE:

Year the study began: 1929

Subject selection process: Subjects, enrolled prenatally or at birth, are children of volunteer families located within a 40-mile radius of Yellow Springs, Ohio. Approximately 25% come from rural areas, 50% from small towns, and 25% from urban areas. Parents are mainly native-born. Forty percent of families have one child in the study; 60% have two or more children in the study.

Total number of subjects at Time 1: The Fels project has enrolled new subjects in to the study *continuously.* In 1929, it began with a sample of 5 infants; an average of 19.4 infants have been added each year since that time (except for the years 1974-1981). As of 1990, 1,034 children have entered the program; they now range in age from zero to 61 years.

Ages at Time 1: 20 weeks gestational age to birth

Sex distribution: Approximately equal numbers of females and males throughout

Socioeconomic status: Family social class of Fels subjects on the five levels (I = high, V = low) of Hollingshead Two Factor Index of Social Position (1957): I, 10.9%; II, 27.5%; III, 32.3%; IV, 29.9%; V, 6.4%.

Race/ethnicity: 100% white

Years of Completed Waves:[a]

Years	N=	Age ranges
1929-1990	1,034	Prenatal-61 yrs.

Comments:
a. Data for this study are not actually collected in discrete waves. (The study is best characterized as using a continuous data collection procedure.) Because subjects' ages at any given time describe a continuous distribution, all forms of data are gathered continuously in accord with an assessment schedule defined by developmental level. From 1929 to 1975, the focus was on the first 18 years of life, and 634 subjects who participated in the study during those years have psychological-social and physical growth data collected on the following schedule: birth (or prenatally); 1, 3, 6, 9, and 12 months; every half-year until age 6; and then annually through age 18. Similar data were gathered from cohorts of 89 and 65 of these subjects who returned for follow-up when they were ages 19-29 and 19-26, respectively. In 1975 the program of psychological tests, home visits, nursery school and day camp observations was terminated; thus, there were no psychological-social data on subjects from that time forward. The study is now devoted to physical development, with a special emphasis on body composition and fat distribution as they relate to disease risk factors. Data are now collected according to the following schedule: 1, 3, 6, 9, and 12 months; every 6 months until age 5; annually until age 10; every 6 months until age 16; annually until age 22 (females) or 24 (males); every 2 years thereafter if subjects live nearby for the remainder of their participation, or irregular visits if they are not local residents.

INFORMATION ON SAMPLE ATTRITION:

During the 61-year period of study, 260 of 1,034 Ss (25.1%) became unavailable for further study. Most of the sample attrition occurred during either the fetal period or the first few months of life. Of the 634 Ss for whom both psychological and physical measures are available from birth (or prenatally) through age 18, a total of 92 Ss (14.5%) are no longer available for future study.

CONSTRUCTS MEASURED: INSTRUMENTS USED

Subjects

Anthropometric, dermatoglyphic, genetic, audiometric, and general health status information: Physical examinations

Skeletal growth, dental growth: Roentgenographic

Amino acids, hemoglobin, glucose, and uric acids monitored: Blood samples

Body composition: Hydrostatic weighing

Child behaviors: Home observations (Narrative reports)

Child social behaviors (e.g. physical aggression, verbal aggression, help-seeking, approval-seeking, imitation of peers, dominance of peers, and so on): Nursery school & day camp observations (Child Behavior Rating Scales and Narrative Reports)

Intelligence: Bayley Scales of Infant Development, Gesell Developmental Scales, Merrill-Palmer Scale of Mental tests; Stanford-Binet Intelligence Test (Form L-M, and L-M), Wechsler Preschool and Primary Scale of Intelligence, Wechsler Intelligence Scale for Children, Wechsler Adult Intelligence Scale, Primary Mental Abilities

Academic achievement: Reading Readiness, Stanford Achievement Test, Metropolitan Achievement Test

Personality, psychological adjustment: Modified Rorschach Ink Blot Test; Thematic Apperception Test, Minnesota Multiphasic Personality Inventory, Fels Q Sort, Self Rating Inventory, French Insight Test, Vineland Social Maturity Scale, Kuder Preference Test

Parents

Anthropometric, genetic, health history and health status information: Physical examinations of parents

Body composition: Hydrostatic weighing

Maternal behaviors and attitudes: Home observations of parents (Narrative Reports and Fels Parent Behavior Rating Scales)

Maternal attitudes; maternal reports of child's behaviors and development: Mother interviews (semistructured)

Parents' intelligence: Otis Test of Mental Ability; Wechsler-Bellevue Intelligence Scale; Wechsler Adult Intelligence Scale

Parents' personality and psychological adjustment: Minnesota Multiphasic Personality Inventory; Rotter Incomplete Sentences Blank; Bernreuter Personality Inventory

Additional information available on Fels subjects, their parents and spouses: Birth histories, family composition, educational and occupational histories, marital histories, date and cause of death

REPRESENTATIVE REFERENCES:

Crandall, V. C. (1972). The Fels Study: Some contributions to personality development and achievement in childhood and adulthood. *Seminars in Psychiatry, 1*(4), 383-398.

Crandall, V. C., & Battle, E. S. (1970). The antecedents and adult correlates of academic and intellectual achievement and effort. In J. P. Hill (Ed.), *Minnesota symposium on child psychology: Vol. 4,* 36-93. Minneapolis: University of Minnesota Press.

Kagan, J., & Moss, H. A. (1962). *Birth to maturity: A study in psychological development.* New York: John Wiley.

McCall, R., Appelbaum, M., & Hogarty, P. (1973). Developmental changes in mental performance. *Monographs of the Society for Research in Child Development, 38*(3).

CURRENT STATUS OF THE STUDY:

a. Further data collection is planned.

b. Some data are in machine-readable format.

c. Psychological-social data from birth to 19-26 years of age for a cohort of 65 Ss (see Comments under "Years of Completed Waves") are conditionally available for secondary analysis through the Henry A. Murray Research Center, Radcliffe College, 10 Garden Street, Cambridge, MA 02138.

■ Oberlin Longitudinal Survey, 1970

Cutler, Stephen J.

Contact Person: Stephen J. Cutler
Address: Department of Sociology
                  University of Vermont
                  31 South Prospect
                  Burlington, VT 05405
Telephone No.:   (802) 656-2217

SUBSTANTIVE TOPICS COVERED:

This study assessed the status and needs of older residents of Oberlin, Ohio.

CHARACTERISTICS OF THE ORIGINAL SAMPLE:

Year the study began: 1970
Subject selection process: Random sample of Ss 65 years of age and older in Oberlin, Ohio
Total number of subjects at Time 1: N = 170
Ages at Time 1: 65-90 yrs.
Sex distribution: 70% female, 30% male (approximately)
Socioeconomic status: 66% middle/upper middle class, 34% working class
Race/ethnicity: 80% white, 20% African-American

Years of Completed Waves:

Years	N=	Age ranges
1970	170	65-90 yrs.
1973	106	68-93 yrs.

INFORMATION ON SAMPLE ATTRITION:

During the 3-year period of study, 64 of 170 Ss (37.6%) were not retrieved for further study. Reasons for attrition include refusal to participate (23%), illness (22%), Ss moved away (20%), death (14%), unable to contact (11%), and Ss residing in nursing homes (9%). The core sample consists of 106 Ss.

CONSTRUCTS MEASURED: INSTRUMENTS USED

Sociodemographic information, life satisfaction, perceived prestige loss, friendship, relations with relatives, health, functional limitations, political concerns (efficacy, orientations, affiliations), and religious beliefs: Structured interview (based on 25-page questionnaire)

REPRESENTATIVE REFERENCES:

Cutler, S. J. (1973). Voluntary association participation and life satisfaction: A cautionary research note. *Journal of Gerontology, 28,* 96-100.

Cutler, S. J. (1975). Transportation and changes in life satisfaction. *The Gerontologist, 15,* 155-159.

Cutler, S. J. (1976). Age differences in voluntary association memberships. *Social Forces, 55,* 43-58.

Cutler, S. J. (1985). Aging and voluntary association participation. In E. Palmore, E. W. Busse, G. L. Maddox, J. B. Nowlik, & I. C. Siegler (Eds.), *Normal aging III* (pp. 415-428). Durham, NC: Duke University Press.

CURRENT STATUS OF THE STUDY:

a. No further waves of data collection are planned.

b. Most of the data are in machine-readable format.

c. Data are available for secondary analysis through the study contact person.

D

Career Plans and Experiences of June 1961 College Graduates, 1961

Davis, James A.; Spaeth, Joe L.; & Greeley, Andrew M.

Contact Person: Patrick Bova
Address: NORC Library
                1155 East 60th Street
                Chicago, IL 60637
Telephone No.: (312) 702-1213

SUBSTANTIVE TOPICS COVERED:

This study examined the future career plans of college graduates.

CHARACTERISTICS OF THE ORIGINAL SAMPLE:

Year the study began: 1961
Subject selection process: Students receiving a baccalaureate degree from an eligible institution in June, 1961
Total number of subjects at Time 1: N = 33,782
Ages at Time 1: 18-22 yrs.
Sex distribution: 60% male, 40% female
Socioeconomic status: 52% middle/upper middle class, 27% poverty class, 21% working class
Race/ethnicity: 94% white, 3% African-American, 2% Asian-American, 1% other

Years of Completed Waves:

Years	N=	Age ranges
1961	33,782	18-22 yrs.
1962	31,075	19-23 yrs.
1963	29,738	20-24 yrs.
1964	24,385	21-25 yrs.
1968	4,868	25-29 yrs.

INFORMATION ON SAMPLE ATTRITION:

During the 7-year period of study, 9,397 of 33,782 Ss (27.8%) were not retrieved for further study. The core sample consists of 24,385 Ss. At the fifth wave, questionnaires were administered to a subsample (6,005 Ss) of the original sample with 4,868 respondents.

CONSTRUCTS MEASURED: INSTRUMENTS USED

Future plans, career aspirations: Questionnaires (self-administered)
Career satisfaction, comparison of actual and predicted plans: Follow-up questionnaire (self-administered)

REPRESENTATIVE REFERENCES:

Davis, J. A. (1964). Great aspirations: The graduate school plans of America's college seniors. *NORC Monographs in Social Research, 1.* Chicago: Aldine.
Davis, J. A. (1965). Undergraduate career decisions: Correlates of occupational choice. *NORC Monographs in Social Research, 2.* Chicago: Aldine.
Spaeth, J. L., & Greeley, A. M. (1970). *Recent alumni and higher education: A survey of college graduates.* New York: McGraw-Hill.
Warkov, S. (1965). Lawyers in the making. *NORC Monographs in Social Research, 7.* Chicago: Aldine.

CURRENT STATUS OF THE STUDY:

a. No further waves of data collection are planned.
b. Most of the data are in machine-readable format.
c. Data are available for secondary analysis through the Inter-University Consortium for Political and Social Research (ICPSR), Institute for Social Research, University of Michigan, P.O. Box 1248, Ann Arbor, MI 48106.

■ Colorado Adoption Project, 1976

DeFries, John C.; Plomin, Robert; and Fulkes, David W.

Contact Person: Sally Ann Rhea
Address: Institute for Behavioral Genetics
Box 447
Boulder, CO 80309
Telephone No.: (303) 492-2822

SUBSTANTIVE TOPICS COVERED:

The study examines genetic and environmental influences on behavioral development, and includes measures that sample broadly the major domains of behavioral development, such as cognitive ability and personality.

CHARACTERISTICS OF THE ORIGINAL SAMPLE:

Year the study began: 1976

Subject selection process: Biological and adoptive parents were contacted through two private adoption agencies in Colorado. Participation in the project was encouraged if it was considered likely that the biological parents would relinquish their child for adoption. Of the biological parents initially tested, approximately 75% later decided to relinquish their child. Comparison of nonparticipating parents with participating parents reveals no important differences in either cognitive or personality variables. Control group subjects were contacted through local hospitals in Colorado. Records of recently born children were surveyed by hospital staff members to identify couples who had a singleton birth and had no more than two other children in the home. Control families were matched to adoptive families on the basis of sex of proband, number of children in the family, age of father, occupation of father, father's level of education. Data were collected, but not compiled. Each birth year is represented as a separate cohort, which may contain siblings from earlier cohorts.

Total number of subjects at Time 1: N = 48

Ages at Time 1: 1 yr.

Sex distribution: Approximately equal numbers of females and males throughout

Socioeconomic status: Information was gathered, but not available in terms of percent distribution by socioeconomic class.

Race/ethnicity: 95% white, 5% Hispanic and Asian-American

Years of Completed Waves:

Years	N=	Age ranges
(Cohort 1)		
1977	48	1 yr.
1978	51	2 yrs.
1979	48	3 yrs.
1980	49	4 yrs.
1981	49	5 yrs.
1982	45	6 yrs.
1983	31	7 yrs.
1984	31	8 yrs.
1985	31	9 yrs.
1986	31	10 yrs.
1987	29	11 yrs.
1988	31	12 yrs.
(Cohort 2)		
1978	107	1 yr.
1979	98	2 yrs.
1980	92	3 yrs.
1981	88	4 yrs.
1982	90	5 yrs.
1983	86	6 yrs.
1984	51	7 yrs.
1985	50	8 yrs.
1986	51	9 yrs.
1987	49	10 yrs.
1988	50	11 yrs.
(Cohort 3)		
1979	88	1 yr.
1980	84	2 yrs.
1981	85	3 yrs.
1982	90	4 yrs.
1983	77	5 yrs.
1984	87	6 yrs.
1985	95	7 yrs.
1986	101	8 yrs.
1987	95	9 yrs.
1988	97	10 yrs.
(Cohort 4)		
1980	112	1 yr.
1981	110	2 yrs.
1982	107	3 yrs.
1983	101	4 yrs.
1984	112	5 yrs.
1985	106	6 yrs.
1986	73	7 yrs.
1987	73	8 yrs.
1988	73	9 yrs.
(Cohort 5)		
1981	97	1 yr.
1982	96	2 yrs.

Years of Completed Waves, Continued:

Years	N=	Age ranges
1983	93	3 yrs.
1984	95	4 yrs.
1985	87	5 yrs.
1986	89	6 yrs.
1987	99	7 yrs.
1988	106	8 yrs.
(Cohort 6)		
1982	50	1 yr.
1983	48	2 yrs.
1984	49	3 yrs.
1985	46	4 yrs.
1986	49	5 yrs.
1987	46	6 yrs.
1988	56	7 yrs.
(Cohort 7)		
1983	80	1 yr.
1984	81	2 yrs.
1985	78	3 yrs.
1986	77	4 yrs.
1987	80	5 yrs.
1988	61	6 yrs.
(Cohort 8)		
1984	49	1 yr.
1985	50	2 yrs.
1986	50	3 yrs.
1987	50	4 yrs.
1988	49	5 yrs.
(Cohort 9)		
1985	19	1 yr.
1986	18	2 yrs.
1987	18	3 yrs.
1988	17	4 yrs.
(Cohort 10)		
1986	19	1 yr.
1987	22	2 yrs.
1988	20	3 yrs.
(Cohort 11)		
1987	18	1 yr.
1988	15	2 yrs.
(Cohort 12)		
1988	6	1 yr.
Generations		
Biological mother	289	19.8 yrs.
Biological father	55	21.3 yrs.
Adoptive mother	247	32.6 yrs.
Adoptive father	247	34 yrs.
Control, mother	244	29.3 yrs.
Control, father	245	31.5 yrs.

Years of Completed Waves, Continued:

Years	N=	Age ranges
Adoptive Children		
Probands	247	*
Sibs, also probands	42	*
Sibs, adopted	41	*
Sibs, born in family	30	*
Control Ss		
Probands	245	*
Sibs	113	*

INFORMATION ON SAMPLE ATTRITION:

The core sample consists of 490 families, 245 adoptive and 245 matched controls. Of these families, 31 have chosen not to continue participation in the project, and principal investigator has lost contact with another 20 families whom they are now attempting to recontact.

CONSTRUCTS MEASURED: INSTRUMENTS USED

Adult Measures

Cognition: Specific Cognitive Tests, Remote Associates, Gray Oral Reading Test
Personality: Cattell's Sixteen Personality Factor Questionnaire (Form A: 16PF), EASI (Emotionality, Activity, Sociability, Impulsivity) Temperament Survey, spouses's EASI, fears, mood and depression
Environment: Television watching, reading, family demographics, education, occupation, religion and religiosity
Handedness, smoking, musical interests, interests and talents, personal rhythms (sleep, coffee), height, weight, headaches, food preferences, motion sickness, speech history and problems, specific medical history: CAP test booklet
Information about birth parents and grandparents: Birth history forms

Year 1

Cognition: The Bayley Mental Scale, Bayley Motor Scale, Uzgiris-Hunt Ordinal Scales of Psychological Development, Imitations, Word Diary
Personality: Enjoyment of movement, response to tester, Infant Behavior Record, Colorado Child Temperament Inventory (CCTI), mother and father; nine NYLS temperament dimensions, mother and father
Environment: Caldwell HOME, Home environment, global ecological ratings, variety of objects, responsiveness and restrictions, and Moos' Family Environment Scale (FES)
Miscellaneous data: Health questions from mother, pediatrician's report, and uncharacteristic behavior

Additional sources of information: Videotape segments which have been scored on handedness, maternal interactions (J. Dunn), Infant Behavior Record (IBR) equivalents (D. Daniels), language transcripts (K.H.B.)

Year 2

Cognition: The Bayley Mental Scale, Bayley Motor Scale, Sequenced Inventory of Communication Development (SICD) Expressive & Receptive, Language Interview with Mother, Stanford-Binet Intelligence Scale (Form L-M) Vocabulary, 18-month interview (word usage), 18-month interview (imitations)

Personality: Enjoyment of movement, response to tester, Infant Behavior Record, CAP behavioral interview, Colorado Child Temperament Inventory (CCTI), mother and father; NYLS mother and father

Environment: Caldwell HOME, home environment, global ecological ratings, Variety of Objects, Responsiveness and restrictions, major family changes, number of children played with

Miscellaneous data: Health questions from mother, pediatrician's report, uncharacteristic behavior, handedness questions

Additional sources of information: Videotaped segments which have been scored on handedness, maternal interactions (J. Dunn), Infant Behavior Record (IBR) equivalents (D. Daniels), language transcripts (K.H.B.)

Year 3

Cognition: Stanford-Binet Intelligence Test, Stanford-Binet items, Specific Cognitive Abilities, Language Usage Interview, Sequenced Inventory of Communication Development (SICD) Expressive & receptive, 30-month motor interview (language use)

Personality: Enjoyment of movement, response to tester, Modified Infant Behavior Record; Colorado Child Temperament Inventory (CCTI), mother and father; nine NYLS temperament dimensions, mother and father; 30-month interview (behavioral assess), 30-month interview (kid interactions)

Environment: Caldwell HOME, global ecological ratings, variety of objects, responsiveness & restrictions, Moos' Family Environment Scale (FES), television watching total, changes in family, mother's current occupation, number of children played with

Health questions from mother, pediatrician's report, uncharacteristic behavior, motor battery, handedness items, 30 month motor items: CAP test booklet

Additional sources of information: Handedness, maternal interactions (J. Dunn)

Years 4, 5, and 6

Cognition: Stanford-Binet Intelligence Test, Stanford-Binet items, specific cognitive abilities; school readiness (years 5 and 6)

Personality: Enjoyment of movement, response to tester, Modified Infant Behavior Record, Colorado Child Temperament Inventory (CCTI), mother only; Colorado Child Temperament Inventory (CCTI), male and female (years 5 and 6); 83-item Carey, mother only; General Temperament Survey, 100-item Carey and GTS (year 6), Child Behavior Checklist

Environment: Modified Caldwell HOME, home environment, variety of objects, Moos' Family Environment Scale (FES), male and female (year 5); television watching (year 5), television at item level (year 6), changes in family, number of children played with, Cumulative Day Care information (year 5), Day Care information (year 6)

Health questions from mother, uncharacteristic behavior, hand preference, some birth history information; father and mother norc (year 5); health, height, weight (year 5); health, height, weight (year 6); sibling interactions (year 5), food preferences (year 5), interests (years 5 and 6): CAP test booklet

Year 7

Child cognition: Revised Wechsler Intelligence Scale for Children (WISC-R), Specific Cognitive Abilities, PIAT Reading Recognition, Key Math, CELF (language functioning), Token (language functioning)

Child personality: Parent Colorado Child Temperament Inventory, Parent Carey, Parent Peer Interactions & Social Competency, parent Child Behavior Checklist, Teacher Colorado Child Temperament Inventory, Teacher Peer Interaction & Social Competency, teacher Child Behavior Checklist, tester Colorado Child Temperament Inventory, tester Social Competency, tester Child Behavior Checklist

Environment: First Grade and Life Events (Stress), television watching at item level, parent Family Environment Scale, Child Family Environment Scale, Dibble & Cohen

Child additional data: Laterality, Bruininks (motor test), health questions from parent, parent interview on sibling, child interview on sibling, parent report on interests and activities, child report on interests and activities, parent report on imagination, child report on food preferences

Additional sources: Human figure drawing, audiotape of child describing human figure drawing; videotape of parent measuring child for height and weight, parent and child playing "Stadium Checkers," parent and child constructing "Crazy Puzzle"

Parent Measure: Revised Wechsler Adult Intelligence Scale (WAIS-R), Peabody Individual Achievement Test (PIAT)—Reading Recognition, Demographics, Laterality, Interests and talents

Year 8

(Data collected via telephone interview with parent or questionnaire to parent or teacher)

Personality: Parent Colorado Child Temperament Inventory, Super-short parent Child Behavior Checklist, teacher Colorado Child Temperament Inventory, Teacher Peer Interaction & Social Competency, teacher Child Behavior Checklist

Environment: Family Events, television watching at item level, Day Care

Miscellaneous data: Health Inquiry, Activities and interests, Sibling interview

Years 9-11

(Data collected via telephone interview to child, except as noted "parent" or "teacher")

Cognition: Specific Cognitive Abilities

Personality: Harter's Self Perception Profile*, Ascher's Loneliness Scale*, Colorado Child Temperament Inventory*, Kandel's Depressive Mood Inventory*, parent Colorado Child Temperament Inventory, parent Child Behavior Checklist, teacher Colorado Child Temperament Inventory, Teacher Peer Interaction and Social Competency, teacher Child Behavior Checklist Environment: Family Environment Scale* (FES), SIQYA*, Stress (9 & 10 only), Brooks-Gunn Life Events Scale, television watching at item level, parent Family Environment Scale, parent Dibble & Cohen

Parent health inquiry, musical interest, interests and activities, parent and child pubertal development: CAP test booklet

Year 12

(Data was collected in person)

Cognition: Specific Cognitive Abilities, Revised Wechsler Intelligence Scale for Children (WISC-R)

Personality: Harter's Self Perception Profile*, Ascher's Loneliness Scale*, Colorado Child Temperament Inventory*, Kandel's Depressive Mood Inventory*, parent Colorado Child Temperament Inventory, parent Child Behavior Checklist, teacher Colorado Child Temperament Inventory, Teacher Peer Interaction and Social Competency, teacher Child Behavior Checklist

Environment: Family Environment Scale* (FES), SIQYA*, Stress (9 & 10 only), Brooks-Gunn Life Events Scale, television watching at item level, parent Family Environment Scale, parent Dibble & Cohen

Parent health inquiry, musical interest, musical abilities test, interests and activities, parent and child pubertal development, social attitudes questionnaire, photo of child: CAP test booklet

Comments:
*These questionnaires are modified and intermixed into one questionnaire.

REPRESENTATIVE REFERENCES:

Plomin, R., & DeFries, J. C. (1983). The Colorado Adoption Project. *Child Development, 54,* 276-289.

Plomin, R., & DeFries, J. C. (1985). *Origins of individual differences in infancy: The Colorado Adoption Project.* New York: Academic Press.

Plomin, R., DeFries, J. C., & Fulkes, D. W. (1988). *Nature and nurture during infancy and early childhood.* New York: Cambridge University Press.

Plomin, R., & Dunn, J. F. (1986). *The study of temperament: Changes, continuities and challenges.* Hillsdale, NJ: Lawrence Erlbaum.

CURRENT STATUS OF THE STUDY:

   a. Further waves of data collection are planned.
   b. Most of the data are in machine-readable format.
   c. The data are conditionally available for secondary analysis.

■ Families, Peers and Schools, 1987

Dornbusch, Sanford M.; and Leiderman, P. Herbert

Contact Person: Sanford M. Dornbusch
Address: Department of Sociology
                  Stanford University
                  Stanford, CA 94305
Telephone No.:   (415) 723-1706

SUBSTANTIVE TOPICS COVERED:

   This study examines family and peer influences on academic performance, extra-curricular activities, and differentiated self-esteem, among several cohorts of students in six San Francisco Bay Area high schools, and among students attending high school in Madison, Wisconsin. The ethnic, neighborhood, and school contexts within which family and peer processes take place are the central foci of the study.

CHARACTERISTICS OF THE ORIGINAL SAMPLE:

Year the study began: 1987

Subject selection process: All students at six high schools in five San Francisco-Bay Area School Districts

Total number of subjects at Time 1: N = 10,016 (7,606, California; 2,410 Wisconsin)

Ages at Time 1: 14-18 yrs. (Cohorts 1 and 2), 15-18 yrs. (Cohort 3)

Sex distribution: Equal numbers of females and males throughout

Socioeconomic status: 100% student

Race/ethnicity: 50% white, 20% Hispanic, 20% Asian-American, 5% African-American, 5% other

Years of Completed Waves:

Years	$N=$[a]	Age ranges
California Site		
(Cohort 1A: Freshmen in 1987-1988)		
1987-1988	1,888	14 yrs.
1988-1989	1,889 (1,308)	15 yrs.
1989-1990	1,800 (900)[b]	16 yrs.
(Cohort 2A: Sophomore in 1987-1988)		
1987-1988	1,984	15 yrs.
1988-1989	1,831 (1,263)	16 yrs.
1989-1990	1,800[b]	17 yrs.
(Cohort 3A: Junior in 1987-1988)		
1987-1988	1,957	16 yrs.
1988-1989	1,768 (1,222)	17 yrs.
(Cohort 4A: Seniors in 1987-1988)		
1987-1988	1,777	17 yrs.
Wisconsin Site		
(Cohort 1B: Freshmen in 1987-1988)		
1987-1988	642	14 yrs.
1988-1989	623	15 yrs.
1989-1990	571	16 yrs.
(Cohort 2B: Sophomores in 1987-1988)		
1987-1988	602	15 yrs.
1988-1989	535	16 yrs.
1989-1990	442	17 yrs.
(Cohort 3B: Juniors in 1987-1988)		
1987-1988	561	16 yrs.
1988-1989	461	17 yrs.
(Cohort 4B: Seniors in 1987-1988)		
1987-1988	605	17 yrs.

Comments:
a. Sample sizes listed in parentheses represent subjects whose student identification numbers, in follow-up, have been verified as matched to numbers they provided at the previous time of data collection. Sample sizes not listed in parentheses represent the number of unmatched students followed at each wave, some of whom could be new students included in the study.
b. Estimated number of subjects followed up.

INFORMATION ON SAMPLE ATTRITION:

During the 3-year period of study, approximately 792 of 7,634 Ss (10.4%) across six cohorts followed in California and Wisconsin were not retrieved for further study: in California, 88 of 1,888 Ss (4.7%) (Cohort 1A); 184 of 1,984 Ss (9.3%) (Cohort 2A); and 189 of 1,957 Ss (9.7%) (Cohort 3A); in Wisconsin 71 of 642 Ss (11.1%) (Cohort 1B); 160 of 602 Ss (26.6%) (Cohort 2B); and 100 of 561 Ss

(17.8%) (Cohort 3B). Rates of attrition are approximations based on the number of subjects tested at each data point, though not necessarily based on subject verified as the same subject tested at several data points ("matched subjects"). Main reasons for attrition included students' graduating, dropping out, or transferring. For California students, core sample, based on estimates of matched subjects, consisted of approximately 3,385 Ss: 900 Ss (Cohort 1A); 1,263 Ss (Cohort 2A); and 1,222 Ss (Cohort 3A). No information was available on the number of matched subjects for Wisconsin students, and therefore core sample could not be estimated.

CONSTRUCTS MEASURED: INSTRUMENTS USED

Academic work; academic performance; student effort, student grades, stressful events, parenting styles, communication in home, susceptibility to peer pressure, family decision making, family relationships; family-school relationship (e.g., level of parental education, extent of parental involvement with adolescent's educational process; and parental expectations for adolescent academic achievement); ethnicity, background, and language use; aspect of student's life; employment; extracurricular activities (e.g., memberships, and sports), and peer relationships: Student Questionnaire

REPRESENTATIVE REFERENCES:

Dornbusch, S. M. (1988). Parents of high school students: A neglected resource. *Educational Horizons, 66*, 75-77.
Dornbusch, S. M. (in press). Family decision-making and academic performance in a diverse high school population. *Journal of Adolescent Research.*
Dornbusch, S. M. (in press). Family influences on dropout behavior: An exploratory study of a single high school. *Sociology of Education.*
Dornbusch, S. M. (in press). Family processes and educational achievement. In William J. Weston (Ed.), *Education and the American family: A research synthesis.* New York: New York University Press.

CURRENT STATUS OF THE STUDY:

a. No further waves of data collection are planned.
b. Most of the data are in machine-readable format.
c. Data will eventually be available for secondary analysis from the study contact person.

E

Epidemiologic Study of Behavior Problems in Children, 1977

Earls, Felton; and Garrison, William

Contact Person: Felton Earls
Address: Department of Maternal and Child Health
School of Public Health
Harvard University
677 Huntington Avenue
Boston, MA 02115
Telephone No.: (617) 432-1227

SUBSTANTIVE TOPICS COVERED:

The study examines stress in family life and its impact upon young children and the prevalence and course of behavior problems detected early in childhood.

CHARACTERISTICS OF THE ORIGINAL SAMPLE:

Year the study began: 1977-1978
Subject selection process: All children born over a 14-month period during 1974-1975 and living in families in permanent residence were asked to participate in the study.
Total number of subjects at Time 1: N = 100
Ages at Time 1: 1-3 yrs.
Sex distribution: Approximately equal numbers of females and males throughout
Socioeconomic status: 60% working class, 40% middle/upper middle class (approximately)
Race/ethnicity: 95% white, 5% African-American

Years of Completed Waves:

Years	N=	Age ranges
(1974/1975 Birth Cohort)		
1977-1978	100	3 yrs.
1980-1981	83	6-7 yrs.
(1978 Birth Cohort)[a]		
1981	155	3 yrs.

Years of Completed Waves, Continued:

Years	N=	Age ranges
(1979 Birth Cohort)[a]		
1981	134	18-24 mos.
1982	134	3 yrs.
(1980 Birth Cohort)[a]		
1981	134	1 yr.
1982	134	2 yrs.
1983	134	3 yrs.

Comments:
a. Subjects were selected through a birth register of all births to permanent residents living in the community in question. The register was compiled and used a sampling frame. The total number of children born during a 3-year period between 1978-1980 was asked to participate.

INFORMATION ON SAMPLE ATTRITION:

During the 9-year period of study, 17 of 368 Ss (4.6%) across three cohorts were not retrieved for further study. The core sample across three cohorts consists of 351 Ss.

CONSTRUCTS MEASURED: INSTRUMENTS USED

Acute and chronic stress in families: Stressful life events interview
Developmental progress and problems: Array of standardized tests and checklists for behavior problems
Self-esteem and perceived competence: Perceived Competence Scale
Personality and emotional development: Play interview
Demographic information, stressors and social support, mother's mental status, quality of parents' marriage: Family interview
Child's temperament: Temperament questionnaire
Behavior adjustment: Preschool Behavior Checklist (self-administered form of the Behavior Screening Questionnaire)

REPRESENTATIVE REFERENCES:

Barron, A., & Earls, F. (1984). The relation of temperament and social factors to behavior problems in three-year old children. *Journal of Child Psychology and Psychiatry, 25,* 23-33.
Earls, F. (1987). Sex differences in psychiatric disorders: Origins and developmental influences. *Psychiatric Developments, 5,* 1-23.
Earls, F., & Jung, K. (1987). Temperament and home environment characteristics as causal factors in the early development of child psychopathology. *Journal of the American Academy of Child and Adolescent Psychiatry, 26,* 491-498.
Garrison, W., & Earls, F. (1983). Life events and social supports in families with a two-year old: Methods and preliminary findings. *Comprehensive Psychiatry, 24,* 439-452.

CURRENT STATUS OF THE STUDY:

a. Further waves of data collection are planned for 1992.
b. Most of the data are in machine-readable format.
c. The data are available for secondary analysis from the study contact person.

■ Adolescent Health Care Evaluation Study, 1984

Earls, Felton; Robins, Lee; and Stiffman, Arlene

Contact person: Felton Earls
Address: Department of Maternal and Child Health
School of Public Health
Harvard University
677 Huntington Avenue
Boston, MA 02115
Telephone No.: (617) 432-1227

SUBSTANTIVE TOPICS COVERED:

This study was designed to evaluate the effectiveness of comprehensive outpatient care for adolescents at high risk for a variety of lifestyle morbidities. Topics included adolescent medicine, health care utilization, and risk assessment.

CHARACTERISTICS OF THE ORIGINAL SAMPLE:

Year the study began: 1984
Subject selection process: Sample was derived from 10 health care programs throughout the country.
Total number of subjects at Time 1: N = 2,788
Ages at Time 1: 13-18 yrs.
Sex distribution: 76% female, 24% male (Cohort 1); approximately equal numbers of females and males (Cohort 2)
Socioeconomic status: 60% working class, 30% poverty class, 10% middle/upper middle class
Race/ethnicity: 71% African-American, 16% white, 12% Hispanic, 1% other (Cohort 1); 60% African-American, 40% Hispanic (Cohort 2)

Years of Completed Waves:

Years	N=	Age ranges
(Cohort 1)		
1984-1985	2,788	13-18 yrs.
1985-1986	2,415	14-19 yrs.
(Cohort 2)[a]		
1988-1989	650	17-22 yrs.

Comments:
a. Cohort 2 is a subgroup of Cohort 1, chosen for follow-up because they are at varying degrees of risk for HIV infection.

INFORMATION ON SAMPLE ATTRITION:

During the 2-year period of study, 372 of 2,787 Ss (13.3%) were not retrieved for further study. The core sample consists of 2,415 Ss.

CONSTRUCTS MEASURED: INSTRUMENTS USED

Home environment, family history, school adjustment, peer relationships, physical and mental health, reasons for seeking health care, substance use/abuse/dependence: Closed-ended interview

REPRESENTATIVE REFERENCES:

Earls, F., & Powell, J. (1988). Patterns of substance use and abuse in inner-city adolescent medical patients. *The Yale Journal of Biology and Medicine, 61*, 233-242.

Earls, F., Robins, L. N., Stiffman, A., & Powell, J. (1989). Comprehensive health care for high-risk adolescents. *American Journal of Public Health, 79*, 999-1005.

Stiffman, A., & Earls, F. (1990). Behavioral risks for HIV infection in adolescent medical patients. *Pediatrics, 85*(3), 303-310.

Stiffman, A. R., Earls, F., Robins, L. N., Jung, K. G., & Kulbok, P. (1987). Adolescent sexual activity and pregnancy: Socioenvironmental problems, physical health and mental health. *Journal of Youth and Adolescence, 16*(5), 497-509.

CURRENT STATUS OF THE STUDY:

a. Further waves of data collection are planned for 1991 and 1993.

b. Most of the data are in machine-readable format.

c. Data are available for secondary analysis from the study contact person or from the Henry A. Murray Research Center, Radcliffe College, 10 Garden Street, Cambridge, MA 02138.

■ Early Adolescent Peer Culture and Peer Relations, 1984

Eder, Donna

Contact Person: Donna Eder
Address: Department of Sociology
Indiana University
Ballantine Hall
Bloomington, IN 47405
Telephone No.: (818) 855-2569

SUBSTANTIVE TOPICS COVERED:

This study examines peer relationships to understand the processes of friendship, popularity, and peer status as these processes change throughout middle school.

CHARACTERISTICS OF THE ORIGINAL SAMPLE:

Year the study began: 1984
Subject selection process: Subjects attended a middle school located in a medium-size midwestern community. Subjects from a broad range of socioeconomic backgrounds were selected.
Total number of subjects at Time 1: N = 700
Ages at Time 1: 11-12 yrs.
Sex distribution: Approximately equal numbers of females and males throughout
Socioeconomic status: 50% working class, 25% poverty class, 25% upper middle class/middle class
Race/ethnicity: 95% white, 5% African-American

Years of Completed Waves:

Years	N=	Age ranges
1984	700	11-12 yrs.
1985	690	12-13 yrs.
1986	660	13-14 yrs.

INFORMATION ON SAMPLE ATTRITION:

During the 2-year period of study, 40 of 700 Ss (57.1%) were not retrieved for further study. The core sample consists of 690 Ss. Attrition was due to subjects' change of residence.

CONSTRUCTS MEASURED: INSTRUMENTS USED

Peer interactions: Observation of extracurricular and informal activities
Peer status: In-depth interviews with group members
Factors contributing to whom peers interacted with, peer activities: Sociometric
    Questionnaire
Extracurricular activities, scholastic honors: School records

REPRESENTATIVE REFERENCES:

Eder, D. (1985). The cycle of popularity: Interpersonal relations among female adolescents. *Sociology of Education, 58,* 154-165.
Eder, D., & Parker, S. (1987). The cultural production and reproduction of gender: The effect of extracurricular activities on peer group culture. *Sociology of Education, 60,* 200-213.
Eder, D., & Sanford, S. (1988). The development and maintenance of interactional norms among early adolescents. In P. Adler & P. Adler (Eds.), *Sociological studies of child development.* Greenwich, CT: JAI Press.
Sanford, S., & Eder, D. (1984). Adolescent humor during peer interaction. *Social Psychology Quarterly, 47,* 235-243.

CURRENT STATUS OF THE STUDY:

a. No further waves of data collection are planned.
b. Most of the data are in machine-readable format.
c. Data are not available for secondary analysis.

■ Mother-Child Research Project, 1975

Egeland, Byron; and Sroufe, Alan

Contact Person: Byron Egeland
Address: Institute of Child Development
                 University of Minnesota
                 Minneapolis, MN 55455
Telephone No.:   (612) 624-6864

SUBSTANTIVE TOPICS COVERED:

This study examines the continuity of early development; social-emotional development; effects of child maltreatment and its antecedents; the relation between mother-infant attachment and later behavior; effects of divorce; continuity of parental behavior; social-emotional development in preschool children; developmental psychopathology; continuity and discontinuity of development; predicting competence in middle childhood.

CHARACTERISTICS OF THE ORIGINAL SAMPLE:

Year the study began: 1975

Subject selection process: Primiparous women enrolled from the Minneapolis Public Health Clinics in the last trimester of pregnancy were contacted for participation in the study.

Total number of subjects at Time 1: N = 267

Ages at Time 1: Last trimester of pregnancy; mothers' ages were 12-32 yrs.

Sex distribution: Approximately equal numbers of females and males throughout

Socioeconomic status: 100% poverty class at the time of enrollment in the study

Race/ethnicity: 85% white, 10% African-American, 3% Native American, 2% Hispanic

Years of Completed Waves:

Years	N=	Age ranges
1975	267	Last trimester of pregnancy
1975	267	7 days
1975	267	10 days
1975	250	3 mos.
1975-1976	250	6 mos.
1976	240	9 mos.
1976	225	12 mos.
1976	225	18 mos.
1977	215	24 mos.
1977-1978	215	30 mos.
1978-1979	210	42 mos.
1980	210	48 mos.
1980-1981	210	54 mos.
1981-1982	194	66 mos.
1982	194	6 yrs., 3 mos.
1983	194	7 yrs., 10 mos.
1983-1984	190	6-7 yrs. (1st grade)
1984-1985	190	7-8 yrs. (2nd grade)
1985-1986	190	8-9 yrs. (3rd grade)
1988-1989	190	11-12 yrs.(6th grade)

INFORMATION ON SAMPLE ATTRITION:

During the 14-year period of study, 77 of 267 Ss (28.8%) were not retrieved for further study. Rate of attrition from 1983-1989 was close to zero. Families who dropped out of the study do not differ from the families remaining. The primary reasons for attrition are death of a parent or child, residence changes, and refusals. The core sample consists of 190 subjects.

CONSTRUCTS MEASURED: INSTRUMENTS USED

Mother

Mother's relationship status, support, and demographic information: Mother's Information and Interview Sheet

Amount of environmental stress on mother: Life Stress Scale (Cockran & Robertson)

Mother's feelings regarding pregnancy (fear for self, desire for pregnancy, dependency, fear for baby, maternal feelings, and irritability and tension): Pregnancy Research Questionnaire (Schaefer & Manheimer)

General medical information on pregnancy: Hennepin County General Hospital Newborn Data Base

General medical information on delivery: Delivery Room Assessment of Newborn

Mother's feelings on delivery and her newborn: First Days Questionnaire

Mother's feelings regarding infant: Enjoyment of Baby Scale

Mother's expectations of child ability: Mother's expectation of child's performance on Bayley Scale, Baby's Activity Scale

Mother's expectation: Neonatal Perception Inventory (Broussard & Hartner)

Mother's attitude toward developing mother-child relationship (appropriate versus inappropriate, control of child's aggression, encouragement versus discouragement of reciprocity, and acceptance versus denial of emotional complexity in child care): Maternal Attitude Scale (Cohler)

Mother's style of discipline: Prohibition of Forbidden Objects

Mother's expectations: Mother's Perception of Toddler

Mother's knowledge of child development norms: Child Development Scale

Mother's knowledge (knowledge of child care and expectations of child development): Questionnaire, interview

Source of knowledge about child rearing: Source of Information Questionnaire

Where mother acquired information: Acquiring Child-care Information

Mother's relationship status, support, and history of her childhood; knowledge of child development, and life circumstances; knowledge of child-care practices; relationship status, life circumstances, contact with social agencies; general information, relationship status, and so on; involvement with social agencies, and child care: Interview

Mother's personality: 16 PF (Cattell)

Personality characteristics of mothers; aggression, dependency, impulsivity, and succorance: Personality Research Form

Locus of control of mother: Inventory of Beliefs (Rotter)

Mother's affective mood states: Profile of Moods (McNair, Loor & Droopleman)

Anxiety of mother: IPAT Anxiety Scale Questionnaire (Cattell & Scheier)

Tendency toward alcoholism: MacAndrew Alcoholism Scale (MacAndrew)

Mother's depression: Beck Depression Inventory

Intelligence (mother): Shipley Hartford Vocabulary Test (Shipley & Hartford), Wechsler Adult Intelligence Scale (WAIS)

Parent's rating of child's behavior problems and social competence: Child Behavior Checklist (Parent's Form) (Achenbach)

Family and work status, feelings about present life situation and child, social life, etc.; mother's feelings, expectations and perceptions of school, mother's life circumstances, family life circumstances: Mother interview

Infant/Child

Attentional development of child: Habituation Task

Cognitive development: Uzgiris and Hunt Assessment in Infancy Scale

Infant's mental and motor development: Bayley Scales of Infant Development

Psychological and physiological characteristics of newborn: Brazelton Behavioral and Neurological Assessment Scale

Measure of infant temperament: Carey Infant Temperament Scale

Infant temperament and characteristics: Nurse's Ratings of Newborn (Ferreira)

Competence, quality of play, quality of problem solving, maternal support and assistance: Tool Using and Problem Solving (Sroufe & Matas)

Involvement, and quality of play: Curiosity Box Assessment (Modified version of Banta's Curiosity Box)

Symptoms of emotional disturbance: Preschool Behavior Questionnaire (Behar & Stringfield)

Intelligence (child): Wechsler Preschool and Primary Scale of Intelligence (WPPSI), Wechsler Intelligence Scale for Children (WISC)

Agency and self-confidence, ego control, dependency, social skills, positive and negative affect, and compliance: Preschool Rating Scales

Behavioral adjustment: Preschool Interpersonal Problem-Solving Test (Shure & Spivack)

Child's ego control: Delay of Gratification—Gift Delivery

Child's ego resiliency: Competing Set (Block & Block)

Ego resiliency: Dual Focus Test (Block & Block)

Child temperament: EASI Temperament Survey (Buss & Plomin)

Child's adaptation to frustration: Barrier Box Task (Harrington, Block & Block)

Child's planfulness and imagination: Lowenfeld Mosaic Test (Block & Block)

Planfulness and impulse control, reflection and planning: Porteus Maze Test

Gender identity and stability over time, and gender constancy across various situations: Gender Constancy Test (Slaby & Frey)

Child behavior problems: Symptom Checklist

Child's problem-solving: Teaching Task

General cognitive ability: Draw-A-Person

Language development: Preschool Language Scale (Zimmerman, Steiner & Pond)

General expressive language: Tell-A-Story

Child's self-help, social and language skills: Developmental Profile (Alpern & Boll)

Self-esteem: Mastery Motivation-Perceived Competence Scale for Children (Harter)

Perceived competence and self-esteem: Pictorial Scale of Perceived Competence and Acceptance

Child's social competence: Observation and interview

Childhood depression: Children's Depression Rating Scale

Child's friendships and peer relations: Observation and interview

Peer acceptance and social competence: Teacher Nomination Procedure

Social support: Social Network Inventory (Staff; Belle-Longfellow; Pattison, Lamas & Jurd)

Mother-Infant Interaction

Observation of mother-infant interaction: Observation of feeding and play, Doctor's Rating Scale, Waiting Room Rating Scale, observation of mother and infant during Bayley Scale

Quality of child-care: Child-care Rating Scale

Security of attachment: Strange Situation (Ainsworth and Wittig)

School Adjustment

Child's general adjustment, and progress and behavior change; child's school adjustment and academic success: Teacher interview

School and classroom adjustment: Devereux Elementary School Rating Scale (Spivack & Swift), school observations

Agency, self-control, positive affect, and negative emotional tone: Kindergarten Social Behavior Scales

Perceived competence: Teacher Rating of Actual Competence and Acceptance

School attendance, referral for special programs: Information from school file

Classroom ecology: Classroom climate

School behavior problems: Child Behavior Checklist (Teacher Form) (Achenbach & Edelbrock)

Motivational orientation: Mastery Motivation-Intrinsic versus Extrinsic Orientation in the Classroom (Harter)

Academic achievement: Peabody Individual Achievement Test (Dunn & Markwordt)

Family and Home Environment

Family interaction: Laboratory observation

Quality of home environment; social, emotional and cognitive and environmental stimulation: Home Observation for Measurement of the Environment (HOME) Inventory (Caldwell, Herder & Kaplan, and Caldwell & Bradley)

Family stressful events: Life Stress Inventory

REPRESENTATIVE REFERENCES:

Egeland, B., Jacobvitz, D., & Sroufe, L. A. (1988). Breaking the cycle of abuse. *Child Development, 59,* 1080-1088.

Egeland, B., & Kreutzer, T. (in press). In E. M. Cummings, A. L. Greene, & K. H. Karraker (Eds.), *Life-span prospectives on stress and coping.* New York: John Wiley.

Egeland, B., Kalkoske, M., Gottesman, N., & Erickson, M. (1990). Preschool behavior problems: Stability and factors accounting for change. *Journal of Child Psychology and Psychiatry, 31*(6), 891-910.

Sroufe, L. A. (in press). An organizational perspective on the self. In D. Cicchetti & M. Beeghly (Eds.), *The self in transition: Infancy to childhood.* Chicago: University of Chicago Press.

CURRENT STATUS OF THE STUDY:

a. Further waves of data collection are planned through 1991 to follow up the children through adolescence.
b. Most of the data are in machine-readable format.
c. Data are not available for secondary analysis.

■ Berkeley Growth Study (B), 1928

Eichorn, Dorothy H. (retired); Bayley, Nancy (retired); Wolff, Lotte V. (deceased)

Contact Person: Intergenerational Studies Archivist
Address: University of California
Institute of Human Development
1203 Tolman Hall
Berkeley, CA 94720
Telephone No.: (415) 642-2022

SUBSTANTIVE TOPICS COVERED:

The study examines mental, motor, and physical growth; skeletal maturation; personality characteristics; occupational history; interrelationships of biological, psychological, and social variables. (See also Clausen, J. A., *Oakland Growth Study*; and Huffine, C., *Guidance Study*.)

CHARACTERISTICS OF THE ORIGINAL SAMPLE:

Year the study began: 1928
Subject selection process: Subjects participating in the study were healthy, full-term infants born in two Berkeley hospitals (one county, one private) to white, English-speaking parents; middle-class families; primarily Protestant. The

sample is of above average socioeconomic status. Offspring of the subjects are also followed from 6 months through 18 years, and spouses of the subjects are followed in adulthood.

Total number of subjects at Time 1: N = 61
Ages at Time 1: Birth
Sex distribution: Approximately equal numbers of females and male throughout
Socioeconomic status: 100% middle class
Race/ethnicity: 100% white

Years of Completed Waves:[a]

Year	N=	Age ranges
1928	61	Birth
1946	41	18 yrs.
1964	54	36 yrs.
1981-1983	49	54 yrs.

Comments:
a. Data were collected continuously from birth through late adolescence. By age 18, 41 of the original 61 Ss were still being seen. Some additional material was obtained from available Ss while they were in their 20s, and two full adult follow-ups have been conducted, one in 1964 and one in 1981-1983. Forty-nine subjects took part in some or all of the 1982 follow-up data collection procedures. The original 61 Ss were born between September 27, 1928, and May 12, 1929. The sample was augmented by eight Ss born between December 1, 1929, and September 18, 1930, and five Ss born between February 26, 1931, and March 29, 1933. Two of the last Ss added were siblings of an original study member, and the other three Ss were triplets.

INFORMATION ON SAMPLE ATTRITION:

After the 54 years of study, 11 of 61 Ss (18.0%) were not retrieved for a follow-up. Principal investigators report that sample attrition occurred primarily when Ss were children and as a result of families moving.

CONSTRUCTS MEASURED: INSTRUMENTS USED

Mental development: California First Year Mental Scale; Preschool A, B (Jaffa); Stanford-Binet (1916, L,M); Wechsler (W-B,WAIS); Specific Tests, Vocab, T-M (c,d), Concept Mastery; Form Boards, Dearborn Puzzles, Mazes
Motor development: Reflexes; body control and motor coordination; motion pictures of creeping and early walking; manual dexterity tasks; ratings of child and notes on mother; Bayley California Scale of Motor Development
Personality development: Ratings of Mother; Rating Scale for Reactions (2 forms); Note on Child's Behavior (during tests)
Self-reports: Food Preference, POP (F Test): ICW Interest Record, UC Inventory, Edwards Personal Preference Scale, Kuder '44, PBI, California Psychological Inventory (CPI), Smoking Survey, Rigidity Scale; Interviews: Bretnal (of mother), Nursery School Follow-up, Leisure Time, Schedule Q (21 yr.), 25-year Information, 36-year Interview

Projective Tests: Thematic Apperception Test, Rorschach Inkblot Test, Picture Interview, Amen Silhouettes, Voice Recording
Physical development: Daily routine and feeding, anthropometrics, physical examination, vegetative functions, skeletal X rays; photographs (stills); footprints; androgyny, immunization (Schick); physiological (shock) responses
School and home background information: School attendance records, interview

REPRESENTATIVE REFERENCES:

Bayley, N. (1949). Consistency and variability in the growth of intelligence from birth to eighteen years. *Journal of Genetic Psychology, 75,* 165-196.
Bayley, N. (1970). Development of mental abilities. In P. H. Mussen (Ed.), *Carmichael's manual of child psychology: Vol. 1.* New York: John Wiley.
Eichorn, D. H., Hunt, J. V., & Honzik, M. P. (1981). Experience, personality, and IQ: Adolescence to middle age. In D. H. Eichorn, J. A. Clausen, N. Haan, M. P. Honzik, & P. H. Mussen (Eds.), *Present and past in middle life.* New York: Academic Press.
McCall, R., Eichorn, D., & Hogarty, P. (1977). Transitions in early mental development. *Monographs of the Society for Research in Child Development, 44*(3).

CURRENT STATUS OF THE STUDY:

a. Further waves of data collection are planned.
b. Some data are in machine-readable format.
c. Data are available for secondary analysis through the study contact person.

■ Longitudinal Study of Prosocial Development, 1977

Eisenberg, Nancy

Contact Person: Nancy Eisenberg
Address: Department of Psychology
                  Arizona State University
                  Tempe, AZ 85282
Telephone No.:   (602) 966-6142

SUBSTANTIVE TOPICS COVERED:

The study examines the development of prosocial moral judgment; its relation to prohibition-oriented moral judgment; prosocial behavior, religious training, role taking, and maternal practices.

CHARACTERISTICS OF THE ORIGINAL SAMPLE:

Year the study began: 1977
Subject selection process: All children 4-to-5 years old in a particular preschool
    were selected for participation in the study.
Total number of subjects at Time 1: N = 52
Ages at Time 1: 46 mos.- 67 mos.
Sex distribution: Approximately equal numbers of females and males throughout
Socioeconomic status: 100% middle/upper middle class
Race/ethnicity: 94% white, 4% Hispanic, and 2% Native American

Years of Completed Waves:

Years	N=	Age ranges
(Cohort 1)		
1977	36	3.8-5.3 yrs.
1978	34	5.3-6.3 yrs.
1980	33	6.8-8.3 yrs.
1982	32	8.8-10.3 yrs.
1984	32	12.8-14.3 yrs.
1988	32	14.8-16.3 yrs.
(Cohort 2)		
1978	16	4.1-5.6 yrs.
1980	16	5.1-6.6 yrs.
1982	14	7.1-8.6 yrs.
1984	14	9.1-12.6 yrs.
1986	11	11.2-12.6 yrs.

INFORMATION ON SAMPLE ATTRITION:

During the 11-year period of study, 9 of 52 Ss (17.3%) across two cohorts were
not retrieved for further study. For Cohort 1, 4 of 36 Ss (11.1%) and for Cohort 2,
5 of 16 Ss (31.3%) were not retrieved for further study. The core sample of each
group is: Cohort 1, 32 Ss; Cohort 2, 11 Ss.

CONSTRUCTS MEASURED: INSTRUMENTS USED

Prosocial moral judgment: Index of prosocial moral judgment (Eisenberg)
Moral judgment: Kohlberg's Moral Judgment Interview
Prosocial behavior: Observations of prosocial behavior, self-report of prosocial be-
    havior, maternal report of prosocial behavior, responses to contrived helping
    situations
Religious training: Maternal report of religious training
Role taking: 7-Picture role taking task

Empathy: Bryant's empathy measure; adapted Davis Empathy scale

Social desirability: Social Desirability Questionnaire (Crandall et al.); Crandall's social desirability scale

Maternal discipline: Block Q-sort for maternal practices, maternal report of discipline (when child does not assist in hypothetical situations)

Self-monitoring: Graziano Self-monitoring Scale

REPRESENTATIVE REFERENCES:

Eisenberg, N. (1986). *Altruistic emotion, cognition, and behavior.* Hillsdale, NJ: Lawrence Erlbaum.

Eisenberg, N., Shell, R., Pasternack, J., Lennon, R., Beller, R., & Mathy, R. M. (1987). Prosocial development in middle childhood: A longitudinal study. *Developmental Psychology, 23,* 712-718.

Eisenberg, N., & Roth, K. (1980). Development of young children's prosocial moral judgment: A longitudinal follow-up. *Developmental Psychology, 16*(4), 375-376.

Eisenberg, N. (1983). The development of prosocial moral reasoning. *Developmental Psychology, 19,* 846-855.

CURRENT STATUS OF THE STUDY:

    a. A further wave of data collection is planned.

    b. Most of the data are not in machine-readable format.

    c. Some of the data are available for secondary analysis from the study contact person.

■ Infant Care Project, 1981

Elias, Marjorie

Contact person: Marjorie Elias
Address: 102 Raymond Street
Cambridge, MA 02140
Telephone No.: (617) 354-5593

SUBSTANTIVE TOPICS COVERED:

This study examines the effect of La Leche League (LL), an international support network to promote breast-feeding and very frequent nursing for many months, and Standard Care (SC), "western" styles of child rearing (i.e., nursing for four to six times daily with earlier weaning) on infant development, using two groups of middle class American mothers and their children.

CHARACTERISTICS OF THE ORIGINAL SAMPLE:

Year the study began: 1981

Subject selection process: Selection criteria included a healthy mother and baby at birth; the family having at least one older child (than the newborn); mother's intention to breast feed and to refrain from full-time employment outside the home for the duration of the study. La Leche subjects were recruited by letter to League leaders, while Standard Care mothers were recruited through birth announcements in local newspapers of the towns in which La Leche League mothers resided.

Total number of subjects at Time 1: N = 32

Ages at Time 1: 2 mos.

Sex distribution: Equal numbers of female and male infants throughout

Socioeconomic status: 100% middle/upper middle class

Race/ethnicity: 100% white

Years of Completed Waves:

Years	N=	Age ranges
(Cohort 1: La Leche League)		
1981-1982	16	2 mos.
1981-1982	16	4 mos.
1981-1982	16	7 mos.
1981-1982	16	10 mos.
1982-1983	16	13 mos.
1982-1983	16	16 mos.
1982-1983	16	20 mos.
1982-1983	16	24 mos.
(Cohort 2: Standard Care)		
1981-1982	16	2 mos.
1981-1982	16	4 mos.
1981-1982	16	7 mos.
1981-1982	16	10 mos.
1982-1983	16	13 mos.
1982-1983	16	16 mos.
1982-1983	16	20 mos.
1982-1983	16	24 mos.

INFORMATION ON SAMPLE ATTRITION:

During the 2-year period of the study, all subjects in both groups participated in each wave. The core sample consists of 32 Ss.

CONSTRUCTS MEASURED: INSTRUMENTS USED

Family health, infant sleeping patterns, introduction of supplementary food, weaning age, resumption of mother's menstrual cycle: Brief home interview (each data point)
Mother-infant interaction: 90-minute observation (each home visit)
trange situation (12 and 24 months), interaction of infant with unfamiliar peers (23 months), mother-infant interaction (4 months): Videotape observation
Breast-feeding frequency and duration: Mother's diary (each data point)
Temperament: Rothbart Infant Behavior Questionnaire (9 months)
Language development and vocabulary: Testing (20 months)
Motor and mental development: Bayley Scales of Infant Development (10 and 24 months), Kagan Cognitive Tests, Draw-a-Free Tests (22 months)
Ainsworth strange situation, reaction to unfamiliar peers, sociability, mother-infant interaction: Videotape observation

REPRESENTATIVE REFERENCES:

Elias, M., Teas, J., Johnston, J., & Bora, C. (1986). Nursing practices and lactation amenorrhoea. *Journal of Biosocial Science, 18*(1), 1-10.

CURRENT STATUS OF THE STUDY:

a. No further waves of data collection are planned.
b. Most data are not in machine-readable format.
c. Data are available for secondary analysis through the Henry A. Murray Research Center, Radcliffe College, 10 Garden Street, Cambridge, MA 02138.

■ The Beginning School Study, 1982

Entwisle, Doris; and Alexander, Karl

Contact Person: Doris Entwisle
Address: Department of Sociology
Johns Hopkins University
304 Barton Hall
Baltimore, MD 21218
Telephone No.: (301) 338-7016

SUBSTANTIVE TOPICS COVERED:

The study examines how social structural factors, in schools and at home, and social-psychological factors affect young children's cognitive, social, and emotional development; the reciprocal influences of cognitive and affective factors;

and how children's position in the social structure and society affect the cognitive and motivational development of children over time.

CHARACTERISTICS OF THE ORIGINAL SAMPLE:

Year the study began: 1982

Subject selection process: Subjects were selected from a probability sample of first graders in Baltimore, Maryland. Subjects were chosen to be reasonably representative of children in the country as a whole, that is, 20 schools in which Ss span a wide range of socioeconomic status for African-Americans and whites.

Total number of subjects at Time 1: N = 790

Ages at Time 1: 5-6 yrs.

Sex distribution: Approximately equal numbers of females and males throughout

Socioeconomic status: 66% poverty class, 20% middle/upper middle class, 14% working class

Race/ethnicity: 54.8% African-American, 45.2% white

Years of Completed Waves:

Years	N=	Age ranges
1982	790	5-6 yrs.
1983	642	6-7 yrs.
1984	612	7-8 yrs.
1985	560	8-9 yrs.
1988-1990[a]	657	11-13 yrs.

Comments:
a. A large majority of those followed-up in 1985 continued to be followed in 1986 and 1987. Starting in 1988, all of the original Ss were resought. By 1990, 657 of the original 790 Ss had been located.

INFORMATION ON SAMPLE ATTRITION:

During the 8-year period of study, not all of the original 838 students were followed continuously. Attrition was mostly due to students' leaving the school system. Most analyses are based on 790 students who were in first grade for the first time (not repeaters) in 1982. Of these, there are current data (1990) on 657 of the original respondents (83%). About one quarter of these are in schools outside Baltimore City.

CONSTRUCTS MEASURED: INSTRUMENTS USED

Background information, expectation of child's school achievements, beliefs about school achievement: Parent interviews

Expectations for children's school achievement, teaching strategies, evaluation criteria: Teacher questionnaires

General ability measure: Cognitive Abilities Test
Reading and mathematical skills: California Achievement Test
Expectations of children's school achievements by peers, popularity ratings: Peer ratings of target children
Achievement expectations: Child interviews
Child's self-esteem: Self-esteem Test (Dickstein)
Grades, attendance, conduct, academic skills: School records
Personal efficacy: Perceived Competence Scale (Harter)

REPRESENTATIVE REFERENCES:

Alexander, K. L., & Entwisle, D. R. (1988). Achievement in the first two years of school: Patterns and processes. *Monographs of the Society for Research in Child Development, 53*(2).

Entwisle, D. R., & Alexander, K. L. (in press). Children's transition into full-time schooling: Black/white comparisons. *Early Education and Development.*

Entwisle, D. R., Alexander, K. L., Pallas, A. M., & Cadigan, D. (1988). A social psychological model for the schooling process over first grade. *Social Psychology Quarterly, 51,* 173-189.

Pallas, A. M., Entwisle, D. R., Alexander, K. L., & Cadigan, D. (1987). Children who do exceptionally well in first grade. *Sociology of Education, 60,* 257-271.

CURRENT STATUS OF THE STUDY:

a. Further waves of data collection are planned for each year until 1993.
b. Most data are in machine-readable format.
c. The data are not available for secondary analysis.

■ Early Schooling, 1971

Entwisle, Doris; and Hayduk, Leslie A.

Contact Person: Doris Entwisle
Address: Department of Sociology
Johns Hopkins University
304 Barton Hall
Baltimore, MD 21218
Telephone No.: (301) 338-7016

SUBSTANTIVE TOPICS COVERED:

The study examines children's ideas about their own level of performance, and how this perception influences actual performance; parents' ideas about children's level of performance; school differences (socioeconomic status, race) and differences in the process of early schooling; and, overall, it is the aim of the investigators to develop a conceptual model for the early schooling process.

CHARACTERISTICS OF THE ORIGINAL SAMPLE:

Year the study began: 1971

Subject selection process: All students beginning first grade in three schools were invited to participate in the study every year, and remained in the sample through third grade or until they transferred out of the school. The white middle-class school started in 1971, (N = 557); the integrated lower-class school started in 1972, (N = 604); and the African-American lower-class school started in 1973 (N = 406).

Total number of subjects at Time 1: N = 1,568[a]

Ages at Time 1: 5-6 yrs.

Sex distribution: Approximately equal numbers of females and males

Socioeconomic status: 63% working class, 37% middle class/upper middle class

Race/ethnicity: 60% white, 40% African-American

Comments:

a. This figure combines yearly cohorts of all three schools from 1971-1976.

Years of Completed Waves:

Years	N=	Age ranges
White Middle-Class School (N - 557)		
(Cohort 1)		
1971	114	6 yrs.
1972	114	7 yrs.
1973	114	8 yrs.
(Cohort 2)		
1972	114	6 yrs.
1973	114	7 yrs.
1974	114	8 yrs.
(Cohort 3)		
1973	114	6 yrs.
1974	114	7 yrs.
1975-1976	114	8 yrs.
(Cohort 4)		
1974	114	6 yrs.
1975-1976	97	7 yrs.
(Cohort 5)		
1975-1976	102	6 yrs.
Integrated Lower-Class School (N = 604)		
(Cohort 1)		
1972	151	6 yrs.
1973	151	7 yrs.
1974	151	8 yrs.

Years of Completed Waves, Continued:

Years	N=	Age ranges
(Cohort 2)		
1973	151	6 yrs.
1974	151	7 yrs.
1975-1976	151	8 yrs.
(Cohort 3)		
1974	151	6 yrs.
1975-1976	79	7 yrs.
(Cohort 4)		
1975-1976	151	6 yrs.
African-American Lower-Class School (N = 406)		
(Cohort 1)		
1972	138	6 yrs.
1973	*	7 yrs.
1974	95	8 yrs.
(Cohort 2)		
1973	138	6 yrs.
1974	*	7 yrs.
1975-1976	30	8 yrs.
(Cohort 3)		
1975-1976	130	6 yrs.

INFORMATION ON SAMPLE ATTRITION:

During the 6-year period of the study, the Ss in each of the six semesters of schooling (two semesters each in grades 1, 2, and 3) were pooled across years. The data consist of pooled two-wave panels for each semester. A new first grade cohort of children was added for each successive year of the study, and the study terminated while some children were only in first or second grade. Given the research design and data collection procedures, the "core sample" could not be computed in a meaningful way.

CONSTRUCTS MEASURED: INSTRUMENTS USED

Expectations for performance in reading, arithmetic, and conduct: Interview with the child
Self-esteem: Self-esteem Test
Parents' expectations for child's performance in reading, arithmetic, and conduct: Interview with parents
Parents' estimate of child's general ability to do schoolwork: Interview with parents
Peer popularity rating: Interview with class peers
Academic performance, grades, conduct, attendance, arithmetic and reading skills: School records

Parents' knowledge of child's social network: Face-to-face interviews and mail
   questionnaires
School aptitude: Cognitive Abilities Test
Achievement in math: Iowa Test of Basic Skills
Achievement in English: California Achievement Test

REPRESENTATIVE REFERENCES:

Entwisle, D. R., & Hayduk, L. A. (1981). Academic expectations and the school attainment of
   young children. *Sociology of Education, 54,* 34-50.
Entwisle, D. R., & Hayduk, L. A. (1982). *Early schooling.* Baltimore: The Johns Hopkins
   University Press.
Entwisle, D. R., & Hayduk, L. A. (1988). Lasting effects of elementary school. *Sociology of Edu-
   cation, 61,* 147-159.
Entwisle, D. R., & Webster, M. (1974). Expectations in mixed racial groups. *Sociology of Educa-
   tion, 47,* 301-318.

CURRENT STATUS OF THE STUDY:

   a. No further waves of data collection are planned.
   b. Most of the data are in machine-readable format.
   c. The data are unavailable for secondary analysis.

■ Longitudinal Study of School and Family Effects, 1973

Epstein, Joyce

Contact Person: Joyce Epstein
Address: Johns Hopkins University
                 The Center for Social Organization and Schools
                 3505 North Charles Street
                 Baltimore, MD 21218
Telephone No.:   (301) 338-7570

SUBSTANTIVE TOPICS COVERED:

   The study examines the effects of open and traditional secondary schools on affect and achievement outcomes; distinctions between formal and informal organization of student decision making; school and family effects on student outcomes;
interaction effects of school and family on student outcomes; effects of school organization on peer and friendship groups; influence of friends on each others' academic and nonacademic behaviors; the relation of quality of school life to student
attitudes.

CHARACTERISTICS OF THE ORIGINAL SAMPLE:

Year the study began: 1973

Subject selection process: The total population of children in selected grade levels was asked to participate. The sample of schools was selected for its diversity of school organization. Each school year, all students in the targeted grades were tested, regardless of whether they had participated in the study in the previous year. Part of the research design is cross-sectional. The additional Ss are reflected in the sample increase of the second data wave.

Total number of subjects at Time 1: N = 7,249

Ages at Time 1: 9-17 yrs.

Sex distribution: Approximately equal numbers of females and males throughout

Socioeconomic status: 44% working class, 41% middle/upper middle class, 15% poverty class

Race/ethnicity: 89% white, 11% African-American

Years of Completed Waves:

Years	N=	Age ranges
(Cohort 1)		
1973	1,680	9-10 yrs.
1974	1,700	11-12 yrs.
(Cohort 2)		
1973	1,603	10-11 yrs.
1974	1,698	12-13 yrs.
(Cohort 3)		
1973	1,519	11-12 yrs.
1974	1,570	13-14 yrs.
(Cohort 4)		
1973	1,398	12-13 yrs.
1974	1,457	14-15 yrs.
(Cohort 5)		
1973	1,049	16-17 yrs.
1974	935	17-18 yrs.

INFORMATION ON SAMPLE ATTRITION:

During the 2-year period of study, 1,795 of 7,249 Ss (24.8%) were not retrieved for further study. The core sample consists of 5,454 Ss. Information about the attrition rate for each age group was not available. Ss were added to the study at the second data point.

CONSTRUCTS MEASURED: INSTRUMENTS USED

Information on educational program characteristics, architectural design, and classroom decision-making style; background information (family background, education, and demographic information): Teacher mail survey

Academic achievement: School records (standardized intelligence tests, grades, standardized mathematics and English scores on the Iowa Test of Basic Skills (ITBS) and Test of Academic Progress (TAP) Achievement Test

Teacher-student decision-making practices, self-reliance, quality of school life, college plans, school anxiety, disciplinary adjustment in the classroom, prosocial classroom behavior, self-esteem, control of environment, friendship and peer status, family background, and family decision-making practices: Student survey

Evaluation of student's self-reliance and satisfaction with school conditions: Teacher reports

REPRESENTATIVE REFERENCES:

Epstein, J. (1983). Longitudinal effects of person-family-school interactions on student outcomes. In A. Kerckhoff (Ed.), *Research in sociology of education and socialization: Vol. 4.* Greenwich, CT: JAI Press.

Epstein, J. (1984). A longitudinal study of school and family effects on student development. In S. A. Mednick, M. Harway, & K. M. Finello (Eds.), *Handbook of longitudinal research: Vol 1.* New York: Praeger.

Epstein, J. L., & McPartland, J. M. (1976). The concept and measurement of the quality of school life. *American Education Research Journal, 50,* 13-30.

McPartland, J., & Epstein, J. (1977). Open schools and achievement: Extended tests of a finding of no relationship. *Sociology of Education, 50,* 133-144.

CURRENT STATUS OF THE STUDY:

a. No further waves of data collection are planned.

b. Data are not in machine-readable format.

c. Data are not available for secondary analysis.

■ The New York High-Risk Project, 1971

Erlenmeyer-Kimling, L.

Contact Person: L. Erlenmeyer-Kimling
Address: Department of Medical Genetics
                 New York State Psychiatric Institute
                 722 West 168th Street
                 New York, NY 10032
Telephone No.:   (212) 960-2475

SUBSTANTIVE TOPICS COVERED:

The study examines the relation of genetic factors to biobehavioral, psychosocial, and clinical deviances; attempts to identify both biobehavioral predictors of heightened risk for psychopathology and positive aspects of the environment that might serve to buffer a genetically predisposed high-risk child from psychopathological development.

CHARACTERISTICS OF THE ORIGINAL SAMPLE:

Year the study began: 1971

Subject selection process: Children of schizophrenic and depressed parents were located through their parents' hospitalization records. Children of normal parents were located through schools in the first sample. In the second sample, children of normal parents were identified by a population sampling firm.

Total number of subjects at Time 1: N = 206[a]

Ages at Time 1: 7-12 yrs.

Sex distribution: Approximately equal numbers of females and males throughout for both cohorts

Socioeconomic status: Predominantly middle/upper middle class and working class

Race/ethnicity: Predominantly white

Comments:

a. Cohort 1 refers to children who entered the study in 1971-1972; their parents were later rediagnosed according to the Research Diagnostic Criteria (RDC). Cohort 2 refers to children who entered the study in 1977-1979; their parents were diagnosed according to the RDC.

Years of Completed Waves:

Years	N=	Age ranges (approximate)
(Cohort 1)		
1971-1972	206	7-12 yrs.
1973-1975	189	9-16 yrs.
1977-1979	194	13-20 yrs.
1982-1984	186	18-25 yrs.
1986-1987	191	21-28 yrs.

Years of Completed Waves, Continued:

Years	N=	Age ranges (approximate)
(Cohort 2)		
1977-1979	150	7-12 yrs.
1980-1981	136	10-16 yrs.
1983-1984	136	12-19 yrs.
1986-1987	137	14-21 yrs.

INFORMATION ON SAMPLE ATTRITION:

During the 20-year period of study, 34 of 356 Ss (9.6%) across two cohorts were not retrieved for further study. By cohort, 20 of 206 Ss (9.7%) for Cohort 1, and 14 of 150 Ss (9.3%) for Cohort 2. Information on core samples was not available.

CONSTRUCTS MEASURED: INSTRUMENTS USED

Attention, information processing and memory: Visual aural design test (VADS), Computerized vigilance test (CPT1), Computerized discrimination task (CPT2), Continuous Performance Test—Identical Pairs Version (CPT-1P), Attention Span Test, Short-term Memory Lag Test (STM-Lag), Information Overload Test (IOT)

Concept attainment: Wisconsin Card Sorting

Developmental level and emotional disturbance: Figure Drawing Test

Developmental level and neurological organization: Bender-Gestalt Visual-Motor Test

Neuromotor functioning: Neurological examination, Lincoln-Oseretzky Test of Motor Impairment, Purdue Pegboard, Dichotic Listening Test

Autonomic nervous system functioning: Skin conductance, heart rate

Central nervous system processing: Event-related cortical evoked potentials

Verbal ability, intelligence: Wechsler Intelligence Scale for Children, or Revised Wechsler Intelligence Scale for Children

Amino acid screening: Urinalysis

Family history, child development, child health, child psychopathology, and child reactions to mentally ill parent: Parent interview

Child's view of parents, sibs, peers, school, and the like: Child interview

Psychiatric disturbances and level of functioning: Videotaped psychiatric interview, Mental Health Assessment Form (Kestenbaum & Bird), Behavioral Global Adjustment Scale (Cornblatt), Minnesota Multiphasic Personality Inventory (MMPI), Schedule for Affective Disorders and Schizophrenia (Lifetime version), structured videotaped interview, friendship and intimacy interview (Kreisman)

Thought disorder: 4-card Rorschach Ink Blot Test

Schizotype, borderline personality: Schizotypal features scale, Personality Disorder Examination (PDE, Lovanger et al.)
Social adjustment: Social adjustment scale
Friendship and intimacy patterns: Friendship and intimacy scale
School behavior, peer relations: Teacher's evaluations
School behavior and performance: School grades
Anhedonia: Physical Anhedonia Scale
Stress and life events: Life events questionnaire
Neuropsychological measure: Smooth pursuit eye movement
Diagnosis of Axis I psychiatric disorders: Schedule for Affective Disorders and Schizophrenia—Lifetime
Diagnosis of personality disorders (Axis II): Personality Disorder Examination
Psychophysiology: Conditioning paradigm, Galvanic Skin Response, resting electroencephalogram, auditory event-related potentials to repetitive stimulation, auditory event-related potentials to task-relevant stimulation, visual evoked potentials to CPT1 and CPT2, auditory thresholds (absolute and aversion), heart rate and skin conductance, magnitude estimation and psycho-physical judgments, stimulus level intensity gradients

REPRESENTATIVE REFERENCES:

Erlenmeyer-Kimling, L. (1975). A prospective study of children at risk for schizophrenia: Methodological considerations and some preliminary findings. In R. Wirt, G. Winokur, & M. Roff (Eds.), *Life history research in psychopathology: Vol. 4* (pp. 22-46). Minneapolis: University of Minnesota Press.

Erlenmeyer-Kimling, L., & Cornblatt, B. (1987). The New York High-Risk Project: A follow-up report. *Schizophrenia Bulletin,* 451-463.

Erlenmeyer-Kimling, L., Cornblatt, B., & Golden, R. (1983). Early indicators of vulnerability to schizophrenia in children at high genetic risk. In S. B. Guze, F. J. Earles, & J. E. Barrett (Eds.), *Childhood psychopathology and development* (pp. 247-261). New York: Raven.

Erlenmeyer-Kimling, L., Marcuse, Y., Cornblatt, B., Friedman, D., Rainer, J. D., & Rutschmann, J. (1984). The New York High-Risk Project. In N. Watt, E. J. Anthony, L. Wynne, & J. Rolf (Eds.), *Children at risk for schizophrenia: A longitudinal perspective* (pp. 169-189). New York: Cambridge University Press.

CURRENT STATUS OF THE STUDY:

a. Further data collection is ongoing.
b. Most data are in machine-readable format.
c. Some data are available for secondary analysis from the study contact person.

F

Indian Adoption Project, 1960

Fanshel, David

Contact Person: David Fanshel
Address: School of Social Work
Columbia University
622 West 113th Street
New York, NY 10025
Telephone No.: (212) 854-3250

SUBSTANTIVE TOPICS COVERED:

This study followed the experiences of white adoptive parents and their Native American adoptive children through the first 5 years of adoption. Annual interviews were conducted with parents to gather information relating to family motives for transracial adoption; social and family relationships; and to monitor the adopted child's developmental progress as well as physical and emotional health status and behavioral tendencies.

CHARACTERISTICS OF THE ORIGINAL SAMPLE:

Year the study began: 1960
Subject selection process: Families who adopted children through the Indian Adoption Project between 1958 and 1967, and who lived near a participating city (e.g., St. Louis) were selected.
Total number of subjects at Time 1: N = 98 families
Ages at Time 1: Adoptive mothers, 33 yrs; Adoptive fathers, 35 yrs.; Children, 2.6 yrs.
Sex distribution: Approximately equal numbers of females and males throughout
Socioeconomic status: 66% middle upper/middle class, 30.9% working class, 3.1% poverty class
Race/ethnicity: 100% white

Years of Completed Waves:

Years	N=	Age ranges
1960-1966	98	33-35 yrs. (Mothers and fathers)
1961-1966	97	34 yrs. (Mothers)
1962-1966	94	37 yrs. (Fathers)
1964-1967	88	37-39 yrs. (Mothers and Fathers)
1965-1968	60	38 yrs. (Mothers)

INFORMATION ON SAMPLE ATTRITION:

During the 9-year period of study, 38 of 98 (38.8%) families were not retrieved for further study. The core sample consists of 88 couples, 60 mothers, and 88 fathers.

CONSTRUCTS MEASURED: INSTRUMENTS USED

Time 1: Background for Adoption and Early Experience

Motivation for adoption, experiences with the agencies, child's entry into the home, and beginning experiences: Interview with both parents

Time 2: Social Perspectives on Transracial Parenthood

Progress of child's integration within the family and his/her adjustment, nature of family's deliberations about adopting an Indian child, child-rearing orientations of adoptive mother, social attitudes and lifestyles of mother: Structured interview

Mother's perception of child's progress: Index of Child Adjustment

Child behavior characteristics: Adjective Checklist

Child temperament: Index of child activity level, Index of child's friendliness and outgoingness

Characteristics of acceptable children: Synopsis of Adoptive Mother's responses

Adoptive mothers' orientation to the adoption of handicapped children; children with psychological problems; African-American children: Factor analytic indices

Adoptive mother's description of child's Indian appearance: Index of child's Indian appearance

Security of adoptive mothers: Index of security of adoptive mothers' parental outlooks

Adoptive mothers' child-rearing orientation: Index of strict versus permissive child-rearing orientation

Account of religious activities: Index of religiosity of adoptive mothers

Adoptive mothers' political orientation: Index of adoptive mothers' liberal versus conservative political orientation

Sex-role orientation: Index of traditional versus modern female ideology

Viewpoints of women's roles: Index of adoptive mothers' lifestyles

Adoptive mothers' experience of deprivation: Index of deprivation in adoptive mothers' backgrounds

Time 3: Adoptive Fathers' Views

Adoptive fathers' descriptions of adoptee's behavioral dispositions: Synopsis of adoptive fathers' responses

Child temperament, degree of quietness and shyness: Factor Analytic Indices

Adoptive fathers' perception of adoptive child's adjustment: Index of Child Adjustment

Adoptive fathers' orientation to the adoption of various types of children: Factor Analytic Indices

Adoptive fathers' support for Indian adoption: Index of background support for Indian adoption

Adoptive fathers' description of child's Indian appearance: Index of child's Indian appearance

Security of adoptive father: Index of security of parental outlook

Adoptive fathers' child-rearing orientation: Index of strict versus permissive child-rearing orientation

Social perspectives of adoptive fathers: Index of lower class-rural background, index of religiosity of adoptive families

Adoptive fathers' political orientation: Index of adoptive fathers' liberal versus conservative political orientation

Adoptive fathers' social problem orientation: Index of social problem orientation of adoptive fathers

Adoptive fathers' views on masculinity: Index of traditional masculine ideology

Adoptive fathers' experience of deprivation: Index of deprivation in adoptive fathers' backgrounds

Time 4: How Fare the Children

Child's developmental progress, health status, Indian background, personality and general disposition, social relationships, problem attributed to his/her Indian or adoptive status, school adjustment, child-rearing patterns, family climate, future plans: Structured interview

Child's health and physical growth and development, intellectual and cognitive competence; personality and behavior patterns, family relationships: Child Progress Scale

Child symptomatology: Parental reports of frequency of symptoms

Time 5: Adoptive Mothers' Views

Child's characteristics: Parent's descriptions of child

Child's symptoms: Frequency of symptoms reported

Child's health and physical growth and development; intellectual and cognitive competence; personality and behavior patterns; social relationships; and family relationships: Child Progress Scale

REPRESENTATIVE REFERENCES:

Fanshel, D. (1972). *Far from the reservation*. Matuchen, New Jersey: Scarecrow Press.
Fanshel, D. (1964). Indian Adoption Research Project (news from the field), *Child Welfare, 43*(9), 486-488.

CURRENT STATUS OF THE STUDY:

a. No further waves of data collection are planned.
b. Data are not in machine-readable format.
c. Data are not available for secondary analysis.

■ Columbia University Longitudinal Study: Children in Foster Care, 1966

Fanshel, David

Contact person: David Fanshel
Address: School of Social Work
                  Columbia University
                  622 West 113th Street
                  New York, NY 10025
Telephone No.:   (212) 854-3250

SUBSTANTIVE TOPICS COVERED:

The purpose of this study is to examine, over time, the personal and social adjustment of children placed in foster care. (See also Jenkins, S., *Columbia University Longitudinal Study: Family Welfare Research Program—Mothers View Foster Care*; and Shapiro, D., *Columbia University Longitudinal Study: Child Welfare Research Program—Nature of Agency Services.*)

CHARACTERISTICS OF THE ORIGINAL SAMPLE:

Year the study began: 1966
Subject selection process: A sequential sampling procedure was used to identify children entering the foster care system of New York City in 1966. Subjects selected for inclusion ranged from birth to 12 years of age; had no physical, emotional, or social handicaps; had not either been placed for adoption or ever been placed in any form of foster care for more than 90 days or had any siblings in any form of placement care.
Total number of subjects at Time 1: N = 624+
Ages at Time 1: Birth-12 yrs.
Sex distribution: Approximately equal numbers of females and males throughout
Socioeconomic status: 41.6% middle/upper middle class, 31.4% working class, 27% poverty class
Race/ethnicity: 41.5% African-American, 32.3% Hispanic, 26.2% white

Years of Completed Waves:

Years	N=[a]	Age ranges
1966-1967	577	Birth-12 yrs.
1967-1968	490	3-14 yrs.
1971	403	5-17 yrs.

Comments:
a. The initial sample consisted of 624 participants. However, the follow-up rates indicated are based upon the number of Ss who completed psychological testing.

INFORMATION ON SAMPLE ATTRITION:

During the 5-year period of study, 221 of the original 624 Ss (35.4%) were not retrieved for further study. The core sample consists of 392 Ss. Attrition was due to subjects' moving and/or refusing to continue participation, and maternal disability.

CONSTRUCTS MEASURED: INSTRUMENTS USED

Developmental history: Interviews (with mothers or caretakers prior to placement), health index, emotional problem index, developmental problem index

Intelligence: The Psyche Cattell Infant Scale (3 mos. to 2 yrs., 11 mos.); The Minnesota Preschool Scale (3 yrs. to 5 yrs., 11 mos.); Wechsler Intelligence Scale for Children (6 yrs. and older)

Self-concept, concept of family: Projective Tests (Draw-a-Person, Draw-a-Family, Michigan Picture Test)

Child's perception of separation, sense of identification and self-identity: Structured interview with child, Sentence-completion Test

Emotional condition, intellectual capability: Clinical assessment (by psychologist)

School performance and achievement: School Report Form, Rating Scale for Pupil Adjustment (teacher rating)

Child profiles: Child Profile Form, Symptomatic Behavior (ratings), Attachments (caseworker ratings), Parent reports on child Symptomatic Behavior

Child behavior: Child Behavior Characteristics Form (Borgatta-Fanshel)

Parent influences: Principal preplacement child care person, stability of care before placement, index of evaluation of mother, parental visiting style, reasons for placement

Agency influences: Index of the total average monthly contact invested by caseworker, index of caseworker's skill

Appraising foster parents: Foster Parent Appraisal Form (Fanshel) (by caseworker)

Institutional care: Routine of institutional care, experience of institutional staff, evaluation of institutional counselor, school setting

REPRESENTATIVE REFERENCES:

Fanshel, D. (1971). The exit of children from foster care: An interim research report. *Child Welfare, 50*, 65-81.

Fanshel, D. (1975). Parental failure and consequences for children: The drug-abusing mother whose children are in foster care. *American Journal of Public Health, 65*, 604-612.

Fanshel, D. (1976). Status changes of children in foster care: Final results of the Columbia University Longitudinal Study. *Child Welfare, 55*, 143-171.

Fanshel, D., & Shinn, E. B. (1978). *Children in foster care: A longitudinal investigation.* New York: Columbia University Press.

CURRENT STATUS OF THE STUDY:

a. No further waves of data collection are planned.

b. Most of the data are in machine-readable format.

c. Data are available for secondary analysis from the study contact person.

■ The Longitudinal Study of Transitions in Four Stages of Life, 1969

Fiske, Marjorie L.; Thurnher, Majda; and Chiriboga, David

Contact Person: David Chiriboga
Address: Graduate Studies
                 School of Allied Health Sciences
                 Route J28
                 University of Texas Medical Branch
                 Galveston, TX 77550
Telephone No.:   (409) 761-3038

SUBSTANTIVE TOPICS COVERED:

The study examines consistencies and inconsistencies in coping processes and related cognitive, emotional, and social characteristics at successive adult life states; situational factors associated with change in psychological and physical well-being; patterns and variations of development and regression; perceptions of social change.

CHARACTERISTICS OF THE ORIGINAL SAMPLE:

Year the study began: 1969
Subject selection process: A representative sample of middle and lower-middle classes was used to create four subsamples. Participants live in the central city of a metropolitan area on the West Coast.
Total number of subjects at Time 1: N = 216
Ages at Time 1: 16-60+ yrs.
Sex distribution: Approximately equal numbers of females and males throughout
Socioeconomic status: 100% middle/lower middle class
Race/ethnicity: 86.6% white, 9.6% Asian-American, 2% African-American, 2% Hispanic (Cohort 1); 100% white (Cohorts 2 & 3); 100% white (Cohort 4)

Years of Completed Waves:

Years	N=	Age ranges
(Cohort 1: High School Seniors)		
1969	52	16-18 yrs.
1971	52	17-19 yrs.
1975	50	21-23 yrs.
1977	47	23-25 yrs.
1979-1980	43	25-27 yrs.
(Cohort 2: Newlyweds)		
1969	50	20-38 yrs.
1971	50	21-39 yrs.
1975	48	25-43 yrs.

Years of Completed Waves, Continued:

Years	N=	Age ranges
1977	44	27-45 yrs.
1979-1980	41	29-47 yrs.
(Cohort 3: Middle-Aged Parents)		
1969	54	48 yrs.[a]
1971	47	50 yrs.
1975	44	54 yrs.
1977	44	57 yrs.
1979-1980	41	59 yrs.
(Cohort 4: Pre-Retirees)		
1969	60	58 yrs.[a]
1971	54	60 yrs.
1975	51	64 yrs.
1979	48	68 yrs.
1979-1980	40	68 yrs.

Comments:
a. Average age.

INFORMATION ON SAMPLE ATTRITION:

During the 12-year period of study, 39 of 202 Ss (19.3%) across four cohorts were not retrieved for further study: 8 of 51 Ss (15.7%), Cohort 1; 9 of 50 Ss (18%), Cohort 2; 8 of 47 Ss (17.1%), Cohort 3; and 14 of 54 Ss (25.9%), Cohort 4. Reasons for sample attrition include Ss refusal to participate, inability to locate Ss, and death. The core sample consists of 163 Ss: 43 Ss (Cohort 1); 41 Ss (Cohort 2); 41 Ss (Cohort 3); and 40 Ss (Cohort 4).

CONSTRUCTS MEASURED: INSTRUMENTS USED

Demographic and sociostructural data, past and present physical and emotional illness in family; daily, weekly, and yearly activities and problems and satisfaction, and meanings attached to them; past, present and future values and goals; relationship with family, dating experiences and events preceding marriage, attitudes toward sex and sexual experience, friendship patterns, organizational membership and participation; perceptions of neighborhood, social groups, and local and national problems and issues; timing, nature, and past life events: Interview

Overall mental health: Bradburn Morale Scales, Thematic Apperception Test, Neugarten and Gutmann's Kansas City Thematic Apperception Test (TAT) card, Wechsler Adult Intelligence Scale Vocabulary Subtest, Wechsler Adult Intelligence Scale Block Subtest, Adjective Rating List derived from Block's Modified Q-Sort, Presumed Stress Checklist (modification of Holmes and Rahe Social Readjustment Scale), Hassles Checklist

REPRESENTATIVE REFERENCES:

Chiriboga, D. A., & Dean, H. (1978). Dimensions of stress: Perspectives from a longitudinal study. *Journal of Psychosomatic Research, 22*, 47-55.

Fiske, M., & Chiriboga, D. (1990). *Change and continuity in adult life.* San Francisco: Jossey-Bass.

Lowenthal, M. F., & Chiriboga, D. A. (1973). Social stress and adaptation: Toward a life course perspective. In C. Eisdorfer & M. P. Lawton (Eds.), *The psychology of adult development and aging* (pp. 281-310). Washington, DC: American Psychological Association.

Lowenthal, M. F., Thurnher, M., Chiriboga, D., et al. (1975). *Four stages of life: A comparative study of women and men facing transitions.* San Francisco: Jossey-Bass.

CURRENT STATUS OF THE STUDY:

a. Further waves of data collection are possible.

b. Most of the data are in machine-readable format.

c. Data are available for secondary analysis through the Henry A. Murray Research Center, Radcliffe College, 10 Garden Street, Cambridge, MA 02138.

■ Baltimore Longitudinal Study of Aging (BLSA), 1958

Fozard, James L.; and Andres, Reuben

Contact Person: James L. Fozard
Address: Gerontology Research Center
                  4940 Eastern Avenue
                  Baltimore, MD 21224
Telephone No.:   (301) 550-1766

SUBSTANTIVE TOPICS COVERED:

The purpose of the BLSA is to examine, both cross-sectionally and longitudinally, the physiological and psychological aspects of aging in persons who live in their communities; to understand the mechanisms underlying the changes; to relate the measures of one another; and to distinguish them from the effects of disease processes, cohort changes, and secular changes. The overall scientific goals of the BLSA are to identify differences among individuals of different ages, and changes that occur in the serial observations of these individuals with the passage of time; to determine the relative contribution of aging, disease processes, cohort effects, and secular effects in producing observed differences and changes; and to establish the degree of interrelation and/or interaction among these factors; to expand the scientific understanding about predictors and risk factors for specific diseases and for other end points related to successes and failures of adaptation to aging processes. The BLSA consists of a series of longitudinal studies of varying duration and degrees of interrelationships as well as several cross-sectional studies.

CHARACTERISTICS OF THE ORIGINAL SAMPLE:

Year the study began: 1958

Subject selection process: Subject selection involves the recruitment of generally healthy and active community-dwelling people of all ages, who would be willing to undergo thorough and repeated testing over a major portion, if not the remainder, of their lives. The BLSA research participants represent an open panel of highly dedicated men and women who are mostly recruited into the program by other volunteers. New volunteers are admitted from a waiting list of approximately 468 men and 627 women applicants. The total size of the group varies from year to year. The goal is to maintain enough volunteers so that there will be a total of 30 men and 30 women in each age decade who have had a minimum of 12 years of observation (6 years for participants entering in their 80s) at any point in time. Accordingly, recruitment is designed to replace participants who die or become inactive. Once in the BLSA, participants agree to return every other year for 2-1/2 days for an undetermined period of time. The BLSA participants as a group are highly educated (63% and 67% of male and female participants, respectively, have at least one college degree), mostly married, and describe themselves as financially comfortable or better. Of the group that returned for their fifth visit, 90% rated their health as good or excellent on both the first and fifth visits. Participants are recruited according to the ages needed. There are no formal admission criteria related to demographic characteristics. Subjects must be able to come to the Gerontology Research Center at their own expense without monetary compensation.

Total number of subjects at Time 1: N = 358

Ages at Time 1: 20-90 yrs.

Sex distribution: 100% male initially; approximately equal numbers of females and males since 1978

Socioeconomic status: 90.6% middle/upper middle class, 8.6% working class, 0.8% student

Race/ethnicity: 96.7% white, 3.3% African-American

Years of Completed Waves:[a]

Years	N=	Age ranges
(Male Ss)		
1958	52	20-90 yrs.
1978	676	20-90 yrs.
1990	461	20-90 yrs.
(Women Ss)		
1978	132	20-90 yrs.
1990	430	20-90 yrs.

Comments:

a. The figures above represent the number of Ss (and their ages) followed at the start of BLSA (1958), at the point at which data collection on women began (1978), and at present (1990). Most Ss participated in BLSA for a minimum of a 12-year "horizon," and with an average length of participation of 17 years. A "core sample" of 30 women, and 30 men within each 10-year age cohort (e.g., 20-29 yrs; 40-49 yrs.) is rigorously maintained through an "open panel" design, which allows for the inclusion of new Ss for each age cohort as needed. The sample of women added to the study in 1978 consists mostly of wives or daughters of the male Ss in the study, although some are volunteers.

INFORMATION ON SAMPLE ATTRITION:

It is difficult to describe this study in terms of attrition because new subjects were added to the study at each data point. As of August 1990, BLSA has 461 men and 36 women deceased participants. Those who have withdrawn or have had three or more years since their last visit total 415—124 women and 291 men. The latter group has been contacted through a telephone survey designed to re-enroll them either as active participants or to be followed periodically by telephone and mail communication.

CONSTRUCTS MEASURED: INSTRUMENTS USED

Clinical evaluation: Physical examination, pelvic examination, neurological examination, Pap smear, urinalysis, hemogram, serological test (syphilis), sedimentation rate, chest X ray, medical history (Q), Cornell Medical Index (Q), medications lists (Q), CES-D Depression (Q), and Mini-mental status examination

Genetic factors: Dermatoglyphics, lateral dominance, lateral dominance (Q), family history (Q), abbreviated genetics (Q), and DNA minisatellites

Metabolic function: Fasting plasma glucose, oral glucose tolerance (1.75 g/kg body wt), intravenous glucose test, intravenous tolbutamide test, cortisone oral glucose, hyperglycemic glucose clamp, oral glucose tolerance (40 g/m2 surface area), cholesterol and triglycerides, high density lipoprotein-cholesterol (HDL-C), HDL2 & HDL3, urinary 24-hr. sodium and potassium excretion, calcium-serum concentration and 24-hr. urinary excretion; and uric acid-serum concentration and 24-hr. urinary excretion

Body composition: Anthropometry, basal metabolism, creatinine excretion (24-hr.)

Nutrition status: Diet interview, 7-day dietary record (Q), vitamin A & E levels, vitamin C levels, trace mineral levels, and food frequency quest

Bone status: Photon scanning (single and double), biochemical parameters/calciotropic hormones, hand X rays, and knee X rays

Neuromuscular function: Tapping test, simple and choice reaction time, strength test, low-level crank-turning ergometer, and maximum work rate-brief

Activity and function: Activity II (Q), Physical activity (Q), computerized activity monitor, Arthritis Symptom Scales (Q), Joint Pain Scales (Q), Musculoskeletal Symptoms (Q), Activities and Functioning (Q), and Pfeiffer Functional (Q)

Pulmonary function: Vital capacity, Forced expiratory volume, Expiratory flow rates, maximum breathing capacity, diaphragmatic-breathing training, post inhalation challenge spriometry, American Thoracic Society/NHBLBI Epidemiological (Q), Personal smoking history (Q), and Pulmonary Disease Forms (Q)

Renal function: 24-hr. creatinine clearance, and Water-load test

Cardiovascular function: Resting electrocardiogram, maximum exercise stress ECG w/oxygen consumption, maximum exercise thallium scan of heart, gated blood pool scan (exercise and rest), echocardiography [M mode (rest), and 2 D (exercise and rest)], volume plethysmography, His-bundle recording (noninvasive), 24-hr. ambulatory electrocardiogram, 24-hr. ambulatory blood pressure, Plasma catecholamines (exercise), Prolonged exercise, Gated blood pool scan w/beta adrenergic blockage (exercise and rest), Magnetic resonance imaging, and pulse wave velocity

Immunologic function: HLA typing, Rosettes, Monoclonal analysis of subsets, NK cell function, Granulocyte function, Mitogen reactivity, Lymphocyte counts, PWM-T+B Ig synthesis, RNA production, IL-2 production, IL-2 receptor, Titers, EBV studies

Skin: Fibroblast culture, and allergy skin testing

Oral function: Oral tissue examination, oral motor function, salivary function, dental/oral history (Q), taste thresholds, taste intensity (4 qualities; 4 qualities, updated method; 2 qualities), viscosity and temperature intensity, pressure intensity, and olfactory recognition

Endocrine function: Reproductive hormone assessment, thyroid hormone assessment and prolactin secretion, pituitary adrenal axis assessment, and growth hormone somatomedin concentration

Vision: Acuity (stereopsis and color vision), acuity (pupils dilated), lens photography, contrast sensitivity, and Your Vision (Q)

Auditory function and speech: Hearing thresholds (Bekesey procedure, Constant stimuli), Speech recognition, acoustic immittance measures, Hearing History (Q), and Hearing Handicap (Q)

Cognitive function: Wechsler Adult Intelligence Scale-WAIS (Vocabulary only), Benton Visual Retention Test, Serial & paired-associate learning, Logical problem solving, Concept problem solving, Everyday problem solving, Everyday memory, Memory & response time, Sentence memory, Raven's Advanced Progressive Matrices, Wechsler Adult Intelligence Scale (excluding vocabulary), and Army Alpha, Forms A & B

Personality & coping assessment: GZTS (Q), TAT & Holtzman Inkblot Tests, California Q-Sort, Minnesota Multiphasic Personality Inventory, Stress and coping interview, Chicago AAI (Q), Mail Questionnaire Project [Schedule of Life Events (Q), EPI (Q), Daily Events Checklist (Q), Well-Being Assessment (Q), POMS (Q), Recalled Parent-Child Relations Inventory (Q), NEO Inventory & Rating (Q), DMI (Q), Marlowe-Crown (Q), Coping Questionnaire and Self-Interview (Q), Holland SDS (Q), Holland SDS (Q), Stress Symptoms Inventory (Q), GWB (Q), SIRS (Q), State-Trait Personality (Q), EPQ - P Scale (Q), Agreeableness & Conscientiousness (Q), Adjective Rating Scales (Q), Twenty Statements test (Q), TAS (Q), SSI-IV (Q); Adjective Check List (Q), MBTI (Q), BDHI (Q), California Psychological Inventory (Q), Gough ACL (Q), Defense Style Questionnaire (Q), and MCMI], Personal interview (marital and sexual history), and Electroencephalogram (evoked potential, and reaction time and Galvanic Skin Response)

Daydreaming and vigilance: Mackworth clock test, Task-unrelated thought, Imagi-
nal Processes (Q), Shadow tasking, and Vigilance (sustained attention)
Death information: Autopsy (brain chemistry, cause-of-death, and special cardiac
protocol), and Death file

REPRESENTATIVE REFERENCES:

Costa, P. T., Jr., McCrae, R. R., & Norris, A. H. (1981). Personal adjustment to aging: Longitudinal prediction from neuroticism and extroversion. *Journal of Gerontology, 36,* 78-85.
Fozard, J. L., Metter, E. J., Brant, L. J. (1990). Next steps in describing aging and disease in longitudinal studies. *Journal of Gerontology: Psychological Sciences, 45,* 116-127.
McCrae, R. R., Costa, P. T., Jr., & Arenberg, D. (1980). Constancy of adult personality structure
in males: Longitudinal, cross-sectional and times-of-measurement analyses. *Journal of Gerontology, 35,* 877-883.
Shock, N. (1984). *Normal human aging: The Baltimore Longitudinal Study of Aging.* (NIH Publication No. 84-2450). Washington, DC: U.S. Department of Health and Human Services.

CURRENT STATUS OF THE STUDY:

a. Further waves of data collection are planned.
b. Most data are in machine-readable format.
c. Data are available for secondary analysis through James L. Fozard, Ph.D., Associate Scientific Director, NIA, for the Baltimore Longitudinal Study of Aging, Gerontology Research Center, 4940 Eastern Avenue, Baltimore, MD 21224.

■ The Baltimore Study: Adolescent Parenthood and the Transmission of Social Disadvantage, 1966

Furstenberg, Frank F., Jr.; and Brooks-Gunn, Jeanne

Contact Person: Frank F. Furstenberg, Jr.
Address: Department of Sociology
                  University of Pennsylvania
                  Philadelphia, PA 19104
Telephone No.:   (215) 898-6718

SUBSTANTIVE TOPICS COVERED:

The study examines the long-term impact of ameliorative programs on the adolescent parent and her child, and their possible effect on the known negative consequences of early childbearing; the costs of existing social programs and how these
programs may be restructured to reduce their undesirable side effects; the long-
term impact of informal support systems on adjustment to early childbearing; the
consequences of maintaining negative stereotypes about adolescent parents.

CHARACTERISTICS OF THE ORIGINAL SAMPLE:

Year the study began: 1966-1967

Subject selection process: All pregnant teenagers enrolling at a hospital in Baltimore were asked to participate; one half of those Ss who responded were assigned to a special program and one half attended a clinic.

Total number of subjects at Time 1: N = 754 (Cohorts 1 and 2)

Ages at Time 1: 14-18 yrs.

Sex distribution: 100% female (Cohorts 1 and 2); approximately equal numbers of females and males (Cohorts 3 and 4)

Socioeconomic status: 50% working class, 50% poverty class

Race/ethnicity: 91% African-American, 9% white

Comments

The mothers of the adolescents (Generation I) were also assessed at data points 1 and 5. The figures below refer to the sample characteristics for the adolescents and their offspring only.

Years of Completed Waves:

Years	N=	Age ranges
(Cohort 1: Grandmothers)		
Generation I		
1966-1968	350	30-50 yrs.
1983-1984	280	47-67 yrs.
1987	263	51-71 yrs.
(Cohort 2: Adolescent Mothers)		
Generation II		
1966-1968	404	14-18 yrs.
1968-1979	382	16-20 yrs.
1970	363	17-21 yrs.
1972	331	18-22 yrs.
1983-1984	300	29-33 yrs.
(Cohort 3: Children)		
Generation III		
1972	306	4-5 yrs.
1983-1984	300	15-17 yrs.
1986	250	18-20 yrs.
(Cohort 4: Classmates)		
1970	268	17-21 yrs.
1972	221	19-23 yrs.

INFORMATION ON SAMPLE ATTRITION:

During the 21-year period of study, approximately 294 of 1,328 Ss (22.1%), across four cohorts, were not retrieved for further study: 87 of 350 Ss (24.9%) in Generation/Cohort 1; 104 of 404 Ss (25.7%) in Generation/Cohort 2; 56 of 306 Ss (18.3%) in Generation/Cohort 3; and 47 of 268 Ss (17.5%) in Cohort 4. The core sample consists of 1,034 Ss: 263 Ss (Cohort 1); 300 Ss (Cohort 2); 250 Ss (Cohort 3); and 221 Ss (Cohort 4).

CONSTRUCTS MEASURED: INSTRUMENTS USED

Reproductive history (sexual attitudes, sexual behavior, contraceptive use, pregnancies, and use of health services), vocational history (aspirations and experience), family relationships (mother, father, siblings, and grandparents): Adolescent Surveys

Body image and self-esteem: Achenbach Scales

Reproductive history (number of children, sexual attitudes, use of health services, and contraceptive use), educational history (educational aspirations for their child, and own education), marital status (residence living patterns, marital status change, attitudes about marriage-self, and attitudes about marriage-child), vocational history (aspirations and job record), social support (use of public assistance and health services, and support network), child's school performance (school achievement, educational aspirations, school attendance, school behavioral problems, and use of special educational services): Adult surveys

REPRESENTATIVE REFERENCES:

Furstenberg, F. F., Jr. (1976). Premarital pregnancy and marital instability. *Journal of Social Issues, 32,* 67-86.

Furstenberg, F. F., Jr. (1976). The social consequences of teenage parenthood. *Family Planning Perspectives, 8,* 148-166.

Furstenberg, F. F., Jr. (1976). *Unplanned parenthood.* New York: Free Press.

Furstenberg, F. F., Jr., Brooks-Gunn, J., & Morgan, S. P. (1987). *Adolescent mothers in later life.* New York: Cambridge University Press.

CURRENT STATUS OF THE STUDY:

a. Further waves of data collection are tentatively planned.

b. The data are in machine-readable format.

c. The data are available for secondary analysis from the Data Archive on Adolescent Pregnancy and Pregnancy Prevention (DAAPPP), Sociometrics Corporation, 170 State Street, Suite 260, Los Altos, CA 94022-2812.

■ The Central Pennsylvania Study, 1977

Furstenberg, Frank F., Jr.; and Spanier, Graham B.

Contact Person: Frank F. Furstenberg, Jr.
Address: Department of Sociology
                 University of Pennsylvania
                 3718 Locust Walk CR
                 Philadelphia, PA 19104
Telephone No.:   (215) 898-6718

SUBSTANTIVE TOPICS COVERED:

The purpose of this 2-year follow-up study was to investigate the changing patterns of remarriage and to examine the possibility that the form and functioning of first and second marriages might be different.

CHARACTERISTICS OF THE ORIGINAL SAMPLE:

Year the study began: 1977
Subject selection process: Subjects recently separated or divorced were selected from public documents at the county courthouse.
Total number of subjects at Time 1: N = 210
Ages at Time 1: 20-67 yrs.
Sex distribution: Approximately equal numbers of females and males throughout
Socioeconomic status: 72% middle class, 28% working class (approximately)
Race/ethnicity: 100% white

Years of Completed Waves:

Years	N=	Age ranges
(Cohort 1)		
1977	210	20-67 yrs.
1979	181[a]	22-69 yrs.
(Cohort 2)[b]		
1979	60	20-67 yrs.

Comments:
a. Case study sample of 25 Ss were followed in greater depth.
b. Eligible spouses and partners of Ss were interviewed.

INFORMATION ON SAMPLE ATTRITION:

During the 2-year period of study, 18 of 210 Ss (13.8 %) were not retrieved for further study. Sample attrition occurred because of Ss who could not be located and those who refused to participate in the study. The core sample consists of 181 Ss.

CONSTRUCTS MEASURED: INSTRUMENTS USED

Background information on current relationship, children living in household, parenting and division of responsibilities for child-rearing, visitation of children not living in household, attitudes toward stepchildren, plans for more children, relationship with former and current spouse, social network, plans for and attitudes about remarriage, physical and mental health, economics, circumstances leading up to decision to remarry, relations between partners, contact between former and current spouses, management of power after remarriage, quality and quantity of contact with extended kin: Interview

Styles of communication, marriage, former relationship, relations with children and stepchildren, managing work and family responsibilities: Delayed probe interview (subsample)

REPRESENTATIVE REFERENCES:

Furstenberg, F. F., & Spanier, G. B. (1984). *Recycling the family: Remarriage after divorce.* Beverly Hills, CA: Sage.

Spanier, G. B., & Furstenberg, F. F. (1982). Remarriage after divorce: A longitudinal analysis of well-being. *Journal of Marriage and the Family, 44,* 709-720.

Spanier, G. B., & Thompson, L. (1983). Relief and distress after marital separation. *Journal of Divorce, 7*(1), 31-49.

Spanier, G. B., & Thompson, L. (1984). *Parting: The aftermath of separation and divorce.* Beverly Hills, CA: Sage.

CURRENT STATUS OF THE STUDY:

a. No further waves of data collection are planned.
b. Most of the data are in machine-readable format.
c. Data are available for secondary analysis from the Henry A. Murray Research Center, Radcliffe College, 10 Garden Street, Cambridge, MA 02138.

G

Early Symbolization Project, 1974

Gardner, Howard; and Wolf, Dennie

Contact Person: Dennie Wolf
Address: Harvard Project Zero
Harvard University
326 Longfellow Hall
Cambridge, MA 02138
Telephone No.: (617) 495-4540

SUBSTANTIVE TOPICS COVERED:

The study examines how individuals master symbol systems in different ways, the course of growth in a number of symbol systems, and the relations among symbolic competencies.

CHARACTERISTICS OF THE ORIGINAL SAMPLE:

Year the study began: 1974
Subject selection process: Children were selected from a relatively homogeneous group of middle-class firstborns. A second cohort of relatively homogeneous firstborns was added to the original sample in 1976.
Total number of subjects at Time 1: N = 5[a]
Ages at Time 1: 10 mos.-18 mos.
Sex distribution: 80% female, 20% male
Socioeconomic status: 100% middle class
Race/ethnicity: 88.9% white, 11.1% biracial
Comments:
a. This figure refers to Cohort 1. In addition to the two cohort groups studied longitudinally, a cross-sectional sample of 69 children, ages 2-5 years, was used to verify the findings of the longitudinal study.

Years of Completed Waves:

Years	N=	Age ranges[b]
(Cohort 1)		
1974-1975	5	10-18 mos.
1976	5	22-30 mos.
1977	5	34-43 mos.
1978	5	36-55 mos.
1979	5	48-67 mos.
1980	5	50-79 mos.
1981-1982	5	7-8 yrs.

Years of Completed Waves, Continued:

Years	N=	Age ranges[b]
(Cohort 2)		
1976	4	1 yr.
1977	4	2 yrs.
1978	4	3 yrs.
1979	4	4 yrs.
1980	4	5 yrs.
1982	4	6 yrs., 6 mos.

Comments:
b. The study is difficult to characterize in terms of data waves. While data were collected at specific time periods, it must be emphasized that the data collection procedure is best described as continuous.

INFORMATION ON SAMPLE ATTRITION:

All Ss in both cohort groups were followed for the full 8 years of the study. The core sample consists of 9 Ss: 5 Ss (Cohort 1), and 4 Ss (Cohort 2).

CONSTRUCTS MEASURED: INSTRUMENTS USED

Symbolic competencies such as use of media and symbolic play: Observations made during a free-use play session in the home (child was offered a range of toys with which to play)

Child's symbolic activities, new interests and skills: Face-to-face interviews with parents about observations of the target child

Skill development: Items selected from the Bender Visual-Motor Gestalt Test and McCarthy's Scales of Children's Abilities

Present level of symbolic potential for different media: Observations

Work style (i.e., how the child interacts with materials, task demands, and other people): Ratings by observer

Language functions and use, use of materials in play: Checklist by observer

Competency with different media, subskills particular to each medium across tasks, problem solving, imitation, elicited symbolic activities: Observations (audiotaped) of child in different task situations

Cognitive capacities: Ordinal Scales of Psychological Development (Uzgiris-Hunt), Bayley Scales of Infant Development, McCarthy Scales of Children's Abilities

Individual differences among children for organizing and remembering information: Novel tests and standardized measures

REPRESENTATIVE REFERENCES:

Wolf, D. (1985). Ways of telling: Text repertories in elementary school children. *Journal of Education, 167*(1), 71-87.

Wolf, D., & Gardner, H. (Eds.). (1979) *Early symbolization.* San Francisco: Jossey-Bass.

Wolf, D. & Gardner, H. (1979). Style and sequence in symbolic play. In N. Smith & M. Franklin (Eds.), *Symbolic functioning in early childhood.* Hillsdale, NJ: Lawrence Erlbaum.

Wolf, D., Rygh, J., & Altshuler, J. (1984). Agency and experiences: Children's representations of people in play narratives. In I. Bretherton (Ed.), *Symbolic play: A social-cognitive approach*. New York: Academic Press.

CURRENT STATUS OF THE STUDY:

a. No further waves of data collection are planned.
b. Some data are available in machine-readable format.
c. The data are conditionally available for secondary analysis.

■ Lifestyles of Educated Women, 1961

Ginzberg, Eli; and Yohalem, Alice

Contact Person: Eli Ginzberg
Address: Conservation of Human Resources
2880 Broadway, 4th Floor
New York, NY 10025
Telephone No.: (212) 280-2301

SUBSTANTIVE TOPICS COVERED:

This study examines factors that influence the life patterns of highly educated women, with special emphasis on the role of work in these women's lives.

CHARACTERISTICS OF THE ORIGINAL SAMPLE:

Year the study began: 1961
Subject selection process: Subjects selected were women who received fellowships or scholarships in the arts and sciences, as well as some women who attended graduate professional schools at Columbia University between 1945 and 1951.
Total number of subjects at Time 1: N = 311
Ages at Time 1: 28-55 yrs.
Sex distribution: 100% female
Socioeconomic status: 100% middle/upper middle class
Race/ethnicity: Predominantly white

Years of Completed Waves:

Years	N=	Age ranges
1961-1963	311	28-55 yrs.
1974	226	41-66 yrs.

INFORMATION ON SAMPLE ATTRITION:

During the 3-year period of study, 85 of 311 Ss (27.3%) were not retrieved for further study. The sample attrition may be attributed to death of subjects. Core sample size consists of 226 Ss.

CONSTRUCTS MEASURED: INSTRUMENTS USED

Role of work, educational and employment histories, problem combining work and family, satisfaction with present lifestyle, present home life, sex discrimination in employment: Structured Questionnaire

REPRESENTATIVE REFERENCES:

Ginzberg, E. (1966). *Lifestyles of educated women.* New York: Columbia University Press.

Ginzberg, E. (1966). *Educated American women: Self portraits.* New York: Columbia University Press.

Mueller, M. W. (1975). Economic determinants of volunteer work by women. *Signs, 1*(2), 325-334.

Yohalem, A. (1978). *The careers of professional women: Commitment and conflict.* Montclair, NJ: Allenheld, Osmun.

CURRENT STATUS OF THE STUDY:

a. No further waves of data collection are planned.
b. Most data are in machine-readable format.
c. Data are available for secondary analysis from the Henry A. Murray Research Center, Radcliffe College, 10 Garden Street, Cambridge, MA 02138.

■ **The Massachusetts Reformatory Study, 1911**

Glueck, Sheldon (deceased); and Glueck, Eleanor (deceased)

Contact Person: Henry A. Murray Research Center
Address: Radcliffe College
                 10 Garden Street
                 Cambridge, MA 02138
Telephone No.:   (617) 495-8140

SUBSTANTIVE TOPICS COVERED:

The study evaluates the effectiveness of penal corrections on men released from the Massachusetts Reformatory in Concord, Massachusetts, in 1921 and 1922, by examining the subjects' life histories.

CHARACTERISTICS OF THE ORIGINAL SAMPLE:

Year the study began: 1911

Subject selection process: Subjects were male juvenile offenders sentenced to the Massachusetts Reformatory for offenses ranging from property crimes (92%) to homicides (3%).

Total number of subjects at Time 1: N = 510

Ages at Time 1: 16-41 yrs. (approximately)

Sex distribution: 100% male

Socioeconomic status:[a] 56.4% working class, 28.8% middle class, 14.8% poverty class (approximately)

Race/ethnicity: 100% white

Comments:

a. Approximation based on 447 Ss.

Years of Completed Waves:

Years	N=	Age ranges
1916-1921	510	16-41 yrs.
1921-1922	477	21-46 yrs.
1922-1926	454	22-47 yrs.
1926-1931	439	26-52 yrs.

INFORMATION ON SAMPLE ATTRITION:

During the 15-year period of study, 71 of 510 Ss (13.8%) were not retrieved for further study. The core sample consists of 439 Ss. The main reason for sample attrition was death of Ss. Investigators also were unable to locate five Ss.

CONSTRUCTS MEASURED: INSTRUMENTS USED

Conduct, mental health: Case records, school records

Mental and physical health: Hospital records

Background, family life: Employment and parole information

History prior to sentencing, behavior changes upon release: Field investigations

Family background, occupational history, behavior and employment during parole: Case records

Family relations, living conditions, occupational history, reformatory influences, criminal record: Interview with subject

Family relations, living conditions, occupational history, reformatory influences, criminal record: Interview with family, friends, employers

Family history: Public office records, occupational history, health, living conditions, criminal record

Marital history, family relationships, industrial history, leisure and habits, delinquencies, economic responsibilities, environmental conditions, attitudes and reactions of subject, community's attitudes and reactions to subject, investigator's attitudes and reactions to subject: Interview

REPRESENTATIVE REFERENCES:

Glueck, S., & Glueck, E. (1930). *Five hundred criminal careers*. New York: Kraus Reprint.
Glueck, S., & Glueck, E. (1937). *Later criminal careers*. New York: Kraus Reprint.
Glueck, S., & Glueck, E. (1943). *Criminal careers in retrospect*. New York: Kraus Reprint.
Glueck, S., & Glueck, E. (1945). *After-conduct of discharged offenders* (Reprint 6). New York: Kraus Reprint.

CURRENT STATUS OF THE STUDY:

a. No further waves of data collection are planned.
b. Most of the data are in machine-readable format.
c. Data are available for secondary analysis from the Henry A. Murray Research Center, Radcliffe College, 10 Garden Street, Cambridge, MA 02138.

■ The Women's Reformatory Study, 1920

Glueck, Sheldon (deceased); and Glueck, Eleanor (deceased)

Contact Person: Henry A. Murray Research Center
Address: Radcliffe College
                 10 Garden Street
                 Cambridge, MA 02318
Telephone No.:   (617) 495-8140

SUBSTANTIVE TOPICS COVERED:

This study assesses the overall effectiveness of correctional treatment on women sentenced to the Women's Reformatory in Framingham, Massachusetts.

CHARACTERISTICS OF THE ORIGINAL SAMPLE:

Year the study began: 1920
Subject selection process: Subjects included those women who had been sentenced to the Women's Reformatory. The majority of Ss were imprisoned for prostitution.
Total number of subjects at Time 1: N = 500
Ages at Time 1: 18-60 yrs. (approximately)
Sex distribution: 100% female
Socioeconomic status: 93.3% poverty class, 6.7% working class
Race/ethnicity: 94% white, 5% African-American, 1% other

Years of Completed Waves:

Years	N=	Age ranges
1920-1925	500 (During parole)	18-60 yrs.
1920-1925	500 (After sentence)	18-60 yrs.

INFORMATION ON SAMPLE ATTRITION:

It is not appropriate to describe this study in terms of discrete data waves since data were collected continuously. The data collected, however, can be divided into the two following parts: information covering the time up to the end of the parole period, and information covering the 5-year period after expiration of the reformatory sentence. In only 21 (4.2%) of the 500 original Ss was no information obtained at the 5-year follow-up. The core sample consists of 479 Ss.

CONSTRUCTS MEASURED: INSTRUMENTS USED

Reformatory and parole history: Reformatory and parole records
Personal history, family history, parole history: Interview with subject
Personal and family history of subject: Interview with relatives, acquaintances, employers

REPRESENTATIVE REFERENCES:

Glueck, E., & Glueck, S. (1934). *Five hundred delinquent women.* New York: Kraus Reprint.

CURRENT STATUS OF THE STUDY:

a. No further waves of data collection are planned.
b. Most of the data are not in machine-readable format.
c. Data are available for secondary analysis through the Henry A. Murray Research Center, Radcliffe College, 10 Garden Street, Cambridge, MA 02138.

■ The UCLA High-Risk Project, 1964

Goldstein, Michael J.

Contact Person: Michael J. Goldstein
Address: Department of Psychology
                 University of California at Los Angeles
                 1283 Franz Hall
                 Los Angeles, CA 90024
Telephone No.:   (213) 825-3367 or 825-2619

SUBSTANTIVE TOPICS COVERED:

The study examines a variety of intrafamilial attributes in the families of disturbed adolescents in order to identify familial marker variables that were related to the subsequent onset of schizophrenia and related disorders. Among the variables studied were the following: parental communication deviance; affective attitudes and styles; family role structure and nonverbal behavior; autonomic reactivity; and genetic history of mental illness.

CHARACTERISTICS OF THE ORIGINAL SAMPLE:

Year the study began: 1964
Subject selection process: Families were contacted through the UCLA Psychology
    Clinic, where they had sought help for their non-psychotically disturbed adolescent.
Total number of subjects at Time 1: N = 64
Ages at Time 1: 13-18 yrs.
Sex distribution: Approximately equal numbers of females and males throughout
Socioeconomic status: 100% middle/upper middle class
Race/ethnicity: Predominantly white

Years of Completed Waves:

Years	N=	Age ranges
1964	64	13-18 yrs.
1969	53	18-23 yrs.
1979	51	28-33 yrs.

INFORMATION ON SAMPLE ATTRITION:

During the 15-year period of study, 13 of 64 Ss (20.3%) were not reinterviewed in person during the third wave. However, diagnostic status of 54 of these cases were available, based on relatives reports and hospital records. The core sample consists of 51 Ss.

CONSTRUCTS MEASURED: INSTRUMENTS USED

Background information about child and parents: Interview with parents and adolescents

Intelligence: Wechsler Adult Intelligence Scale (child and parents)

Communication deviance of adolescent and parent: Thematic Apperception Test (TAT), Zulliger Inkblot Test

To rule out organic abnormalities at original assessment: Bender Gestalt

Subclinical thought disorder: Word Association Test, Thematic Apperception Test, communication deviance scoring system

Affective style, role structure, acknowledgement of others, and nonverbal behavior: Directive interaction tasks

Autonomic reactivity: Galvanic Skin Response

Task focusing: Videotape feedback session

Family attitudes: Adjective checklist

Psychiatric diagnoses: UCLA follow-up interview at 5- and 15-year follow-up

Information about child's psychosocial functioning: UCLA follow-up interview collected from parents

Family history of mental illness: UCLA history of mental illness interview collected from parents

Social competence: Social adjustment rating scales

Attitudes toward interpersonal relationships on Thematic Apperception Test: Interpersonal attitude scale

REPRESENTATIVE REFERENCES:

Goldstein, M. J. (1985). Family factors that antedate the onset of schizophrenia and related disorders: The results of a fifteen year prospective longitudinal study. *Acta Psychiatrica Scandinavica, 71*(Supp. 319), 7-18.

Goldstein, M. J. (1987). The UCLA High-Risk Project. *Schizophrenia Bulletin, 13*(3), 505-514.

Goldstein, M. J., Judd, L. L., Rodnick, E. H., Alkire, A., & Gould, E. (1968). A method for studying social influence and coping patterns within families of disturbed adolescents. *Journal of Nervous and Mental Disease, 147*, 233-251.

Lewis, J. M., Rodnick, E. H., & Goldstein, M. J. (1981). Intrafamilial interactive behavior, parental communication deviance, and risk for schizophrenia. *Journal of Abnormal Psychology, 90*, 448-457.

CURRENT STATUS OF THE STUDY:

a. No further waves of data collection are planned.

b. All data are in machine-readable format.

c. The data are not available for secondary analysis.

■ Iowa Older-Workers Panel Study, 1964

Goudy, Willis J.; Keith, Patricia M.; and Powers, Edward A.

Contact Person: Willis J. Goudy
Address: Sociology & Anthropology Department
                 Iowa State University of Science and Technology
                 107 East Hall
                 Ames, IA 50011
Telephone No.:   (515) 294-8337

SUBSTANTIVE TOPICS COVERED:

The study examines work and retirement history; work and retirement attitudes; perceptions of change (work, family, community, health, and finances); social networks (family, friends, community); social-psychological attitudes (e.g., life satisfaction, self-esteem, anomie, and attitudes toward death); financial information; religious participation; and sociodemographic characteristics (including extended information on widowers).

CHARACTERISTICS OF THE ORIGINAL SAMPLE:

Year the study began: 1964
Subject selection process: Selection required employment in one of five occupational categories: farmers, blue-collar workers, small businessmen, salaried, and self-employed professionals. Subjects were Iowan males, 50 years of age or older, living in or near towns with populations ranging from 2,500 to 10,000.
Total number of subjects at Time 1: N = 1,870
Ages at Time 1: 50-82 yrs.
Sex distribution: 100% male
Socioeconomic status: 50% middle/upper middle class, 33.3% working class, 16.7% poverty class
Race/ethnicity: 100% white

Years of Completed Waves:

Years	N=	Age ranges
1964	1,870	50-82 yrs.
1974	1,332	60-92 yrs.

INFORMATION ON SAMPLE ATTRITION:

During the 10-year period of study, 538 of 1,870 Ss (28.8%) were not retrieved for further study. Reasons for sample attrition included deaths (21.7%); refusing the second interview (3.7%); illness or incompetence to be reinterviewed (1.7%); or nonlocatable (1.7%). The core sample consists of 1,332 Ss.

CONSTRUCTS MEASURED: INSTRUMENTS USED

Work history, household mobility, living arrangements and visiting patterns, demographic information, work satisfaction, retirement, and morale: Face-to-face interview schedules

REPRESENTATIVE REFERENCES:

Goudy, W. J., Powers, E. A., & Keith, P. M. (1975). The work-satisfaction, retirement-attitude typology: Profile examination. *Experimental Aging Research, 1,* 267-279.
Goudy, W. J., Powers, E. A., Keith, P. M., & Reger, R. A. (1980). Changes in attitudes toward retirement: Evidence from a panel study of older males. *Journal of Gerontology, 35,* 942-948.
Keith, P. M., Goudy, W. J., & Powers, E. A. (1979). Work-nonwork orientations among older men in nonmetropolitan communities. *Sociological Symposium, 26,* 83-101.
Powers, E. A., Goudy, W. J., & Keith, P. M. (1985). *Later life transitions: Older males in rural America.* Boston: Kluwer-Nijhoff.

CURRENT STATUS OF THE STUDY:

    a. No further waves of data collection are planned.
    b. Most data are in machine-readable format.
    c. Data are not available for secondary analysis.

■ National Institute of Mental Health Study, 1957

Granick, Samuel; Birren, James E.; and Kleban, Morton H.

Contact Person: Samuel Granick
Address: 404 Waring Road
                 Elkins Park, PA 19117
Telephone No.: (215) 635-0404

SUBSTANTIVE TOPICS COVERED:

This study examines medical factors in human aging; cerebral circulation and electroencephalogram changes; psychological test functioning; psychiatric aspects; social adaptation; and psychobiological interrelationships.

CHARACTERISTICS OF THE ORIGINAL SAMPLE:

Year the study began: 1957
Subject selection process: Subjects were volunteers who responded to publicity released through the Philadelphia Geriatric Center and the Association of Retired Civil Employees in Washington, D.C. Ss chosen were 65 years of age or older, showed no significant medical or psychiatric problems, and resided in the community.
Total number of subjects at Time 1: N = 47
Ages at Time 1: 65-92 yrs.
Sex distribution: 100% male
Socioeconomic status: 56% working class, 44% middle/upper middle class
Race/ethnicity: 98% white, 2% African-American

Years of Completed Waves:

Years	N=	Age ranges
1957	47	65-92 yrs.
1961-1962	29	71-97 yrs.
1967-1968	19	78-89 yrs.

INFORMATION ON SAMPLE ATTRITION:

During the 11-year period of study, 28 of 47 Ss (59.5%) were not retrieved for further study. Attrition was due to illness, death, subjects' loss of interest in the study, and the inability to contact subjects.

CONSTRUCTS MEASURED: INSTRUMENTS USED

Social adaption, psychiatric status (symptoms), life satisfaction, mental status: Interviews (Psychiatric Social Adjustment)
Personal history, attitudes toward future, aging self, death: Questionnaires, levels of aspiration
Medical health: Medical history, physical examination, complete neurological examination
Physiological functioning: Hematology, blood chemistry, urinalysis, chest X ray, skull X ray, electrocardiogram, electroencephalogram, pulmonary-function studies, cerebral-blood-flow studies, audiometric examination, click-perception tests, delayed auditory feedback tests
Personality tests (mostly projective): Draw-A-Person Test, Emotional projection test, Minnesota Multiphasic Personality Inventory, Rorschach, Thematic Apperception Test, Sentence-completion Test
Cognitive abilities: Addition rate, arithmetic alternation rate, mirror tracing, perception of the line difference, reaction time, speed of card sorting, speed of

copying words, Stroop Test, Weigl Color Sorting, Wisconsin Card Sorting, word fluency, homonyms

Intelligence: Raven's Progressive Matrices, Wechsler Adult Intelligence Scale

Family history (or interval history), family scene, educational history, occupational history, retirement planning and activities, marital history, living arrangements, use of time, social relations and interaction, attitudes toward life, goals and aspirations, critical turning points of life, significant losses, observed physical and mental changes in aging: Social-psychological interview

History of psychiatric contact, personal-social history (or interval history), psychiatric-symptom check list, mental-status evaluation; assessment of attitudes about futurity, death, self, aging: Psychiatric interviews

REPRESENTATIVE REFERENCES:

Birren, J. E., Butler, R. N., Greenhouse, S., Sokoloff, L., & Yarrow, M. R. (Eds.). (1963). *Human aging* (PHS Publication No. 986). Washington, DC: Government Printing Office.

Granick, S., & Kleban, M. H. (1977). Data file of NIMH study of healthy aged males. *The Gerontologist, 47*(6), 531-536.

Granick, S., Kleban, M. H., & Weiss, A. D. (1976). Relationships between hearing loss and cognition in normally hearing aged persons. *Journal of Gerontology, 31*(4), 434-440.

Granick, S., & Patterson, R. D. (1971). *Human aging II* (DHEW Publication No. HSM 71-9037). Washington, DC: Government Printing Office.

CURRENT STATUS OF THE STUDY:

a. No further waves of data collection are planned.

b. Most data are in machine-readable format.

c. Data are available for secondary analysis from the study contact person, and through the National Archive of Computerized Data, P.O. Box 1248, Ann Arbor, MI 48106.

■ The Early Training Project, 1961

Gray, Susan; and Klaus, Rupert

Contact person: Susan Gray
Address: JFK Center for Research on Education
and Human Development
George Peabody College for Teachers
Vanderbilt University
Nashville, TN 37203
Telephone No.: (617) 383-1441 or (615) 322-8239

SUBSTANTIVE TOPICS COVERED:

This study was designed to test whether it is possible to offset the progressive retardation in schooling commonly observed in children from low-income homes. The study specifically focused on intellectual development, school achievement, school adjustment, social and vocational orientations.

CHARACTERISTICS OF THE ORIGINAL SAMPLE:

Year the study began: 1961

Subject selection process: Census was made of all African-American children born in 1958. Children were selected according to indices of educational disadvantage. All families were below the poverty level.

Total number of subjects at Time 1: N = 90 (42 experimental, 21 local, and 27 distal controls)

Ages at Time 1: 3.5-4.5 yrs.

Sex distribution: Approximately equal numbers of females and males throughout

Socioeconomic status: 100% poverty class

Race/ethnicity: 100% African-American

Years of Completed Waves:

Years	N=	Age ranges
(Cohort 1: Experimental Group 1)		
1962 (Summer)	21	3-4 yrs.
1962-1963 (Winter)	21	4-5 yrs.
1963 (Summer)	21	4-5 yrs.
1963-1964 (Winter)	21	5-6 yrs.
1964 (Summer)	21	5-6 yrs.
1964-1965 (Winter)	21	6-7 yrs.
1965 (Summer)	19	6-7 yrs.
1966 (Summer)	19	8 yrs.
1968 (Summer)	19	10 yrs.
1975	18[a]	17 yrs.
1975-1976	18[a]	17-18 yrs.

Years of Completed Waves, Continued:

Years	N=	Age ranges
1976-1977	18[a]	18-19 yrs.
1978-1980	21	20-22 yrs.
(Cohort 2: Experimental Group 2)		
1963 (Summer)	21	4-5 yrs.
1963-1964 (Winter)	21	5-6 yrs.
1964 (Summer)	21	5-6 yrs.
1964-1965 (Winter)	21	6-7 yrs.
1965 (Summer)	19	6-7 yrs.
1966 (Summer)	19	8 yrs.
1968 (Summer)	19	10 yrs.
1975	18[a]	17 yrs.
1975-1976	18[a]	17-18 yrs.
1976-1977	18[a]	18-19 yrs.
1978-1980	21	20-22 yrs.
(Cohort 3: Local Control Group [Abbotfield: Town A])		
1962 (Summer)	21	3-4 yrs.
1962-1963 (Winter)	21	4-5 yrs.
1963 (Summer)	21	4-5 yrs.
1963-1964 (Winter)	21	5-6 yrs.
1964 (Summer)	21	5-6 yrs.
1964-1965 (Winter)	21	6-7 yrs.
1965 (Summer)	18	6-7 yrs.
1966 (Summer)	18	8 yrs.
1968 (Summer)	18	10 yrs.
1975	18[a]	17 yrs.
1975-1976	18[a]	17-18 yrs.
1976-1977	17[a]	18-19 yrs.
1978-1980	21	20-22 yrs.
(Cohort 4: Distal Control Group [Bakersville: Town B])		
1962 (Summer)	27	3-4 yrs.
1962-1963 (Winter)	27	4-5 yrs.
1963 (Summer)	27	4-5 yrs.
1963-1964 (Winter)	27	5-6 yrs.
1964 (Summer)	27	5-6 yrs.
1964-1965 (Winter)	27	6-7 yrs.
1965 (Summer)	23	6-7 yrs.
1966 (Summer)	23	8 yrs.
1968 (Summer)	23	10 yrs.
1975	21[a]	17 yrs.
1975-1976	21[a]	17-18 yrs.
1976-1977	21[a]	18-19 yrs.
1978-1980	23	20-22 yrs.

Comments:
a. Sample sizes are approximations for these years.

INFORMATION ON SAMPLE ATTRITION:

During the 19-year period of study, 4 of 90 Ss (4.4%) were not retrieved for further study. Attrition was due to death, disability, refusal to participate, and change of residence. The core sample consists of 86 Ss.

CONSTRUCTS MEASURED: INSTRUMENTS USED

Intelligence: Stanford-Binet Intelligence Scale, Wechsler Intelligence Scale for Children

Language development: Illinois Test of Psycholinguistic Abilities, Peabody Picture Vocabulary Test

Child's academic performance: Metropolitan Achievement Test (MAT), Stanford Test of Academic Skills (TASK)

Self-esteem: Piers-Harris Self-Concept Test, Rosenberg Test of Self-Esteem

Reputation of child among schoolmates: "Who Are They?" Test

Subject's social adjustment, leadership, participation in activities, and general productivity: Counselor ratings

Locus of control: Rotter's Locus of Control Scale

Household enumeration; ages of subjects and parents' educational levels, and occupations, and relationship to participant; subject's birth order, and number of siblings: Demographic data

Family structure, friendship, attitudes toward family, questions on identification figures, locus of control, activities when alone, extracurricular activities, attitudes toward school, occupation orientation, attitudes toward social protest: Subject interviews

Parent's educational and occupational aspirations for the child, parent's awareness of social differences among African-Americans, general positive and negative feelings toward the child, perceptions of opportunities for African-Americans in their local city, attitudes toward desegregation in school and work settings, general health status of child over time, and child's participation in any "unusual" educational programs: Parental interviews

School mobility, retention in grade, course failure, graduation, dropouts, grade point average, grades in specific courses, placement in special education courses, suspensions and expulsions, absences: School records

REPRESENTATIVE REFERENCES:

Gray, S. W., & Klaus, R. A. (1970). The Early Training Project: A seventh year report. *Child Development, 41,* 909-924.

Gray, S. W., Klaus, R. A., Miller, J. O., & Forrester, B. J. (1966). *Before first grade.* New York: Teachers College Press, Columbia University.

Gray, S. W., Ramsey, B. K., & Klaus, R. A. (1982). *From 3 to 20: The Early Training Project.* Baltimore: University Park Press.

Klaus, R. A., & Gray, S. W. (1968). The Early Training Project for disadvantaged children. *Monographs of the Society of Research in Child Development, 33*(4).

CURRENT STATUS OF THE STUDY:

a. No further waves of data collection are planned.
b. Most of the data are in machine-readable format.
c. Data are available for secondary analysis from the Henry A. Murray Research Center, Radcliffe College, 10 Garden Street, Cambridge, MA 02138.

■ Longitudinal Study of the Psychosocial Effects of Disaster: Buffalo Creek Survivors in the Second Decade, 1973

Green, Bonnie L.; Grace, Mary C.; Lindy, Jacob D.; and Gleser, Goldine C.

Contact Person: Mary C. Grace
Address: Department of Psychiatry
                  University of Cincinnati
                  School of Medicine
                  7110 College of Medicine
                  Cincinnati, OH 45267
Telephone No.:   (513) 558-5857

SUBSTANTIVE TOPICS COVERED:

The study seeks to describe the trauma-related psychopathology in flood survivors who are experiencing problems at follow-up. The study examines the extent to which individual survivor experiences are predictive of long-term psychopathology. Finally, the study identifies the incidence of posttraumatic stress disorder in this sample.

CHARACTERISTICS OF THE ORIGINAL SAMPLE:

Year the study began: 1974
Subject selection process: All of the original plaintiffs in a law suit against the Pittston Coal Company in regard to a flood in Buffalo Creek, West Virginia
Total number of subjects at Time 1: N = 381
Ages at Time 1: 16-74 yrs.
Sex distribution: Approximately equal numbers of females and males throughout
Socioeconomic status: Approximately 90% working class, 10% middle/upper middle class
Race/ethnicity: 87.3% white, 12.7% African-American

Years of Completed Waves:

Years	N=	Age ranges
1974 (April)	381	16-74 yrs.
1974 (Oct.)	381	16-74 yrs.
1975-1977	102	17-77 yrs.
1979	*	21-61 yrs.
1986	121	28-68 yrs.

INFORMATION ON SAMPLE ATTRITION:

During the 12-year period of study, 279 of 381 Ss (73.2%) were not retrieved for further study. The core sample consists of 121 Ss. Attrition was due to refusals, Ss moving away, and death due to black lung disease.

CONSTRUCTS MEASURED: INSTRUMENTS USED

Subjective distress: Hopkins Symptoms Checklist-90-R (Self-report)
Family disruption (e.g., arguments, divorce, separation): Checklist of Family Disruption Indicators
Degree of psychological impairment: Clinical Impairment Rating (by social worker and psychiatrist)
Presence of psychopathology: Medical-Psychiatric Report
Psychological functioning: Open-ended clinical interview, Psychiatric Evaluation Form Scales (semistructured clinical interview)
Stressors due to flood (degree of threat to life, degree of injury, degree of damage to house): Stress scale
Clinical diagnosis: The Structured Clinical Interview for the Diagnostic & Statistical Manual III-R

REPRESENTATIVE REFERENCES:

Gleser, G. C., Green, B. L., & Winget, C. N. (1981). *Prolonged psychosocial effects of disaster.* New York: Academic Press.

Green, B. L., & Gleser, G. C. (1983). Stress and long-term psychopathology in survivors of the Buffalo Creek disaster. In D. F. Ricks & B. S. Dohrenwend (Eds.), *Origins of psychopathology* (pp. 73-90). Cambridge, U.K.: Cambridge University Press.

Green, B. L., Grace, M. C., Lindy, J. D., Gleser, G. C., Leonard, A. C., & Kramer, T. L. (1990). Buffalo Creek survivors in the second decade: Comparison with unexposed and nonlitigant groups. *Journal of Applied Social Psychology, 20,* 1033-1050.

Green, B. L., Lindy, J. D., Grace, M. C., Gleser, G. C., Leonard, A. C., Koral, M., & Winget, C. (1990). Buffalo Creek survivors in the second decade: Stability of stress symptoms. *American Journal of Orthopsychiatry, 60,* 43-54.

CURRENT STATUS OF THE STUDY:

a. No further waves of data collection are planned.
b. Most data are in machine-readable format.
c. Data are conditionally available for secondary analysis from the study contact person, to be negotiated on a case-by-case basis.

■ Mother-Infant Project, 1980

Greenberg, Mark T.; and Crnic, Keith

Contact Person: Mark T. Greenberg
Address: Department of Psychology
                  NI-25 University of Washington
                  Seattle, WA 98195
Telephone No.:   (206) 543-4339

Contact Person: Keith Crnic
Address: Department of Psychology
                  612 Moore Building
                  Pennsylvania State University
                  University Park, PA 16802
Telephone No.:   (814) 863-1745

SUBSTANTIVE TOPICS COVERED:

This 5-year study compared the social, cognitive, linguistic, and family development of a sample of preterm and full-term children and their families.

CHARACTERISTICS OF THE ORIGINAL SAMPLE:

Year the study began: 1980

Subject selection process: Full-term infants were case-matched to preterms. Preterms selected weighed under 1,800 grams, had no serious brain damage, and did not return to the hospital for more than 3 days during their first year of life. They were small but relatively healthy preterm babies.

Total number of subjects at Time 1: N = 105 (52 preterms, 53 full-terms)

Ages at Time 1: 1 month.

Sex distribution: Equal numbers of females and males throughout

Socioeconomic status: 50% middle/upper middle class, 25% working class, and 25% poverty class (both cohorts)

Race/ethnicity: Predominantly white

Years of Completed Waves:

Years	N=	Age ranges
(Cohort 1: Preterm Ss)		
1980	52	1 mos.
1980	45	4 mos.
1980	41	8 mos.
1981	37	1 yrs.
1982	30	2 yrs.
1984	38	4 yrs.
1985	31	5 yrs.
(Cohort 2: Full-Term Ss)		
1980	53	1 mos.
1980	47	4 mos.
1980	43	8 mos.
1981	41	1 yrs.
1982	40	2 yrs.
1984	45	4 yrs.
1985	44	5 yrs.

INFORMATION ON SAMPLE ATTRITION:

During the 5-year period of study, 30 of 105 Ss (28.6%), across both cohorts, were not retrieved for further study: 21 of 52 Ss (40.4%) in Cohort 1, and 9 of 53 Ss (17%) in Cohort 2. The main reason for sample attrition among preterm Ss was dropping out. The core sample consists of 75 Ss from both cohorts: 31 Ss (Cohort 1), and 44 Ss (Cohort 2).

CONSTRUCTS MEASURED: INSTRUMENTS USED

Attachment: Strange situation (modified)
Mother and infant behavior: Nursing Child Assessment Teaching Scale (NCATS)
Mother-child interaction: Ratings of affect of mother and infant language development, videotaped behavioral observations
Maternal attitude: Satisfaction with Parenting Scale (SWPS), Index of General Life Satisfaction
Mother's perception of infant temperament: Sostek and Anders' Temperament Measure
Maternal and family style: Barnard's Questionnaire version of the Home Observation for Measurement of the Environment (HOME) Scale
Social support, stress: Inventory of parent experiences
Daily stress: Parenting daily hassles
Psychosocial family functioning: Structured Home Interviews
Mother's life stress: The Life Experience Survey (LES)
Infant's prelinguistic behavior: Receptive-Expressive Emergent Language Scale (REEL)

Language development: Peabody Picture Vocabulary Test, Mean Length Utterance
Cognitive development: Bayley Scales of Infant Development, Stanford-Binet Intelligence Test, Wechsler Preschool and Primary Scale of Intelligence, Sequenced Inventory of Communication Development (comprehension subscale)

REPRESENTATIVE REFERENCES:

Crnic, K. A., & Greenberg, (1990). Minor parenting stresses with young children. *Child Develop-
ment, 61,* 1628-1637.
Crnic, K. A., Ragozin, A. S., Greenberg, M. T., Robinson, N. M., & Basham, R. (1983). Social in-
teraction and development competence of preterm and full-term infants in the first year of
life. *Child Development, 54,* 1199-1210.
Greenberg, M. T. (1984). Pragmatics and social interaction: The unrealized nexus. In L. Feagans,
R. Golinkoff, & C. Garvey (Eds.), *The origins and growth of communication* (pp. 208-223).
Norwood, NJ: Albex.
Greenberg, M. T., & Crnic, K. A. (1988). Longitudinal predictors of developmental status and social
interaction in premature and full-term infants at age two. *Child Development, 59,* 544-570.

CURRENT STATUS OF THE STUDY:

a. No further waves of data collection are planned.
b. Most data are in machine-readable format.
c. Data are available for secondary analysis from the study contact person.

■ Pregnancy and Parenthood Project, 1975

Grossman, Frances K.

Contact Person: Frances K. Grossman
Address: Department of Psychology
                  Boston University
                  64 Cummington Street
                  Boston, MA 02215
Telephone No.:   (617) 353-2538

SUBSTANTIVE TOPICS COVERED:

The purpose of this study is to increase understanding of the process of childbearing; to identify factors early in pregnancy that are predictive of future problems with childbirth and child rearing; and to compare the experiences of first-time
parents with those of parents who have already had children.

CHARACTERISTICS OF THE ORIGINAL SAMPLE:

Year the study began: 1975

Subject selection process: In 1975, 100 women and the husbands of 90 of them were recruited from the clinics of two teaching hospitals in Boston and from private obstetricians' offices early in their first or later pregnancy. In 1981 a sample of Chinese-American families was added to the study as a comparison group.

Total number of subjects at Time 1: N = 100 families

Ages at Time 1: 21-38 yrs.

Sex distribution: Approximately equal numbers of females and males throughout

Socioeconomic status: Predominantly middle/upper middle class

Race/ethnicity: 75.7% white, 24.3% Chinese-American

Years of Completed Waves:

Years	N=	Age ranges
(Cohort 1: White families)		
1975	100	21-34 yrs.
1975	85	21-34 yrs.
1976	76	22-39 yrs.
1976	81	22-39 yrs.
1977	82	23-40 yrs.
1978	53	24-41 yrs.
1981	58[a]	27-44 yrs.
(Cohort 2: Chinese-American families)		
1981	32	34 yrs.

Comments:

a. Fourteen additional families were added to the remaining 44 families in 1981.

INFORMATION ON SAMPLE ATTRITION:

During the 6-year period of study, 56 of 100 Ss (56%) followed over time, were not retrieved for further study. (As noted above, 14 families were added in 1981.) The core sample consists of 44 Ss. Attrition was due to miscarriage, relocation, or withdrawal for personal reasons.

CONSTRUCTS MEASURED: INSTRUMENTS USED

Life history: Biographical data sheet, Life Adaptation Interview

Anxiety, depression and anxiety in the puerperim: State-Trait Anxiety Scale, Pitt Anxiety and Depression Scale

Adaptation to pregnancy: Adaptation to Pregnancy Interview

Motivation for pregnancy: Motivation for Pregnancy Questionnaire

Personality: Rorschach Index of Repressive Style, Modified Thematic Apperception Test

Sex-role identification, identification with mother: Bem Sex Role Inventory

Identification with mother: Scale

Identification with father: Scale

Remembered nurturance: Remembered Nurturance Scale, (variation of Biller and
Reuter scale)

Physical health and history: Medical Questionnaire (women only), Relationship
Questionnaire, Social Adjustment Scale

Sexual history: Sexual Experience Questionnaire

Marital adjustment: Marital Adjustment Questionnaire

Motivation for pregnancy: Conscious Motivation for Pregnancy Questionnaire

Maternal adaptation to labor and delivery: Maternal Adaptation to Labor and Delivery Interview

Adaptation to self, adaptation to pregnancy, adaptation to spouse, couple prepared-
ness, complications of labor and delivery: Semistructured Interview

Parental adaptation, medication (mother): Observed parental adaptation

Infant alertness, motor maturity, irritability, reciprocity: Brazelton Alertness,
Motor Maturity, Irritability

Neonatal perception: Neonatal Perception Inventory

Infant adaptation: Observed Adaptation (infant)

Intelligence, physiological adaptation (infant): Bayley Scales of Infant Development (infant)

Personality: Carey Infant Temperament Scale, Thorndike Dimensions of Temperament

Maternal attachment: Klaus Maternal Attachment Measures (Observational)

Repression-Sensitization: Repression-Sensitization (Byrne)

Marital adjustment, sexual activity and satisfaction: Spanier's Marital Adjustment
Scale

Health; remembered nurturance and remembered involvement from father (men
only): Health and Opinion Survey

Family closeness: Family Closeness and Distance Questionnaire

Family closeness and distance: Observation

Child development: Minnesota Child Development Inventory, Parent Perception
Questionnaire, Situation Questionnaire

Interpersonal awareness, locus of control (child): Carnegie-Mellon Interpersonal
Awareness Test (child)

Preschool attainment: Preschool Attainment Record (child)

Intelligence: Peabody Picture Vocabulary Test

Interpersonal relations: Preschool Interpersonal Problem Solving Test, Acculturation Questionnaire

Premenstrual tension: Premenstrual Tension Questionnaire (women only)

REPRESENTATIVE REFERENCES:

Grossman, F. K. (1987). Separate and together: Men's autonomy and affiliation in the transition to parenthood. In P. Berman & F. Pederson (Eds.), *Men's transition to parenthood.* Hillsdale, NJ: Lawrence Erlbaum.

Grossman, F. K., Eichler, L. S., Winickoff, S. A., Anzalone, M. K., Gofseyeff, M. H., & Sargent, S. P. (1980). *Pregnancy, birth, and parenthood: Adaptations of mothers, fathers and infants.* San Francisco: Jossey-Bass.

Grossman, F. K., Pollack, W. S., & Golding, E. (1988). Fathers and children: Predicting the quality and quantity of fathering. *Developmental Psychology, 24*(1), 82-91.

Grossman, F. K., Pollack, W. S., Golding, E., & Fedele, N. (1987). Affiliation and autonomy in the transition to parenthood. *Family Relations, 36,* 263-269.

CURRENT STATUS OF THE STUDY:

    a. No further waves of data collection are planned.

    b. Most of the data are in machine-readable format.

    c. Data are available for secondary analysis through the Henry A. Murray Research Center, Radcliffe College, 10 Garden Street, Cambridge, MA 02138.

■ Michigan Student Study: A Study of Students in a Multiversity, 1962

Gurin, Gerald

Contact Person: Gerald Gurin
Address: 2117 School of Education Building
               610 East University Street
               University of Michigan
               Ann Arbor, MI 48109
Telephone No.:   (313) 764-9300

SUBSTANTIVE TOPICS COVERED:

The study assesses the impact of college experience on students and vice versa. (See also Mortimer, J. T., *The Michigan Study: Male Follow-Up*; and Tangri, S. S., *Longitudinal Study of Career Development in College-Educated Women.*)

CHARACTERISTICS OF THE ORIGINAL SAMPLE:

Year the study began: 1962

Subject selection process: Sample included freshmen entering a large midwestern university in 1962-1963.

Total number of subjects at Time 1: N = 2,207

Ages at Time 1: 18-19 yrs.
Sex distribution: Approximately equal numbers of females and males
   throughout
Socioeconomic status: 100% student
Race/ethnicity: Predominantly white

Years of Completed Waves:

Years	N=	Age ranges
(Cohort 1: Graduating class of 1966)		
1962	2,207[a]	18-19 yrs.
1966	450[b]	21-22 yrs.
(Cohort 2: Graduating class of 1967)[c]		
1963	2,161[a]	18-19 yrs.
1967	450[b]	21-22 yrs.

Comments:
a. 400 Ss, half from both cohorts, received extensive interviews in the second semester of their freshman year, and in the second semester of their senior year.
b. 450 Ss, half female and half male, were followed up in each cohort at the end of their senior year.
c. 300 subjects who were seniors in 1967 were added to offset sample attrition.

INFORMATION ON SAMPLE ATTRITION:

   During the 5-year period of study, 900 of 4,368 Ss from both cohorts were followed in depth; 3,468 Ss (73.6%) were not retrieved for further study.

CONSTRUCTS MEASURED: INSTRUMENTS USED

College plans of siblings, contributors to the financial cost of subject's education,
   level of importance of various college expectations, factors influencing decision to attend this university, academic major, perceived ability to handle university workload, anticipated grade point average, expectation of
   post-graduate education, specific activities of interest, living arrangement
   preferences and characteristics, desire to affiliate with Greek system, self-ex-
   pression during high school, friendship patterns and relationships, relationship
   with parents, feelings about parental practices, future goals, parental influence
   on career choice, frequency of identity seeking, level of self-criticism, desired
   change in self; feelings towards death, life, illness, dreams, cheating, stealing,
   and unkindness; feelings toward African-Americans: Initial Freshman Questionnaire
Personality: Standardized Omnibus Personality Inventory
Readiness to handle the academic demands at university: College Entrance Examination Board Scholastic Aptitude Test
Feelings about academic aspects of college, level of interest in specific subject
   areas, preference for various classroom procedures, level of participation in

and evaluation of honors program, academic standing and achievement, feelings toward academic major and how it was chosen, satisfaction with living arrangements, reaction to and perceptions of the university, relationship to and feelings about faculty, level of satisfaction with academic aspects, experience and feelings toward beliefs being challenged, level of change and university's effect on changes, future goals, level of importance of various life spheres, changes in career choice since beginning of college, feelings towards present and future marital status, desire to marry, when and how many children are desired, feelings toward relationships, level of agreement with various new issues, attitudes toward African-Americans, feelings toward university experience; changes in ideas, beliefs, or values while in college; perception of self as student; contact with and relationship to parents: Senior Questionnaire

Expectation of work after marriage and children: Senior Questionnaire (women)

Feelings about marrying career-oriented women: Senior Questionnaire (men)

REPRESENTATIVE REFERENCES:

Feldman, K. A., & Newcombe, T. M. (1969). *The impact of college on students.* San Francisco: Jossey-Bass.

Gurin, G. (1968). *A study of students in multiversity.* Office of Education, U.S. Department of Health, Education and Welfare (Project No. 5-0901). Ann Arbor: Survey Research Center, Institute for Social Research, University of Michigan.

Gurin, G. (1971). The impact of the college experience. In S. B. Whithey (Ed.), *A degree and what else? Correlates and consequences of a college education* (pp.25-54). New York: McGraw-Hill.

Gurin, G., Newcomb, T. M., & Cope, R. G. (1968). *Characteristics of entering freshmen related to attrition in the literacy college of a large state university.* Office of Education, U.S. Department of Health, Education and Welfare (Project No. 1938). Ann Arbor: Survey Research Center, Institute for Social Research, University of Michigan.

CURRENT STATUS OF THE STUDY:

a. An additional wave of data collection is currently in progress.

b. Most data are in machine-readable format.

c. Data are available for secondary analysis through the Henry A. Murray Research Center, Radcliffe College, 10 Garden Street, Cambridge, MA 02138.

H

Early Patterns of Cognitive Development, 1973

Hall, Vernon; and Kaye, Daniel

Contact Person: Vernon Hall
Address: Department of Psychology
                 Syracuse University
                 150 Marshall Street
                 Syracuse, NY 13210
Telephone No.:   (315) 423-2353

SUBSTANTIVE TOPICS COVERED:

The study examines the similarities and differences in cognitive development of four subcultural groups of boys, with the purpose of testing Jensen's theory of differential readiness by race and socioeconomic status. Specifically, it focuses on memory, intelligence and transfer abilities, and children's level of performance and rate of development, according to age, cohort, race, socioeconomic status, and practice effects. Hall and Kaye concluded that all subcultural groups improved at the same rate on memory and intelligence tasks with age, thereby calling into question many conclusions drawn from Jensen's theory.

CHARACTERISTICS OF THE ORIGINAL SAMPLE:

Year the study began: 1973

Subject selection process: The sample was randomly selected from several schools in an eastern metropolitan area. Ss were all male, and all sample groups were balanced for race and socioeconomic status. Additional age groups were added to the study in the second and third waves. Some of these age groups were followed longitudinally and some were not. All Ss in the additional groups were randomly selected from schools in the same eastern metropolitan area, were male, and were balanced for age and socioeconomic status.

Total number of subjects at Time 1: N = 898[a]

Ages at Time 1: 6-8 yrs.

Sex distribution: 100% male

Socioeconomic status: 50% middle class, 50% working class

Race/ethnicity: 50% African-American, 50% white

Comments:

a. The research design included a total of four longitudinal and two cross-sectional samples: 599 Ss followed longitudinally and 299 Ss tested cross-sectionally. The supplemental sample groups were added to the original sample over the 4-year period of the study. Only one age group of the original sample was followed from 6 to 9 years of age.

Years of Completed Waves:

Years	N=	Age ranges
(Cohort 811: MCW)[b]		
1973-1974	50	8 yrs.
(Cohort 811: LCW)[b]		
1973-1974	50	8 yrs.
(Cohort 811: MCB)[b]		
1973-1974	50	8 yrs.
(Cohort 811: LCB)[b]		
1973-1974	50	8 yrs.
(Cohort 711: MCW)		
1973-1974	50	7 yrs.
1974-1975	43	8 yrs.
(Cohort 711: LCW)		
1973-1974	50	7 yrs.
1974-1975	47	8 yrs.
(Cohort 711: MCB)		
1973-1974	50	7 yrs.
1974-1975	46	8 yrs.
(Cohort 711: LCB)		
1973-1974	50	7 yrs.
1974-1975	44	8 yrs.
(Cohort 611: MCW)		
1973-1974	50	6 yrs.
1974-1975	44	7 yrs.
1975-1976	41	8 yrs.
1976-1977	36	9 yrs.
(Cohort 611: LCW)		
1973-1974	50	6 yrs.
1974-1975	44	7 yrs.
1975-1976	41	8 yrs.
1976-1977	36	9 yrs.
(Cohort 611: MCB)		
1973-1974	50	6 yrs.
1974-1975	48	7 yrs.
1975-1976	46	8 yrs.
1976-1977	45	9 yrs.
(Cohort 611: LCB)		
1973-1974	50	6 yrs.
1974-1975	45	7 yrs.
1975-1976	42	8 yrs.
1976-1977	42	9 yrs.
(Cohort 721: MCW)		
1974-1975	25	7 yrs.
1975-1976	24	8 yrs.
1976-1977	20	9 yrs.
(Cohort 721: LCW)		
1974-1975	25	7 yrs.
1975-1976	23	8 yrs.
1976-1977	21	9 yrs.

Years of Completed Waves, Continued:

Years	N=	Age ranges
(Cohort 721: MCB)		
1974-1975	25	7 yrs.
1975-1976	23	8 yrs.
1976-1977	22	9 yrs.
(Cohort 721: LCB)		
1974-1975	25	7 yrs.
1975-1976	23	8 yrs.
1976-1977	22	9 yrs.
(Cohort 821: MCW)		
1974-1975	25	8 yrs.
(Cohort 821: LCW)		
1974-1975	25	8 yrs.
(Cohort 821: MCB)		
1974-1975	25	8 yrs.
(Cohort 821: LCB)		
1974-1975	24	8 yrs.
(Cohort 831: MCW)		
1975-1976	25	8 yrs.
1976-1977	22	9 yrs.
(Cohort 831: LCW)		
1975-1976	24	8 yrs.
1976-1977	24	9 yrs.

Comments:
b. MCW: Middle Class White
  LCW: Lower Class White
  MCB: Middle Class Black
  LCB: Lower Class Black

INFORMATION ON SAMPLE ATTRITION:

During the 4-year period of study, 107 of 599 Ss (17.9%) across 16 cohorts were not retrieved for further study. Information on core samples was not available.

CONSTRUCTS MEASURED: INSTRUMENTS USED

Memory (Jensen's Level I): Digit Span Forward Test (adapted from the Stanford-Binet I.Q. Test), free recall (adapted from AA Thorndike-Lorge 1944 list of high frequency words)

Intelligence (Jensen's Level II): Raven's Coloured Progressive Matrices, Peabody Picture Vocabulary Test

Learning and learning transfer: Paired-associate learning of visual stimuli (from AA or A Thorndike-Lorge 1944 list of high frequency words) using 3 different lists, Matrices Solving Ability (Matrices Proficiency Test and Matrices Training Tests); matrices training and transfer; Esper paradigm rule learning test

REPRESENTATIVE REFERENCES:

Hall, V. C., Huppertz, J. W., & Levi, A. (1977). Attention and achievement exhibited by middle- and lower-class black and white elementary school boys. *Journal of Educational Psychology, 69*(2), 115-120.

Hall, V., & Kaye, D. (1980). Early patterns of cognitive development. *Monographs of the Society for Research in Child Development, 45.*

Hall, V., & Kaye, D. (1977). Patterns of early cognitive development among boys in four subcultural groups. *Journal of Educational Psychology, 69,* 66-87.

Kaye, D., Hall, V. C., & Barron, M. B. (1979). Factors influencing rule discovery in children. *Journal of Educational Psychology, 71*(5), 115-120.

CURRENT STATUS OF THE STUDY:

a. No further waves of data collection are planned.
b. The data are in machine-readable format.
c. The data are available for secondary analysis from the study contact person.

■ The Vermont Longitudinal Research Project, 1955

Harding, Courtenay M.; Brooks, George W.; Ashikaga, Takamaru; Strauss, John S.; and Breier, Alan

Contact person: Courtenay M. Harding
Address: University of Colorado School of Medicine
                 Department of Psychiatry
                 UCHSC Box C-249
                 4200 East 9th Avenue
                 Denver, CO 80262
Telephone No.:   (303) 270-8313

SUBSTANTIVE TOPICS COVERED:

This study follows the re-entry into the community of 269 back ward patients from Vermont State Hospital, after a planned deinstitutionalization effort in the mid-1950s, to document their lives across multiple domains of functioning.

CHARACTERISTICS OF THE ORIGINAL SAMPLE:

Year the study began: 1955

Subject selection process: Initially all subjects were referred from back wards; however, the following groups were excluded from the sample: major cases of retardation, those over 62 years of age, and those on legal mandate. During

1980-1982 the entire initial sample was followed, but subjects with organic disorders were not included in the analyses.

Total number of subjects at Time 1: N = 269

Ages at Time 1: 40 yrs.

Sex distribution: Approximately equal numbers of females and males throughout

Socioeconomic status: 60% poverty class, 40% working class (approximately)

Race/ethnicity: 100% white

Years of Completed Waves:

Years	N=	Average age
(Cohort 1: Vermont Ss)		
1955-1960	269	40 yrs.
1965-1967	269	50 yrs.
1980-1982	262	61 yrs.
(Cohort 2: Comparison Ss)[a]		
1986-1989	269	late 50s

Comments:

a. Baseline data were gathered on inpatients from Augusta State Hospital to replicate data collected from the Vermont cohort. Ss were matched on age, gender, diagnosis, and length of chronicity. Ss also had not received any rehabilitation.

INFORMATION ON SAMPLE ATTRITION:

During the 22-year period of study, 7 of 269 Ss (2.6%) were not retrieved for further study. Attrition was due to deaths, subjects' refusal to participate, and inability to locate subjects. The core sample consists of 262 Ss.

CONSTRUCTS MEASURED: INSTRUMENTS USED[1]

Current psychiatric status, social and vocational functioning: Interview with subject

Verification of information: Interview with subject's family or acquaintances, and double set of prospectively gathered hospital and vocational rehabilitation program records

Status of patient (current comprehensive status): Vermont Community Questionnaire-C

Retrospective data over the intervening 20 years: Vermont Community Questionnaire-Longitudinal (VCQ-L)

Patient's current state and historical data (verified): Verinform

1,800 variables extracting data across multiple domains, first Index Episodes and course information: Hospital record review form

Patterns, shifts, and trends in life course: Life Chart (Meyer, Leighton, and Harding)

Comments:

1. Restriction of space and format prevent a full description of the constructs and measures used.

REPRESENTATIVE REFERENCES:

Harding, C. M. (1988). Course types in schizophrenia: An analysis of European and American studies. *Schizophrenia Bulletin, 14*(4), 633-643.
Harding, C. M., Brooks, G. W., Ashikaga, T., Strauss, J. S., & Breier, A. (1987). The Vermont longitudinal study of persons with severe mental illness: I. Methodology, study sample, and overall status 32 years later. *American Journal of Psychiatry, 144*(6), 718-726.
Harding, C. M., Brooks, G. W., Ashikaga, T., Strauss, J. S., & Breier, A. (1987). The Vermont longitudinal study: II. Long-term outcome of subjects who retrospectively met DSM-III criteria for schizophrenia. *American Journal of Psychiatry, 144*(6), 727-735.
Harding, C. M., McCormick, R. V., Strauss, J. S., Ashikaga, T., & Brooks, G. W. (1989). Investigating mediating factors in the long-term course of DSM-III schizophrenia with computerized life chart methods. *British Journal of Psychiatry, 155*(Supp. 5), 100-106.

CURRENT STATUS OF THE STUDY:

a. No further waves of data collection are planned.
b. Most of the data are in machine-readable format.
c. Data are available for secondary analysis from the study contact person.

■ Terman Life Cycle Study of Children with High Ability, 1921

Hastorf, Albert H.; Horowitz, Leonard; Holahan, Carol K.; and Sears, Robert R. (deceased); Sears, Pauline; Cronbach, Lee; and Terman, Lewis (deceased)

Contact Person:	Albert H. Hastorf
Address:	Department of Psychology
	Stanford University
	Palo Alto, CA 94305
Telephone No.:	(415) 725-2451

SUBSTANTIVE TOPICS COVERED:

The study examines the physical, intellectual, and social characteristics of children who are gifted, as compared with nongifted children. Specific characteristics studied include the following: cognitive abilities, marital history and satisfaction, occupational history and satisfaction, fertility and family history, and life satisfaction.

CHARACTERISTICS OF THE ORIGINAL SAMPLE:

Year the study began: 1921
Subject selection process: Children were selected from California public school systems. The gifted Ss were chosen on the basis of having an IQ within the

top 1% of tested intelligence (135 or higher). Samples of nongifted children were obtained from test norm populations, census, or other surveys for comparisons with the gifted sample at the initial data point. Comparisons with the gifted sample at later data points employed data bases for the population at large from the U.S. Census data. The gifted group was not randomly selected. Children were chosen from grades 3 to 8 and high school. Members from the "outside Binet group" consisted of a sample of gifted Ss of the same age range as the original sample, chosen from smaller communities in California. The same IQ criterion was used. In 1927-1928, 58 Ss (siblings) were added to the study as a comparison group.

Total number of subjects at Time 1: N = 1,470[a]

Ages at Time 1: 2-22 yrs.

Sex distribution: Approximately equal numbers of females and males throughout

Socioeconomic status: 75% middle/upper middle class, 25% working class (approximately)

Race/ethnicity: 100% white

Comments:

a. This figure refers to the gifted children at the initial data point. The comparison groups of nongifted children are not included in this figure.

Years of Completed Waves:

Years	N=	Age ranges[a]
1921-1923	1,512	2-22 yrs.
1928[b]	1,486	8-27 yrs.
1936	1,450	17-35 yrs.
1940	1,433	20-39 yrs.
1945	1,415	26-44 yrs.
1950	1,385	31-49 yrs.
1955	1,375	36-54 yrs.
1960	1,231	41-59 yrs.
1972	1,060	53-71 yrs.
1977	960	58-76 yrs.
1982	870	63-81 yrs.
1985-1986	707	66-85 yrs.

Comments:

a. Figures are an approximation.

b. A control sample of 58 Ss was tested in 1927-1928.

INFORMATION ON SAMPLE ATTRITION:

During the 64-year period of study, 484 of 1,512 Ss (32%) were not retrieved for further study. Main reasons for sample attrition included deaths (408 Ss), dropouts (309 Ss), and Ss not found for follow-up (104 Ss). The core sample consists of 1,028 Ss.

CONSTRUCTS MEASURED: INSTRUMENTS USED

Intelligence: Stanford-Binet Intelligence Test, National Intelligence Test, Army Alpha, National Intelligence Test, Otis Group Test, Terman Group Test

Academic achievement: Stanford Achievement Test

Breadth of knowledge: General Information Test

High level verbal intelligence: Concept Mastery Test

Masculinity/Femininity, social interests, intellectual interests: Play behaviors and games

Amount of reading: Books reported read during 2 months

Personality, honesty, self-estimation: Wyman Character Test, character and personality trait tests

Scholastic, occupational, and other interests: General and domain specific interests

Physical growth: Anthropometric measures

Health status: Medical examination

Demographic data, intellectual and social educational interests, health: Home information blank, school information blank, home "annual report"

Home environment: Whittier Scale of Home Conditions

Findings from the medical examination: Report to parents, medical

Personality: Report to parents, interest, personality tests; trait rating blank

Family relationships, child's progress: Report on home visit, report on conference with teachers, report on conference with subject

Biographical information: General information

Personality and temperament: Personality and temperament assessments

Marital satisfaction: Marriage blank

Occupational interest: Strong Vocational Interest Blank

Biographical information: Supplementary biographical questionnaire

Areas in which subjects had sought and found life-satisfaction; occupational success; family life, friendships, richness of cultural life, and total service to society and joy in living; demographic information (with gerontological focus—retirement, health, avocations, living arrangements, and social networks): Mail questionnaires

REPRESENTATIVE REFERENCES:

Oden, M. H. (1968). The fulfillment of promise: 40-year follow-up of the Terman gifted group. *Genetic Psychology Monographs, 77,* 3-93.

Sears, R. R. (1977). Sources of life satisfactions among Terman's gifted women. *American Psychologist, 32,* 119-128.

Sears, R. R., & Holahan, C. K. (in press). *The later maturity of the gifted group.* Palo Alto, CA: Stanford University Press.

Terman, L. M. (1925). *Genetic studies of genius: Vol. I. Mental and physical traits of a thousand gifted children.* Palo Alto, CA: Stanford University Press.

CURRENT STATUS OF THE STUDY:

a. A further wave of data collection is planned for 1991.

b. Most data are in machine-readable format.

c. The data are available for secondary analysis through the study contact person or from the Henry A. Murray Research Center, Radcliffe College, 10 Garden Street, Cambridge, MA 02138.

■ Adolescence and Family Development Project, 1978

Hauser, Stuart T.; Powers, Sally; Jacobson, Alan; and Noam, Gil G.

Contact Person: Stuart T. Hauser
Address: Department of Psychiatry
                  Harvard Medical School
                  74 Fenwood Road
                  Boston, MA 02115
Telephone No.:   (617) 232-2690

SUBSTANTIVE TOPICS COVERED:

The study examines adolescent psychosocial development (ego development, moral development); adolescent personality dimensions, and their changes (self-esteem, self-images, and ego processes); family interaction over time; adult (parent) development (ego and moral development) and its relationship to adolescent change.

CHARACTERISTICS OF THE ORIGINAL SAMPLE:

Year the study began: 1978

Subject selection process: The study follows three samples: 1) High school students, originally volunteers from a freshman class, who were then selected to match the other subsamples on socioeconomic status, age, and gender; 2) adolescent psychiatric patients, who were successive admissions to an in-patient unit and are neither psychotic nor organically impaired; 3) adolescent diabetic patients, who were successive admissions to a diabetes treatment unit.

Total number of subjects at Time 1: N = 201

Ages at Time 1: 12-16 yrs.

Sex distribution: Approximately equal numbers of females and males throughout

Socioeconomic status: 100% upper middle/middle class

Race/ethnicity: 100% white

Years of Completed Waves:

Years	N=	Age ranges
(Cohort 1: High school adolescents)		
1978	76	14-16 yrs.
1979	65	15-17 yrs.
1980	58	16-18 yrs.
1981[a]	45	17-19 yrs.
1989-1990[b]	*	25-27 yrs.
(Cohort 2: Psychiatric hospitalized adolescents)		
1978	70	12-16 yrs.
1979	61	13-17 yrs.
1980	56	14-18 yrs.
1981	38	15-19 yrs.
1989-1991[b]	*	23-27 yrs.
(Cohort 3: Diabetic adolescents)		
1978	55	12-16 yrs.
1979	42	13-17 yrs.

Comments:

a. Year 4 of the study was selectively truncated, as described below. Samples from Cohorts 1 and 2 were selectively followed in order to achieve a full range of individual differences with regard to ego development. Subjects from Cohort 3 were not systematically followed beyond the 2nd year.

b. Follow-up of Ss in Cohort 1 and Cohort 2 is in progress. As of November 1990, 98% of the original high school sample and 95% of the original psychiatric sample have been relocated.

INFORMATION ON SAMPLE ATTRITION:

Within the first 3 years of the study, 32 of the 146 Ss (21.9%) from Cohorts 1 and 2 did not continue with the study: 18 of 76 Ss (23.6%) in Cohort 1; 14 of 70 Ss (20%) in Cohort 2. In the 4th year of the study, a smaller set of subjects from both Cohorts, selected on the basis of ego development contrasts, was deliberately chosen to be followed. Thirteen of the Ss (23.6%) from Cohort 3 were not retrieved for the 2nd year of the study.

CONSTRUCTS MEASURED: INSTRUMENTS USED

Ego development: Washington University Sentence Completion Test (Loevinger) (parents and adolescents)

Moral judgment development: Moral Judgment Interview (Kohlberg) (parents and adolescents)

Self-esteem: Coopersmith Self-Esteem Inventory (adolescents)

Self-image perspectives: Q-Sort (adolescents) (Hauser et al.)

Intelligence: Shipley-Hartford Intelligence Test (adolescents), California Test of Basic Skills (adolescents), Wechsler Intelligence Scale for Children (psychiatric adolescents)

Behavior symptoms and social competence: Achenbach-Edelbrock Behavior Checklist (parents), Achenbach-Edelbrock Youth Self-Report (adolescents)

Coping behavior: McCubbin Coping-Health Inventory for Parents (CHIP) (designed for families with a child who is chronically ill or having to manage a physical illness for an extended period of time) (parents)

Adolescent coping behaviors: McCubbin Adolescent Coping Orientation for Problem Experiences (A-COPE) (adolescents)

Family coping behaviors: McCubbin Family Crises Oriented Personal Scales (parents and adolescents)

Family coping processes: Family Coping Coding System (FCCS) (parents and adolescents) (Hauser et al.)

Family interactions: Constraining and Enabling Coding System (CECS), operational codes applied to transcripts of family discussions which were stimulated by a revealed differences task (parents and adolescents) (Hauser et al.)

Interaction variables derived from structural-developmental theory as influencing moral development: Developmental Environments Coding System (DECS), operational codes applied to the transcripts of family discussions which were stimulated by a revealed differences task (parents and adolescents) (Powers)

Ego processes, coping and defense: Q-Sort of Ego Processes (Haan), operational codes applied to transcripts of clinical research interviews (adolescents)

REPRESENTATIVE REFERENCES:

Hauser, S. T., Borman, E. H., Jacobson, A. M., Powers, S. I., & Noam, G. G. (in press). Understanding family contexts of adolescent coping: A study of parental ego development and adolescent coping strategies. *Journal of Early Adolescence.*

Hauser, S. T., Jacobson, A. M., Noam, G. G., & Powers, S. (1983). Ego development and self-image complexity in early adolescence: Longitudinal studies of psychiatric and diabetic patients. *Archives of General Psychiatry, 40,* 325-332.

Leaper, C., Hauser, S. T., Kremen, A., Powers, S., Jacobson, A., Noam, G., Weiss-Perry, B., & Follansbee, D. (1989). Adolescent parent-interactions in relation to adolescents' gender and ego development pathway: A longitudinal study. *Journal of Early Adolescence, 9,* 335-361.

Noam, G., Hauser, S., Santostefano, S., Garrison, R., Jacobson, A., Powers, S., & Mead, M. (1984). Ego development and psychopathology: A study of hospitalized adolescents. *Child Development, 55,* 184-194.

CURRENT STATUS OF THE STUDY:

a. A follow-up study of Cohorts 1 and 2 is progress.
b. Data are in machine-readable format.
c. The data are available for secondary analysis through the Henry A. Murray Research Center, Radcliffe College, 10 Garden Street, Cambridge, MA 02138.

■ The Study of Adult Development, 1960s

Heath, Douglas H.

Contact Person: Douglas H. Heath
Address: Heath Consultants
223 Buck Lane
Haverford, PA 19041
Telephone No.: (215) 649-7037

SUBSTANTIVE TOPICS COVERED:

This study examined the meaning of competence and psychological maturity of college men, their course and causes through the adult years, and the differences between males and females and their maturation.

CHARACTERISTICS OF THE ORIGINAL SAMPLE:

Year the study began: 1960s (early)[a]
Subject selection process: Students judged most and least effective in functioning by 18 teachers, students, counselors, and coaches were included in the study along with a random selection of students of intermediate levels of effective functioning.
Total number of subjects at Time 1: N = 80
Ages at Time 1: 17 yrs. (males); 29-52 yrs. (females)
Sex distribution: 100% male initially. At Wave 3 a cohort of women was included.
Socioeconomic status: 100% middle/upper middle class for males; mixed for females
Race/ethnicity: 100% white; mixed for females
Comments:
a. Exact years of study were withheld at the request of the principal investigator to maintain subject confidentiality.

Years of Completed Waves:

Years	N=	Age ranges
(Cohort 1: men)		
1960s (early)	80	17 yrs.
1960s (mid)	80	20-21 yrs.
1970s (mid)	68	33-34 yrs.
1980s (early)	65	43-47 yrs.
(Cohort 2: women)		
1980s (early)	41	29-52 yrs.

INFORMATION ON SAMPLE ATTRITION:

During the approximately 25-year period of study, 15 of 80 male Ss (18.8%) were not retrieved for further study. The core sample consists of 65 male SS, and 40 female Ss.

CONSTRUCTS MEASURED: INSTRUMENTS USED

Developmental history: Developmental history questionnaire

Personality functioning: Minnesota Multiphasic Personality Inventory, Self-Image Questionnaire, Perceived Self Questionnaire, Loevinger's Washington University Sentence Completion Test of Ego Development, Rorschach Ink Blot Test, selected Thematic Apperception Test cards

Temperamental similarity to successful and happy men and women: Strong Campbell Interest Inventory

Health: Self-rated body symptoms and change, self-rated, spouse-, friend-, and colleague-rated physical and mental health

Satisfaction with 30 attributes of vocational adaptation: Vocational Adaptation Scale; self, spouse, and colleague ratings

Marital relationships: Marital Adjustment Scale, numerous measures of sexual behavior and communication

Interpersonal communication: 20-item scale for varied types of relationships

Parental satisfaction and competence: Parental Adaptation Scale, Self-spouse ratings

Judged personality: Spouse, friend, and colleague ratings

Dimensional maturity of the self-concept: Self-image questionnaire, Perceived Self Questionnaire

Value Maturity: Valuator Test, Perceived Self Questionnaire

Preferences for way of life: Study of values

Maturity: Perceived Self Questionnaire, Judge ratings

Adult success and maturity: Washington University Sentence Completion Test (Loevinger)

Child's psychological maturity and adaptability: Parental ratings

Defenses, models of coping, intellectual strengths, qualities of relationships: Rorschach Ink Blot Test, focused interview

Relationships, feelings about death, unfulfilled wishes: Selected Thematic Apperception Test cards, extensive questionnaire ratings, focused interview

Changes in attitudes and behavior: Sex-role interview, repeated focused interview and identification of determinants; comparisons of repeated tests from Waves 1 through 4.

REPRESENTATIVE REFERENCES:

Heath, D. H. (1965). *Explorations of maturity.* New York: Appleton-Century-Crofts.
Heath, D. H. (1977). *Maturity and competence: A transcultural view.* New York: Gardner Press.

Heath, D. H. (1977). Some possible effects of occupation on the maturing of professional men. *Journal of Vocational Behavior, 11,* 263-281.
Heath, D. H. (in press). *Growing up to succeed: A study of middle-aged men and women.* San Francisco, CA: Jossey-Bass.

CURRENT STATUS OF THE STUDY:

a. Further waves of data collection are planned.
b. Most of the data are in machine-readable format.
c. Data are available for secondary analysis from the study contact person.

■ Mills Longitudinal Study, 1958

Helson, Ravenna

Contact person:　Ravenna Helson
Address:　　　　Institute of Personality Assessment & Research
　　　　　　　　University of California
　　　　　　　　Berkeley, CA 94720
Telephone No.:　(415) 642-5050

SUBSTANTIVE TOPICS COVERED:

This study examines women's personality development, from the senior year of college through young and middle adulthood, with wide-ranging personality inventories and questionnaires about work, relationships, and other aspects of life, with regard for the interpersonal environment and sociohistorical context.

CHARACTERISTICS OF THE ORIGINAL SAMPLE:

Year the study began: 1958
Subject selection process: All Mills College graduating seniors were invited to participate in a study of creativity, leadership, and young women's plans for the future, by attending one of two testing sessions.
Total number of subjects at Time 1: N = 142
Ages at Time 1: 21 yrs.
Sex distribution: 100% female
Socioeconomic status: 100% student
Race/ethnicity: 95% white, 4% Asian-American, 1% other

Years of Completed Waves:

Years	N=	Age ranges
1958-1960[a]	142	20-22 yrs. (Total)
1963-1964	99	25-27 yrs.
1981	130	42-45 yrs.
1989	123	51-54 yrs.

Comments:
a. The sample size listed (N = 142) combines Ss from the class of 1958 (N = 65) and 1960 (N = 77) respectively. The class of 1958 was retested in 1963, and the class of 1960 in 1964, but the two groups were then merged and have been merged since.

INFORMATION ON SAMPLE ATTRITION:

During the 31-year period of study, 10 of the original 142 Ss (7%) provided no further information. Inventory and questionnaire data are available for 109 Ss at age 43, 107 at age 52. Core sample consists of 82 Ss.

CONSTRUCTS MEASURED: INSTRUMENTS USED

Demographic Data

Feminine social clock, traditionality of feminine role, masculine occupational clock: Demographic Data Sheet (age 43)
Number of roles: Demographic Data Sheet (ages 43 & 51)

Inventories

Social personality traits: California Psychological Inventory (CPI) (ages 21, 27, 43, & 52)
Originality, needs and transactional analysis scales: Adjective Checklist (ages 27, 43, & 52)
Psychopathology: Minnesota Multiphasic Personality Inventory (ages 21 & 27)
Jungian personality typologies: Myers-Briggs Type Indicator (ages 27 & 43)
Values: Allport-Vernon-Lindzey Study of Value (age 27)
Simplicity-complexity: Barron-Welsh Art Scale (age 27)
Attitudes expressing various forms of hostility or need to control in the context of homemaker: Parental Attitudes Research Instrument (age 27)
Ego development: Washington University Sentence Completion Test (Loevinger) (age 43)
Defense mechanisms: Coping and defending scales (ages 21, 27, 43, & 52)
Originality, complexity of outlook, ego strength, overcontrol and undercontrol: IPAR scales (ages 21 & 27)
Developmental status, social maturity: Vassar scales (ages 21 & 27)

Questionnaire Data

Health ratings: Health scale (ages 27, 43, & 52)
Psychological distress: Scale (age 43)
Energy: Rating scale (ages 27 & 43)
Total amount of participation in labor force: Work scale (age 43)
Status level of paid work: Rating (ages 43 & 52)
Adult adjustment: Index (up to age 43)
Relationships with parents past and present, factor scores: Scale (age 43)
Childhood activities: Checklist (age 21)
Imaginative-artistic and activities, tomboy activities, and individual activities: Checklist (age 21)
Marital tensions: Checklist (ages 27 & 52)
Marital satisfaction, feelings about life now and 10 years ago: Checklist (ages 43 and 52)
Social networks: Checklist (age 43)
Health and health practices: Checklist (ages 27, 43, & 52)
Aspects of work: Checklist (Different questions at ages 43 & 52)
Conflict and cohesiveness in home environment: Checklist (age 43)
Influence of cohort and social climate: Checklist (ages 43 & 52)
Political and religious attitudes: Checklist (age 52)

Observer and File-rater Data

Prototype scores on narcissism; ego-identity status, introversion, shyness, and soundness: File rater Q-sorts
Personality type scores: Q sort-derived

Data from Parents, Partners, and Siblings

Self-descriptions from parents: Adjective checklist (age 21)
Self-descriptions from partners: Adjective checklist (ages 27 & 52)
Parental and partners' values: Allport-Vernon-Lindzey Study of Values (age 27)
Sibling data: California Psychological Inventory, childhood activities, art scale

REPRESENTATIVE REFERENCES:

Helson, R., Mitchell, V., & Moane, G. (1984). Personality and patterns of adherence and non-adherence to the social clock. *Journal of Personality and Social Psychology, 46,* 1079-1096.

Helson, R., & Moane, G. (1987). Personality change in women from college to midlife. *Journal of Personality and Social Psychology, 53,* 176-186.

Helson, R., & Picano, J. (in press). Is the traditional role bad for women? *Journal of Personality and Social Psychology, 59.*

Helson, R., & Wink, P. (1987). Two conceptions of maturity examined in the findings of a longitudinal study. *Journal of Personality and Social Psychology, 53,* 531-541.

CURRENT STATUS OF THE STUDY:

a. The 4th wave of data collection is being concluded.
b. Much of the data are in machine-readable format.
c. Data are currently not available for secondary analysis.

■ A Longitudinal Study of the Consequences of Child Abuse, 1975

Herrenkohl, Roy C.; and Herrenkohl, Ellen C.

Contact Person: Roy C. and Ellen C. Herrenkohl
Address: Lehigh University
Center for Social Research
203 East Packer Ave.
Bethlehem, PA 18015
Telephone No.: (215) 758-3800

SUBSTANTIVE TOPICS COVERED:

The study examines the relation of maltreatment of children to indicators of child development (e.g., school performance, cognition, behavior, health status, personality, and social relations between children and their parents); the child-family setting, and the broader community setting in which maltreatment occurs. An ecological perspective is emphasized.

CHARACTERISTICS OF THE ORIGINAL SAMPLE:

Year the study began: 1975
Subject selection process: Subjects selected to participate in the study were children, ages 16 months to 6 years, from families served by abuse centers of two county child welfare agencies. Comparison groups from neglect units of the same child welfare agencies and from day-care centers, Head Start centers, and nursery schools were also included in the study.
Total number of subjects at Time 1: N = 439
Ages at Time 1: 1-6 yrs.
Sex distribution: Approximately equal numbers of females and males throughout
Socioeconomic status: 75% poverty class, 15% working class, and 10% middle/upper middle class
Race/ethnicity: 83% white, 12% Hispanic, and 5% African-American

Years of Completed Waves:

Years	N=	Age ranges
(Cohort 1: Maltreatment Ss)		
1975-1977	439	1-6 yrs.
1980-1982	152	6-12 yrs.
(Cohort 2: Control Ss)		
1975-1977	250	1-6 yrs.
1980-1982	201	6-12 yrs.

INFORMATION ON SAMPLE ATTRITION:

During the 5-year period of study, 86 of 439 Ss (19.6%) across both cohorts were not retrieved for further study. The core sample consists of 353 Ss. Primary reasons for sample attrition included inability to locate Ss, refusal, and Ss having moved away from the geographic area of study.

CONSTRUCTS MEASURED: INSTRUMENTS USED

Antecedents of abuse: Interview with parent
Quality of parent-child interaction: Parent-child observation
Condition at birth: Birth record from hospital
Quality of child's peer interaction: Preschool classroom observation
Cognitive ability: McCarthy Scales of Children's Abilities, Revised Wechsler Intelligence Scale for Children (WISC-R)
Family violence and services: Child welfare case records
Factors influencing child's development: Interview with parent
Grades, IQ, achievement scores, number of schools: School record
Locus of control: Children's locus of control
Behavior of child as perceived by parent and teacher (social competence): Child Behavior Inventory
Parent and child's frustration tolerance: Rosenzweig Picture-Frustration Test
Rating of child and family stress violence: Caseworker evaluations

REPRESENTATIVE REFERENCES:

Herrenkohl, R. C. (1990). Research directions related to child abuse and neglect. In R. Ammerman & M. Hersen (Eds.), *Children at risk: An evaluation of factors contributing to child abuse and neglect* (pp. 85-108). New York: Plenum.

Herrenkohl, R. C., & Herrenkohl, E. C. (1981). Some antecedents and development consequences of child maltreatment. *New Directions for Child Development, 11,* 57-76.

Herrenkohl, R. C., Herrenkohl, E. C., & Egolf, B. (1983). Circumstances surrounding the occurrence of child maltreatment. *Journal of Consulting and Clinical Psychology, 51*(3), 424-431.

Herrenkohl, E. C., & Herrenkohl, R. C., Toedter, L., & Yanushefski, A. M. (1984). Parent-child interactions in abusive and non-abusive families. *Journal of American Academy of Child Psychiatry, 23,* 641-648.

CURRENT STATUS OF THE STUDY:

a. A third wave of data collection is currently in progress.
b. Most data are in machine-readable format.
c. Data are available for secondary analysis from the study contact person.

■ Longitudinal Study of Temperament in Low Birthweight of Infants, 1963

Hertzig, Margaret E.

Contact Person: Margaret E. Hertzig
Address: Cornell University Medical Center
                  Payne Whitney Psychiatric Clinic Building
                  525 East 68th Street, Basement Level
                  New York, NY 10021
Telephone No.:   (212) 746-3714

SUBSTANTIVE TOPICS COVERED:

This study examines the relationship of neurologic status to the following: (a) antecedent conditions during pregnancy, birth, and delivery; (b) academic school performance and the presence of psychiatric disturbance; and (c) temperamental organization.

CHARACTERISTICS OF THE ORIGINAL SAMPLE:

Year the study began: 1962
Subject selection process: A continuous series of socially advantaged low birthweight infants was recruited between 1962 and 1965. Infants weighed between 1,000 and 1,750 grams and were cared for in two premature centers in New York City.
Total number of subjects at Time 1: N = 71
Ages at Time 1: Newborn
Sex distribution: Equal numbers of females and males
Socioeconomic status: 90% middle/upper middle class, 10% working class
Race/ethnicity: 93% white, 7% African-American

Years of Completed Waves:

Years	N=	Age ranges
1962	71	Newborn
1962	53	6 mos.
1963	50	1 yr.
1963	*	1.5 yrs.
1964	57	2 yrs.
1965	62	3 yrs.
1966	*	4 yrs.
1967	63	5 yrs.
1968	*	6 yrs.
1969	*	7 yrs.
1970	66	8 yrs.
1974	66	12 yrs.

Comments:
Data on temperament was collected on 66 children at ages 1, 2, and 3.

INFORMATION ON SAMPLE ATTRITION:

During the 12-year period of study, 5 of 71 Ss (7.0%) were not retrieved for further study. Attrition was due to death and families moving out of the area. The core sample consists of 66 Ss.

CONSTRUCTS MEASURED: INSTRUMENTS USED

Behavioral characteristics of children: Parental interviews
Medical history: Medical consultation reports
Psychiatric history: Psychiatric consultation reports
Academic progress: School records, observations
Neurological functioning (localizing and nonfocal signs): Neurological examinations
Intelligence: Wechsler Intelligence Scale for Children
Reading achievement: Wide-Range Achievement Test Reading (8 yrs.)
Arithmetic achievement: Wide-Range Achievement Test Arithmetic (8 yrs.)
Temperament (nine categories): Content analysis of parent interviews; annual reports
Neurologic status: Clinical Neurologic Assessment

REPRESENTATIVE REFERENCES:

Hertzig, M. E. (1981). Neurologic "soft signs" in low birthweight children. *Developmental Medicine Child Neurology, 23,* 778-791.

Hertzig, M. E. (1983). Temperament and neurological status. In M. Rutter (Ed.), *Developmental neuropsychiatry.* New York: Guilford Press.

Hertzig, M. E. (1987). Non focal neurologic signs in low birthweight children. In D. E. Tupper
    (Ed.), *Soft neurologic signs.* New York: Gruner Stratton.
Hertzig, M. E., & Mittleman, M. (1984). Temperament in low birthweight children. *Merrill
    Palmer Quarterly, 30,* 201-211.

CURRENT STATUS OF THE STUDY:

a. No further waves of data collection are planned.
b. Data are not in machine-readable format.
c. Data is available for secondary analysis from the study contact person.

■ Longitudinal Study of Adaptation to Remarriage in Stepfamilies, 1980

Hetherington, E. Mavis; and Clingempeel, Glen

Contact Person: E. Mavis Hetherington
Address: Department of Psychology
                  University of Virginia
                  102 Gilmer Hall
                  Charlottesville, VA 22903
Telephone No.:   (804) 924-0644

SUBSTANTIVE TOPICS COVERED:

The study examines family responses to remarriage and the dynamic process of family reorganization over the 6-year period following remarriage; the relation between the structural type of stepfamily, various dimensions of family functioning, and successful and unsuccessful outcomes for parents and children; comparisons of family interaction patterns and psychological adjustment of family members in three types of stepfamilies with a nondivorced nuclear control group and with a divorced, mother-custody, and non-remarried group; the impact of marriage-engendered kin who live outside the stepfamily (e.g., quasi-kin, and stepkin) in intrafamily relationships and adjustment of stepfamily members.

CHARACTERISTICS OF THE ORIGINAL SAMPLE:

Year the study began: 1980
Subject selection process: Potential subject families were identified through marriage license records and human service organizations such as churches and Scout groups. Families also responded to random telephone calls, advertisements, and media coverage. Selection criteria include: socioeconomic status (minimum of $15,000 as total annual income); high school education for both

spouses; race, Caucasian; reason first marriage ended (divorce only); number of previous marriages (no more than one previous marriage for either spouse); number of children in household not mentioned; age of spouse (neither spouse over 45 years of age); age of target child (between 9 and 13 years of age).

Total number of subjects at Time 1: N = 210[a]
Ages at Time 1: 9-13 yrs.
Sex distribution: Equal numbers of females and males throughout
Socioeconomic status: 100% middle/upper middle class
Race/ethnicity: 100% white
Comments:
a. This figure is an approximation, reflecting intact, mother-custody, and stepfather families, and excluding data from stepmother and blended families. Information about cohorts was not available.

Years of Completed Waves:

Years	N=	Age ranges
1981-1983	210	9-13 yrs.
1987-1988	180	15-18 yrs.

INFORMATION ON SAMPLE ATTRITION:

During the 7-year period of study, 30 of 210 Ss (14.3%) were not retrieved for further study. Reasons for sample attrition were not available. The core sample consists of 180 Ss.

CONSTRUCTS MEASURED: INSTRUMENTS USED

Active kindness versus unkindness; anger; avoidance and embarrassment, involvement, empathy and concern: Sibling Inventory of Behavior (short form; Aaronson & Schaefer)

Somatic complaints, schizoid uncommunicativeness, immaturity, obsessive-compulsiveness, hostile withdrawal, delinquency, aggression, hyperactivity, sex problems, cruelty, anxious-obsessiveness, and depressed withdrawal: Child Behavior Checklist (Achenbach & Edelbrock) (C-depression subscale only)

Routinized/chaotic household environment: Family Organization Subscale of the Family Environment Scale (Moos)

Attitudes and beliefs about stepparenting role: Stepparent's Role Questionnaire (Goetting et al.)

Division of child-rearing responsibilities; feelings about housekeeping responsibilities: Child-rearing Questionnaire (Baumrind)

Division of decision-making roles; feelings about decision-making roles: Decision making (Baumrind)

Stressful life events: Life Events Checklist (Sarason et al.)

Depression: Depression Inventory (Beck et al.)

Fatalism, social system control: Internal-External Locus of Control Scale (Reid & Ware)

Marital satisfaction, expressiveness, cohesiveness, and consensus: Marital Adjustment Scale (Spanier)

Cognitive competence, social competence, physical competence, and general self-esteem: Teacher's Rating Scale of Child Competence (Harter)

Stressors occurring immediately prior to each of the interviews in each data wave: Family 24-hr event list

Personality variables of adults (traditionality, social responsibility, ego strength, social agency, cognitive agency, mood, and physical fitness): Personal attributes Q-Sort, and attributes of spouse Q-Sort

Prosocial and acting-out behavior in the last 24 hours; social responsibility, ego strength, social agency, cognitive agency, mood and physical fitness: Child outcome measures (school assessment of child, behavior events inventory, attributes of child Q-Sort; personal attributes of child, satisfaction with life and self)

Major stresses that the child experienced in the past year; adjustment to divorce, adolescent family life, employment history, residential history, child-care history; divorce-related court settlements and legal issues; target child's response to divorce of natural parents; target child's response to remarriage of residential parent; target child's response to remarriage of nonresidential parent; marital status variables (e.g., length of previous marriage); child pubertal status; number of children living outside household; plans for future children; religious preference: Family Interview

Involvement of each parent and members of extrafamilial support system in child-rearing; child's assessment of parental compatibility and consensus agreement on rules for children; level of conflict; encapsulated versus open conflict; agreement on rules, disciplinary practices, and parenting style, parental control, expressive involvement, and instrument involvement regarding household organization; marital relationship (e.g., relationship between residential parents, child-rearing issues); parent (mother, father/stepparent, nonresidential parent-child relationships (e.g., relationship with custodial parent, relationship with residential stepparent, relationship with nonresidential parent and residential parent's assessment of self and child); relations with stepchildren, stepparent self assessment; relations with stepchildren (residential parent's assessment of stepparent; plans for adoption), sibling and stepsibling-target child relationship (e.g., relationship with siblings, relationship with stepsiblings); residential parent-nonresidential parent relationship (e.g., relations with former spouse, relationship between biological parents): Family Interview

REPRESENTATIVE REFERENCES:

Anderson, E. R., Hetherington, E. M., & Clingempeel, W. G. (1989). Transformations in family relations at puberty: Effects of family context. *Journal of Early Adolescence, 9*(3), 310-334.

Hetherington, E. M. (1985). Long-term effects of divorce and remarriage on the adjustment of children. *Journal of the American Academy of Child Psychiatry, 24*(5), 518-530.

Hetherington, E. M. (1989). Coping with family transitions: Winners, losers, and survivors. *Child Development, 60*(1), 1-14.

Hetherington, E. M., & Camara, K. A. (1984). Families in transition: The process of dissolution and reconstruction. In R. Parke (Ed.), *Review of child development research: Vol. 7* (pp. 398-439). Chicago: University of Chicago Press.

CURRENT STATUS OF THE STUDY:

a. Further waves of data collection are currently in progress.
b. Most of the data are in machine-readable format.
c. The data are not available for secondary analysis.

■ Virginia Longitudinal Study of Divorce, 1971

Hetherington, E. Mavis; Cox, Martha; and Cox, Roger

Contact Person: E. Mavis Hetherington
Address: Department of Psychology
102 Gilmer Hall
University of Virginia
Charlottesville, VA 22903
Telephone No.: (804) 924-0644

SUBSTANTIVE TOPICS COVERED:

The study examines responses to the family crisis of divorce; patterns of reorganization and alterations in functioning of the family over the 6-year period following divorce; the stresses, support systems, and patterns of family functioning that were associated with positive and negative outcomes for members of divorced families; compares the stresses, support systems, family functioning, and developmental status of children in divorced and non-divorced families.

CHARACTERISTICS OF THE ORIGINAL SAMPLE:

Year the study began: 1971

Subject selection process: Divorced parents were identified and contacted through court records and lawyers. Only families with a child attending nursery school—who could serve as the target child—were included in the study. Non-divorced Ss were selected on the basis of having a child of the same sex, age, and birth order as a target child from a divorced family. Parents were matched on age, education, and length of marriage. Only first- and second-born children were included in the sample. Families with stepparents were excluded.

Year the study began: N = 144[a]
Ages at Time 1: 3 yrs., 7 mos. to 4 yrs., 4 mos.
Sex distribution: Equal numbers of females and males throughout
Socioeconomic status: 100% middle/upper middle class
Race/ethnicity: 100% white
Comments:
a. This figure refers to the number of children in the study. The ages of the parents were as follows: mothers, 27-29 yrs.; fathers, 27-30 yrs.

Years of Completed Waves:

Years	N=	Age ranges
Cohort 1: Divorced Family		
1971-1974	72	3 yrs., 7 mos.(2 mos. post-divorce)
1972-1975	64	4 yrs., 6 mos.-5 yrs., 2 mos. (1 year post-divorce)
1973-1976	43	5 yrs., 6 mos.-5 yrs., 4 mos. (2 years post-divorce)
1977-1980	42	9 yrs., 6 mos.-10 yrs., 4 mos. (6 years post-divorce)
Cohort 2: Nondivorced Family		
1971-1974	72	3 yrs., 7 mos.
1972-1975	66	4 yrs., 6 mos.-5 yrs., 2 mos.
1973-1976	59	5 yrs., 6 mos.-6 yrs., 4 mos.
1977-1980	59	9 yrs., 6 mos.-10 yrs., 4 mos.

INFORMATION ON SAMPLE ATTRITION:

During the 6-year period of study, 43 of 144 Ss (42.6%) across both cohorts were not retrieved for further study. The core sample consists of 101 Ss: 42 Ss from the divorced family cohort, and 59 Ss from the nondivorced family cohort.

CONSTRUCTS MEASURED: INSTRUMENTS USED

Discipline practices and parent-child relationship; support systems outside the household; social, emotional, and heterosexual relationships; quality of relationship with spouse, attitude toward self: Parent interview (face-to-face structured interview schedule)

Personality: Personal adjustment scale of the adjective check list (Gough & Heilbrun), Socialization Scale and Masculinity-Femininity Scale of California Personality Inventory (Gough)

Internal-external locus of control: Rotter I-E Scale (Rotter)

Anxiety: Speilberger's State-Trait Anxiety (Speilberger, Goruch, & Lushene)

Activities, situations, people and moods (anxious-relaxed); hostile-friendly, unhappy-happy, helpless-competent, unloved-loved: Structured diary record for 3 days by mothers and fathers

Quality of the parent-child relationship along a number of interaction dimensions; aggression, requests, affiliation, independence: Free play interaction (each parent interacts separately with child for 1/2 hour each; also interaction was observed in a structured play situation using block building, bead stringing, sorting tasks)

Prosocial/antisocial behaviors: Checklist of child behavior by parents

Aggression, inhibition, distractibility, task orientation, prosocial behavior, habit disturbances, and self-control: Parent rating of child's behavior

Intelligence: Wechsler Preschool and Primary Scale of Intelligence

Impulsivity/reflectivity measures: Matching Familiar Figures Test

Field dependence-independence: Embedded Figures Test

Sex role typing: Preference for toys, activities, and vocations (card sort)

Sex role orientation: Draw-a-Person Test

Sex role adoption (masculine-feminine behaviors, amount of time spent in play with same- or opposite-sex peers, participation in activities, social behaviors, and use of toys as preferred by one sex over another): Teacher and parent ratings of child

Types of play, participants involved, affect being experienced, initiation and termination of play sequences, imaginative play: Free play observation in school classroom and playgrounds (6 half-hour sessions at first three time points)

Types of behavior interactions and types of activities: Social interactions observed in school classroom and playground (eighteen 10-minute sessions which sampled free play, small group activities, and teacher-controlled activities)

Task orientation (purposive, aimless, impulsive, and distractible behaviors; cooperative and defiant behaviors): Teacher ratings

Child's social status among peers: Peer nomination inventory (seven photos of seven children, one including a target subject; photographs of all the children in the class; Ss asked to pick the child he/she liked the best, next best, and so on)

Assignment of responsibility and maturity demands, structure and predictability, responsiveness to child, control, affection ambience: Observations and rating of teacher behaviors

Physical setting of school: number and sex of children, room size, number of teachers in classroom, ratio of teachers to children, separation of classroom areas, amount and type of equipment and accessibility, and room decorations: Observations and descriptions

REPRESENTATIVE REFERENCES:

Hetherington, E. M. (1976). Divorced fathers. *Family Coordinator, 25*(4), 417-428.

Hetherington, E. M. (1981). Children and divorce. In R. Henderson (Ed.), *Parent-child interaction: Theory, research and prospect.* New York: Academic Press.

Hetherington, M., Cox, M., & Cox, R. (1981). Effects of divorce on parents and children. In M. Lamb (Ed.), *Non-traditional families.* Hillsdale, NJ: Lawrence Erlbaum.

Hetherington, M., Cox, M., & Cox, R. (1979). Play and social interaction of children following divorce. *Journal of Social Issues, 35*(4), 26-49.

CURRENT STATUS OF THE STUDY:

a. Further waves of data collection are currently in progress.

b. Most of the data are in machine-readable format.

c. The data are not available for secondary analysis.

■ The Tecumseh, Michigan, Community Health Study, 1957

Higgins, Millicent W.; Ostrander, Leon D., Jr.; Monto, Arnold S.; Garn, Stanley M.; Harburg, Ernest; House, James S.; Metzner, Helen L.; and Sing, Charles F.

Contact Person: Ruth Little
Address: Department of Epidemiology
                 School of Public Health
                 University of Michigan
                 109 Observatory Street
                 Ann Arbor, MI 48109
Telephone No.:   (313) 764-7407

SUBSTANTIVE TOPICS COVERED:

The study attempts to detect characteristics of individuals and their environments that relate to health, resistance and susceptibility to disease, and onset and course of disease. Conditions of major interest are coronary heart disease, hypertension, chronic lung disease, diabetes mellitus, arthritis, and obesity.

CHARACTERISTICS OF THE ORIGINAL SAMPLE:

Year the study began: 1959

Subject selection process: The subjects were the entire population of a defined community, which included the city of Tecumseh and a rural area around Tecumseh (approximately 3-4 miles out in each direction, where it was determined that 90% or more of the population used Tecumseh for shopping, medical services, and social/religious activities).

Total number of subjects at Time 1: N = 8,641

Ages at Time 1: 16-90s.

Sex distribution: Equal numbers of females and males throughout

Socioeconomic status: 100% middle/upper middle class

Race/ethnicity: 99.6% white, 0.4% Hispanic

Years of Completed Waves:[a]

Years	N=	Age ranges
1959-1960	8,641	16-90s
1962-1965	9,226	19-90s
1967-1969	6,012	24-90s
1978+	9,226	35-90s
(Subsample 1: High blood pressure)		
1978	5,000	16-36 yrs.
(Subsample 2: Hypoglycemia, Diabetes, Cardiovascular disease)		
1978[b]	2,500	30-64 yrs.

Comments:

a. In 1959-1960 interviewers visited every dwelling unit in the community, collected medical history interviews for all persons in the household, and scheduled a medical examination in a clinic that was set up in the local hospital. Interviews were completed for 95% of the population, and 88% of the community (or 8,641 persons) visited the clinic for the examination. In 1962-1965 a second round of examination was completed, with persons new to the community added to those previously examined. A total of 9,266 persons were examined in the second examination cycle. Subsequent to 1965, the emphasis shifted from a study of a total community to a study of a cohort of previously examined persons. With the exception of a 10% community sample that was completed as part of Round III in 1967-1969, no new persons were added to the study population after 1965.

In 1977 a *Study of High Blood Pressure in Young People in Tecumseh* was conducted. This was a follow-up of approximately 5,000 persons who were less than age 19 when they were examined in the clinic in 1959-1960 and 1962-1965.

The 1977 *Study of Hyperglycemia, Diabetes and Cardiovascular Disease* included approximately 2,500 men and women between ages 30-64 who had three previous glucose tolerance tests in Rounds I, II, and III.

b. The 1978 *Epidemiological Study of Chronic Lung Disease* was a follow-up of the entire 9,226 persons seen in the clinic in Round II.

INFORMATION ON SAMPLE ATTRITION:

During the 11-year period of the study, most of the 8,641 Ss were retrieved for further study. The core sample size consists of 4,312 Ss.

CONSTRUCTS MEASURED: INSTRUMENTS USED

General health status: Medical history questionnaire

Physical health: Self-administered health questionnaire, simplified physician's history, electrocardiography

Pulmonary adequacy and effects of aging: Pulmonary function measurements

Body build, body fatness, skeletal dimension, strength: Anthropometric measurements

Blood pressure: Sphygmomanometer

Skeletal formation of chest, spine, hand: X rays

Determinations of uric acid, various rheumatoid factors, fasting levels of serum triglycerides: Blood tests

Determinations of levels of glucose, protein, acetone, occult blood and acidity: Urine tests

Changes in the composition of the population due to births, deaths, marriages, divorces, or movements away from or into the Tecumseh Community: Household Interview (annual)

Update of medical histories: Annual health report

Current activities and attitudes; occupation, physical activities on the job; attitudes towards aspects of the job; leisure activities, memberships; worries, problems; life goals; occupational history, residential history; nativity, education, religious preference; occupation of parents: Interview

Vegetation and land use in Tecumseh: Observation

Contamination of atmosphere, radioactivity in air and soil: Environmental tests

Mineral content of drinking water: Monthly samples

REPRESENTATIVE REFERENCES:

Francis, T., Jr. (1961). Aspects of the Tecumseh Study. *Public Health Report, 76,* 963-965.

Higgins, M. W., Kjelsberg, M. O., & Metzner, H. L. (1967). Characteristics of smokers and non-smokers in Tecumseh, Michigan. I. The distribution of smoking habits in persons and families and their relationship to social characteristics. *American Journal of Epidemiology, 86,* 45-59.

Napier, J. A. (1962). Field methods and response rates in the Tecumseh Community Health Study. *American Journal of Public Health, 52,* 208-216.

Napier, J. A., Johnson, B. C., & Epstein, F. H. (1970). The Tecumseh, Michigan, Community Health Study. In I. I. Kessler, & M. L. Levin (Eds.), *The community as an epidemiologic laboratory: A casebook of community studies.* Baltimore: The Johns Hopkins University Press.

CURRENT STATUS OF THE STUDY:

a. Further waves of data collection are planned for subsample of the original cohort.

b. Most of the data are in machine-readable format.

c. A subset of the data are available for secondary analysis through the Inter-University Consortium for Political and Social Research, University of Michigan, Ann Arbor, MI 48106. Nonarchived data are available upon approval of the study's management committee.

■ Austin-Mexico City Project, 1962

Holtzman, Wayne; and Diaz-Guerrero, R.

Contact Person: Wayne Holtzman
Address: The Hogg Foundation for Mental Health
                  University of Texas
                  Austin, TX 78713-7998
Telephone No.:   (512) 471-5041

SUBSTANTIVE TOPICS COVERED:

The study examines cultural influences on personality, cognition, and perception.

CHARACTERISTICS OF THE ORIGINAL SAMPLE:

Year the study began: 1962

Subject selection process: Children in Austin, Texas, were selected from six elementary schools and one junior high school. The sample is a broad range of working-class, business, and professional families. Only white, English-speaking families were chosen for inclusion in the American sample. Children in Mexico City, Mexico, were selected from three school systems—two public and one private. These subjects were Mexican nationals. Families were chosen to approximate the socioeconomic status of the American sample, and nearly two thirds of the children were matched on socioeconomic status between samples.

Total number of subjects at Time 1: N = 860

Ages at Time 1: 6-12 yrs.

Sex distribution: Approximately equal numbers of females and males throughout

Socioeconomic status: 60% middle/upper middle class, 40% working class

Race/ethnicity: 50% white, 50% Hispanic (Mexican nationals)

Years of Completed Waves:

Years	N=	Age ranges
(Cohort 1: American 6-year-olds)		
1962	133	6 yrs.
1963	109	7 yrs.
1964	105	8 yrs.
1965	102	9 yrs.
1966	101	10 yrs.
1967	89	11 yrs.
(Cohort 2: Mexican 6-year-olds)		
1962	150	6 yrs.
1963	142	7 yrs.
1964	142	8 yrs.

Years of Completed Waves, Continued:

Years	N=	Age ranges
1965	136	9 yrs.
1966	133	10 yrs.
1967	52	11 yrs.
(Cohort 3: American 9-year-olds)		
1962	142	9 yrs.
1963	125	10 yrs.
1964	121	11 yrs.
1965	111	12 yrs.
1966	107	13 yrs.
1967	96	14 yrs.
(Cohort 4: Mexican 9-year-olds)		
1962	143	9 yrs.
1963	132	10 yrs.
1964	132	11 yrs.
1965	129	12 yrs.
1966	121	13 yrs.
1967	67	14 yrs.
(Cohort 5: American 12-year-olds)		
1962	142	12 yrs.
1963	131	13 yrs.
1964	128	14 yrs.
1965	122	15 yrs.
1966	121	16 yrs.
1967	113	17 yrs.
(Cohort 6: Mexican 12-year-olds)		
1962	150	12 yrs.
1963	138	13 yrs.
1964	138	14 yrs.
1965	127	15 yrs.
1966	111	16 yrs.
1967	49	17 yrs.

INFORMATION ON SAMPLE ATTRITION:

During the 6-year period of study, 394 of 860 (45.8%) Ss across six cohorts were not retrieved for further study. Sample attrition ranged from 20.4% (Cohort 5) to 67.3% (Cohort 6). The sudden drop from the fifth to sixth wave in the Mexican children was due to the fact that in Mexico only cases in the matched cross-cultural sample were tested during the 6th year. Most other attrition was due to families moving. Information on core samples was not available.

CONSTRUCTS MEASURED: INSTRUMENTS USED

Demographic information, family information, and home information: Structured interviews

Personality: Holtzman Inkblot Technique, Human Figure Drawing, Test Anxiety Scale for Children, Filled Time Estimation, Test Behavior Ratings, Family and home rating from interviews with mothers, Parental Attitude Scales (mother), Occupational Values Inventory, Personality Research Form, Survey of Study Habits and Attitudes, Views of Life and Sociocultural Premises

Cognition: Vocabulary (Wechsler Intelligence Scale for Children or Wechsler Adult Intelligence Scale), Block Design (WISC or WAIS), Time Estimation, Object Sorting Test, Embedded Figures Test, Stroop Color-Word Test, Conceptual Styles Test, Word Association Test, WISC or WAIS Arithmetic and Picture Completion, WISC Subtests, Academic Summary (School record data), Manuel's Reading Test

Perception: Visual Fractionation Test, Perceptual Maturity Scale, Stroop Color-Word Test

REPRESENTATIVE REFERENCES:

Holtzman, W. H. (1979). Concepts and methods in the cross-cultural study of personality development. *Human Development, 22*(5), 281-295.

Holtzman, W. H. (1979). Culture, personality development, and mental health in the Americas. *Revista Interamericana de Psicologia, 13*(1-2), 27-49.

Holtzman, W. H., Diaz-Guerrero, R., & Swartz, J. D. (1975). *Personality development in two cultures: A cross-cultural longitudinal study of school children in Mexico and the United States.* Austin: University of Texas Press.

Reyes-Lagunes, I., Morales, M. L., & Velazquez de Tonorio, A. (1979). Cognitive development, cross-cultural and sub-cultural comparisons. *Human Development, 22*(5), 332-339.

CURRENT STATUS OF THE STUDY:

a. No further waves of data collection are planned.

b. Most of the data are in machine-readable format.

c. The data are available for secondary analysis from the study contact person.

■ The AT&T Longitudinal Studies of Managers: Management Progress Study (MPS), 1956

Howard, Ann; and Bray, Douglas W.

Contact Person: Ann Howard
Address: Leadership Research Institute
                 21 Knoll Road
                 Tenafly, NJ 07670
Telephone No.:   (201) 894-5289

SUBSTANTIVE TOPICS COVERED:

This study examines the relationship between career success and life satisfactions; selection and development of successful managers; changes in abilities, motivation, personality, and life interests over time; work characteristics, stress, and medical and emotional outcomes; integration of work and the family; early retirement. (See also Howard, A., *The AT&T Longitudinal Studies of Managers: Management Continuity Study*.)

CHARACTERISTICS OF THE ORIGINAL SAMPLE:

Year the study began: 1956
Subject selection process: Young managers in six Bell Telephone companies, including college graduates recently hired into general management and high school graduates promoted into management by age 32.
Total number of subjects at Time 1: N = 422
Ages at Time 1: 21-33 yrs.
Sex distribution: 100% male
Socioeconomic status: 100% middle/upper middle class
Race/ethnicity: 100% white

Years of Completed Waves:

Years	N=	Age ranges
(Cohort 1: College Graduates)		
1956-1960	274	21-31 yrs.
1957-1961	201	22-32 yrs.
1958-1962	185	23-33 yrs.
1959-1963	196	24-34 yrs.
1960-1964	192	25-35 yrs.
1961-1965	180	26-36 yrs.
1962-1966	168	27-37 yrs.
1963-1967	167	28-38 yrs.
1964-1968	167	29-39 yrs.
1966-1970	148	31-41 yrs.

Years of Completed Waves, Continued:

Years	N=	Age ranges
1969-1973	133	34-44 yrs.
1972-1976	134	37-47 yrs.
1975-1979	130	40-50 yrs.
1976-1980	137	41-51 yrs.
1981-1985	114	46-56 yrs.
(Cohort 2: High School Graduates)		
1958-1960	148	23-33 yrs.
1959-1961	148	24-34 yrs.
1960-1961	148	25-35 yrs.
1961-1963	147	26-36 yrs.
1962-1964	145	27-37 yrs.
1963-1965	145	28-38 yrs.
1964-1966	59	29-39 yrs.
1965-1967	142	30-40 yrs.
1966-1968	142	31-41 yrs.
1968-1970	128	33-43 yrs.
1971-1973	121	36-46 yrs.
1974-1976	127	39-49 yrs.
1977-1979	117	42-52 yrs.
1978-1980	129	43-53 yrs.
1983-1985	68	48-58 yrs.

INFORMATION ON SAMPLE ATTRITION:

During the years 0-20 of the study, 156 of 422 Ss (40%) from both cohorts were not retrieved for further study: 137 of 274 Ss (50%) in Cohort 1, and 19 of 148 Ss (12.8%) in Cohort 2. Main reasons for sample attrition included Ss finding new employment, and death. The core sample for this period consists of 266 Ss: 137 from Cohort 1 and 129 from Cohort 2. An additional wave of data collection during Year 25 of the study resulted in additional attrition of 84 of 422 Ss (20%) from both cohorts: 23 of 274 Ss (8%) from Cohort 1, and 61 of 148 Ss (41%) from Cohort 2. The primary reason for the additional sample attrition was retirement.

CONSTRUCTS MEASURED: INSTRUMENTS USED

Assessment Center Data (Years 0, 8, and 20)

Administrative skills, interpersonal skills, cognitive ability, stability of performance, advancement motivation, work involvement, independence: Ratings of dimensions by psychologists and company executives based on assessment center performance
Administrative skills: In-basket
Interpersonal skills: Leaderless group discussions, business games

Cognitive ability: School and College Ability Test, Critical Thinking in Social Science test, tests of knowledge of contemporary affairs
Personality/motivation—questionnaires: Edwards Personal Preference Schedule, Guilford-Martin Survey of Factors GAMIN, Opinion Questionnaire (version of California F-Scale), Sarnoff Survey of Attitudes Toward Life
Personality/motivation—projectives: Thematic Apperception Test (6 pictures), Rotter Incomplete Sentences Blank, Business Incomplete Sentences Test
Biographical data: Questionnaire, interview

Medical Data (Years 0, 8, and 20)

Physiological development: Blood, urine, chest X ray, physical examination
Medical history: Questionnaire

Follow-up Data (Years 1-7, 10, 13, 16, 19, and 25)

Perceptions of and reactions to company, job, and supervisor; future career expectations; family life, recreational and social activities, community activities, religious involvement: Interview; questionnaires (years 16, 19, 25)
Job attitudes: Expectations Inventory, Management Attitude Questionnaire
Perceptions of individual on the job: Interview with supervisor (years 1-6, 11, 14, 17, 20, 25)

REPRESENTATIVE REFERENCES:

Bray, D. W., Campbell, R. J., & Grant, D. L. (1974). *Formative years in business: A long-term AT&T study of managerial lives.* New York: John Wiley.
Bray, D. W., & Howard, A. (1980). Career success and life satisfactions of middle-aged managers. In L. A. Bond & J. C. Rosen (Eds.), *Coping and competence during adulthood.* Hanover, NH: University Press of New England.
Bray, D. W., & Howard, A. (1983). The AT&T longitudinal studies of managers. In K. W. Schaie (Ed.), *Longitudinal studies of adult psychological development.* New York: Guilford Press.
Howard, A., & Bray, D. W. (1988). *Managerial lives in transition: Advancing age and changing times.* New York: Guilford Press.

CURRENT STATUS OF THE STUDY:

a. No further waves of data collection are planned.
b. Much of the data are in machine-readable format. Interview summaries are available for additional coding.
c. Data are available for secondary analysis in collaboration with the study contact person.

■ The AT&T Longitudinal Studies of Managers: Management Continuity Study (MCS), 1977

Howard, Ann; and Bray, Douglas W.

Contact Person: Ann Howard
Address: Leadership Research Institute
                 21 Knoll Road
                 Tenafly, NJ 07670
Telephone No.:   (201) 894-5289

SUBSTANTIVE TOPICS COVERED:

The Management Continuity Study is generally parallel to the first 6 years of the Management Progress Study, permitting comparison of managers over two generations. Topics include selection and development of successful managers; changing work values; race and sex differences among managers; work characteristics and individual development in the early career; integration of work and the family. (See also Howard, A., *The AT&T Longitudinal Studies of Managers: Management Progress Study*.)

CHARACTERISTICS OF THE ORIGINAL SAMPLE:

Year the study began: 1977
Subject selection process: College graduates hired within the previous year for general management jobs at 18 Bell System telephone companies and AT&T
Total number of subjects at Time 1: N = 391
Ages at Time 1: 21-43 yrs.
Sex distribution: 54% male, 46% female
Socioeconomic status: 100% middle/upper-middle class
Race/ethnicity: 68.3% white, 23.5% African-American, 6.9% Hispanic, 1.3% other

Years of Completed Waves:

Years	N=	Age ranges
(Cohort 1: 1970s Hires)		
1977-1979	226	21-43 yrs.
1979-1981	189	23-45 yrs.
1981-1983	163	25-47 yrs.
1983-1985	134	27-49 yrs.
(Cohort 2: 1980s Hires)		
1981-1982	165	21-42 yrs.
1983-1985	116	23-45 yrs.
1985-1987	110	25-47 yrs.

INFORMATION ON SAMPLE ATTRITION:

During the years 0-4, 118 of 391 Ss (30%) were not retrieved for further study: 63 of 226 Ss (28%) in Cohort 1, and 55 of 165 Ss (33%) in Cohort 2. Over this period, the core sample consists of 273 Ss: 163 in Cohort 1, and 110 in Cohort 2. Additional data collection for Cohort 1 in Year 6 resulted in additional attrition of 29 of 226 Ss (13%). The primary reason for sample attrition at all time periods was finding new employment.

CONSTRUCTS MEASURED: INSTRUMENTS USED

Assessment Center Data (Year 0)

Administrative skills, interpersonal skills, cognitive ability, stability of performance, advancement motivation, work involvement, independence, company loyalty, external self-development, social liberalism: Ratings of dimensions by psychologists and company executives based on assessment center performance

Administrative skills: In-basket

Cognitive ability: School and College Ability Test, general knowledge test

Personality/motivation—questionnaires: Edwards Personal Preference Schedule, Guilford-Zimmerman Temperament Survey, Opinion Questionnaire (version of California F-Scale), Sarnoff Survey of Attitudes Toward Life, California Psychological Inventory, Rokeach Value Survey

Personality/motivation—projectives: Thematic Apperception Test (9 pictures), Rotter Incomplete Sentences Blank, Business Incomplete Sentences Test

Biographical data: Questionnaire, interview

Follow-up Data (Years 2, 4, and 6)

Perceptions of and reactions to company, job, and supervisor, future career expectations, family life, recreational and social activities, community activities, religious involvement: Interview, questionnaire

Job attitudes: Expectations Inventory, Management Attitude Questionnaire

Perceptions of individual on the job: Interview with supervisor

REPRESENTATIVE REFERENCES:

Bray, D. W., & Howard, A. (1983). The AT&T longitudinal studies of managers. In K. W. Schaie (Ed.), *Longitudinal studies of adult psychological development.* New York: Guilford Press.

Bray, D. W., & Howard A. (1988). Management career motivation: Life changes and social vicissitudes. In M. London & E. M. Mone (Eds.), *The human resources professional and employee career development.* Westport, CT: Greenwood.

Howard, A., & Bray, D. W. (1988). *Managerial lives in transition: Advancing age and changing times.* New York: Guilford Press.

Howard, A., & Wilson, J. A. (1982). Leadership in a declining work ethic. *California Management Review, 23*(4), 33-46.

CURRENT STATUS OF THE STUDY:

a. No further waves of data collection are planned.
b. Much of the data are in machine-readable format. Interview summaries are available for additional coding.
c. Data are available for secondary analysis in collaboration with the study contact person.

■ Development of Aggressive Behavior, 1960

Huesmann, L. Rowell; and Eron, Leonard D.

Contact Person: L. Rowell Huesmann
Address: Department of Psychology
                  University of Illinois at Chicago
                  Box 4348
                  Chicago, IL 60680
Telephone No.:   (312) 996-4453

SUBSTANTIVE TOPICS COVERED:

The study examines aggression in relation to socioeconomic status, television media, intelligence, stability of behavior, child-rearing factors, and peer relations.

CHARACTERISTICS OF THE ORIGINAL SAMPLE:

Year the study began: 1960
Subject selection process: All children registered in the third grade in Columbia County, New York State, were selected for participation.
Total number of subjects at Time 1: N = 875 (children); mothers = 527, fathers = 424
Ages at Time 1: 8 yrs.
Sex distribution: Approximately equal numbers of females and males throughout
Socioeconomic status: 30% poverty class, 44% working class, 26% middle/upper middle class
Race/ethnicity: 97% white, 3% other

Years of Completed Waves:

Years	N=	Age ranges
1960[a]	875	8 yrs.
1970	427	19 yrs.
1981[b]	409	29 yrs.
1981[c]	632	29-30 yrs.

Comments:
a. In 1960, 75% of the mothers and fathers were interviewed.

b. In 1981, 165 spouses of the target Ss, and 82 of their children (approximately 8 yrs. of age) were also interviewed.
c. In 1981, New York State archival data was obtained on these subjects.

INFORMATION ON SAMPLE ATTRITION:

During the 21-year period of study, 243 of 875 Ss (27.8%) were not retrieved for further study. The core sample consists of 632 Ss.

CONSTRUCTS MEASURED: INSTRUMENTS USED

Aggression, anxiety, popularity: Peer rating
Intelligence: California Mental Maturity Test
Child-rearing practices and attitudes: Parent questionnaire
Psychopathology and aggression: Minnesota Multiphasic Personality Inventory
Leadership, good citizen: Questionnaire
History of criminal acts, mental illness, and traffic violations: Public records
Verbal and quantitative achievement: Wide Range Achievement Test
Exposure to violence and judgment of realism of violence: Television viewing habits
Harshness of punishment of children: Parental punishment
Aggression toward spouse: Strauss Spouse Abuse
Ego development: Washington University Sentence Completion Test (Loevinger)
Risk for psychopathology: Ulman & Giovanni Risk

REPRESENTATIVE REFERENCES:

Eron, L. D., Walder, L. O., & Lefkowitz, M. M. (1971). *Learning of aggression in children.* Boston: Little, Brown.

Huesmann, L. R., Eron, L. D., Lefkowitz, M. M., & Walder, L. O. (1984). The stability of aggression over time and generations. *Developmental Psychology, 20*(6), 1120-1134.

Huesmann, L. R., Eron, L. D., & Yarmel, P. (1987). Intellectual functioning and aggression. *Journal of Personality and Social Psychology, 52*(1), 232-240.

Lefkowitz, M. M., Eron, L. D., Walder, L. O., & Huesmann, L. R. (1977). *Growing up to be violent.* New York: Pergamon.

CURRENT STATUS OF THE STUDY:

a. Further waves of data collection are planned.
b. Most data are in machine-readable format.
c. Data are available for secondary analysis from the study contact person.

■ Prospective Study of 500 Second Graders, 1965

Huessy, Hans R.

Contact Person: Hans R. Huessy
Address: University of Vermont
Department of Psychiatry
150 Prospect Street
Burlington, VT 05401
Telephone No.: (802) 656-4563

SUBSTANTIVE TOPICS COVERED:

The study examines the stability and predictive power of hyperkinetic types of behaviors, and the outcomes of hyperkinetic children regarding academic achievement, employment and social-interpersonal development, as compared to non-hyperkinetic children.

CHARACTERISTICS OF THE ORIGINAL SAMPLE:

Year the study began: 1965
Subject selection process: All subjects participating in the study were second graders selected from 18 rural schools in Northwestern Vermont.
Total number of subjects at Time 1: N = 501
Ages at Time 1: 6-8 yrs.
Sex distribution: Approximately equal numbers of females and males
Socioeconomic status: 80% working class, 20% poverty class (approximately)
Race/ethnicity: 100% white

Years of Completed Waves:

Years	N=	Age ranges
1965	501	6-8 yrs.
1967	430	8-10 yrs.
1968	352	9-11 yrs.
1972	318	13-15 yrs.
1975	318	16-18 yrs.
1979	369	20-22 yrs.

INFORMATION ON SAMPLE ATTRITION:

During the 15-year period of study, 132 of 501 Ss (26.3%) were not retrieved for further study. Information on the core sample was not available.

CONSTRUCTS MEASURED: INSTRUMENTS USED

Classification of hyperkinetic behaviors: Huessy-Marshall Teacher Rating Scales

Academic development (interests, behavioral problems, grades repeated): School records

Social development, employment, military status, social relations, interaction with police and other authorities, drug use, satisfaction with life: Structured interview, questionnaire

REPRESENTATIVE REFERENCES:

Howell, D. C., & Huessy, H. R. (1981). Hyperkinetic behavior followed from 7 to 21 years of age. In M. Gittelman (Ed.), *Intervention strategies with hyperactive children*. New York: M. E. Sharpe.

Howell, D. C., Huessy, H. R., & Hassuk, B. (1985). Fifteen year follow-up of a behavioral history of attention deficit disorder. *Pediatrics, 26*(2), 185-190.

Huessy, H. R. (1967). Study of the prevalence and therapy of the choreatiform syndrome or hyperkinesis in rural Vermont. *Acta Paedopsychiatrica, 34*(4/5), 130-135.

Huessy, H. R., Marshall, C. D., & Gendron, R. A. (1973). Five hundred children followed from grade 2 through grade 5 for the prevalence of behavior disorder. *Acta Paedopsychiatrica, 39*(11), 301-309.

CURRENT STATUS OF THE STUDY:

a. Further waves of data collection are planned.

b. The data are in machine-readable format.

c. The data are available for secondary analysis through the Henry A. Murray Research Center, Radcliffe College, 10 Garden Street, Cambridge, MA 02138.

■ Guidance Study (G), 1928

Huffine, Carol; Honzik, Marjorie; and Macfarlane, Jean W. (deceased)

Contact Person: Intergenerational Studies Archivist
Address: University of California
                 Institute of Human Development
                 1203 Tolman Hall
                 Berkeley, CA 94720
Telephone No.:   (415) 642-2022

SUBSTANTIVE TOPICS COVERED:

The study was initially designed as a study of the effect of parental counseling on the incidence of behavioral problems among preschool children. The study has developed as an examination of interactions of psychological, social, and biological factors in personality development. (See also Clausen, J. A., *Oakland Growth Study*; and Eichorn, D. H., *Berkeley Growth Study*.)

CHARACTERISTICS OF THE ORIGINAL SAMPLE:

Year the study began: 1928

Subject selection process: Subjects participating in the study were selected from a regional socioeconomic survey involving every third birth in Berkeley, California. Parents, especially mothers, of subjects were frequently included in studies through interviews and questionnaires; more recently, as the "children" became adults and then parents, their children and spouses have sometimes been studied.

Total number of subjects at Time 1: N = 248

Ages at Time 1: 3 mos.

Sex distribution: Approximately equal numbers of females and males throughout

Socioeconomic status: Representative sample

Race/ethnicity: 95.2% white, 4.8% African-American

Years of Completed Waves:[a]

Years	N=	Age ranges
1928	248	3 mos.
1929-1930	248	21 mos.
1946	150	18 yrs.
1958	171	30 yrs.
1970	143	42 yrs.
1981-1982	157	53-54 yrs.

Comments:

a. Data were collected continuously from age 21 months through late adolescence. By age 18, more than 150 study members were still being seen. Three full adult follow-ups have been conducted, one in 1958, one in 1970, and one in 1982. More than 140 subjects took part in some or all of the 1982 data collection procedures. The original 248 Ss were born between January 1, 1928, and June 30, 1929.

INFORMATION ON SAMPLE ATTRITION:

After 52 years of study, 91 of 248 Ss (36.7%) were not retrieved for a follow-up. Sixteen study members are known to be deceased as of November 1990.

CONSTRUCTS MEASURED: INSTRUMENTS USED

Physical development and health information: Physical examination and health history, anthropometrics (M.D.), skeletal development (X ray), body build pictures, physical rating scale, diet summary, menstrual history

Motor development: Strength-Grip-Thrust-Dexterity

Physiological development: Heart rate, blood pressure

Mental development: California Preschool Schedule or II, Stanford Tests, S-B, L or M; Wechsler-Bellevue, Gray's Oral, Porteus Maze, Healy P.C. II, Kuder Preference Test

Personality development: Behavior & Personality Interviews, Personality development with mother, Recapitulation Interviews, Behavior & Personality, Reputation Test, Ratings of Observed Behavior—Mental Test, Physical Exams (M.D.), and Interviews, Occupational Interests, Things You Talk About, Thematic Apperception Test, Rorschach Ink Blots

Academic achievement: Grades from School Records

REPRESENTATIVE REFERENCES:

Eichorn, D. H., Clausen, J. A., Haan, N., Honzik, M., & Mussen, P. H. (Eds.), (1981). *Present and past in middle life.* New York: Academic Press.

Mussen, P., Honzik, M. P., Eichorn, D. H. (1982). Early antecedents of life satisfaction at age 70. *Journal of Gerontology, 37*(3), 316-322.

Macfarlane, J. W. (1938). Studies in child guidance. I. Methodology of data collection and organization. *Monographs of the Society for Research in Child Development, 3*(6).

Macfarlane, J. W., Allen, L., & Honzik, M. P. (1954). A developmental study of the behavior problems of normal children between twenty-one months and fourteen years. *University of California Publications in Child Development, 2,* 1-222.

CURRENT STATUS OF THE STUDY:

a. Further waves of data collection are planned.
b. Some data are in machine-readable format.
c. Data are available for secondary analysis through the study contact person.

■ Longitudinal Study of Family Relationships, 1981

Huston, Ted; McHale, Susan; and Crouter, Ann

Contact Person: Ted Huston
Address: The University of Texas, Austin
                 Division of Child Development
                 and Family Relationship
                 Mary Gearing Hall
                 Austin, TX 78712
Telephone No.:   (512) 471-4682

SUBSTANTIVE TOPICS COVERED:

The study examines men's and women's premarital and early marital experiences with regard to feelings and attitudes about themselves, their lives, and their interpersonal relations; how and why parents take on particular roles when they have children; and identifies what happens when mothers and fathers assume their parental roles in different ways.

CHARACTERISTICS OF THE ORIGINAL SAMPLE:

Year the study began: 1981

Subject selection process: Newlyweds residing in four counties in central Pennsylvania were contacted by marriage license records from county courthouses. Subjects were solicited by letters and telephone. All participants were married for the first time.

Total number of subjects at Time 1: N = 168 couples[a]

Ages at Time 1: 16-38 yrs.

Sex distribution: Equal numbers of females and males throughout

Socioeconomic status: 60% working class, 40% middle class (approximately)

Race/ethnicity: 98.2% white, 0.6% African-American, 1.2% Asian-American

Comments:
a. The sample includes children born to couples during the first 24-27 months of their marriage.

Years of Completed Waves:[b]

Years	N=	Age ranges
1981	168	16-38 yrs.
1982	139	17-39 yrs.
1983	123	18-40 yrs.

Comments:
b. A subsample of 13 divorced couples were followed up in 1984.

INFORMATION ON SAMPLE ATTRITION:

During the 3-year period of study, 34 of 168 couples (20.2%) were not retrieved for further study. Main reasons for sample attrition included separation or divorce (8.4%), and couples moving or dropping out of the study. The core sample consists of 123 couples.

CONSTRUCTS MEASURED: INSTRUMENTS USED

Data collected during nine phone calls; household tasks performed in previous 24 hours, child-care tasks performed in previous 24 hours, leisure activities performed in previous 24 hours, interaction events in previous 24 hours, conflicts with spouse in previous 24 hours, conversations in previous 24 hours, time with child, child illnesses: Daily record of activities (For additional information on measures derived from this procedure, see Huston, McHale, & Crouter, 1986)

Demographic and life history information, perceptions of partner's personality change in early marriage, satisfaction with division of child care, satisfaction with relationship with child, child-care arrangements: Questionnaire

Masculinity/femininity: Personal Attributes Questionnaire (Spence and Helmrich)

Sex-role attitudes: Attitude questionnaire (Spence, Helmrich, Stapp)

Standard personality questionnaire written at seventh grade reading level: Self Description Questionnaire (Cattell 16 PF)

Preferences regarding organization of tasks household responsibilities: Preferred activities—household

Interest in various leisure activities: Preferred activities—leisure

Extent to which person believes each is skilled at performing various household tasks; comparison or relative competence of husband and wife: Household Task Skills

Perception of parents' relative child-care competency: Child-Care Task Skills

Preferences regarding having children, their sex and spacing; employment hours (i.e., when to return to work); wife's involvement in employment as opposed to homemaking: Child preferences

Job satisfaction over the previous 2 months: Job opinion questionnaire (Campbell, Converse, et al.)

Moods and feelings after work: Moods and Feelings (Eight State Questionnaire, Cattell)

Assessing features of social networks maintained by spouses separately and together to assess whether cohesiveness and stability of marriage depends in part on the extent and nature of the partners' involvement with others: Social Networks Questionnaire

Subjective well-being: Questionnaire (Campbell, Converse, et al.)

Identify recent events that may have disrupted or affected the relationship (e.g., birth of a child): Couple Life Events Survey (adapted from Holmes and Rahe)

Previous dating experience: Dating History Questionnaire

Features of courtship (e.g., rate at which a couple progressed toward commitment to marriage, and downturns in commitment during courtship): Relationship Graph and Graph Recording Sheet

Explanation of change in commitment in the premarital relationship: Explanation of Graph

Identifying phases in relationship (e.g., regularly dating, cohabiting) and timing of particular events (e.g., first intercourse, pregnancy): Premarital Relationship Events Chart

Report of amount of conflict, ambivalence, love, and maintenance (self-disclosure of their relationship during time when participants were a couple but not committed to marriage): Relationship Questionnaire—Premarital Couple (Braiker & Kelley)

Marital satisfaction over previous 2 months: Marriage Opinion Questionnaire (Campbell, Converse, et al.)

Comparable to Relationship Questionnaire—Premarital Couple, except couple is asked about the previous 2 months of their marriage: Relationship Questionnaire—Marriage (Braiker & Kelley)

Extent to which a person would like pleasurable activities to occur more frequently and unpleasurable activities to occur less frequently in the relationship: Preferred Activities—Interaction

Satisfaction in nine domains of marriage during the 2-month periods prior to the second and third interviews (e.g., own leisure time, division of household tasks, communication, influence in decisions, sexual relationships, amount of time spent with spouse, amount of contact with friends and kin, financial situation, division of child-care tasks): Assessing Satisfaction with Aspects of Marriage (9-point scale)

REPRESENTATIVE REFERENCES:

Atkinson, J., & Huston, T. L. (1984). Sex role orientation and division of labor early in marriage. *Journal of Personality and Social Psychology, 46*(2), 330-345.

Huston, T. L., & McHale, S. M. (1984). Men and women as parents: Sex role orientation, employment, and parental role with infants. *Child Development, 5*(4), 1349-1361.

Huston, T. L., McHale, S. M., & Crouter, A. C. (1986). When the honeymoon's over: Changes in the topography and satisfactoriness of marriage over the first year. In R. Gilmour & S. Duck (Eds.), *The emerging field of personal relationships*. Hillsdale, NJ: Lawrence Erlbaum.

Huston, T., Robins, E., Atkinson, J., & McHale, S. (1987). Surveying the landscape of marital behavior: A behavioral self-report approach to studying marriage. In S. Oskamp (Ed.), *Family processes and problems: Social psychological aspects* (pp.45-72). Beverly Hills, CA: Sage.

CURRENT STATUS OF THE STUDY:

a. Further waves of data collection are planned.

b. The data are in machine-readable format.

c. The data are available for secondary analysis through the study contact person. Manuals pertaining to this study may be obtained by contacting Dr. Huston.

I

Retirement History Study, 1969

Irelan, Lola M.

Contact Person: Linda George
Address: Center for the Study of Aging and Human Development
Box 3003
Duke University Medical Center
Durham, NC 27710
Telephone No.: (919) 684-3204

SUBSTANTIVE TOPICS COVERED:

The study examines work lives, health, living arrangements, financial resources and assets, expenditures, leisure activities, retirement plans, family composition, travel, life satisfaction, and the spouse's labor force history.

CHARACTERISTICS OF THE ORIGINAL SAMPLE:

Year the study began: 1969
Subject selection process: Three subsamples were taken from a national multistage area probability sample of the following Americans: married couples, unmarried men, unmarried women.
Total number of subjects at Time 1: N = 11,153
Ages at Time 1: 58-63 yrs.
Sex distribution: 73% males, 27% females
Socioeconomic status: Information gathered, but not available in terms of percentage distribution by socioeconomic class
Race/ethnicity: 90% white, 10% African-American (approximately)

Years of Completed Waves:

Years	N=	Age ranges
1969	11,153	58-63 yrs.
1971	10,169	60-65 yrs.
1973	9,423	62-67 yrs.
1975	8,693	64-69 yrs.
1977	7,079	66-71 yrs.
1979	6,270	68-73 yrs.

INFORMATION ON SAMPLE ATTRITION:

Over the 10-year period of the study 5,583 of 11,853 Ss (43.8%) were lost due to death, refusal, and relocation. The core sample consists of 6,270 Ss.

CONSTRUCTS MEASURED: INSTRUMENTS USED

Health, respondent's labor force history, retirement plans, household, family, and social activities; income, assets, and debts; spouse's labor force history: Longitudinal Retirement History Survey Questionnaire

REPRESENTATIVE REFERENCES:

Irelan, L. M. (1972). Retirement history study: Introduction (RHS Report No. 1). *Social Security Bulletin, 35* 3-8.

Irelan, L. M., & Motley, D. K. (1972). Health on the threshold of retirement. *Industrial Gerontology, 12,* 16-19.

Irelan, L. M., & Schwab, K. (1981). The Social Security Administration's retirement history study. *Research on Aging, 3*(4), 381-386.

Schwab, K. (1974). Early labor-force withdrawal of men: Participants and nonparticipants aged 58-63 (RHS Report No. 4). *Social Security Bulletin, 37*(8), 24-28.

CURRENT STATUS OF THE STUDY:

a. No further waves of data collection are planned.
b. All data are in machine-readable format.
c. Data are available for secondary analysis from Machine Readable Records Branch, National Archives and Records Administration, Washington, DC 20409, or Center for the Study of Aging and Human Development, Box 3003, Duke University Medical Center, Durham, NC 27710.

J

Stanford Longitudinal Study, 1973

Jacklin, Carol Nagy; and Maccoby, Eleanor

Contact person: Carol Nagy Jacklin
Address: Department of Psychology
University of Southern California
Los Angeles, CA 90089-1061
Telephone No.: (213) 740-2203

SUBSTANTIVE TOPICS COVERED:

This study examines the development of gender differences and the relations of birth hormones to later behavior. It also examines parent-child relationships from an interactionist view, that is, how the child affects the parent and how the parent affects the child; and the interaction between the child's temperament and the adult's attitudinal and behavioral responses.

CHARACTERISTICS OF THE ORIGINAL SAMPLE:

Year the study began: 1973

Subject selection process: Subjects selected were all normal births on which 15cc of cord blood had been collected by delivery room nurses and had an Apgar 3-minute score of 7 or above. The initial design of the study included three cohorts. In 1976, Cohorts 1 and 2 were merged. All subjects were English-speaking.

Total number of subjects at Time 1: N = 76

Ages at Time 1: Birth; 26 yrs. (mothers)

Sex distribution: Approximately equal numbers of females and males throughout

Socioeconomic status: 100% middle/upper middle class

Race/ethnicity: Predominantly white

Years of Completed Waves:

Years	N=	Age ranges
(Cohort 1)		
1973	76	Birth
1974	53	6 mos.
1974	45	12 mos.
1975	48	18 mos.

Years of Completed Waves, Continued:

Years	N=	Age ranges
(Cohort 2)		
1974	74	Birth
1974	56	3 mos.
1974	44	9 mos.
1975	37	18 mos.
1976	33	26 mos.
(Cohorts 1 & 2 merged)		
1976	66	33 mos.
1978	54	4-5 yrs.
1980-1981	50	6 yrs.
(Cohort 3)		
1975	107	Birth
1976	90	6 mos.
1976	85	9 mos.
1976	74	12 mos.
1976-1977	98	14 mos.
1977	86	18 mos.
1977-1978	64	26 mos.
1978	68	33 mos.
1979	63	45 mos.
1979-1980	43	4-5 yrs.
1982	51	6 yrs.

INFORMATION ON SAMPLE ATTRITION:

During the 9-year period of study, 156 of 257 Ss (60.7%) across three cohorts were not retrieved for further study.

CONSTRUCTS MEASURED: INSTRUMENTS USED

Mother's age, family composition, socioeconomic status: Demographic fact sheet

At Birth

Five sex-steroid hormones (testosterone, androstenedione, estrone, estradiol, progesterone), length of labor, obstetrical drugs used, tactile sensitivity, grip strength, prone head response, length and weight: Cord-blood assays (all cohorts); Aesthesiometer, standardized observation; Spring Scale (Cohorts 1 and 2)

At 3 Months

Grip strength, sleep pattern, total crying, Q [activity, negative affect, positive affect, and soothability (Cohort 2)]: Spring Scale, at-home observations, mother questionnaire, sleep-wake diary

At 6 Months

Auditory habituation, localization, visual habituation; attention to social, non-social stimuli; timidity, sleep pattern, maturity, positive and negative arousal; infant fuss-cry, mother (latency to respond, response to fuss-cry, and caretaking); waking moods, activity: Standardized presentation of visual and auditory stimuli (laboratory), Spring Scale, observation (waiting room), timidity test, sleep-wake diary (Cohort 1); mother interview, questionnaire, state-mood diary (Cohort 3)

At 9 Months

Timidity (observed, questionnaire), sleep pattern, maturity, infant crying, proximity to mother, activity (observed and questionnaire); infant (positive and negative bids to mother), relative intensity (child and mother), mother responsiveness, mother calming behavior; Q (child resistiveness, difficulty, intensity), negative arousal, soothability, grip strength, visual attention, fuss-cry (observed), waking moods: Observation of mother and child in standardized laboratory situation, timidity test, mother questionnaire, sleep-wake diary; Spring Scale (Cohorts 2 and 3), state-mood diary (Cohort 3)

At 12 Months

Soothability, height, weight, timidity, negative arousal, resistiveness (observed, questionnaire); grip strength, waking mood, sleep pattern, maturity, child task orientation, compliance, parent teaching style, teaching effort, child mischievous exploration (waiting room behaviors), father prohibitions, proximity to parent, mother and father's positive and negative interaction with child, word comprehension, roughness of father play with child, waking moods, activity, difficulty, resistiveness, irritability: Observations of father-child interaction in waiting room, teaching; observations of mother-child interaction, teaching; questionnaires for mother and father; sleep-wake diary, timidity test, Spring Scale, mother report (word comprehension) (Cohorts 1 and 3); state-mood diary (Cohort 3)

At 18 Months

Sleep patterns and maturity, waking moods, activity, Q (difficulty, negative arousal, resistiveness); timidity, child bids to mother, child task orientation, mother teaching style, teaching effort, child (total positive to experimenter); height, weight, child pull strength; mother-child positive distal interaction, mother-child proximal interaction, mother responsiveness, mischief, roughness of father-child play, Q (mother firmness and maturity demands), waking mood: State-mood diary, mother questionnaire (all cohorts); assessment (minor physical anomalies), light box (for measurement of pull strength), timidity test, observation (mother-child interaction, home visit) (Cohorts 2 and 4)

At 26 Months

Height, weight, sleep pattern, maturity, activity level, percent (each waking mood); Q (difficulty, negative arousal, resistiveness, amount of mother-child conflict, mother firmness, and mother maturity demands): Observation in preschool play yard, mother questionnaire, state-mood diary

At 33 Months

Pull strength, child orientation (compliance), child confront frustration, activity level, social behavior toward peer, social withdrawal, passive toward peer (watch), child (negative coercion toward mother, mother (teaching style, teaching effort), mother (positive, negative responses), Q (mother efficacy, mother-child conflict, and child resistiveness, negative affect, difficultness, waking moods): Lab observation (mother-child in standardized frustrating situations and in tasks), sleep-wake diary, mother questionnaire, lab observation (child interaction with unfamiliar peer); light-box, state-mood diary

At 45 Months

Child's sex-typing; with each parent (amount of thematic play, amount of rough-and-tumble play, mutual compliance, amount of parental sex-typing pressure, amount of child's sex-typed play initiations, extent to which parent arouses child), observer rating (parent skill), each parent questionnaire (degree of child's masculinity, femininity, parental efficacy, parental firmness, and parent-child conflict, method of dealing with conflict): Observation (child with mother and child with father), toy-choice (sex-typing measure), questionnaires (mother, father, observe rating), interviews with mother and father

At 4-5 Years

Partners' playful attacks on target child; in mobile lab (activity level, amount of rough-and-tumble play, target child yields to partners' dominance attempts, partners yield to target child's dominance attempts, and amount of responsible suggesting, rule-quoting); during free play (amount of solitary, parallel and interactive play, preference for same-sex play partners, onlooker behavior, activity level, social approach to adults, egoistic demands to other children); and suggestions to other children; child resistiveness, mother firmness, maturity demands, and mother efficacy: In mobile lab (observation of interaction with two same-sex peers); observation of free play, nursery school during indoor and outdoor play; mother questionnaire

At 6 Years

Q-sort composites (agentic, cooperative, positive social, positive mood, aggressive, impulsive, and inhibited); cognitive scores (total, verbal, quantitative, space); interaction session (number of influence attempts by mother, father, difference between mother and father in influence attempts, ratio of parental suggestions to demands, amount of positive or negative feedback, and communication accuracy, mother and child, father and child); school observations (orientation to task, classroom); free play (amount of rough-and-tumble, preference for same-sex peers, solitary, parallel, interactive, social approach to adults); demanding versus suggestion (to peers, and activity level); amount of parent-child conflict (with mother, with father, mother firmness, father firmness, methods used to get compliance, child assertiveness, parent efficacy), after-school supervision; closeness (parent standard child cooperation, and parent permissiveness for child argument): In lab session, observations of interaction with mother and father, in task situation and during free "snack" time; referential communication task, with mother and father; standardized cognitive test, test for cerebral lateralization (recognition of familiar face when presented to each hemisphere); handedness test; Q-sorts (completed by mother, father, and teacher); teacher questionnaire (school task orientation), mother and father interviews, questionnaires (mother and father), school observations (free play during recess, during classroom work time)

Affect, mothers' teaching style, mother firmness and maturity demands, amount of mother-child conflict, parent efficacy, method of dealing with conflict, method used to get compliance, parent permissiveness for child argument, positive and negative interaction with the child: Questionnaires, observations of mothers via mother/child interactions

Comments:
All "Q" variables throughout this section are derived from questionnaires.

REPRESENTATIVE REFERENCES:

Jacklin, C. N. (1989). Female and male: Issues of gender. *American Psychologist, 44,* 127-133.

Jacklin, C. N., Maccoby, E. E., & Doering, C. H. (1983). Neonatal sex-steroid hormones and timidity in 6-18 month old boys and girls. *Developmental Psychobiology, 16,* 163-168.

Jacklin, C. N., Maccoby, E. E., Doering, C. H., & King, D. R. (1984). Neonatal sex-steroid hormones and muscular strength of boys and girls in the first three years. *Developmental Psychobiology, 17,* 301-310.

Jacklin, C. N., Wilcox, K., & Maccoby, E. E. (1988). Neonatal sex-steroid hormones and cognitive abilities at six years. *Developmental Psychobiology, 21,* 567-574.

CURRENT STATUS OF THE STUDY:

a. No further waves of data collection are planned.

b. Most data are in machine-readable format.

c. Data are available for secondary analysis from the study contact person.

■ Longitudinal Study of Aging Human Twins, 1947

Jarvik, Lissy F.

Contact Person: Lissy F. Jarvik
Address: UCLA Neuropsychiatric Institute and Hospital
                  37-431 NPI
                  Center for the Health Sciences
                  760 Westwood Plaza
                  Los Angeles, CA 90024-1759
Telephone No.:   (213) 825-3885, or (213) 824-4350

SUBSTANTIVE TOPICS COVERED:

The study examines the associations between hereditary aspects of aging, mental functioning, and longevity.

CHARACTERISTICS OF THE ORIGINAL SAMPLE:

Year the study began: 1946

Subject selection process: Subjects are age 60 or over and come from the English-speaking, literate white population residing in communities in or near New York State. Health had to be good enough to participate in an extensive testing program.[1] The 268 twins studied constitute 134 intact pairs. The twins of each pair are of the same sex.

Total number of subjects at Time 1: N = 268

Ages at Time 1: 60-89 yrs.

Sex distribution: Higher percentage of females than males throughout

Socioeconomic status: Data were collected, but information in terms of percent distribution by socioeconomic class were not available

Race/ethnicity: 100% white

Comments:
1. Education closely resembled the total white population of New York State. In terms of occupation, farmers and their wives were heavily over-represented; factory and clerical workers were under-represented.

Years of Completed Waves:

Years	$N=$[a]	Age ranges
1946-1949	268[b]	60-89 yrs.
1955	79	c
1957	17	c
1967	68	78-94 yrs.
1973	22	84-100 yrs.

Comments:
a. Sample sizes listed represent Ss tested, not the number of surviving subjects.
b. Sample represents 134 twin pairs.
c. Information about age ranges was not available for the 1955 and 1957 follow-ups.

INFORMATION ON SAMPLE ATTRITION:

During the 31-year period of study, 256 of 268 Ss were not retrieved for further study. Main reasons for sample attrition were death, and the lack of study funds.

CONSTRUCTS MEASURED: INSTRUMENTS USED

Cognitive functioning: Wechsler-Bellevue Intelligence Test (Scale I) (digits forward, digits backward, similarities; block design, digit symbol substitution, picture arrangement, picture completion), Stanford-Binet Vocabulary List 1, Stroop Color-Word test, Memory for Designs Test
Hand-eye coordination and psychomotor speed: Paper and Pencil Tapping Test
Health and activity: Physical examination, medical records
Family, past history, activities, and interests: Interview

REPRESENTATIVE REFERENCES:

Jarvik, L. F., Altshuler, K. Z., Kato, T., & Blumner, B. (1971). Organic brain syndrome and chromosome loss in aged twins. *Diseases of the Nervous System, 32,* 159-170.
Jarvik, L. F., Blum, J. E., & Varma, A. O. (1972). Genetic components and intellectual functioning during senescence: A 20-year study of aging twins. *Behavior Genetics, 2,* 159-171.
Jarvik, L. F., & Falek, A. (1963). Intellectual stability and survival in the aged. *Journal of Gerontology, 18,* 173-176.
LaRue, A., & Jarvik, L. F. (1987). Cognitive function and prediction of dementia in old age. *International Journal of Aging and Human Development, 25,* 79-89.

CURRENT STATUS OF THE STUDY:

a. No further waves of data collection are possible due to lack of survivors.
b. The data are not in machine-readable format.
c. Data are available for secondary analysis through the study contact person.

■ Columbia University Longitudinal Study: Family Welfare Research Program-Mothers View Foster Care, 1966

Jenkins, Shirley; and Norman, Elaine

Contact Person: Shirley Jenkins
Address: Columbia University School of Social Work
                  Office 708
                  New York, NY 10032
Telephone No.:   (212) 854-5155

SUBSTANTIVE TOPICS COVERED:

This longitudinal study of families of children placed in foster care shows the changes that occurred in the circumstances of these families over the 5 years after initial foster care. Changes in maternal feelings about placement were also examined and compared with mothers' feelings on entry, as well as with their feelings when children were discharged. (See also Fanshel, D., *Columbia University Longitudinal Study: Children in Foster Care*; and Shapiro, D., *Columbia University Longitudinal Study: Child Welfare Research Program—Nature of Agency Services.*)

CHARACTERISTICS OF THE ORIGINAL SAMPLE:

Year the study began: 1966

Subject selection process: The sample included children who experienced their first foster care placement between January and October of 1966. They did not become part of the sample until they had been in care for 90 days.

Total number of subjects at Time 1: N = 517 parents

Ages at Time 1: Birth-12 yrs. (children)

Sex distribution: 75% mothers, 25% fathers

Socioeconomic status: 66% poverty class, 34% working class (approximately)

Race/ethnicity: 39% African-American, 38% Puerto Rican, 23% white

Years of Completed Waves:[a]

Years	$N=$[b]	Age ranges
1966	390	20-40 yrs.
1968	304	22-42 yrs.
1971	257	25-45 yrs.

Comments:

a. Number of mothers interviewed at three time points is presented here.

b. For 88 cases, both mother and father were interviewed separately. Some fathers were seen in the initial 1966 interviews, others in a special father survey that followed, bringing the total of fathers seen to 127, including 88 interviews of both parents and 49 of fathers alone.

INFORMATION ON SAMPLE ATTRITION:

During the 5-year period of study, 133 of 390 Ss (29.3%) were not retrieved for further study. Attrition was due to subjects' refusal to continue participation, the inability to locate Ss, death of child, illness, institutionalization, and casework reasons. The core sample consists of 257 Ss.

CONSTRUCTS MEASURED: INSTRUMENTS USED

Socioeconomic and demographic information, placement experience, agency related attitudes and experiences, expectations for child, preferred child traits, child-rearing practice, conception of parenthood, marital role expectations, marital role performance, social attitudes, family functioning, community resources and primary prevention: Interview

REPRESENTATIVE REFERENCES:

Jenkins, S. (1969). Separation experiences of parents whose children are in foster care. *Child Welfare, 48,* 334-340.

Jenkins, S., & Norman, E. (1969). Families of children in foster care. *Children, 16,* 155-159.

Jenkins, S., & Norman, E. (1972). *Filial deprivation and foster care.* New York: Columbia University Press.

Jenkins, S., & Norman, E. (1975). *Beyond placement: Mothers view foster care.* New York: Columbia University Press.

CURRENT STATUS OF THE STUDY:

a. No further waves of data collection are planned.

b. Data are not in machine-readable format.

c. Data are not available for secondary analysis.

■ Youth-Parent Socialization Panel Study, 1965

Jennings, M. Kent

Contact Person: M. Kent Jennings
Address: Institute for Social Research
                  426 Thompson Street
                  University of Michigan
                  Ann Arbor, MI 48106
Telephone No.:   (313) 763-1347

SUBSTANTIVE TOPICS COVERED:

This study examines socialization on a variety of dimensions, including politics, family life, education, and attitudes toward other generation members; the aging process as it is reflected in the development of sociological orientations within two biologically linked generations, with a focus on the following: quantity, quality, and timing of political participations; public policy preferences and goals; and evaluations of public institutions, actors, and processes.

CHARACTERISTICS OF THE ORIGINAL SAMPLE:

Year the study began: 1965
Subject selection process: Subjects were selected by a national probability sample of second semester seniors in public and private high schools, and their parents.
Total number of subjects at Time 1: 1,669 students, 1,562 parents
Ages at Time 1: 17-18 yrs. (offspring/students); 37-66 yrs. (parents)
Sex distribution: Approximately equal numbers of females and males throughout
Socioeconomic status: 54.5% working class, 45.5% middle class
Race/ethnicity: 90% white, 9% African-American, 1% other

Years of Completed Waves:

Years	N=	Age ranges
(Cohort 1: Offspring)		
1965	1,669	17-18 yrs.
1973	1,348	25-26 yrs.
1982	1,135	34-35 yrs.
(Cohort 2: Parents)		
1965	1,562	37-66 yrs.
1973	1,179	45-74 yrs.
1982	898	54-83 yrs.

INFORMATION ON SAMPLE ATTRITION:

During the 17-year period of study, 1,198 of 3,231 Ss (37.1%), from both co-horts, were not retrieved for further study: 534 of 1,669 (32%) offspring, and 664 of 1,562 (42.5%) parents. The core sample consists of 2,033 Ss: 1,135 offspring and 898 parents.

CONSTRUCTS MEASURED: INSTRUMENTS USED

Political participation, public policy preferences and goals, and evaluations of public institutions, politicians, and processes; demographic information and life
  histories: Personal interviews

REPRESENTATIVE REFERENCES:

Jennings, M. K. (1987). Residues of a movement: The aging of the American protest generation. *American Political Science Review, 81,* 367-382.

Jennings, M. K., & Markus, G. (1988). Political involvement in the later years: A longitudinal survey. *American Journal of Political Science, 32,* 302-316.

Jennings, M. K., & Neimi, R. (1974). *The political character of adolescence.* Princeton, NJ: Princeton University Press.

Jennings, M. K., & Neimi, R. (1981). *Generations and politics: A panel study of young adults and their parents.* Princeton, NJ: Princeton University Press.

CURRENT STATUS OF THE STUDY:

a. A fourth wave of data collection is planned, pending additional funding.
b. Most data are in machine-readable format.
c. Data are available for secondary analysis through both the Inter-University Consortium for Political and Social Research, University of Michigan, Ann Arbor, MI
   48106. The third wave was released in Fall 1990.

■ The Socialization of Problem Behavior in Youth, 1969

Jessor, Richard; and Jessor, Lee

Contact Person: Richard Jessor
Address: Institute of Behavioral Science
                 University of Colorado
                 Campus Box 483
                 Boulder, CO 80309
Telephone No.:   (303) 492-6921

SUBSTANTIVE TOPICS COVERED:

The study examines problem behavior and psychosocial development with the aims of predicting the onset of developmental transition behaviors; exploring the continuity between early and late developmental stages; and testing the usefulness of problem-behavior theory.

CHARACTERISTICS OF THE ORIGINAL SAMPLE:

The High School Study

Year the study began: 1969
Subject selection process: Subjects participating in the study were female and male
    junior high school (grades 7, 8, and 9) students from a small city in the Rocky
    Mountain region. All Ss were selected through a 75% random sampling proce-
    dure in which Ss were stratified by gender and grade level.
Total number of subjects at Time 1: N = 589 (432 in core 4-year sample)
Ages at Time 1: 13-15 yrs.
Sex distribution: 56% female, 44% male (approximately)
Socioeconomic status: Predominantly middle class
Race/ethnicity: 89% white, 7% African-American and Native American, 4% Hispanic

Years of Completed Waves:[a]

Years	N=	Age ranges
(1956 Birth Cohort: Seventh Grade Females)		
1969	96[b]	13 yrs.
1970[c]	96	14 yrs.
1971	96	15 yrs.
1972	96	16 yrs.
1979	87	23 yrs.
1981	81	25 yrs.

Years of Completed Waves, Continued:[a]

Years	N=	Age ranges
(1956 Birth Cohort: Seventh Grade Males)		
1969	75[b]	13 yrs.
1970[c]	75	14 yrs.
1971	75	15 yrs.
1972	75	16 yrs.
1979	66	23 yrs.
1981	60	25 yrs.
(1955 Birth Cohort: Eighth Grade Females)		
1969	82[b]	4 yrs.
1970[c]	82	15 yrs.
1971	82	16 yrs.
1972	82	17 yrs.
1979	80	24 yrs.
1981	77	26 yrs.
(1955 Birth Cohort: Eighth Grade Males)		
1969	60[b]	14 yrs.
1970[c]	60	15 yrs.
1971	60	16 yrs.
1972	60	17 yrs.
1979	54	24 yrs.
1981	53	26 yrs.
(1954 Birth Cohort: Ninth Grade Females)		
1969	66[b]	15 yrs.
1970[c]	66	16 yrs.
1971	66	17 yrs.
1972	66	18 yrs.
1979	64	25 yrs.
1981	64	27 yrs.
(1954 Birth Cohort: Ninth Grade Males)		
1969	53[b]	15 yrs.
1970[c]	53	16 yrs.
1971	53	17 yrs.
1972	53	18 yrs.
1979	52	25 yrs.
1981	49	27 yrs.

Comments:
a. The High School Study utilized a cohort-sequential design.
b. This figure refers to the core sample on whom there were four consecutive waves of data by 1972. Other Ss were tested, but these Ss are not represented in the present figure of 432 Ss.
c. A third study, The Family Interview Study, included 200 mothers from a randomly selected subsample of high school youth.

INFORMATION ON SAMPLE ATTRITION:

During the 12-year period of data collection, 157 of 589 Ss (27%) tested in Year I (1969) were not retrieved by Year IV (1972). An additional 48 Ss were not retrieved by Year VI (1981).

The College Study

Year the study began: 1970
Subject selection process: Subjects were stratified by gender and drawn from a
   10% random sample of freshman students enrolled in the college of arts and
   sciences at a major Rocky Mountain state university in 1969.
Total number of subjects at Time 1: N = 276 (205 in core 4-year sample)
Ages at Time 1: 19 yrs.
Sex distribution: Approximately equal numbers of females and males
Socioeconomic status: Predominantly middle class
Race/ethnicity: 96% white, 2% Hispanic, 1% African-American, 1% Asian-American

Years of Completed Waves:

Years	N=	Age ranges
(1951 Birth Cohort: Females)		
1970	113	19 yrs.
1971	113	20 yrs.
1972	113	21 yrs.
1973	113	22 yrs.
1979	105	28 yrs.
1981	100	30 yrs.
(1951 Birth Cohort: Males)		
1970	92	19 yrs.
1971	92	20 yrs.
1972	92	21 yrs.
1973	92	22 yrs.
1979	86	28 yrs.
1981	84	30 yrs.

INFORMATION ON SAMPLE ATTRITION:

During the 11-year period of data collection, 71 of 276 Ss (26%) were not retrieved
by Year IV (1973). An additional 21 Ss were not retrieved by Year VI (1981).

CONSTRUCTS MEASURED: INSTRUMENTS USED

Demographic-social structure of the family; Socialization (parental ideology, home
   climate, peer influence, and media influence); personality system (motiva-
   tional-instigation structure, personal belief structure, and personal control
   structure); perceived environment system (distal-social structure and proxi-
   mal-social structure); behavior system (problem behavior structure and con-
   ventional behavior structure): Structured questionnaire[1]

Comments:
1. The High School Study and The College Study measured similar constructs, using a similar questionnaire
adapted for high school and college-aged samples.

REPRESENTATIVE REFERENCES:

Jessor, R. (1987). Problem-behavior theory, psychosocial development, and adolescent problem drinking. *British Journal of Addiction, 82,* 435-446.

Jessor, R., Donovan, J. E., & Costa, F. M. (in press). *Beyond adolescence: Problem behavior and young adult development.* New York: Cambridge University Press.

Jessor, R., & Jessor, S. (1977). *Problem behavior and psychosocial development: A longitudinal study of youth.* New York: Academic Press.

Jessor, R., & Jessor, S. (1984). Adolescence to young adulthood: A twelve year prospective study of problem behavior and psychosocial development. In S. Mednick, M. Harway, & K. M. Finello (Eds.), *Handbook of longitudinal research in the United States: Vol. 2. Teenage and adult cohorts.* New York: Praeger.

CURRENT STATUS OF THE STUDY:

a. Further waves of data collection are planned.

b. Most of the data are in machine-readable format.

c. The data are not yet available for secondary analysis.

■ Houston Parent-Child Development Center Project, 1970

Johnson, Dale L.

Contact person: Dale L. Johnson
Address: Department of Psychology
                  University of Houston
                  Houston, TX 77204-5341
Telephone No.:   (713) 749-2961

SUBSTANTIVE TOPICS COVERED:

The purpose of this study was to develop and evaluate a program for low-income families designed to prevent school failure and behavioral problems.

CHARACTERISTICS OF THE ORIGINAL SAMPLE:

Year the study began: 1970

Subject selection process: Community surveys were conducted to locate low-income Mexican-American families with a one-year-old child who was not neurologically impaired. Participants were randomly assigned to program or control groups after they had been fully apprised.

Total number of subjects at Time 1: N = 88[a]

Ages at Time 1: 1 yr.

Sex distribution: Approximately equal numbers of females and males throughout

Socioeconomic status: 100% poverty class
Race/ethnicity: 100% Hispanic (Mexican-American)
Comments:
a. Cohort D was part of a pilot study; the study formally began with Cohort F.

Years of Completed Waves:

Years	N=	Age ranges
(Cohort 1 [D])		
1971-1972	88[b]	1 yr.
1972-1973	*	2 yrs
1973-1974	20	3 yrs.
1976-1989[c]	*	6-19 yrs.

Comments:
b. Experimental Group (Program), N = 53; Control, N = 35
c. Ss were also followed in 1976, 1978-1979, 1985-1986, and 1987-1989.

(Cohort 2 [F])		
1972	104[b]	1-3 yrs.
1973	*	2-4 yrs.
1974-1975	83	3-5 yrs.
1977-1989[c]	*	6-18 yrs.

Comments:
b. Experimental Group (Program), N = 50; Control, N = 54
c. Ss were followed in 1977, 1978-1979, 1982-1983, 1985-1986, 1987-1988, and 1987-1989.

(Cohort 3 [G])		
1973	94[b]	1-3 yrs.
1974	*	2-4 yrs.
1975	62	3-5 yrs.
1978-1989[c]	*	6-19 yrs.

Comments:
b. Experimental Group (Program), N = 55; Control, N = 39
c. Ss were also followed in 1978, 1980, 1985-1986, and 1987-1989.

(Cohort 4 [H])		
1974	65[b]	1-3 yrs.
1975	*	2-4 yrs.
1976	48	3-5 yrs.
1979-1989[c]	*	7-17 yrs.

Comments:
b. Experimental Group (Program), N = 34; Control, N = 31
c. Ss were also followed in 1979, 1981, 1985-1986, and 1987-1989.

Years of Completed Waves, Continued:

Years	N=	Age ranges
(Cohort 5 [I])		
1975	68[b]	1-3 yrs.
1976	*	2-4 yrs.
1977	51	3-5 yrs.
1980-1989[c]	*	6-17 yrs.

Comments:
b. Experimental Group (Program), N = 40; Control, N = 28
c. Ss were also followed in 1980, 1982, 1985-1986, and 1987-1989.

(Cohort 6 [J])		
1976	52[b]	1-3 yrs.
1977	*	2-4 yrs.
1978	40	3-5 yrs.
1981-1989[c]	*	6-16 yrs.

Comments:
b. Experimental Group (Program), N = 33; Control, N = 19
c. Ss were also followed in 1981, 1983, 1985-1986, and 1987-1989.

(Cohort 7 [K])		
1977	66[b]	1-3 yrs.
1978	*	2-4 yrs.
1979-1989[c]	54	3-14 yrs.

Comments:
b. Experimental Group (Program), N = 40; Control, N = 26
c. Ss were also followed in 1979, 1982, 1985-1986, and 1987-1989.

(Cohort 8 [L])		
1978	76[b]	1-3 yrs.
1979	*	2-4 yrs.
1980	59	3-5 yrs.
1983-1989[c]	*	6-12 yrs.

Comments:
b. Experimental Group (Program), N = 36; Control, N = 40
c. Ss were also followed in 1983, 1985-1986, and 1987-1989.

INFORMATION ON SAMPLE ATTRITION:

During the 19-year period of study, 127 of 390 Ss (32.5%) were not retrieved for further study. Attrition was due to families moving out of the target area; dropouts due to mothers' having to work; and inability to re-locate families for interviews.

CONSTRUCTS MEASURED: INSTRUMENTS USED

Mother

Home environment: Home Observation for Measurement of the Environment (HOME), Home Behavior Inventory, Home Environment
Family functioning: Comprehensive Family Data Inventory, Traditional Family Ideology, Family Update, Modernity, Acculturation
Child rearing: Child Rearing Beliefs, Index of Achievement Values, Parent Practices Inventory, Cornell Child Rearing Report, Parent Interview
Child behavior: Behavioral Assessment Interview, Child Behavior Checklist
Mother-child interaction: Mother-Child Interaction (Observation), Structured Situations (waiting room, teaching, nonsocial stress situations: videotaped)
Maternal satisfaction: Psychological Well-being
Maternal Self-perception: Parental Self-Efficacy, Self-esteem
Internalization: Psychological Mindedness, Locus of Control
Language development: Mother Language Assessment, Mother Language Questionnaire
History of substance use: Alcohol and Drug Interview

Child

Cognitive abilities: Palmer Concept Familiarity Index, Pacific Test Series, Boehm Concepts, Stickers Creativity, Circus Quantitative, Children's Embedded Figures Test, Rod and Frame Test, Locus of Control
Intelligence: Bayley Infant Scales of Development, Uzgiris-Hunt Scales of Infant Ordinal Development, Emmons Full-Range Picture Vocabulary Test, Stanford-Binet Intelligence Test (Form LM), McCarthy Scales of Children's Abilities, Wechsler Preschool and Primary Scales of Intelligence, Revised Wechsler Intelligence Scales for Children (WISC-R)
Language development: Bilingual Syntax Measure, Test of Auditory Comprehension of Language, Receptive Language Inventory
Neurological functioning: Satz Battery (Finger Localization, Recognition Discrimination, Alphabet)
Personality: Children's Manifest Anxiety Scale, Thematic Apperception Test (Need Achievement), Effectance Motivation
Self-Perception: Purdue Self-Concept Scale, Coopersmith Self-Esteem Inventory; What Am I Like?
Perception of parents: Parental Acceptance-Rejection Questionnaire, Cornell Child Rearing Report
Ego development: Loevinger's Washington University Sentence Completion Test
Aspirations: Educational and Career Goals
Interpersonal relationships: Children's Self-Efficacy of Peer Interaction Scale, Family and Peer Relations
Symptoms: Youth Self Report
Substance use history: Alcohol and Drug Questionnaire

School

Child behavior problems: Classroom Behavior Inventory (teacher ratings), Teacher Interview, AML (Aggressive, Mood and Learning difficulties) screening instrument

Academic progress: Achievement Test Scores, School Grades, Retention in Grade, Special Education Class Assignment

REPRESENTATIVE REFERENCES:

Andrews, S. R., Blumenthal, J. B., Johnson, D. L., Ferguson, C. J., Kahn, A. J., Lasater, T. M., Malone, P. E., & Wallace, D. B. (1982). The skills of mothering: A study of the Parent-Child Development Centers. *Monographs of the Society for Research in Child Development,* *47*(6).

Johnson, D. L. (1975). The development of a program for parent-child education among Mexican-Americans in Texas. In B. Friedlander, G. Sterritt, & G. Kirk (Eds.), *The exceptional infant: Vol. III* (chap. 18). New York: Brunner/Mazel.

Johnson, D. L., & Breckenridge, J. N. (1982). The Houston Parent-Child Development Center and the primary prevention of behavior problems in young children. *American Journal of Community Psychology, 10,* 305-316.

Johnson, D. L., & Walker, T. (1987). The primary prevention of behavior problems in Mexican-American children. *American Journal of Community Psychology, 15,* 375-385.

CURRENT STATUS OF THE STUDY:

a. Further waves of data collection are planned.

b. Most of the data are in machine-readable format.

c. Data may be available for secondary analysis from the study contact person.

■ Monitoring the Future: A Continuing Study of Lifestyles and Values of Youth, 1976

Johnston, Lloyd D.; Bachman, Jerald G.; and O'Malley, Patrick

Contact Person: Patrick O'Malley
Address: University of Michigan
P.O. Box 1248
Ann Arbor, MI 48106-1248
Telephone No.: (313) 763-5043

SUBSTANTIVE TOPICS COVERED:

The study examines the changing behaviors, plans, and preferences of American youth: views about lifestyles, intergroup and interpersonal attitudes, public concerns, drug and alcohol use, and other social and ethical issues.

CHARACTERISTICS OF THE ORIGINAL SAMPLE:

Year the study began: 1976

Subject selection process: Subjects were selected by a stratified, clustered random sampling of high school seniors in public and private high schools in the coterminous United States. A total of 130 high schools was sampled: nationally representative of high school seniors. A new cohort of high school seniors is selected every year.

Total number of subjects at Time 1: N = 1,200

Ages at Time 1: 17-18 yrs.

Sex distribution: Approximately equal numbers of females and males throughout

Socioeconomic status: National representative sample

Race/ethnicity: 77% white, 12% African-American, 5.5% Hispanic, 5.5% Native American and Asian-American

Years of Completed Waves:[a]

Years	N=	Age ranges
Cohort 1: Class of 1976		
(Cohort 1A)		
1976	1,200	17-18 yrs.
1978	978	19-20 yrs.
1980	990	21-22 yrs.
1982	965	23-24 yrs.
1984	898	25-26 yrs.
1986	893	27-28 yrs.
1988	882	29-30 yrs.
1990	*	31-32 yrs.

Years of Completed Waves, Continued:[a]

Years	N=	Age ranges
(Cohort 1B)		
1977	1,200	18-19 yrs.
1979	925	20-21 yrs.
1981	931	22-23 yrs.
1983	930	24-25 yrs.
1985	876	26-27 yrs.
1987	870	28-29 yrs.
1989	*	30-31 yrs.
Cohort 2: Class of 1977		
(Cohort 2A)		
1977	1,200	17-18 yrs.
1979	1,004	19-20 yrs.
1981	985	21-22 yrs.
1983	965	23-24 yrs.
1985	918	25-26 yrs.
1987	895	27-28 yrs.
1989	*	29-30 yrs.
(Cohort 2B)		
1978	1,200	18-19 yrs.
1980	994	20-21 yrs.
1982	967	22-23 yrs.
1984	899	24-25 yrs.
1986	898	26-27 yrs.
1988	854	28-29 yrs.
1990	*	30-31 yrs.
Cohort 3: Class of 1978		
(Cohort 3A)		
1978	1,200	17-18 yrs.
1980	1,019	19-20 yrs.
1982	982	21-22 yrs.
1984	932	23-24 yrs.
1986	917	25-26 yrs.
1988	871	27-28 yrs.
1990	*	29-30 yrs.
(Cohort 3B)		
1979	1,200	18-19 yrs.
1981	988	20-21 yrs.
1983	974	22-23 yrs.
1985	900	24-25 yrs.
1987	894	26-27 yrs.
1989	*	28-29 yrs.
Cohort 4: Class of 1979		
(Cohort 4A)		
1979	1,200	17-18 yrs.
1981	991	19-20 yrs.
1983	938	21-22 yrs.
1985	883	23-24 yrs.
1987	890	25-26 yrs.
1989	*	27-28 yrs.

Years of Completed Waves, Continued:[a]

Years	N=	Age ranges
(Cohort 4B)		
1980	1,200	18-19 yrs.
1982	1,000	20-21 yrs.
1984	941	22-23 yrs.
1986	946	24-25 yrs.
1988	888	26-27 yrs.
1990	*	28-29 yrs.
Cohort 5: Class of 1980		
(Cohort 5A)		
1980	1,200	17-18 yrs.
1982	1,015	19-20 yrs.
1984	937	21-22 yrs.
1986	938	23-24 yrs.
1988	911	25-26 yrs.
1990	*	27-28 yrs.
(Cohort 5B)		
1981	1,200	18-19 yrs.
1983	992	20-21 yrs.
1985	931	22-23 yrs.
1987	921	24-25 yrs.
1989	*	26-27 yrs.
Cohort 6: Class of 1981		
(Cohort 6A)		
1981	1,200	17-18 yrs.
1983	1,005	19-20 yrs.
1985	914	21-22 yrs.
1987	910	23-24 yrs.
1989	*	25-26 yrs.
(Cohort 6B)		
1982	1,200	18-19 yrs.
1984	966	20-21 yrs.
1986	952	22-23 yrs.
1988	878	24-25 yrs.
1990	*	26-27 yrs.
Cohort 7: Class of 1982		
(Cohort 7A)		
1982	1,200	17-18 yrs.
1984	1,000	19-20 yrs.
1986	938	21-22 yrs.
1988	884	23-24 yrs.
1990	*	25-26 yrs.
(Cohort 7B)		
1983	1,200	18-19 yrs.
1985	938	20-21 yrs.
1987	917	22-23 yrs.
1989	*	24-25 yrs.
Cohort 8: Class of 1983		
(Cohort 8A)		
1983	1,200	17-18 yrs.

Years of Completed Waves, Continued:[a]

Years	N=	Age ranges
1985	956	19-20 yrs.
1987	929	21-22 yrs.
1989	*	23-24 yrs.
(Cohort 8B)		
1984	1,200	18-19 yrs.
1986	949	20-21 yrs.
1988	876	22-23 yrs.
1990	*	24-25 yrs.
Cohort 9: Class of 1984		
(Cohort 9A)		
1984	1,200	17-18 yrs.
1986	982	19-20 yrs.
1988	894	21-22 yrs.
1990	*	23-24 yrs.
(Cohort 9B)		
1985	1,200	18-19 yrs.
1987	926	20-21 yrs.
1989	*	22-23 yrs.
Cohort 10: Class of 1985		
(Cohort 10A)		
1985	1,200	17-18 yrs.
1987	965	19-20 yrs.
1989	*	21-22 yrs.
(Cohort 10B)		
1986	1,200	18-19 yrs.
1988	887	20-21 yrs.
1990	*	22-23 yrs.
Cohort 11: Class of 1986		
(Cohort 11A)		
1986	1,200	17-18 yrs.
1988	886	19-20 yrs.
1990	*	21-22 yrs.
(Cohort 11B)		
1987	1,200	18-19 yrs.
1989	*	20-21 yrs.
Cohort 12: Class of 1987		
(Cohort 12A)		
1987	1,200	17-18 yrs.
1989	*	19-20 yrs.
(Cohort 12B)		
1988	1,200	18-19 yrs.
1990	*	20-21 yrs.
Cohort 13: Class of 1988		
(Cohort 13A)		
1988	1,200	17-18 yrs.
1990	*	19-20 yrs.
(Cohort 13B)		
1989	1,200	18-19 yrs.

Years of Completed Waves, Continued:[a]

Years	N=	Age ranges
Cohort 14: Class of 1989		
(Cohort 14A)		
1989	1,200	17-18 yrs.
(Cohort 14B)		
1990	1,200	18-19 yrs.
Cohort 15: Class of 1990		
(Cohort 15A)		
1990	1,200	17-18 yrs.
(Cohort 15B)		
1991	1,200[b]	18-19 yrs.

Comments:
a. Sample sizes are approximations based on weighted response rate percentages.
b. Planned for 1,200 Ss.

INFORMATION ON SAMPLE ATTRITION:

During the 14-year period of study, 6,372 of 30,000 Ss (21.3%), across 25 cohorts of graduating seniors, were not retrieved for further study. Attrition ranged from 19.6% (Cohort 10A) to 28.8% (Cohort 2B). The core sample consists of 23,628 Ss across 25 cohorts, ranging from 854 Ss (Cohort 2B) to 1,200 Ss (Cohorts 11B-13A) per cohort. Additional cohorts (Cohorts 13B-15A) were excluded from attrition and core sample figures because their second data points are still pending (in 1990 or 1991).

CONSTRUCTS MEASURED: INSTRUMENTS USED

Drug behaviors, attitudes, and related factors (exposure to and availability of various drugs, use of licit and illicit drugs, frequency of use in different settings, drug-related problems, reasons for use, abstention, and termination of use; attitudes and beliefs regarding the use of various drugs, attitudes of significant others, drug counseling—rating of various help-giving sources), exposure to drug education; values, attitudes, and behavior (life-style values, attitudes and behaviors, views about social institutions, personality characteristics (self-esteem, internal control), intergroup and interpersonal attitudes, delinquent behavior, victimization, life satisfaction/happiness, person characteristics, home environment, large social environment); high school experiences, role behaviors, and satisfactions (educational experiences, employment experiences, military service, marriage and parenthood, sources of financial support): Questionnaire[1]

Comments
1. Self-administered, optically scanned questionnaires, administered in group settings in and by mail after that. There were five different forms with a common core of questions. (Individual respondents in the panel studies retain the same form of the questionnaire).

REPRESENTATIVE REFERENCES:

Bachman, J. G., & Johnston, L. D. (1987). *Monitoring the future: Questionnaire responses from the nation's high school seniors, 1986.* Ann Arbor: Institute for Social Research.

Bachman, J. G., Johnston, L. D., & O'Malley, P. M. (1987). *Monitoring the future: Questionnaire responses from the nation's high school seniors, 1986.* Ann Arbor: Institute for Social Research.

Johnston, L. D., O'Malley, P. M., & Bachman, J. G. (1989). *Drug use, drinking, and smoking: National survey results from high school, college, and young adult populations: 1975-1988.* Washington, DC: National Institute on Drug Abuse.

O'Malley, P. M., Bachman, J. G., & Johnston, L. D. (1988). Period, age, and cohort effects on substance use among young Americans: A decade of change, 1976-1986. *American Journal of Public Health, 78,* 1315-1321.

CURRENT STATUS OF THE STUDY:

    a. Further waves of data collection are planned for all cohorts; data collection for Cohort 15B (Class of 1990) is planned for 1991.

    b. The data are in machine-readable format.

    c. Longitudinal data are not yet available. Cross-sectional data are available for secondary analysis through the Inter-University Consortium for Political and Social Research (ICPSR) Institute for Social Research, University of Michigan, P. O. Box 1248, Ann Arbor, MI 48106.

■ St. Louis Baby Study, 1966

Jordan, Thomas E.

Contact Person: Thomas E. Jordan
Address: University of Missouri-St. Louis
                 8001 Natural Bridge Road
                 St. Louis, MO 63121
Telephone No.:   (314) 553-5732

SUBSTANTIVE TOPICS COVERED:

The purpose of this study was to develop a data base by prospective, individual study from birth, permitting a developmental approach to the study of children's problems including mental retardation, reading problems, juvenile pregnancies, and adjudicated delinquency.

CHARACTERISTICS OF THE ORIGINAL SAMPLE:

Year the study began: 1966

Subject selection process: Selection criterion was defined as biological risk, using the International Classification of Diseases (ICDA) for experimental Ss; controls were the next case seriatim not meeting the ICDA condition. A full range of SES levels, including inner city and minority poor families, was incorporated.

Total number of subjects at Time 1: N = 1,008

Ages at Time 1: Birth

Sex distribution: Equal numbers of females and males

Socioeconomic status: 57% working class, 36% poverty class, 17% middle/upper middle class

Race/ethnicity: 50% African-American, 50% white

Years of Completed Waves:[a]

Year	N=	Age ranges
1966	1,008	Birth
1966-1967	800	6 mos.
1967-1968	580	1-1.5 yrs.
1968-1969	724	2-2.5 yrs.
1969-1970	756	3-3.5 yrs.
1970-1971	825	4-4.5 yrs.
1971-1972	806	5-5.5 yrs.
1972-1973	766	6-6.5 yrs.
1973-1974	284	7 yrs.
1974-1975	221	8 yrs.
1975-1976	327	9 yrs.
1976-1977	260	10 yrs.
1977-1978	180	11 yrs.
1978-1979	146	12 yrs.
1979-1980	199	13 yrs.
1980-1981	150	14 yrs.
1981-1982	146	15 yrs.
1982-1983	130	16 yrs.
1983-1984	96	17 yrs.
1984-1985	123	18 yrs.

Comments:
a. These are approximations.

INFORMATION ON SAMPLE ATTRITION:

During the 19-year period of study, 912 of 1,008 Ss (94.7%) were not retrieved for further study. During the 19-year period of the study, there was a core sample of approximately 700 case studies from birth to age 9 years. In the remaining years to age 18, the core sample was deliberately reduced to 100-200 cases. At most ages, it was not the goal to take identical data from all Ss; a common test battery was given to all, with additional tests administered to some, and additional different tests given to others. The concept of a core group needs to be understood in the context of prospective programmatic study resulting in a broad range of developmental criteria, and a data base of about 450,000 items. Due to broad fluctuations in sample size at each wave, it was not possible to define a core sample. Attrition due to Ss progressive refusal to participate resulted from the burden of semiannual data taking, and the principal investigator eliminated some cases due to risk of violence to caseworkers.

CONSTRUCTS MEASURED: INSTRUMENTS USED

Early development: Apgar Score, Preschool Attainment Record (PAR), Biosocial risk ratings (5)

Intelligence: Peabody Picture Vocabulary Test (PPVT); Wechsler's Primary and Preschool Scale of Intelligence (WPPSI); Wechsler's Intelligence Scale for Children (WISC); Coloured Progressive Matrices (CPM)

Verbal language development: Verbal Language Development Scale (VLDS)

Picture vocabulary: Full Range Picture Vocabulary Test (FRPVT)

School readiness: Preschool Inventory

Psycholinguistic abilities: Illinois Test of Psycholinguistic Abilities (ITPA)

Auditory comprehension, spoken language: Myklebust Pupil Rating Scale

Articulation: Denver Test of Articulation

Receptive auditory discrimination: Wepman Test of Auditory Discrimination (X-error score)

Attitude towards school: Attitude Towards School (Total score + 3 subscores) (Darrington & Gumm)

Scholastic motivation: Scholastic Motivation Test (Russell)

Time orientation: Future Time Perspective Test (Sarbin & Kolik)

Test anxiety: Test Anxiety Scale (Sarason)

Social stress: Life Changes Inventory (Coddington)

The world of adolescents: *HS & B* "Sophomore Questionnaire"

Verbal ability: Word Knowledge Test (Lorge-Thorndike)

Child-rearing values: Authoritarian Child Rearing Ideology "AFI 68" (Loevinger)

Self-concept: Self Concept Scale (Wallace)

N Achievement: N Achievement Scale (Smith) (Ray)

Self-esteem: Performance Self-Esteem Scale (Stake)

Extroversion: Extroversion Scale (Eysenck)

Neuroticism: Neuroticism Scale (Eysenck)

Delinquency: Delinquency Questionnaire (Janson)

Delinquency (non-adjudicated): Self-Reported Delinquency (Elliot)

Self-acceptance: *HS & B* Self-Acceptance Scale

Knowledge about jobs: Knowing About Jobs Scale (Crites)

Vocational choice: Choosing Jobs Scale (Crites)

Students' perceptions of school: *HS & B* Rating of School

Social stress: *HS & B* Life Events (Newcomb)

Life satisfaction: Life Satisfaction Index (Neugarten, S. & B.)

Familiarity with computers: Familiarity with computers

REPRESENTATIVE REFERENCES:

Jordan, T. E. (1976). Developmental factors influencing exceptional status at age six years. *Contemporary Educational Psychology, 1,* 4-19.

Jordan, T. E. (1980). *Development in the preschool years.* New York: Academic Press.

Jordan, T. E. (1984). The St. Louis Baby Study: Theory, practice, and findings. In S.A. Mednick, M. Harway, & K. M. Finello (Eds.), *Handbook of longitudinal research: Vol. 1. Birth and childhood cohorts.* New York: Praeger.

Jordan, T. E. (1991). From birth to eighteen: Modelling self-reported delinquency. *International Review of Comparative and Applied Criminal Justice, 15,* 1.

CURRENT STATUS OF THE STUDY:

a. No further waves of data collection are planned.

b. All of the data are in machine-readable format.

c. Data are available for secondary analysis from the study contact person.

■ Time Allocation Study, 1975

Juster, F. Thomas; Hill, Martha; and Stafford, Frank

Contact Person: F. Thomas Juster
Address: Institute for Social Research
University of Michigan
Box 1248
Ann Arbor, MI 48106
Telephone No.: (313) 764-4207

SUBSTANTIVE TOPICS COVERED:

The purpose of this study was to provide detailed longitudinal data on the time use patterns of American households.

CHARACTERISTICS OF THE ORIGINAL SAMPLE:

Year the study began: 1975

Subject selection process: The population for the original study in 1975-1976 was drawn from a national probability survey. Those respondents for whom three or four waves of data were collected in the first study, and who were heads of households or the wives of household heads, were eligible for the 1981 follow-up.

Total number of subjects at Time 1: N = 1,519

Ages at Time 1: 18-97 yrs.

Sex distribution: Equal numbers of females and males throughout
Socioeconomic status: National representative sample of the adult population
Race/ethnicity: National representative sample of the adult population

Years of Completed Waves:

Years	N=	Age ranges
(Cohort 1: Adults)		
1975 (Oct.)	1,519	18 yrs. and above
1976 (Feb.)	1,147	18 yrs. and above
1976 (May)	1,007	18 yrs. and above
1976 (Sept.)	947	18 yrs. and above
1981 (Feb.)	620	23 yrs. and above
1981 (May)	554	23 yrs. and above
1981 (Aug.)	511	23 yrs. and above
1981 (Nov.)	493	23 yrs. and above
(Cohort 2: Spouses)		
1975 (Oct.)	887	18 yrs. and above
1976 (Feb.)	644	18 yrs. and above
1976 (May)	556	18 yrs. and above
1976 (Sept.)	500	18 yrs. and above
1981 (Feb.)	376	23 yrs. and above
1981 (May)	297	23 yrs. and above
1981 (Aug.)	258	23 yrs. and above
1981 (Nov.)	241	24 yrs. and above
(Cohort 3: Children)[a]		
1981 (Feb.)	492	3-17 yrs.

Comments:
a. Further information was gathered about the children in the study from 202 of their teachers in November 1981.

INFORMATION ON SAMPLE ATTRITION:

During the 6-year period of study, 1,026 of 1,519 Ss (67.5%) were not retrieved for further study. The core sample consists of 493 Ss.

CONSTRUCTS MEASURED: INSTRUMENTS USED

Waves 1-4 (1981 data collection)

Time use: Time diary collected at each wave

Wave 1

Life satisfaction, housing, employment (job status, hours, training, wages, etc.); skills, talents; household organization, employment of activities: Personal Interview

Wave 2

Employment, life satisfaction, job income, family income, employments plans of wife, sex-role attitudes, family-making decisions, attitudes towards time, sex, role sharing; sex-role attitudes (women's independence), quality of marriage, social support, family's health: Telephone Interview

Wave 3

Neighborhood characteristics, employment status, satisfaction with household outputs and household help, effort expenditure, decision making, male-female expectations, television use, child's school performance, household rules, child's role models; child's goals, values, and expectations; child's sex-role expectations, child's work experience: Personal or Telephone Interview
Word recognition (child): Wide Range Achievement Test (Jastak & Jastak)

Wave 4

Family finances; employment (status, wages, emotional support for job); life satisfaction: Telephone Interview
Child's school performance: Teacher ratings

REPRESENTATIVE REFERENCES:

Hill, C. R. (1980). Parental care of children: Time diary estimates of quantity, predictability and variety. *Journal of Human Resources, 15*, 220-239.

Juster, F. T. (1986). Response errors in the measurement of time use. *Journal of the American Statistical Association, 81*, 390-402.

Juster, F. T., & Stafford, F. P. (Eds.). (1985). *Time, goods, and well-being.* Ann Arbor: Survey Research Center, Institute for Social Research, University of Michigan.

Stafford, F. P., & Duncan, G. J. (1980). The use of time and technology by households in the United States. In R. G. Ehrenberg (Ed.), *Research in labor economics (Vol. III).* Greenwich, CT: JAI Press.

CURRENT STATUS OF THE STUDY:

a. No further waves of data collection are planned.
b. Data are in machine-readable format.
c. Data are available for secondary analysis through the Inter-University Consortium for Political and Social Research (ICPSR).

Intergenerational Transmission of Deviance, 1971

Kandel, Denise

Contact Person: Denise Kandel
Address: Department of Psychiatry
                  College of Physicians & Surgeons
                  Columbia University
                  722 West 168th Street, Box 20
                  New York, NY 10032
Telephone No.:   (212) 568-2570

SUBSTANTIVE TOPICS COVERED:

The study examines psychosocial development in adolescence and young adulthood; the natural history, antecedents, and consequences of drug use; the intergenerational transmission of deviance; processes of interpersonal influences; and the antecedents and consequences of adolescent depression.

CHARACTERISTICS OF THE ORIGINAL SAMPLE:

Year the study began: 1971

Subject selection process: Subjects were selected by a two-stage random sampling of adolescents who were representative of public secondary school students in grades 9-12 in New York state during Fall 1971. A stratified sample of 18 high schools was first chosen, and a subsequent sampling of home rooms within schools was conducted. The total cross-section of Ss to whom the questionnaires were administered was 8,209 Ss. In 1980 a long-term follow-up of a subsample was conducted. The target population was drawn from the enrollment lists of half the home rooms from grades 10 and 11 and includes students absent from school at the time of the initial study. The cohort was reinterviewed in 1984 and 1990. At Time 4, a mailed survey was conducted of all spouse/partners (73% participated, N = 561). In 1990 personal interviews were conducted with spouses and partners of focal respondents who were parents of a child 6 years of age and over (N = 336, representing an 82% completion rate); oldest (N = 264, 87%) and second-oldest (N = 106, 85%) children 9-17 years old. Data were also collected by mail from 1) spouse/partners when there was no child 6 years of age and older in the household (N = 300, 71%); and 2) teachers of children 9-17 years of age, who were interviewed, and the oldest child 6-8, who was not interviewed (N = 420, 89%, completion rate of teachers for whom parents gave permission to contact); 96% of focals interviewed at Time 4 and still alive at Time 5 were reinterviewed, for a 72% completion rate 19 years later of those alive from the original 1971 target school enrollment list.

Total number of subjects at Time 1: N = 1,651 (1,333 regular students and 318 absentees)[a]

Ages at Time 1: 14-17 yrs.

Sex distribution: 54% females, 46% male

Socioeconomic status: Data were gathered, but specific information about percent distribution by class was not available.

Race/ethnicity: 80% white, 10% African-American, 7% Hispanic, 0.6% Asian-American, 0.8% Native American

Years of Completed Waves:

Years	N=	Age ranges
1971	1,651	14-17 yrs.
1980	1,325[b]	23-27 yrs.
1984	1,222[c]	27-31 yrs.
1990	1,160[d]	33-37 yrs.

Comments:

a. The 1,651 Ss represent a subsample of the 8,209 Ss who participated in the original school survey.

b. In 1980 data were collected on Ss of the initial (1971) 10th-11th graders who participated in the school survey (sampled at the rate of 53%), adolescents enrolled in the same home rooms as the initial 1971 survey, but had not participated in the study (sampled at the rate of 56%).

c. In 1984 all Ss interviewed in 1980 were targeted for follow-up.

d. In 1990 all Ss interviewed in 1984 were targeted for follow-up.

INFORMATION ON SAMPLE ATTRITION:

During the 19-year period of study, 462 of 1,622 Ss (28.5%) were not retrieved for further study. Twenty-nine Ss had died. The core sample consists of 1,160 Ss.

CONSTRUCTS MEASURED: INSTRUMENTS USED

Background information on parent and adolescent, adolescent drug behaviors, drug-related attitudes, self-image, norms, depression, personal growth orientation, academic orientation, lifestyle values, delinquent involvement, quality of parent-adolescent relations, parental drug behaviors, perceived peer drug behaviors and attitudes, drug availability, peer-adolescent relations: Self-administered, structured questionnaires; telephone interviews and mail questionnaires

Educational, occupational, and marital and parental histories; detailed histories of use of 12 classes of legal, illegal, and medically prescribed drugs; depression, self-image, quality of relationship with spouse/partner, parents and children; characteristics of three best friends, drug-related problems, psychophysiological symptoms, medical and psychiatric hospitalizations, delinquent behaviors, short measure of IQ; marital and parent-child interactions; children's academic performance, problem behaviors and delinquency: Structured personal interviews and drug and life history charts

REPRESENTATIVE REFERENCES:

Kandel, D. (1990). Parenting styles, drug use and children's adjustment in families of young adults. *Journal of Marriage and the Family, 52,* 183-196.

Kandel, D., Singer, E., & Kessler, R. (1976). The epidemiology of drug use among New York State high school students: Distribution, trends and changes in rates of use. *American Journal of Public Health, 66,* 43-53.

Kandel, D. B., & Yamaguchi, K. (1985). Developmental patterns of the use of legal, illegal and medically prescribed psychotropic drugs from adolescence to young adulthood. In C. L. Jones & R. Battjes (Eds.), *Etiology of drug abuse: Implications for prevention* (NIDA Research Monograph No. 56) (DHHS Publication No. ADM 85-1335). Washington, DC: Government Printing Office.

Yamaguchi, K., & Kandel, D. (1985). On the resolution of role incompatibility: Life event history analysis of family roles and marijuana use. *American Journal of Sociology, 90,* 1284-1325.

CURRENT STATUS OF THE STUDY:

a. Further waves of data collection are tentatively planned.
b. Most data are in machine-readable format.
c. Data are not available for secondary analysis from the study contact person.

■ Alameda County Human Population Laboratory Study, 1965

Kaplan, George

Contact Person: George Kaplan
Address: Human Population Laboratory
                California State Department of Health Services
                2151 Berkeley Way
                Annex 2, Room 300
                Berkeley, CA 94704
Telephone No.: (415) 540-2396

SUBSTANTIVE TOPICS COVERED:

The aims of the Human Population Laboratory consist of evaluating the degree of health (mental, social, and physical) of residents of Alameda County, California; determining to what extent degrees of health in one health area correspond with similar degrees of health in another area; and in discerning the relationships between specific demographic characteristics, various lifestyles (i.e., common health practices and social relationships), and degrees of physical health.

CHARACTERISTICS OF THE ORIGINAL SAMPLE:

Year the study began: 1965

Subject selection process: A three-stage, stratified, random, area probability sample of households was drawn from residents of Alameda County (including the cities of Oakland and Berkeley). Participants were non-institutionalized, 20 years of age or older, and married. The sample constitutes 86% of the total population (N = 8,083).

Total number of subjects at Time 1: N = 6,928

Ages at Time 1: 17-94 yrs.

Sex distribution: Approximately equal numbers of females and males throughout

Socioeconomic status: Data gathered, but information on percent distribution by socioeconomic status was not available.

Race/ethnicity: 81.1% white, 12.4% African-American, 3.1% Asian-American, 2.4% Hispanic, 1% other

Years of Completed Waves:

Years	N=	Age ranges
1965	6,928	17-94 yrs.
1974	4,864	26-103 yrs.
1983	1,799[a]	34-99+ yrs.

Comments:
a. The third follow-up was a 50% subsample of subjects from Wave 2. In 1974, a new sample of Alameda County residents was drawn to study changes in the County between 1965 and 1974. Mortality data were also collected for the 1965 sample spanning 1965-1985 (1,565 deaths), and for the 1974 sample spanning 1974-1985 (347 deaths).

INFORMATION ON SAMPLE ATTRITION:

During the 18-year period of study, 2,064 of 6,928 Ss (29.8%) were not retrieved for study. The primary reasons for sample attrition were death and failure to re-locate subjects. The core sample size, based on the first two data points, consists of 4,864 Ss.

CONSTRUCTS MEASURED: INSTRUMENTS USED

Alcohol consumption, cigarette smoking, weight relative to height, physical activity, breakfast and snack habits: Health Practices Index

Functional disabilities, chronic conditions and symptoms, energy level: Health status

Marital status, contact with friends and relatives, group memberships: Social networks

Depression: 18 self-reported feeling-state items

Habits of daily life (smoking, alcohol use, patterns of eating, amount of physical activity), biological factors to health (age, height, weight, use of medical services), mental health, psychological well-being, ego resiliency, degree of experienced alienation (anomie), neurotic traits, and psychiatric history: "Health and Ways of Living" questionnaire (1965)

Social well-being: Social Network Index (from 1965 questionnaire)

Disability, chronic conditions, impairments, energy level, and recurrent symptoms: Physical Health Index (from 1965 questionnaire)

Stressful events (1965-1974), use of health care services: 1974 Panel Study questionnaire

REPRESENTATIVE REFERENCES:

Berkman L. F., & Breslow, L. (1983). *Health and ways of living: The Alameda County Study.* New York: Oxford University Press.

Berkman, L. R., & Syme, S. L. (1979). Social networks, host resistance, and mortality: A nine year follow-up study of Alameda County residents. *American Journal of Epidemiology, 109*(2), 186-204.

Kaplan, G. A. (1985). Psychosocial aspects of chronic illness: Direct and indirect associations with ischemic heart disease mortality. In R. M. Kaplan & M. H. Criqui (Eds.), *Behavioral epidemiology and disease prevention* (pp. 237-269). New York: Plenum.

Kaplan, G. A., Roberts, R. E., Camacho, T. C., & Coyne J. C. (1987). Psychosocial predictors of depression: Prospective evidence from the Human Population Laboratory Studies. *American Journal of Epidemiology, 125*(2), 206-220.

CURRENT STATUS OF THE STUDY:

a. Further waves of data collection are planned.

b. Most data are in machine-readable format.

c. The data are available for secondary analysis from the study contact person.

■ The Woodlawn Mental Health Longitudinal Community Epidemiological Project, 1963

Kellam, Sheppard; Ensminger, Margaret; and Branch, Jeannette

Contact Person: Margaret Ensminger
Address: Johns Hopkins University
                School of Hygiene and Public Health
                Health Policy and Management
                624 North Broadway
                Baltimore, MD 21205
Telephone No.: (301) 955-2312

SUBSTANTIVE TOPICS COVERED:

The study examines first grade children in an urban ghetto community. The study focuses on the evolving relationships between psychological well-being and social adaptational status within and across stages of life. Of major concern is the role that environmental characteristics (such as family structure and atmosphere, and neighborhood and classroom characteristics) play in mental health over the life cycle. Specific concerns address the examination of developing family structure, long-term consequences of teenage motherhood for the mother and child, evaluation of preventive trials on first graders, participation in a broad-based teenage treatment program, explanations of sex differences, and applications of social control theory.

CHARACTERISTICS OF THE ORIGINAL SAMPLE:

Year the study began: 1963
Subject selection process: The epidemiologic studies were done on all first graders from nine public schools and three parochial schools of the 1964-1965 class through the 1967-1968 class. All first grade children from this poor African-American community on the South Side of Chicago were assessed periodically in four consecutive total cohorts.
Total number of subjects at Time 1: N = 1,700
Ages at Time 1: 6-7 yrs.
Sex distribution: Approximately equal numbers of females and males throughout
Socioeconomic status: 53% poverty class, 40% working class, 7% upper middle/middle class
Race/ethnicity: 100% African-American

Years of Completed Waves:

Years	$N=$[a]	Age ranges
(Cohort 1)		
1964-1965	1,700	6 yrs.
(Cohort 2)		
1965-1966	1,600	6 yrs.
(Cohort 3A)		
1967-1968	1,242	6 yrs.
1975	705	15 yrs.
(Cohort 3B)[b]		
1967	1,242	20-50 yrs.
1975	939	30-60 yrs.

Comments:
a. A breakdown of each cohort group by year, N, age, and sex distribution was not available. However, the principal investigators report that data were collected three times in first grade at time of first report card, mid-year, end-of-year, and again in third grade. Data are currently being collected on "official" records for the 1966-1967 cohort of first graders. Motor vehicle records, criminal justice records, and drug- and alcohol-treatment records are being collected for the 1,242 cases. The records will be used as indicators of alcohol and drug problems and criminality. The investigators hope to do face-to-face interviews with the population.
b. Ss from Cohort 3B are the mothers of Ss in Cohort 3A.

INFORMATION ON SAMPLE ATTRITION:

During the 11-year period of study, 437 of 1,242 Ss (35.2%) in Cohort 3A were not retrieved for further study. Of the 1,242 mothers of Cohort 3B Ss, 303 Ss (24.4%) were also not retrieved. The sample included children who moved out of Woodlawn and new children who moved in. The core sample consists of 705 children and 939 mothers.

CONSTRUCTS MEASURED: INSTRUMENTS USED

Adults present in the household, child-rearing role specification, affection and rule setting and enforcing, value orientations around purposes of education, sense of potency, internality/externality, formal and informal social integration of family, involvement with school, plus other areas: Interviews with mother
Assessment of readiness for learning in school: Metropolitan Readiness Test
Psychiatric symptom status: Direct clinical observation
Psychiatric symptom status in first grade: Mother Symptom Inventory
Tension, nervousness, and sadness, how child feels he or she is doing at school tasks in third grade: Children's "How I Feel"
Adequacy of the child's performance on each of the social task demands set by teacher in first and third grades: Teacher's Observation of Classroom Adaptation (TOCA)
Aptitude: Grades, intelligence tests, readiness for school and achievement tests
Psychiatric symptoms, self-esteem, self-perception of social adaptational status in important social fields, and satisfaction with social adaptational status—at age 16 or 17: Adolescent's "How I Feel"

Criminality: Criminal justice (police arrest) records
Frequency of drug use, reports of family practices and values around affection and
rules, self-reports of delinquency, sexual behavior and attitudes, and other
areas—at age 16 or 17: Adolescent's "What's Happening"

REPRESENTATIVE REFERENCES:

Ensminger, M. E. (1990). Sexual activity and problem behaviors among black, urban adolescents. *Child Development, 61*(6).

Kellam, S., Brown, C. H., Rubin, B. R., & Ensminger, M. (1983). Paths leading to teenage psychiatric symptoms and substance use: Developmental epidemiological studies in Woodlawn. In S. B. Guze, F. L. Earls, & J. E. Barrett (Eds.), *Child psychopathology and development*. New York: Raven Press.

Kellam, S. G., Ensminger, M. E., Branch, J., Brown, C. H., & Fleming, J. P. (1984). The Woodlawn Mental Health Longitudinal Community Epidemiological Project. In S. A. Mednick, M. Harway, & K. M. Finello, (Eds.), *Handbook of longitudinal research: Vol. 2. Teenage and adult cohorts*. New York: Praeger.

Pearson, J. L., Hunter, A. G., Ensminger, M. E., & Kellam, S. G. (1990). Black grandmothers in multigenerational households: Diversity in family structure and parenting involvement in the Woodlawn community. *Child Development, 61*(2), 434-442.

CURRENT STATUS OF THE STUDY:

a. Further waves of data collection are planned.
b. Most data are in machine-readable format.
c. The data are available for secondary analysis from the study contact person.

■ Project REACH Longitudinal Study, 1977

Keogh, Barbara; and Bernheimer, Lucinda

Contact Person: Lucinda Bernheimer
Address: University of California, Los Angeles
UCLA Sociobehavioral Group
760 Westwood Plaza
47-438C NPI
Los Angeles, CA 90024-1759
Telephone No.: (213) 825-2861

SUBSTANTIVE TOPICS COVERED:

Project REACH was designed to document the development of children diagnosed as developmentally delayed with uncertain or unknown etiology. Family adaptation over time has been addressed.

CHARACTERISTICS OF THE ORIGINAL SAMPLE:

Year the study began: 1977

Subject selection process: Subjects were selected from referrals made by pediatricians, referral centers, intervention programs, and community preschools. Subjects had developmental delays of one year or more in at least one area. Excluded were children with chromosomal problems or children whose delay resulted either from maternal alcohol or drug abuse or primarily from emotional pathology.

Total number of subjects at Time 1: N = 44

Ages at Time 1: 26-42 mos.

Sex distribution: 65.9% male, 35.1% female

Socioeconomic status: 70% middle class/upper middle class, 30% working class

Race/ethnicity: 100% white

Years of Completed Waves:

Years[a]	N=	Age ranges
1979-1981	44	25-42 mos.
1983-1984	37	5-7 yrs.
1985	37	7-9 yrs.
1986	37	8-10 yrs.
1987	37	9-11 yrs.
1988	37	10-12 yrs.

Comments:
a. Data were collected at 6-month intervals.

INFORMATION ON SAMPLE ATTRITION:

During the 9-year period of study, 7 of 44 Ss (15.9%) were not retrieved for further study. Attrition was due to Ss moving. The core sample consists of 37 Ss.

CONSTRUCTS MEASURED: INSTRUMENTS USED

Cognitive status: Bayley Scales of Infant Development, McCarthy Scales of Children's Abilities, Stanford-Binet Intelligence Test

Developmental status: Gesell Developmental Schedules

Language: Sequenced Inventory of Communication Development

Temperament: Thomas and Chess Temperament Scale (Parent Form), Thomas and Chess Temperament Scale (Teacher Form)

Self-help skills: Alpern-Bolls Developmental Profile

Behavior problems: Achenbach Child Behavior Checklist (parent and teacher)

Social competence: Gesten Health Resources Inventory (parent and teacher)

Home environment: Caldwell's Home Observation for Measurement of the Environment Scale; Resources and Support Systems Interview

REPRESENTATIVE REFERENCES:

Bernheimer, L. P., & Keogh, B. K. (1986). Developmental delays and developmental disabilities in preschool children. In B. K. Keogh (Ed.), *Advances in special education: Vol. 5* (pp. 61-94). Greenwich, CT: JAI Press.

Bernheimer, L. P., & Keogh, B. K. (1987). Developmental delays in preschool children: Assessment over time. *European Journal of Special Needs Education, 2*(4), 211-220.

Bernheimer, L. P., & Keogh, B. K. (1988). The stability of cognitive performance of developmentally delayed children. *American Journal of Mental Retardation, 92*(6), 539-542.

Bernheimer, L. P., Young, M. S., & Winston, P. J. (1984). Stress over time: Parents with young handicapped children. *Journal of Developmental and Behavioral Pediatrics, 4*(3), 177-181.

CURRENT STATUS OF THE STUDY:

a. Further waves of data collection are planned.[1]

b. Most of the data are in machine-readable format.

c. Data are not currently available for secondary analysis.

Comments:

1. The study will focus increasingly on competence in the subject population, as well as family adaptation as the Ss move through adolescence into young adulthood.

■ The Precursors Study, 1947

Klag, Michael J.

Contact Person:　Michael J. Klag
Address:　　　　School of Medicine
　　　　　　　　The Johns Hopkins University
　　　　　　　　550 North Broadway
　　　　　　　　Suite 502
　　　　　　　　Baltimore, MD 21205
Telephone No.:　(301) 955-0496

SUBSTANTIVE TOPICS COVERED:

The Precursors Study consists of an integrated body of information concerning 1,337 former Johns Hopkins medical students in classes graduating in the years 1948 through 1964. These data, both longitudinal and cross-sectional, have been collected over a period of 43 years (January 1947 through 1990). The purpose of the study is to identify youthful characteristics of the subjects that are importantly associated with subsequent disease and death—by mid-life and at older ages.

The study also examines factors preceding the onset of hypertension and coronary heart disease, and ways to predict suicide, death, and premature diseases. The study also focuses on physicians as an occupational group in terms of job stress, career achievements, and malpractice.

CHARACTERISTICS OF THE ORIGINAL SAMPLE:

Year the study began: 1947

Subject selection process: Subjects were Johns Hopkins University medical students in classes graduating in 1948 through 1964. Ages ranged from 21 to 38 at graduation.

Total number of subjects at Time 1: N = 1,337

Ages at Time 1: 21-38 yrs.

Sex distribution: 91% male, 9% female

Socioeconomic status: 100% middle/upper class

Race/ethnicity: 97.3% white, 2.7% other

Years of Completed Waves:[a]

Years	N =	Age ranges
1947-1990	1,337	21-38 yrs.

Comments:
a. There have been 35 annual follow-ups since 1953.

INFORMATION ON SAMPLE ATTRITION:

During the 43-year period of the study, 95% of the subjects have responded within any 3-year period.

CONSTRUCTS MEASURED: INSTRUMENTS USED

Genetic, Physiological, Metabolic, and Environmental Data

Age, ancestry, education, religion, marital status, jobs, military service, and medical specialty interest: General background

Medical history, physical and cardiovascular examination, teleoroentgenogram, urinalysis, and STS: Medical examination

Detailed parental history, and detailed history on grandparents, aunts and uncles: Family studies

Casual blood pressure and heart rate, resting blood pressure and heart rate: Electrocardiogram, cold pressor test, double master exercise test, oximeter-controlled anoxemia test (1948-1953), ballistiocardiographic smoking test (1953-1964), and timed vital capacity (1948-1957; 1961-1964)

Height, weight, ponderal index, total serum cholesterol (1949), circulating eosinophil count (1950-1064), and sodium withdrawal test (1984-1954; 1957)

Anthropometry, constitutional photograph, and somatotype: Anthropologic studies (chiefly 1960-1964):

Psychological Data[1]

Habits of sleeping, eating, smoking, drinking, medication, nervous tension, work, recreation and exercise: Habit survey questionnaire

Interpersonal family attitudes, religious background, educational background: Questionnaire

Personality: Rorschach Inkblot Test scores and interpretations (individual protocols, group protocols); figure-drawing test and interpretations (1952-1964)

Vocational interests: Strong Vocational Interest Blank and score (1958-1964)

Stress: Stress sheets

Comments:
1. Classes of 1948 through 1964 unless otherwise indicated.

REPRESENTATIVE REFERENCES:

Graves, P. L., & Thomas, C. B. (1985). Correlates of midlife career achievement among women physicians. *Journal of the American Medical Association, 254*(6), 781-787.

LaCroix, A. Z., Mead, L. A., Liang, K.-Y., Thomas, C. B. & Pearson, T. A. (1986). Coffee consumption and incidence of coronary heart disease. *New England Journal of Medicine, 315*(8), 549-563.

Shaffer, J. W., Graves. P. L., Mead, L. A., Thomas, C. B., & Pearson, T. A. (1986). Development of alternate methods for scoring the Rorschach interaction scale. *Educational and Psychological Measurement, 46,* 837-844.

Thomas, J., Semenya, K., Thomas, C. B., Thomas, D. J., Neser, W. B., Pearson, T. A., & Gillum, R. F. (1987). Precursors of hypertension in black compared to white medical students. *Journal of Chronic Disease, 40*(7), 721-727.

CURRENT STATUS OF THE STUDY:

a. Further waves of data collection are planned.

b. Most of the data are in machine-readable format.

c. Data are available for secondary analysis from the study contact person.

■ Childhood Depression: Nosologic Developmental Aspects, 1978

Kovacs, Maria

Contact person: Maria Kovacs
Address: Western Psychiatric Institute and Clinic
                 3811 O'Hara Street
                 Pittsburgh, PA 15213
Telephone No.:   (412) 624-2043

SUBSTANTIVE TOPICS COVERED:

This study examines the course and outcome of childhood onset depressive disorder; psychosocial and family correlates, functional consequences, and young adult outcomes.

CHARACTERISTICS OF THE ORIGINAL SAMPLE:

Year the study began: 1978

Subject selection process: Subjects selected met the following criteria: (a) Ss were between 8 and 13 years of age; (b) Ss were not mentally retarded; (c) Ss had no major systemic illness; (d) Ss had ambulatory psychiatric and medical status; (e) Ss were living with parents or legal guardians; and (f) Ss resided within commuting distance of greater Pittsburgh.

Total number of subjects at Time 1: N = 134 depressed controls; N = 49 pathologic non-depressed controls

Ages at Time 1: 8-13 yrs.

Sex distribution: 53% females, 47% males (Cohort 1); 24% females, 76% males (Cohort 2)

Socioeconomic status: 74% middle/upper middle class, 26% lowest class (for cohorts combined)

Race/ethnicity: 62% white, 34% African-American, 4% multiracial (Cohort 1); 63% white, 29% African-American, 4% multiracial, 4% other (Cohort 2)

Years of Completed Waves:

Years	N=	Age ranges
1978-1990	134[a]	8-25 yrs. (Cohort 1)
1978-1990	49[a]	8-25 yrs. (Cohort 2)

Comments:

a. Baseline samples were drawn from 1978 to 1984 for both cohorts during which time Ss were 8-13 years of age. Subsequent follow-up has been continuous yearly for both cohorts. Ss were followed at 2 months, 6 months, 1 year, and at 6-month intervals thereafter.

INFORMATION ON SAMPLE ATTRITION:

Due to the continuous nature of follow-up, exact figures on attrition cannot be provided. However, average attrition for both cohorts has been estimated at 15% at any given time. Subjects who had dropped out of the study had refused to participate any further. Other Ss had moved away, or were currently unavailable for follow-up. Due to fluctuations in the size of the participating samples, specifying a core sample carries little value.

CONSTRUCTS MEASURED: INSTRUMENTS USED

Psychiatric/psychologic symptoms, psychiatric diagnoses: Interview Schedule for Children (ISC) (semi-structured child psychiatric interview)
Psychological well-being: Standardized clinical assessment of parents
Background: Demographic data collection
Symptoms, cognitive stage, intelligence, family adjustment, social support: Parent and child self-rated scales
Pubertal stage, height and weight: Physical examination

REPRESENTATIVE REFERENCES:

Kovacs, M., & Gatsonis, C. (1989). Stability and change in childhood-onset depressive disorders: Longitudinal course as a diagnostic validator. In L. Robins, J. Fleiss, & J. Barrett (Eds.), *The validity of psychiatric diagnosis*. New York: Raven Press.

Kovacs, M., Gatsonis, C., Paulauskas, S., & Richards, C. (1989). Depressive disorders in childhood. IV. A longitudinal study of comorbidity with and risk for anxiety disorders. *Archives of General Psychiatry, 46*, 776-782.

Kovacs, M., & Paulauskas, S. (1984). Developmental stage and the expression of depressive disorders. In D. Cicchetti and K. Schneider-Rosen (Eds.), *Childhood depression: New directions for child development* (No. 26). San Francisco: Jossey-Bass.

Kovacs, M., Paulauskas, S., Gatsonis, C., & Richards, C. (1988). Depressive disorders in childhood. III. A longitudinal study of comorbidity with and risk for conduct disorders. *Journal of Affective Disorders, 15*, 205-217.

CURRENT STATUS OF THE STUDY:

a. Further data collection is planned.
b. Most of the data are in machine-readable format.
c. Data are not available for secondary analysis.

■ Longitudinal Study of Children from Kindergarten into the Adult Years, 1953

Kraus, Philip E.

Contact Person: Philip E. Kraus
Address: Hunter College
                 40 East 84th Street
                 New York, NY 10028
Telephone No.:   (212) 628-1593

SUBSTANTIVE TOPICS COVERED:

This study examines children's early and middle school years, allowing discernment of individual patterns of academic success or failure, and also examines children's' learning and adjustment over time.

CHARACTERISTICS OF THE ORIGINAL SAMPLE:

Year the study began: 1953
Subject selection process: Children in five New York City schools were originally selected for study. Schools chosen were those where opportunities for research and study were deemed greatest.
Total number of subjects at Time 1: N = 294
Ages at Time 1: 4-7 yrs.
Sex distribution: Approximately equal numbers of females and males throughout
Socioeconomic status: 50% middle/upper middle class, 50% working class
Race/ethnicity: 52% white, 46% African-American, 2% Hispanic

Years of Completed Waves:

Years	N=	Age ranges
1953-1954	294	4-7 yrs.
1954-1955	290[a]	5-8 yrs.
1955-1956	290[a]	6-9 yrs.
1956-1957	190[a]	7-10 yrs.
1957-1958	185[a]	8-11 yrs.
1958-1959	165	9-12 yrs.
1959-1960	165[a]	10-13 yrs.
1960-1961	160[a]	11-14 yrs.
1961-1962	148	12-15 yrs.
1963-1964	138[a]	13-16 yrs.
1964-1965	105[a]	14-17 yrs.
1965-1966	64	15-18 yrs.

Comments:
a. Estimated number of Ss followed-up.

INFORMATION ON SAMPLE ATTRITION:

During the 13-year period of study, attrition was due to families moving out of the school district, community efforts to racially balance junior high schools, and the elimination of three of the original five schools due to budgetary cuts.

CONSTRUCTS MEASURED: INSTRUMENTS USED

Reading achievement: The New York Reading Readiness Test (Grade 1), New York Test of Growth in Reading (Grade 2), Gates Primary Reading Test (Grade 2), Metropolitan achievement tests (primary, elementary, intermediate and advanced) (Grades 3-9), Stanford Achievement Test-intermediate (Grade 5)

Math achievement: New York Inventory of Mathematical Concepts (Grades 1-5), Metropolitan Achievement Tests-intermediate (Grade 6)

Intelligence: Pintner-Cunningham Primary Test (Grade 1), Otis Quick Scoring Mental Ability Test-Alpha (Grade 3), Otis Quick Scoring Mental Ability Test-Beta (Grade 6), Pintner General Ability Test (Grade 9), Wechsler Intelligence Scale for Children, Revised Stanford-Binet Intelligence Scale, Henmon-Nelson Tests of Mental Ability

Behavior and personality: Haggerty-Olson-Wickman Behavior Rating Schedules, California Test of Personality, Ohio Social Acceptance Scale

Achievement and interest in reading: Teacher's estimate of reading development

Child's level of potential: Teacher's estimate of intelligence

Children's reactions to and participation in classroom activity: Attitude toward classroom activity

Extent of behavioral adjustment of each child and teacher recommendations for special services where indicated: General adjustment rating scale

Reactions and attitudes of children toward various phases of school environment and personal lives: Children's questionnaires

Interrelationships among children: Sociogram Scale

Degree to which child is accepted by classmates and extent to which child reaches out and seeks the friendship of other children: Ohio Social Acceptance Scale

Parental attitudes toward the schools: Parent questionnaires

REPRESENTATIVE REFERENCES:

Kraus, P. E. (1973). *Yesterday's children: A longitudinal study of children from kindergarten into the adult years*. New York: John Wiley.

Kraus, P. E. (1984). A longitudinal study of children from kindergarten into the adult years. In S. A. Mednick, M. Harway, & K. M. Finello (Eds.), *Handbook of longitudinal research: Vol. I. Birth and childhood cohorts* (pp. 353-363). New York: Praeger.

CURRENT STATUS OF THE STUDY:

a. No further waves of data collection are planned.
b. Most data are not in machine-readable format.
c. Data are not available for secondary analysis from the study contact person.

■ Patterns of Concrete Operational Development, 1971

Kuhn, Deanna

Contact Person: Deanna Kuhn
Address: Columbia University
                 Teacher's College
                 Box 119
                 520 120th Street
                 New York, NY 10027
Telephone No.:   (212) 678-3885

SUBSTANTIVE TOPICS COVERED:

The study examines the development of concrete operations in children, focusing on a variety of logical, physical, and social concepts; assesses whether progress with respect to one concept coincides with progress on other concepts; assesses within- and inter-task continuities and changes in processes and performances; tests Piaget's structural assertions about development.

CHARACTERISTICS OF THE ORIGINAL SAMPLE:

Year the study began: 1971

Subject selection process: Subjects were selected from kindergarten through second grades in a middle-class, urban public school. Subjects were pretested and classified into one of three groups regarding the attainment of concrete operations.

Total number of subjects at Time 1: N = 56

Ages at Time 1: 5-8 yrs.

Sex distribution: Approximately equal numbers of females and males throughout

Socioeconomic status: 100% middle/upper middle class

Race/ethnicity: 100% white

Years of Completed Waves:

Years	N=	Age ranges
1971	56	5 yrs., 5 mos.-8 yrs., 2 mos.[a]
1972	56	5 yrs., 11 mos.-8 yrs., 9 mos.
1972	56	6 yrs., 5 mos.-9 yrs., 3 mos.

Comments:

a. A breakdown of the ages was available only for the core sample. Information on the ages of all Ss (N = 68) at the first data point was not available.

INFORMATION ON SAMPLE ATTRITION:

During the one-year period of study, all Ss were retrieved for further study. The core sample consists of 56 Ss.

CONSTRUCTS MEASURED: INSTRUMENTS USED[1]

Intelligence: Wechsler Intelligence Scale for Children
Cognitive development: Classification, seriation, multiple classification, multiple seriation, and conservation
Egocentric thought and causal relations: Floating objects task (Piaget)
Development of moral judgment: Kohlberg's Moral Judgment Interview
Social perspective taking: Flavell's Social Perspective Risk Taking Task
Comments:
1. A battery of experimental tasks was used to assess all constructs. Some tasks were devised by Kuhn and some were developed by other researchers.

REPRESENTATIVE REFERENCES:

Kuhn, D. (1976). Relation of two Piagetian stage transitions to IQ. *Developmental Psychology, 12,* 156-161.
Kuhn, D. (1976). Short-term longitudinal evidence for the sequentiality of Kohlberg's early stages of moral judgment. *Developmental Psychology, 12,* 162-166.
Kuhn, D., Langer, J., Kohlberg, L., & Haan, N. S. (1977). The development of formal operations in logical and moral judgment. *Genetic Psychology Monographs, 95*(1), 97-188.

CURRENT STATUS OF THE STUDY:

a. No further waves of data collection are planned.
b. Most data are not in machine-readable format.
c. The data are available for secondary analysis from the study contact person.

L

Rutgers Health and Human Development Project, 1979

Labouvie, Erich; and Pandina, Robert

Contact person: Erich Labouvie
Address: Center of Alcohol Studies
                Rutgers University
                New Brunswick, NJ 08903
Telephone No.: (201) 932-3580

SUBSTANTIVE TOPICS COVERED:

This study examines the development of alcohol and drug use in adolescence and young adulthood, including consequences and correlates of use.

CHARACTERISTICS OF THE ORIGINAL SAMPLE:

Year the study began: 1979
Subject selection process: A random household sample of subjects were selected.
Total number of subjects at Time 1: N = 1,380 (Cohorts 1-3)
Ages at Time 1: 12 yrs., 15 yrs., and 18 yrs.
Sex distribution: Approximately equal numbers of females and males throughout
Socioeconomic status: 55% working class, 35% middle/upper middle class, 10% poverty class (Cohort 1); 52% working class, 40% middle/upper middle class, 8% poverty class (Cohort 2); 51% working class, 42% middle/upper middle class, 7% poverty class (Cohort 3)
Race/ethnicity: 90% white, 8% African-American, 2% other

Years of Completed Waves:

Years	N=	Age ranges
(Cohort 1: Birth yrs. 1967-1969)		
1979	447	12 yrs.
1982	437	15 yrs.
1985	437	18 yrs.
(Cohort 2: Birth yrs. 1964-1966)		
1979	475	15 yrs.
1982	455	18 yrs.
1985	450	21 yrs.

Years of Completed Waves, Continued:

Years	N=	Age ranges
(Cohort 3: Birth yrs. 1961-1963)		
1979	458	18 yrs.
1982	416	21 yrs.
1985	416	24 yrs.

INFORMATION ON SAMPLE ATTRITION:

During the 6-year period of study, 77 of 1,380 Ss (5.6%) across three cohorts were not retrieved for further study: 10 of 447 Ss (2.3%) in Cohort 1; 25 of 475 Ss (5.3%) in Cohort 2; and 42 of 458 Ss (9.2%) in Cohort 3. The core sample consists of 1,303 Ss across three cohorts: 437 Ss in Cohort 1; 450 Ss in Cohort 2; and 416 Ss in Cohort 3.

CONSTRUCTS MEASURED: INSTRUMENTS USED

Sociodemographic information: Anonymous telephone interview, self-report questionnaires, Zuckerman Sensation Seeking Scale
Family life: Personal interview
Degree of interaction, social controls, behavior and attitudes of significant others: Questionnaire about relations with parents, siblings, friends; SCL-90R
Personality: Abbreviated version of the Personality Research Form
Physiological, behavioral-cognitive measures: Rod and frame (field independence/ dependence), autonomic level and reactivity, perceptual reactance and impulse control
Physiological measures: Pre- and post-test skin conductance and finger volume
Physical health: Medical examination
Frequency and quantity: Alcohol/drug use
Reasons for use, consequences of use: Use experiences
Self-esteem, sources of stress, coping behaviors, delinquency, school performance: Questionnaire

REPRESENTATIVE REFERENCES:

Labouvie, E. W. (1984). The Rutgers Health and Human Development Project: A longitudinal study of alcohol and drug use. In S. A. Mednick, M. Harway, & K. M. Finello (Eds.), *Handbook of longitudinal research: Vol. 2. Teenage and Adult Cohorts.* New York: Praeger.

Labouvie, E. W. (1986). Alcohol and marijuana use in relation to adolescent stress. *International Journal of Addictions, 21,*(3), 333-345.

Labouvie, E. W., & McGee, C. R. (1986). Relation of personality to alcohol and drug use in adolescence. *Journal of Consulting and Clinical Psychology, 54*(3), 289-293.

Pandina, R. J., Labouvie, E. W., & Raskin White, H. (1984). Potential contributions of the life span developmental approach to the study of adolescent alcohol and drug use: The Rutgers Health and Human Development Project, a working model. *Journal of Drug Issues, 14,* 253-268.

CURRENT STATUS OF THE STUDY:

a. Further waves of data collection are planned.

b. Most of the data are in machine-readable format.

c. Data are not available for secondary analysis.

■ The Family Research Project, 1966

Langner, Thomas S.

Contact person: Dr. Thomas S. Langner
Address: 202 Riverside Drive
               Apartment 3C
               New York, NY 10025
Telephone No.: (212) 865-0257

SUBSTANTIVE TOPICS COVERED:

The study investigates the etiology of psychiatric impairment and behavior disorders in children, with special emphasis on the role of environmental stressors and strain in contributing to mental disorders in children.

CHARACTERISTICS OF THE ORIGINAL SAMPLE:

Year the study began: 1966

Subject selection process: The cross-sectional sample was a representative sample of 1,034 children, ages 6-18 years. Ss were randomly selected from a cross-section of Manhattan households between 125th and Houston streets. Within that area of the city, a cluster of eight dwelling units was randomly selected from each health area designated by the City Planning Commission, after which every 30th cluster was selected within those designated health areas. Eligible families included those that had at least one child between the ages of 6 and 18. Eligible families within a cluster were enumerated and selected through a stratified systematic cluster-sampling method, which yielded an equal probability of selection. The Welfare AFDC sample consisted of 1,000 children ages 6-18 years from families who received Aid to Dependent Children support through the use of Aid to Dependent Children rolls from four welfare centers; households were randomly selected within racial/ethnic groups, yielding equal numbers of white, Hispanic, and African-American Ss. The target area was the same as that of the cross-sectional sample.

Total number of subjects at Time 1: N = 2,034

Ages at Time 1: 6-18 yrs.

Sex distribution: Approximately equal numbers of females and males throughout

Socioeconomic status: Varied (Cohort 1); 100% poverty class (Cohort 2)
Race/ethnicity: 56% white, 29% Hispanic, 14% African-American, 1% other (Cohort 1); 33.4% African-American, 33.3% white, 33.3% Hispanic (Cohort 2)

Years of Completed Waves:

Years	N=	Age ranges
(Cohort 1: Cross-sectional Ss)		
1966-1967	1,034	6-18 yrs.
1971	732	11-23 yrs.
(Cohort 2: Welfare AFDC Ss)		
1966-1967	1,000	6-18 yrs.
1971-1972	661	11-23 yrs.

INFORMATION ON SAMPLE ATTRITION:

During the 16-year period of study, 641 of 2,034 Ss (31.5%) combining both cohorts were not retrieved for further study: 302 of 1,034 Ss (25.2%) in Cohort 1; and 33% of 1,000 (33.9%) in Cohort 2. The core sample consists of 732 Ss for Cohort 1, and 661 Ss for Cohort 2. Attrition was due to many of the families moving out of the area.

CONSTRUCTS MEASURED: INSTRUMENTS USED

Development and current behavior of child subject, aspects of parental character, marital relationship, child-rearing practices, demographic information, welfare-related attitudes and behavior (for Cohort 2 mothers): Mother's Interview (structured questionnaire)
Parental character, child-rearing practices, marital relationship: Psychiatrists' Total Impairment Ratings (based on questionnaire)

REPRESENTATIVE REFERENCES:

Langner, T. S. (1984). City children: The Family Research Project. In S. A. Mednick, M. Harway, and K. M. Finello (Eds.), *Handbook of longitudinal research: Vol. 2. Teenage and adult cohorts.* New York: Praeger.
Langner, T. S., Gersten, J. C., Greene, E. L., Eisenberg, J. G., Hersen, J. H., & McCarthy, E. D. (1974). Treatment of psychological disorders among urban children. *Journal of Consulting and Clinical Psychology, 42*(2), 170-179.
Langner, T. S., Gersten, J. C., Wills, T. A., & Simcha-Fagan, O. (1983). The relative roles of early environment and early behavior as predictors of later child behavior. In D. Ricks & B. Dohrenwend (Eds.), *Origins of psychopathology: Problems in research and public policies.* New York: Cambridge University Press.

CURRENT STATUS OF THE STUDY:

a. No further waves of data collection are planned.
b. Most of the data are in machine-readable format.
c. Data are not available for secondary analysis.

■ **Early Environmental Experience Study, 1978**

Laosa, Luis M.

Contact Person: Luis M. Laosa
Address: Educational Testing Service
                  Research Building 08-R
                  Princeton, NJ 08541
Telephone No.:   (609) 734-5524

SUBSTANTIVE TOPICS COVERED:

The study examines the relation of cultural experiences to task-specific performances. Emphasis is on description, the predictability of these performances based on early childhood experiences, the stability of performances, and relations of performances and meaning of activities across time.

CHARACTERISTICS OF THE ORIGINAL SAMPLE:

Year the study began: 1978
Subject selection process: Subjects were contacted by mailings to all families registered as having given birth during 1975-1976. Families that responded were screened on the basis of income and educational level. All Ss were Mexican-Americans. All families were intact, mothers were not employed outside the home, and children had no physical and cognitive deficiencies. Preference was given to Ss who were going to stay in south-central Texas for an extended period of time. The principal investigator collected parallel data in 1977 on non-Hispanic, white, English-speaking Ss and Hispanic, English- and Spanish-speaking subjects in the same geographic area. The same subject selection process was used.
Total number of subjects at Time 1: N = 100
Ages at Time 1: 2 yrs., 6 mos.
Sex distribution: Approximately equal numbers of females and males throughout
Socioeconomic status: Information was not available in terms of percent distribution by socioeconomic class
Race/ethnicity: 100% Hispanic (Cohort 1); 100% white (Cohort 2)

Years of Completed Waves:

Years	N=	Age ranges
(Cohort 1: Mexican-American)		
1978-1979	100	2 yrs., 6 mos.
1979	100	3 yrs.
1979-1980	97	3 yrs., 6 mos.
1980	94	4 yrs.
(Cohort 2: White American)		
1977	100	2 yrs., 6 mos.

INFORMATION ON SAMPLE ATTRITION:

During the 2-year period of study, 6 of 100 Ss (6.0%) were not retrieved for further study. The core sample consists of 94 Ss.

CONSTRUCTS MEASURED: INSTRUMENTS USED

General and specific descriptions of the child in the home and his/her development observations (all the child's behaviors and verbalizations—to whom he/she spoke, what was said, what was done in reaction to the child's utterances, and how the child responded); the frequency of behaviors, activities, and duration a child engaged in an activity: Repeated observations (made by trained observers) in the home with the child and both parents

Details about the family history and current family activities affecting the child, mother's aspirations for the child, caretaking activities and practices, contacts the child has with others outside the immediate family, household activities and environment, and an intergenerational history of the family: Interview with the mother (semistructured)

Child's performance on standardized American tests: McCarthy Scales of Children's Abilities

Child's performance on school-related tasks: Caldwell Preschool Inventory

Attention assessment, relation to the interviewer and task, and task persistence: Ratings by an examiner of the child's interpersonal relations with the examiner during the test sessions and with the task, for the McCarthy Scales and Caldwell preschool inventory only

Child temperament: Behavioral Style Questionnaire (McDevitt & Carey) to mother about the child

Parents' intelligence: Cattell Culture Fair

REPRESENTATIVE REFERENCES:

Laosa, L. M. (1980). Maternal teaching strategies in Chicana and Anglo-American families: The influence of culture and education on maternal behavior. *Child Development, 51,* 759-765.

Laosa, L. M. (1982). Psychometric characteristics of Chicano and non-Hispanic white children's performance on the preschool inventory. *Journal of Applied Developmental Psychology, 3*(3), 217-245.

Laosa, L. M. (1982). School, occupation, culture, and family: The impact of parental schooling on the parent-child relationship. *Journal of Educational Psychology, 74*(6), 791-827.

Laosa, L. M. (1984). Ethnic, socioeconomic, and home language influences upon early performance on measures of abilities. *Journal of Educational Psychology, 76*(6), 1178-1198.

CURRENT STATUS OF THE STUDY:

a. No further waves of data collection are planned.

b. The data are in machine-readable format.

c. The data are conditionally available for secondary analysis through the study contact person.

■ The Impact of Home Placement Versus Foster Care, 1978

Leiderman, P. H.; and Wald, M. S.

Contact Person: Michael S. Wald
Address: School of Law
                  Stanford University
                  Palo Alto, CA 94305
Telephone No.:   (415) 723-4933

SUBSTANTIVE TOPICS COVERED:

The study examines the consequences of placement alternatives for child development; policy decisions regarding what type of intervention is most appropriate in abuse or neglect cases; the effects of child abuse or neglect on development.

CHARACTERISTICS OF THE ORIGINAL SAMPLE:

Year the study began: 1978

Subject selection process: Cohort 1 consists of new cases of physical abuse and neglect of children between the ages of 4 and 10 years in three Bay Area counties in California. Cohort 2 children were randomly selected from schools where abuse or neglect referrals are significant.

Total number of subjects at Time 1: N = 151

Ages at Time 1: 4-11 yrs.

Sex distribution: Approximately equal numbers of females and males throughout

Socioeconomic status: 60% poverty class, 30% working class, 10% middle/upper middle class

Race/ethnicity: 59% white, 25% African-American, 12% Hispanic, and 4% Asian-American

Years of Completed Waves:

Years	N=	Age ranges
1978-1982	70	4-10 yrs. (Cohort 1)[a]
1978-1982	81	5-11 yrs. (Cohort 2)[a]

Comments:
a. Cohorts 1 and 2 are not grouped in waves. Data collection is best described as continuous.

INFORMATION ON SAMPLE ATTRITION:

The subjects have been studied for a 4-year period. Sample attrition and core sample statistics cannot be computed, based on information at discrete data collection periods. The main reason for sample attrition was Ss moving out of the area of study without a forwarding address. The core sample consists of 145 Ss.

CONSTRUCTS MEASURED: INSTRUMENTS USED

Cognitive development: Revised Wechsler Intelligence Scale for Children (WISC-R), Wechsler Preschool and Primary Scale of Intelligence (WPPSI)
Problem behavior: Child Behavior Scale
Social competence: Social Competence Scale
Social competence for peer relations: Social Behavior Scale
Social climate: Family Environment Scale (Moos)
Physical environment: Physical environment checklist
Child's perceptions: Child interview
Parent perceptions of child's adjustment: Parent interview
Foster parent perception: Foster parent interview
Peer relations: School observations
Academic progress: School record
Social worker's perceptions of the child: Social worker interview
Major life events: Significant events interview

REPRESENTATIVE REFERENCES:

Wald, M. S. (1975). State intervention on behalf of neglected children: A search for realistic standards. *Stanford Law Review, 27,* 985-1040.

Wald, M. S. (1976). State intervention on behalf of neglected children: Standards for removal of children from their homes, monitoring the status of children in foster care, and termination of parental rights. *Stanford Law Review, 28,* 625-706.

Wald, M. S., Carlsmith, J. M., Leiderman, P. H., & Smith, C. (1983). Intervention to protect abused and neglected children. In M. Perlmutter (Ed.), *Minnesota Symposium on Child Psychology* (Vol. 16). Hillsdale, NJ: Lawrence Erlbaum.

Wald, M. S., et al. (1988). *Protecting abused and neglected children.* Palo Alto, CA: Stanford University Press.

CURRENT STATUS OF THE STUDY:

a. No further waves of data collection are planned.
b. Most of the data are in machine-readable format.
c. The data are available for secondary analysis from the study contact person.

■ Cardiovascular Disease Project at the University of Minnesota, 1947

Leon, Gloria; Murray, David; and Keys, Ancel

Contact Person: Gloria Leon
Address: Department of Psychology
                         University of Minnesota
                         Minneapolis, MN 55455
Telephone No.:   (612) 625-2546

SUBSTANTIVE TOPICS COVERED:

The study determines various personality, social, and physical factors associated with the onset and course of cardiovascular and other chronic diseases, as measured by the Minnesota Multiphasic Personality Inventory.

CHARACTERISTICS OF THE ORIGINAL SAMPLE:

Year the study began: 1947
Subject selection process: Subjects were emotionally stable, physically healthy business and professional males.
Total number of subjects at Time 1: N = 281
Ages at Time 1: 49 yrs. (mean age)
Sex distribution: 100% male
Socioeconomic status: 100% middle/upper middle class
Race/ethnicity: 100% white

Years of Completed Waves:

Years	N=	Age ranges
1947	281	49 yrs.
1953	261	55 yrs.
1960	194	62 yrs.
1977	99	79 yrs.

INFORMATION ON SAMPLE ATTRITION:

During the 30-year period of study, 182 of 281 Ss (64.7%) were not retrieved for further study. The core sample consists of 99 Ss. Attrition was due to death (62% cardiac disease, 32% cancer, 7.6% arterial deaths, and 9% other causes).

CONSTRUCTS MEASURED: INSTRUMENTS USED

Health, physiological functioning: Medical examination, blood pressure, blood sample, electrocardiogram, chest X ray, urinalysis
Personality: Minnesota Multiphasic Personality Inventory, Thurstone Temperament Schedule
Life stress events: Social Interest and Physical Activity Questionnaire

REPRESENTATIVE REFERENCES:

Keys, A., Taylor, H. L., Blackburn, H., Brozek, J., Anderson, J. T., & Simonson, E. (1963). Coronary heart disease among Minnesota business and professional men followed fifteen years. *Circulation, 28,* 381-395.

Keys, A., Taylor, H. L., Blackburn, H., Brozek, J., Anderson, J. T., & Simonson, E. (1971). Mortality and coronary heart disease among men studied for 23 years. *Archives of Internal Medicine, 128,* 201-214.

Leon, G. R., Gillum, B., Gillum, R. F., & Gouze, M. (1979). Personality, stability, and change over a 30-year period—Middle age to old age. *Journal of Consulting and Clinical Psychology, 47*(3), 517-524.

Leon, G. R., Finn, S. E., Murray, D., & Bailey, J. M. (1988). Inability to predict cardiovascular disease from hostility score of MMPI items related to Type A behavior. *Journal of Consulting and Clinical Psychology, 56,* 597-600.

CURRENT STATUS OF THE STUDY:

a. No further waves of data collection are planned.
b. Data are not in machine-readable format.
c. Data are available for secondary analysis from the study contact person.

■ Longitudinal Study of Cognitive, Social and Affective Development, 1974

Lewis, Michael

Contact Person: Michael Lewis or Candice Feiring
Address: Institute for the Study of Child Development
                 Robert Wood Johnson Medical School
                 Medical Education Building, CN-19
                 New Brunswick, NJ 08903-0019
Telephone No.:   (201) 937-7901, (201) 937-7902

SUBSTANTIVE TOPICS COVERED:

The study examines cognitive, social, and emotional development from infancy into childhood and adolescence. The study currently focuses on the degree of emotional adjustment of school-age children and how the adjustments are related to other competencies during childhood and adolescence; the relation of emotional competencies in childhood and adolescence to emotional competencies in infancy; and the stability and changes in emotional, social, and cognitive competencies.

CHARACTERISTICS OF THE ORIGINAL SAMPLE:

Year the study began: 1974

Subject selection process: The sample was solicited through newspaper advertisements, pediatricians' offices, and birth announcements in the Princeton, New Jersey, area.

Total number of subjects at Time 1: N = 198

Ages at Time 1: 3 mos.

Sex distribution: Approximately equal numbers of females and males throughout

Socioeconomic status: 100% middle/upper middle class

Race/ethnicity: 100% white

Years of Completed Waves:

Years	N=	Age ranges
1974-1975	198	3 mos.
1975-1976	174	1 yr.
1976-1977	160	2 yrs.
1977-1978	142	3 yrs.
1980-1981	132	6 yrs.
1983-1984	130	9 yrs.
1987-1988	116	13 yrs.

INFORMATION ON SAMPLE ATTRITION:

During the 13-year period of the study, 82 of 198 Ss (41.4%) were not retrieved for further study. The core sample consists of 116 Ss.

CONSTRUCTS MEASURED: INSTRUMENTS USED

Attachment behavior, emotional expression, maternal teaching style, parent-child interaction: Videotaped interviews of child-mother interactions in playroom situations

Cognitive abilities: Bayley Infant Scales of Development

Block design, evaluation of children's abilities in areas related to school achievement, pre-reading skills, mathematics concepts and general knowledge: Circus (Bogatz)

Intelligence: Peabody Picture Vocabulary Test, Stanford-Binet Intelligence Test, Wechsler Preschool and Primary Scales of Intelligence, Wechsler Intelligence Scales for Children-Revised

Behavior problem, internalizing and externalizing behavior: Child Behavioral Profile (Achenbach & Edelbrock)

Depressive mood: Child Depression Inventory (Kovacs & Beck)

Social network, contacts with relatives, adults, and peers: Pattison Psychosocial Network Questionnaire (1975)

Self concept: Self Interview, Self Q-Sort (adapted from Block & Block)

School adjustment, social development, verbal intelligence, curiosity/creativity, apathy distractibility, task orientation: Child Behavior Inventory

Strategies for problem solving, problem solving, effectiveness of problem-solving strategies: Interpersonal Problem-solving Measure (Spivak & Shure)

Mother measures of social interaction with child, child measures of social interaction with mother: Mother-Child Interaction Measure

Family environment: Family Environment Scale (Moos), videotape of family interactions at dinner

Health history: Health Questionnaire

Child temperament: Carey & McDevitt Temperament Scales

Family and child stress events and reaction to events: Stress Questionnaire

Friend contacts at home and school: Friendship Interview

Prosocial behavior in the classroom: Prosocial Questionnaire (Weir, Stevenson & Graham)

Child attribution style: Child Attribution Questionnaire (Kastan)

Mother attribution style: Mother Attribution Questionnaire

Mothers' depressive mood: Beck Depression Inventory

School achievement and performance: School achievement and grades

Teacher rating behavior problems: Teacher Child Behavior Profile

Physiological state: Salivary cortisol, heart rate

Pubertal body changes (e.g., menses, body hair, growth): Petersen Maturation Questionnaire

Masculinity/femininity/androgyny: Bem Sex Role Inventory

Self-concept (social, scholastic, moral, and athletic competence): Harter Scales
Peer pressure: What Would You Do? (Steinberg)
Social life: Dating-popularity interview
Emotional autonomy: Mom & I, Dad & I (Steinberg)
Ideal and self-perceived body image: Lerner Body Image Questionnaire

REPRESENTATIVE REFERENCES:

Feiring, C., & Lewis, M. (1989). The social networks of girls and boys from early through middle childhood. In D. Belle (Ed.), *Children's social networks and social supports* (pp. 119-150). New York: John Wiley.

Lewis, M., Feiring, C. (1989). Infant, mother and mother-infant interaction behavior and subsequent attachment. (1989). *Child Development, 60,* 831-837.

Lewis, M., Feiring, C., McGuffog, C., & Jaskir, J. (1984). Predicting psychopathology in six year olds from early social relations. *Child Development, 55,* 123-136.

Lewis, M., & Krietzberg, V. S. (1979). Effects of birth order and spacing on mother-infant interactions. *Developmental Psychology, 15,* 617-625.

CURRENT STATUS OF THE STUDY:

a. The study is active, and a follow-up of Ss at age 16 is planned.
b. Most data are in machine-readable format.
c. The data are available for secondary analysis from the study contact person.

■ The Collaborative Perinatal Project: Providence Site, 1959

Lipsitt, Lewis P.; Buka, Stephen L.; and Tsuang, Ming T.

Contact Person: Stephen L. Buka
Address: Child Study Center, Brown University
                 Box 1836
                 Providence, RI 02912
Telephone No.:   (401) 421-8241

SUBSTANTIVE TOPICS COVERED:

The study examines those factors during pregnancy, and the conditions of birth and the perinatal period, that are related to development over the first 7 years of life, as assessed by pediatric, psychological, speech, and hearing examinations. Of special interest are the following: fetal loss; infant and early childhood mortality and premature births; the dynamics of physical and mental development in early childhood and relationships to genetic, biological, and environmental factors; and the evaluation of the significance of events in the postnatal environment in relation to the later development and functioning of the nervous system. (See also Broman, S., *The Collaborative Perinatal Project*.)

CHARACTERISTICS OF THE ORIGINAL SAMPLE:

Year the study began: 1959

Subject selection process: Women were selected for participation in the study over a 7-year period (1959-1965). Subject selection criteria included patients' admittance to the hospital clinic for care, Ss' geographical area of residence, and exclusion of Ss whose prognosis for follow-up was poor.

Comments:
Data collected at the Providence Lying-In Hospital was a portion of a total of 58,828 women contacted in a nationwide sample of pregnancies, centered at 12 university-affiliated hospitals. (For more information see Broman, pp. 59-69). The study was conducted under the sponsorship and direction of the National Institute of Neurological Diseases and Blindness (NINDB), now known as NINCDS. The hospitals were chosen by NINDB on a non-random basis. The selection procedure for actual inclusion in the study and the size of the sample frames did vary with each medical center. The general objective of the sample selection procedure was to cover the broad spectrum of pregnancy conditions. After the selection procedure from each hospital in the national project was complete, approximately 53,000 pregnancies constituted the nationwide sample. The information presented below refers to the sample enrolled through the Providence, Rhode Island, study site.

Total number of subjects at Time 1: N = 4,140

Ages at Time 1: Prenatal

Sex distribution: Approximately equal numbers of females and males throughout

Socioeconomic status: Data were gathered, but not presented in terms of percent distribution by socioeconomic class.

Race/ethnicity: 77.1% white, 21% African-American, 1.4% biracial, 0.2% Asian-American

Years of Completed Waves:[a]

Years	N=	Age ranges
1959-1965	4,140	Prenatal
1959-1960	4,120	Birth
1960	3,058	4 mos.
1960	3,041	8 mos.
1961	2,900	1 yr.
1963	2,327	3 yrs.
1964	2,894	4 yrs.
1967	3,130	7 yrs.
1967-1969[b]	840	8 yrs.
1983[b]	700	17-27 yrs.
1987[b]	200	21-22 yrs.

Comments:
a. The Brown University Child Study Center conducted two major follow-up investigations of Ss between 1983 and 1989. One study examined the relationship between perinatal complications and psychiatric disorder, the second study investigated reproductive outcomes among low-birthweight and small-for-gestational-age women. Additional research includes a study of family migration patterns, an analysis of developmental risk factors in the natural histories of delinquent young people, and a follow-up of project subjects who had learning disabilities and/or required special education services.
b. Three separate follow-up subsamples.

INFORMATION ON SAMPLE ATTRITION:

During the initial 8-year period of study, 1,010 of 4,140 Ss (24.4%) were not retrieved for further study. Information on the core sample was not available.

CONSTRUCTS MEASURED: INSTRUMENTS USED

Medical history, socioeconomic status, genetic information about the mother, the child's father, and their respective families: Interviews with the mother at a clinic

Physical health of the child and mother, including history of the delivery: Physical examination by obstetricians

Events surrounding the labor and delivery, health status of the neonate: Observation by a pediatrician every 24 hours in the nursery

Cause of death: Autopsy when infants died at birth

Health status of the child: Neurological exam, nurse's evaluation, diagnostic summary, pediatric examination

Cognitive and psychomotor functions: Bayley Infant Scales of Development, Stanford-Binet Intelligence Test, Wechsler Intelligence Scale for Children

Demographic changes, health status of the child: Interviews with parents

Speech, language, and hearing: Specially devised protocol, audiometric examinations

Family and social history information: Special protocol

Assessment of severity of special problems: Neurological, ophthalmological, psychological, and/or psychiatric exams, as required

Psychiatric disorders (DSM-III): Diagnostic Interview Schedule-III

Verbal and conceptual abilities: Shipley Vocabulary and Abstraction Tests

Academic, vocational, relationship attainment: Social history interview

Antisocial behavior: Juvenile court records

Academic achievement: School records

REPRESENTATIVE REFERENCES:

Buka, S. L., Lipsitt, L. P., & Tsuang, M. T. (1988). Birth complications and psychological deviancy: A 25-year prospective inquiry. *Acta Pediatrica Japonica, 30,* 537-546.

Buka, S. L., Lipsitt, L. P., & Tsuang, M. T. (in press). Social and emotional development of low birthweight infants and children. In S. L. Friedman & M. D. Sigman (Eds.), *The psychological development of low birthweight children.* Norwood, NJ: Adlex.

Lipsitt, L. P., Sturner, W. Q., & Burke, P. (1979). Perinatal indicators and subsequent crib death. *Infant Behavior and Development, 2,* 325-328.

Niswander, K. R., & Gordon, M., et al. (1972). *The women and their pregnancies.* Philadelphia: W. B. Saunders.

CURRENT STATUS OF THE STUDY:

a. Further waves of data collection are planned.
b. Most data are in machine-readable format.

c. Data are available for secondary analysis from the study contact person or from the References Services Center for Electronic Records, National Archives and Records Administration, Washington, DC 20408.

■ The Iowa HABIT Project, 1967

Loney, Jan; Paternite, Carl E.; and Langhorne, John E., Jr.

Contact Person: Jan Loney
Address: Department of Psychiatry and Behavioral Sciences
State University at Stony Brook
South Campus, Putnam Hall
Stony Brook, NY 11794
Telephone No.: (516) 632-8830

SUBSTANTIVE TOPICS COVERED:

This study describes outcomes of medicated and unmedicated hyperactive/ADD boys at adolescence, young adulthood (21-23 yrs.), and later adulthood (28-32 yrs.).

CHARACTERISTICS OF THE ORIGINAL SAMPLE:

Year the study began: 1967
Subject selection process: Subjects selected were boys referred to outpatient psychiatric clinic for evaluation and treatment, ages 6-12, IQ ≥ 70.
Total number of subjects at Time 1: N = 135
Ages at Time 1: 4-12 yrs.
Sex distribution: 100% male
Socioeconomic status: 59% working class, 21% upper middle/middle class, 20% poverty class
Race/ethnicity: 98% white, 2% African-American

Years of Completed Waves:

Years	N=	Age ranges
1967-1972	135	4-12 yrs.
1973-1976	124	10-16 yrs.
1980-1984	100	21-23 yrs.
1987-1989	77	28-32 yrs.

INFORMATION ON SAMPLE ATTRITION:

During the 22-year period of study, approximately 92% of the sample was followed-up in adolescence. Approximately 79% of the sample was followed up at the young adult phase. Percentage follow-up is not currently available for the later adult phase.

CONSTRUCTS MEASURED: INSTRUMENTS USED

Development of child's problem behavior, events surrounding referral, details about the pregnancy, birth, and neonatal period, developmental milestones, and social, behavioral, and learning patterns at home and at school: Child Intake Form (163 items)

Child's present condition, school progress, peer relationships, trouble with the law; child's feelings of self-worth; self-control; aspirations for adulthood: Structured Child Interview

Child's intelligence: Wechsler Intelligence Scale for Children (WISC), Wide Range Achievement Test (WRAT)

Child's physical health status: Physical-neurological examinations, Electroencephalogram

Child's personality: Cattell's High School Personality Questionnaire; Sines Missouri Children's Picture Series

Child's self-esteem: Piers-Harris Test, Draw-A-Car Test, Adjective Checklist (ACL)

Locus of control: Locus of Control Scale (Nowicki-Strickland)

Reflection-Impulsivity: Matching Familiar Figures (Kagan)

Child's perception of parents: Children's Report of Parental Behavior (Schaefer)

Child symptomatology: Primary-Secondary Symptom Checklist, Examiner ratings of primary and secondary symptoms

Child's academic performance, child's social behavior in the classroom: School Intake Form (81 items) (Teacher's assessment)

Standardized achievement and performance: Gray Oral Reading Test, The Iowa Test of Basic Skills, The Gettysburg Normed Handwriting Scale, Bender-Gestalt Visual-Motor Test

Background, demographic, marital, and socioeconomic information, family structure and relationships, parental child-rearing styles (29 items): Mother Intake Form, Father Intake Form

Child's present condition, child's school progress, child's peer relationships, child's encounters with legal authorities; parents' attitudes about discipline, reinforcement practices, and expressions of affection, child's progress on medication (e.g., side effects, attitudes, circumstances of termination): Structured Parent Interview

Parent's view of child: Conners Parent's Rating Scale

Teacher's impressions of child: Structured Teacher Questionnaire

REPRESENTATIVE REFERENCES:

Langhorne, J. E., Jr., & Loney, J. (1979). A four-fold model for subgrouping the hyperkinetic/MBD syndrome. *Child Psychiatry and Human Development, 9*(3): 153-159.

Loney, J., Kramer, J., & Milich, R. (1984). The hyperkinetic child grows up: Predictors of symptoms, delinquency, and achievement at follow-up. In S. A. Mednick, M. Harway, & S. M. Finello (Eds.), *Handbook of longitudinal research: Vol. 1. Birth and childhood cohorts.* New York: Praeger.

Loney, J., Langhorne, J. E., Jr., Paternite, C. E.; Whaley-Klahn, M. A., Blair-Broeker, C. T., & Hacker, M. (1980). The Iowa HABIT: Hyperkinetic/aggressive boys in treatment. In S. B. Sells, R. Crandall, M. Roff, J. S. Strauss, & W. Pollin (Eds.), *Human functioning in longitudinal perspective: Studies of normal and psychopathic populations.* Baltimore/London: Williams and Wilkins.

Loney, J., & Paternite, C. E. (1980). Childhood hyperkinesis: Relationships between symptomatology and home environment. In C. K. Whalen & B. Henker (Eds.), *Hyperactive children: The social ecology of identification and treatment.* New York: Academic Press.

CURRENT STATUS OF THE STUDY:

a. No further waves of data collection are planned.
b. Most data are in machine-readable format.
c. Data are available for secondary analysis from the study contact person.

■ Longitudinal Study of the Socialization and Development of Twin Boys, 1970

Lytton, Hugh; Watts, Denise; and Dunn, Bruce E.

Contact Person: Hugh Lytton
Address: Department of Educational Psychology
                University of Calgary
                2500 University Drive N.W.
                Calgary, Alberta T2N 1N4
                Canada
Telephone No.: (403) 220-5652

SUBSTANTIVE TOPICS COVERED:

This study examines the development of compliance, attachment, independence, and language ability in twin boys, in relation to parents' rearing practices and to genetic factors from age 2 to age 9. A comparison of child characteristics and parents' socialization practices for twin and singleton boys was also conducted.

CHARACTERISTICS OF THE ORIGINAL SAMPLE:

Year the study began: 1970
Subject selection process: Subjects selected were pairs of male twins available in Calgary. A control group of singleton boys, matched for mother's education, was also selected; however, the control group was not studied longitudinally.
Total number of subjects at Time 1: N = 136
Ages at Time 1: 2 yrs.
Sex distribution: 100% male
Socioeconomic status: 67% working class, 33% middle/upper middle class
Race/ethnicity: 100% white

Years of Completed Waves:

Years	*N =*	*Age ranges*
(Cohort 1: Twins)		
1970-1973	92	2-3 yrs.
1978-1980	76	8-10 yrs.
(Cohort 2: Singleton boys)		
1970-1973	44	2-3 yrs.

INFORMATION ON SAMPLE ATTRITION:

During the 10-year period of study, 16 of 92 twin Ss (17.4%) were not retrieved for further study. The core sample consists of 76 Ss. Sample attrition was due to families' moving and subjects' refusing to participate in the follow-up.

CONSTRUCTS MEASURED: INSTRUMENTS USED

Social characteristics of children; socialization practices of parents: Naturalistic observation, interview with mother (Wave 1), interview with mother and father (Wave 2)
Language and cognitive ability: Peabody Picture Vocabulary Test, observation (Wave 1), Crichton Vocabulary Scale, Raven's Coloured Progressive Matrices (Wave 2)
Social adjustment: Teacher ratings, Child Behavior Questionnaire (Rutter) (Wave 2)

REPRESENTATIVE REFERENCES:

Lytton, H. (1986). *Parent-child interaction: The socialization process observed in twin and singleton families.* New York: Plenum.
Lytton, H., Watts, D., & Dunn, B. E. (1987). Stability and predictability of cognitive and social characteristics from age 2 to age 9. *Genetic, Social, and General Psychology Monographs, 112,* 363-398.

Lytton, H., Watts, D., & Dunn, B. E. (1987). Twin and singleton differences in verbal ability: Where do they come from? *Intelligence, 11,* 359-369.

Lytton, H., Watts, D., & Dunn, B. E. (1988). Stability of genetic determination from age 2 to age 9: A longitudinal twin study. *Social Biology, 35,* 62-73.

CURRENT STATUS OF THE STUDY:

a. No further waves of data collection are planned.

b. Most of the data are in machine-readable format.

c. Data are not available for secondary analysis.

M

Duke Longitudinal Study of Aging (Duke First Longitudinal Study), 1955

Maddox, George L.; Busse, Ewald W.; Siegler, Ilene C.; George, Linda; Palmore, Erdman; and Nowlin, John B.

Contact Person: George L. Maddox
Address: Box 2920
Duke University Medical Center
Durham, NC 27710
Telephone No.: (919) 684-6118

SUBSTANTIVE TOPICS COVERED:

The study examines physiological functioning (e.g., of cardiovascular system); physical and mental health; cognitive, psychomotor, and perceptual functioning (e.g., intelligence, memory, hearing, reaction time); activities and satisfactions; marital and family relations; sexual behavior; health and illness behaviors; lifestyle; work status and history; and predictors of morbidity and mortality. (See also Busse, E. W., *Duke Adaptation Study: Duke Second Longitudinal Study.*)

CHARACTERISTICS OF THE ORIGINAL SAMPLE:

Year the study began: 1955

Subject selection process: Subjects were a sample of volunteers, ages 60 and over, who were offered a free annual physical examination. The primary consideration in selection was the likelihood of continued participation. Subsequently, efforts were made to recruit numbers of African-Americans and whites, lower and upper socioeconomic groups, and age groups so that cell sizes would be adequate for data analysis.

Total number of subjects at Time 1: N = 267

Ages at Time 1: 60-94 yrs.

Sex distribution: Approximately equal numbers of females and males throughout

Socioeconomic status: Full range.

Race/ethnicity: 65.2% white, 34.8% African-American

Years of Completed Waves:

Years	N=	Age ranges
1955-1959	267	60-94 yrs.
1959-1961	182	61-95 yrs.
1964-1965	140	64-98 yrs.
1966-1967	110	65-99 yrs.
1968-1969	93	66-100 yrs.
1970	92	67-101 yrs.
1972	60	69-102 yrs.
1973	57	70-102 yrs.
1974	52	71-102 yrs.
1974-1975	47	72-102 yrs.
1976	42	76-102 yrs.

INFORMATION ON SAMPLE ATTRITION:

During the 21-year period of study, 225 of 267 Ss (84.3%) were not retrieved for further study. The core sample consists of 42 Ss. Main reasons for attrition included death, refusal to participate further, serious illness, and moving.

CONSTRUCTS MEASURED: INSTRUMENTS USED

Activities and satisfactions, marital and family relations, sexual behavior, health and illness behaviors, lifestyle, work status and history: Personal interview
Intelligence: Wechsler Adult Intelligence Scale (WAIS)
Cognitive or mental functioning: Rorschach Ink Blot Test
Memory: Modified Wechsler Memory Scale
Audition: Pure-tone audiometry, spondee words
Reaction time: Simple and choice reaction time and Continuous Performance Task
Happiness, use of free time, emotional security: Cavan Adjustment Rating
Usefulness and work satisfaction: Chicago Inventory of Activities and Attitudes
Physical health, physiological functioning, psychomotor and perceptual functioning, systolic and diastolic blood pressure; extent of obesity, serum cholesterol level, cardiovascular impairment, visual acuity, auditory acuity: Physical and laboratory examinations
Sleep patterns: Beckman Electroencephalograph

REPRESENTATIVE REFERENCES:

Palmore, E. (1970). *Normal aging: Reports from the Duke Longitudinal Study, 1955-1969.* Durham, NC: Duke University Press.
Palmore, E. (1974). *Normal aging, II: Reports from the Duke Longitudinal Study, 1970-1973.* Durham, NC: Duke University Press.

Palmore, E., Busse, E. W., Maddox, G. L., Nowlin, J. B., & Siegler, I. (1985). *Normal aging, III: Reports from the Duke Longitudinal Study, 1975-1984.* Durham, NC: Duke University Press.

Siegler, I. C. (1983). Psychological aspects of the Duke longitudinal studies. In K. W. Schaie (Ed.), *Longitudinal studies of adult psychological development.* New York: Guilford Press.

CURRENT STATUS OF THE STUDY:

a. No further data collection is planned.
b. Most data are in machine-readable format.
c. Data are available through the Archive of Data on Adult Development and Aging, Duke University Medical Center, Box 3003, Durham, NC 27710.

■ Emotional Socialization and Expressive Development in Preterm and Full-Term Infants, 1981

Malatesta, Carol Zander

Contact Person: Carol Zander Malatesta
Address: Long Island University
                  Psychology Department
                  1 University Plaza
                  Brooklyn, NY 11201
Telephone No.:   (718) 403-1068

SUBSTANTIVE TOPICS COVERED:

This study examines emotional expressive development in preterm and full-term infants.

CHARACTERISTICS OF THE ORIGINAL SAMPLE:

Year the study began: 1981
Subject selection process: Subjects were recruited via announcements and contacts with their pediatrician.
Total number of subjects at Time 1: N = 111 (77 full-term, 34 preterm)
Ages at Time 1: 2.5 mos. (infants); 33.8 yrs. (mothers)
Sex distribution: Approximately equal numbers of females and males
Socioeconomic status: 100% middle/upper middle class
Race/ethnicity: 88.3% white (including 10 Israeli Ss), 9% Asian-American, 2.7% African-American

Years of Completed Waves:[a]

Year	N=	Age ranges
(Cohort 1: Full-term Ss)		
1981	77	2.5 mos.
1981	64	5 mos.
1981	63	7.5 mos.
1983	31	22 mos.
1984	40	3.6 yrs.
1986	20	5 yrs.
(Cohort 2: Preterm Ss)		
1981	34	2.5 mos.
1981	25	5 mos.
1981	24	7.5 mos.
1983	15	22 mos.
1984	15	3.6 yrs.
1986	15	5 yrs.

Comments:
a. Ss were recontacted at 3.6 yrs. and at 5 yrs. Data have not yet been fully analyzed.

INFORMATION ON SAMPLE ATTRITION:

During the 5-year period of study, 22% of the Ss dropped out between waves one and three. Five percent of the Ss dropped out between wave three and wave four. Another 5% of the Ss dropped out between wave four and wave five. However, a few Ss, who did not participate at wave four, rejoined at wave five. The core sample consists of 35 Ss.

CONSTRUCTS MEASURED: INSTRUMENTS USED

Expressive behaviors of babies and their mothers: Videotaped observation of face-to-face interaction
Expressive behaviors of children and their mothers (age 2): Ainsworth Strange Situation, videotaped observation of play, separation, and reunion episodes

REPRESENTATIVE REFERENCES:

Malatesta, C. Z. (1982). The expression and regulation of emotion: A lifespan perspective. In T. Field & A. Fogel (Eds.), *Emotion and early interaction* (pp. 1-24). Hillsdale, NJ: Lawrence Erlbaum.

Malatesta, C. Z. (1986). Emotion socialization and expressive development in pre-term and full-term infants. *Child Development, 57,* 316-330.

Malatesta, C. Z., Culver, C., Tesmon, J. R., & Shepard, B. (1989). The development of emotion expression during the first 2 years of life. *Monographs of the Society for Research on Child Development, 54,* 1-104.

Malatesta, C. Z., & Haviland, J. M. (1982). Learning display rules: The socialization of emotion expression in infancy. *Child Development, 53,* 991-1003.

CURRENT STATUS OF THE STUDY:

a. No further waves of data collection are planned.

b. Data are not in machine-readable format.

c. Data are not currently available for secondary analysis.

■ **Transition from Adolescence to Adulthood: Follow-Up Study, 1973**

Marini, Margaret Mooney; Temme, Lloyd; and Coleman, James

Contact Person: Margaret M. Marini
Address: Department of Sociology
                  University of Minnesota
                  909 Social Sciences
                  267 19th Avenue South
                  Minneapolis, MN 55455
Telephone No.:   (612) 624-5296
Comments:
The first data wave was collected by James Coleman, and the subsequent follow-up of the sample was conducted by Margaret Marini and Lloyd Temme.

SUBSTANTIVE TOPICS COVERED:

The initial study examined the nature and consequences of high school status systems; the relation between status systems of high schools and the values and activities of students. The follow-up study examines the long-term effects of adolescent experiences and the effects of differences in the process of role transference on adult outcomes.

CHARACTERISTICS OF THE ORIGINAL SAMPLE:

Year the study began: 1957

Subject selection process: Subjects were students from 10 northern Illinois high schools. All students attending these schools were asked to participate. Schools were selected to provide variation in size of school, type of community location, and adolescent status system.

Total number of subjects at Time 1: N = 8,617

Ages at Time 1: 13-18 yrs.

Sex distribution: Approximately equal numbers of females and males throughout

Socioeconomic status: Data were gathered, but specific information about percent distribution by socioeconomic class was not available.

Race/ethnicity: Predominantly white

Years of Completed Waves:

Years	N=	Age ranges
1957	8,617	13-18 yrs.
1973	6,498	29-34 yrs.

INFORMATION ON SAMPLE ATTRITION:

During the 16-year period of study, 2,119 of 8,617 Ss (24.6%) were not retrieved for further study. The core sample consists of 6,498 Ss.

CONSTRUCTS MEASURED: INSTRUMENTS USED

Influences related to the high school (community and school environment, peer influences, academic experiences, school involvement, involvement in the high school as a social system, and dating behavior); personal adjustment and values, future plans and aspirations; family structure (socioeconomic status, family size, birth order of children): Student questionnaire

Parental role models, family socialization: Mail questionnaire (parents)

Grades and academic history: Student records

Intelligence: Standardized intelligence test

Information on current activities and life satisfaction; retrospective data over a 15-year period, which includes (a) employment, marriage, educational, and fertility experiences, and residence changes; (b) personal well-being in adulthood (occupational attainment and social mobility); (c) satisfaction (job, marital, parental, and community satisfaction) and (d) personal esteem: Mail questionnaire to subjects or telephone interview

REPRESENTATIVE REFERENCES:

Marini, M. M. (1978). The transition to adulthood: Sex differences in educational attainment and age at marriage. *American Sociological Review, 43,* 483-507.

Marini, M. M. (1980). Sex differences in the process of occupational attainment: A closer look. *Social Science Research, 9,* 307-361.

Marini, M. M. (1987). Measuring the process of role change during the transition to adulthood. *Social Science Research, 16,* 1-38.

Marini, M. M., Olsen, A. R., & Rubin, D. B. (1979). Maximum-likelihood estimation in panel studies with missing data. In K. F. Schuessler (Ed.), *Sociological Methodology 1980* (pp. 314-357). San Francisco: Jossey-Bass.

CURRENT STATUS OF THE STUDY:

a. No further waves of data collection are planned.

b. Most data are in machine-readable format.

c. The data are not available for secondary analysis.

■ The Prediction and Prevention of Marital and Family Distress, 1980

Markman, Howard J.; and Stanley, Scott

Contact person: Howard J. Markman
Address: Center for Marital and Family Studies
                  University of Denver
                  Denver, CO 70208
Telephone No.:   (303) 871-3370

SUBSTANTIVE TOPICS COVERED:

This study investigated the causes of divorce and marital distress; evaluated the long-term effects of a communication program (PREP-Premarital Relationship Enhancement Program) designed to prevent divorce and marital stress; evaluated the effects of premarital and marital communication on child development; and followed people, who divorce in their first marriage, into their second marriage to assess similarities and differences in communication problems.

CHARACTERISTICS OF THE ORIGINAL SAMPLE:

Year the study began: 1980

Subject selection process: Subjects were couples who were planning marriage or couples who were already engaged. They were selected through community-wide media advertisement.

Total number of subjects at Time 1: N = 135 couples

Ages at Time 1: 23 yrs. (females), 24 yrs. (males)

Sex distribution: Equal numbers of females and males throughout

Socioeconomic status: 70% middle/upper middle class, 20% working class, 10% student

Race/ethnicity: 87% white, 8% Hispanic, 5% African-American

Comments:
The study also includes the children of the subjects. This cohort currently consists of 110 children, ranging from 1 month to 7 years of age. Couples with children are assessed yearly on child and family functioning.

Years of Completed Waves:[a]

Years	N=	Age ranges
1980	135	18-35 yrs.
1981	100	19-36 yrs.
1983	100	21-37 yrs.
1984	100	22-38 yrs.
1985	100	23-39 yrs.

Years of Completed Waves, Continued:[a]

Years	N=	Age ranges
1986	100	24-40 yrs.
1987	100	25-41 yrs.
1988	100	26-42 yrs.
1989	98	27-43 yrs.

Comments:
a. The number of couples followed-up between 1981 and 1988 are based on approximations.

INFORMATION ON SAMPLE ATTRITION:

During the 10-year period of study, 37 of 135 Ss (27.4%) were not retrieved for further study. The core sample consists of 85 Ss. Attrition was due to couples who broke up before marriage, to separation or divorce, and to Ss who declined participation or were lost to follow-up.

CONSTRUCTS MEASURED: INSTRUMENTS USED

Marital satisfaction: Locke-Wallace Marital Adjustment Test
Problem intensity, relationship efficacy: Knox Problem Inventory Marital Agenda's Protocol
Individual adjustment: Hopkins Symptom Checklist
Verbal-physical aggression: Conflict Tactics Scale
Self-reported communication quality: Communication Box
Couples interaction (i.e., conflict, withdrawal): Interaction Dimension Grouping System (a behavioral observation system)
Division of labor: Who Does What?
Gender roles: Personal Attribute Scale
Attachment (child measure): Attachment Q-Sort
Self-esteem: Harter Self-esteem Scale
Child and family functioning: Family Interaction Global Sensing System

REPRESENTATIVE REFERENCES:

Liudahl, K., & Markman, H. J. (in press). The impact of marital communication on the development of children. In E. Blechman (Ed.), *Emotions and families*. New York: Plenum.

Markman, H. J., Duncan S. W., Storaasli, R., & Howes, P. (1987). The prediction and prevention of marital distress: A longitudinal investigation. In K. Hahlweg & M. Goldstein (Eds.), *Understanding major mental disorders: The contribution of family interaction research* (pp. 266-289). New York: Family Process Press.

Markman, H. J., Floyd, S., Stanley, S., & Storaasli, R. (1988). The prevention of marital distress: A longitudinal investigation. *Journal of Consulting and Clinical Psychology, 56,* 210-217.

Markman, J. H., Stanley, S., Floyd, S., & Blumberg, S. (in press). The Premarital Relationship Enhancement Program (PREP): Current status. *International Programs of Psychotherapy Research*. American Psychological Association-Society for Psychotherapy Research.

CURRENT STATUS OF THE STUDY:

a. Further waves of data collection are planned through the first 15 years of marriage.
b. Most of the data are in machine-readable format.
c. Data are available for secondary analysis from study contact person.

■ Louisville Twin Study, 1959

Matheny, Adam P., Jr.; and Wilson, Ronald (deceased)

Contact Person: Adam P. Matheny, Jr.
Address: Child Development Unit
                Pediatric School of Medicine
                University of Louisville
                Louisville, KY 40292
Telephone No.: (502) 588-1090

SUBSTANTIVE TOPICS COVERED:

This study examines the contributions of genetic and environmental factors to physical growth and mental development. The focus of the study has shifted to the study of the origin and stability of temperament, and of social development.

CHARACTERISTICS OF THE ORIGINAL SAMPLE:

Year the study began: 1959
Subject selection process: Twin families were recruited from the Board of Health records in the metropolitan Louisville area. The sample includes monozygotic (MZ) and dizygotic (DZ) twins, and siblings of twins. A general effort was made to make the sample as representative as possible.
Total number of subjects at Time 1: N = 324
Ages at Time 1: 3 mos.
Sex distribution: Approximately equal numbers of females and males throughout
Socioeconomic status: 43% middle/upper middle class, 35% working class, 22% poverty class
Race/ethnicity: 80% white, 18% African-American, 2% biracial

Years of Completed Waves:

Years[a]	N=[b]	Age ranges
1959	324 (144=MZ, 180=DZ)	3 mos.
1959-1960	364 (162=MZ, 202=DZ)	6 mos.
1960	350 (166=MZ, 184=DZ)	1 yrs.

Years of Completed Waves, Continued:

Years[a]	N=[b]	Age ranges
1960-1961	410 (184=MZ, 226=DZ)	18 mos.
1961-1962	330 (144=MZ, 186=DZ)	30 mos.
1962	458 (208=MZ, 250=DZ)	3 yrs.
1963	450 (210=MZ, 240=DZ)	4 yrs.
1964	534 (258=MZ, 276=DZ)	5 yrs.
1965	560 (278=MZ, 282=DZ)	6 yrs.
1966-1968	568 (292=MZ, 276=DZ)	7-9 yrs.
1974	284 (156=MZ, 128=DZ)	15 yrs.
1975-1988	520 (276=MZ, 244=DZ)	3 mos.-16 yrs.[c]
1985-1988	150 (80=MZ, 70=DZ)	20-25 yrs.

Comments:
a. Approximately 30 to 40 twin pairs were added each year to the main sample. Also, years of data waves are approximations based on the ages of the subjects.
b. These figures refer to twins. Thus, half of the N for each data point is the number of twin pairs tested. Approximately 600 siblings have also been tested.
c. Roughly 220 Ss were added during these years, and followed annually.

INFORMATION ON SAMPLE ATTRITION:

The sample was followed for a 29-year period. The attrition rate for the original sample of 1959 could not be calculated because the sample size of subsequent data points includes supplementary samples. Ongoing recruitment shows core sample steadily increasing.

CONSTRUCTS MEASURED: INSTRUMENTS USED

Physical status: Neonatal assessment and hospital data on delivery and medical status

Intelligence and mental abilities: Bayley Scales of Infant Development, Stanford-Binet L-M, McCarthy Scales of Mental Abilities, Wechsler Preschool and Primary Scale of Intelligence (WPPSI), Wechsler Intelligence Scale for Children (WISC), Wechsler Adult Intelligence Scale (WAIS)

Temperament and social development: Mother's interviews regarding child's behavior; experimenter's observations and ratings; subscale of Bayley's Infant Behavior Record (social orientation, emotional tone, attention span, fearfulness, goal directedness); Carey Scales; social interactions with the experimenter and twins together, then alone; measures of cuddling; visible barrier behavior (from Cattell Infant Intelligence Scale); mirror vignettes based on Bertenthal & Fischer (1978); imitation games

Social development: Social interaction assessments, mother's interviews, Carey Scales, teacher temperament questionnaire

Emotional tone, attention, activity, and orientation to staff: Behavioral ratings by experimenter from videotapes

Physical status: Measures of weight, height, and head circumference

Locus of control for health and injuries: Health-Accident Locus of Control
Adult personality: Multidimensional personality questionnaire
Family environment: Family Environment Scale
Home environment: (Home visits at 7, 36, 72 months), Home inventory, Appraisals
   of Basic Opportunities for Developmental Experiences (ABODE)
Child self-esteem and competence: Perceived Competence Scale for Children
Injury behaviors: Accident Behavior Checklist
Adult temperament: Thurstone Temperament Schedule, Dimensions of Tempera-
   ment Survey-Revised (DOTS-R)

REPRESENTATIVE REFERENCES:

Matheny, A. P., Jr. (1989). Developmental behavioral genetics: The Louisville Twin Study. In M.
   Hahn, J. Hewitt, N. Henderson, & R. Benno (Eds.), *Genes, development and behavior*. New
   York: Oxford.
Wilson, R. (1978). Synchronies in mental development: An epigenetic perspective. *Science, 202*,
   939-948.
Wilson, R. (1983). The Louisville Twin Study: Developmental synchronies in behavior. *Child De-
   velopment, 54*, 298-316.
Wilson, R. S., & Matheny, A. P., Jr. (1986). Behavior-genetic research in infant temperament:
   The Louisville Twin Study. In R. Plomin, & J. Dunn (Eds.), *The study of temperament:
   Changes, continuities and challenges*. Hillsdale, NJ: Lawrence Erlbaum.

CURRENT STATUS OF THE STUDY:

   a. Further waves of data collection are planned; subjects will be recontacted yearly.
   b. Most of the data are in machine-readable format.
   c. Data are available for secondary analysis from the study contact person.

■ Longitudinal Study of Male Medical Students and Alumni, 1935

Mawardi, Betty Hosmer

Contact person: Betty Hosmer Mawardi
Address: School of Medicine
Case Western Reserve University
2119 Abington Road
Cleveland, OH 44106
Telephone No.: (216) 368-2830

SUBSTANTIVE TOPICS COVERED:

The study examines the satisfactions, dissatisfactions, and stresses of Case Western Medical School alumni who entered into medical practice.

CHARACTERISTICS OF THE ORIGINAL SAMPLE:

Year the study began: 1935
Subject selection process: Subjects were Case Western Reserve Medical school alumni who had received medical education.
Total number of subjects at Time 1: N = 153
Ages at Time 1: mid 20s-mid 30s
Sex distribution: 100% male
Socioeconomic status: 100% middle/upper middle class
Race/ethnicity: 97% white, 3% African-American

Years of Completed Waves:

Years	N=	Age ranges
1935-1945	153	Mid 20s-mid 30s
1962-1970	153	Mid 50s-mid 60s

INFORMATION ON SAMPLE ATTRITION:

During the 35-year period of study, no sample attrition was reported. The core sample consists of 153 Ss.

CONSTRUCTS MEASURED: INSTRUMENTS USED

Personal history, socioeconomic status, interests, values: Booklet
Job satisfaction: Brayfield Job Satisfaction Blank (from booklet)
Values: Study of Values (Allport-Vernon-Lindzey)

Risk-taking propensity, decision-making abilities: Wallach and Kogan's Dilemmas of Choice

Location of practice, type of practice, medical society memberships, age at obtaining MD degree, Medical Aptitude Test score, number of medical school honors, failures and promotions, type of internship held, type of residency, orientation to practice (patient or problem), qualifications of office assistants, records kept on patients, amount of time scheduled for new patients and repeat patients, participation in local medical activities, participation in local civic activities, strictness of authoritarianism in patient's failure to follow regimen, flexibility in treatment of patients, amount of medical consultation done and sought, amount of research consulting done, academic appointments held in medical schools, teaching appointments held in hospitals, professional advancement and mobility, number of papers published, number of refresher courses taken, number of local, state, and national meetings attended; income from medical profession, income expected in 10 years, self-image in relation to "physician" image, amount of vacation taken: Interview

Awards or honors, Medical Aptitude Test score, problems or failures, class rank, grade point average, military service: Medical school records

REPRESENTATIVE REFERENCES:

Mawardi, B. H. (1963). A study of careers of physicians: Progress report. *Journal of Medical Education, 38*(9), 793-794.

Mawardi, B. H. (1965). A career study of physicians. *Journal of Medical Education, 40*(7), 658-666.

Mawardi, B. H. (1966). Relation of student learning to physician performance. *Journal of American Medical Association, 198,* 767-769.

Mawardi, B. H. (1979). *Physicians and their careers.* Ann Arbor, MI: University Microfilms International.

CURRENT STATUS OF THE STUDY:

a. Further waves of data collection are planned.

b. Most of the data are in machine-readable format.

c. Data are available for secondary analysis through the study contact person.

■ Longitudinal Study of Male and Female Medical Students and Alumni, 1956

Mawardi, Betty Hosmer

Contact person: Betty Hosmer Mawardi
Address: School of Medicine
Case Western Reserve University
2119 Abington Road
Cleveland, OH 44106
Telephone No.: (216) 368-2830

SUBSTANTIVE TOPICS COVERED:

The study examines the satisfactions, dissatisfactions, and stresses of Case Western Medical School alumni who entered into medical practice.

CHARACTERISTICS OF THE ORIGINAL SAMPLE:

Year the study began: 1956
Subject selection process: Subjects were Case Western Reserve Medical school alumni who were randomly chosen according to nine different specialties. Subjects had received the revised medical education program at Case Western.
Total number of subjects at Time 1: N = 200
Ages at Time 1: Mid 20s-mid 30s
Sex distribution: 90% male, 10% female
Socioeconomic status: 100% middle/upper middle class
Race/ethnicity: Predominantly white

Years of Completed Waves:

Years	N=	Age ranges
1956-1965	200	Mid 20s-mid 30s
1973-1981	198	Mid 40s-mid 50s

INFORMATION ON SAMPLE ATTRITION:

During the 25-year period of study, 2 of 200 Ss (1.0%) were not retrieved for further study. The core sample consists of 198 Ss.

CONSTRUCTS MEASURED: INSTRUMENTS USED

Personal history, socioeconomic status, interests, values: Booklet
Job satisfaction: Brayfield Job Satisfaction Blank (from booklet)

Values: Study of Values (Allport-Vernon-Lindzey)

Risk-taking propensity, decision-making abilities: Wallach and Kogan's Dilemmas of Choice

Location of practice, type of practice, medical society memberships, age at obtaining MD degree, Medical Aptitude Test score, number of medical school honors, failures and promotions, type of internship held, type of residency, orientation to practice (patient or problem), qualifications of office assistants, records kept on patients, amount of time scheduled for new patients and repeat patients, participation in local medical activities, participation in local civic activities, strictness of authoritarianism in patient's failure to follow regimen, flexibility in treatment of patients, amount of medical consultation done and sought, amount of research consulting done, academic appointments held in medical schools, teaching appointments held in hospitals, professional advancement and mobility, number of papers published, number of refresher courses taken, number of local, state and national meetings attended; income from medical profession, income expected in 10 years, self-image in relation to "physician" image, amount of vacation taken: Interview

Awards or honors, Medical Aptitude Test score, problems or failures, class rank, grade point average, military service: Medical school records

REPRESENTATIVE REFERENCES:

Mawardi, B. H. (1976). New sources of stress in the practice of medicine. *Medical Alumni Bulletin, 2,* 4-7.

Mawardi, B. H. (1979). Satisfactions, dissatisfactions, and causes of stress in medical practice. *Journal of the American Medical Association, 241*(14), 1483-1486.

CURRENT STATUS OF THE STUDY:

a. Further waves of data collection are planned.

b. Most of the data are not in machine-readable format.

c. Data are available for secondary analysis through the study contact person.

■ Denver Study of Human Development, 1927

McCammon, Robert; and Tennes, Katherine

Contact Person: Jane Gardner
Address: Department of Maternal and Child Health
                  Harvard School of Public Health
                  677 Huntington Avenue
                  Boston, MA 02115
Telephone No.:   (615) 432-1080

SUBSTANTIVE TOPICS COVERED:

The study examines changes in structure during growth, development, and adaptation; changes in physiological functioning throughout life; and personality development.

CHARACTERISTICS OF THE ORIGINAL SAMPLE:

Year the study began: 1927
Subject selection process: Subjects were chosen on the basis of permanence of residence in Denver area; willingness to participate for the entire life span; availability of good medical care; middle-class social status. Ss were volunteers who were solicited through community institutions. Ss were added throughout the duration of the study.
Total number of subjects at Time 1: N = 334
Ages at Time 1: Birth
Sex distribution: Approximately equal numbers of females and males throughout
Socioeconomic status: 100% middle class
Race/ethnicity: 100% white

Years of Completed Waves:[a]

Years	N=	Ages ranges
1927-1966	334	Birth-55 yrs.

Comments:
a. The study is not conceptualized in data waves. Data collection was continuous. Ss were added to the sample from 1927 through 1966.

INFORMATION ON SAMPLE ATTRITION:

Because the study is not conceptualized in data waves, sample attrition and core sample information could not be calculated in the standard manner. Of the total 334 Ss, 78 were born before 1930. Nineteen of the 78 Ss were still being followed up at the end of 1966. Of the remaining 256 Ss who were born after 1930, 24 were not retrieved for further study beyond a 5-year period of time. Attrition for these Ss was primarily due to relocation outside the Denver area. An additional 41 Ss withdrew from the study. At the end of 1966, 179 Ss were still actively being studied. (See McCammon, 1970)

CONSTRUCTS MEASURED: INSTRUMENTS USED

Personality: Projective personality tests, non-projective personality tests
Infant development: Stanford-Binet Intelligence Test
Ability to predict from early experience: Systemized-experimental conditions
Physical growth and physical status, perception: Anthropometry and skull measurements, ossification, fusion, and skeletal maturation; pubertal growth and development; ergometry, blood pressure and pulse after ergometry; orthodontic studies of cranio-facial development; routine physical (EENT, CV, respiratory, orthopedic); Roentgenography (heart measurement, large bone length, bone, muscle, and fat width); serum cholesterol, hematology, plasma and serum protein; electrocardiograms and vital capacity, stress response of cardiovascular system; reaction time; eye-body coordination; grip strength; maximum ventilatory capacity; critical flicker fusion; nutrition intake

REPRESENTATIVE REFERENCES:

Benjamin, J. D. (1959). Prediction and psychopathological theory. In L. Jessner & E. Pavenstedt (Eds.), *Dynamic psychopathology in childhood*. New York: Grune & Stratton.

McCammon, R. W. (1970). *Human growth and development*. Springfield, IL: Charles C. Thomas.

Tennes, K., Downey, K., & Vernadakis, A. (1974). Urinary cortisal excretion rates and anxiety in normal 1-year-old infants. *Psychosomatic Medicine, 39*, 178-187.

Tennes, K., Emde, R., Kisley, A., & Metcalf, D. (1974). The stimulus barrier in early infancy: An exploration of some formulations of John Benjamin. In R. Holt & E. Peterfreund (Eds.), *Psychoanalysis and contemporary science: Vol. 1*. New York: MacMillan.

CURRENT STATUS OF THE STUDY:

a. No further waves of data collection are planned.
b. Data are in machine-readable format.
c. The data are available for secondary analysis through Dr. Jane Gardner, Department of Maternal and Child Health, Harvard School of Public Health, 677 Huntington Avenue, Boston, MA 02115.

■ Cambridge-Somerville Youth Study, 1936[a]

McCord, Joan

Contact Person: Joan McCord
Address: Department of Criminal Justice
Temple University
Philadelphia, PA 19122
Telephone No.: (215) 787-8080

SUBSTANTIVE TOPICS COVERED:

The study examines continuities in behavior, effects of child-rearing and parental characteristics on personality development (e.g., aggressiveness, antisocial behavior, alcoholism), and effects of various types of intervention on antisocial behavior.
Comment:
a. The study was initiated by Dr. Richard C. Cabot.

CHARACTERISTICS OF THE ORIGINAL SAMPLE:

Year the study began: 1936
Subject selection process: Youths were selected on the basis of age and the fact that two similar boys could be found. Both high-risk and low-risk boys from neighborhoods known to have high crime rates were eligible for inclusion. Boys were placed into pairs matched for age, background, and personality; one member of each pair was randomly selected for a treatment program.
Total number of subjects at Time 1: N = 506 (253 matched pairs)
Ages at Time 1: 4-11 yrs.
Sex distribution: 100% male
Socioeconomic status: Predominantly poverty and working class
Race/ethnicity: 95% white, 5% African-American

Years of Completed Waves:

Years	N=	Age ranges
(Cohort 1: Experimental Condition)		
1936-1937	253	4-11 yrs.
1939-1945[a]	253[b]	6-16 yrs.
1975-1976	235	43-50 yrs.
(Cohort 2: Control Condition)		
1936-1937	253	4-11 yrs.
1939-1945	253	6-16 yrs.
1975-1976	235	43-50 yrs.

Comments:
a. These subjects were randomly selected for inclusion in a treatment program. Records on child-rearing are available only for Ss in the experimental condition. The 1976-1979 wave traced official records for all 506 Ss.
b. Parents of Ss (N = 253) were followed during the 1939-1945 period of data collection.

INFORMATION ON SAMPLE ATTRITION:

Subjects were studied for a period of 41 years. The core sample consists of 232 Ss (one from each family in Cohort 1). Because of the data collection procedures, the use of a percentage for attrition does not adequately describe the sample over time, due to a selection of best data which utilized only one child per family.

CONSTRUCTS MEASURED: INSTRUMENTS USED

Criminal behavior: Criminal and court records
Alcoholism: CAGE Test
Mental illness: Mental hospital records
Occupational information, authoritarianism, marital history, self-confidence, psychosomatic illnesses, use of time, and addiction: Questionnaires
Aggression, dependency, addiction, self-confidence, parent-child interactions (in three generations), achievement orientation, social mobility, illnesses, sex-role attitudes, and recall biases: Personal interviews
Self-esteem: Modified Rosenberg Scale of Self-Esteem
Classroom behavior: Teacher's check lists
Home environment: Case records of home visits

REPRESENTATIVE REFERENCES:

McCord, J. (1978). A thirty year follow-up of treatment effects. *American Psychologists, 33*(3), 284-289.

McCord, J. (1979). Some child-rearing antecedents of criminal behavior in adult men. *Journal of Personality and Social Psychology, 37*(9), 1477-1486.

McCord, J. (1988). Identifying developmental paradigms leading to alcoholism. *Journal of Studies on Alcohol, 49*(4), 357-362.

McCord, J., & McCord, W. (1959). A follow-up report on the Cambridge-Somerville Youth Study. *Annals of the American Academy of Political and Social Science, 322*, 89-96.

CURRENT STATUS OF THE STUDY:

a. Further waves of data collection are planned, focusing on interviews with wives and children of subjects.
b. Most of the data are in machine-readable format.
c. The data are available for secondary analysis from the study contact person.

■ The Development of Representational Play and Language, 1979

McCune, Lorraine

Contact Person: Lorraine McCune
Address: Graduate School of Education
Rutgers University
10 Seminary Place
New Brunswick, NJ 08903
Telephone No.: (201) 932-8297

SUBSTANTIVE TOPICS COVERED:

The study examines the development of representational play, language, and mother-child interactions.

CHARACTERISTICS OF THE ORIGINAL SAMPLE:

Year the study began: 1979
Subject selection process: Subjects were solicited through newspaper and radio advertisements.
Total number of subjects at Time 1: N = 10
Ages at Time 1: 8 mos.
Sex distribution: Approximately equal numbers of females and males throughout
Socioeconomic status: 75% middle class, 25% working class
Race/ethnicity: 100% white

Years of Completed Waves:

Years	N=	Age ranges
1979	10	8 mos.
1980	10	1 yr.
1981	10	2 yrs.
1982	9	3 yrs.
1984	9	5 yrs.

INFORMATION ON SAMPLE ATTRITION:

During the 5-year period of study, 1 of 10 Ss (10.0%) was not retrieved for further study at the last data point. The core sample consists of 9 Ss.

CONSTRUCTS MEASURED: INSTRUMENTS USED

Development of symbolic play: McCune-Nicolich Symbolic Play Assessment
Sensory-motor development: Object Permanence Task
Cognitive development: Bayley Scales of Infant Development
Mother-child interaction behaviors: Videotape of mother-child interactions

REPRESENTATIVE REFERENCES:

McCune, L. (1990). First words: A dynamic systems view. In C. Ferguson & C. Stoel-Gammon
    (Eds.), *Child psychology: Models, research, and application*. Barkton, MD: York Press.

CURRENT STATUS OF THE STUDY:

    a. No further waves of data collection are planned.
    b. The data are not in machine-readable format.
    c. The data are available for secondary analysis through the study contact person.

■ Longitudinal Study of Preschool Programs, 1968

Miller, Louise (deceased); Dyer, Jean; Bizell, Rondell; & Sullivan, Sara

Contact Person: Sara Sullivan
Address: Department of Psychology
                  University of Wisconsin
                  La Crosse, WI 54601
Telephone No.:   (608) 785-6885

SUBSTANTIVE TOPICS COVERED:

The study examined the differential effects of four preschool programs: The Bereiter-Engelmann remedial program, the Demonstration and Research Center for Early Education (DARCEE) Early Intervention Program, the Montessori program, and the Official Head Start (Traditional) program. The study assessed the effects of each of these programs on subjects' "cognitive, motivational and perceptual development," and attempted to establish "predictive relationships from prekindergarten through high school" (see Miller & Dyer, 1975).

CHARACTERISTICS OF THE ORIGINAL SAMPLE:

Year the study began: 1968
Subject selection process: The experimental sample was derived from 14 of 48 prekindergarten classes held in Louisville, Kentucky. Of these 14 classes, 4

classes utilized the Bereiter-Engelmann program; 4 classes used the Demonstration and Research Center for Early Education (DARCEE) program; 4 classes utilized the Official Head Start (Traditional) program, while 2 other classes focused on the Montessori method of instruction. Programs were conducted at 10 different schools in four areas of the city. Children were enrolled by random assignment to experimental and nonexperimental classes. Control subjects originated from low-income backgrounds and were enrolled in the same school districts.

Total number of subjects at Time 1: N = 214
Ages at Time 1: 4 yrs.
Sex distribution: Approximately equal numbers of females and males, but varies from year to year
Socioeconomic status: 85% poverty class, 15% working class (approximately)
Race/ethnicity: 90% African-American, 10% white (approximately)

Years of Completed Waves:

Years	N=	Age ranges
Cohorts 1-4: Experimental Groups [a]		
1968-1969	214	4 yrs.(Preschool)
1968-1969	214	4 yrs.(Preschool: 8 weeks into program)
1968-1971[b]	*	5-6 yrs. (Kindergarten-1st grade)
1971-1972	175	7 yrs.(2nd grade)
1975-1976	152	11 yrs. (6th grade)
1976-1977	176	12 yrs. (7th grade)
1977-1978	109	13 yrs. (8th grade)
1978-1979	91	14 yrs. (9th grade
1979-1980	126	15 yrs. (10th grade
1980-1981	126	16 yrs. (11th grade)
1981-1982	119	17 yrs. (12th grade)
Cohort 5: Controls: No preschool experience (living at home with mothers)		
1968-1969	34	4 yrs.(Preschool)
1968-1971[c]	*	4-6 yrs. (Preschool-1st grade)
1971-1972	40[d]	7 yrs.(2nd grade)
1975-1976	35	11 yrs. (6th grade)
1976-1977	22	12 yrs. (7th grade)
1977-1978	22	13 yrs. (8th grade)
1978-1979	25	14 yrs. (9th grade)
1979-1980	38	15 yrs. (10th grade)
1980-1981	31	16 yrs. (11th grade)
1981-1982	29	17 yrs. (12th grade)

Comments:
a. The experimental groups comprised subjects enrolled in one of four preschool programs: 1) the Bereiter-Engelmann remedial program, which emphasizes acquiring academic learning skills; 2) the Demonstration and Research Center for Early Education (DARCEE), Early Intervention Program, which focuses on remediation and on "intermediate goals for all children"; 3) the Montessori program, which emphasizes long-term development in the areas of developing senses, conceptual development, development of competence in daily activities, character development, and cognitive development; and 4) the Official Head Start (Traditional) program, which emphasizes enhancing all areas of a child's development at the natural pace of the child.

b. Ss were also followed twice in 1968-1969 while in kindergarten (5 yrs.), and in 1970-1971 while in first grade (6 yrs.)

c. Ss were also followed twice in 1968-1969: 8 weeks into the preschool program at 4 yrs. of age, and in kindergarten at 5 yrs. of age; in 1969-1970 at the end of kindergarten (5 yrs.); and in 1970-1971 in first grade (6 yrs.).

d. Includes 29 of the original subjects plus 11 out of 15 follow-up controls added in 1969-1970.

INFORMATION ON SAMPLE ATTRITION:

During the 11-year period of study, approximately 88 of 214 Ss enrolled in experimental intervention programs (41.1%) were not retrieved for further study. Essentially all of the control Ss were retained throughout. Attrition was due to absenteeism, inability to locate subjects, loss of school records, and insufficient funds. The core sample consists of 126 Ss, from the experimental programs, and 34 control Ss.

CONSTRUCTS MEASURED: INSTRUMENTS USED

Cognitive and Achievement Measures

Vocabulary, knowledge of basic numerical and sensory concepts, and child's knowledge of his or her own personal world (pre-K—grade 2): The Preschool Inventory (PSI)

Listening vocabulary, knowledge of linguistic structure, and logic (pre-K—grade 2): The Basic Concept Inventory

Achievement (grades 2-3): California Achievement Test

Achievement (grades 4-6): Stanford Achievement Test, Intermediate Battery (Form B)

Achievement (grades 7-8): Stanford Achievement Test, Advanced Battery (Form B)

Reading, math, and general achievement (grades 9-12): Comprehensive Test of Basic Skills (CTBS)

Verbal intelligence (pre-K—grade 2): Peabody Picture Vocabulary Test

General intelligence (pre-K—grade 2, grade 8, grade 10, grade 12): Stanford-Binet Intelligence Test

General intelligence (grade 7, grade 9, grade 11): Revised Wechsler Intelligence Scale for Children (WISC-R)

Reasoning ability, fluid intelligence (grades 9-12): Raven's Progressive Matrices

Language skills, extent of mastery of standard English: The Parallel Sentence Production Inventory, The Expressive Vocabulary Inventory

Ability to count and to add: The Arithmetic Test

Language and math skills (grades 9-12): STEP-Locator (STEP)

Divergent thinking ability (grades 9-12): "Unusual Uses for Boxes" (Verbal Form A), "Picture Completion" (Figural Form B) (subtests of the Torrance Tests of Creative Thinking)

Motivational Measures

Autonomous behavior (pre-K—grade 2): The Cincinnati Autonomy Test Battery
Child's ability to explore, to manipulate, to investigate, and to discover when presented with novel stimuli (pre-K—grade 2): The Curiosity Box
Persistence and distractibility (pre-K—grade 2): The Replacement Puzzle
Persistence on an externally imposed task (grades 9-11): Bizzell's Persistence Puzzle (BPP)
Innovative behavior (pre-K—grade 2): The Dog and Bone Test
Child's classroom behavior (pre-K—grade 2): The Behavior Inventory
Adequacy of test-taking behavior and attitude (pre-K, grade 2, grades 6-12): The Face Sheet of the Stanford-Binet
Tester ratings of child's task absorption, task interest, confidence, and rapport with tester (grades 9-12): Proctor's Observation Scale for Testers (POST)
Sex role identification, and self-esteem (grades 9-12): PRF-Andro
Self-esteem (grades 9-10): Coopersmith Self-Esteem Inventory

Perceptual Measures

Field dependence/independence: The Early Childhood Embedded Figures Test
Youth's household, school experience, work experience, future educational aspirations and expectations, future occupational aspirations and expectations, attitudes about work, and self-esteem (grades 9-12)

REPRESENTATIVE REFERENCES:

Miller, L. B., & Bizzell, R. P. (1983). Long-term effects of four preschool programs: Sixth, seventh, and eighth grades. *Child Development, 54*, 727-741.
Miller, L. B., & Bizzell, R. P. (1984). Long-term effects of four preschool programs: Ninth- and tenth-grade results. *Child Development, 55*(4), 1570-1587.
Miller, L. B., & Dyer, J. L. (1975). Four preschool programs: Their dimensions and effects. *Monographs of the Society for Research in Child Development, 40*(5-6).
Miller, L. B., & Medley, S. S. (1984). *Preschool intervention: Fifteen years of research.* Paper presented at the American Psychological Association Meeting, Toronto, Canada.

CURRENT STATUS OF THE STUDY:

a. No further waves of data collection are planned.
b. Data are in machine-readable format.
c. Data will be available for secondary analysis through the Henry A. Murray Research Center, Radcliffe College, 10 Garden Street, Cambridge, MA 02138.

■ Continuities and Discontinuities in the Development of 64 Very Small Premature Infants to 4 Years of Age, 1980

Minde, Klaus K.

Contact Person: Klaus K. Minde
Address: Montreal Children's Hospital
                  Department of Psychiatry
                  2300 Tupper Street
                  Montreal, Quebec H3H 1P3
                  Canada
Telephone No.:   (514) 934-4449

SUBSTANTIVE TOPICS COVERED:

The psychiatric, psychological, school, and overall family functioning of 64 small premature infants was assessed from birth to 48 months of age. The study attempted to answer whether prematurely born children are more likely to have behavioral problems by age 48 months, as assessed by maternal and teacher rating scales as well as by psychiatric interview, and to what extent we can predict problematic children from their perinatal histories, early attachment patterns, temperament ratings, and family functioning measures.

CHARACTERISTICS OF THE ORIGINAL SAMPLE:

Year the study began: 1980-1981
Subject selection process: The sample was initially drawn from the population of small premature twins and singletons admitted within 12 hours of birth to the neonatal intensive care unit at the Toronto Hospital for Sick Children. To be eligible for the study, infants had to weigh less than 1,501 grams and had to be free of major physical malformations. In addition, the investigators required that the parents spoke English, lived within 25 miles of the hospital, intended to keep their babies, and gave verbal consent to participate in this study.
Total number of subjects at Time 1: N = 77
Ages at Time 1: 3 months
Sex distribution: 57.8% male, 42.2% female
Socioeconomic status: 60% middle/upper middle class, 40% working class
Race/ethnicity: 75% white, 10% Hispanic, 10% black, 5% Asian

Years of Completed Waves:

Years	N=	Age ranges
1980-1981	77	3 mos.
1980-1981	77	6 mos.
1980-1981	77	9 mos.
1981-1982	72	1 yr.
1985-1986	64	4 yrs.

INFORMATION ON SAMPLE ATTRITION:

During the 6-year period of study, 7 of 77 Ss (9.1%) were not retrieved for further study. At 48 months, seven children could not be followed-up because the families had left the country (one twin pair); one twin pair refused to be seen again; and three children could not be traced. Six more children were not included because they were significantly delayed in their development. The core sample consists of 64 Ss.

CONSTRUCTS MEASURED: INSTRUMENTS USED

Child's and family's medical, psychological and social functioning: Psychiatric interview and family rating
Temperament: Toddler Temperament Scale
Developmental status: Bayley Infant Scales of Development, Stanford-Binet Intelligence Scale
Attachment status: Ainsworth Strange Situation
Maternal emotions, psychological and physical state: Malaise Inventory
Child behavior: Behavior Check List
Teacher reports to help identify children at risk for psychopathology: Preschool Behavior Questionnaire

REPRESENTATIVE REFERENCES:

Minde, K., Corter, C., & Goldberg, S. (1984). The contribution of twinship and early biological impediments to early interaction and attachment between premature infants and their mothers. In J. D. Call, E. Galenson, & R. L. Tyson (Eds.), *Frontiers of infant psychiatry II* (pp. 160-176). New York: Basic Books.
Minde, K., Goldberg, S., Perrotta, M., et al. (1989). Continuities and discontinuities in the development of 64 very small premature infants to 4 years of age. *Journal of Child Psychology and Psychiatry, 30*(3), 391-404.
Minde, K., Perrotta, M., & Hellmann, J. (1988). The impact of delayed development in premature infants on mother-infant interaction: A prospective investigation. *Journal of Pediatrics, 112*, 136-142.
Minde, K., Whitelaw, H., Brown, J., & Fitzhardinge, P. (1983). Effect of neonatal complications in premature infants on early parent-infant interaction. *Developmental Medicine and Child Neurology, 25*, 763-777.

CURRENT STATUS OF THE STUDY:

a. No further waves of data collection are planned.
b. Data are in machine-readable format.
c. Data are available for secondary analysis.

■ Repatriated Prisoner of War Program, 1974

Mitchell, Robert E.

Contact person: Captain Robert E. Mitchell
Address: Naval Aerospace Medical Institute
                 Naval Air Station
                 Pensacola, FL 32500-5600
Telephone No.:   (904) 452-8066

SUBSTANTIVE TOPICS COVERED:

The study examines the extent of harmful psychological and physical effects upon individuals who had been held captive as prisoners of war.

CHARACTERISTICS OF THE ORIGINAL SAMPLE:

Year the study began: 1974

Subject selection process: All subjects were Navy and Marine Corps personnel who were prisoners of war in Vietnam. Control Ss consisted of a computer-matched group of Navy personnel who were generally identical to the prisoner of war Ss, except for not having been held as prisoners of war.

Total number of subjects at Time 1: N = 168

Ages at Time 1: 20-50 yrs.

Sex distribution: 100% male

Socioeconomic status: Information not available

Race/ethnicity: 97% white, 1% African-American, 1% Hispanic, 1% Asian-American (Cohort 1); 99% white, 1% Hispanic (Cohort 2)

Years of Completed Waves:[a]

Years	N=	Age ranges
(Cohort 1: Former Prisoners of War)		
1974	168	20-50 yrs.
1975	164	21-51 yrs.
1976	164	22-52 yrs.
1977	164	23-53 yrs.
1978	160	24-54 yrs.
1979	160	25-55 yrs.
1980	155	26-56 yrs.
1981	155	27-57 yrs.
1982	155	28-58 yrs.
1983	155	29-59 yrs.
1984	155	30-60 yrs.
1985	155	31-61 yrs.
1986	155	32-62 yrs.
1987	155	33-63 yrs.

Years of Completed Waves, Continued:[a]

Years	N=	Age ranges
1988	155	34-64 yrs.
1989	155	35-65 yrs.
1990	155	36-66 yrs.
(Cohort 2: Control Ss)		
1976	92	30-50 yrs.
1977	90	31-51 yrs.
1978	90	32-52 yrs.
1979	85	33-53 yrs.
1980	80	34-54 yrs.
1981	80	35-55 yrs.
1982	80	36-56 yrs.
1983	80	37-57 yrs.
1984	80	38-58 yrs.
1985	80	39-59 yrs.
1986	80	40-60 yrs.
1987	80	41-61 yrs.
1988	80	42-62 yrs.
1989	80	43-63 yrs.
1990	80	44-64 yrs.

Comments:
a. Sample sizes are approximations throughout.

INFORMATION ON SAMPLE ATTRITION:

During the 16-year period of study, approximately 23 of 260 Ss (8.8%), from both cohorts, were not retrieved for further study. The core sample consists of 235 Ss: 155 Ss (Cohort 1), 80 Ss (Cohort 2). Attrition was due to death, Ss dropping out of the program, and their inability to attend examinations due to deployment.

CONSTRUCTS MEASURED: INSTRUMENTS USED

Physical health, medical evaluation, complete history, physical examination, Anthropometrics, laboratory tests, X rays, electrocardiograms, medical tests, visual function tests, vestibular function tests, audiologic tests, sleep questionnaire, neurologic examination (Time 1), Dermatologic examination (Time 1), complete chronology of POW experience (Time 1): Repatriated Prisoners of War Program Initial Evaluation Protocol.

Psychological well-being: Psychiatric Interview Questionnaire, Personality Research Forms (1974, 1976,1978, 1981), Basic Temperament Scale (1977), Halstead-Reitan (1977, 1978, 1979, 1984), Wechsler Adult Intelligence Scale, (1977, 1978, 1979, 1984), Fifth-Year Repatriated Prisoners of War Program (RPOW) Questionnaire (1978), Minnesota Multiphasic Personality Inventory (1981, 1984), FIBO-B (1983), Mooney Problem Checklist (1984), Self-Assessment Questionnaire (1984), Mental Health Assessment Questionnaire (1985)

REPRESENTATIVE REFERENCES:

Dahl, B. B., McCubbin, H. I., & Lester, G. R. (1976). War-induced father absence: Comparing the adjustment of children in reunited, non-reunited and reconstituted families. *International Journal of Sociology of the Family, 6*(1), 99-108.

McCubbin, H. I., Dahl, B., Lester, G., & Ross, B. (1975). The returned prisoner of war: Factors in family reintegration. *Journal of Marriage and the Family, 37*(3), 471-478.

McCubbin, H. I., Hunter, E. J., & Dahl, B. B. (1975). Residuals of war: Families of prisoners of war and servicemen missing in action. *Journal of Social Issues, 31*(4).

Rutledge, H., Hunter, E. J., & Dahl, B. (1979). Human values and the prisoner of war. *Environment and Behavior, 11*(2), 227-244.

CURRENT STATUS OF THE STUDY:

    a. Further annual waves of data collection are planned.
    b. Most of the data are in machine-readable format.
    c. Data are not available for secondary analysis.

■ Pensacola Study of Naval Aviators, 1940

Mitchell, Robert E.; Graybiel, Ashton; Harlan, William R., Jr.; and Oberman, Albert

Contact Person: Captain Robert E. Mitchell
Address: Naval Aerospace Medical Institute
               Naval Air Station
               Pensacola, FL 32500-5600
Telephone No.: (904) 452-8066

SUBSTANTIVE TOPICS COVERED:

    The study explored the value of psychological and physiological testing in the prediction of success in the flight training program. Subsequent studies have been concerned with the effects of the stresses of an aviation environment and with the aging of the group of aviators.

CHARACTERISTICS OF THE ORIGINAL SAMPLE:

Year the study began: 1940
Subject selection process: Officers and cadets in classes entering the flight training program and a group of instructors.
Total number of subjects at Time 1: N = 1,312
Ages at Time 1: 20-30 yrs.
Sex distribution: 100% male

Socioeconomic status: Information not available
Race/ethnicity: 100% white

Years of Completed Waves:

Years	N=	Age ranges
1940	1,312	20-30 yrs.
1951	1,049	31-41 yrs.
1957	836	37-47 yrs.
1963	811	43-53 yrs.
1969-1971	718	49-59 yrs.
1988	450[a]	66-76 yrs.

Comments:
a. This number is an estimate. 708 questionnaires were sent to the last known addresses; 132 questionnaires were returned as not forwardable; 335 responded.

INFORMATION ON SAMPLE ATTRITION:

Attrition was due to aviators dropping out of the program, failed aviator training, Ss not answering or returning questionnaires (172 Ss), and death (69 Ss). The core sample consists of 335 Ss.

CONSTRUCTS MEASURED: INSTRUMENTS USED

Health, occupation, military status: Questionnaire
Physical health: Physical examinations, Medical tests (cardiovascular, laboratory tests, pulmonary and metabolic tests); anthropometry (somatotype, and physical measurements); Interview (personal and medical histories, including alcohol, smoking, and exercise histories)
Psychological well-being: Psychiatric Interview
Psychologic-Psychomotor assessments: Guilford-Zimmerman Temperament Survey, Ataxia test, Tilt Chair
Neurophysiological functioning: Electroencephalogram, skin resistance
Perceptual abilities: Vision tests, audiometry

REPRESENTATIVE REFERENCES:

Gunderson, E. K. E., Mitchell, R. E., & Biersner, R. J. (1984). Longitudinal health research in the U.S. Navy. In Mednick, S. A., Harway, M., & Finello, K. M. (Eds.). *Handbook of longitudinal research: Vol. 2. Teenage and adult cohorts.* New York: Praeger.
Mitchell, R. E. (1976). The thousand aviators—thirty-three years later. In C. L. Rose (Ed.), *Collaboration among longitudinal studies* (Research Report Series, Publication No. 8). Boston: Veterans Administration Outpatient Clinic.
Mitchell, R. E. (1990). The thousand aviators—a half century. *Foundation, 11*(2), 76-83.

Oberman, A., Lane, N. E., Mitchell, R. E., & Graybiel, A. (1965). *The Thousand Aviator Study. Distributions and inter-correlations of selected variables* (Monograph 12). Pensacola, FL: United States Naval School of Aviation Medicine.

CURRENT STATUS OF THE STUDY:

    a. Further waves of data collection are planned.

    b. Most of the data are in machine-readable format.

    c. Data are not available for secondary analysis.

■ Panel Study of Income Dynamics (PSID), 1968

Morgan, James N.; Duncan, Gregory J.; and Hill, Martha

Contact Person: Greg J. Duncan/Martha Hill
Address: P.O. Box 1248
                 Survey Research Center
                 Institute for Social Research
                 University of Michigan
                 Ann Arbor, MI 48104
Telephone No.:   (313) 763-5186

SUBSTANTIVE TOPICS COVERED:

PSID generates data on individuals and families concerning economy, behavior, and attitude information required to analyze factors affecting changes in well-being. The annual interviews gather information on income, education, labor force participation, occupation, work hours, family composition, housing, commuting, changing jobs or residences, housework, child care, and food expenditures. Environmental data from counties where respondents live, economic behavior patterns, attitudes, and home production (first 5 years); achievement motivation and cognitive ability (5th year), housing and neighborhood (8th year), interviews with wives and family heads (9th year), how people got jobs, the disabilities of each family member, and retirement plans and coverage of older workers and retirement experiences of the retired (11th year), do-it-yourself activities (12th year), emergency help in terms of time and money to or from friends or relatives (13th year), participation in the food stamp program and participation in SSI, unemployment and periods out of the labor force, re-asks expected retirement age, and number of days in the hospital, and number of days in the hospital or sick in bed at home (14th year).

CHARACTERISTICS OF THE ORIGINAL SAMPLE:

Year the study began: 1968

Subject selection process: The panel study surveyed representative American families. All members of the original probability sample of families interviewed in 1968 (N = 4,802) define eligible families.

Total number of subjects at Time 1: N = 4,802 families

Ages at Time 1: All ages

Sex distribution: Equal numbers of females and males throughout

Socioeconomic status: 60% national representative sample for 1968, 40% poverty and working class

Race/ethnicity: 70% white (initially), 30% African-American; 55.6% white, 22.2% African-American, 22.2% Hispanic (1990)

Years of Completed Waves:

Years	N=	Age ranges
1968	4,802	All ages
1969	4,460	All ages
1970	4,665	All ages
1971	4,840	All ages
1972	5,060	All ages
1973	5,185	All ages
1974	5,517	All ages
1975	5,725	All ages
1976	5,862	All ages
1977	6,007	All ages
1978	6,154	All ages
1979	6,373	All ages
1980	6,533	All ages
1981	6,620	All ages
1982	6,742	All ages
1983	6,852	All ages
1984	7,153	All ages
1985	7,032	All ages
1986	7,018	All ages
1987	7,061	All ages
1988	7,114	All ages
1989	7,114	All ages
1990[a]	7,327	All ages

Comments:

a. A sample of roughly 2,000 Hispanic households was added in 1990.

INFORMATION ON SAMPLE ATTRITION:

During the 23-year period of study, the total number of participants has grown from roughly 16,000 to more than 38,000 Ss due to yearly enrollment of new Ss. Yearly response rates have ranged between 97% and 98%. The cumulative response rate over the 23-year period of study is approximately 62%.

CONSTRUCTS MEASURED: INSTRUMENTS USED

Housing; family composition; education of children; car ownership; car behavior; debt; health insurance; assets, consumption (food, clothing, cigarettes, alcohol); occupation and employment of head; marital status; education of wife, occupation and employment of wife, family planning; family income, occupation of others in family, other income and financial information; time use: "feelings" questions; background questions for head; interviewer's observation section including who was respondent, impressions of respondent and dwelling unit, and location and type of dwelling relative to an SMSA: Family Economics Questionnaire (Wave 1)

REPRESENTATIVE REFERENCES:

Duncan, G. J. (1984). *Years of poverty, years of plenty: The changing economic fortunes of American workers and families.* Ann Arbor, MI: Survey Research Center, Institute for Social Research, University of Michigan.

Morgan, James N., et al. *Five thousand American families—patterns of economic progress: Analyses and special studies of the Panel Study of Income Dynamics* (Vols. I-X). Ann Arbor, MI: Survey Research Center, Institute for Social Research, University of Michigan.

Survey Research Center. (1972-1990). *A Panel Study of Income Dynamics: Procedures and tape codes, wave I-XX.* Survey Research Center/Inter-University Consortium for Political and Social Research, Institute for Social Research. Ann Arbor, MI: University of Michigan.

Survey Research Center. (1984). *User guide to the Panel Study of Income Dynamics, Vols. I & II.* Inter-University Consortium for Political and Social Research, Ann Arbor: University of Michigan.

CURRENT STATUS OF THE STUDY:

a. Further waves of data collection are planned.
b. Data are in machine-readable format.
c. Data are available for secondary analysis through the Inter-University Consortium for Political and Social Research, University of Michigan, Ann Arbor, MI 48106.

■ The Michigan Student Study: Male Follow-Up, 1962

Mortimer, Jeylan T.

Contact person: Jeylan T. Mortimer
Address: University of Minnesota
                  909 Social Science Tower
                  267 19th Avenue South
                  Minneapolis, MN 55455
Telephone No.:   (612) 624-6333

SUBSTANTIVE TOPICS COVERED:

The purpose of this follow-up study was to assess the implications of work experience for personal development early in one's career. (See also Gurin, G., *Michigan Student Study: A Study of Students in a Multiversity*; and Tangri, S. S., *Longitudinal Study of Career Development in College-Educated Women*.)

CHARACTERISTICS OF THE ORIGINAL SAMPLE:

Year the study began: 1962

Subject selection process: Subjects initially selected by Dr. Gerald Gurin in 1962 were students in their first year. One fourth were chosen randomly from the entering student classes of the University of Michigan in 1962 and 1963. Four years later (1966, 1967) 150 additional seniors were chosen randomly to compensate for first year sample attrition. In 1976, 512 members of the senior sample were located and followed up. These constituted 74% of the target group.

Total number of subjects at Time 1: N = 650

Ages at Time 1: 18-19 yrs.

Sex distribution: 100% male

Socioeconomic status: 91% middle/upper middle class, 9% working class

Race/ethnicity: 100% white

Years of Completed Waves:

Years	N=	Age ranges
1962-1963	650	18-19 yrs.
1966-1967[a]	694	22-23 yrs.
1976	512	32-33 yrs.

Comments:
a. 150 seniors were added to compensate for first year student attrition.

INFORMATION ON SAMPLE ATTRITION:

During the 14-year period of study, 138 of 650 Ss (21.2%) were not retrieved for further study. The core sample consists of 512 Ss. The main reason for sample attrition was difficulty in locating graduates because of the mobility of the sample.

CONSTRUCTS MEASURED: INSTRUMENTS USED

Self-concept: Semantic Differential Scale
Occupational values: Rosenberg Scale
Commitments: Likert-type scale
Work autonomy: Kohn and Schooler Survey
Career stability, parental support, work-family strain: Questionnaire

REPRESENTATIVE REFERENCES:

Mortimer, J. T., Finch, M. D., & Kumka, D. (1982). Persistence and change in development: The multi-dimensional self-concept. In P. D. Bates & O. G. Brim, Jr. (Eds.), *Life span development and behavior: Vol. 4* (pp. 263-313). New York: Academic Press.
Mortimer, J. T., & Lorence, J. (1979). Work experience and occupational value socialization: A longitudinal study. *American Journal of Sociology, 84,* 1361-1385.
Mortimer, J. T., & Lorence, J. (1979). Occupational experience and the self-concept: A longitudinal study. *Social Psychology Quarterly, 42,* 307-323.
Mortimer, J. T., Lorence, J., & Kumka, D. (1986). *Work, family, and personality: Transition to adulthood.* Norwood, NJ: Ablex.

CURRENT STATUS OF THE STUDY:

a. No further waves of data collection are planned.
b. Most data are in machine-readable format.
c. Data are available for secondary analysis from the study contact person.

■ Multiform Assessments of Personality Development Among Gifted College Men, 1941

Murray, Henry A. (deceased)

Contact person: Henry A. Murray Research Center
Address: Radcliffe College
                  10 Garden Street
                  Cambridge, MA 02138
Telephone No.:   (617) 495-8140

SUBSTANTIVE TOPICS COVERED:

The purpose of this study is to further understand the personality by combining the use of standardized tests and projective measures with intensive study of social interaction, responses to stress, and memory.

CHARACTERISTICS OF THE ORIGINAL SAMPLE:

Year the study began: 1941
Subject selection process: Subjects selected were male undergraduates at Harvard University.
Total number of subjects at Time 1: N = 11
Ages at Time 1: 18-19 yrs.
Sex distribution: 100% male
Socioeconomic status: 100% middle/upper middle class

Years of Completed Waves:

Years	N=	Age ranges
(Cohort 1)		
1942-1943	11	18-19 yrs.
1943-1944	11	19-20 yrs.
1944-1945	11	20-21 yrs.
(Cohort 2)		
1951-1952	20	18-19 yrs.
1952-1953	20	19-20 yrs.
1953-1954	20	20-21 yrs.
(Cohort 3)		
1954-1955	20	18-19 yrs.
1955-1956	20	19-20 yrs.
1956-1957	20	20-21 yrs.
(Cohort 4)		
1959-1960	23	18-19 yrs.
1960-1961	23	19-20 yrs.
1961-1962	23	20-21 yrs.

Years of Completed Waves, Continued:

Years	N=	Age ranges
(Cohort 5)		
1962-1963	22	18-19 yrs.
1963-1964	22	19-20 yrs.
1964-1965	22	20-21 yrs.

INFORMATION ON SAMPLE ATTRITION:

During the 23-year period of study, all Ss from each wave were retained for further study. The core sample consists of 96 Ss across five cohorts.

CONSTRUCTS MEASURED: INSTRUMENTS USED

Marital status, college information (class, best course, college address), extracurricular activities, family background: Face sheet
Personal and academic history: Personal History Questionnaire
Academic performance: Transcript
School history, academic performance: Harvard application
Personal history written by subject: Autobiography
Subject's idea of long-term future: View of the Future Essay
Religious history, attitudes: Jewish Interview
List of ego ideal components (dominance, achievement, nurturance, and so on): Reading History Essay
Psychiatric treatment, mental functioning: Clinical record
Anxiety, attitudes toward women, outlook on life, deference: Essay of Psychodrama

REPRESENTATIVE REFERENCES:

Murray, Henry A. (1955). American Icarus. In A. Burton & R. E. Harris (Eds.), *Clinical studies in personality: Vol. 2* (pp. 615-641). New York: Harper & Row.
Murray, Henry A. (1963). Studies of stressful interpersonal disputations. *American Psychologist, 18,* 23-36.
Murray, Henry A. (1965). Estimates of the intensity of anxiety, anger, and drive during a stressful dyadic disputation. *Conference on Emotion and Feeling,* New York.

CURRENT STATUS OF THE STUDY:

a. No further waves of data collection are planned.
b. Most of the data are not in machine-readable format.
c. Data are available for secondary analysis through the Henry A. Murray Research Center, Radcliffe College, 10 Garden Street, Cambridge, MA 02138.

■ Third Harvard Growth Study, 1922

Must, Aviva; Bajema, Carl J.; Johnston, Francis; and Scott, Eugenie C.

Contact person: Aviva Must
Address: Human Nutrition Center
Tufts University
711 Washington Street
Boston, MA 02111
Telephone No.: (617) 556-3325

SUBSTANTIVE TOPICS COVERED:

The original Harvard Growth Study monitored the physical and mental growth of school children. The mid-life follow-up collected data on health and reproductive histories as well as basic sociodemographic data. The current elderly follow-up is concerned with the health and mortality outcomes relative to childhood obesity. The current study population is a subsample of the original study selected on the basis of childhood weight status.

CHARACTERISTICS OF THE ORIGINAL SAMPLE:

Year the study began: 1922
Subject selection process: The original study population consisted of all Medford, Massachusetts, public school first graders in 1922, and second graders in 1923, and Beverly and Revere, Massachusetts, public school first graders in 1923. The study later expanded to include siblings of Ss.
Total number of subjects at Time 1: N = 3,592
Ages at Time 1: 5 yrs.
Sex distribution: Approximately equal numbers of females and males throughout
Socioeconomic status: 94% working class, 6% middle class (approximately)
Race/ethnicity: 97% white, 3% African-American

Years of Completed Waves:

Years	N=	Ages ranges
1922-1923	3,592	5 yrs.
1923-1924	3,569	6 yrs.
1924-1925	3,400	7 yrs.
1925-1926	3,172	8 yrs.
1926-1927	2,899	9 yrs.
1927-1928	2,729	10 yrs.
1928-1929	2,571	11 yrs.
1929-1930	2,443	12 yrs.
1930-1931	2,322	13 yrs.
1931-1932	2,105	14 yrs.

Years of Completed Waves, Continued:

Years	N=	Ages ranges
1932-1933	1,829	15 yrs.
1933-1934	1,468	16 yrs.
1934-1935	889	17 yrs.
1935-1936	384	18 yrs.
1936-1937	284	19 yrs.
1937-1938	267	20 yrs.
1938-1939	265	21 yrs.
1968	1,222	45-48 yrs.
1989[a]	508	72-74 yrs.

Comments:
a. In 1989, a subsample of 508 Ss were followed-up, focusing upon the aftereffects of childhood obesity (roughly 254 obese Ss and 254 non-obese Ss).

INFORMATION ON SAMPLE ATTRITION:

During the 67-year period of study, 2,370 of 3,592 Ss (66%) were not retrieved for further study. The core sample consists of 1,222 Ss.

CONSTRUCTS MEASURED: INSTRUMENTS USED

Phase I: Initial Study (1922-1934)

Intelligence and educational achievement:

Year 1: Dearborn Group Test of Intelligence, General Examination A, (also B in some instances); Detroit First-Grade Intelligence Test, Form A; Stanford-Binet Individual Intelligence Test (selected cases), Otis Group Intelligence Scale, Primary Examination, Form A, (selected groups); Peet-Dearborn Progress Tests in Arithmetic, for Primary and Intermediate Grades; Haggerty Reading Examination, Sigma 1

Year 2: Dearborn Group Test of Intelligence, General Examination A; Stanford-Binet Intelligence test (selected cases), Peet-Dearborn Progress Tests in Arithmetic, Form for Primary and Intermediate Grades

Year 3: Dearborn Group Test of Intelligence, General Examination A; Myers Mental Measure; Stanford-Binet Individual Intelligence Test (selected cases), Otis Primary Intelligence Test, Form A; Peet-Dearborn Progress Tests in Arithmetic, Form for Primary and Intermediate Grades, Haggerty Reading Examination, Sigma 1

Year 4: Dearborn Group Test of Intelligence, General Examination C; Otis Primary Intelligence Test, Form A; Stanford-Binet Individual Intelligence Test (selected cases), Peet-Dearborn Progress Tests in Arithmetic, Form for Primary and Intermediate Grades; Dearborn-Westbrook Reading Test, No. 2, Form 1; Ayres' Scale for Measuring Ability in Silent Reading, P.S. 2

Year 5: Dearborn Group Test of Intelligence, General Examination C; Otis Self-administering Test of Mental Ability, Form A; Stanford-Binet Individual Intelligence Test (selected cases), Peet-Dearborn Progress Tests in Arithmetic, Form for Primary and Intermediate Grades; Chapman-Cook Speed of Reading Test (Grades 4-8), Chapman Unspeeded Reading Comprehension Test, Burgess Scale for Measuring Ability in Silent Reading, P.S. 2; Dearborn-Westbrook Reading Test, No. 2, Form 1

Year 6: Dearborn Group Test of Intelligence, General Examination C; Otis Self-administering Test of Mental Ability, Form B; Stanford-Binet Individual Intelligence Test (selected cases), Peet-Dearborn Progress Tests in Arithmetic, for Advanced Grades; Chapman Unspeeded Reading Comprehension Test (Grades 5-12), Chapman-Cook Speed Reading Comprehension Test (Grades 5-12), Chapman-Cook Speed of Reading Test, for Grades 4-8; Burgess Scale of Measuring Ability in Silent Reading, P.S. 2

Year 7: Haggerty Intelligence Test, Delta 2; Dearborn Group Intelligence, Old Form 4 and 5; Stanford Achievement Test, Reading and Arithmetic; Stanford-Binet Individual Intelligence Test (all cases)

Year 8: Terman Group Test of Mental Ability, Form A or B; Haggerty Intelligence Examination, Delta 2; Stanford-Binet Individual Intelligence Test (selected cases), New Stanford Arithmetic Examination, Form V; New Stanford Reading Examination, Form V

Year 9: Terman Group Test of Mental Ability, Form B (grades 7 and above); National Intelligence Tests (for pupils below the 7th grade); Kuhlmann-Anderson Intelligence Tests, forms appropriate for the grade in which the child was placed; Stanford-Binet Individual Intelligence Test (selected cases), New Stanford Achievement Test (entire), Form W

Years 10-12: Kuhlmann-Anderson Intelligence Test, Detroit Advanced Intelligence Test, Form A; National Intelligence Test, Scale A-1; Stanford-Binet Intelligence Test; New Stanford Achievement Test, Primary, Form X; New Standard Achievement Test, Advanced, Form X; Morrison-McCall Spelling Scale, Sones-Harry High School Achievement Test, Form A or B; American Council French Grammar Test, Form A; A Silent Reading Test in French, Form A; Iowa Silent Reading Test, Form A (revised); English Minimum Essentials Test, Tressler, Form A; Schorling-Clark-Potter Arithmetic Test, Form A (revised); Elwell-Fowlkes Bookkeeping Test, Form 2A; A Series of Tests in Gregg Shorthand (Reading, A-1; Speed Writing, B-1; Vocabulary, C-2); Detroit Advanced Intelligence Test (Form V) (Year 10); Detroit Advanced Intelligence Test (Form W) (Year 11); Revised Alpha Examination (Form VII) (Year 11); Revised Alpha Examination (Form V) (Year 12)

Anthropometric measurements: Stature, porion height, supra-sternal notch height, sitting height, iliac diameter, breadth of the chest (The Transverse Diameter), chest depth (The Antero-Posterior Diameter), head length, head circumference, head width, weight, number of teeth, leg length, trunk length, X ray hand and wrist, wrist width, wrist depth, skeletal maturity, and arm length

Home conditions, language spoken in the home, language spoken by pupil, ability to speak and understand English, examination ability (group or individual), and home handicaps: Sociological information (based on first grade teacher's ratings)

Name, birth, date and place, town residence, father's birthplace, mother's birthplace, club memberships (jr. high school), office held in club (jr. high school), sports taken part in (jr. high school), other activities (jr. high school); Junior, Senior Prom Committee (high school), sports (high school), office held while a member of club (high school), hobbies (high school), class officer, socioeconomic status, birth order, marital condition of parents, attitude toward unemployment (1935), attitude toward existing conditions (1935): Sociological Questionnaire

Intelligence, ability to get explanations and directions, concentration, work habits, study habits, cooperation, leadership, nervous condition, ability in plays and games, general standing in school, ability in arithmetic, ability in reading, ability in expression, behavior, and handwork: Psychological information (based on first grade teacher's ratings)

Age at school entrance, number of years in school, highest grade reached, name of school attended, one arithmetic test each school year, one reading test each school year, music lessons, instrument played, vocal lessons, dancing lessons, elocution lessons, studying outside of school, instrument played in an orchestra, school attendance records (absences each year), school marks (during entire school career), teachers' conduct rating (each year), reasons for leaving school, reason for attending school, occupational training, most valuable school subject, most enjoyable school subject, training most desired, attitude toward education, and subjects best liked in high school: Educational Questionnaire

Father's occupation, mother's occupation, work after school hours for pay, kind of work, vocational plans (while in high school), preference of occupation after leaving school, employment status, July 1, 1935 (13 yrs. after school entrance), employment status, means used in trying to obtain employment, means by which employment was obtained, type of present position, success since leaving school, salary level (present), future occupational plans (lowest acceptable salary to change, lowest acceptable salary to begin), and attitude toward present position: Economic Questionnaire

Physical handicaps, annual health rating, puberty: Medical Questionnaire

Phase II: Follow-up (conducted by Dr. Carl J. Bajema)

Health history, educational history, and occupational history: Questionnaire (8 pages)

1989 Subsample Follow-up: Obesity Study (conducted by Ms. Aviva Must)

Current health, health history, body mass index, blood pressure: Questionnaire, measurement of height, weight, sphygmomanometer

REPRESENTATIVE REFERENCES:

Bajema, C. J., & Damon, A. (1974). Age at menarche: Accuracy of recall after 39 years. *Human Biology, 46,* 381-384.

Dearborn, W. F., & Rothney, J. W. M. (1941). *Predicting the child's development.* Cambridge, MA: Sci-Art.

Dearborn, W. F., Rothney, J. W., & Shuttleworth, F. K. (1938). Data on the growth of school children (from the materials of the Third Harvard Growth Study). *Monographs of the Society for Research in Child Development, 3,* 1-136.

Scott, E. C., & Bajema, C. J. (1982). Height, weight and fertility among the participants of the Third Harvard Growth Study. *Human Biology, 54,* 501-516.

CURRENT STATUS OF THE STUDY:

a. No further waves of data collection are planned.

b. Most of the data are in machine-readable format.

c. Data are available for secondary analysis through Dr. Francis E. Johnston, Department of Anthropology, University of Pennsylvania, Philadelphia, PA 19104-6398.

N

Longitudinal Study of the Development of Formal Operations, 1967

Neimark, Edith D.

Contact Person: Edith D. Neimark
Address: Psychology Department, Rutgers University
Kilmer Campus
New Brunswick, NJ 08903
Telephone No.: (201) 932-4636

SUBSTANTIVE TOPICS COVERED:

This study traces child development from concrete to formal operations, as reflected in a diagnostic problem-solving task as well as Piagetian Tasks, and relates performance to two measures of cognitive style.

CHARACTERISTICS OF THE ORIGINAL SAMPLE:

Year the study began: 1967
Subject selection process: All children in the school (grades 4-6) who met the following criteria were selected: (a) parents gave written permission for child's participation, (b) Otis IQ was 90-115, and (c) performance on diagnostic problem-solving task allowed room for improvement.
Total number of subjects at Time 1: N - 53
Ages at Time 1: 9-11 yrs.
Sex distribution: Approximately equal numbers of females and males throughout
Socioeconomic status: Predominantly middle class
Race/ethnicity: Predominantly white

Years of Completed Waves:

Years	N=	Age ranges
(Cohort 1)[a]		
1967 (Sept.)	53	9-11 yrs.
1967-1970[b]	*	9-13 yrs.
1971 (Jan.)	42	12-14 yrs.

Comments:
a. Fourth, fifth, and sixth graders with average intelligence, and "bright" fourth graders
b. Ss were also followed in 1967 (Dec.); 1968 (Mar., June, Sept., Nov.), 1969 (Mar.), and 1970 (Apr. & May).

Years of Completed Waves, Continued:

Years	N=	Age ranges
(Cohort 2)[a]		
1968 (Sept.)	28	9-10 yrs.
1969-1970[b]	*	9-11 yrs.
1970 (Nov.)	24	11-12 yrs.

Comments:
a. Fourth and fifth graders with average intelligence
b. Ss were also followed in 1969 (Jan., May, Sept.), and 1970 (Mar.).

Years	N=	Age ranges
(Cohort 3)[a]		
1969 (Jan.)	24	8 yrs.
1969-1971[b]	*	8-10 yrs.
1971 (June)	18	10 yrs.

Comments:
a. Third graders with average intelligence
b. Ss were also followed in 1969 (Apr. & Oct.), 1970 (Jan., May, Oct.), and 1971 (Apr.).

Years	N=	Age ranges
(Control)[a]		
1970 (Apr.)	52	9-11 yrs.

Comments:
a. Fourth, fifth, and sixth graders with average intelligence

INFORMATION ON SAMPLE ATTRITION:

During the 4-year period of study, 73 of 157 Ss (46.5%), across the three cohorts followed, were not retrieved for further study. The core sample consists of 84 Ss: 42 Ss for Cohort 1, 24 Ss for Cohort 2, and 18 Ss for Cohort 3. Attrition was due to children moving out of the area.

CONSTRUCTS MEASURED: INSTRUMENTS USED

Planning, development of information gathering strategy: Eight diagnostic problems (Neimark)
Early formal operations: Combinations (Piaget)
Formal operations: Correlations (Piaget)
Information-gathering strategy: Matrix (20 questions)
Early formal operations conceptual classification: Construct matrix of blocks (Wohlwill)
Later formal operations: Permutations
Reflection, impulsivity, field dependence, independence: Matching familiar figures embedded figures test

REPRESENTATIVE REFERENCES:

Neimark, E. D. (1970). A preliminary search for formal operations structure. *Journal of Genetic Psychology, 116,* 223-232.

Neimark, E. D. (1975). Longitudinal development of formal operations and thought. *Genetic Psychology Monograph, 91,* 171-225.

Neimark, E. D., & Lewis, N. (1968). Development of logical problem-solving: A one-year retest. *Child Development, 39,* 527-536.

Neimark, E. D., Slotnick, N. S., & Ulrich, T. (1971). Development of memorization strategies. *Development Psychology, 5,* 427-432.

CURRENT STATUS OF THE STUDY:

a. No further waves of data collection are planned.
b. Most data are in machine-readable format.
c. Data are available for secondary analyses from the study contact person.

■ Structure and Strategy in Learning to Talk, 1970

Nelson, Katherine

Contact Person: Katherine Nelson
Address: Developmental Psychology Department
                  The Graduate Center of
                  the City University of New York
                  33 West 42nd Street
                  New York, NY 10036
Telephone No.:   (212) 790-4457

SUBSTANTIVE TOPICS COVERED:

The study examines the acquisition and use of early lexical development in relation to later stages of language development, learning and general cognitive development, individual differences, and environmental variables.

CHARACTERISTICS OF THE ORIGINAL SAMPLE:

Year the study began: 1970

Subject selection process: Infants were selected from a pool of 160 mothers who participated in a previous experiment in the Yale Laboratory of Infant Study. Mothers were volunteers, identified either through the birth records of the Yale-New Haven Hospital or through newspaper announcements of birth.

Total number of subjects at Time 1: N = 19

Ages at Time 1: 10-15 mos. The principal investigator divided the sample into three age cohorts. These age groups are identified as Cohort 1, Cohort 2, and Cohort 3.

Sex distribution: 61.1% females, 38.9% males (Total sample); 50% females, 50% males (Cohort 1); 60% females, 40% males (Cohort 2); 71.4% females, 28.6% males (Cohort 3)

Socioeconomic status: 84% middle/upper middle class, 16% working class

Race/ethnicity: 95% white, 5% African-American

Years of Completed Waves:

Years	N=	Age range
(Cohort 1)		
1970-1971	6	10-11 mos.
1970-1971	6	17 mos.
1970-1971	6	18 mos.
1970-1971	6	19 mos.
1970-1971	6	20 mos.
1970-1971	6	21 mos.
1970-1971	6	22 mos.
1970-1971	6	23 mos.
1970-1971	6	24 mos.
1970-1971	6	25 mos.
1971	6	30 mos.
(Cohort 2)		
1970-1971	5	12-13 mos.
1970-1971	5	19 mos.
1970-1971	5	20 mos.
1970-1971	5	21 mos.
1970-1971	5	22 mos.
1970-1971	5	23 mos.
1970-1971	5	24 mos.
1970-1971	5	25 mos.
1971	5	30 mos.
(Cohort 3)		
1970-1971	7	14-15 mos.
1970-1971	7	21 mos.
1970-1971	7	22 mos.
1970-1971	7	23 mos.
1970-1971	7	24 mos.
1970-1971	7	25 mos.
1971	7	30 mos.

Comments:

The study began with 19 Ss; however, information about age and sex distributions was available only for the core sample of 18 Ss.

INFORMATION ON SAMPLE ATTRITION:

During the 20-month period of study, 1 of 19 Ss (5.3%) across three cohorts was not retrieved for further study. The core sample consists of 17 Ss: 6 Ss (Cohort 1); 5 Ss (Cohort 2); and 6 Ss (Cohort 3).

CONSTRUCTS MEASURED: INSTRUMENTS USED

Background information about child and family: Interview
Mother-child interaction: Structured observations
Comprehension: Comprehension tests
Sensorimotor cognition: Probes of object permanence
Linguistic and conceptual development: Categorization tests
General information about child's activities at home, with others and alone: Home
    activity interview
Language: Toy play, mother-child talk
Imitative competency: Imitation tests
Categorization: Grouping experiment
Attention: Structured play observation
General developmental level: Bayley Scales of Infant Development
Vocabulary: Peabody Picture Vocabulary Test
First 50 words of child's language acquisition: Vocabulary diaries (kept by mother)

REPRESENTATIVE REFERENCES:

Nelson, K. (1973). Structure and strategy in learning to talk. *Monographs of the Society for Research in Child Development, 38*(1-2).

Nelson, K. (1975). Individual differences in early semantic and syntactic development. *Annals of the New York Academy of Sciences, 263*, 132-139.

Nelson, K. (1975). The nominal shift in early language development. *Cognitive Psychology, 7*, 461-479.

Nelson, K. (1976). Some attributes of adjectives used by young children. *Cognition, 4*, 13-30.

CURRENT STATUS OF THE STUDY:

    a. No further waves of data collection are planned.
    b. Data are not in machine-readable format.
    c. Limited data are available for secondary analysis from the study contact person.

■ Adolescent Personality Development and Historical Change, 1970

Nesselroade, John; and Baltes, Paul B.

Contact Person:　John Nesselroade
Address:　　　　　Pennsylvania State University
　　　　　　　　　College of Human Development
　　　　　　　　　University Park, PA 16802
Telephone No.:　(814) 865-3253

SUBSTANTIVE TOPICS COVERED:

The study examines the relationship between ontogenetic and sociocultural change in adolescent personality and social development. In particular, it focuses on the nature and direction of change regarding quantitative and structural aspects of social development.

CHARACTERISTICS OF THE ORIGINAL SAMPLE:

Year the study began: 1970

Subject selection process: Subjects were junior and senior high school students selected from 32 West Virginia public school systems in three counties, representing a base population of 20,000 adolescents. The sample was stratified by grade, sex, and home room unit, and was selected at random from 32 school rosters. Approximately 2,000 students were contacted for participation in the study.

Total number of subjects at Time 1: N = 1,580[a]

Ages at Time 1: 13-16 yrs.

Sex distribution: Approximately equal numbers of females and males throughout

Socioeconomic status: Information was not available

Race/ethnicity: 95% white, 5% African-American

Comments:
a. Two control groups were included in the design: 1) a control group (in 1972) to assess the effect of repeated measures; 2) a "dropout" group consisting of Ss who participated in the 1970 data wave, but did not participate in subsequent data waves. A comparison of the scores of the dropout group in 1970 with the scores of Ss who remained in the study was used to assess sample bias.

Years of Completed Waves:

Years	N=	Age ranges
1970	1,580	13-16 yrs.
1971	1,214	14-17 yrs.
1972	816	15-18 yrs.

INFORMATION ON SAMPLE ATTRITION:

During the 2-year period of study, 716 of 1,580 Ss (48.4%) were not retrieved for further study. However, the principal investigators did not intend to follow up the entire initial sample. Specific information on attrition was not available, though attrition did occur. The core sample consisted of 816 Ss.

CONSTRUCTS MEASURED: INSTRUMENTS USED

Primary mental abilities: Primary Mental Abilities Battery (Thurstone & Thurstone, 1962)

Personality: High School Personality Questionnaire Form A (Cattell & Cattell, 1969), Personality Research Form E (Jackson, 1968)

REPRESENTATIVE REFERENCES:

Baltes, P. B., & Nesselroade, J. R. (1972). Cultural change and adolescent personality development. *Developmental Psychology, 7*, 244-256.

Labouvie, E., Bartsch, T., Nesselroade, J., & Baltes, P. (1974). On internal and external validity of simple longitudinal designs. *Child Development, 45*, 282-290.

Nesselroade, J., & Baltes, P. (1974). Adolescent personality development and historical change: 1970-1972. *Monographs of the Society for Research in Child Development, 39*(1).

Nesselroade, J., & Baltes, P. (Eds.). (1979). *Longitudinal research in the study of behavior and development.* New York: Academic Press.

CURRENT STATUS OF THE STUDY:

a. No further waves of data collection are planned.

b. Most data are in machine-readable format.

c. The data are conditionally available for secondary analysis from the study contact person.

■ UCLA Study of Adolescent Growth, 1976

Newcomb, Michael D.; and Bentler, Peter M.

Contact Person: Michael D. Newcomb
Address: University of California at Los Angeles
Department of Psychology
405 Hilgard Avenue
Los Angeles, CA 90024-1563
Telephone No.: (213) 825-5735

SUBSTANTIVE TOPICS COVERED:

The study examines adolescent and adult drug use, etiology and consequences; personality, peer cultures, and pressure related to drug use; drug intentions, deviance, and perceived drug availability; educational functioning; physical and mental health, social support; adult roles and socialization.

CHARACTERISTICS OF THE ORIGINAL SAMPLE:

Year the study began: 1976
Subject selection process: Subjects were selected from Los Angeles County school districts. All students were invited to participate.
Total number of subjects at Time 1: N = 1,634
Ages at Time 1: 13-15 yrs.
Sex distribution: 64% female, 36% male
Socioeconomic status: Information was not available.
Race/ethnicity: 60% white, 18% African-American, 15% Hispanic, 7% Asian-American

Years of Completed Waves:

Years	N=	Age ranges
1976	1,634	13-15 yrs.
1977	1,177	14-16 yrs.
1979	1,068	16-18 yrs.
1980	896	17-19 yrs.
1984	739	22-24 yrs.
1988	614	26-28 yrs.

INFORMATION ON SAMPLE ATTRITION:

During the 12-year period of study, 1,020 of 1,634 Ss (62.4%) were not retrieved for further study. The core sample consists of 614 Ss.

CONSTRUCTS MEASURED: INSTRUMENTS USED

Self-acceptance, extroversion, law abidance, liberalism, attractiveness, diligence, deliberateness, orderliness, depression, thought disorder, generosity, trustfulness, and achievement: Personality inventory

Peer culture involvement, time spent with friends, peer-adult compatibility, peer drug use: Peer culture questionnaire

Drug use (liquor, cigarettes, marijuana, cocaine, hard drugs, and hashish): Self drug use questionnaire

Intended use of substances: Drug use intentions questionnaire

Adult use (beer, wine, liquors, marijuana, and pills), drug use in the work place: Adult drug use questionnaire

REPRESENTATIVE REFERENCES:

Newcomb, M. D., & Bentler, P. M. (1988). *Consequences of adolescent drug use: Impact of the lives of young adults*. Newbury Park, CA: Sage.

Newcomb, M. D., & Bentler, P. M. (1988). Impact of adolescent drug use and social support on problems of young adults: A longitudinal study. *Journal of Abnormal Psychology, 97*, 64-75.

Newcomb, M. D., Chou, C., Bentler, P. M., & Huba, G. J. (1988). Cognitive motivations for drug use among adolescents: Longitudinal tests of gender differences and predictors of change in drug use. *Journal of Counseling Psychology, 35*(4), 426-438.

Newcomb, M. D., Huba, G. J., & Bentler, P. M. (1986). Desirability of various life change events among adolescents: Effects of exposure, sex, age, and ethnicity. *Journal of Research in Personality, 20*(2), 207-227.

CURRENT STATUS OF THE STUDY:

a. Further waves of data collection are planned.

b. All data are in machine-readable format.

c. The data are not yet available for secondary analysis through the principal investigator.

■ Trajectories of Health and Illness: A Longitudinal Follow-Up Study of Child Psychiatric Patients, 1984

Noam, Gil G.

Contact person: Gil G. Noam
Address: Hall Mercer Laboratory of Developmental Psychology
                  and Developmental Psychopathology
                  115 Mill Street
                  Belmont, MA 02178
Telephone No.:   (617) 855-2884

SUBSTANTIVE TOPICS COVERED:

This study investigates the developmental causes and consequences of such child psychiatric problems as conduct and affective disorders, examines factors that support the amelioration of psychiatric illness in children and adolescents over time, and assesses the impact of hospitalization on patients and their families in the alleviation of emotional and behavioral dysfunctioning and in the promotion of recovery.

CHARACTERISTICS OF THE ORIGINAL SAMPLE:

Year the study began: 1984
Subject selection process: A sample of subjects consecutively admitted to a child
    and adolescent psychiatric unit were selected for study.
Total number of subjects at Time 1: N = 229
Ages at Time 1: 12-16 yrs.
Sex distribution: Approximately equal numbers of females and males throughout
Socioeconomic status: Working class and middle class
Race/ethnicity: Predominantly white

Years of Completed Waves:

Years	N=	Age ranges
(Cohort 1)[a]		
1984-1985	44	12-16 yrs.
1986-1987	44	13-17 yrs.
(Cohort 2)[a]		
1984-1986	185	12-16 yrs.
1988-1990	50[b]	13-17 yrs.

Comments:
a. Cohort 1: Long-term Ss (hospitalized 9 months or more). Cohort 2: Short-term Ss (hospitalized less than 9 months).
b. Data collection for Cohort 2 is currently in progress; to date, 50 subjects have been followed up.

INFORMATION ON SAMPLE ATTRITION:

During the 6-year period of study, no attrition was reported for Cohort 1, yielding a core sample of 44 Ss. Data collection for the second wave of Cohort 2 is still in progress.

CONSTRUCTS MEASURED: INSTRUMENTS USED

Child and adolescent symptoms and competencies: Youth Self Report and Child Behavior Checklist (Achenbach and Edelbrock)

Current DSM-III diagnoses and symptom levels: Diagnostic Interview Schedule for Children (Child and Parent versions)

Ego development: Washington University Sentence Completion Test (Loevinger)

Defense styles: Defense Mechanism Inventory (Gleser and Ilevitch)

Parents and peer relationships: Developmental Self Interview (Noam, Kilkenny, Borst, Kurens)

Coping strategies: Adolescent Coping-Orientation for Problem Experiences (A-COPE)

Moral development: Moral Judgment Interview (Kohlberg)

Demographic variables, education, and treatment before hospitalization: Hall-Mercer Baseline Questionnaire

Demographic variables, education, and treatment since hospitalization: Hall-Mercer Follow-Up Questionnaire

Family functioning: Family Environment Scale (Moos)

Adolescent functioning: Social Adjustment Interview of Children and Adolescents (SAICA)

Interpersonal relationships, and coping skills: Vineland Adaptive Behavior Scales (Socialization Scale)

Stressful life events: Family Inventory of Life Events

REPRESENTATIVE REFERENCES:

Borst, S. R., & Noam, G. G. (1989). Suicidality and psychopathology in hospitalized children and adolescents. *Acta Paedopsychiatrica, 52,* 165-175.

Noam, G. G. (1988). A constructivist approach to developmental psychopathology. *Developmental psychopathology and its treatment. New Directions for Child Development,39* (pp. 91-121). San Francisco: Jossey-Bass.

Noam, G., & Houlihan, J. (1990). Developmental dimensions of DSM-III diagnoses in adolescent psychiatric patients. *American Journal of Orthopsychiatry, 60*(3), 371-378.

Noam, G. G., & Recklitis, C. J. (1990). The relationship between defenses and symptoms in adolescent psychopathology. *Journal of Personality Assessment, 54*(1 & 2), 311-327.

CURRENT STATUS OF THE STUDY:

a. Further waves of data collection are planned.

b. Most of the data are in machine-readable format.

c. Data are not yet available for secondary analysis.

O

National Longitudinal Survey of Youth Labor Market Experience (NLSY), 1979

Olsen, Randall

Contact Person: Randall Olsen
Address: Center for Human Resource Research
Ohio State University
921 Chatham Lane, Suite 200
Columbus, OH 43221
Telephone No.: (614) 442-7300

SUBSTANTIVE TOPICS COVERED:

These yearly surveys examine three aspects of labor in relation to the following historical factors: (a) labor market experience variables (e.g., current labor force and employment status, characteristics of current or last job, and work experience prior to and since last interview); (b) human capital and other socioeconomic variables (e.g., early formative influences, migration, education, vocational training, government jobs and training programs, health and physical conditions, marital and family characteristics, income and assets, military service, job and work attitudes, educational/occupational aspirations, psychological factors (Rotter locus of control; Rosenberg self-esteem), and child care arrangements; and (c) environmental variables (e. g., region of residence, characteristics of current residence, local unemployment rate). In addition, respondents in these surveys have been the subject of the following special surveys: (a) high school transcripts collection and a survey of last secondary school attended; (b) the administration of the Armed Services Vocational Aptitude Battery (ASVAB); (c) special collections on alcohol, substance use, and illegal activities; and (d) a battery of cognitive-socioemotional-physiological and home environment assessment instruments administered to NLSY mothers and their children. (Note: These NLSY children are hereafter referred to as the "child sample.") Finally, constructed data files offer detailed work histories, supplemental geocode data, supplemental fertility data, and a women's support network file.

CHARACTERISTICS OF THE ORIGINAL SAMPLE:

Year the study began: 1979
Subject selection process: The following three independent probability samples, designed to be representative of the entire population of youth born in the United States between 1957 and 1964, were drawn for the NLSY: (a) a cross-sectional

359

sample of 6,111 respondents representing the noninstitutionalized civilian segment of American young people ages 14-21 on 1/1/79; (b) a supplemental sample of 5,295 respondents designed to oversample civilian Hispanic, African-American, and economically disadvantaged non-Hispanic, non-African-American youth; and (c) a military sample of 1,280 respondents representing the population ages 17-21 as of 1/1/79, who were serving in the military as of 9/30/78. The children surveyed in 1986 and 1988 can be considered as representative of all children born to a nationally representative cross-section of women ages 23-30 on 1/1/88.

Total number of subjects at Time 1: N = 12,686
Ages at Time 1: 14-21 yrs.
Sex distribution: Approximately equal numbers of females and males throughout
Socioeconomic status: Information was gathered, but not available in terms of percent distribution by socioeconomic class.
Race/ethnicity: 59.1% white, 25.2% African-American, 15.7% Hispanic

Years of Completed Waves:

Years	N=	Age ranges
(Civilian Sample)		
1979	11,406	14-21 yrs.
1980	10,948	15-22 yrs.
1981	11,000	16-23 yrs.
1982	10,912	17-24 yrs.
1983	10,995	18-25 yrs.
1984	10,854	19-26 yrs.
1985	10,708	20-27 yrs.
1986	10,472	21-28 yrs.
1987	10,306	22-29 yrs.
1988	10,291	23-30 yrs.
(Military Sample)		
1979	1,280	14-21 yrs.
1980	1,193	15-22 yrs.
1981	1,195	16-23 yrs.
1982	1,211	17-24 yrs.
1983	1,226	18-25 yrs.
1984	1,212	19-26 yrs.
1985	184[a]	20-27 yrs.
1986	183	21-28 yrs.
1987	179	22-29 yrs.
1988	175	23-30 yrs.
(Child Sample)		
1986	4,971	Birth-16 yrs.
1988	6,266	Birth-18 yrs.

Comments:
a. Beginning in 1985, 1,079 of 1,280 respondents in the military subsample ceased to be interviewed: 201 military respondents were retained for continued interviewing.

INFORMATION ON SAMPLE ATTRITION:

During the 10-year period of study, 1,115 of 11,406 civilian Ss (9.8%) and 65 of 1,280 military Ss (5.1%) (until 1985) were not retrieved for further study. Reasons for sample attrition included inability to re-locate Ss; subject refusal to further participate; and dropping the majority of the military sample. The remaining core sample consists of 11,607 Ss: 11,406 Ss in Cohort 1, 201 Ss in Cohort 2.

CONSTRUCTS MEASURED: INSTRUMENTS USED

NLSY Civilian and Military Samples

Labor market experience, human capital and other socioeconomic variables, and environmental variables: Yearly questionnaires

Information on household composition including, for each member of the Ss household, sex, relationship to respondent, age, highest grade completed, and work experience in last year: Household Interview Forms

Detailed job information on up to five employers for whom each respondent worked since last interview: Employer Supplement

High school transcripts and school profiles: High School Survey (1979) and Transcript Surveys (1980-1983)

Aptitude scores: 1980 national administration of the Armed Services Vocational Aptitude Battery (ASVAB)

Illegal activities, arrest records, and police contacts: 1980 questionnaire and confidential illegal activities supplement

Use of marijuana, cocaine, and other controlled substances: 1984 and 1988 questionnaire and drug use supplement

Abortion reports: Confidential abortion forms 1984, 1986, and 1988

Childhood residences of Ss who did not reside with both biological parents from birth to age 18: Childhood Residence Calendar and 1988 questionnaire

Child Sample

Nature and quality of child's home environment: Home Observation for Measurement of the Environment (HOME)

Ability of child to recognize various body parts: Body Parts Recognition

Hearing vocabulary knowledge: Peabody Picture Vocabulary Test Revised

Ability of child to remember location of object: Memory for Location

Short-term verbal memory: McCarthy Verbal Memory Scale

Ability to remember and repeat numbers sequentially in forward and reverse order: Memory for Digit span (component for Wechsler Intelligence Scale for Children)

Achievement in mathematics: Peabody Individual Achievement Test, Math Subscale

Attained reading knowledge: Peabody Individual Achievement Test, reading comprehension, reading recognition

Temperament or behavioral style: How My Child Usually Acts

Mother ratings of problem behavior; hyperactivity, anxiety, dependency, depression and aggressiveness: Behavior Problems Index

Perceived Competence Scale for Children: Self-Perception Profile

Motor-social-cognitive development: Motor and Social Development Scale

Child's health limitations, accidents, injuries, medical treatment: Child Questionnaire

Perceived self-competence in academic skill domain and sense of general worth: What Am I Like (two scales from Harter's Self-Perception Profile for Children)

Attitudes of child toward testing, child's general psychiatric condition, events that may have interfered with the assessment: Interviewer Evaluation of Testing Conditions

REPRESENTATIVE REFERENCES:

Baker, P. C., & Mott, F. L. (1989). *NLSY child handbook*. Columbus: Center for Human Resource Research, Ohio State University.

Center for Human Resources Research. (1990). NLS handbook. Columbus: Ohio State University.

Center for Human Resource Research. (1989). *NLS annotated bibliography: 1968-1989*. Columbus: Ohio State University.

CURRENT STATUS OF THE STUDY:

a. Further waves of data collection are planned.

b. Most of the data are in machine-readable format.

c. Data are available for secondary analysis through the study contact person at the Center for Human Resource Research, Ohio State University, 921 Chatham Lane, Suite 200, Columbus, OH 43221, or from ICPSR, University of Michigan.

■ National Longitudinal Surveys of Labor Market Experience (NLS), 1965

Olsen, Randall; Parnes, Herbert; Borus, Michael; and Wolpin, Kenneth

Contact Person: Randall Olsen
Address: Center for Human Resource Research
                 Ohio State University
                 921 Chatham Lane, Suite 200
                 Columbus, OH 43221
Telephone No.:   (614) 442-7300

SUBSTANTIVE TOPICS COVERED:

These surveys examine the following three aspects of labor in relation to historical factors: (a) labor market experience variables (e.g., characteristics of last or current job, work experience and military experience); (b) human capital and other socioeconomic variables (e.g., early socializing experiences, migration, education, non-formal education experience, health and physical status, marital and family status, child care, level of income, and military status, job and work attitudes, education-market experience, significant others, retirement); and (c) environmental variables (e.g., size of local area labor force, local unemployment rate, and index of demand for female labor).

CHARACTERISTICS OF THE ORIGINAL SAMPLE:

Year the study began: 1965
Subject selection process: Each of four cohort groups was selected using a national probability sample of approximately 5,000 Ss. Samples were drawn by the Bureau of the Census from primary sampling units that had been selected for the study. Monthly labor surveys conducted from early 1964 to 1966 used a multistage probability sample of 485 counties representing every state, with an over-sampling from African-American districts.
Total number of subjects at Time 1: N = 20,487 (Cohorts 1-4)
Ages at Time 1: 14-24 yrs.; 30-59 yrs.
Sex distribution: 100% male (Cohorts 1 & 3); 100% female (Cohorts 2 & 4)
Socioeconomic status: Information was gathered, but was not available by percent distribution of socioeconomic class.
Race/ethnicity: 70% white, 30% African-American (approximately and across cohorts)

Years of Completed Waves:

Years	N=	Age ranges
(Cohort 1: Older Men)		
1966	5,020	45-59 yrs.
1967	4,751	46-60 yrs.
1968	4,661	47-61 yrs.
1969	4,388	48-62 yrs.
1971	4,182	50-64 yrs.
1973	3,951	52-66 yrs.
1975	3,732	54-68 yrs.
1976	3,487	55-69 yrs.
1978	3,219	57-71 yrs.
1980	3,001	59-73 yrs.
1981	2,834	60-74 yrs.
1983	2,634	62-76 yrs.
1990	2,600	69-83 yrs.
(Cohort 2: Mature Women)		
1967	5,083	30-44 yrs.
1968	4,910	31-45 yrs.
1969	4,712	32-46 yrs.
1971	4,575	34-48 yrs.

Years of Completed Waves, Continued:

Years	N=	Age ranges
1972	4,471	35-49 yrs.
1974	4,322	37-51 yrs.
1976	4,172	39-53 yrs.
1977	3,966	40-54 yrs.
1979	3,812	42-56 yrs.
1981	3,677	44-58 yrs.
1982	3,542	45-59 yrs.
1984	3,422	47-61 yrs.
1986	3,335	49-63 yrs.
1987	3,241	50-64 yrs.
(Cohort 3: Young Men)		
1966	5,225	14-24 yrs.
1967	4,790	15-25 yrs.
1968	4,318	16-26 yrs.
1969	4,033	17-27 yrs.
1970	3,993	18-28 yrs.
1971	3,987	19-29 yrs.
1973	4,014	21-31 yrs.
1975	3,977	23-33 yrs.
1976	3,538	24-34 yrs.
1978	3,695	26-36 yrs.
1980	3,438	28-38 yrs.
1981	3,398	29-39 yrs.
(Cohort 4: Young Women)		
1968	5,159	14-24 yrs.
1969	4,930	15-25 yrs.
1970	4,766	16-26 yrs.
1971	4,714	17-27 yrs.
1972	4,625	18-28 yrs.
1973	4,424	19-29 yrs.
1975	4,243	21-31 yrs.
1977	4,071	23-33 yrs.
1978	3,923	24-34 yrs.
1980	3,801	26-36 yrs.
1982	3,650	28-38 yrs.
1983	3,545	29-39 yrs.
1985	3,720	31-41 yrs.
1987	3,639	33-43 yrs.
1988	3,510	34-44 yrs.

INFORMATION ON SAMPLE ATTRITION:

During the 22-year period of study, 7,718 of 20,487 Ss (37.7%) across four co-horts were not retrieved for further study: 2,400 of 5,020 Ss (47.8%) in Cohort 1; 1,842 of 5,083 Ss (36.2%) in Cohort 2; 1,827 of 5,225 Ss (35%) in Cohort 3; and 1,649 of 5,159 Ss (32%) in Cohort 4. Attrition was due to participants' institutionalization, death, and refusals. The remaining core sample consists of 12,783 Ss across four cohorts: 2,634 Ss (Cohort 1); 3,241 Ss (Cohort 2); 3,398 Ss (Cohort 3); and 3,510 Ss (Cohort 4).

CONSTRUCTS MEASURED: INSTRUMENTS USED

Labor Market Experiences (current labor force and employment status, characteristics of current or last job, work experience prior to initial and since previous survey); human capital and other socioeconomic variables (early formative influences, migration, education, training, health and physical condition, marital and family characteristics, financial characteristics, military service, attitudes/perspectives, retirement, hypothetical job offer, volunteer work); environmental variables (residence and local labor market characteristics): Survey Questionnaires

Information of household members including relationship to respondent, household member status, marital status, birth date, sex, military enlistment, as well as type and access to living quarters, availability of kitchen-cooking equipment, whether house is owned or rented, rural acreage, crop information: Household Record Cards

Academic performance, programs and facilities of high schools: 1968 High School Survey (Cohorts 3 and 4)

Labor market experience variables, household composition, human capital and socioeconomic variables, environmental variables: Alternating personal and telephone interviews

REPRESENTATIVE REFERENCES:

Center for Human Resource Research. (1989). *NLS annotated bibliography: 1968-1989.* Columbus: Ohio State University.
Center for Human Resource Research. (1990). *NLS handbook.* Columbus: Ohio State University.

CURRENT STATUS OF THE STUDY:

a. Further waves of data collection are planned.
b. The data are in machine readable format.
c. Data are available for secondary analysis from the study contact person through the Center for Human Resource Research, Ohio State University, 921 Chatham Lane, Suite 200, Columbus, OH 43221.

■ Oral Language Competency and the Acquisition of Literacy Skills, 1979

Olson, David; and Torrance, Nancy

Contact Person: Nancy Torrance
Address: Ontario Institute for Studies in Education
                University of Toronto
                252 Bloor Street
                Toronto, Ontario M5S 1U6
                Canada
Telephone No.: (416) 923-6641

SUBSTANTIVE TOPICS COVERED:

The study examines the development of children's lexicon, communicative skills, and literacy skills; and aspects of oral language that predict competency in learning to read.

CHARACTERISTICS OF THE ORIGINAL SAMPLE:

Year the study began: 1979
Subject selection process: Subjects were selected from two schools in Toronto; one school was in a working-class neighborhood, the other in a middle-class neighborhood.
Total number of subjects at Time 1: N = 40
Ages at Time 1: 5-6 yrs.
Sex distribution: Approximately equal numbers of females and males throughout
Socioeconomic status: 50% middle/upper middle class, 50% working class
Race/ethnicity: 90% white, 5% black, 5% Asian

Years of Completed Waves:

Years	N=	Age ranges
1979-1980	40	5-6 yrs.
1980-1981	40	6-7 yrs.
1981-1982	40	7-8 yrs.

INFORMATION ON SAMPLE ATTRITION:

During the 3-year period of study, all 40 subjects were retrieved at all data points. The core sample consists of 40 Ss.

CONSTRUCTS MEASURED: INSTRUMENTS USED

Language development: Transcribed speech in various tasks

Conversational development: Speech during child-other dialogues, speech during cooperative play

Reading development: Wechsler Intelligence Scale for Children, Vocabulary Test, standardized reading test, Block description test, story retelling

REPRESENTATIVE REFERENCES:

Olson, D. (1980). On language and literacy. *International Journal of Psycholinguistics, 7*(5), 69-84.

Olson D., & Torrance, N. (1983). Literacy and cognitive development: A conceptual revolution in the early school years. In S. Meadows (Ed.), *Developing thinking: Approaches to children's cognitive development.* London: Methuen.

Olson, D. R., & Torrance, N. (1987). Language, literacy, and mental states. Special issue: The language of thinking: Mental state words. *Discourse Processes, 10,* 157-167.

Torrance, N., & Olson, D. R. (1987). Development of the metalanguage and the acquisition of literacy: A progress report. *Interchange, 18*(1-2), 136-146.

CURRENT STATUS OF THE STUDY:

a. No further waves of data collection are planned.

b. Data are not in machine-readable format.

c. The data are available for secondary analysis from the study contact person.

■ Career Development Study, 1966

Otto, Luther B.

Contact Person: Luther B. Otto
Address: Department of Sociology
North Carolina State University
P. O. Box 8107
Raleigh, NC 27695
Telephone No.: (919) 737-3180

SUBSTANTIVE TOPICS COVERED:

The study examines the relation of family life, military service, careers, and education to life-course transitions.

CHARACTERISTICS OF THE ORIGINAL SAMPLE:

Year the study began: 1966
Subject selection process: The subjects were junior and senior high school students in Washington State. The Ss were selected through a stratified random sampling procedure.
Total number of subjects at Time 1: N = 6,729
Ages at Time 1: 16-19 yrs.
Sex distribution: Approximately equal numbers of females and males throughout
Socioeconomic status: Information was gathered, but not available in terms of percentage distribution by socioeconomic class
Race/ethnicity: 98% white, 2% African-American and Hispanic

Years of Completed Waves:

Years	N=	Age ranges
1966	6,729	16-19 yrs.
1979	5,977	28-31 yrs.

INFORMATION ON SAMPLE ATTRITION:

During the 13-year period of study, 752 of 6,729 Ss (11.2%) were not retrieved for further study. The core sample consists of 5,966 Ss. Sources of attrition are as follows: 115 deceased; 31 institutionalized; 127 not located; 272 no response; 207 refused; and information on 11 Ss is not available.

CONSTRUCTS MEASURED: INSTRUMENTS USED

Family characteristics, attitudes, and values; respondent's school activities and achievements (peers' attitudes, aspirations, and achievements), respondent's self-esteem, attitudes toward work and social-psychological constructs: Questionnaires
Replication of selected questionnaire items: Personal interview
Parent-adolescent relationships: Questionnaire to parents
Respondent's educational and occupational aspirations and expectations: Questionnaire to counselor
Event history data on all educational, occupational, family, and military experience since 1966: Telephone interview
Attitudes toward current job, self-esteem, and social-psychological constructs, sex role and marital attitudes, leisure time activities: Mail questionnaire
High School transcripts: All courses, course grades, credit hours, attendance, class rank, grade point average, and standardized test scores: School achievement

REPRESENTATIVE REFERENCES:

Call, V., Otto, L. B., & Spenner, K. I. (1982). *Tracking respondents: A multi-method approach: Vol. II. Entry into careers series*. Lexington, MA: Lexington Books.

Otto, L., Call, V., & Spenner, K. (1981). *Design for a study of entry into careers: Vol. I. Entry into careers series* (pp. 81-92). Lexington, MA: Lexington Books.

Otto, L. B., Spenner, K. I., & Call, V. (1980). *Career line prototypes*. Boys Town, NE: Boys Town Center.

Spenner, K., Otto, L., & Call, V. (1982). *Careers and career lines: Vol. III. Entry into careers series*. Lexington, MA: Lexington Books.

CURRENT STATUS OF THE STUDY:

a. Further waves of data collection are planned.
b. The data are in machine-readable format.
c. The data are conditionally available for secondary analysis.

P

Understanding and Prediction of Delinquent Child Behavior, 1984

Patterson, Gerald R.; Reid, John B.; and Dishion, Thomas J.

Contact Person: Gerald R. Patterson
Address: 207 East 5th Street
Suite 202
Eugene, OR 97401
Telephone No.: (503) 485-2711

SUBSTANTIVE TOPICS COVERED:

The study examines antisocial behavior, substance use, academic skills and depression in boys, family management, family relations, peer involvement, and factors influencing the family structure.

CHARACTERISTICS OF THE ORIGINAL SAMPLE:

Year the study began: 1984
Subject selection process: Males from selected high-risk, fourth-grade classrooms were included in the study.
Total number of subjects at Time 1: N = 206
Ages at Time 1: 9-11 yrs.
Sex distribution: 100% males
Socioeconomic status: 42% poverty class, 29% working class, 23% middle/upper middle class
Race/ethnicity: 90% white, 8% Hispanic, 2% African-American

Years of Completed Waves:

Years	N=	Age ranges
(Cohort 1)		
1984	102	9-11 yrs.
1985	102	10-12 yrs.
1986	102	11-13 yrs.
1987	102	12-14 yrs.
1988	102	13-15 yrs.
1989	102	14-16 yrs.

Years of Completed Waves, continued:

Years	N=	Age ranges
(Cohort 2)		
1984	104	9-11 yrs.
1985	104	10-12 yrs.
1986	104	11-13 yrs.
1987	104	12-14 yrs.
1988	100	13-15 yrs.
1989	101	14-16 yrs.

INFORMATION ON SAMPLE ATTRITION:

During the 5-year period of study, 4 of 206 Ss (1.9%), across two cohorts, were not retrieved for further study. Within Cohort 1, all Ss were retrieved for further study, while 4 of 104 Ss (3.8%) in Cohort 2 were not followed. The core sample for the study consists of 202 Ss: 102 Ss in Cohort 1, and 101 Ss in Cohort 2.

CONSTRUCTS MEASURED: INSTRUMENTS USED

Child

Intelligence: Wechsler Intelligence Scale for Children (vocabulary and performance tests)

Adolescent development (physical): Questionnaire

Child unpleasant event: Child unpleasant event schedule (Hoberman)

Child stress: Junior high life experiences survey (boy questionnaire), child unpleasant events schedule (boy questionnaire)

Anxiety: Diagnostic Interview Schedule for Children (DISC), anxiety (boy questionnaire), Child Behavior Checklist (parent), Child Behavior Checklist (teacher), Anxiety questionnaire (Speilburger et al.)

Self-esteem: Skill checklist (boy questionnaire), self perception (boy questionnaire), Harter self-esteem (boy questionnaire), Harter domain importance (boy questionnaire)

Child depressed mood: Child Behavior Checklist (parent), Child Behavior Checklist (teacher), child depression rating scale (child questionnaire), child depression inventory (child questionnaire), boy telephone interview, observer impressions, coder impressions, Diagnostic Interview Schedule for Children (DISC), CDRS (Birelson), CDI (Beck, et al.)

Other psychopathologies: Diagnostic Interview Schedule for Children (DISC), Child Behavior Checklist (parent), Child Behavior Checklist (teacher), Diagnostic interview (Costello, Edelbrock, & Costello)

Dyadic adjustment: Dyadic adjustment scale (Spanier)

Child psychosocial functioning: Peers and social skills (Walker & McConnell), problem solving, sports and hobbies (child), substance use (parents)

Child social skills: Walker/McConnell Social Skills (teacher and parent questionnaire), relationship characteristics (boy and peer questionnaire), peer interaction task (PIT), PIT coder impressions, quality of interpersonal relationships (boy interview)

Social activities: Social control (social attitudes), sports and hobbies

Child prosocial activities: Sports and hobbies (boy questionnaire), sports and hobbies (parent questionnaire), chores (boy interview), chores (parent interview), inventory of peer activities (boy and peer)

Peer relations: Peer involvement questionnaire (teacher's), Child Behavior Checklist (parent), Child Behavior Checklist (teacher), peer nominations, peer questionnaire, parent/peer attachment (boy and peer questionnaire), peer dyadic adjustment (boy questionnaire), Friend Observation checklist (boy and peer questionnaire), relationship characteristics (boy and peer), peer interaction task (PIT), PIT coder impressions, parent/boy telephone interview, describing friends (peer influences), friend observation checklist, junior high life experience survey (Swearingen & Cohen), inventory of peer activities, peer dyadic adjustment, peer relationship characteristics, parent/peer attachment, problem solving (Armsden & Greenberg)

Early difficulties with boy: Son's early history (parent questionnaire) two scales

Peer instruments: Relationship characteristics, self-report delinquency (Elliot), substance use, school records, juvenile court records

Child behavior: Child Behavior Checklist (parent) (Achenbach & Edelbrock), Overt-Covert antisocial behavior (Elliot)

Child substance use: Parent OCA questionnaire, boy interview, parent interview substance use

Boy's antisocial behavior: Total aversive behavior (TAB), (home observations), family interaction task, boy telephone interview, boy interview (antisocial), boy interview (Elliot), mother/father OCA, parent interview (Elliott), Child Behavior Checklist (parent report), Child Behavior Checklist (teacher report), peer nominations, parent telephone interview, sexual activity and contraceptive use, juvenile court records, division of motor vehicle records

Deviant Peers: Teacher peer involvement (teacher's questionnaire), boy interview (peer antisocial behavior and substance use), boy telephone interview, sibling substance use, peer nominations, Teacher Child Behavior Checklist (boy), Teacher Child Behavior Checklist (peer), peer interactions task (PIT), PIT coder impressions, Child Behavior Checklist (parent), describing friends (boy questionnaire), peer self-reported deviance, inventory of peer activities (boy and peer)

Criminal history: Juvenile court arrest records, Department of Motor Vehicles

Monitoring: Boy interview report (rules), parent interview report (rules), interviewer impressions, parent telephone interview, child telephone interview

Parents

Parent functioning: Parent life events (modified Holmes & Rahe), parent irritability (Caprara et al.), Family activities list (Patterson), issues checklist (family conflict), family event checklist (stress events) (Patterson)

Parental stress: Demographic questionnaire, family life events (parent questionnaire), family event checklist (parent questionnaire), family health history (parent questionnaire)

Parent depression: CES-D (parent questionnaire), Lubin C&D (parent questionnaire), parent telephone interview

Parent alcohol problems: Alcohol problems scale (Skinner & Allen), substance use (parents)

Parent substance use: Self/spouse substance use (parent questionnaire), MAST alcohol use (parent questionnaire), alcohol use (parent questionnaire), Department of Motor Vehicles (DMV) driving under the influence convictions

Parent antisocial behavior: Minnesota Multiphasic Personality Inventory (scales 5 & 7), police records, Department of Motor Vehicles records, irritability

Parent records: Police arrest records, Division of Motor Vehicles records

Family

Parental monitoring, parental rejection, employment and further education, family relations, family problem solving, child attitude (alcohol), child substance use, positive reinforcement, antisocial peers, child chores, discipline, child perception deviancy, educational and performance expectations for child, religious practices, quality of interpersonal relationships, attitude toward absent parent, sibling substance use, self-report delinquency (Elliot), sexual activity and contraceptive use, parent tobacco use, demographic information (on new parent, on siblings) demographic update: Parent Interview

Parent involvement: Family activities checklist (parent and boy questionnaire), boy interview, boy telephone interview

Discipline: Family Interaction Task (FIT), FIT coder impressions, parent telephone interview, boy telephone interview, parent interview, home observations (nattering, and abusive cluster), observer impressions

Positive reinforcement: parent interview, boy interview, parent interviewer impressions, observer impressions, parent telephone interview, probability mother prosocial given boy prosocial (from observations), family interaction task, Family Interaction Task (FIT) coder impressions

Parental rejection: Parent interview, boy interview (family relations), parent/peer attachment (boy questionnaire), boy interview (absent parent)

Problem solving: Family Interaction Task (FIT), FIT (coder impressions), parent interview, boy interview, Family Interaction Task parent/child questionnaire (hot issues checklist)

Videotaped tasks: Family Interaction Task (FIT), Peer Interaction Task (PIT)

FIT and PIT Coder instruments: problem-solving coder impressions, family interaction task (coder impressions); peer interaction task (coder impressions)

School

Academic skills: Child Behavior Checklist (parent), scholastic test scores, Wechsler Reading Achievement Test, verbal intelligence (Peabody Picture Vocabulary Test)

Reading achievement: Wechsler Reading Achievement Test

School instruments: Child Behavior Checklist (teacher) (Achenbach & Edelbrock), peer involvement and social skills, school data form (scholastic test scores)

REPRESENTATIVE REFERENCES:

Dishion, T. J., Patterson, G. R., & Reid, J. B. (1988). Parent and peer factors associated with drug sampling in early adolescence: Implications for treatment. *National Institute on Drug Abuse Research Monograph Series, 77*, 69-93.
Dishion, T. J., Reid, J. B., & Patterson, G. R. (1988). Empirical guidelines for a family intervention for adolescent drug abuse. *Journal of Chemical Dependency Treatment, 1*(2), 189-224.
Loeber, R., & Dishion, T. J. (1984). Boys who fight at home and school: Family conditions influencing cross-setting consistency. *Journal of Consulting and Clinical Psychology, 52*(5), 759-768.
Snyder, J., Dishion, T. J., & Patterson, G. R. (1986). Determinants and consequences of associating with deviant peers during preadolescence and adolescence. *Journal of Early Adolescence, 6*(1), 29-43.

CURRENT STATUS OF THE STUDY:

a. Further waves of data collection are planned.
b. Most data are in machine-readable format.
c. The data are not yet available for secondary analysis.

■ Developmental Study of Adolescent Mental Health, 1978

Petersen, Anne C.

Contact Person: Anne C. Petersen
Address: Pennsylvania State University
                 104 Henderson Building
                 University Park, PA 16802
Telephone No.:   (814) 863-0241 or (814) 863-0053

SUBSTANTIVE TOPICS COVERED:

The study examines the relation of biological, psychological, cognitive, and social development of the young adolescent to parental support and family relationships, and to school change and the environment.

CHARACTERISTICS OF THE ORIGINAL SAMPLE:

Year the study began: 1978
Subject selection process: The sample was randomly selected from two suburban school districts.
Total number of subjects at Time 1: N = 335[a]
Ages at Time 1: 11-12 yrs.

Sex distribution: Approximately equal numbers of females and males throughout
Socioeconomic status: Predominantly middle/upper middle class
Race/ethnicity: Predominantly white
Comments:
a. This figure includes adolescent cohorts starting in 1978 and 1979. Data were also collected at three points in time from the parents of these adolescents. The figure of 335 adolescents does not include two control groups that were part of the initial testing phase.

Years of Completed Waves:

Years	N=	Age ranges
(1967 Birth Cohort)[a]		
1978 (Fall)	188	11-12 yrs.
1979 (Spring)	188	11-12 yrs.
1979 (Fall)	176	12 yrs.
1980 (Spring)	175	12-13 yrs.
1980 (Fall)	166	13 yrs.
1981 (Spring)	160	13-14 yrs.
1984-1985	94	17-18 yrs.
1988-1989	140	21-22 yrs.
(1967 Birth Cohort: Mothers)		
1978-1979	188	32-58 yrs.
1980-1981	149	33-60 yrs.
1984-1985	87	37-63 yrs.
(1967 Birth Cohort: Fathers)		
1978-1979	188	30-64 yrs.
1980-1981	134	35-66 yrs.
1984-1985	87	39-65 yrs.
(1968 Birth Cohort)[a]		
1979 (Fall)	147	11 yrs.
1980 (Spring)	128	11-12 yrs.
1980 (Fall)	134	12 yrs.
1981 (Spring)	135	12-13 yrs.
1981 (Fall)	128	13 yrs.
1982 (Spring)	127	13-14 yrs.
1985-1986	71	17-18 yrs.
1989-1990	105	21-22 yrs.
(1968 Birth Cohort: Mothers)		
1979-1980	129	30-53 yrs.
1980-1981	102	32-51 yrs.
1985-1986	89	36-55 yrs.
(1968 Birth Cohort: Fathers)		
1979-1980	123	31-56 yrs.
1980-1981	82	33-58 yrs.
1985-1986	73	37-59 yrs.

Comments:
a. A cohort-sequential design was used. Interviews and assessments were each conducted twice per school year (Spring and Fall), in 6th through 8th grades and once during the 12th grade and during the latest assessment during young childhood. Because sampling was done by grade, the age ranges presented are estimates only. Data were also collected at three points in time from the parents of these adolescents.

INFORMATION ON SAMPLE ATTRITION:

During the most recent wave of assessments, data were obtained from 245 of the 335 Ss across the two cohorts. This represented an overall return rate of 73%. A total of 140 of 188 Ss (74%) from the 1967 Birth Cohort participated during the most recent wave of data collection, as did 105 of 147 Ss (71%) from the 1968 Birth Cohort. During the last wave of assessment that included parents, 87 of 188 mothers (46%) and 87 of 188 fathers (46%) of the 1967 Birth Cohort Ss participated. A total of 89 of 129 mothers (69%) and 73 of 123 fathers (59%) of the 1968 Birth Cohort Ss also participated during the last wave of parent assessments. Primary sources of attrition included changes of residence, and death. Core samples were based on 1984-1986 data collection as follows: 1967 Birth Cohort, 149 adolescent Ss; mothers, 87 Ss; fathers 87 Ss; 1968 Birth Cohort, 113 adolescent Ss; mothers, 89 Ss; fathers, 73 Ss.

CONSTRUCTS MEASURED: INSTRUMENTS USED

Self-esteem: Self-Image Questionnaire for Young Adolescents (SIQYA), Rosenberg Self-Esteem Inventory
Parent perception of adolescent self-image: Parent Offer Self-Image Questionnaire
Psychopathology: Teenage or Young Adult Schedule (TOYS)
Problem behavior: Child Behavior Checklist (Youth Form)
Depression: Kandel Depression Scale
Life satisfaction: Adjectives, Satisfaction with Life Scale
Ego development: Washington University Sentence Completion Test (Loevinger)
Locus of control: Multidimensional-Multiattributional Causality Scale, Spheres of Control Battery
Pubertal development: Pubertal Development Scale
School performance: Final Course Grades
Cognitive ability (Formal Operations): Equilibrium in a Balance, Advertised Specials, Water Glass Puzzles
Field independence: Group Embedded Figures Test Field
Fluency of production: DAT Clerical Speed & Accuracy
Physical abstract reasoning and formal operations: Linn Equilibrium in a Balance Task
Verbal abstract reasoning and formal operations: Peel Story Completions
Spatial ability: Primary Mental Abilities Space Relations
Family relationships: SIQYA Family Relationships, Personal Relationships Questionnaire, Family Environment Scale, Parent-Adolescent Communication
Perceptions of family relationships: Lowman Inventory of Family Feeling
Peer relationships: SIQYA Peer Relationships, Peer Relationships Questionnaire
Work orientation: Work Aspect Performance Scale
Sex role orientation: Bem Sex Role Inventory, Personal Attributes Questionnaire
Sex role attitudes: Attitudes toward Women Scale for Adolescents
Activities: Activities and Interests Inventory (Swisher)
Social network: Important People Inventory

REPRESENTATIVE REFERENCES:

Crockett, L. J., & Petersen, A. C. (1987). Pubertal status and psychological development: Findings from the Early Adolescence Study. In R. M. Lerner & T. T. Foch (Eds.), *Biological-psychosocial interaction in early adolescence: A life-span perspective* (pp. 173-188). Hillsdale, NJ: Lawrence Erlbaum.

Petersen, A. C. (1983). Menarche: Meaning of measures and measuring meaning. In S. Golub (Ed.), *Menarche.* New York: D. C. Heath.

Petersen, A. C. (Ed.). (1984). The Early Adolescent Study (special issue). *The Journal of Early Adolescence, 4*(2).

Petersen, A. C., & Taylor, B. V. (1980). The biological approach to adolescence: Biological change and psychological adaptation. In J. Adelson (Ed.), *Handbook of adolescent psychology.* New York: John Wiley.

CURRENT STATUS OF THE STUDY:

a. No further waves of data collection are planned.
b. Most of the data are in machine-readable format.
c. The data are available for secondary analysis from the study contact person.

■ Life After 70 in Iowa, 1960

Powers, Edward A.; and Bultena, Gordon L.

Contact Person: Edward A. Powers
Address: School of Human Environmental Sciences
University of North Carolina at Greensboro
Greensboro, NC 27412-5001
Telephone No.: (919) 334-5733

SUBSTANTIVE TOPICS COVERED:

The study assesses general lifestyle, including health, income, interaction, residence, attitudes, division of labor, and helping patterns.

CHARACTERISTICS OF THE ORIGINAL SAMPLE:

Year the study began: 1960
Subject selection process: Subjects resided in household units that were randomly picked from county maps and property-tax lists, and included widely distributed counties selected as representative of the rural-urban distributions and economic levels of Iowa's population.
Total number of subjects at Time 1: N = 611
Ages at Time 1: 60-82 yrs.

Sex distribution: Approximately equal numbers of females and males throughout
Socioeconomic status: 36.6% middle/upper-middle class, 63.4% working class
Race/ethnicity: 100% white

Years of Completed Waves:

Years	N=	Age ranges
1960	611	60-82 yrs.
1971	235	70-93 yrs.

INFORMATION ON SAMPLE ATTRITION:

During the 11-year period of study, 376 of 611 Ss (61.5%) were not retrieved for
further study. Attrition was due to death, inability to locate subjects, subjects' refusal
to participate, and subjects' moving to another state. Core sample consists of 235 Ss.

CONSTRUCTS MEASURED: INSTRUMENTS USED

Need for and use of community programs: Structured Interview (Wave 1)
Age identification, age identity, reference group comparisons (self versus other appraisals),
    interaction patterns, intimate friendships (Wave 2), marital status, education, employ-
    ment status, general outlook on life, life satisfaction, residential mobility, neighbor-
    hood, contact with children, division of labor: Structured interview
Health: Self-reported health questions
Socioeconomic level: Total family income
Social involvement: Interviews (response to clubs and social groups attended and
    how frequently Ss got out of the house for visiting and shopping)

REPRESENTATIVE REFERENCES:

Bultena, G. L., & Powers, E. A. (1978). Denial of aging: Age identification and reference group
    orientations. *Journal of Gerontology, 33*(5), 748-754.
Powers, E. A., & Bultena, G. L. (1972). Characteristics of deceased dropouts in longitudinal re-
    search. *Journal of Gerontology, 27*(4), 530-535.
Powers, E. A., & Bultena, G. L. (1974). Correspondence between anticipated and actual uses of
    public services by the aged. *Social Service Review, 48*(2), 245-254.
Powers, E. A., & Bultena, G. L. (1976). Sex differences in intimate friendships of old age. *Jour-
    nal of Marriage and the Family, 38*(4), 739-747.

CURRENT STATUS OF THE STUDY:

a. No further waves of data collection planned.
b. Data are not in machine-readable format.
c. Data are available for secondary analysis.

Q

Quality of Employment Survey: Panel Study, 1973

Quinn, Robert P.; Mangione, Thomas W.; and Seashore, Stanley E.

Contact Person: Robert P. Quinn
Address: 1721 Abbott Street
Ann Arbor, MI 48103
Telephone No.: (313) 994-1196

SUBSTANTIVE TOPICS COVERED:

This study assesses the frequency and severity of work-related problems experienced by employed people, with special emphasis on those types of problems that were or might become matters of public policy; assesses the impact of working conditions upon the well-being of workers; establishes baseline statistics that might permit subsequent national surveys to reveal any trends in the content areas originally investigated; and establishes normative statistics that might permit other investigators to compare with national norms their data from more limited subsamples of workers (e.g., in particular occupations, organizations, or regions); develops efficient measures of job satisfaction suitable for use with samples of workers in heterogeneous occupations and suitable for use under a variety of conditions of census and research.

CHARACTERISTICS OF THE ORIGINAL SAMPLE:

Year the study began: 1973
Subject selection process: A multistage-area probability sample was selected from 74 different geographic areas of the coterminous United States. The subjects, ages 16 and over, were representative of all employed adults, all occupations, and all industries.
Total number of subjects at Time 1: N = 1,455
Ages at Time 1: 16-65 yrs.
Sex distribution: 61.8% male, 38.2% female
Socioeconomic status: 51.5% middle/upper middle class, 48.5% working class
Race/ethnicity: 89.7% white, 10.3% African-American

Years of Completed Waves:[a]

Years	N=	Age ranges
1973	1,455	16-65 yrs.
1977	1,086	20-69 yrs.

Comments:
a. This study also includes cross-sectional cohorts from years 1969, 1973, and 1977.

INFORMATION ON SAMPLE ATTRITION:

During the 9-year period of study, 369 of 1,455 Ss (25.3%) were not retrieved for follow-up. The core sample consists of 1,086 Ss.

CONSTRUCTS MEASURED: INSTRUMENTS USED

Job satisfaction, job tension, job security, physical health, financial well-being: 1972-1973 Quality of Employment Survey Schedule
Health and safety hazards, inadequate fringe benefits, unpleasant physical conditions, inconvenient or excessive hours, transportation problems, inadequate family income, work-related illness or injury, occupational handicaps, unsteady employment, age discrimination, race or national origin discrimination, sex discrimination, work-related problems, job satisfaction, working conditions, workers' well-being, job stress, physical health, mental health: 1977 Quality of Employment Survey Schedule

REPRESENTATIVE REFERENCES:

Herrick, N. Q., & Quinn, R. P. (1971). The working conditions survey as a source of social indicators. *Monthly Labor Review, 102*(1), 15-24.
Quinn, R. P., & Staines, G. L. (1979). *The 1977 Quality of Employment Survey: Descriptive statistics, with comparison data from the 1969-1970 Survey of Working Conditions and the 1972-1973 Quality of Employment Survey.* Ann Arbor: Institute of Social Research, University of Michigan.
Quinn, R. P., Mangione, T. W., & Baldi de Mandilovich, M. S. (1973). Evaluating working conditions in America. *Monthly Labor Review, 5*(11), 32-40.
Staines, G. L., & Quinn, R. P. (1979). American workers evaluate the quality of their jobs. *Monthly Labor Review, 102*(1), 3-12.

CURRENT STATUS OF THE STUDY:

a. No further waves of data collection are planned.
b. Most data are in machine-readable format.
c. Data are available for secondary analysis from the Inter-University Consortium for Political and Social Research, Institute for Social Research, University of Michigan, P.O. Box 1248, Ann Arbor, MI 48106.

R

The Children of Primary Caregiving Fathers: An 11-Year Follow-Up, 1977

Radin, Norma; Williams, Edith; and Oyserman, Daphna

Contact Person: Norma Radin
Address: University of Michigan
School of Social Work
Ann Arbor, MI 48109
Telephone No.: (313) 763-6257

SUBSTANTIVE TOPICS COVERED:

This study explores some possible antecedents and consequences of high father involvement in child-rearing, such as the impact on adolescents' family and occupational expectations, as well as mathematics ability. In one third of the families studied the father was the primary caregiver; in one third the mother was the primary caregiver; and the remaining one third comprised an intermediate group.

CHARACTERISTICS OF THE ORIGINAL SAMPLE:

Year the study began: 1977
Subject selection process: Subjects were selected via advertising and by word of mouth.
Total number of subjects at Time 1: N = 59
Ages at Time 1: 3-5 yrs.
Sex distribution: Approximately equal numbers of females and males throughout
Socioeconomic status: 100% middle/upper middle class
Race/ethnicity: 100% white (approximately)

Years of Completed Waves:

Years	N=	Age ranges
1977-1978	59	3-5 yrs.
1981-1982	47	7-9 yrs.
1988-1989	32	14-16 yrs.

INFORMATION ON SAMPLE ATTRITION:

During the 12-year period of study, 27 of 59 Ss (45.8%) were not retrieved for further study. The core sample consists of 32 Ss. Sample attrition was due to families who divorced or were no longer intact, families who moved and could not be located, and families who declined further participation.

CONSTRUCTS MEASURED: INSTRUMENTS USED

Amount of father involvement: Paternal Involvement in Child Care Index (PICCI)
Sex-role preferences of mothers and fathers: Bem Sex Role Inventory
Sex-role preferences of adolescents: Shortened version of Spence's PAQ (a personal attributes questionnaire; a measure of sex-role stereotypes and masculinity/femininity)
Parental expectations and aspirations for their children's occupation and education: Cognitive Home Environment Scale (CHES)

REPRESENTATIVE REFERENCES:

Radin, N. (1982). Primary caregiving and role-sharing fathers. In M. E. Lamb (Ed.), *Nontraditional families* (pp. 173-204). Hillsdale, NJ: Lawrence Erlbaum.

Radin, N., & Goldsmith, R. (1985). Caregiving fathers of preschoolers: Four years later. *Merrill-Palmer Quarterly, 31,* 375-383.

Radin, N., & Sagi, A. (1982). Childrearing fathers in intact families in Israel and the USA. *Merrill-Palmer Quarterly, 28,* 111-136.

Williams, E., Radin, N., & Allegro, T. *Children of highly involved fathers: An eleven year follow-up.* Manuscript submitted for publication.

CURRENT STATUS OF THE STUDY:

a. No further waves of data collection are planned.
b. Most of the data are in machine-readable format.
c. Data are available for secondary analysis from the study contact person.

■ A Study of Child Rearing and Child Development in Normal Families and Families with Affective Disorders, 1980

Radke-Yarrow, Marian

Contact Person: Marian Radke-Yarrow
Address: Laboratory of Developmental Psychology
               National Institute of Mental Health
               9000 Rockville Pike
               Bethesda, MD 20892
Telephone No.: (301) 496-1091

SUBSTANTIVE TOPICS COVERED:

The study examines the relation of child-rearing practices and child development in normal and depressed families; relation of parents to child, the parents' belief systems regarding their influences on offspring; psychosocial and physical development of offspring peer relations.

CHARACTERISTICS OF THE ORIGINAL SAMPLE:

Year the study began: 1980
Subject selection process: Parents were selected for the study based on a psychiatric interview; each family having two children: younger child, 15 mos. to 3 years; and older sibling, 5 years to 8 years.
Total number of subjects at Time 1: N = 130[a]
Ages at Time 1: 15 mos.-5 yrs.
Sex distribution: Approximately equal numbers of females and males throughout
Socioeconomic status: 85% middle/upper middle class, 9% poverty class, 6% working class
Race/ethnicity: 89% white, 9% African-American, 2% Hispanic
Comments:
a. 120 families were assessed (4 persons per family: 2 children and 2 parents), and data on both mothers and fathers were collected, but only the children are included in the following sample figures.

Years of Completed Waves:

Years	N=	Age ranges
(Cohort 1: Families with Affective Disorders)		
1980	80	15-36 mos.
1984	75	5-8 yrs.
1988-1991	a	9-12 yrs.
(Cohort 2: Normal Families)		
1980	50	42 mos.-63 mos.
1984	40	7-9 yrs.
1988-1991	a	11-13 yrs.

Comments:
a. Data collection in progress; approximately 95 families interviewed to date.

INFORMATION ON SAMPLE ATTRITION:

During the 11-year period of study, approximately 15 of 130 Ss (11.5%) were not available for further study. Reasons for sample attrition included refusal to participate, families could not be located, and subject was unavailable due to death of both parents. As of 1984 the core sample consisted of 220 families.

CONSTRUCTS MEASURED: INSTRUMENTS USED

Psychiatric evaluation of child DSM III: Child assessment scale (T1, T2), Child Psychiatric Play Interview (T1), Diagnostic Instrument for Children and Adolescents (DICA) (T3)

Psychiatric syndromes; internality-externality symptoms: Achenbach Child Behavior Check List

Cognitive abilities: McCarthy Intelligence Test, Wechsler Intelligence Scale for Children

Attitudes toward self and relation to other family members: Drawings of family

Child-rearing values: Block Q-Sort

Parental belief system: Interview/verbal probe (developed by study's staff)

Self-ratings of mood of mother: Profile of Mood States (POMS)

Life events of acute and chronic stresses and family responses to them: Life Interviews

Family background regarding mental illness: Family history interview

Psychiatric assessment DSM III: Schedule of Affective Disorders and Schizophrenia (SADS) (SCID)—of parents

Dimensions of parental rearing behavior, child behavior, and language: Videotaped parent-child interactions (9 hours of observation)

Personality assessment of parent: Personality Disorder Examination (PDE), (nonpatient version) (SCID)

Competence, self-concept of child, competencies of child: Harter's Self Competence Interview

Development: Developmental history

Physical health: Physical examination

REPRESENTATIVE REFERENCES:

Kochanska, G., Kuczynski, L., & Radke-Yarrow, M., & Welsh, J. D. (1987). Resolutions of control episodes between well and affectively ill mothers and their young children. *Journal of Abnormal Child Psychology, 87*(15), 441-456.

Radke-Yarrow, M., Richters, J., & Wilson, E. E. (1988). Child development in a network of relationships. In R. A. Hinde & J. Stevenson-Hind (Eds.), *Relationships within families*. Oxford, UK: Oxford University Press.

Radke-Yarrow, M. (1989). Family environments of depressed and well parents and their children: Issues of research methods. In G. R. Patterson (Ed.), *Aggression and depression in family interactions* (pp. 169-184). Hillsdale, NJ: Lawrence Erlbaum.

Radke-Yarrow, M., Cummings, E. M., Kuczynski, L., & Chapman, M. (1985). Patterns of attachment in two- and three-year olds in normal families and families with parental depression. *Child Development, 56*, 591-615.

CURRENT STATUS OF THE STUDY:

a. A further wave of data collection is in progress.
b. Most data are in machine-readable format.
c. Data are available for secondary analysis from the study contact person.

■ Carolina Abecedarian Project: Early Adolescent Follow-Up for High Risk Infants, 1972

Ramey, Craig T.

Contact Person: Civitan International Research Center
Address: University of Alabama at Birmingham
P.O. Box 313, UAB Station
Birmingham, AL 35294
Telephone No.: (205) 934-5471

SUBSTANTIVE TOPICS COVERED:

The study examines the effects of early educational intervention on disadvantaged children's cognitive and social development; mother-child interactions; language development, especially adaptive language in disadvantaged children; intellectual development; demographic circumstances in high-risk families; physical growth and health.

CHARACTERISTICS OF THE ORIGINAL SAMPLE:

Year the study began: 1972
Subject selection process: Subjects were referred from local hospitals, obstetrical clinics, other social service agencies; screening by a High Risk Index with criterion score for inclusion. Children were randomly assigned to an experimental condition, which provided day care beginning in infancy, or a control group, which did not provide day-care services. At school-age, subjects in the two groups were re-randomized, creating four groups: those with both preschool and school-age experimental intervention (EE); those with preschool but no school-age intervention (EC); those without preschool but with school-age intervention (CE); those assigned to the control group both times (CC).
Total number of subjects at Time 1: N = 111
Ages at Time 1: 3-6 mos.

Sex distribution: Approximately equal numbers of females and males in most
cases, though the range of differences have been as extreme as 71.4% to
28.6% in some subsamples.

Socioeconomic status: 43% poverty class, 27% working class, 30% undetermined

Race/ethnicity: 98% African-American, 2% white

Years of Completed Waves:

Years	N=	Age ranges
(Cohort 1)[a]		
1972-1973	25	3 mos.-4.5 yrs.
1977-1981	22	5-8 yrs.
1984-1985	22	12 yrs.
1987-1988	22	15 yrs.
(Cohort 2)[a]		
1973-1974	29	3 mos.-4.5 yrs.
1978-1982	23	5-8 yrs.
1985-1986	23	12 yrs.
1988-1989	23	15 yrs.
(Cohort 3)[a]		
1975-1980	29	3 mos.-4.5 yrs.
1980-1983	25	5-8 yrs.
1987-1988	26	12 yrs.
1990	26	15 yrs.
(Cohort 4)[a]		
1977-1981	28	3 mos.-4.5 yrs.
1982-1985	26	5-8 yrs.
1989-1990	[b]	12 yrs.

Comments:
a. Approximately equal numbers of subjects were randomly distributed to experimental and control conditions.
b. Data collection has not been completed.

INFORMATION ON SAMPLE ATTRITION:

During the 16-year period of study, 14 of 111 Ss (12.6%) across four cohorts
were not retrieved for further study: 3 of 25 Ss (12%) in Cohort 1; 6 of 29 Ss
(20.7%) in Cohort 2; 3 of 29 Ss (10.3%) in Cohort 3; and 2 of 28 Ss (7.1%) in Cohort 4. The principal investigators report an average attrition rate for each cohort
sample tested of 1.8% each year. The main source of sample attrition has been subject deaths. The core sample consists of 97 Ss: 22 Ss (Cohort 1); 23 Ss (Cohort 2);
26 Ss (Cohort 3); 26 Ss (Cohort 4).

CONSTRUCTS MEASURED: INSTRUMENTS USED

Cognitive and intellectual development in infancy: Bayley Scales of Infant Development

Development of cognitive structures in late sensorimotor period: Uzgiris-Hunt Ordinal Scales of Psychological Development

McCarthy Scales of Children's Development: Skill levels in different areas of development

Child's intellectual development relative to normative population: Wechsler Preschool and Primary Scale of Intelligence, Revised Wechsler Intelligence Scale for Children, Stanford-Binet Intelligence Scale

Attainment of conservation of number, quantity and weight: Concept Assessment Kit—Conservation

Non-verbal abstract reasoning: Raven's Progressive Matrices

Examiner ratings of infants' behavior during Bayley Infant Test on Infant Behavior Record: Social reactions and task orientation during infant test

Task orientation and cooperativeness: Kohn and Rosman Test Behavior Inventory

Social adjustment, adaptive behavior and pre-academic competence in young children: Classroom Behavior Inventory

Social competence, emotional disturbance: Child Behavior Checklist (Achenbach & Edelbrock)

Teacher views of adaptation in school: Teacher ratings

Child's temperament: Parental ratings of emotionality, activity, sociability; impulsivity temperament survey

Child's self-esteem: Purdue Self Concept Scale, Perceived Competence Scale (Harter)

Actual child-parent interaction in a laboratory setting: Videotaped observation of mother-child interactions and maternal teaching

Child's attitudes toward preschool and school experience: Child Interview

Children's skills with preschool and school experience: Feagans-Farran Adaptive Language Tasks, "Grocery Store" and "Magic Box"

Language competence in elementary school: Adaptive Language Inventory

Language competency in areas considered important for school success: Gordon Psycholinguistic Battery

Language usage as processed through visual and auditory channels: Illinois Test Psycholinguistic Ability

Maternal intellectual level: Wechsler Adult Intelligence Scale

Parent attitudes toward child rearing: Parent Attitude Research Instrument

Parent's locus of control: Rotter's Locus of Control Scale

Information on family background, pregnancy history, opinions on child rearing, sex roles, educational and vocational histories, social supports: Parent Interview

Parent's attitudes, beliefs, and values about child education and child rearing: Parent as Educator Interview

Demographic, parent-child aspirations, parent-child attitudes: Child-Parent Interviews

Family status: Interviews

Family relationships, personal growth, organization and control: Family Environment Scale (Moos & Moos)

Quality of intellectual stimulation and care provided in child's home environment: Home Observation for Measurement of Environment

Play styles, social interaction and verbal behavior in home or neighborhood: Neighborhood Play Observation

School achievement: Peabody Individual Achievement Test, Woodcock Johnson
    Psychoeducational Battery (Part 2)
Time on and off task during academic work periods in class: Schedule of Class-
    room Activity Norms (SCAN)
Social interactions in class and on playground: School Adaptive Behavior Observations
Physical growth: Growth measurements
Development of gross and fine motor skill: Bayley Scales of Infant Development
    (Psychomotor Development Index), Motor Scale Index (McCarthy Scales)

REPRESENTATIVE REFERENCES:

Martin, S. L., Ramey, C. T., & Ramey, S. L. (1990). The prevention of intellectual impairment in
    children of impoverished families: Findings of a randomized trial of educational daycare.
    American Journal of Public Health, 80, 844-847.
Ramey, C. T., & Campbell, F. A. (1984). Preventive education for high-risk children: Cognitive
    consequences of the Carolina Abecedarian Project [Special issue] *American Journal of Men-
    tal Deficiency, 88*(5), 515-523.
Ramey, C. T., & Campbell, F. A. (1987). The Carolina Abecedarian Project: An educational ex-
    periment concerning human malleability. In J. J. Gallagher, & C. T. Ramey (Eds.), *The mal-
    leability of children* (pp. 127-139). Baltimore: Paul H. Brookes.

CURRENT STATUS OF THE STUDY:

   a. Further waves of data collection are planned.
   b. The data are in machine-readable format.
   c. The data are conditionally available for secondary analysis through the study con-
       tact person.

■ Project CARE: Carolina Approach to Responsive Education, 1977

Ramey, Craig T.

Contact Person: Craig T. Ramey
Address: Civitan International Research Center
                 University of Alabama at Birmingham
                 P.O. Box 313, UAB Station
                 Birmingham, AL 35294
Telephone No.:   (205) 934-5471

SUBSTANTIVE TOPICS COVERED:

   The study examines the effects of early educational intervention on disadvantaged children's cognitive and social development; mother-child interactions, lan-

guage development, especially adaptive language in disadvantaged children; intellectual development; demographic circumstances in high-risk families; physical growth and health. The study also contrasts two forms of early intervention, discerning the differential effects of "developmental day care" versus "family education." Study participants were enrolled in one of these home/school resource programs for 3 years from age 5 (kindergarten) to age 8 (second grade).

CHARACTERISTICS OF THE ORIGINAL SAMPLE:

Year the study began: 1977
Subject selection process: The High-Risk Index was used to screen for eligible families in the local area whose infants were at risk for developmental delay. The eligible families were then randomly placed into one of three experimental, family education alone, or an educationally untreated group of controls.
Total number of subjects at Time 1: N = 15
Ages at Time 1: Birth
Sex distribution: Approximately equal numbers of females and males (Cohort 1); 63% male, 37% female (Cohort 2); 65% male, 35% female (Cohort 3)
Socioeconomic status: 100% poverty class
Race/ethnicity: 94% African-American, 6% white (Cohort 1); 96% African-American, 4% white (Cohort 2); 83% African-American, 17% white (Cohort 2)

Years of Completed Waves:

Years	N=	Age ranges
(Cohort 1: Developmental Day care plus Family Education)		
1978	15	Birth
1978	14	6 mos.
1979	15	1 yr.
1979	15	18 mos.
1979	15	20 mos.
1980	15	2 yrs.
1980	15	30 mos.
1981	14	3 yrs.
1981	15	42 mos.
1982	15	4 yrs.
1983	15	5 yrs.
1984	15	6 yrs.
1985	15	7 yrs.
1986	15	8 yrs.
1990	a	12 yrs.
(Cohort 2: Family Education)		
1978	24	Birth
1978	26	6 mos.
1979	26	1 yr.
1979	25	18 mos.
1979	25	20 mos.

Years of Completed Waves, Continued:

Years	N=	Age ranges
1980	26	2 yrs.
1980	25	30 mos.
1981	25	3 yrs.
1981	25	42 mos.
1982	25	4 yrs.
1983	25	5 yrs.
1984	25	6 yrs.
1985	25	7 yrs.
1986	25	8 yrs.
1990	a	12 yrs.
(Cohort 3: Controls)		
1978	23	Birth
1978	23	6 mos.
1979	22	1 yr.
1979	22	18 mos.
1979	22	20 mos.
1980	22	2 yrs.
1980	22	30 mos.
1981	22	3 yrs.
1981	22	42 mos.
1982	22	4 yrs.
1983	22	5 yrs.
1984	22	6 yrs.
1985	22	7 yrs.
1986	22	8 yrs.
1990	a	12 yrs.

Comments:
a. Follow-up of Ss at age 12 is in progress.

INFORMATION ON SAMPLE ATTRITION:

During the 12-year period of study, 1 of 63 Ss (1.6%) was not retrieved for further study. The core sample consists of 62 Ss: 15 Ss (Cohort 1); 25 Ss (Cohort 2); and 22 Ss (Cohort 3).

CONSTRUCTS MEASURED: INSTRUMENTS USED

Mental development: Bayley Mental Development Index
Intelligence: Stanford-Binet Intelligence Test, Wechsler Preschool and Primary Scales of Intelligence, McCarthy Scales of Children's Abilities
Mother's intelligence: Wechsler Adult Intelligence Scale, Infant Behavior Record
Temperament: Infant Temperament Scale, Toddler Temperament Scale, EASI, Demographic Information
Pregnancy and birth data: Pregnancy and birth

Mother-child interaction free-play: Videotape, videotaped Teaching Task, videotaped Strange Situation

Home environment: Caldwell's HOME, Stimulation Inventory, Holmes-Rahe Life Change Scale

Parental locus of control: Rotter's Locus of Control Scale

Parental attitudes: Parental Attitude Research Instrument (PARI), Inventory of Caregiver's Child Development Value and Concepts, Attitude questionnaire, parent evaluation of program

Parent skill and knowledge: Knowledge of Infant Development Inventory, Parent Problem Solving Instrument

Parental support systems: Community Interaction Checklists, Supports interview

REPRESENTATIVE REFERENCES:

Bryant, D. M., Ramey, C. T., Sparling, J. J., Wasik, B. H. (1987). The Carolina approach to responsive education: A model for daycare. *Topics on Early Childhood Special Education, 7,* 48-60.

Ramey, C. T., Bryant, D. M., Sparling, J. J., Wasik, B. H. (1985). Project CARE: A comparison of two early intervention strategies to prevent retarded development. *Topics in Early Childhood Special Education, 5*(2), 12-25.

Wasik, B. H., Ramey, C. T., Bryant, D. M., & Sparling, J. J. (in press). A "longitudinal study" of two early intervention strategies: Project CARE. *Child Development.*

CURRENT STATUS OF THE STUDY:

a. Further waves of data collection are planned.

b. Data are in machine-readable format.

c. Data are available for secondary analysis through the study contact person.

■ Adolescent Research Project, 1976

Reinherz, Helen

Contact Person: Helen Reinherz
Address: Simmons College
School of Social Work
51 Commonwealth Avenue
Boston, MA 02116
Telephone No.: (617) 738-2930

SUBSTANTIVE TOPICS COVERED:

The study examines the relations of predictor variables (domains of health, demography, and so on) to behavior, school adjustment, guidance and special education services received in the early years of school.

CHARACTERISTICS OF THE ORIGINAL SAMPLE:

Year the study began: 1976

Subject selection process: All children registering for kindergarten in the Quincy, Massachusetts, public school system were invited to participate in the study.

Total number of subjects at Time 1: N = 777

Ages at Time 1: 4-6 yrs.

Sex distribution: Approximately equal numbers of females and males throughout

Socioeconomic status: 46.6 % upper middle/middle class, 53.4% working and poverty classes

Race/ethnicity: 99% white, 1% Asian-American

Years of Completed Waves:

Years	N=	Age ranges
1977	777	4-6 yrs.
1978	702	5-7 yrs.
1981[a]	519	8-10 yrs.
1987	404	14-16 yrs.
1990	370	17-18 yrs.

Comments:

a. A supplemental sample of 283 immigrants, not part of the original sample, were tested at this data point. These Ss are not included in the sample N for 1981.

INFORMATION ON SAMPLE ATTRITION:

During the 13-year period of study, 407 of 777 (52.8%) were not retrieved for further study. The core sample consists of 370 Ss.

CONSTRUCTS MEASURED: INSTRUMENTS USED

Information processing, verbal ability: Preschool Screening System (Ainsworth)

Demographics, development, preschool attendance, health, family characteristics: Parent questionnaire

Parental assessment of behavior: Simmons Behavior Checklist, Parent questionnaire

Sensory deficits: Vision and hearing tests

Development, health, life events, and behavior: Parent questionnaire

Social competency, behavior, and cognition: Teacher questionnaire

Teacher assessment of behavior: Preschool behavior questionnaire (Behar & Stringfield), teacher questionnaire

Self-concept: Piers-Harris Children's Self-Concept Scale

Academic achievement: California Achievement Test

Academic aptitude: Short Form Test of Academic Aptitude

Depressive symptoms: Children's Depression Inventory (Kovacs)

Stressful life events: Coddington Life Events
Parental and peer assessment of emotional and behavioral problems: Child Behavior
    Checklist (Achenbach) and Youth Self-Report (Achenbach)
Social support: Inventory of Socially Supportive Behaviors (Barrera)
Health and physical status: Adolescent and parent interview
Family functioning, family structure: Family Adaptability and Cohesion Evaluation
    Scales III (Olson), interview

REPRESENTATIVE REFERENCES:

Anatas, J. W., & Reinherz, H. (1984). Gender differences in learning and adjustment problems in
    school: Results of a longitudinal study. *American Journal of Orthopsychiatry, 54*(1), 110-122.
Kinard, E. M., & Reinherz, H. (1984). Behavioral and emotional functioning of children of ado-
    lescent mothers. *American Journal of Orthopsychiatry, 54*(4), 578-594.
Kinard, E. M., & Reinherz, H. (1986). Birthdate effects on school performance and adjustment: A
    longitudinal study. *The Journal of Educational Research, 79,* 366-372.
Reinherz, H. (1982). Primary prevention of emotional disorders in school settings. In H. C.
    Schulberg & M. Killilea (Eds.), *The modern practice of community mental health.* San Fran-
    cisco: Jossey-Bass.

CURRENT STATUS OF THE STUDY:

a. A further wave of data collection is planned, pending additional funding.
b. Most data are in machine-readable format.
c. The data are not yet available for secondary analysis.

■ Moral Judgment Development and Life Experience, 1972

Rest, James R.

Contact Person: James R. Rest
Address: University of Minnesota
                  206A Burton Hall
                  178 Pillsbury Drive, S.E.
                  Minneapolis, MN 55455
Telephone No.:   (612) 624-0876

SUBSTANTIVE TOPICS COVERED:

The study examines what life experiences and life-adjustment patterns are associated with moral judgment change; how moral judgment development is influ-
enced by the prevailing social-political climate of the culture; how individual
ontogenetic changes are related to cultural historical change; the predictability of
life-adjustment patterns of adults from moral judgment scores in children; the typical

course of moral judgment development in this sample from adolescence to early adulthood.

CHARACTERISTICS OF THE ORIGINAL SAMPLE:

Year the study began: 1972
Subject selection process: Subjects were not randomly selected. Subjects from several high school classrooms were asked to participate.
Total number of subjects at Time 1: N = 160
Ages at Time 1: 14-18 yrs.
Sex distribution: Equal numbers of females and males throughout
Socioeconomic status: 100% middle/lower middle class
Race/ethnicity: 100% white

Years of Completed Waves:

Years	N=	Age ranges
1972	160	14-18 yrs.
1974	128	16-20 yrs.
1976	98	18-22 yrs.
1978	56	20-24 yrs.
1980	40	22-26 yrs.
1983	102	25-29 yrs.

INFORMATION ON SAMPLE ATTRITION:

During the 11-year period of study, 58 of 160 Ss (36.3%) were not retrieved for further study. In 1983, 62 Ss who had missed the 1980 data wave were recontacted. Information about the core sample was not available.

CONSTRUCTS MEASURED: INSTRUMENTS USED

Moral judgment level: Defining Issues Test (Rest)
Understanding of moral concepts: Comprehension of moral concept test
Attitudes toward controversial issues: "Law and Order" attitude scale
Demographic information: Questionnaire
Activities, interests: Structured interview
Characterizing life experience (10 categories): Volker's Checklist
Current life adjustment patterns: Semistructured interview

REPRESENTATIVE REFERENCES:

McColgan, E. B., Rest, J. R., & Pruitt, D. B. (1983). Moral judgment and antisocial behavior in early adolescence. *Journal of Applied Developmental Psychology, 4*(2), 189-199.

Rest, J. (1975). Longitudinal study of the defining issues test of moral judgment: A strategy for analyzing developmental change. *Developmental Psychology, 11*(6), 738-748.

Rest, J. R., & Thoma, S. (1985). Moral judgment development and formal education. *Developmental Psychology, 21*(4), 709-714.

Rest, J. R., et al. (1986). *Moral development: Advances in research and theory.* New York: Praeger.

CURRENT STATUS OF THE STUDY:

a. Further waves of data collection are planned.

b. The data are in machine-readable format.

c. The data are conditionally available for secondary analysis through the study contact person.

■ The National Longitudinal Study of the High School Class of Nineteen Seventy-Two, 1972

Riccobono, John A.; Levinson, Jay R.; and Burkheimer, Graham J.

Contact Person: Paula Knepper
Address: National Center for Education Statistics
Postsecondary Education Statistics Division
555 New Jersey Avenue, N.W.
Washington, DC 20208-5652
Telephone No.: (202) 219-1914

SUBSTANTIVE TOPICS COVERED:

The study examines the vocational activities, plans, aspirations, and attitudes of young adults after they leave high school, and the personal, familial, social, institutional, and cultural factors contributing to the development of educational and career outcomes.

CHARACTERISTICS OF THE ORIGINAL SAMPLE:

Year the study began: 1972

Subject selection process: A national probability sample of high school seniors was drawn from 1,070 public, private, and church-affiliated high schools participating in the base-year survey. Base-year data was collected by the Educational Testing Service (ETS). At Wave 2, additional 1972 high school graduates who had been unable to participate earlier were added to the subject pool. They were drawn from 248 additional schools.

Total number of subjects at Time 1: N = 23,451

Ages at Time 1: 16-21 yrs.

Sex distribution: Approximately equal numbers of females and males throughout
Socioeconomic status: Nationally representative sample
Race/ethnicity: 82% white, 9.5% African-American, 8.5% other

Years of Completed Waves:

Years	N=	Age ranges
1972	23,451	16-21 yrs.
1973-1974	21,350	17-22 yrs.
1974-1975	20,872	18-23 yrs.
1976-1977	20,092	19-24 yrs.
1979-1980	18,630	21-26 yrs.
1986	12,841	28-32 yrs.

INFORMATION ON SAMPLE ATTRITION:

During the 14-year period of study, 10,610 of 23,451 Ss (45.2%) were not retrieved for further study. The core sample consists of 12,841 Ss.

CONSTRUCTS MEASURED: INSTRUMENTS USED

Ability: Base (SAT, ACT, and test scores on vocabulary, reading, math, letter
    groups, mosaic comparison, and picture-number); F-4 (retest on vocabulary
    and mathematics)
Community environment, activity status, educational attainment, school character-
    istics, school experience, school performance, work status, work performance
    and satisfaction, noncognitive traits, goal orientations, marriage and family,
    opinions, military: Questionnaire
Academic achievement: School record information
Verbal and mathematical skills: NLS Student Test (ETS)
Demographic and general descriptive information on student population: School
    Questionnaire (ETS)
Demographic information and information on student problems and faculty contact
    with students: Counselor Questionnaire (ETS)
Plans for after high school, high school experience, attitudes and opinions, family
    plans: Student Questionnaire (ETS)
Plans, attitudes and opinions, career goals, educational goals, family goals, demo-
    graphic information, activity status, vocabulary and mathematics retest,
    school experience (college), military service, school performance, work sta-
    tus, social traits: Adult Questionnaire (ETS)

REPRESENTATIVE REFERENCES:

Burkheimer, G. J., Jaffe, J., Kolstad, A. J. (1982). *Highly able students who did not go to college/Center for Educational Research and Evaluation.* Washington, DC: National Center for Education Statistics.

Dawkins, M. P. (1981). Mobility aspirations of black adolescents: A comparison of males and females. *Adolescence, 16*(63), 701-710.

Munro, B. H. (1981). Dropouts from higher education: Path analysis of a national sample. *American Educational Research Journal, 18*(2), 133-141.

Peng, S. S., & Fetters, W. B. (1978). Variables involved in withdrawal during the first two years of college: Preliminary findings from the National Longitudinal Study of the High School Class of 1972. *American Educational Research Journal, 15*(3), 361-372.

CURRENT STATUS OF THE STUDY:

a. No further waves of data collection are planned.
b. Most data are in machine-readable format.
c. Data are available for secondary analysis through the National Center for Education Statistics, U.S. Department of Education, Data Systems Branch, 555 New Jersey Avenue NW, Washington D.C., 20208.

■ Biopsychosocial Development of Early Adolescent Girls: A Short-Term Longitudinal Study, 1982

Rierdan, Jill E.; and Koff, Elissa

Contact Person: Elissa Koff or Jill E. Rierdan
Address: Center for Research on Women
                Wellesley College
                Wellesley, MA 02181
Telephone No.: (617) 235-0320

SUBSTANTIVE TOPICS COVERED:

The study examines normative female biopsychosocial functioning and development during the junior high school years. The study monitors the onset of menstruation; evaluates such biopsychosocial factors as development of secondary sex characteristics, preparation for menstruation, and level of ego development, in terms of how they mediate the impact of menarche on psychosocial functioning; and examines such psychosocial factors thought to change with menarche as body experience, body image, psychological well-being, self-concept, and experience of self in social contexts. The study explores several key questions: what the biopsychosocial changes are that characterize girls' development over the junior high school years; the psychosocial impact of menarche; the differential psychosocial impact of menarche among early, average, and late maturers; and what factors mediate the responses of early, average, and late maturers to the onset of menstruation.

CHARACTERISTICS OF THE ORIGINAL SAMPLE:

Year the study began: 1982
Subject selection process: Volunteer Ss who received parental permission
Total number of subjects at Time 1: N = 587
Ages at Time 1: 11-14 yrs.
Sex distribution: 100% female
Socioeconomic status: 100% middle/upper middle class
Race/ethnicity: 100% white

Years of Completed Waves:

Years	N=	Age ranges
1982	587	11-14 yrs.
1983	587	12-15 yrs.

INFORMATION ON SAMPLE ATTRITION:

During the one-year period of study, all of the 587 Ss (100%) were retrieved for further study. The core sample consists of 587 Ss.

CONSTRUCTS MEASURED: INSTRUMENTS USED

Depression: Beck Depression Inventory, Short Form
Degree of satisfaction with body: Body Cathexis Scale, Modified Form
Dimensions of Body Experience: Body Experience Scale
Activities related to adolescent maturation: Girls Growing Up Scale
Sexual differentiation: Draw-A-Person Test

REPRESENTATIVE REFERENCES:

Koff, E., Rierdan, J., & Silverstone, E. (1978). Changes in representation of body image as a function of menarcheal status. *Developmental Psychology, 14,* 635-642.

Rierdan, J. (1985). Timing of menarche and initial menstrual experience. [Special issue: Time of maturation and psychosocial functioning in adolescence: I]. *Journal of Youth and Adolescence, 14,* 237-244.

Rierdan, J., Koff, E., & Stubbs, M. L. (1987). Depressive symptomatology and body image in adolescent girls. *Journal of Early Adolescence, 7,* 205-216.

Rierdan, J., Koff, E., & Stubbs, M. L. (1988). Gender, depression, and body image in early adolescents. *Journal of Early Adolescence, 8,* 109-117.

CURRENT STATUS OF THE STUDY:

a. Further waves of data collection are planned.
b. Most data are in machine-readable format.
c. Data are not available for secondary analysis.

■ Biopsychosocial Development of Early Adolescent Girls: A Long-Term Longitudinal Study, 1984

Rierdan, Jill E.; and Koff, Elissa

Contact Person: Elissa Koff or Jill E. Rierdan
Address: Center for Research on Women
                 Wellesley College
                 Wellesley, MA 02181
Telephone No.:   (617) 235-0320, ext. 3006

SUBSTANTIVE TOPICS COVERED:

The main focus of this study is to discern and differentiate adaptive and maladaptive effects of menarche and related pubertal developments through examining preadolescent girls' psychosocial functioning within its biological context. An additional focus of the study pertains to identifying biopsychosocial factors associated with greater risk for adult clinical depression and/or eating disorders through pinpointing the onset of subclinical depression and eating disorders in adolescence in a normative sample of girls. The study specifically investigates menarcheal status and three domains of biopsychosocial functioning: physical development and body experience (i.e., pubertal development; knowledge of, attitudes toward, and experience of menstruation; sense of being developmentally on-or-off-time; physical attractiveness, attitudes toward the body; eating attitudes and behavior); personality (i.e., ego development, self-concept, and affect); and interpersonal functioning (i.e., frequency, variety, and intimacy of interpersonal interactions). Central questions guiding the study pertain to the psychosocial impact of menarche; how the psychosocial impact of menarche varies for early, average, and late maturers; what factors mediate the responses to menarche in early, average, and late maturers; the extent of stability of psychosocial differences among early, average, and late maturers; and to determine the natural history of maladaptive biopsychosocial patterns for girls.

CHARACTERISTICS OF THE ORIGINAL SAMPLE:

Year the study began: 1984
Subject selection process: Volunteer Ss who received parental permission

Total number of subjects at Time 1: N = 220
Ages at Time 1: 11 yrs.
Sex distribution: 100% female
Socioeconomic status: 100% middle/upper middle class
Race/ethnicity: 100% white

Years of Completed Waves:

Years	N=[a]	Age ranges
1984 (Fall)	218	11 yrs.
1985 (Spring)	201	11 yrs.
1985 (Fall)	206	12 yrs.
1986 (Spring)	204	12 yrs.
1986 (Fall)	199	13 yrs.
1987 (Spring)	191	13 yrs.
1987 (Fall)	173	14 yrs.
1988 (Spring)	175	14 yrs.

Comments:
a. Follow-up rates are approximations based upon the number of Ss who completed one measure.

INFORMATION ON SAMPLE ATTRITION:

During the 4-year period of study, authors estimate attrition to be approximately 15%. Main reasons for sample attrition included Ss moving away and changing to other school districts.

CONSTRUCTS MEASURED: INSTRUMENTS USED

Shyness: Revised Check and Buss Shyness Scale
State anxiety: State-Trait Anxiety Inventory for Children (STAIC) (Spielberger)
Weight: Self-reported and nurses' measurements
Fear of fat: The Goldfarb Fear of Fat Scale
Body self-perception: Body self-perception scale (Koff & Rierdan)
Age self-perception: Age self-perception scale (Koff & Rierdan)
Body consciousness: Body Consciousness scale (Miller, Murphy & Buss)
Ego development: Washington University Sentence Completion Test (Loevinger)
Sexual differentiation: Draw-A-Person Test (Haworth & Normington)
Memories: Memory scale (Rierdan & Koff)
Breast development: Self and objective ratings
Menstrual attitudes: The Menstrual Attitude Questionnaire
Sex roles: Bem Sex Role Inventory
Body experience: Body Experience Scale (Rierdan & Koff)
Body satisfaction: The Body Esteem Scale (Franzoi & Shields)
Chumships: Chumship Checklist (Mannarino)
Depression: Beck Depression Inventory

Dieting: The Restraint Scale (adaptation of Herman & Polivy)
Eating attitudes: Eating Disorder Inventory
Life events: Life Events Checklist
Locus of control: Children's Locus of Control Scale, Locus of Control Scale for
    Children
Physical competence: Self-Rating Scale (Physical appearance and physical abilities
    subscales)
Self-consciousness: Self-consciousness Scale (Fenigstein, Scheier, & Buss)
Self-esteem: Rosenberg Self-Esteem Scale

REPRESENTATIVE REFERENCES:

No publications to date.

CURRENT STATUS OF THE STUDY:

a. Further waves of data collection are planned.
b. Most data are in machine-readable format.
c. Data are not available for secondary analysis.

■ Deviant Children Grown Up, 1954

Robins, Lee; and O'Neal, Patricia

Contact Person: Lee Robins
Address: Department of Psychiatry
                 Washington University School of Medicine
                 4940 Audubon Avenue
                 St. Louis, MO 63110
Telephone No.:   (314) 362-2469

SUBSTANTIVE TOPICS COVERED:

The study sought to describe the natural history of Ss displaying antisocial per-sonality and behavior, through examining childhood factors that lead to antisocial behavior and distinguishing these factors from those childhood problem behaviors that remain relatively transient (See Robins, 1966; Preface and Chapter One)

CHARACTERISTICS OF THE ORIGINAL SAMPLE:

Year the study began: 1924
Subject selection process: Consecutive series of a municipal child guidance clinic
    of all white patients, with an IQ 80+ and under 18 years of age, seen from

1924 to 1929 (Cohort 1); white elementary school students of same age and
sex distribution from same census tracts (Cohort 2); subjects' sons, age 18 or
older in 1966, who grew up in St. Louis (Cohort 3)

Total number of subjects at Time 1: N = 524

Ages at Time 1: Median age = 13 yrs.

Sex distribution: 73% male, 27% female (Cohort 1); 70% male, 30% female (Cohort 2); 100% male (Cohort 3)

Socioeconomic status: 54% working class, 20% middle/upper middle class, 15%
poverty class, 11% other (Cohort 1); 68% working class, 29% middle/upper
middle class, 3% poverty class (Cohort 2); 60% working class, 40% mid-
dle/upper middle class (Cohort 3)

Race/ethnicity: 100% white

Years of Completed Waves:

Years	N=	Age ranges
(Cohort 1: Child Guidance Patients)		
1924-1929	524	5-17 yrs.
1955-1960	438	30-55 yrs.
(Cohort 2: Control Ss)		
1924-1929	100	5-17 yrs.
1955-1960	98	30-55 yrs.
(Cohort 3: Sons of Cohorts 1 and 2)		
1966-1967	67	18-30 yrs.

INFORMATION ON SAMPLE ATTRITION:

During the 45-year period of study, 88 of 624 Ss (14.1%), for Cohorts 1 and 2,
were not retrieved for further study. Attrition was due to the inability to locate subjects, subjects' refusal to participate, institutionalization, and death. The core sample consists of 559 Ss: 461 Ss (Cohort 1), and 98 Ss (Cohort 2).

CONSTRUCTS MEASURED: INSTRUMENTS USED

Family life as a child, school success, juvenile delinquency, marital history, job
history, arrest history, psychiatric symptoms, treatment for psychiatric disorders, financial dependency, adult relationships with parents and siblings, participation in formal and informal relationships: Personal Interview (with a
relative if subject is not alive) and abstracts of many adult records, including
police, hospital, social agencies, credit ratings

School problems, level of achievement; criminal history: Abstracts of school records; abstract of juvenile court records; abstract of police records

Psychiatric disorder: Abstracts of child clinic records, psychiatric hospital records,
interview

Changes in deviant behavior, history of physical illness, history of psychiatric illness, history of alcohol and drug use, family history of psychiatric illness: Interview

REPRESENTATIVE REFERENCES:

Robins, Lee. (1966). *Deviant children grown up*. Baltimore: Williams & Wilkins. (Reprinted by Krieger, 1972.)

Robins, L., Bates, W. M., & O'Neal, P. (1962). Adult drinking patterns of former problem children. In D. J. Pittman & C. R. Snyder (Eds.), *Society, culture, and drinking patterns*. New York: John Wiley.

Robins, L., & O'Neal, P. (1958). Mortality, mobility and crime: Problem children thirty years later. *American Sociological Review, 23*, 162-171.

O'Neal, P., & Robins, L. (1958). Childhood patterns predictive of adult schizophrenia 30-year follow-up study. *American Journal of Psychiatry, 115*, 385-391.

CURRENT STATUS OF THE STUDY:

a. No further waves of data collection are planned.
b. Most of the data are in machine-readable format.
c. Data are available for secondary analysis through the Washington University School of Medicine Library.

■ Longitudinal Follow-Up of Very Low Birthweight Preterm Infants: Neurologic, Cognitive, and Behavioral Outcome, 1978

Ross, Gail; Lipper, Evelyn; and Auld, Peter A. M.

Contact Person: Gail Ross
Address: Perinatology Center
New York Hospital
Cornell Medical Center
525 E. 68th Street
New York, NY 10021
Telephone No.: (212) 746-3548

SUBSTANTIVE TOPICS COVERED:

The central purpose of this study is to determine the effects of prematurity and very low birthweight on the neurologic, intellectual, and behavioral development of the child.

CHARACTERISTICS OF THE ORIGINAL SAMPLE:

Year the study began: 1978
Subject selection process: Subjects selected were infants weighing less than or equal to 1,500 grams who were appropriate for gestational age and were admitted to the neonatal intensive care unit at New York Hospital.
Total number of subjects at Time 1: N = 120
Ages at Time 1: Birth
Sex distribution: Approximately equal numbers of females and males throughout
Socioeconomic status: 49% middle/upper middle class, 34% working class, 17% poverty class
Race/ethnicity: Approximately 49% white, 32% African-American, 16% Hispanic, 3% other

Years of Completed Waves:

Year	N=	Age ranges
1978-1979	120	Birth
1979-1980	102	1 yr.
1981-1988	94	3-4 yrs.
1984-1986	88	7-8 yrs.[a]

Comments:
a. A full-term matched control group (matched on age, ethnicity, SES and geographic location) of 80 Ss was included at this time point.

INFORMATION ON SAMPLE ATTRITION:

During the 7-year period of study, 32 of 120 Ss (26.7%) were not retrieved for further study. Reasons for attrition included some subjects' moving; subjects' adoption; parents' refusal to continue participation; and death.

CONSTRUCTS MEASURED: INSTRUMENTS USED

Neurologic development: Amiel-Tison first year exam (Birth-12 mos.)
Neurologic functioning: Standard neurologic exam (3 yrs. and 6 yrs.)
Manual laterality: Purdue Peg Board
Ability to copy designs: Visual-motor Integration Test (Beery)
Mental and motor ability: Bayley Scales of Infant Development (12 mos.)
Intelligence: Revised Stanford-Binet Intelligence Test (Form L-M) (3 yrs.), Revised Wechsler Intelligence Scales for Children (WISC-R)
Auditory memory and comprehension: Wechsler sentences, sound blending, story comprehension
School achievement: Wide Range Achievement Test (Revised)
Social and behavioral competence: Child Behavior Checklist (Achenbach)

REPRESENTATIVE REFERENCES:

Ross, G., Lipper, E. G., & Auld, P. A. M. (1985). Consistency and change in the development of premature infants weighing less than or equal to 1,501 grams at birth. *Pediatrics, 76,* 885-891.

Ross, G., Lipper, E. G., & Auld, P. A. M. (1986). Early predictors of neurodevelopmental outcome of very low-birthweight infants at three years. *Developmental Medicine and Child Neurology, 28,* 171-179.

Ross, G., Lipper, E. G., Auld, P. A. M. (1987). Hand preference of four-year-old children: Its relationship to premature birth and neurodevelopmental outcome. *Developmental Medicine and Child Neurology, 29,* 615-622.

Ross, G., Lipper, E. G., Auld, P. A. M. (1990). Social competence and behavior problems in premature children at school age. *Pediatrics, 86,* 391-397.

CURRENT STATUS OF THE STUDY:

a. No further waves of data collection are planned.
b. Most data are in machine-readable format.
c. Data are available for secondary analysis from study contact person.

■ The Waterloo Longitudinal Project, 1980

Rubin, Kenneth H.; and Hymel, Shelley

Contact Person: Kenneth H. Rubin
Address: Department of Psychology
University of Waterloo
Waterloo, Ontario N2L 3G1
Canada
Telephone No.: (519) 885-3912

SUBSTANTIVE TOPICS COVERED:

This study examines the causes, correlates, and consequences of aggression, social withdrawal, and poor peer relationships in childhood.

CHARACTERISTICS OF THE ORIGINAL SAMPLE:

Year the study began: 1980
Subject selection process: Subjects selected were children attending public schools.
Total number of subjects at Time 1: N = 111
Ages at Time 1: 5 yrs.
Sex distribution: Approximately equal numbers of females and males throughout

Socioeconomic status: 80% middle/upper middle class, 20% working class (Cohort 1);
    70% middle/upper middle class, 20% working, 10% poverty class (Cohort 2)
Race/ethnicity: 85% white, 10% Asian, 5% black (both cohorts)

Years of Completed Waves:

Years	N=	Age ranges
(Cohort 1)		
1980	111	5 yrs.
1982	88	7 yrs.
1984	81	9 yrs.
1985	77	10 yrs.
1989-1990	60	14 yrs.
(Cohort 2)		
1982	79	5 yrs.
1985	45	8 yrs.

INFORMATION ON SAMPLE ATTRITION:

During the 6-year period of study, 85 of 190 Ss (44.7%), combining both co-horts, were not retrieved for further study: 51 of 111 Ss (45.9%) in Cohort 1, and 34 of 79 Ss (43%) in Cohort 2. The main reason for sample attrition was parents moving their children out of the school district under study. The core sample con-sists of 105 Ss for both cohorts: 60 Ss (Cohort 1) and 45 Ss (Cohort 2).

CONSTRUCTS MEASURED: INSTRUMENTS USED

Popularity or acceptability by peers: Sociometric Rating Scale (Asher)
Peer assessments of social behavior: Revised Class Play (Masten, Morison & Pelligrini)
Cognitive, social and physical competence: Perceived Competence Scale
Children's perceptions of their competencies in five domains; cognitive, physical, social, appearance, and conduct: The Self-perception Profile for Children (Harter)
Social problem solving: The Social Problem-Solving Test (SPST)
Depression: Child Depression Inventory (Kovacs)
Behavioral observations: Play sessions
Receptive vocabulary: Peabody Picture Vocabulary Test
Socioeconomic problems as well as various other problems: Teacher ratings, using the Preschool Behavior Questionnaire (Behar & Stringfield) and the T-Cars.

REPRESENTATIVE REFERENCES:

Rubin, K. H. (1982). Social and social-cognitive development characteristics of young isolate, normal and sociable children. In K. H. Rubin & H. S. Ross (Eds.), *Peer relationships and social skills in childhood.* New York: Springer-Verlag.

Rubin, K. H. (1985). Socially withdrawn children: An "at risk" population? In B. H. Schneider, K. H. Rubin, & J. E. Ledingham (Eds.), *Children's peer relations: Issues in assessment and intervention.* New York: Springer-Verlag.

Rubin, K. H., Daniels-Beirness, T., & Bream, L. (1984). Social isolation and social problem solving: A longitudinal study. *Journal of Consulting and Clinical Psychology, 52,* 17-25.

Rubin, K. H., Hymel, S., LeMare, L., & Rowden, L. (1989). Children experiencing social difficulties: Sociometric neglect reconsidered. *Canadian Journal of Behavioral Science, 21,* 94-111.

CURRENT STATUS OF THE STUDY:

a. Further waves of data collection are planned.

b. Most of the data are in machine-readable format.

c. Data are available for secondary analysis from the study contact person at the University of Waterloo, Department of Psychology, Waterloo, Ontario N2L 3G1, Canada.

S

Rochester Longitudinal Study, 1970

Sameroff, Arnold J.; Seifer, Ronald; Zax, Melvin; and Barocas, Ralph

Contact Person: Arnold J. Sameroff
Address: Brown University
Emma Pendleton Bradley Hospital
1011 Veterans Memorial Parkway
Riverside, RI 02915
Telephone No.: (401) 751-8040

SUBSTANTIVE TOPICS COVERED:

The study examines congenital and environmental influences on the etiology of mental disorders; compares the prenatal history and birth experiences of women diagnosed as schizophrenic with women who had other psychiatric diagnoses or no mental disorder; and assesses the cognitive, psychomotor, emotional, and social functioning of the offspring of these women.

CHARACTERISTICS OF THE ORIGINAL SAMPLE:

Year the study began: 1970

Subject selection process: The recruitment of subjects began in 1970 and ended in 1974. Names of all women who were to deliver at a local hospital were checked against the Monroe County Psychiatric Case Register. Those women showing a history of mental illness were recruited. A sample of women with no history of mental illness was also recruited.

Total number of subjects at Time 1: N = 337[a]

Ages at Time 1: Prenatal

Sex distribution: Approximately equal numbers of females and males throughout

Socioeconomic status: 37% upper middle/middle class, 32% poverty class, 31% working class

Race/ethnicity: 67% white, 32% African-American, 1% Hispanic

Comments:

a. This figure refers to the number of mothers who agreed to participate in the study and were tested during the prenatal period. Ages at each data point are reported in terms of the children. Initial age range for the mothers was 15-46 years (mean = 24.4 years).

Years of Completed Waves:

Years	N=	Age ranges
1970	337	Prenatal
1970	263	Birth
1970	262	4 mos.
1971	263	12 mos.
1972	234	30 mos.
1974	214	4 yrs.
1986-1988	180	12-14 yrs.

INFORMATION ON SAMPLE ATTRITION:

During the 18-year period of study, 157 of 337 subjects (46.6%) were not retrieved for further study. The core sample consists of 180 Ss.

CONSTRUCTS MEASURED: INSTRUMENTS USED

History of mental illness: Current and past psychopathology schedule
Anxiety: Personality and Ability Tests Anxiety Scale, Eysenck Personality, Malaise Anxiety Scale
Maternal attitude toward pregnancy: Maternal attitude toward pregnancy questionnaire
Social-medical history: Social-medical history schedule
Mother's perceptions of child's development: Concepts of Development questionnaire
Parenting styles: Cook-Gumperz Parenting Styles
Parental values: Kohn's Parental Values
Social desirability: Marlowe-Crowne Social Desirability Scales
Neonatal status: Neonatal behavioral assessment scales (Brazelton)
Physical abnormalities: Minor physical anomalies
Neurological development: Autonomic levels
Status of the child at birth: Research Obstetric Scale
Developmental level: Bayley Scales of Infant Development
Temperament: Carey Infant Temperament Questionnaire
Attachment: Mother-infant attachment
Intelligence: Stanford-Binet Vocabulary, Peabody Picture Vocabulary Test, Wechsler Preschool and Primary Scale of Intelligence, Verbal Scales
Attention: Delayed match-to-sample
Self-regulation of behavior: Luria verbal regulation
Adaptive behavior: Rochester Adaptive Behavior Inventory
Language development: Verbal production measure
Temperament: Child Temperament Questionnaire
Mother-child interaction: Home observation
Maternal teaching style: Mother-child interaction

Ratings of parental emotional expressiveness about child: Camberwell Variables
Parental styles: Ratings of parenting styles
Stressful life events: Life events inventory
Mothers's mental health: Denver Community Mental Health Inventory, Rutter Malaise Inventory (Parent Mental Health Scale), Beck Scale (parent depression), interviewer's ratings on the parent
Social support: Chisel (social support questionnaire)
Parental values: Kohn Rankings (ranking of parental values)
Concepts of development: Concepts of Development Questionnaire (CODQ), (perspectivistic or categorical)
Parent's intellectual functioning: Shipley-Hartford Test (vocabulary and abstractions), Quick test
Child's intellectual functioning: Wechsler Intelligence Scale for Children (4 subscales; information, similarities, picture arrangement, and block design)
Self-esteem: Harter Self-Perception Scale (What I Am Like)
Locus of control: Connell Perceptions of Control Scale (Why Things Happen)
Social support: Child's Social World Questionnaire (Furman)
Physical and physiological measures: Child's height and weight, judgments of his/her physical maturity (Tanner), and report of menstruation
Physical attractiveness: Rater judgments on attractiveness of each child's photograph
Child's psychological interview rating scale (CHPIRS): Interviewer's ratings on the child personality

REPRESENTATIVE REFERENCES:

Sameroff, A., & Seifer, R. (1981). The transmission of incompetence: The offspring of mentally-ill women. In M. Lewis & L. Rosenblum (Eds.), *The uncommon child*. New York: Plenum.
Sameroff, A., Seifer, R., & Zax, M. (1982). Early development of children at risk for emotional disorder. *Monographs of the Society for Child Development, 44*(7).
Sameroff, A., Seifer, R., Barocas, R., Zax, M., & Greenspan, S. (1987). I.Q. scores of 4-year old children: Social environmental risk factors. *Pediatrics, 79,* 343-350.
Sameroff, A., Seifer, R., Zax, M., & Barocas, R. (1987). Early indices of developmental risk: The Rochester Longitudinal Study. *Schizophrenia Bulletin, 13,* 383-394.

CURRENT STATUS OF THE STUDY:

   a. Further waves of data collection are planned.
   b. Most data are in machine-readable format.
   c. The data are conditionally available for secondary analysis through the study contact person.

■ Boston University Longitudinal Study of Personality Development, 1954

Sander, Louis

Contact Person: Louis Sander
Address: 2525 Madrona Avenue
St. Helena, CA 94574
Telephone No.: (707) 963-0743

SUBSTANTIVE TOPICS COVERED:

The study examines the emerging mother-child relationship to provide an objective documentation of the course of events in a normal population; the effect of maternal maturity upon normal variations in ego organization during development; and the different caretaking behaviors associated with them; and the relation of early ego organization to outcome ego organization 25 years later.

CHARACTERISTICS OF THE ORIGINAL SAMPLE:

Year the study began: 1954
Subject selection process: Mothers were referred from a Massachusetts prenatal hospital clinic. Selection of Ss was based on criteria to obtain mothers within a normal population showing character organization ranging from most-, middle-, and least-mature. 150 Ss were screened to derive the final population.
Total number of subjects at Time 1: N = 30[a]
Ages at Time 1: Prenatal-40 mos.
Sex distribution: Approximately equal numbers of females and males (child cohort)
Socioeconomic status: 100% working class
Race/ethnicity: 90% white, 10% African-American
Comments:
a. This figure represents mother-prenatal pairs because prenatal measures were taken throughout the pregnancy.

Years of Completed Waves:

Years	N=	Age ranges
(Cohort 1: Mothers)		
1954-1959	30	18-40 yrs.
1979-1983	29	43-57 yrs.
(Cohort 2: Offspring)		
1954-1959	30	Prenatal-40 mos.
1961-1964	22[a]	5-7 yrs.
1979-1983	29	24-27 yrs.

Comments:
a. A subsample was followed up 1961-1964.

INFORMATION ON SAMPLE ATTRITION:

During the 29-year period of study, 2 of 60 Ss were not retrieved for further study: 1 of 30 Ss (mother cohort), and 1 of 30 Ss (offspring cohort). The core sample consists of 58 Ss: 29 mothers and 29 offspring.

CONSTRUCTS MEASURED: INSTRUMENTS USED

Mother

Functioning level: Clinical interview by a psychiatric team

Mother's intelligence: Wechsler Adult Intelligence Scale

Personality of mother: Rorschach Ink Blot Test, Thematic Apperception Test, Draw-A-Person Test, social worker interview with husband present

Maturity level of relationships, sexual identity, competence, and control of inner and outer processes: Ratings based on interviews

Physical status of the mother and fetus: Obstetricians interviewed mothers on a biweekly basis during early pregnancy, then on a weekly schedule during the end of pregnancy

Delivery process, newborn state, and behavioral organization: Observations of the delivery process, attitudes and reactions of mothers, reactions of the child, and medical status of the child shortly after birth (obstetricians recorded observations of the labor process)

Current family organization, relationships, and home environment; demographic information, life histories, life adaptations and transitions: Tape-recorded interviews with parents and with children who were 24-27 years old at the time of the outcome interviews

Inner experiences and appraisal of self, life events and conflicts; self-esteem, ego defense strategies: Interviews (6-8 hours) of subject by psychoanalyst

Child

Child play and motor skills: Play session of child with toy

Child behavior in school, classroom atmosphere, and activities-deployment of attention: Classroom observation in first grade

Child's intelligence: Stanford-Binet Intelligence Test or Wechsler Intelligence Scale for Children

Self-concept of child: Draw-A-Person Test

Personality assessment of child: Children's Apperception Test

Mental and physical activity; cognitive evaluation (perceptual organization language functions, arithmetic skills, memory, and so on); personality evaluation (Cognitive style and skills, personality organization, object relations, self-representation, personality style and adaptive capacities): Neuropsychological battery, Rorschach Ink Blot Test, Thematic Apperception Test, Human Figure Drawings, Cole Animal Test, Continuous Performance Test

REPRESENTATIVE REFERENCES:

Sander, L. W. (1964). Adaptive relationships in early mother-child interaction. *Journal of the American Academy of Child Psychiatry, 3*(2), 231-265.

Sander, L. W. (1969). The longitudinal course of early mother-child interaction: Cross-case comparison in a sample of mother-child pairs. In B. M. Moss (Ed.), *Determinants of infant behavior, IV.* New York: Methuen.

Sander, L. W. (1975). A 25-year follow-up: Some reflections on personality over the long term. [Special issue: Papers from the Third Congress of the World Association for Infant Psychiatry and Allied Disciplines]. *Infant Mental Health Journal, 8*(3), 210-220.

Sander, L. W. (1975). Awareness of inner experience: A systems perspective on self regulatory process in early development. [Special issue: Child abuse and neglect]. *Child Abuse and Neglect, 11*(3), 339-346.

CURRENT STATUS OF THE STUDY:

a. A follow-up data collection of a subsample of Ss is underway for 1990-1991.
b. Selected data are in machine-readable format.
c. Availability of data for secondary analysis is currently under negotiation.

■ The Florida Longitudinal Project, 1970

Satz, Paul; Fletcher, Jack; and Morris, Robin

Contact person: Paul Satz
Address: Neuropsychiatric Institute
University of California at Los Angeles
760 Westwood Plaza (C8-747)
Los Angeles, CA 90024-1759
Telephone No.: (213) 825-5360

SUBSTANTIVE TOPICS COVERED:

This study was designed to develop a battery for early detection of reading disabilities with longitudinal validation; to determine long-term prognosis of reading and learning disabilities in children; and to study changes over time in the cognitive and neuropsychological correlates of learning disabilities.

CHARACTERISTICS OF THE ORIGINAL SAMPLE:

Year the study began: 1970
Subject selection process: Subjects selected were white males in Alachua County, Florida; subsequent cohorts represented whole schools with kindergarten classes.
Total number of subjects at Time 1: N = 474
Ages at Time 1: 4-5 yrs.

Sex distribution: 100% male (Cohorts 1 and 2); approximately equal numbers of
 females and males (Cohort 3)
Socioeconomic status: 90.3% middle/upper middle class, 9.7% working class (Cohort 1); 95% middle/upper middle class, 5% working class (Cohort 2); 80%
 middle/upper middle class, 20% working class (Cohort 3)
Race/ethnicity: 100% white (Cohorts 1 and 2); 78.8% white, 21.2% African-American
 (Cohort 3)

Years of Completed Waves:

Years	N=	Age ranges
(Cohort 1)		
1970	474	4-5 yrs.
1971	473	5-6 yrs.
1972	463	6-7 yrs.
1973	459	7-8 yrs.
1974	455	8-9 yrs.
1975	444	9-10 yrs.
1976	419	10-11 yrs.
(Cohort 2)		
1971	175	4-6 yrs.
1972	173	5-7 yrs.
1973	175	6-8 yrs.
1974	168	7-9 yrs.
1975	159	8-10 yrs.
1976	161	9-11 yrs.
(Cohort 3)		
1974	128	4-5 yrs.
1975	114	5-6 yrs.
1976	107	6-7 yrs.

INFORMATION ON SAMPLE ATTRITION:

During the 7-year period of study, 90 of 777 Ss (11.5%), across three cohorts,
were not retrieved for further study: 55 of 474 Ss (11.6%), Cohort 1; 14 of 175 Ss
(8%), Cohort 2; and 21 of 128 Ss (16.4%), Cohort 3. The core sample consists of
687 Ss across three cohorts: 419 Ss (Cohort 1); 161 Ss (Cohort 2); and 107 Ss (Cohort 3).

CONSTRUCTS MEASURED: INSTRUMENTS USED

Receptive language: Peabody Picture Vocabulary Test
Visual-perception: Recognition-Discrimination Task
Perceptual-Motor Coping: Berry Visual-Motor Integration Task
Somatosensory functioning: Finger Localization Task
Verbal cultural functioning: Alphabet recitation

Auditory discrimination: Wepman Auditory Discrimination Test (short version)
Ear asymmetry: Dichotic Listening Task
Verbal fluency: Verbal Fluency Test (modified version)
Fine motor movement: Finger Tapping Task
Visual perception: Embedded Figures Task
Verbal reasoning: Wechsler Preschool and Primary Scale of Intelligence (Similarities subtest)
Auditory-visual integration: Auditory-Visual Integration Task
Right-left discrimination: Right-left Discrimination Task
Child's behavior: Behavior Checklist
Risk of learning disability, child's physical maturity, child's emotional maturity, child's social maturity, activity level: Teacher Rating
Classroom reading level (achievement) (all grades): Teacher specification
Vocabulary achievement (Grade 2): Iota Word Test (Grade 2)
Reading achievement (Grade 5): Wide Range Achievement (Reading Recognition)
Spelling achievement (Grade 5): Wide Range Achievement (Spelling)
Arithmetic achievement (Grade 5): Wide Range Achievement (Arithmetic)
Vocabulary and comprehension achievement (Grade 2): Gates-McGintie Test
Psycholinguistic functioning: Illinois Test of Psycholinguistic Abilities Grammatic Closure subtest, Double Object Comprehension Test, Morphological Knowledge Berry-Talbot Test (Cohort 3)
Verbal fluency: Verbal Fluency Test (Cohort 3)
General neurological functioning: General neurological examination (Cohorts 1 and 2)
Fine and gross motor functioning, Examination of gross body anomalies: Neurological Examination (Cohorts 1 and 2)
Parent reading ability: Wide Range Achievement Test Reading Subtest (Parents)
Parent spelling ability: Wide Range Achievement Test Spelling Subtest (Parents)

REPRESENTATIVE REFERENCES:

Fletcher, J. M., & Satz, P. (1980). Developmental changes in the neuropsychological correlates of reading achievement: A six-year longitudinal follow-up. *Journal of Clinical Neuropsychology, 2*, 23-37.

Fletcher, J. M., & Satz, P. (1984). Teacher versus test-based predictions of reading achievement. *Journal of Pediatric Psychology, 9*, 193-203.

Satz, P., & Fletcher, J. M. (1987). Left-handedness and dyslexia: An old myth revisited. *Journal of Pediatric Psychology, 12*, 291-298.

Satz, P., Taylor, G., Friel, J., & Fletcher, J. M. (1978). Some developmental and predictive precursors of reading disabilities: A six-year follow-up. In A. L. Benton and D. Pearl (Eds.), *Dyslexia: An appraisal of current knowledge* (pp. 457-501). New York: Oxford University Press.

CURRENT STATUS OF THE STUDY:

a. No further waves of data collection are planned.
b. Most data are in machine-readable format.
c. Data are available for secondary analysis from the study contact person.

■ The Ecology of Adolescent Self-Esteem, 1978

Savin-Williams, Ritch C.

Contact Person: Ritch C. Savin-Williams
Address: Human Development and Family Studies
                M.R.V. Hall
                Cornell University
                Ithaca, NY 14853-4401
Telephone No.: (607) 255-6111

SUBSTANTIVE TOPICS COVERED:

This study compared various methods of studying self-esteem, especially in terms of self-report and experiential dimensions. Self-esteem was also examined in terms of its stability from year to year through adolescence, and its contextual variability in naturalistic settings (e.g., activities, physical location, and participants present).

CHARACTERISTICS OF THE ORIGINAL SAMPLE:

Year the study began: 1978
Subject selection process: Subjects were recruited by selecting every third seventh-grade student from a junior high school in Ithaca, New York.
Total number of subjects at Time 1: N = 41
Ages at Time 1: 12-13 yrs.
Sex distribution: Approximately equal numbers of females and males throughout
Socioeconomic status: 80% middle/upper middle class, 20% working class
Race/ethnicity: 90.2% white, 4.9% African-American, 4.9% Asian-American

Years of Completed Waves:

Years	N=	Age ranges
1978	41	12-13 yrs.
1979	39	13-14 yrs.
1980	53	14-15 yrs.
1981	39	15-16 yrs.
1982	35	16-17 yrs.
1983	36	17-18 yrs.
1984	32	18-19 yrs.

INFORMATION ON SAMPLE ATTRITION:

During the 7-year period of study, 9 of 41 Ss (22%) were not retrieved for further study. The core sample consists of 32 Ss.

CONSTRUCTS MEASURED: INSTRUMENTS USED

Self-esteem: Rosenberg Self-Esteem Scale, Coopersmith Self-Esteem Inventory, Self-Esteem Interview, Peer Ratings of Self-Esteem, Observations of Self-esteem, Experiential Sampling Method ("beepers" or paging devices), Block Q-Sort
Academic achievement: Grade point average, questionnaire (educational attainment, attitudes, and aspirations)
Friendship, popularity, athletic ability, leadership: Peer ratings, Interview
Activities, moods: Paging devices (Experiential Sampling Method)
Personality: Block Q-Sort

REPRESENTATIVE REFERENCES:

Demo, D. H., & Savin-Williams, R. C. (in press). Self-concept, stability and change during adolescence. In R. P. Lipka & T. Brinthawpt (Eds.), *Studying the self: Vol 2. Self-perspectives across the life span.* New York: SUNY Press.
Savin-Williams, R. C., & Demo, D. H. (1983). Conceiving or misconceiving the self: Issues in adolescent self-esteem. *Journal of Early Adolescence, 3,* 121-140.
Savin-Williams, R. C., & Demo, D. H. (1984). Developmental change and stability in adolescent self-concept. *Developmental Psychology, 20,* 1100-1110.
Savin-Williams, R. C., & Jaquish, G. A. (1981). The assessment of adolescent self-esteem. *Journal of Personality, 49,* 324-335.

CURRENT STATUS OF THE STUDY:

a. No further waves of data collection are planned.
b. Most of the data are in machine-readable format.
c. Data are available for secondary analysis from the study contact person.

■ An Evaluation of the Verbal Interaction Project in Bermuda, 1978

Scarr, Sandra; and McCartney, Kathleen

Contact Person: Sandra Scarr
Address: Department of Psychology, University of Virginia
                 Gilmer Hall
                 Charlottesville, VA 22901
Telephone No.:   (804) 924-3374

SUBSTANTIVE TOPICS COVERED:

The study examines an early childhood intervention program; mother-child interaction; the development of children's competence from 2 to 4 years.

CHARACTERISTICS OF THE ORIGINAL SAMPLE:

Year the study began: 1978
Subject selection process: All 2-year-olds (within 6-month intervals) in a parish, chosen
        to be representative of Bermuda as a whole, were asked to participate in the study.
Total number of subjects at Time 1: N = 125[a]
Ages at Time 1: 2 yrs.
Sex distribution: Equal numbers of females and males
Socioeconomic status: 33.3% working class, 33.3% poverty class, 33.4% middle class
Race/ethnicity: 60% black, 40% white
Comments:
a. Sample consists of 1978 and 1979 subject cohorts.

Years of Completed Waves:

Years	N=	Age ranges
1978-1979	125	2 yrs.
1981-1982	117	4 yrs.
1987	105	9 yrs.

INFORMATION ON SAMPLE ATTRITION:

During the 9-year period of study, 20 of 125 Ss (16%) were not retrieved for further study. The core sample consists of 105 Ss.

CONSTRUCTS MEASURED: INSTRUMENTS USED

Family constellation, education, and employment: Demographic questionnaire
Substitute care experiences of the child: History of child care questionnaire
Intelligence: Stanford-Binet Intelligence Test
Maternal teaching skills: Maternal teaching test (Hess & Shipman)
Delay of gratification: Delay of gratification test (experimental test)
Personality: Childhood personality test (Cohen & Dibble)
Mother's self-satisfaction and social support systems: Maternal self-esteem/support
        system questionnaire
Child-rearing practices: Maternal discipline strategies questionnaire
Parents' attitudes toward parenting: Parent report (Cohen & Dibble)
Maternal teaching skills: Parent as educator (Schaefer & Edgerton)

REPRESENTATIVE REFERENCES:

McCartney, K., Scarr, S., Phillips, D., & Grajek, S. (1985). Day care as intervention: Comparisons of
        varying quality programs. *Journal of Applied Developmental Psychology, 6*(2-3), 247-260.
Phillips, D., McCartney, K., & Scarr, S. (1987). Child-care quality and children's social develop-
        ment. *Developmental Psychology, 23*(4), 537-543.

Scarr, S. (1984). *Mother care/other care*. New York: Basic Books.

Scarr, S., & McCartney, K. (1988). Far from hone: An experimental evaluation of the Mother-Child Home Program in Bermuda. *Child Development, 59*(3), 531-543.

CURRENT STATUS OF THE STUDY:

a. No further waves of data collection are planned.

b. Data are in machine-readable format.

c. The data are available for secondary analysis through the study contact person.

■ Seattle Longitudinal Study, 1956

Schaie, K. Warner

Contact Person: K. Warner Schaie
Address: Department of Human Development and Family Studies
                 College of Health and Human Development
                 110 Henderson Building South
                 Pennsylvania State University
                 University Park, PA 16802
Telephone No.:   (814) 863-0241

SUBSTANTIVE TOPICS COVERED:

The study investigates adult intellectual development and causes of individual differences in intellectual abilities and development, through examining age changes and cohort differences in psychometric intelligence and rigidity-flexibility (verbal meaning, space, reasoning, number, perceptual speed, verbal memory, and word fluency). The study also investigates the incidence of disease in relation to mental abilities. Research design includes both longitudinal and cross-sectional sequences.[1]

Comments:

1. In addition to the four longitudinal sequences described below, the study includes five cross-sectional sequences (1965, 1963, 1970, 1977, 1984) derived from five independent data sets. These sequences involved data collection from seven cohorts in 1956; eights cohorts in 1963; nine cohorts in 1970; nine cohorts in 1977 and 1984. Subjects were gathered in 7-year age-intervals for each cohort, ranging from 25 to 81 years of age. The 1984 wave included cognitive training of 229 participants. Two panels were also studied once in 1974 and 1975, respectively.

CHARACTERISTICS OF THE ORIGINAL SAMPLE:

1956 Longitudinal Sequence A: 1956-1984

Year the study began: 1956

Subject selection process: Twenty-five men and 25 women for each 5-year interval from 20 to 70 were randomly selected from a pool of 18,000 adult members of a health maintenance organization.

Total number of subjects at Time 1: N = 500

Ages at Time 1: 25-67 yrs.

Sex distribution: Approximately equal numbers of females and males in most cohorts and waves

Socioeconomic status: 58% working class, 37.5% middle/upper middle class, 4.5% poverty class

Race/ethnicity: Predominantly white

Years of Completed Waves: Total Sample:

Years	N=	Age ranges	Birth Year
1956	500	25-67 yrs.	
1963	303	32-74 yrs.	
1970	162	39-81 yrs.	
1977	128	46-88 yrs.	
1984	97	53-95 yrs.	
(Cohort 1)			
1956	76	25 yrs.	1931
1963	40	32 yrs.	1931
1970	21	39 yrs.	1931
1977	19	46 yrs.	1931
1984	15	53 yrs.	1931
(Cohort 2)			
1956	70	32 yrs.	1924
1963	46	39 yrs.	1924
1970	26	46 yrs.	1924
1977	19	53 yrs.	1924
1984	21	60 yrs.	1924
(Cohort 3)			
1956	150	39 yrs.	1917
1963	79	46 yrs.	1917
1970	67	53 yrs.	1917
1977	50	60 yrs.	1917
1984	17	67 yrs.	1917
(Cohort 4)			
1956	65	46 yrs.	1910
1963	40	53 yrs.	1910
1970	32	60 yrs.	1910
1977	31	67 yrs.	1910
1984	24	74 yrs.	1910
(Cohort 5)			
1956	70	53 yrs.	1903
1963	44	60 yrs.	1903
1970	28	67 yrs.	1903
1977	24	74 yrs.	1903
1984	16	81 yrs.	1903

Years of Completed Waves: Total Sample, Continued:

Years	N=	Age ranges	Birth Year
(Cohort 6)			
1956	72	60 yrs.	1896
1963	40	67 yrs.	1896
1970	15	74 yrs.	1896
1977	9	81 yrs.	1896
1984	2	88 yrs.	1896
(Cohort 7)			
1956	76	67 yrs.	1889
1963	48	74 yrs.	1889
1970	14	81 yrs.	1889
1977	5	88 yrs.	1889
1984	2	95 yrs.	1889

INFORMATION ON SAMPLE ATTRITION:

During the 28-year period of the sequence, 403 of 500 Ss (80.6%) were not retrieved. Principle reasons for attrition included subject mobility, lack of interest, death, and disabilities. Core samples ranged from 24 subjects in Cohort 4 to 2 subjects in Cohorts 6 and 7.

1963 Longitudinal Sequence B: 1963-1984

Year the study began: 1963
Subject selection process: Twenty-five men and 25 women for each 5-year interval from 20 to 70 were randomly selected from a pool of 18,000 adult members of a health maintenance organization.
Total number of subjects at Time 1: N = 996
Ages at Time 1: 25-74 yrs.
Sex distribution: Distribution ranged between 75% female and 25% male across cohorts and waves, with approximately equal numbers of females and males in most cohorts and waves.
Socioeconomic status: 67.8% working class, 28.2% middle/upper middle class, 5.0% poverty class
Race/ethnicity: Predominantly white

Years of Completed Waves: Total Sample:

Years	N=	Age ranges	Birth Year
1963	996	25-74 yrs.	
1970	420	32-81 yrs.	
1977	337	39-88 yrs.	
1984	250	46-95 yrs.	

Years of Completed Waves: Total Sample, Continued:

Years	N=	Age ranges	Birth Year
(Cohort 1)			
1963	100	25 yrs.	1938
1970	35	32 yrs.	1938
1977	25	39 yrs.	1938
1984	18	46 yrs.	1938
(Cohort 2)			
1963	122	32 yrs.	1931
1970	61	39 yrs.	1931
1977	55	46 yrs.	1931
1984	45	53 yrs.	1931
(Cohort 3)			
1963	150	39 yrs.	1924
1970	79	46 yrs.	1924
1977	67	53 yrs.	1924
1984	50	60 yrs.	1924
(Cohort 4)			
1963	155	46 yrs.	1917
1970	73	53 yrs.	1917
1977	69	60 yrs.	1917
1984	64	67 yrs.	1917
(Cohort 5)			
1963	143	53 yrs.	1910
1970	74	60 yrs.	1910
1977	67	67 yrs.	1910
1984	50	74 yrs.	1910
(Cohort 6)			
1963	122	60 yrs.	1903
1970	41	67 yrs.	1903
1977	23	74 yrs.	1903
1984	16	81 yrs.	1903
(Cohort 7)			
1963	127	67 yrs.	1896
1970	43	74 yrs.	1896
1977	27	81 yrs.	1896
1984	6	88 yrs.	1896
(Cohort 8)			
1963	77	74 yrs.	1889
1970	14	81 yrs.	1889
1977	4	88 yrs.	1889
1984	1	95 yrs.	1889

INFORMATION ON SAMPLE ATTRITION:

During the 21-year period of the sequence, 746 of 996 Ss (74.9%) were not retrieved. Principle reasons for attrition included subject mobility, lack of interest, death, and disabilities. Core samples ranged from 60 subjects in Cohort 4 to one subject in Cohort 8.

1970 Longitudinal Sequence C: 1970-1984

Year the study began: 1970
Subject selection process: Twenty-five men and 25 women for each 5-year interval from 20 to 70 were randomly selected from a pool of 18,000 adult members of a health maintenance organization.
Total number of subjects at Time 1: N = 705
Ages at Time 1: 25-74 years.
Sex distribution: Approximately equal numbers of females in males in most co-horts and waves
Socioeconomic status: 53.7% working class, 45.7% middle/upper middle class, 0.6% poverty class
Race/ethnicity: Predominantly white

Years of Completed Waves: Total Sample:

Years	N=	Age ranges	Birth Year
1970	705	25-74 yrs.	
1977	340	32-81 yrs.	
1984	224	39-88 yrs.	
(Cohort 1)			
1970	71	25 yrs.	1945
1977	34	32 yrs.	1945
1984	26	39 yrs.	1945
(Cohort 2)			
1970	65	32 yrs.	1938
1977	36	39 yrs.	1938
1984	29	46 yrs.	1938
(Cohort 3)			
1970	84	39 yrs.	1931
1977	45	46 yrs.	1931
1984	31	53 yrs.	1931
(Cohort 4)			
1970	87	46 yrs.	1924
1977	54	53 yrs.	1924
1984	43	60 yrs.	1924
(Cohort 5)			
1970	89	53 yrs.	1917
1977	53	60 yrs.	1917
1984	42	67 yrs.	1917
(Cohort 6)			
1970	80	60 yrs.	1910
1977	46	67 yrs.	1910
1984	33	74 yrs.	1910

Years of Completed Waves: Total Sample, Continued:

Years	N=	Age ranges	Birth Year
(Cohort 7)			
1970	91	60 yrs.	1903
1977	34	74 yrs.	1903
1984	14	81 yrs.	1903
(Cohort 8)			
1970	88	74 yrs.	1896
1977	30	81 yrs.	1896
1984	4	88 yrs.	1896
(Cohort 9)			
1970	50	81 yrs.	1889
1977	8	88 yrs.	1889
1984	2	95 yrs.	1889

INFORMATION ON SAMPLE ATTRITION:

During the 14-year period of the sequence, 481 of 705 Ss (68.2%) were not retrieved. Principle reasons for attrition included subject mobility, lack of interest, death, and disabilities. Core samples ranged from 43 subjects in Cohort 4 to 2 subjects in Cohort 9.

1977 Longitudinal Sequence D: 1977-1984

Year the study began: 1977
Subject selection process: Random sample of subjects from members of a health maintenance organization in 1977
Total number of subjects at Time 1: N = 609
Ages at Time 1: 25-81 yrs.
Sex distribution: Approximately equal numbers of females and males in most cohorts and waves
Socioeconomic status: 54.8% middle/upper middle class, 38.6% working class, 6.6% poverty class
Race/ethnicity: Predominantly white

Years of Completed Waves: Total sample:

Years	N=	Age ranges	Birth Year
1977	609	25-81 yrs.	
1984	294	32-88 yrs.	
(Cohort 1)			
1977	55	25 yrs.	1952
1984	26	32 yrs.	1952

Years of Completed Waves: Total Sample, Continued:

Years	N=	Age ranges	Birth Year
(Cohort 2)			
1977	62	32 yrs.	1945
1984	28	39 yrs.	1945
(Cohort 3)			
1977	73	39 yrs.	1938
1984	42	46 yrs.	1938
(Cohort 4)			
1977	69	46 yrs.	1931
1984	37	53 yrs.	1931
(Cohort 5)			
1977	77	53 yrs.	1924
1984	53	60 yrs.	1924
(Cohort 6)			
1977	72	60 yrs.	1917
1984	44	67 yrs.	1917
(Cohort 7)			
1977	73	67 yrs.	1910
1984	38	74 yrs.	1910
(Cohort 8)			
1977	70	74 yrs.	1903
1984	16	81 yrs.	1903
(Cohort 9)			
1977	58	81 yrs.	1896
1984	10	88 yrs.	1896

INFORMATION ON SAMPLE ATTRITION:

During the 7-year period of the sequence, 315 of 609 Ss (50.1%) were not re-trieved. Principle reasons for attrition included subject mobility, lack of interest, death, and disabilities. Core samples ranged from 53 subjects in Cohort 5 to 10 subjects in Cohort 9.

CONSTRUCTS MEASURED: INSTRUMENTS USED

Intelligence: Primary Mental Abilities Test
Rigidity-flexibility: Test of Behavior Rigidity
Health behavior: Health history abstracts
Personal microenvironment: Life Complexity Inventory

REPRESENTATIVE REFERENCES:

Schaie, K. W. (1983). The Seattle Longitudinal Study: A 21-year exploration of psychometric intelligence in adulthood. In K. W. Schaie (Ed.), *Longitudinal studies of adult psychosocial development*. New York: Guilford Press.

Schaie, K. W. (1988). Internal validity threats in studies of adult cognitive development. In M. L. Howe & C. J. Brainard (Eds.), *Cognitive development in adulthood*. New York: Springer-Verlag.

Schaie, K. W., & Hertzog, C. (1986). Toward a comprehensive model of adult intellectual development: Contributions of the Seattle Longitudinal Study. In R. J. Sternberg (Ed.), *Advances in the psychology of human intelligence*. Hillsdale, NJ: Lawrence Erlbaum.

Schaie, K. W., Labouvie, G. V., & Buech, B. U. (1973). Generational and cohort-specific differences in adult cognitive functioning: A fourteen-year study of independent samples. *Developmental Psychology, 9,* 151-166.

CURRENT STATUS OF THE STUDY:

a. Further waves of data collection are planned.[1]

b. Most of the data are in machine-readable format.

c. The data are available for secondary analysis through the study contact person.

Comments:

1. A study of approximately 1,200 adult children and siblings of the subjects in the longitudinal study was conducted in 1989-1990. This study included an assessment of family environment in the family of origin and in the current family. A follow-up of subjects trained during the 1984 cycle is also in progress. A sixth wave of data collection on subjects in the 1956 Longitudinal Sequence A is scheduled for 1991.

■ Peer Processes in a Newly Desegregated Middle School, 1975

Schofield, Janet

Contact Person: Janet Schofield
Address: University of Pittsburgh
3939 O'Hara Street
816 LRDC Building
Pittsburgh, PA 15260
Telephone No.: (412) 624-7473

SUBSTANTIVE TOPICS COVERED:

This intensive primarily qualitative study explored the development of peer relations between African-American and white students in a newly desegregated middle school. Special attention was focused on the evolution of interracial attitudes and behaviors and the impact of school policies on them.

CHARACTERISTICS OF THE ORIGINAL SAMPLE:

Year the study began: 1975

Subject selection process: Subjects were randomly selected students from randomly selected classes.

Total number of subjects at Time 1: N = 100[a]

Ages at Time 1: 11-12 yrs.

Sex distribution: Equal numbers of females and males throughout

Socioeconomic status: 40% poverty class, 35% working class, 25% middle/upper middle class

Race/ethnicity: 50% African-American, 50% white (Cohort 1); 55% African-American, 45% white (Cohort 2)

Comments:

a. This and all other numbers are very rough approximations. The study was a complex mixture of interrelated studies, some using an entire cohort and others not.

Years of Completed Waves:

Years	N=	Age ranges
(Cohort 1)		
1975-1976	100	11-12 yrs.
1976-1977	100	12-13 yrs.
1977-1978	100	13-14 yrs.
(Cohort 2)		
1976-1977	100	11-12 yrs.
1977-1978	100	12-13 yrs.
1978-1979	100	13-14 yrs.

INFORMATION ON SAMPLE ATTRITION:

During the 3-year period of study, new Ss were added to make up for some attrition. The core sample consists of approximately 150 Ss who remained in the study the entire 3 years.

CONSTRUCTS MEASURED: INSTRUMENTS USED[1]

Interracial peer preference (friendship): Sociometric measures (both peer nomination and roster-and-rating methods)

Peer interaction patterns: Cambell, Kruskal, & Wallace's formula for estimating extent to which seating patterns (obtained from daily maps of seating patterns in school cafeteria) deviate from randomness

Peer classroom behavior: Reliable quantitative measure of affective tone, task orientation, and mutuality in peer interactions

Comments:

1. The primary data-gathering methodology was the full field note method, a commonly used technique in anthropology. However, quantitative measures were utilized on subsamples, as was necessary or appropriate. Thus, the instruments listed above were generally used with a subsample of the cohorts listed.

REPRESENTATIVE REFERENCES:

Schofield, J. W. (1979). The impact of positively structured contact on intergroup behavior: Does it last under adverse conditions? *Social Psychology Quarterly, 42,* 280-284.

Schofield, J. W. (1989). *Black and white in school: Trust, tension or tolerance?* New York: Teachers College Press.

Schofield, J. W., & Sagar, H. A. (1977). Peer interaction patterns in an integrated middle school. *Sociometry, 40,* 130-138.

Schofield, J. W., & Whitley, B. E., Jr. (1983). Peer nomination versus rating scale measurement of children's peer preferences. *Social Psychology Quarterly, 46,* 242-251.

CURRENT STATUS OF THE STUDY:

a. No further waves of data collection are planned.

b. Most of the data are not in machine-readable format.

c. Some of the data are available for secondary analysis from the study contact person.

■ Patterns of Child Rearing, 1951

Sears, Robert (deceased); Maccoby, Eleanor E.; and Levin, Henry

Contact Person: Henry A. Murray Research Center
Address: Radcliffe College
               10 Garden Street
               Cambridge, MA 02138
Telephone No.: (617) 495-8140

SUBSTANTIVE TOPICS COVERED:

The study examines how different child-rearing practices and values affect children's development; the factors that determine the use of a method by parents; the effect of early childhood experiences on personality development.

CHARACTERISTICS OF THE ORIGINAL SAMPLE:

Year the study began: 1951

Subject selection process: The sample is stratified by socioeconomic status, husband's occupation, and sex and ordinal position of the child. Families were contacted through enrollment at public kindergartens in two suburban towns in a metropolitan area of Massachusetts. One child per mother was chosen. The selection process maximized the homogeneity of the sample by controlling for social class, religious background, and other dimensions thought to be important variables for child-rearing practices and values. All families were intact. The study was originally a cross-sectional design that was later expanded into a longitudinal design.

Total number of subjects at Time 1: N = 379 dyads

Ages at Time 1: 5 yrs. (children); 24-42 yrs. (mothers)

Sex distribution: Approximately equal number of females and males throughout

Socioeconomic status: 53.2% middle class, 46.8% working class
Race/ethnicity: 100% white

Years of Completed Waves:

Years	N=	Age ranges
1951-1952	379	5 yrs.
1958	160	12 yrs.
1964	83[a]	18 yrs.
1964-1965	83[a]	18-19 yrs.
1968	64[a]	22 yrs.
1977-1979	160	30-32 yrs.
1987-1989	89	40-42 yrs.

Comments:
a. A subsample of the original 379 Ss was followed from 1964 to 1979.

INFORMATION ON SAMPLE ATTRITION:

During the 26-year period of study, 219 of 379 subjects (57.8%) were not retrieved for further study. The core sample consists of 160 Ss.

CONSTRUCTS MEASURED: INSTRUMENTS USED

Child-rearing practices, personality indicators to assess the effects of those practices, and a profile (by socioeconomic status, and so on) of the kinds of mothers using certain kinds of child-rearing practices; techniques of discipline, permissiveness, and tolerance for changeworthy behavior; severity of techniques for purpose of eliminating changeworthy behavior; temperamental qualities of mother, and positive encouragement of more mature behavior to replace that which is changeworthy; demographic and personality information; reward and punishment in teaching; leisure time activities and financial matters; effects of becoming a mother on outside activities; personal differences between respondent's current child-rearing method and her experiences as a child: Face-to-face, semistructured interview

Aggressive acts, thematically neutral acts, and which one of the five dolls was used to perform it: Three 20-minute sessions of doll play with each of the children [first two sessions were permissive, the third session was a series of uncompleted stories describing a child's transgression—Ss had to complete the story using five dolls (father, mother, boy, girl, and baby)]

Resistance to temptation: "Raygun" marksmanship task in which Ss scored own performance, giving the child a chance to cheat

Identification: Series of described situations for which alternative adultlike or childlike behavior was offered to the child as solutions—child made choice of solution

Aggressive feelings; self-concepts, self-criticism, ideas of reference, hypersensitivity to others, and self-evaluation; masculinity-femininity: Questionnaire scales

Perceived child-rearing experiences: Retrospective child-rearing experiences

Hypnotizability of subjects: Trancelike experiences

Level of aspiration categories: Rotter level of aspiration board

Psychopathological patterns, neurotic or psychotic symptoms, anxiety, hypochondria: Minnesota Multiphasic Personality Inventory (MMPI)

Need for affiliation; Need for achievement; Need for power: Thematic Apperception Test (TAT)

Non-verbal sensitivity: Rosenthal's PONS, Ambiguous voice test

Adult behavioral qualities: Interviews

Home life, marriage, income, education, employment, job history, relationship to others: Life Patterns Questionnaire

Stress: Ways of coping

Work changes, school changes, financial changes, health changes: Life Changes Questionnaire

Work and family climate: Work and family climate questionnaire

Social support: Social support measure

Participation in athletic events, extracurricular activities: Activities Questionnaire

Self-Image: Self-descriptions

Ego development: Washington University Sentence Completion Test (Loevinger)

Physical symptoms: Symptoms questionnaire

Moral orientation toward justice or caring: Porcupine and Moles

Substance use, exercise, relaxation, diet, major illnesses: Health questionnaire

Worst experience in last 3 years, religious beliefs: Life-Orientation Questionnaire

REPRESENTATIVE REFERENCES:

McClelland, D., Constantian, C., Pilon, D., & Stone, C. (1980). Effects of child-rearing practices on adult maturity. In D. C. McClelland (Ed.), *The development of social maturity*. New York: Irvington.

Sears, R. R. (1984). Patterns of child rearing. In S. A. Mednick, M. Harway, & K. M. Finello (Eds.), *Handbook of longitudinal research: Vol. 1. Birth and childhood cohorts*. New York: Praeger.

Sears, R., Maccoby, E., & Levin, H. (1957). *Patterns of childrearing*. Palo Alto, CA: Stanford University Press.

Sears, R. R., Whiting, J. W. M., Nowlis, V., & Sears, P. S. (1953). Some childrearing antecedents of aggression and dependency in young children. *Genetic Psychology Monographs, 47*, 135-234.

CURRENT STATUS OF THE STUDY:

a. No further waves of data collection are planned.

b. Most data are in machine-readable format.

c. The first six waves of data are available for secondary analysis at the Henry A. Murray Research Center, Radcliffe College, 10 Garden Street, Cambridge, MA 02138.

■ Wisconsin Longitudinal Study of Social and Psychological Factors in Aspiration and Achievements, 1957

Sewell, William H.; and Hauser, Robert M.

Contact Person: Robert M. Hauser
Address: University of Wisconsin, Madison
                  Department of Sociology
                  1180 Observatory Drive
                  Madison, WI 53706
Telephone No.:   (608) 262-2182

SUBSTANTIVE TOPICS COVERED:

The study examines the process that connects socioeconomic background and family structure with academic achievement in high school, social influences of parents, teachers, and peers, postsecondary schooling, occupational careers, family formation, and social participation.

CHARACTERISTICS OF THE ORIGINAL SAMPLE:

Year the study began: 1957
Subject selection process: Subjects were selected from a random sample of Wisconsin youths who were high school seniors. The WLS began as a short-term panel study of college entry, but later turned into a long-term study of social and psychological factors in achievement.
Total number of subjects at Time 1: N = 10,317
Ages at Time 1: 18 yrs.
Sex distribution: Approximately equal numbers of females and males throughout
Socioeconomic status: Sample was representative of the state of Wisconsin.
Race/ethnicity: 98% white, 2% African-American

Years of Completed Waves:[a]

Years	N =	Age ranges
1957	10,317	18 yrs.
1964	9,007	25 yrs.
1975	9,141	36 yrs.

Comments:
a. In 1977, 2,000 siblings of the original respondents were randomly selected and interviewed. These Ss will be reinterviewed in 1992.

INFORMATION ON SAMPLE ATTRITION:

During the 18-year period of study, approximately 1,176 of 10,317 (11.4%) were not retrieved for further study. The main reasons for sample attrition were death and refusal to participate. The supplemental sample of Ss added in 1977 has not been followed-up to date.

CONSTRUCTS MEASURED: INSTRUMENTS USED

Educational plans; curriculum followed; perceptions of encouragement to go to college by parents; perception of college plans by best friend; size of place of residence; information on parents' occupations, level of education; size of school: Questionnaire survey (1957)

Mental ability, rank in high school graduating class: School and state records, Henmon-Nelson test

Information about (colleges or schools attended after high school), occupations; educational degrees; marital and military status; place of residence: Parent questionnaire/survey (1964)

Income of students' parents; parents' occupations; students' occupations; family's income: Department of Taxation records

Men's earnings for 1957-1971; occupations; parents' ages: Social Security records

Occupations, educational attainment; marital and military status; jobs held, work satisfaction; work authority and job complexity; occupational aspirations; earnings; educational/work aspirations for children; family formation and fertility; social participation: Telephone interviews (1975/1977)

REPRESENTATIVE REFERENCES:

Hauser, R. M., & Mossel, P. A. (1985). Fraternal resemblance in educational attainment and occupational status. *American Journal of Sociology, 91,* 650-673.

Hauser, R. M., & Sewell, W. H. (1986). Family effects in simple models of education, occupational status, and earnings: Findings from the Wisconsin and Kalamazoo Studies. *Journal of Labor Economics, 4*(part 2), S83-S115.

Sewell, W. H., & Hauser, R. M. (1980). Sex, schooling, and occupational status. *American Journal of Sociology, 86*(3), 551-583.

Sewell, W. H., & Hauser, R. M. (1980). The Wisconsin Longitudinal Study of Social and Psychological Factors in Aspirations and Achievements. *Research in Sociology of Education and Socialization, 1,* 59-99.

CURRENT STATUS OF THE STUDY:

a. A further wave of data collection is planned for 1992.

b. The data are in machine-readable format.

c. The data are available for secondary analysis from Data and Program Library Service, The University of Wisconsin-Madison, 1180 Observatory Drive, Madison, WI 53706.

■ Columbia University Longitudinal Study: Child Welfare Research Program—Nature of Agency Services, 1966

Shapiro, Deborah

Contact Person: Deborah Shapiro
Address: Rutgers University
             School of Social Work
             327 Cooper Street
             Camden, NJ 08102
Telephone No.: (609) 757-6347

SUBSTANTIVE TOPICS COVERED:

This study addresses the outcomes of foster care, and the factors in the agency system most likely to influence such outcomes. More specifically, the purpose was to assess the extent of the welfare agency's commitment to its foster care clients. (See also Fanshel, D., Columbia University Longitudinal Study: *Children in Foster Care;* and Jenkins, S., Columbia University Longitudinal Study: *Family Welfare Research Program—Mothers View Foster Care.*)

CHARACTERISTICS OF THE ORIGINAL SAMPLE:

Year the study began: 1966
Subject selection process: The sample included the social workers handling the cases of study subjects. Of the 87 agencies eligible for the study, only 3 drew no subjects during the 5-year period the children were in placement, and therefore, no workers from these 3 agencies were in the sample. The total social worker sample was 1,074 Ss.
Total number of subjects at Time 1: N = 511 caseworkers (the interviews covered 616 children)
Ages at Time 1: 25-35 yrs.
Sex distribution: 76% female, 24% male
Socioeconomic status: 100% middle class
Race/ethnicity: 76% white, 15% African-American, 9% Hispanic

Years of Completed Waves:

Years	$N=$[a]	Age ranges
1966-1967	511	25-35 yrs.
1968	363	26-36 yrs.
1969-1970	352	27-37 yrs.
1970-1971	231	28-38 yrs.

Comments:
a. In 1966-1967, 40% of workers were interviewed more than once. In 1968, the need for multiple interviews was reduced to 18% of the respondents and remained at that level for each of the remaining waves.

INFORMATION ON SAMPLE ATTRITION:

Each wave involved interviews with caseworkers who had participated earlier and with workers new to the study; the latter outnumbered the former each time. Altogether, 1,107 workers were required to give 2,274 interviews in order to obtain a reasonably complete picture of agency investment in the study children over the 5-year period.

CONSTRUCTS MEASURED: INSTRUMENTS USED

Time worker spent with study subject, training and professional experience, how knowledgeable worker was about the case, how interested worker was in subject and his/her family, how much worker identified with subject and family, worker's judgments of quality of care, placement process, relation with other agencies, work atmosphere, size of caseload, pressures of job, amount of time spent in administrative tasks, job satisfaction: Telephone interview

REPRESENTATIVE REFERENCES:

Shapiro, D. (1972). Agency investment in foster care: A study. *Social Work, 17,* 20-28.

Shapiro, D. (1973). Agency investment in foster care: A follow-up. *Social Work, 18,* 3-9.

Shapiro, D. (1974). Occupational mobility and child welfare workers: An exploratory study. *Child Welfare, 53,* 5-13.

Shapiro, D. (1976). *Agencies and foster children.* New York: Columbia University Press.

CURRENT STATUS OF THE STUDY:

a. No further waves of data collection are planned.

b. Data in machine-readable format.

c. Data may be available for secondary analysis through David Fanshel, School of Social Work, Columbia University, 622 West 113th Street, New York, NY 10025.

■ The Educational Testing Service Head Start Longitudinal Study (HSLS), 1968

Shipman, Virginia

Contact Person:	Virginia Shipman
Address:	Counseling and Family Studies
	University of New Mexico
	Albuquerque, NM 87131
Telephone No.:	(505) 277-4316, ext. 7222

SUBSTANTIVE TOPICS COVERED:

The study examines the components of early education that facilitate or interfere with the cognitive, personal, and social development of disadvantaged children; the environmental and background variables that moderate these effects; and how these moderators produce their influence. Also, extensive information on measures for assessing young children and their environment was collected.

CHARACTERISTICS OF THE ORIGINAL SAMPLE:

Year the study began: 1968

Subject selection process: Four regionally distinct communities were selected that had sufficient numbers of children in grade school; expressed community and school cooperation; expected mobility rates were low; offered variation in preschool and primary grade experiences. (These school programs include, but are not limited to, Head Start.) Children from each of the four sites (multiple school districts in every site) who were tested met the following criteria: non-physically handicapped, English-speaking, and expected to be enrolled in first grade in Fall 1971 (i.e., 3 yrs., 6 mos.-4 yrs., 6 mos.)

Total number of subjects at Time 1: N = 1,875

Ages at Time 1: 3 yrs., 6 mos.-4 yrs., 6 mos.

Sex distribution: Approximately equal numbers of females and males throughout

Socioeconomic status: Information was gathered, but not available in terms of percentage distribution by socioeconomic class.

Race/ethnicity: 62% African-American, 38% white

Years of Completed Waves:

Years	N=	Age ranges
1968-1969	1,875	3 yrs., 6 mos.-4 yrs., 6 mos.
1969-1970	1,275	4 yrs., 6 mos.-5 yrs., 6 mos.
1970-1971	1,179	5 yrs., 6 mos.-6 yrs., 6 mos.
1971-1972	1,086	6 yrs., 6 mos.-7 yrs., 6 mos.
1973-1974	1,017	8 yrs., 6 mos.-9 yrs., 6 mos.
1974-1975	[a]	9 yrs., 6 mos.-10 yrs., 6 mos.

Comments:
a. One of the four testing sites was dropped from the study after the third data point.

INFORMATION ON SAMPLE ATTRITION:

In addition to the longitudinal sample, several hundred children attending participating schools were tested each year. Thus, the sample described above includes both subjects followed longitudinally for differing periods and subjects examined cross-sectionally. A study of attrition effects for the Year 6 sample indicated no significant effects of attrition in child or family variables, with the exception that the longitudinal sample had a higher proportion of African-American and low-income families. Information about the attrition rate and core sample was not available.

CONSTRUCTS MEASURED: INSTRUMENTS USED

Parents

Child's school experiences; community and personal and family information, description of physical environment by interviewer, feelings of control over environment, differentiation of the environment (knowledge, attributes, and beliefs), encouragement of school-related achievement and general cognitive development, potential stress conditions, child's possessions, material objects and living space, achievement pressure, aspiration level, alienation, attitudes toward preschool, individuation of child, illness, hospitalizations; feelings of powerlessness, extent and nature of preschool participation; attitudes toward preschool; knowledge and utilization of community resources, availability of community resources; crowding; dental care, family structure; mobility, maternal warmth, medical status; social status (demographic characteristics of household members, physical characteristics of dwelling place and neighborhood, home resources, language spoken in home): Parent interview
Maternal warmth: Hess and Shipman Eight Block Sorting, Etch-a-Sketch and Toy Sorting Interaction Task, Parent interview
Mothers' perceptions of their children, mother-child joint activities: Semistructured interview with each child's mother or mother surrogate in the home
Aspiration level: Hess and Shipman Etch-a-Sketch Interaction Task, Parent interview
Availability of community resources: Community Questionnaire, Parent interview

Language

Articulation (phoneme and words): Massad Mimicry Test
Spontaneous verbalization: Hess and Shipman Eight Block Sorting, Etch-a-Sketch and Toy Sorting Interaction Tasks, Modified Hertzig Procedure, Open Field Task
Encouragement of verbalization: Global Classroom Ratings, Hess and Shipman Eight Block Sorting, Etch-a-Sketch and Toy Sorting Interaction Tasks

Specificity of verbalization: ETS Story Sequence, Global Classroom Ratings, Hess and Shipman Eight Block Sorting, Etch-a-Sketch and Toy Sorting Interaction Tasks

Nonverbal elaboration: Human Figure Drawings, Modified Hertzig Procedure, Sticker Task

Comprehension and interpretation (verbal skills): ETS Story Sequence Task (Part II)

Listening comprehension: Cooperative Preschool Inventory (Caldwell), Cooperative Primary Tests (Listening, Forms 12B, 23A, 23B), ETS Story Sequence Task (Part I)

Listening: Receptive skill, recognition of word and sentence properties through listening

Reading: Recognition of word meaning through reading; recognition of word properties through reading

Reading comprehension: Cooperative Primary Tests (Reading, Forms 12B, 23A, 23B)

Recognition of word meaning: Peabody Picture Vocabulary Test

Word discrimination: Cooperative Primary Tests (Word Analysis, Forms 13A, 13B)

Recognition of word properties through reading: Cooperative Primary Tests (Word Analysis, Forms 13A, 13B)

Recognition of word and sentence properties through writing: Cooperative Primary Tests (Writing Skills, Forms 23A, 23B)

Letter discrimination: Cooperative Primary Tests (Word Analysis, Forms 13A, 13B)

Writing: Knowledge of sentence properties through writing; recognition of word and sentence properties through writing

Spelling: Cooperative Primary Tests (Writing Skills, Forms 23A, 23B)

Punctuation-capitalization: Cooperative Primary Tests (Writing Skills, Forms 23A, 23B)

Stimulus differentiation: Fixation time, Open Field Test

Ability to verbalize sorting rationale: ETS Linguistic Structure Test, Hess and Shipman Eight Block Sorting Task, Hess and Shipman Toy Sorting Task, Sigel Object/Picture Categorization Task

Knowledge of word and sentence properties: Cooperative Primary Tests (Writing Skills, Forms 23A, 23B), ETS Linguistic Structures Test, ETS 2 Story Sequence Task, Massad Mimicry Test

Recognition of word and sentence properties through listening: Cooperative Preschool Inventory (Caldwell), ETS Matched Pictures Comprehension Task

Knowledge of word properties through story telling: ETS Story Sequence

Comprehension of functor words: ETS Matched Pictures Tests, ETS Test of Linguistic Structures

Verbal facility: Verbal Facility Test by OEO in Equal Opportunity Survey 1966 (Teacher Questionnaire)

Verbal skills, oral productive: General ability; labeling, letter naming, verbal facility; encouragement of verbalization; specificity of verbalization, spontaneous verbalization, ability to verbalize sorting reaction; knowledge of word and sentence properties; word naming

Perception

Audition: Auditory Screening
Auditory-discrimination: Auditory Discrimination Test (Wepman), Children's Auditory Discrimination Inventory (Stern)
Auditory-visual integration: Auditory-Visual Integration Test (Birch)
Vision (acuity, motility): Vision screening
Visual-motor integration: Bender-Gestalt Test

Cognition

General ability: Cooperative Preschool Inventory (Caldwell), Raven's Colored Progressive Matrices, TAMA General Knowledge, Wechsler Intelligence Scale for Children (WISC)—(Block Design, Picture Completion), Wechsler Preschool Primary Scale of Intelligence (WPPSI)—(Block Design, Picture Completion)
Analytic functioning: Children's Embedded Figures Test, Preschool Embedded Figures Test, WPPSI and WISC (Block Designs, Picture Completion subtests)
Concept formation: Hess and Shipman Eight Block Sorting, Etch-a-Sketch and Toy Sorting Interaction Tasks
Concept of geometry, concept of symbolism: Cooperative Primary Tests (Mathematics, Forms 12B, 23A, 23B)
Concept of number: Conservation of Discontinuous Quantity, Cooperative Primary Test (Mathematics, Forms 12B, 23A, 23B), ETS Spontaneous Correspondence Task, ETS Enumeration (Spatial Enumeration, Seriation and Ordinal Correspondence)
Concept of operation: Cooperative Primary Tests (Mathematics, Forms 12B, 23A, 23B)
Conservation of identity: Boy-Girl Identity Task
Arithmetic computation: Cooperative Primary Tests
Quantitative concepts: Concept of approximation, concept of estimation, concept of junction and relation, concept of geometry, concept of measurement, concept of number, concept of operation, concept of symbolism
Concept of measurement: Cooperative Primary Tests (Mathematics, Forms 12B, 23A, 23B)
Concept of function and concept of relations: Cooperative Primary Tests (Mathematics, Forms 12B, 23A, 23B)
Concept of estimation: Cooperative Primary Tests (Mathematics, Forms 12B, 23A, 23B)
Configurations, form discrimination: Johns Hopkins Perceptual Test, Matching Familiar Figures Test
Spatial relations and rotations: Spatial Relations Test (Thurstone)
Form reproduction: Bender-Gestalt Developmental Test of Visual-Motor Integration, Geometric Designs (WISC), Metropolitan Readiness Test
Eye-hand motor coordination: Sequin Form Board

Copying skill: Hess and Shipman Etch-a-Sketch Interaction Task

Creativity: Naming Category Instances, Open Field Test, PROSE, Stickers Task, Story Sequence Task, What Could It Be?, What Can You Use It For?

Orientation: Hess and Shipman Eight Block Sorting, Etch-a-Sketch and Toy Sorting Interaction Tasks

Fixation time: Fixation Time Task, Schaefer Classroom Behavior Inventory, Test Situation Ratings

Distractibility: Open Field Test, Test Situation Ratings

Attention: Digit span, Relevant Redundant Cue Concept Task

Labeling: Preschool Inventory (Caldwell), Peabody Picture Vocabulary Test, Sigel Object/Picture Categorization Task

Information processing/transmission: Hess and Shipman Eight Block Sorting, Etch-a-Sketch and Toy Sorting Interaction Tasks

Cognitive styles (preferred categorizing mode): Sigel Object/Picture Categorization Task

Egocentrism: ETS Spatial Egocentrism Tasks, ETS Story Sequence Task

Rote memory: Wechsler Intelligence Scale for Children Digit Span

Associative memory: Stanford Memory Test

Personality

Ability to delay gratification: Mischel Technique

Frustration tolerance: Classroom Observation Rating Scales, Test Situation Ratings

Impulsivity: Motor Inhibition Test

Reflection-impulsivity: Matching Familiar Figures Tests, Sigel Object/Picture Categorization Task

Planfulness: Hess and Shipman Eight Block Sorting, Etch-a-Sketch and Toy Sorting Interaction Tasks, Open Field tasks, teacher questionnaire

Risk taking: Risk-taking Test

Vigor: Vigor measure (crank-turning, hopping, running)

Energy level: Vigor Task

Self-concept: Brown IDS Self-Concept Referents Test, Classroom Observation Rating Scale, Global Classroom Ratings, Gumpgookies, parent interview, school perception interview, Self-Esteem Inventory (Coopersmith), Test Situation Ratings

Locus of control: Locus of Control Picture Story Task (Shipman), school perception Interview

Interests: Classroom Observation Rating Scales, Fixation Time (selective attention), Open Field Test, parent interview, PROSE, School Perception Interview

Perception of parental influence: Self-Esteem Inventory (Coopersmith), teacher questionnaire

Medical

Birth condition: Health record

Height and weight at birth and at age 4: Health record, physical examination

Hemoglobin level: Physical examination
Medical status: Child and Family Medical History Report Form, Physical Examination, parent interview

School

Attitudes towards school: First Day of School Questionnaire, parent interview, school perception interview
Attitudes towards education: First Day of School Questionnaire, parent interview, teacher questionnaire
Preschool resources and facilities: Preschool Center Inventory, PROSE
Grade school resources and facilities: Classroom Facilities Inventory, school inventory
Goals for school effectiveness: Parent interview, teacher questionnaire
School description, per-pupil expenditure: School inventory
Attitude (interpersonal, racial): Social Schemata, school perception interview
Instructional group size: Assessment of classroom programs, Global Classroom Ratings, PROSE
Classroom composition, classroom size: Class rosters, Global Classroom Ratings, school inventory
Classroom atmosphere: Global Classroom Ratings
Perception of class: Enhancement of Learning Inventory, teacher questionnaire
Special class placement: Class rosters
Nature and extent of questioning, response to questioning: Global Classroom Ratings, Hess and Shipman Eight Block Sorting, Etch-a-Sketch and Toy Sorting Interaction Tasks, Individual Pupil Observation
Arithmetic computation: Cooperative Primary Tests
Use of commands: First Day of School Questionnaire, Hess and Shipman Eight Block Sorting, Etch-a-Sketch and Toy Sorting Interaction Tasks
Frequency and type of punishment: Global Classroom Ratings, Hess and Shipman Eight Block Sorting; Etch-a-Sketch and Toy Sorting Interaction Tasks, parent interview
Appeal system: Hess and Shipman Eight Block Sorting, Etch-a-Sketch and Toy Sort Interaction Tasks, Global Classroom Ratings
Achievement-Motivation: Classroom Observation Rating Scales, Gumpgookies
Adult versus peer orientation: Classroom Observation Rating Scales, Individual Pupil Observation
Compliance; dependency; responsiveness to social reinforcement: Classroom Observation Rating Scales, Global Classroom Ratings
Cooperation: Classroom Observation Rating Scales, Global Classroom Ratings, Hess and Shipman Eight Block Sorting, Etch-a-Sketch and Toy Sort Interaction Tasks, PROSE, Test Situation Ratings
Involvement, classroom: Global Classroom Ratings
Positive reinforcement: Enhancement of Learning Inventory, Global Classroom ratings, Hess and Shipman Eight Block Sorting, Etch-A-Sketch and Toy Sorting Interaction Tasks, Individual Pupil Observation, parent interview, PROSE

Negative reinforcement: Enhancement of Learning Inventory, Global Classroom ratings, Hess and Shipman Eight Block Sorting, Etch-A-Sketch and Toy Sorting Interaction Tasks, Individual Pupil Observation, parent interview, PROSE

Test-taking behaviors: Modified Hertzig Procedure, Test Situation Ratings

Social motives: California Social Competency Scale, Classroom Observation Rating Scale, Gumpgookies, Hess and Shipman Block Sorting, Etch-a-Sketch and Toy Sorting Interaction Tasks, Individual Pupil Observations, Open Field Test, parent interview, Schaefer Classroom Behavior Inventory, School Perception Interview, Test Situation Ratings

Group membership: Parent interview, teacher questionnaire

Peer preference: Individual Pupil Observation, PROSE, school perception interview

Special class placement: Class roster

Hostility: Classroom Observation Rating Scales, Global Classroom Ratings, Individual Pupil Observations

Aggression: Classroom Observation Rating Scales, Global Classroom Ratings, Individual Pupil Observation, PROSE, Schaefer Classroom Behavior Inventory

Emphasis on affective discrimination: Global Classroom Ratings

Cognitive-perceptual stimulation: Global Classroom Ratings, PROSE

Teacher

Teacher education, teacher experience: School inventory, teacher questionnaire

Teacher-pupil ratio: Global Classroom Ratings, Preschool Center Inventory, school inventory

Teacher individuation of pupils: Enhancement of Learning Inventory, Global Classroom Ratings

Teacher warmth: Global Classroom Ratings

Teaching time for various activities: Global Classroom Ratings, PROSE

Perception of the disadvantaged, perception of principal performance: Teacher questionnaire

Teaching time estimates: Estimates of time spent on certain instructional activities

REPRESENTATIVE REFERENCES:

Bridgeman, B., & Shipman, V. C. (1975). *Disadvantaged children and their first school experience: Predictive value of measures of self-esteem and achievement motivation in four-to-nine-year-old low-income children* (PR 75-24). Princeton, NJ: Educational Testing Service.

Shipman, V. C. (1971). *Disadvantaged children and their first school experiences: Structure and development of cognitive competencies and styles prior to school entry* (PR 71-19). Princeton, NJ: Educational Testing Service.

Shipman, V., et al. (1976). *Disadvantaged children and their first school experiences: Notable early characteristics of high and low achieving black low-SES children* (PR 76-21). Princeton, NJ: Education Testing Service.

Shipman, V., et al. (1976). *Disadvantaged children and their first school experiences: Stability and change in family status, situational, and process variables and their relationship to children's cognitive performance* (PR 75-82). Princeton, NJ: Educational Testing Service.

CURRENT STATUS OF THE STUDY:

a. No further waves of data collection are planned.
b. Most of the data are in machine-readable format.
c. The data are conditionally available for secondary analysis through the study contact person.

■ The Family Life Project: A Longitudinal Adoption Study, 1970

Shireman, Joan F.; and Johnson, Penny R.

Contact Person: Joan F. Shireman
Address: School of Social Work
                Portland State University
                P.O. Box 751
                Portland, OR 97207
Telephone No.: (503) 229-4712

SUBSTANTIVE TOPICS COVERED:

The study examines child and family adjustment; exploration of strengths and weaknesses of single-parent and transracial adoption; racial and sexual identity formation; handling of adoption issues and exploration of identity issues unique to adopted children; assessment of family members' ability to form social relations and cope with stress.

CHARACTERISTICS OF THE ORIGINAL SAMPLE:

Year the study began: 1970
Subject selection process: The sample was selected from single-parent, transracial, and traditional adoptive placements made by two Chicago agencies; three groups of approximately equal size were selected.
Total number of subjects at Time 1: N = 118
Ages at Time 1: Birth-2 yrs.
Sex distribution: Approximately equal numbers of females and males throughout
Socioeconomic status: 75% upper middle/middle class, 25% working class
Race/ethnicity: 100% African-American children (33% of the adopting families were white).

Years of Completed Waves:[a]

Years	N=	Age ranges
(Cohort 1: Single Adoptees)		
1970	31	Birth-2 yrs.
1974	27	3-4 yrs.
1978	23	7-8 yrs.
1984-1985	15	12-13 yrs
(Cohort 2: Transracial Adoptees)		
1970	42	Birth-2 yrs.
1974	36	3-4 yrs.
1978	27	7-8 yrs.
1984-1985	36	12-13 yrs.
1987-1988	35	16 yrs.
(Cohort 3: Traditional Adoptees)		
1970	45	Birth-2 yrs
1974	36	3-4 yrs.
1978	27	7-8 yrs.
1984-1985	19	12-13 yrs.
1987-1988	20	16 yrs.

Comments:

a. A cohort of children living with their biological parents—50 African-American families, 25 two-parent families, and 25 single-parent families—will be added to the original sample and followed longitudinally. The focus of the study will remain the same. However, the principal investigators will also focus on the extent to which non-adopted adolescents experience crises similar to or different from those of children from adoptive homes.

INFORMATION ON SAMPLE ATTRITION:

During the 18-year period of study, 48 of 118 Ss (40.7%) were not retrieved for further study: 16 of 31 Ss (51.6%), Cohort 1; 7 of 42 Ss (16.7%) Cohort 2; and 25 of 45 Ss (55.6%), Cohort 3. The core sample consists of 70 Ss: 15 (Cohort 1: Single adoptees); 35 (Cohort 2: Transracial adoptees); and 20 (Cohort 3: Traditional adoptees).

CONSTRUCTS MEASURED: INSTRUMENTS USED

Child and family adjustment, handling of adoption issue: Interview with family, interview with parents, interview with child
Self-concept: Piers-Harris self-concept scale
Racial identity and preference: Morland Social Distance, Morland Black Preference, Morland Racial Attitudes Scales
Background information on child and parents: Records from social workers
Sexual identity and preference: Several measures of sexual identity
Perceptions of similarities: Perceived Similarities (Patricia Basaal)
Gender identity: Masculinity and Femininity Psychological Correlates (Spence, Helmrich, and Stapp)

REPRESENTATIVE REFERENCES:

Shireman, J., & Johnson, P. (1980). *Adoption: Three alternatives* (Part II). Chicago: Chicago Child Care Society.

Shireman, J., & Johnson, P. (1985, Winter). Single parent adoptions. *Children and Youth Services Review, 7.*

Shireman, J., & Johnson, P. (1986, May-June). A longitudinal study of black adoptions. *Social Work, 3*(3), 172-176.

Shireman, J., Johnson, P., & Watson, K. (1987). Transracial adoptions and the development of black identity. *Child Welfare, LXVI*(1).

CURRENT STATUS OF THE STUDY:

a. The principal investigators plan to follow up the families in 1990-1991, when subjects are 20 years of age.

b. Most data are in machine-readable format.

c. The data are available for secondary analysis from the study contact person.

■ Educating the Young Thinker Program: A Distancing Model, 1970

Sigel, Irving E.; and Cataldo, Christine Z. (deceased)

Contact Person: Irving E. Sigel
Address: Education Policy Research Division
                   Educational Testing Service
                   Rosedale Road
                   Princeton, NJ 08541
Telephone No.:   (609) 734-5788

SUBSTANTIVE TOPICS COVERED:

The study examines intervention procedures to foster the development of an interpersonal and intrapersonal sense of competence in representational thinking, and the understanding of imitation, pantomime, classification, seriation, memory, and conception; effects of a cognitively oriented intervention are evaluated; and long-term impacts on mathematics, reading skills, and personality traits are examined; effects of home environment and school program environments (teacher, curriculum, and peers) on cognitive and social competencies are also studied.

CHARACTERISTICS OF THE ORIGINAL SAMPLE:

Year the study began: 1970
Subject selection process: African-American children of a lower socioeconomic
    status background were selected; families were solicited on a house-to-house
    basis in the inner city of Buffalo.
Total number of subjects at Time 1: N = 22
Ages at Time 1: 27-28 mos.
Sex distribution: Approximately equal numbers of females and males throughout
Socioeconomic status: 75% poverty class, 25% working class
Race/ethnicity: 100% African-American

Years of Completed Waves:

Years	N=	Age ranges
1970	22	27-28 mos.
1971	20	34-39 mos.
1972	18	4-5 yrs.
1973	18	6-7 yrs.

INFORMATION ON SAMPLE ATTRITION:

During the 4-year period of study, 4 of 22 Ss (18.2%) were not retrieved for further study. The core sample consists of 18 Ss.

CONSTRUCTS MEASURED: INSTRUMENTS USED[1]

Perception: Bayley R Scale (nine hole form board), Stanford-Binet three hole form
    board, rotated; Kagan Embedded Figures Task; stacking blocks to reach candy
    task, fitting toys into box task
Memory: Invisible transportation task, delayed response task, simple bridge build-
    ing with model present and absent, Sigel memory matching test, Illinois Test
    of Psycholinguistic Abilities, auditory sequential memory task (digit span),
    seriation task, complex invisible transportation task
Language: Stanford-Binet identifying parts of the body, Bayley U Scale (3-D doll
    task), Bayley (name pictures), Bayley (points to pictures), Stanford-Binet pic-
    ture vocabulary, Stanford-Binet understanding objects by use, Bayley Z Scale
    (understanding prepositions), Stanford-Binet Comprehension I Test, Stanford-
    Binet Comprehension II Test; comprehension of simple commands, verbal im-
    itation of four-word sentences, judgment of grammatical correctness,
    comprehension of simple commands, verbal imitation of seven-to-eight-word
    sentences, verbal imitation of nine-word sentences

Imitation and pantomime: Bayley block building of train task, pantomime task (touching object), Bayley M Scale (imitation), pantomime with object in view, pantomime with picture cue, pantomime with verbal cue

Classification: Piaget's identity matching task, Piaget's intersecting classes task, Piaget's large-small classification task, concept of "one" task, Sigel's object categorization task, non-scorable; Sigel's non-grouping and grouping task

Problem solving: Stacking blocks to reach candy task, fitting toys into box task

Achievement: "Mathematics and reading" tasks, Stanford Early School Achievement Test, reading and math 6 & 7 years (Grade 1), school reading and grades

Personality rating by teachers: Achievement, personal traits and stability of personality

Perceptions of program effects: Parent and teacher interviews

Personal and environmental trends: Biographies

Comments:
1. Many of the assessment techniques employed experimental tasks. For further descriptions of these measures, consult publications from the study or contact the principal investigators.

REPRESENTATIVE REFERENCES:

Copple, C., Sigel, I., & Saunders, R. (1987). *Educating the young thinker.* Hillsdale, NJ: Lawrence Erlbaum.

Sigel, I. (1979). Consciousness raising of individual competence in problem-solving. In N. Kent & J. Rolf (Eds.), *Primary prevention of psychopathology: Vol. III. Social competence in children.* Hanover, NH: University Press of New England.

Sigel, I., Secrist, A., & Forman, G. (1973). Psycho-educational intervention beginning at age two: Reflections and outcomes. In J. C. Stanley (Ed.), *Compulsory education for children, ages two to eight: Recent studies of educational intervention.* Baltimore: The Johns Hopkins University Press.

Sigel, I., Secrist, A., Sorce, J., Priebe, K., & Norris, J. (1973). *Changes in cognitive structure between ages two and four: A longitudinal study of twenty black boys and girls.* Paper presented at the meeting of the Society for Research in Child Development, Philadelphia.

CURRENT STATUS OF THE STUDY:

a. No further waves of data collection are planned.

b. Most of the data are in machine-readable format.

c. The data are available for secondary analysis through the study contact person.

■ Transition into Adolescence: A Longitudinal Study, 1974

Simmons, Roberta; and Blyth, Dale

Contact Person: Roberta Simmons
Address: Department of Psychiatry and Sociology
                 University of Pittsburgh, School of Medicine
                 Western Psychiatric Institute and Clinic
                 3811 O'Hara Street
                 Pittsburgh, PA 15213
Telephone No.:   (412) 621-9444

SUBSTANTIVE TOPICS COVERED:

This study examines the transition from late childhood to early adolescence, focusing on the effect of this transition upon the following five areas of social and psychological development: self and body image, peer relationships, independence, future-plans, and conformity-related behavior (including academic achievement). These five areas are evaluated in relation to gender and in relation to two major transition variables (biological factors and school environmental factors).

CHARACTERISTICS OF THE ORIGINAL SAMPLE:

Year the study began: 1974

Subject selection process: Subjects were sixth graders selected from a pool of 18 elementary public schools in Milwaukee, Wisconsin. A stratified random sample of schools by race and school size was selected, based on the following sources: (a) eight schools with K-6th grades from predominantly white or integrated populations; (b) four schools with K-6th grades from predominantly African-American populations; and (c) six schools with K-8th grades from predominantly white or integrated populations. All sixth graders in each school were asked to participate, and 82% volunteered. Only subjects staying in the Milwaukee public schools were followed through Grade 10.

Total number of subjects at Time 1: N = 919

Ages at Time 1: 10-14 yrs.

Sex distribution: Approximately equal numbers of females and males throughout

Socioeconomic status: 36.5% poverty class, 32.4% working class, 31.1% middle/upper middle class

Race/ethnicity: 67.4% white, 28.2% African-American, 3.1% Hispanic, 1.1% Native American, 0.1% Asian-American

Years of Completed Waves:

Years	N=	Age ranges
(Cohort 1)		
1974-1975	4	10 yrs.
1975-1976	3	11 yrs.
1976-1977	1	12 yrs.
1977-1978	1	13 yrs.
1978-1979	1	14 yrs.
(Cohort 2)		
1974-1975	515	11 yrs.
1975-1976	489	12 yrs.
1976-1977	235	13 yrs.
1977-1978	229	14 yrs.
1978-1979	250	15 yrs.
(Cohort 3)		
1974-1975	373	12 yrs.
1975-1976	284	13 yrs.
1976-1977	320	14 yrs.
1977-1978	312	15 yrs.
1978-1979	271	16 yrs.
(Cohort 4)		
1974-1975	25	13 yrs.
1975-1976	20	14 yrs.
1976-1977	43	15 yrs.
1977-1978	34	16 yrs.
1978-1979	29	17 yrs.
(Cohort 5)		
1974-1975	2	14 yrs.
1976-1977	1	16 yrs.
1977-1978	1	17 yrs.
1978-1979	1	18 yrs.

INFORMATION ON SAMPLE ATTRITION:

During the 5-year period of study, 371 of 919 Ss (40.4%) across five cohorts were not available for further study. Attrition by cohort was as follows: Cohort 1, 3 of 4 Ss (75%); Cohort 2, 265 of 515 Ss (51.5%); Cohort 3, 102 of 373 Ss (27.3%); Cohort 4, no attrition; Cohort 5, 1 of 2 Ss (50%). The core sample consists of 522 Ss across five cohorts.

CONSTRUCTS MEASURED: INSTRUMENTS USED

Self-esteem: 6-Item Guttman Scale (Rosenberg & Simmons)
Female puberty: Onset of menstruation—a survey interview by a nurse
Dating behavior: 3-Item Guttman scaled questionnaire
Self-image, perception of others' expectations, importance of different characteristics, attitudes towards school, behavioral questions, satisfaction with body

image, problem behavior in school, parent and peer relations, participation in extracurricular activities, future/plans, independence behavior: Structured interview

Physical development: Body type, weight, and height measured by project's registered nurse

Academic achievement: Four subsets of the Iowa tests of basic skills, Grade Point Average, reading test, vocabulary test, arithmetic concept tests, and arithmetic problem-solving test

Victimization: Three separate self-report questions combining to yield a single score

Perceived anonymity of school environment: Four-item scale of subjects' perceptions of school environment

Demographic information: Questionnaire and interview

REPRESENTATIVE REFERENCES:

Blyth, D. A., Simmons, R. G., & Carlton-Ford, S. (1983). The adjustment of early adolescents to school transitions. *Journal of Early Adolescence, 3*, 105-120.

Simmons, R. G., & Blyth, D. A. (1987). *Moving into adolescence: The impact of pubertal change and school context.* New York: Aldine.

Simmons, R., Blyth, D., Van Cleave, E., & Bush, D. (1979). Entry into early adolescence: The impact of school structure, puberty and early dating on self-esteem. *American Sociological Review, 44*, 948-967.

Simmons, R. G., Marine, S. K., & Simmons, R. L. (1987). *Gift of life.* New Brunswick, NJ: Transaction Books.

CURRENT STATUS OF THE STUDY:

a. No further waves of data collection are planned.

b. Most data are in machine-readable format.

c. Data are available for secondary analysis from the study contact person.

■ Longitudinal Study of Television, Imagination and Aggression, 1977

Singer, Dorothy G.; and Singer, Jerome L.

Contact Person: Dorothy G. Singer
Address: Television Research Center
                  405 Temple Street
                  New Haven, CT 06511
Telephone No.:   (203) 432-4565

SUBSTANTIVE TOPICS COVERED:

The study examines television viewing within the family setting and the possible influences of such viewing patterns on conscious experience, social interaction patterns, and behavior in the family.

CHARACTERISTICS OF THE ORIGINAL SAMPLE:

Year the study began: 1977
Subject selection process: Thirteen preschools in New Haven, Connecticut, participated in the study. Children were randomly assigned to experimental and control groups for the intervention phase in 1978.
Total number of subjects at Time 1: N = 141
Ages at Time 1: 3-4 yrs.
Sex distribution: Approximately equal numbers of females and males throughout
Socioeconomic status: 75% middle/upper middle class, 25% working class
Race/ethnicity: 72.4% white, 23.6% African-American, 3% Hispanic, 1% Asian-American

Years of Completed Waves:

Years	N=	Age ranges
1977	141	3-4 yrs.
1978	200[a]	3-5 yrs.
1978-1979	91	5-6 yrs.
1980-1982	63	7-9 yrs.

Comments:
a. Approximately 58 additional subjects were added to the original sample, most of whom were 3-year-olds.

INFORMATION ON SAMPLE ATTRITION:

During the 6-year period of study, 137 of 200 Ss (68.5%) were not retrieved for further study. Attrition was due to subjects having moved out of the area. The core sample consists of 63 Ss.

CONSTRUCTS MEASURED: INSTRUMENTS USED

Aggression (e.g., direct acts of hitting, fighting, physical disruption, and so on): Observations of children during play on at least six occasions over a year's time

Children's television viewing (for a 2-week period three times during the same year): Parents' daily logs

Children's television viewing (for a 2-week period four times during the year), daily family routines, cultural activities, child's sleep patterns, stress, and so on: Interviews with parents in their homes

Parental discipline and control of children, and power assertion in child-rearing: Hoffman Child-rearing Questionnaire

Parents' physical punishment of children (frequency): "Questionnaire"

Description of mother's household routines; family recreational and cultural activities, child's mealtime and bedtime patterns: Interviews with mothers

Parental values (resourcefulness, and desirable traits, activity, social orientation, responsibility): Self-description of positive and desirable traits

Family's television use, restrictions on television use, parental television viewing, number and location of television sets: "Questionnaires (parents)"

Intelligence: Peabody Picture Vocabulary Test

Child's knowledge of television characters: Interview with child

Child's belief system; Continuum of danger to fairness outside the home as perceived by the child: "Scary World" Questionnaire (child)

Child's motor behavior: Observations of restlessness, self-restraint task

School behavioral adjustment: Interviews with parents, school reports

Estimate of imaginative predisposition: Barron Movement Threshold Inkblots

Records of programs child watched at home, favorite programs, hours watched, and kinds of shows: Television viewing patterns

Imagery comparisons, play style: Intervention on imaginative play

Ratings made on 5-point scale to measure specific behavior: Observation variables (14)

REPRESENTATIVE REFERENCES:

Singer, J. L., & Singer, D. G. (1981). *Television, imagination, and aggression: A study of preschoolers.* Hillsdale, NJ: Lawrence Erlbaum.

Singer, J. L., Singer, D. G., & Rapaczynski, W. (1984). Children's imagination as predicted by family patterns and television viewing: A longitudinal study. *Genetic Psychology Monographs, 110,* 43-69.

Singer, J. L., Singer, D. G., & Rapaczynski, W. (1984). Family patterns and television viewing as predictors of children's beliefs and aggression. *Journal of Communication, 42*(2), 73-89.

CURRENT STATUS OF THE STUDY:

a. Further waves of data collection are planned.
b. Most of the data are in machine-readable format.
c. The data are available for secondary analysis from the study contact person.

■ Longitudinal Study of Family Mediation and Children's Cognition, Aggression, and Comprehension of Television, 1982

Singer, Jerome L.; Singer, Dorothy G.; Desmond, Roger; Hirsch, Bennett; and Nicol, Anne

Contact person: Jerome L. Singer
Address: Family Television Research and Consultation Center
                Department of Psychology, Yale University
                Box 11A, Yale Station
                New Haven, CT 06525
Telephone No.: (203) 432-4527

SUBSTANTIVE TOPICS COVERED:

This study examines the effects of television on children's cognition, aggression, and comprehension of television controlling for family style, using Power/Assertion/Discussion and Explanation as the two variables.

CHARACTERISTICS OF THE ORIGINAL SAMPLE:

Year the study began: 1982
Subject selection process: Representative sample of urban children
Total number of subjects at Time 1: N = 66
Ages at Time 1: 5-6 yrs.
Sex distribution: Equal numbers of females and males throughout
Socioeconomic status: 70% middle/upper middle class, 30% working class
Race/ethnicity: 75% white, 15% African-American, 10% Hispanic

Years of Completed Waves:

Years	N=	Age ranges
1982	66	5-6 yrs.
1983	66	6-7 yrs.

INFORMATION ON SAMPLE ATTRITION:

During the one-year period of study, all Ss were retrieved for further study. The core sample consists of 66 Ss.

CONSTRUCTS MEASURED: INSTRUMENTS USED

Parent Measures

Television viewing and activities: Family activity log, family information questionnaire
General patterns of parent-child communication: Parent-child interaction questionnaire
Parental disciplinary orientation: Parental disciplinary questionnaire
General mediation: Parent's report of television mediation

Child Measures

Child's verbal intelligence: Peabody Picture Vocabulary Test (Form M)
Reading, recognition, comprehension, and general knowledge: Peabody Individual Achievement Test
Reality-fantasy identification: Questions based in part on fantasy depictions
Television comprehension: Comprehension test of television show
Child's ability to perceive parent's mediation: The Family Interaction Picture Story Test
Aggression: Parent's rating scale
Restlessness: Staff observation

REPRESENTATIVE REFERENCES:

Desmond, R., Singer, J., Calam, R., & Colimore, K. (1985). Family, mediation patterns and television viewing: Young children's use and grasp of the medium. *Human Communication Research, 11,* 461-481.
Singer, J. L., et al. (1988). Family mediation and children's cognition, aggression, and comprehension of television: A longitudinal study. *Journal of Applied Developmental Psychology, 9,* 329-347.

CURRENT STATUS OF THE STUDY:

a. No further waves of data collection are planned.
b. Most of the data are in machine-readable format.
c. Data are available for secondary analysis from the Family Television and Consultations Center, Department of Psychology, Yale University, Box 11A, Yale Station, New Haven, CT 06525.

■ Early Intervention and Its Effects on Maternal and Child Development, 1973

Slaughter-Defoe, Diana T.

Contact person: Diana T. Slaughter-Defoe
Address: School of Education and Social Policy
                 Northwestern University
                 2003 Sheridan Road
                 Evanston, IL 60208
Telephone No.:   (708) 491-3787

SUBSTANTIVE TOPICS COVERED:

The purpose of this study was to test the thesis that sociocultural background influences early development in educationally significant ways. This background was assumed mediated, partially, by maternal attitudes and behaviors.

CHARACTERISTICS OF THE ORIGINAL SAMPLE:

Year the study began: 1973

Subject selection process: Subjects were selected from three Chicago housing project sites. Random, multistage, stratified cluster samplings were conducted in August and September 1974; mothers of children 18 to 24 months old were selected as of October 1, 1974.

Total number of subjects at Time 1: N = 132

Ages at Time 1: 18-24 mos. (infants), 24.3 yrs. (mothers)

Sex distribution: Approximately equal numbers of females and males throughout (infants); 100% female (mothers)

Socioeconomic status: 100% poverty class

Race/ethnicity: 100% African-American

Years of Completed Waves:[a]

Years	N=[a]	Age ranges
.(Cohort 1: Levenstein Toy Demonstration Program)		
1974	41	18.6 mos
1975	26	19.6 mos.
(Cohort 2: Mothers' Discussion Group Program)		
1974	53	19.5 mos.
1975	26	20.5 mos.
(Cohort 3: Control Ss)		
1974	38	18.8 mos.
1975	31	19.8 mos.

Comments:
a. N values refer to mother-infant dyads, though age ranges report only infant mean ages.

INFORMATION ON SAMPLE ATTRITION:

During the 2-year period of study, 49 of 132 Ss (37.1%) across three cohorts were not retrieved for further study: 15 of 41 Ss (36.6%), Cohort 1; 27 of 53 Ss (50.9%), Cohort 2; and 7 of 38 Ss (18.4%), Cohort 3. The core sample consists of 83 Ss: 26 Ss (Cohort 1), 26 Ss (Cohort 2), and 31 Ss (Cohort 3). Reasons for sample attrition included family pressures, "altered program commitment," residential relocation of family, and occupation.

CONSTRUCTS MEASURED: INSTRUMENTS USED

Maternal Teaching Style/Child Play Behavior

Personal-subjective interactive maternal teaching style, child nonplay (inactive play/social contact), child attention span (transition), child object uses (nonverbal/verbal), child grouping (nonverbal/verbal), child verbal expressiveness, child imitation, child representation: Videotaped observation

Maternal Child-rearing Attitudes and Practices

Maternal individuation: Maternal Individuation Scale (Interview rating)
Developmental explanations for child behaviors; teaching perspectives: Maternal report on child-rearing: (Interview rating)
Value for school achievement: Value for School Achievement Scale

Maternal Personality Process

Ego development: Washington University Sentence Completion Test (Loevinger)
Self-esteem: Self-esteem scale
Personal control: Personal-Environmental Control Scale

Intellectual Development

Intellectual development: Cattell Infant Intelligence Scale, Peabody Picture Vocabulary Test, McCarthy Scales of Mental Abilities

REPRESENTATIVE REFERENCES:

Slaughter, D. T. *Modernization through education of mother-child dyads* (1978, 1979). Final reports 1 and 2 to the National Institute of Child Health and Human Development, Grant Foundation of New York, and the University Research Committee of Northwestern University, December 1978 and June 1979.

Slaughter, D. T. (1988). Black children, schooling, and educational interventions. In D. T. Slaughter (Ed.), *Black children and poverty: A developmental perspective. New directions for child development, 42.* San Francisco: Jossey-Bass.

Slaughter, D. (1990). The expressed values scale: Assessing traditionalism in lower socioeconomic status black American women. In R. Jones (Ed.), *Handbook of tests and measurements for black populations*. Berkeley, CA: Cobb & Henry.

CURRENT STATUS OF THE STUDY:

a. No further waves of data collection are planned.
b. Most data are in machine-readable format.
c. Data are available for secondary analysis from the study contact person.

■ Nurses' Health Study (NHS I), 1976

Speizer, Frank; Willet, Walter; and Colditz, Graham

Contact Person: Frank Speizer
Address: Harvard Medical School
                 Channing Laboratory
                 180 Longwood Avenue
                 Boston, MA 02115
Telephone No.:   (617) 732-2275

SUBSTANTIVE TOPICS COVERED:

The purpose of this study is to examine chronic disease in women.

CHARACTERISTICS OF THE ORIGINAL SAMPLE:

Year the study began: 1976
Subject selection process: Subjects were selected from a registration list of registered nurses in several states.
Total number of subjects at Time 1: N = 121,700
Ages at Time 1: 30-55 yrs.
Sex distribution: 100% female
Socioeconomic status: Information not available
Race/ethnicity: Predominantly white
Comments:
a. In 1989 a second Nurses' Health Study (NHS II) began, and will follow the same format as NHS I.

Years of Completed Waves:

Years	N=	Age ranges
(Cohort 1)		
1976	121,700	30-55 yrs.
1978	121,700	32-57 yrs.
1980	121,700	34-59 yrs.
1982	121,700	36-61 yrs.
1984	121,700	38-63 yrs.
1986	121,700	40-65 yrs.
1988	121,700	42-67 yrs.
(Cohort 2)[a]		
1989	120,000	25-42 yrs.

INFORMATION ON SAMPLE ATTRITION:

During the 11-year period of study, virtually all of the 121,700 Ss from Cohort 1 were retrieved for further study. The core sample consists of 121,700 Ss (Cohort 1) and 120,000 Ss (Cohort 2).

CONSTRUCTS MEASURED: INSTRUMENTS USED

Disease outcome: Questionnaires, hospital and doctors' records

REPRESENTATIVE REFERENCES:

Belanger, C. F., Hennekens, C. H., Rosner, B., & Speizer, F. E. (1978). The Nurses' Health Study. *American Journal of Nursing, 78,* 1039-1040.

Myers, A. H., Rosner, B., Abbey, H., Willett, W. C., Stampfer, M. J., Bain, C., Lipnick, R., Hennekens, C., & Speizer, F. (1987). Smoking behavior among participants in the Nurses' Health Study. *American Journal of Public Health, 77,* 628-630.

Willett, W. C., Green, A., Stampfer, M. J., Speizer, F. E., Colditz, G.A., Rosner, B., Monson, R., Stason, W., & Hennekens, C. H. (1987). Relative and absolute excess risks of coronary heart disease among women who smoke cigarettes. *New England Journal of Medicine, 317,* 1303-1309.

Willett, W. C., Stampfer, M. J., Colditz, G. A., Rosner, B., Hennekens, C. H., & Speizer, F. E. (1987). Moderate alcohol consumption and risk of breast cancer. *New England Journal of Medicine, 315,* 1174-1180.

CURRENT STATUS OF THE STUDY:

a. Further data collection is planned for every two years.

b. Most data are in machine-readable format.

c. Data may be available for secondary analysis from study contact person.

■ Personal and Social Adjustment of Minority Status Children, 1978

Spencer, Margaret

Contact Person: Margaret Spencer
Address: Emory University
                 Division of Educational Studies
                 201 Fishburne Building
                 Atlanta, GA 30322
Telephone No.:   (404) 727-0610

SUBSTANTIVE TOPICS COVERED:

The study examines the social and cognitive development of minority status children, with a focus on expressive and receptive language; play and spontaneous social behavior; cultural variables such as racial attitudes and preferences; global and academic self-esteem; interpersonal competence; locus of control; parental socialization techniques.

CHARACTERISTICS OF THE ORIGINAL SAMPLE:

Year the study began: 1978
Subject selection process: Stratification techniques for socioeconomic status were
    used to select subjects for participation.
Total number of subjects at Time 1: N = 384
Ages at Time 1: 3-9 yrs.
Sex distribution: Equal numbers of females and males throughout
Socioeconomic status: 50% middle class, 50% poverty class
Race/ethnicity: 100% African-American

Years of Completed Waves:

Years	N=	Age ranges
(Cohort 1)		
1978-1979	95	3 yrs.
1981-1982	13	6 yrs.
(Cohort 2)		
1978-1979	97	5 yrs.
1981-1982	29	8 yrs.
(Cohort 3)		
1978-1979	96	7 yrs.
1981-1982	57	10 yrs.
(Cohort 4)		
1978-1979	96	9 yrs.
1981-1982	51	12 yrs.

INFORMATION ON SAMPLE ATTRITION:

During the 4-year period of study, 150 of 384 Ss (39.1%) were not retrieved for further study across four cohorts.

CONSTRUCTS MEASURED: INSTRUMENTS USED

Self-esteem and personal assessment: Primary Self Concept Test, Thomas Self Concept Values Test, Hare General and Area Specific Self Esteem

Cultural values and group identity: Racial Attitude and Preference Assessment Interview, Color Concept Assessment, Race Awareness Assessment

Decentration: Flavell's Cube, Little Bear Test of Affect Differentiation, Perspective Taking Measure

Vocabulary and general language abilities: Peabody Picture Vocabulary Test, McCarthy Scales of Children's Abilities

Social competence: Kohn Social Competence Scale (Teacher rating), Schaefer Classroom Behavior Inventory, Achenbach and Edelbrock Social Competencies and Symptomatology (Parent rating)

Locus of control: Nowicke-Strickland Locus of Control

Social skills and play: Free-play observation (preschool)

Child-rearing practices and values: Parental Interviews

Personal, social values regarding the five "Atlanta child killings" in the 1980s: Adolescent Interviews

REPRESENTATIVE REFERENCES:

Spencer, M. (1983). Children's cultural values and parental child rearing strategies. *Developmental Review, 3,* 351-370.

Spencer, M. (1985). Cultural cognition and social cognition as identity correlates of black children's personal-social development. In M. Spencer, G. Brookins, & A. Allen (Eds.), *Beginnings: Social and affective development of black children.* Hillsdale, NJ: Lawrence Erlbaum.

Spencer, M. B., Dobbs, B., & Swanson, D. P. (1988). African American adolescents: Adaptational processes and socioeconomic diversity in behavioral outcomes. [Special Issue: Mental health research and service issues for minority youth.] *Journal of Adolescence, 11,* 117-137.

CURRENT STATUS OF THE STUDY:

a. No further waves of data collection are planned.

b. Data are in machine-readable format.

c. The data are conditionally available for secondary analysis from the study contact person.

■ The Seattle and Denver Income Maintenance Experiment (SIME/DIME), 1970

Spiegelman, Robert G.

Contact Person: Robert G. Spiegelman
Address: Upjohn Institute for Employment Research
                  300 Southwestnedge
                  Kalamazoo, MI 49007
Telephone No.:   (616) 343-5541

SUBSTANTIVE TOPICS COVERED:

The study examines the impact of a negative income tax program on work effort and labor supply; income transfers and family structure; marital dissolution and family interaction.

CHARACTERISTICS OF THE ORIGINAL SAMPLE:

Year the study began: 1970

Subject selection process: Families in Denver and Seattle were eligible to participate if the following were met: (a) the head of the family was between the ages of 18 and 58 at enrollment, (b) the family contained at least an adult with a dependent child or a married couple, (c) earnings of the family in 1970 were less than $9,000 for a family of four with one working head, and less than $11,000 for a family of four with two working heads (dollar amount adjusted for family size), and (d) the family heads were not permanently disabled.

Total number of subjects at Time 1: N = 4,727 families

Ages at Time 1: 20-55 yrs.

Sex distribution: Approximately equal numbers of females and males throughout

Socioeconomic status: 66% working class, 34% poverty class

Race/ethnicity: 50% African-American, 50% white (Seattle); 33.4% African-American, 33.3% Chicano, 33.3% white (Denver)

Years of Completed Waves:[a]

Years	N=	Age ranges
(Seattle Cohort)		
1970-1971	2,028	20-55 yrs.
1970-1971	1,964	20-55 yrs.
1970-1971	1,897	20-55 yrs.
1970-1971	1,820	20-55 yrs.
1971-1972	1,799	21-56 yrs.
1971-1972	1,720	21-56 yrs.
1972-1973	1,689	22-57 yrs.

Years of Completed Waves, Continued:[a]

Years	N=	Age ranges
1972-1973	1,590	22-57 yrs.
1972-1973	1,537	22-57 yrs.
1973-1974	1,602	23-58 yrs.
1973-1974	1,661	23-58 yrs.
1974-1975	1,336	24-59 yrs.
1974-1975	895	24-59 yrs.
1974-1975	580	24-59 yrs.
1975-1976	562	25-60 yrs.
1975-1976	545	25-60 yrs.
1975-1976	400	25-60 yrs.
(Denver Cohort)		
1971-1972	2,699	20-55 yrs.
1971-1972	2,660	20-55 yrs.
1971-1972	2,588	20-55 yrs.
1971-1972	2,541	20-55 yrs.
1972-1973	2,483	21-56 yrs.
1972-1973	2,425	21-56 yrs.
1973-1974	2,419	22-57 yrs.
1973-1974	2,398	22-57 yrs.
1973-1974	2,394	22-57 yrs.
1973-1974	2,375	22-57 yrs.
1974-1975	2,327	23-58 yrs.
1974-1975	2,186	23-58 yrs.
1974-1975	1,431	23-58 yrs.
1975-1976	1,076	24-59 yrs.
1975-1976	1,033	24-59 yrs.
1975-1976	988	24-59 yrs.
1976-1977	976	24-59 yrs.
1976-1977	479	25-60 yrs.

Comments:
a. Participants were interviewed once prior to enrollment, at enrollment, and then once every 4 months throughout the study. About 75% of the eligible families were enrolled for 3 years. The remainder were enrolled for 5 years. A small group of about 100 families was enrolled for 20 years.

INFORMATION ON SAMPLE ATTRITION:

For the Seattle sample, 385 families were dropped from the experiment, and 261 families moved out of the area. Interview completion rates at any given time point ranged from 95.7% to 99.9%. For the Denver sample, 426 families were dropped from the experiment, and 285 families moved out of the area. Interview completion rates ranged from 96.7% to 100%.

CONSTRUCTS MEASURED: INSTRUMENTS USED

Work history for new members; employment history, social ethics of work; Assets and Debt Data (net worth, real property, sale of real property, attitudes toward use of credit, time horizon and planning, budget attitudes); Education and Training Data (educational and training of family members, education history, job training history, training and education update, attitudes toward training); Family Composition and Stability (family composition, introperiodic composition changes, secondary unit identification, relationships of family heads and children, family opinions, family roles, family arguments, family leisure time); Housing Data (subsidized housing, housing, housing expenditure, housing rent update); Respondent Behavior Data (fertility history, household chores, utilization of child care, job counseling, children's paying jobs [10-15 yrs.], educational status of children); Quality of Life Data (mental health status, nondurable consumption, community ties, educational and occupational expectations for children); Background and Attitudinal Data (marital status and history, ethnicity, mobility history, verbal awareness, occupation and education of parents, attitudes toward welfare, self-perception of socioeconomic status, perception of discrimination): Family Interview

REPRESENTATIVE REFERENCES:

Keeley, M. C. (1976). *The impact of income maintenance on geographical mobility: Preliminary analysis and empirical results from the Seattle and Denver Income Maintenance Experiments.* Menlo Park, CA: Center for the Study of Welfare Policy, Stanford Research Institute.

Robins, P. K., Spiegel, R. G., Weiner, S., & Bell., J. G. (Eds.). (1980). *A guaranteed annual income: Evidence from a social experiment.* New York: Academic Press.

Spiegelman, R. G., et al. (1980). *The Journal of Human Resources, XV*(4) (entire volume).

Thoits, P., & Hannau, M. (1979). Income and psychological distress: The impact of an *income maintenance* experiment. *Journal of Health and Social Behavior, 20*(2), 120-138.

CURRENT STATUS OF THE STUDY:

a. No further waves of data collection are planned.

b. Data are in machine-readable format.

c. Data are available for secondary analysis through the principal investigator.

■ Longitudinal Study of Early Classroom Behaviors and Later Misconduct, 1968

Spivack, George

Contact person: George Spivack
Address: Institute for Graduate Clinical Psychology
Widener University
Chester, PA 19013
Telephone No.: (215) 499-1211

SUBSTANTIVE TOPICS COVERED:

This study identifies early at-risk signs of subsequent life failures among urban minority youth.

CHARACTERISTICS OF THE ORIGINAL SAMPLE:

Year the study began: 1968
Subject selection process: Subjects were selected as a stratified sample of 659 female and male kindergarten children from Philadelphia public school files in the fall of 1968. Subsequent follow-up continued until cohort reached 20 years of age.
Total number of subjects at Time 1: N = 659
Ages at Time 1: 4-6 yrs.
Sex distribution: Equal numbers of females and males throughout
Socioeconomic status: Predominantly poverty class
Race/ethnicity: 80% African-American, 10% Hispanic, 10% white

Years of Completed Waves:

Years	N=	Age ranges
1968	659	4-6 yrs.
1969	548	5-7 yrs.
1969	428	5-7 yrs.
1970	427	6-8 yrs.
1971	472	7-9 yrs.
1972	506	8-10 yrs.
1976	403	12-14 yrs.
1977	476	13-15 yrs.
1978	417	14-16 yrs.
1982	380	18-20 yrs.

INFORMATION ON SAMPLE ATTRITION:

During the 14-year period of study, 279 of 659 Ss (42.3%) were not retrieved for further study. Attrition was random in so far as early at-risk factors are concerned and was primarily due to subjects' moving to new neighborhoods or attending new schools, and teachers' unwillingness to participate. The core sample consists of 380 Ss.

CONSTRUCTS MEASURED: INSTRUMENTS USED

Classroom disturbance, disrespect-defiance, external blame, achievement anxiety, external reliance, comprehension, inattentiveness-withdrawness, irrelevant responsiveness, creative initiative, need for closeness to teacher: Devereux Elementary School Behavior Rating Scale
Criminal behavior: Sellin-Wolfgang Scoring Method, Juvenile Police Records
Classroom conduct disturbance: Teacher Rated Adjustment Scale, Hahnemann High School Behavior Scale (HHSB)
Current functioning and work history, drug/alcohol use, self-reported delinquency, marital and economic status: Interviews
Absenteeism, dropout, conduct disturbance, counselor contact, subject grades and citizenship guides, school transfers, special school placements, CMH contacts: School records
Mental health at age 20: Minnesota Multiphasic Personality Inventory

REPRESENTATIVE REFERENCES:

Spivack, G. (1984). Related behavioral difficulties: A longitudinal study. In S. A. Mednick, M. Harway, & K. M. Finello (Eds.), *Handbook of longitudinal research: Vol. 1. Birth and childhood cohorts*. New York: Praeger.

Spivack, G., & Cianci, N. (1989). High risk early behavior pattern and later delinquency. In J. D. Burchard & S. N. Burchard (Eds.), *Prevention of antisocial and delinquent behavior*. Washington, DC: Government Printing Office.

Spivack, G., & Marcus, J. (1987). Marks and classroom adjustment as early indicators of mental health at age 20. *American Journal of Community Psychology, 15*, 35-56.

Spivack, G., Marcus, J., & Swift, M. (1986). Early classroom behavior and later misconduct. *Developmental Psychology, 22*(1), 124-131.

CURRENT STATUS OF THE STUDY:

a. Further waves of data collection are planned.
b. Most of the data are in machine-readable format.
c. Data are available for secondary analysis from the study contact person.

■ Project Talent, 1960

Steel, Lauri; and Wise, Laurie

Contact Person: Lauri Steel
Address: American Institutes for Research
in the Behavioral Sciences
P.O. Box 1113
Palo Alto, CA 94302
Telephone No.: (415) 493-3550

SUBSTANTIVE TOPICS COVERED:

The study examines the development of knowledge and skills necessary for adult roles and responsibilities; factors that encourage or discourage subpopulations regarding career and educational goals; how people can be best prepared for transitions between different aspects of their lives; the relation of high school interests, abilities, activities, background, and environmental factors to subsequent occupational choice and achievements.

CHARACTERISTICS OF THE ORIGINAL SAMPLE:

Year the study began: 1960
Subject selection process: Subjects consisted of individuals in grades 9-12 during
1960. A nationally representative sample of more than 1,000 high schools was used as the primary population source. With some exceptions, all students within the selected schools were surveyed. In addition, supplementary subsamples (e.g., all 15-year-olds) were surveyed.
Total number of subjects at Time 1: N = 377,015[a]
Ages at Time 1: 14-18 yrs.
Sex distribution: Approximately equal numbers of females and males throughout
Socioeconomic status: Data were gathered, but percent distributions by socioeconomic class were not available.
Race/ethnicity: 87.3% white, 7.4% African-American, 5.3% Asian-American and Hispanic (approximation)
Comments:
a. This figure includes only the four grade cohort groups in the probability sample. Including supplementary subsamples increased the sample size to more than 400,000.

Years of Completed Waves:[a]

Years	N=	Age ranges
(Cohort 1)		
1960	103,893	14 yrs.
1963	7,678	17 yrs.
1964	49,275	19 yrs.

Years of Completed Waves, Continued:[a]

Years	N=	Age ranges
1968	29,260	23 yrs.
1974	23,042	29 yrs.
(Cohort 2)		
1960	99,573	15 yrs.
1963	44,856	19 yrs.
1967	33,636	23 yrs.
1973	21,792	29 yrs.
(Cohort 3)		
1960	92,419	16 yrs.
1962	46,171	19 yrs.
1966	34,407	23 yrs.
1972	25,039	29 yrs.
(Cohort 4)		
1960	81,130	17-18 yrs.
1961	51,753	19 yrs.
1965	32,550	23 yrs.
1971	24,161	29 yrs.

Comments:
a. The Project Talent follow-up design called for general efforts to survey all members of a cohort, combined with an intensive effort to locate and survey a representative subsample of approximately 2,500 members of a cohort. Response rates for these special subsamples average 79.3%, with a low of 62.3% for the 5-year follow-up of Cohort 4, and a high of 99.5% for the one-year follow-up of Cohort 1. Response rates were much lower, however, for the sample as a whole.

INFORMATION ON SAMPLE ATTRITION:

During the 14-year period of study, the following Ss per cohort group were not retrieved for further study: Cohort 1, 80,851 of 103,893 Ss (77.8%); Cohort 2, 77,781 of 99,573 Ss (78.1%); Cohort 3, 67,380 of 92,419 Ss (72.9%); Cohort 4, 56,969 of 81,130 Ss (70.2%). The core sample for each cohort group is approximately: Cohort 1, 24,161 Ss; Cohort 2, 25,039 Ss; Cohort 3, 21,792 Ss; Cohort 4, 23,042 Ss.

CONSTRUCTS MEASURED: INSTRUMENTS USED

Language aptitude and ability (8 scales); mathematics ability (3 scales); visualization ability (2 scales); complex intellectual aptitude (3 scales); general and specific knowledge (37 scales): Aptitude, ability, and school achievement

Family (parents' education and occupation, economic status, and number of siblings and their educational experience), health, current activities, school courses and grades, extracurricular activities, hobbies, reading and study habits, and social activities, plans (college, military, career, and marital): Background Questionnaire

Occupational and activity interest inventory: Preference for activities and occupations

Dispositional traits: Self-descriptive adjectives (10 scales)

Description of school and general characteristics (e.g., kind, size, urban-rural, economic level, retention ratio, percent minority, region, and programs offered): School principal and counselor questionnaires

Educational experience (kind and amount), degrees, occupational training in high school, noncollege training, colleges and dates attended, reasons for stopping, financial support during college, and perceived value of education, career; work experience, occupation, income; job satisfaction (15-25 dimensions), evaluations of job, career plans, and reasons for stopping work; race, marital status and history, spouse's education and career, childbearing history, ideal and expected family size, quality of life (15 areas), geographical mobility, health, leisure and civic activities, military status and experience, discrimination experienced, and political behavior: Follow-up survey questionnaire

REPRESENTATIVE REFERENCES:

Steel, L., Wise, L. L., & Abeles, R. P. (1984). Project Talent: A longitudinal study of the development and utilization of individuals' capabilities. In S. A. Mednick, M. Harway, K. M. Finello (Eds.), *Handbook of longitudinal research: Vol. 2. Teenage and adult cohorts* (pp. 77-98). New York: Praeger.

Wise, L. (1979). Project Talent: Studying the development of human resources. *New Directives for Testing and Measurement, 2,* 1-26.

Wise, L. & Steel, L. (1980). Educational attainment of the high school classes of 1960 through 1963: Findings from Project Talent. *Research in Sociology of Education and Socialization, 1,* 101-126.

CURRENT STATUS OF THE STUDY:

a. No further waves of data collection are planned.

b. The data are in machine-readable format.

c. The data are available for secondary analysis through the Inter-University Consortium of Political and Social Research, Institute for Social Research, University of Michigan, P.O. Box 1248, Ann Arbor, MI 48106.

■ Pediatric Ambulatory Care Treatment Study, 1977

Stein, Ruth E. K.; and Jessop, Dorothy Jones

Contact Person: Ruth E. K. Stein
Address: Pediatric Ambulatory Care Division, Room 1N17
                Albert Einstein College of Medicine
                Bronx Municipal Hospital Center
                Pelham Parkway and Eastchester Road
                Bronx, NY 10461
Telephone No.: (212) 918-5304

SUBSTANTIVE TOPICS COVERED:

The study examines the effects of a unique pediatric home care program as compared to standard care in managing children with chronic physical illnesses. Research focuses on which mode of care reduces secondary social and psychological sequelae of illness for the child and the family; the psychosocial correlates of chronic illness in childhood; the characteristics of those children who cope well and those who do not.

CHARACTERISTICS OF THE ORIGINAL SAMPLE:

Year the study began: 1977
Subject selection process: Patients were referred by "providers" from those being seen in primary care clinics, specialty clinics, and in-patient services at Bronx Municipal Hospital Center and the Hospital of Albert Einstein College of Medicine. All children lived in Bronx, New York, and have chronic physical conditions, which are heterogeneous with respect to diagnosis. Ss were recruited from June 1978 to January 1980.
Total number of subjects at Time 1: N = 219
Ages at Time 1: Birth-11 yrs.
Sex distribution: Approximately equal numbers of females and males throughout
Socioeconomic status: 50% working class, 50% poverty class
Race/ethnicity: 61% Hispanic, 35% African-American, 4% white

Years of Completed Waves:

Years	N=	Age ranges
1977-1978	219	Birth-11 yrs.
1977-1978	188	6 mos.-11.5 yrs.
1978-1979	179	1 yr.-12-yrs.
1985	55	9.5-16 yrs.

INFORMATION ON SAMPLE ATTRITION:

During the 8-year period of study, 40 of 219 Ss (18.3%) were not retrieved for further study. The core sample consists of 174 Ss. The 1985 follow-up focused on a subsample of Ss.

CONSTRUCTS MEASURED: INSTRUMENTS USED

Mother's mental health: Psychiatric Symptoms Index (Ilfeld)
Child's mental health: Personal Adjustment and Roles Skill Scale (Ellsworth)
Impact of illness on the family: Impact of Chronic Illness on the Family (Stein & Riessman)
Functional status of the child: Functional Status (Stein & Jessop)
Satisfaction with care: Rand (Ware & Eisen) (modified)
Burden of care: Clinicians Overall Burden Index (Stein & Jessop)
Resources for coping: Judged Ability to Cope Scale
Utilization of services, self-care and self-health knowledge, and health needs: Interviews (Kantor, modified version)

REPRESENTATIVE REFERENCES:

Jessop, D. J., & Stein, R. E. K. (1985). Uncertainty and its relation to psychological and social correlates of chronic illness in children. *Social Science and Medicine, 20,* 993-997.

Stein, R. E. K., & Jessop, D. J. (1984). Delivery of care to inner-city children with chronic conditions. In N. Hobbs & J. Perrin (Eds.), *Chronically ill children: Issues and policies.* San Francisco: Jossey-Bass.

Stein, R. E. K., & Jessop, D. J. (1984). Does pediatric home care make a difference for children with chronic illness in children? Findings from the Pediatric Ambulatory Care Treatment Study. *Pediatrics, 73,* 845-853.

Stein, R. E. K., & Jessop, D. J. (1984). Relationship between health status and psychological adjustment among children with chronic conditions. *Pediatrics, 73,* 169-174.

CURRENT STATUS OF THE STUDY:

a. Further waves of data collection are tentatively planned.
b. Most data are in machine-readable format.
c. Data are available for secondary analysis from the study contact person.

■ Longitudinal Study of the Life Patterns of College-Educated Women, 1960

Stewart, Abigail

Contact Person: Abigail Stewart
Address: Department of Psychology
                  University of Michigan
                  Ann Arbor, MI 48104
Telephone No.:   (313) 764-6571

SUBSTANTIVE TOPICS COVERED:

The study examines the effects of personality and situations on the life outcomes of college-educated women.

CHARACTERISTICS OF THE ORIGINAL SAMPLE:

Year the study began: 1960
Subject selection process: Sample consisted of women from the class of 1964 at a prestigious women's college in the eastern United States.
Total number of subjects at Time 1: N = 244
Ages at Time 1: 18-22 yrs.
Sex distribution: 100% female
Socioeconomic status: 100% middle/upper middle class
Race/ethnicity: 100% white

Years of Completed Waves:

Years	N=	Age ranges
1960	244	18-22 yrs.
1974	122	32-36 yrs.
1976	96	34-38 yrs.
1979	59	37-41 yrs.

INFORMATION ON SAMPLE ATTRITION:

During the 19-year period of study, 185 of 244 Ss (75.8%) were not retrieved for further study. Information about sample attrition was not available. The core sample consists of 59 Ss.

CONSTRUCTS MEASURED: INSTRUMENTS USED

Background, college experience, future aspirations: Life-patterns Questionnaire
Initial personality variables: Thematic Apperception Test
Recent activities: Open-ended Recent Activities Questionnaire
Life changes: Recent Life Changes Questionnaire
Physical health: Health Questionnaire
Stressful events: Telephone interview (Wave 2, N = 57)

REPRESENTATIVE REFERENCES:

Stewart, A. J. (1975). *Longitudinal prediction from personality to life outcomes among college-educated women.* Doctoral dissertation, Harvard University.

Stewart, A. J. (1978). A longitudinal study of coping styles in self-defining and socially defined women. *Journal of Consulting and Clinical Psychology, 46*(5), 1079-1084.

Stewart, A. J. (1980). Personality and situation in the prediction of women's life patterns. *Psychology of Women Quarterly, 5*(2), 195-206.

Stewart, A. J., Lykes, M., & La France, M. (1982). Educated women's career patterns. *Journal of Social Issues, 38*(1), 97-117.

CURRENT STATUS OF THE STUDY:

a. Further waves of data collection are planned.
b. Most data are in machine-readable format.
c. Data are available for secondary analysis through the Henry A. Murray Research Center, Radcliffe College, 10 Garden Street, Cambridge, MA 02138.

■ Experience-Induced Affective Development in Children and Adults, 1976

Stewart, Abigail

Contact Person: Abigail Stewart
Address: Department of Psychology
University of Michigan
Ann Arbor, MI 48104
Telephone No.: (313) 764-6571

SUBSTANTIVE TOPICS COVERED:

This study tests the theory of experience-induced affective development, which links the individuals' subjective experience with their external environmental changes.

CHARACTERISTICS OF THE ORIGINAL SAMPLE:

Year the study began: 1976

Subject selection process: Subjects selected were about to experience a life change, had very recently experienced a life change, or had experienced a life change fairly recently and had made some adaptation to it.

Total number of subjects at Time 1: N = 475

Ages at Time 1: 4-7 yrs. (Cohort 1); 10-15 yrs. (Cohort 2); 18-20 yrs. (Cohort 3); 20-24 yrs. (Cohort 4); 25-35 yrs. (Cohorts 6 & 7)

Sex distribution: Approximately equal numbers of females and males throughout, except for Cohort 3 (73.7% female, 26.3% male), and Cohort 4 (72.2% female, 27.8% male)

Socioeconomic status: Predominantly middle class (each cohort)

Race/ethnicity: 100% white

Years of Completed Waves:

Years	N=	Age ranges
(Cohort 1: Young Children)		
1977	62	4-7 yrs.
1978	55	5-8 yrs.
(Cohort 2: School Children: 5th-10th Grades)		
1976	342	10-15 yrs.
1977	136	11-16 yrs.
1978	148	12-18 yrs.
(Cohort 3: College Students: Freshmen and Sophomores)		
1976	99	18-20 yrs.
1977	39	19-21 yrs.
1978	39	20-22 yrs.
Cohort 4: Engaged Couples)		
1976	48	20-24 yrs.
1977	35	21-25 yrs.
(Cohort 5: Newly Married)		
1977	60	a
1978	41	a
(Cohort 6: Expectant Parents)		
1977	40	25-35 yrs.
(Cohort 7: New Parents)		
1977	41	25-31 yrs.

Comments:

a. Data not available.

INFORMATION ON SAMPLE ATTRITION:

During the 3-year period of study, at least 279 of 597 Ss (46.7%), followed-up in five of seven cohorts, were not retrieved for further study. The core sample consists of 279 Ss for those followed up, and 360 Ss across all seven cohorts.

CONSTRUCTS MEASURED: INSTRUMENTS USED

Emotional stance or orientation to environment: Thematic Apperception Test (4 cues), Kelly Repertory Grid (People I Know)
Ability, adjustment to school environment, transitions: Teacher ratings
Self-evaluation: Who Am I?
School, family, activities: Basic Facts Questionnaire
Future goals: Future Goals Questionnaire
College experience: College Experience Questionnaire
Marital relations: Spanier Marital Inventory
Child's assessment of marriage: Parents' Marriage Questionnaire
Marriage experiences: Marriage Experience Questionnaire
Experiences with new child: Experiences As A New Parent Questionnaire

REPRESENTATIVE REFERENCES:

Healy, J. M., & Stewart, A. J. (1984). Adaptation to life changes in adolescence. *Advances in Child Behavioral Analysis and Therapy, 3,* 39-60.

Stewart, A. J., et al. (1982). Adaptation to life changes in children and adults: Cross-sectional studies. *Journal of Personality and Social Psychology, 43*(6), 1270-1281.

Stewart, A. J., Sokol, M., Healy, J. M., & Chester, N. L. (1986). Longitudinal studies of psychological consequences of life changes in children and adults. *Journal of Personality and Social Psychology, 50*(1), 143-151.

CURRENT STATUS OF THE STUDY:

a. No further waves of data collection are planned.
b. Most of the data are in machine-readable format.
c. Data are available for secondary analysis through the Henry A. Murray Research Center, Radcliffe College, 10 Garden Street, Cambridge, MA 02138.

■ International Pilot Study of Schizophrenia: Washington, D.C., Site, 1966

Strauss, John S.; Carpenter, William; and Bartko, John

Contact Person: John S. Strauss
Address: Department of Psychiatry, Yale University
                 25 Park Street
                 New Haven, CT 06519
Telephone No.:   (203) 789-7417

SUBSTANTIVE TOPICS COVERED:

This cross-cultural study was designed to investigate diagnosis, prognosis, and outcome in schizophrenia and to develop interview schedules and rating scales for cross-national research.

CHARACTERISTICS OF THE ORIGINAL SAMPLE:

Year the study began: 1966

Subject selection process: Subjects selected were hospitalized patients from nine sites internationally: Aarhus, Denmark; Agra, India; Cali, Colombia; Ibadan, Nigeria; London, England; Moscow, U.S.S.R.; Taipei, Taiwan; Prague, Czechoslovakia; and Washington, D.C., U.S.A. The selection of the field centers was based on the existence of a network of services able to detect a substantial proportion of the likely cases of schizophrenia occurring in the population at risk; the presence of several well-trained psychiatrists; possibility of setting up a simple reporting system; recognition of a fairly distinct local culture; availability of census data; and the absence of very high death or emigration rates or a high prevalence of masking organic diseases that might make the diagnosis of schizophrenia difficult. All patients contacting the psychiatric services of each center were screened. Subjects selected were young patients with functional psychoses of recent onset, ranged from 15 to 44 years of age, and with an onset of the illness within 5 years of admission to the study. Subjects typically presented with delusions, inappropriate behavior, hallucination, gross psychomotor disorder (overactivity, or underactivity), social withdrawal, disorders of thinking (other than delusions), overwhelming fear, disorders of affect, depersonalization, and/or self-neglect. Excluded subjects presented with severe psychotic symptoms present for 3 continuous years; a total hospitalization of 2 years or more in the last 5 years; regular abuse of alcohol or drugs; mental retardation (IQ less than 70); endocrine-related, metabolic-related, organically related, or nutritionally related psychoses; epilepsy; hearing impairment; and/or speech or language impairment.

Total number of subjects at Time 1: N = 131 (Washington, D.C., Site)

Ages at Time 1: 15-44 yrs.

Sex distribution: Approximately equal numbers of females and males throughout

Socioeconomic status: 70% working class, 15% poverty class, 15% middle/upper
middle class
Race/ethnicity: 97% white, 3% African-American

Years of Completed Waves:

Years	N=	Age ranges
1967-1969	131	15-44 yrs.
1969-1970	111	17-46 yrs.
1970-1971	61	18-47 yrs.

INFORMATION ON SAMPLE ATTRITION:

During the 5-year period of study, 70 of 131 Ss (53.4%) were not retrieved for
further study. The core sample consists of 61 Ss.

CONSTRUCTS MEASURED: INSTRUMENTS USED

Mental status: Present State Examination (PSE)
Past history of patient and his illness: Psychiatric History Form (PH)
Social and demographic information: Social Descriptive Form (SD)
Physical health status: Physical and neurological examination
Diagnosis and prognosis of patients: Diagnostic Assessment Form (DA)
Initial patient assessment and follow-up: Present State Examination, psychiatric history
    and social description schedules, Level of Function Scale (Strauss & Carpenter),
    Prognostic Scale (Strauss & Carpenter), Follow-up history schedule

REPRESENTATIVE REFERENCES:

Strauss, J. S., & Carpenter, W. T., Jr. (1972). Prediction of outcome in schizophrenia: I. Charac-
    teristics of outcome. *Archive of General Psychiatry, 27,* 739-746.
Strauss, J. S., & Carpenter, W. T., Jr. (1974). The prediction of outcome in schizophrenia: II. Relation-
    ships between predictor and outcome variables. *Archive of General Psychiatry, 31,* 37-42.
Strauss, J. S., & Carpenter, W. T., Jr. (1977). Prediction of outcome in schizophrenia. *Archive of
    General Psychiatry, 34,* 159-163.
World Health Organization. (1973). *The International Pilot Study of Schizophrenia. Vol. 1.* Ge-
    neva: World Health Organization Press.

CURRENT STATUS OF THE STUDY:

a. No further waves of data collection are planned.
b. Most of the data are in machine-readable format.
c. Data are available for secondary analysis from the study contact person. (Approval
    of specific projects requires agreement of collaborating investigators.)

■ Yale Longitudinal Study, 1978

Strauss, John S.; Hisham, Hafez; Lieberman, Paul; Rakfeldt, Jack; and Harding, Courtenay M.

Contact Person: John S. Strauss
Address: Department of Psychiatry, Yale University
                 25 Park Street
                 New Haven, CT 06519
Telephone No.:   (203) 789-7417

SUBSTANTIVE TOPICS COVERED:

This study examines the nature of psychiatric disorder and treatment effects and focuses on understanding the course of disorder, patterns of improvement, factors in the person, the environment, and interactions that affect course.

CHARACTERISTICS OF THE ORIGINAL SAMPLE:

Year the study began: 1978
Subject selection process: Subjects selected were hospitalized adult patients with severe mental disorders, exclusive of substance abuse and organic brain disease.
Total number of subjects at Time 1: N = 78 (both cohorts)
Ages at Time 1: 18-55 yrs.
Sex distribution: Approximately equal numbers of males and females throughout
Socioeconomic status: 70% working class, 15% poverty class, 15% middle/upper middle class
Race/ethnicity: 95% white, 5% African-American (Cohort 1); 90% white, 10% African-American (Cohort 2)

Years of Completed Waves:

Year	N=	Age ranges
(Cohort 1)[a]		
1978-1979	28	18-55 yrs.
1979	22	19-56 yrs.
(Cohort 2)[b]		
1986	50	18-45 yrs.
1987	40	19-46 yrs.

Comments:
a. Cohort 1: Bimonthly for one year then at the end of year 2.
b. Cohort 2: Monthly, then bimonthly, then every 4 mos., and so on, for 2 yrs.

INFORMATION ON SAMPLE ATTRITION:

During the 2-year period of study, approximately 80% of subjects from both cohorts were retrieved for further study. The core sample consists of 78 Ss.

CONSTRUCTS MEASURED: INSTRUMENTS USED

Social functioning: Open-ended and structured interview
Work: Narrative description of the previous 2 months
Symptoms, helping self, treatment, family support, phases of course: Standard scales

REPRESENTATIVE REFERENCES:

Breier, A., & Strauss, J. S. (1984). Social relationships in the recovery from psychotic disorder. *American Journal of Psychiatry, 141*(8), 949-955.

Strauss, J. S. (1989). Subjective experiences of schizophrenia: Towards a new dynamic psychiatry. *Schizophrenia Bulletin, 15*(2), 179-187.

Strauss, J. S., Hafez, H., Lieberman, P., & Harding, C. (1985). The course of psychiatric disorder, III: Longitudinal principles. *American Journal of Psychiatry, 142*(3), 289-296.

Strauss, J. S., Rakfeldt, J., Harding, C. M., & Lieberman, P. (in press). Psychological and social aspects of negative symptoms. *British Journal of Psychiatry.*

CURRENT STATUS OF THE STUDY:

a. Further waves of data collection are planned to study intensively those patients who have improved.
b. Most of the data are in machine-readable format.
c. Data are available for secondary analysis from the study contact person.

■ The Cornell Study of Occupational Retirement, 1952

Streib, Gordon F.

Contact Person: Gordon F. Streib
Address: Department of Sociology
                University of Florida
                Gainesville, FL 32611
Telephone No.: (904) 392-0254

SUBSTANTIVE TOPICS COVERED:

The study examines the retirement decision; the influence of retirement on physical health; the economics of retirement; the social psychology of retirement; the adjustment to retirement; the rejection of the retiree role.

CHARACTERISTICS OF THE ORIGINAL SAMPLE:

Year the study began: 1952

Subject selection process: The nonrepresentative sample comprised of volunteer Ss, residing in urban centers recruited from 231 organizations across the United States, at or near 64 years of age (retirement).

Total number of subjects at Time 1: N = 3,793

Ages at Time 1: 63-65 yrs.

Sex distribution: 75.5% male, 24.5% female

Socioeconomic status: 52.5% upper/middle class, 47.5% working class (approximately)

Race/ethnicity: 96.7% white, 3.3% African-American

Years of Completed Waves:

Years	*N=*	*Age ranges*
1952-1953	3,793	63-65 yrs.
1954	2,857	65-67 yrs.
1956	2,465	67-69 yrs.
1957	*	68-70 yrs.
1958-1959	1,969	69-71 yrs.

INFORMATION ON SAMPLE ATTRITION:

During the 7-year period of study, 1,824 of 3,793 Ss (48.1%) were not retrieved for further study. The main reason for sample attrition was subject dropouts. The core sample consists of 1,969 Ss.

CONSTRUCTS MEASURED: INSTRUMENTS USED

Demographic characteristics, work history, attitudes toward retirement, adjustment to retirement, age identification, leisure activities, health, and economic factors: Wave I Questionnaire, Wave II Working Questionnaire, Wave III Retired Questionnaire, Wave IV Retired-Working Questionnaire, Wave IV Retired Questionnaire, Wave IV Retired Questionnaire

Health in the past year: Wave III Follow-up Health Questionnaire, Wave IV Follow-up Health Questionnaire

REPRESENTATIVE REFERENCES:

Streib, G. F. (1963). Longitudinal studies in social gerontology. In R. H. Williams, C. Tibbitts, & W. Donahue (Eds.), *Processes of aging: Vol. II* (pp. 25-39). New York: Atherton Press.

Streib, G. F. (1966). Participants and drop-outs in a longitudinal study. *Journal of Gerontology, 21,* 200-209.

Streib, G. F., & Schneider, C. J. (1971). *Retirement in American society*. Ithaca, NY: Cornell University Press.

Streib, G. F., Thompson, W. E., & Suchman, E. A. (1958). The Cornell Study of Occupational Retirement. *Journal of Social Issues, 14,* 3-17.

CURRENT STATUS OF THE STUDY:

a. No further waves of data collection are planned.
b. Data are in machine-readable format.
c. Data are available for secondary analysis through Newberry Library, 60 West Walton Street, Chicago, IL 60610.

■ Seattle Longitudinal Prospective Study on Alcohol and Pregnancy, 1974

Streissguth, Ann P.; Martin, Donald C.; Martin, Joan C.; Barr, Helen; and Sampson, Paul D.

Contact Person: Ann P. Streissguth
Address: Department of Psychiatry and Behavioral Sciences
                         University of Washington, GG-20
                         2707 Northeast Blakeley
                         Seattle, WA 98105
Telephone No.:   (206) 543-7155

SUBSTANTIVE TOPICS COVERED:

To study the long-term consequences of social drinking during pregnancy in a population-based cohort of 500 children examined periodically between day 1 and year 14.

CHARACTERISTICS OF THE ORIGINAL SAMPLE:

Year the study began: 1974
Subject selection process: A screening sample consisting of 1,529 consecutively consenting pregnant women, in prenatal care by the 5th month of pregnancy at two Seattle hospitals whose combined populations were representative of the Seattle population. Participation rate was 86%. The mothers were primarily white, married, and middle class. They were low-risk in the sense that they were all in prenatal care by the 5th month of pregnancy. The study was identified as a "Pregnancy and Health Study" and women were interviewed in private in their own home about many factors associated with healthy pregnancies. The children were born across a 13-month period in 1975-1976. Approximately 500 children were selected at delivery, according to maternal

drinking history obtained at the 5th month of pregnancy. The follow-up cohort was identified at delivery according to their ORDEXC code, a 4-point code deriving from 19 different self-reported alcohol use patterns during and in the month or so prior to pregnancy or pregnancy recognition. The follow-up co-hort was stratified for alcohol and smoking, but retained the same sociodemographic characteristics as the screening sample.

Total number of subjects at Time 1: N = 1,529

Ages at Time 1: 13-45 yrs. (mothers).

Sex distribution: Approximately equal numbers of females and males (infants) throughout

Socioeconomic status: 57.9% middle/upper middle class, 33.3% working class, 8.8% poverty class

Race/ethnicity: 85.5% white, 9.1% African-American, 1.5% Asian-American, 0.7% Native American, 3.2% other

Years of Completed Waves:[a]

Years	N=	Age ranges
1974-1975	1,529	5th month in-utero
1975-1976	506[a]	Birth, day 1, day 2
1975	462	8 mos.
1976	490	18 mos.
1978-1979	457	4 yrs., 3 mos.
1981-1982	486	6.5-8.5 yrs.
1985-1986	461	10.2-11.8 yrs.
1989-1990	465	14 yrs., 4 mos.

Comments

a. Starting at birth, sample size reflects the number of singleton liveborn children in the cohort at that wave of data collection. Subject selection is determined by level of maternal alcohol use (abstainer, infrequent, moderate, low-priority alcohol exposed, and high-priority alcohol exposed). Data on up to four sets of twins were also obtained at several follow-ups. Outcome data and additional assessments of the environment were obtained at the following waves of data collection: Day 1, Day 2, Months 8 and 18, and Years 4, 7, 11, and 14. Follow-up is 82% of the original sample at 14 years. Outcome data has been obtained and edited "blind" by examiners trained to a high degree of reliability, with subjects seen within a specified window of time for each examination period, and tested under standardized laboratory conditions. Covariates have been assessed both pre- and post-natally. Approximately 150 potential covariates are routinely examined with each new data set, and entered into the analyses as appropriate.

INFORMATION ON SAMPLE ATTRITION:

A follow-up cohort of approximately 500 children was selected at birth from the screening study sample of 1,529 mothers interviewed during pregnancy. Actual at-trition in the cohort from birth to age 14 years was 18%. Additional children were occasionally added to the cohort from the screening study mothers, as needed, to keep cohort size close to 500.

CONSTRUCTS MEASURED: INSTRUMENTS USED

Predictor Variables and Covariates

Maternal alcohol use, caffeine consumption during pregnancy, tobacco use, diet, prescription and nonprescription drug use during pregnancy: Maternal Interview (at 5th month of pregnancy)

Neonatal Outcomes

Course and outcome of pregnancy: Medical records

Orientation, reactivity/irritability, habituation, tremulousness/motor immaturity, low arousal, and activity/muscle tone: Brazelton Neonatal Behavioral Assessment Scale

Eye movements, facial expressions and vocalizations, head movements, and limb activities: Naturalistic Observation

Operant Learning (sucking, head-turning): Electronic Monitoring Device

Non-nutritive sucking (latency and pressure): Pressure Transducer

Abnormalities of growth, development, and morphogenesis: Dysmorphology assessments (by pediatricians)

Infant Outcomes

Intelligence: Bayley Scales of Infant Mental & Motor Development

Infant and mother-infant behavior: Infant Behavior Ratings

Height, weight, head circumference, and palpebral fissures: Physical measurements

Maternal behavior (feeding, sleeping, behavior problems with infants), and history (hospitalization, separation from infant, employment outside of home, head injuries and high fevers in infants, major life changes in household): Maternal Questionnaire

Preschool Outcomes

Intelligence: Wechsler Preschool and Primary Scales of Intelligence (WPPSI)

Fine motor behavior: Wisconsin Motor Steadiness Battery

Laterality, and errors of localization: Tactual-Performance Test

Balance, coordination, and strength: Gross-Motor Test (adaptation)

Reaction time, Errors of Omission, Errors of Commission: Vigilance Test

Gross motor movement: Gross-Motor Test (adaptation)

Body activity: Body activity, physical measurements and morphological assessments

Preschool behavior: Behavior Ratings, Maternal Questionnaire, Dsymorphology Examinations

School-age Outcomes

Intelligence: Revised Wechsler Intelligence Scale for Children (WISC-R)
Reading, spelling, and arithmetic: Wide Range Achievement Test
Neuropsychological functioning: Neuropsychological Tests, physical measurements, be-
    havior ratings, maternal interview, teacher ratings and reports, standardized testing

REPRESENTATIVE REFERENCES:

Streissguth, A. P. (1978). Fetal alcohol syndrome: An epidemiologic perspective. *American Journal of Epidemiology, 107*(6), 467-478.
Streissguth, A. P., Barr, H. M., Martin, D. C., & Herman, C. S. (1980). Effects of maternal alcohol, nicotine, and caffeine use during pregnancy on infant mental and motor development at eight months. *Alcoholism: Clinical and Experimental Research, 4,* 152-164.
Streissguth, A. P., Martin, D. C., Barr, H. M., Sandman, B. M., Kirchner, G. L., & Darby, B. L. (1983). Intrauterine alcohol and nicotine exposure: Attention and reaction time in four-year-old children. *Developmental Psychology, 20*(4), 533-541.
Streissguth, A. P., Martin, D. C., Martin, J. C., & Barr, H. M. (1981). The Seattle Longitudinal Prospective Study on Alcohol and Pregnancy. *Neurobehavioral Toxicology and Teratology, 3,* 223-233.

CURRENT STATUS OF THE STUDY:

a. Further waves of data collection are planned.
b. Data are in machine-readable format.
c. Data are conditionally available for secondary analysis at the research site.

T

Longitudinal Study of Career Development in College-Educated Women, 1967

Tangri, Sandra S.

Contact Person: Sandra S. Tangri
Address: Department of Psychology
Howard University
525 Bryant Street, N.W.
C. B. Powell Building
Washington, DC 20059
Telephone No.: (202) 806-6806

SUBSTANTIVE TOPICS COVERED:

This study examines the background, personality, and college experience characteristics that distinguish those women who aspire to enter occupations dominated by men from those women who choose female-dominated careers. (See also Gurin, G., *Michigan Student Study: A Study of Students in a Multiversity*; and Mortimer, J. T., *The Michigan Student Study: Male Follow-Up.*)

CHARACTERISTICS OF THE ORIGINAL SAMPLE:

Year the study began: 1967

Subject selection process: A follow-up sample of 200 women seniors was chosen from those who were tested as freshmen in 1963 in the *Michigan Student Study: A Study of Students in a Multiversity* (Gurin, 1971).

Total number of subjects at Time 1: N = 200

Ages at Time 1: 18-22 yrs.

Sex distribution: 100% female

Socioeconomic status: 100% student

Race/ethnicity: Predominantly white

Years of Completed Waves:

Years	N=	Age ranges
1967	200	18-22 yrs.
1970	152	21-25 yrs.
1981	118	32-36 yrs.

INFORMATION ON SAMPLE ATTRITION:

During the 14-year period of study, 82 of 200 Ss (41%) were not retrieved for further study. Attrition was due to deaths and inability to locate current addresses of subjects. The core sample size consists of 118 Ss.

CONSTRUCTS MEASURED: INSTRUMENTS USED

Childhood; college experiences, interests, attitudes, desires, expectations: Questionnaire, Interview (for some Ss in 1970)
Need for achievement, motive to avoid success: Projective tests (N = 109)

REPRESENTATIVE REFERENCES:

Tangri, S. (1972). Determinants of occupational role-innovation among college women. *Journal of Social Issues, 28*(2), 177-200.
Tangri, S. (1974). *Effects of background, personality, college and post-college experiences on women's post-graduate employment* (Final report). Washington, DC: U.S. Department of Labor (Manpower Administration).
Tangri, S. (1975). Implied demand character of the wife's future and role-innovation: Patternings of achievement orientation in women. In M. Mednick, S. Tangri, & L. Hoffman (Eds.), *Women and achievement: Social and motivational analyses* (pp. 239-253). New York: John Wiley.
Tangri, S. S., & Jenkins, S. R. (1986). Stability and change in role innovation and life plans. *Sex Roles, 14,* 647-662.

CURRENT STATUS OF THE STUDY:

a. A further wave of data collection is planned for 1991.
b. Most of the data are in machine-readable format.
c. Data are available for secondary analysis through the Henry A. Murray Research Center, Radcliffe College, 10 Garden Street, Cambridge, MA 02138.

■ Mother-Infant Interaction in Normal and High Risk Infants, 1973

Thoman, Evelyn B.

Contact Person: Evelyn B. Thoman
Address:　　　　Box U-154
　　　　　　　　3107 Horsebarn Hill
　　　　　　　　Department of Biobehavioral Science
　　　　　　　　University of Connecticut
　　　　　　　　Storrs, CT 06268
Telephone No.: (203) 486-4042

SUBSTANTIVE TOPICS COVERED:

The study examines the socio-emotional development of full-term and premature infants, the quality of their mother-child interactions, the infants' sleep-wake states, and state-related respiration.

CHARACTERISTICS OF THE ORIGINAL SAMPLE:

Year the study began: 1973
Subject selection process: Initially, normal infants were enrolled during the last trimester of pregnancy, but are currently enrolled during the first 2 weeks after birth. Prematurely born infants are enrolled postnatally.
Total number of subjects at Time 1: N = 52
Ages at Time 1: Birth
Sex distribution: Approximately equal numbers of females and males throughout
Socioeconomic status: Data were gathered, but specific information about percent distribution by socioeconomic class was not available.
Race/ethnicity: 100% white

Years of Completed Waves:

Years	N=	Age ranges
(Cohort 1: Full-Term Infants)		
1973	29	Birth
1975-1976	27	3 yrs.
1976-1977	29	4 yrs.
1977-1978	29	5 yrs.
1978-1979	29	6 yrs.
1979-1980	29	7 yrs.
1980-1981	29	8 yrs.
1981-1982	29	9 yrs.
1982-1983	29	10 yrs.
1983-1984	29	11 yrs.

Years of Completed Waves, Continued:

Years	N=	Age ranges
1984-1985	29	12 yrs.
1985-1986	29	13 yrs.
1986-1987	29	14 yrs.
1987-1988	29	15 yrs.
1988-1989	29	16 yrs.
(Cohort 2: Premature Infants)		
1973	10	Birth
1975-1976	9	3 yrs.
1976-1977	9	4 yrs.
1977-1978	9	5 yrs.
1978-1979	9	6 yrs.
1979-1980	9	7 yrs.
1980-1981	9	8 yrs.
1981-1982	9	9 yrs.
1982-1983	9	10 yrs.
1983-1984	9	11 yrs.
1984-1985	9	12 yrs.
1985-1986	9	13 yrs.
1986-1987	9	14 yrs.
1987-1988	9	15 yrs.
1988-1989	9	16 yrs.
(Cohort 3: Siblings)[a]		
1973	13	Birth
1975-1976	12	3 yrs.
1976-1977	13	4 yrs.
1977-1978	13	5 yrs.
1978-1979	13	6 yrs.
1979-1980	13	7 yrs.
1980-1981	13	8 yrs.
1981-1982	13	9 yrs.
1982-1983	13	10 yrs.
1983-1984	13	11 yrs.
1984-1985	13	12 yrs.
1985-1986	13	13 yrs.
1986-1987	13	14 yrs.
1987-1988	13	15 yrs.
1988-1989	13	16 yrs.

Comments:
a. Siblings of the firstborn full-term subjects were included in the study. These infants were also full-term.

INFORMATION ON SAMPLE ATTRITION:

During the 15-year period of study, 1 of 52 Ss (1.9%), across three cohorts, was not retrieved for further study: 1 of 10 Ss (Cohort 2). Three of 4 Ss not tested at the second data point were available for further testing; 1 infant died. The core sample consists of 48 Ss.

CONSTRUCTS MEASURED: INSTRUMENTS USED[1]

Infant state of premature infants: 7-hour weekly home observations after discharge from hospital during preterm period

Infant status at term: Brazelton Neonatal Assessment Scale

Gestation age: Dubowitz Assessment Scale

Mother-infant interaction and infant states: Observation of two feeding intervals at term, 7-hour weekly home observations from 2-5 weeks of age post-term, three weekly home observations (2 hours) at 1 year

Ratio of body length and body weight: Ponderal Index

Infant's state during the evening: Observations of sleeping infant

Parental perception of infant temperament: Carey Questionnaire for Parents

Mental and motor development: Bayley Mental and Motor Scales

Neurological development: Neurological examination at 1 year

Mental development: McCarthy Middle Evaluation Test at 3 years

General health: Questionnaire sent to parents every 6 months

Handedness (left or right): Questionnaire every year

Behavioral style: Behavioral Style Questionnaire (McDevitt & Carey) every year

Middle childhood temperament: Middle Childhood Temperament Questionnaire (Hegvik, McDevitt & Carey) every year

Likes and dislikes; how subjects feel about their world in various ways: Questionnaire sent to the teenage subjects

Comments:
1. While most measures were used for both full-term and premature infants, some measures were employed for one group but not the other.

REPRESENTATIVE REFERENCES:

Thoman, E. (1974). Some consequences of early infant-mother interaction. *Early Child Development and Care, 3,* 249-261.

Thoman, E., & Acebo, C. (1984). The first affections of infancy. In R. Bell, J. Elias, R. Greene, & J. Harvey (Eds.), *Interfaces in psychology* (pp.17-55). Lubbock: Texas Tech Press.

Thoman, E., Acebo, C., & Becker, P. (1983). Infant crying and stability in the mother-infant relationship: A systems analysis. *Child Development, 54,* 653-659.

Thoman, E., Korner, A., & Kraemer, H. (1976). Individual consistency in behavioral states in neonates. *Developmental Psychology, 9,* 271-283.

CURRENT STATUS OF THE STUDY:

a. Further waves of data collection are planned.

b. Most data are in machine-readable format.

c. Data are available for secondary analysis from the study contact person.

■ New York Longitudinal Study, 1956

Thomas, Alexander; Chess, Stella; Lerner, Jacqueline; and Lerner, Richard

Contact Person: Jacqueline Lerner or Richard Lerner
Address: College of Health & Human Development
                  Pennsylvania State University
                  University Park, PA 16802
Telephone No.:   Jacqueline Lerner (814) 865-0530, Richard Lerner (814) 863-0530

SUBSTANTIVE TOPICS COVERED:

This study was initially designed to examine child temperament, but the data set also includes longitudinal data pertinent to the following: personality variables other than temperament (e.g., anxiety, adjustment, self-image); cognitive development and academic achievement; family structure and function and parent-child relations; health and physical development; the development of clinical symptomatology; peer relationships; the development of sexuality; drug use and abuse; and vocational interests and career development.

CHARACTERISTICS OF THE ORIGINAL SAMPLE:

Year the study began: 1956
Subject selection process: Subjects were selected from middle- (MC) or upper-middle-class (UMC) backgrounds with parents of higher educational levels. A total of 84 families participated. Some families had more than one child in the study. Supplemental samples of mentally retarded children and Puerto Rican children were used as comparison groups.
Total number of subjects at Time 1: N = 133 (Excludes supplemental samples)
Ages at Time 1: 3 mos.
Sex distribution: Approximately equal numbers of females and males throughout
Socioeconomic status: 100% middle/upper middle class
Race/ethnicity: 98% white, 2% other

Years of Completed Waves:

Years	N=	Age ranges
1956-1962	133	3 mos.-6 yrs.
1972-1974	107	16-18 yrs.
1978-1980	133	17-24 yrs.
1986-1988	131	28-32 yrs.
Supplemental Samples		
(Cohort 2: Mentally Retarded Ss)		
1956-1960	52	5-11 yrs.
(Cohort 3: Puerto Rican Ss)		
1961-1968	97	1-7 yrs.

INFORMATION ON SAMPLE ATTRITION:

During the 32-year period of study, 131 of 133 subjects (98.4%) were retrieved for further study. However, 26 Ss (19.5%) were not tested at the second data wave. The core sample consists of 107 Ss.

CONSTRUCTS MEASURED: INSTRUMENTS USED

Family background information (family size, birth order, and demographic information): Face-to-face interviews with parents

Obstetrical history (information about neonatal and birth complications): Interview information from mother

Child's behavior (sleeping, feeding, bathing, toileting, social responsibility, and sensorimotor functioning): Semistructured face-to-face interviews with parents

Temperament: Semistructured face-to-face interviews with parents regarding child's behavior

Temperament, adjustment, and life events during adolescence and adulthood: Semistructured interviews and questionnaires with Ss

Family dynamics and child-rearing practices: Audiotaped parental interviews

Parental discipline and consistency of child and family dynamics: Parental attitude research instruments (Schaeffer & Bell)

Contextual information (significant life events and family history): Interviews with parents

Adaptation and overall functioning in school: Face-to-face interviews with teachers

Play and problem-solving activities: School behavioral observations

Academic performance and achievement: School grades measured from school records

Cognitive functioning and arithmetic achievement: Stanford-Binet IQ, Wechsler Intelligence Scale for Child (WISC), reading and arithmetic achievement tests, Wide Range Achievement Test

Social family background: Home environment observation

Behavioral disorders: Psychiatric evaluation

Intelligence: Gesell Test or Bayley Scales of Infant Development, Revised Stanford-Binet Preschool Form-L, Wechsler Intelligence Scale for Children (WISC), psychological reports and/or direct observations of testing situation

Self-image and self-esteem: Offer Self-image Questionnaire

Development of parents as parents: Early adult life face-to-face interviews with parents

General development: Early adult life face-to-face interviews with Ss

Early adult temperament (adaptation level, approach-withdrawal behavior, intensity, sensorimotor threshold, quality of mood, attention span/persistence, activity level, distractibility and rhythmicity of biological functions): Early adult temperament questionnaire

Adolescent and adult temperament, work, substance use, and psychological and social functioning: Open-ended interview and semistructured interview

Knowledge of Ss level of functioning: Parent interviews, open-ended and semistructured

Self-image/self-evaluation, changes in life, medical problems, routines, goals, athletics, hobbies, religion, family structure, school history, work functioning, social functioning, sexual functioning, marital status, communication problems, expressiveness (with anger and such), adaptability to new situations, self-motivation, anxiety, de-

pression, psychosomatic problems, substance use, temperament questionnaire, nine characteristics of temperament: Face-to-face interview
Nine characteristics of temperament: Temperament Questionnaire

REPRESENTATIVE REFERENCES:

Lerner, J. V., Hertzog, C., Hooker, K. A., Hassibi, M., & Thomas, A. (1988). A longitudinal study of negative emotional-behavioral states and adjustment for early childhood through adolescence. *Child Development, 59,* 356-366.
Thomas, A., & Chess, S. (1977). *Temperament and development.* New York: Brunner/Mazel.
Thomas, A., & Chess, S. (1980). *The dynamics of psychological development.* New York: Brunner/Mazel.
Vicary, J. R., & Lerner, J. V. (1983). Longitudinal predictors of drug use: Analyses from the New York Longitudinal Study. *Journal of Drug Education, 13,* 275-285.

CURRENT STATUS OF THE STUDY:

a. Further waves of data collection may be planned.
b. Most data are not in machine-readable format.
c. Data are available for secondary analysis from the New York Longitudinal Study archive: c/o Jacqueline V. Lerner, Department of Individual and Family Studies, College of Health & Human Development, Pennsylvania State University, University Park, PA 16802.

■ Study of American Families, 1961

Thornton, Arland

Contact Person: Arland Thornton
Address: Institute for Social Research
University of Michigan
426 Thompson Street
Ann Arbor, MI 48106-1248
Telephone No.: (313) 763-5015

SUBSTANTIVE TOPICS COVERED:

The study examines geographical mobility, education, paid employment, attitudes about jobs, sex-role attitudes, marriage, childbearing, desired lifestyle.

CHARACTERISTICS OF THE ORIGINAL SAMPLE:

Year the study began: 1961
Subject selection process: White women, who either recently had a new baby (their first, second, or fourth child) or had recently married, were chosen by random sampling from the birth and marriage records of the Detroit metropolitan area.

Total number of subjects at Time 1: N = 1,113
Ages at Time 1: 15-39 yrs.
Sex distribution: 100% female
Socioeconomic status: 76% middle class, 24% working class (approximately)
Race/ethnicity: 100% white

Years of Completed Waves:[a]

Years	N=	Age ranges
1961-1963	1,113	15-39 yrs.
1966	1,113	18-42 yrs.
1977	1,015	29-53 yrs.
1980	996	31-56 yrs.
1985	929	57-61 yrs.

Comments:
a. In 1980 subjects' children, born in 1962, were also interviewed.

INFORMATION ON SAMPLE ATTRITION:

During the 24-year period of study, 184 of 1,113 Ss (16.5%) were not retrieved for further study.

CONSTRUCTS MEASURED: INSTRUMENTS USED

Family's demographic and social characteristics; economic standing, asset holdings, economic expectations and attitudes; care and home ownership, educational aspirations for children, work experience, sharing of family responsibilities; young people's attitudes about marriage, children, and work; opinions, interests, and activities of subjects' children; appropriate roles of men and women: Interview

REPRESENTATIVE REFERENCES:

Alwin, D. F., & Thornton, A. (1984). Family origins and the schooling process: Early versus late influence of parental characteristics. *American Sociological Review, 49,* 784-803.

Coombs, L. C., Freedman, R., Friedman, J., & Pratt, W. (1970). Premarital pregnancy and status before and after marriage. *American Journal of Sociology, 75,* 800-820.

Freedman, D. S., & Thornton, A. (1979). The long-term impact of pregnancy at marriage on the family's economic circumstances. *Family Planning Perspectives, 11,* 6-21.

Thornton, A. (1985). Changing attitudes toward separation and divorce: Causes and consequences. *American Journal of Sociology, 90*(4), 856-872.

CURRENT STATUS OF THE STUDY:

a. Further waves of data collection are planned.
b. Most of the data are in machine-readable format.
c. Data are available for secondary analysis through the study contact person.

■ Longitudinal Study of Creative Behavior, 1959

Torrance, E. Paul

Contact Person: E. Paul Torrance
Address: 183 Cherokee Avenue
                 Athens, GA 30606
Telephone No.:   (404) 543-9679

SUBSTANTIVE TOPICS COVERED:

The study examines the prediction of creative behavior, the struggle for identity, career patterns, and sex differences in children regarded as creative.

CHARACTERISTICS OF THE ORIGINAL SAMPLE:

Year the study began: 1959
Subject selection process: Subjects were selected from the total high school population in Minneapolis, Minnesota, grades 7 through 12.
Total number of subjects at Time 1: N = 392
Ages at Time 1: 13-18 yrs.
Sex distribution: Approximately equal numbers of females and males throughout
Socioeconomic status: 95% middle/upper middle class, 5% working class
Race/ethnicity: 95% white, 5% African-American

Years of Completed Waves:

Years	N=	Age ranges
1959	392	13-18 yrs.
1971	264	25-30 yrs.
1979-1980	220	33-39 yrs.
1990	150[a]	43-49 yrs.

Comments:
a. Data collection is still in progress.

INFORMATION ON SAMPLE ATTRITION:

During the 22-year period of study, 172 of 392 Ss (43.9%) were not retrieved for further study. The core sample consists of 220 Ss; core sample by age cohort was not available.

CONSTRUCTS MEASURED: INSTRUMENTS USED

Creative abilities: Torrance Tests of Creative Thinking, Checklists of creative activities, biographical inventory, creative writing samples
Creative adult achievement: Questionnaire
Creative promise: Sociometric (peer nominations)
Intelligence: Stanford-Binet Intelligence Tests, Lorge-Thorndike Intelligence Test, Wechsler Intelligence Scales for Children, California Test of Mental Maturity, Buck's House-Tree-Person Test
Educational achievement: Iowa Tests of Educational Skill

REPRESENTATIVE REFERENCES:

Torrance, E. P. (1965). *Gifted children in the classroom.* New York: Macmillan.
Torrance, E. P. (1968). A longitudinal examination of fourth grade slump in creativity. *Gifted Child Quarterly, 12,* 195-199.
Torrance, E. P. (1980). Growing up creatively gifted: A 22-year longitudinal study. *Creative Child and Adult Quarterly, 5,* 148-158.
Torrance, E. P. (1981). Predicting the creativity of elementary school children (1958-1980)—and the teacher who "made a difference." *Gifted Child Quarterly, 25,* 55-62.

CURRENT STATUS OF THE STUDY:

a. No further waves of data collection are planned.
b. The data are not in machine-readable format.
c. The data are conditionally available for secondary analysis.

V

The Grant Study of Adult Development, 1938

Vaillant, George E.

Contact Person: George E. Vaillant
Address: Department of Psychiatry
Dartmouth Medical School
Hanover, NH 03756
Telephone No.: (603) 646-7560

SUBSTANTIVE TOPICS COVERED:

The study includes psychiatric interviews of early sexual development; social histories and family histories from parents; retrospective histories of child development from mothers; and post-graduation mail questionnaires on employment, family, health, leisure, and political attitudes. A subsample was reinterviewed concerning defense mechanisms; occupational, social, and psychological adjustment; and marital and sexual adjustment. Wives were also interviewed.

CHARACTERISTICS OF THE ORIGINAL SAMPLE:

Year the study began: 1938
Subject selection process: Subjects were males from the Harvard classes of 1942-1944 (N = 204) and of 1939-1941 (N = 64). Ten percent were selected on a semi-random basis. The other 90% were chosen on the basis of above-average grades and excellent health and on recommendation by college deans.
Total number of subjects at Time 1: N = 268
Ages at Time 1: 18 yrs. average
Sex distribution: 100% male
Socioeconomic status: 93% middle/upper middle class, 7% working class
Race/ethnicity: 100% white

Years of Completed Waves:

Years	N=	Age ranges
1938-1942	268	18-20 yrs.
1943-1949	241	19-30 yrs.
1950-1967	250	25-48 yrs.
1968-1978	236	43-59 yrs.
1979-1989	203	54-71 yrs.
1990	203	68-72 yrs.

Comments:
After college graduation, Ss received annual questionnaires until 1955. Since 1956 Ss have received questionnaires every 2 years. The rate of questionnaire return ranged from 50% to 70% at any given data point. Ss who continually failed to return questionnaires were contacted by telephone every 6 years. Complete physical examinations were conducted in 1969, 1974, 1979, 1984, and 1989 in 95% of the surviving participants. Future follow-ups will focus on the natural history of marriages and the relation of mental health to physical health.

INFORMATION ON SAMPLE ATTRITION:

During the 52-year period of study, 20 of 268 Ss (7%) have withdrawn and 45 of 268 Ss (17%) have died before age 68. The core sample now consists of 203 active Ss who have survived until age 68.

CONSTRUCTS MEASURED: INSTRUMENTS USED

Military (WWII) history: Personal Interview (1946)
Family life, work history: Home visit (cultural anthropological field observation: 1950-1952)
Work history, marital history, physical health, style of adaptation, and psychological problems: Psychiatric Interview (1967-1977)[a]
Physical status: Physical examination (chest X ray, electrocardiogram, blood chemistry, blood count, and neurological examination)
Intelligence: Harvard Block Test, Army Alpha, Scholastic Achievement Test
Personality: Thematic Apperception Test (Morgan & Murray), Brief Rorschach Ink Blot Test
Ego development: Washington University Sentence Completion Test (Loevinger)
Comments:
a. During the years 1967-1977, a random sample comprising 200 of the surviving participants received psychiatric interviews.

REPRESENTATIVE REFERENCES:

Heath, C. W. (1946). *What people are*. Cambridge, MA: Harvard University Press.
Vaillant, G. E. (1977). *Adaptation to life*. Boston: Little, Brown.
Vaillant, G. E. (1983). *The natural history of alcoholism: Causes, patterns, and paths to recovery*. Cambridge, MA: Harvard University Press.
Vaillant, G. E., & Schnurr, P. (1988). What is a case? A forty-five year follow-up of a college sample selected for mental health. *Archives of General Psychiatry, 45*, 313-319.

CURRENT STATUS OF THE STUDY:

a. Further waves of data collection are planned in 1991.
b. The data are not in machine-readable format.
c. Data are not available for secondary analysis.

■ Crime Causation Study: Unraveling Juvenile Delinquency, 1940

Vaillant, George; Glueck, Sheldon (deceased); Glueck, Eleanor (deceased)

Contact Person: George A. Vaillant
Address: Department of Psychiatry, Dartmouth Medical School
                 Hanover, NH 03756
Telephone No.:   (603) 646-7560

SUBSTANTIVE TOPICS COVERED:

Originally this study examined the causes of delinquency up to age 32, in terms of social (socioeconomic), somatic, and psychological (intellectual and emotional-temperamental) influences. A sample of 500 juvenile delinquents and 500 non-delinquent controls were followed. Later, up to age 47, the study did the same for alcohol abuse in the non-delinquent sample. Since then the study has studied physical aging, retirement, and mental health in the non-delinquent cohort.

CHARACTERISTICS OF THE ORIGINAL SAMPLE:

Year the study began: 1940
Subject selection process: Delinquents were selected from the Lyman School for Boys, and from the Shirley Industrial School for Boys, and had originated from underprivileged neighborhoods in the Boston area. Non-delinquent controls were matched with delinquents on age, intelligence, ethnicity, and area of residence.
Total number of subjects at Time 1: N = 1,000
Ages at Time 1: 10-17 yrs.
Sex distribution: 100% male
Socioeconomic status: 50% working class, 50% poverty class
Race/ethnicity: 100% white (varied ethnicity)

Years of Completed Waves:

Years	N=	Age ranges
(Delinquent Cohort)		
1940-1948	500	10-17 yrs.
1948-1956	461[a]	18-25 yrs.
1954-1963	439	24-32 yrs.
(Non-Delinquent Cohort)		
1940-1948	500	10-17 yrs.
1948-1956	456[a]	18-25 yrs.
1954-1963	456	24-32 yrs.
1969-1978	393	39-47 yrs.
1978-1988	288	48-57 yrs.

Comments:
a. The decrease in sample size from Time 1 is due to randomly dropping 10% of the youngest Ss from the original sample.

INFORMATION ON SAMPLE ATTRITION:

Since age 32 the 500 members of the delinquent cohort have not been recontacted. Around age 47 all but 4 of the surviving 423 members of the non-delinquent cohort (N = 456) were relocated, and 393 agreed to cooperate (367 interviewed, 9 completed questionnaires, and, in 22 cases, next of kin were interviewed). As of 1988, 288 Ss continue to cooperate (complete biennial questionnaires and return physical examinations every 5 years). Seventy Ss have died, 50 Ss have dropped out, 48 Ss are lost or not answering mail.

CONSTRUCTS MEASURED: INSTRUMENTS USED

Identifying information: Request forms, identification transcripts, home contact reports
Academic achievement: Stanford Achievement Test (Reading and Arithmetic)
Club membership, military history: Official records
Criminal history: Delinquency and arrest records, index of chronological treatment experiences, court case reports, official records
Family history and background: Interview, official records
Clinical impressions of subject: Psychiatric interview, Rorschach Ink Blot Test (The non-delinquent cohort was reinterviewed for 2 hours at age 47. Since then, they have returned biennial questionnaires and received physical examinations every 5 years.)
Intelligence: Wechsler/Bellevue Intelligence Test; Terman-McNemar Test of Mental Ability; Dearborn Group Tests
Vital Statistics of Family, family background; mobility of boy, environmental circumstances; "home atmosphere in which boy reared"; health history of boy; conduct of boy; and school history of boy: Social Investigation Schedule, Interview, Official Records
Since age 47 for the non-delinquent sample: Health Sickness Rating Scale, Washington University Sentence Completion Test (Loevinger), Bond's Defense Style Questionnaire

REPRESENTATIVE REFERENCES:

Glueck, S., & Glueck, E. (1950). *Unraveling juvenile delinquency*. New York: The Commonwealth Fund.

Glueck, S., & Glueck, E. (1968). *Delinquents and non-delinquents in perspective*. Cambridge, MA: Harvard University Press.

Sampson, R. J., & Laub, J. H. (1990). Crime and deviance over the life course: The salience of adult social bonds. *American Sociological Review, 55*, 609-627.

Vaillant, G. E. (1983). *The natural history of alcoholism: Causes, patterns, and paths to recovery*. Cambridge, MA: Harvard University Press.

CURRENT STATUS OF THE STUDY:

a. Biennial waves of data collection have been carried out for the non-delinquent cohort by Dr. Vaillant since 1977 and will be continued.
b. Most of the data are in machine-readable format.
c. Original records and machine-readable data from the delinquent cohort, and machine-readable data up to age 32 for the non-delinquent group are available from
   the Henry A. Murray Research Center, Radcliffe College, 10 Garden Street, Cambridge, MA 02138.

■ The Stuart Study, 1930

Valadian, Isabelle; Gardner, Jane; Dwyer, Joanna; and Stuart, Harold
(deceased)

Contact Person: Isabelle Valadian
Address: Department of Maternal and Child Health
                Harvard School of Public Health
                Kresge Building, Third Floor
                677 Huntington Avenue
                Boston, MA 02115
Telephone No.: (617) 432-1080

SUBSTANTIVE TOPICS COVERED:

The purpose of this study was to examine the ways in which the rate of mental
development varies from age to age; whether some children develop more rapidly
than the norm at one end and less rapidly at another; whether the effects of mental
status are permanent.

CHARACTERISTICS OF THE ORIGINAL SAMPLE:

Year the study began: 1930
Subject selection process: Subjects were white, full-term children whose mothers
    had been patients of the Boston Lying-In Hospital.
Total number of subjects at Time 1: N = 309
Ages at Time 1: Prenatal to birth
Sex distribution: Approximately equal numbers of females and males throughout
Socioeconomic status: 100% middle/upper middle class
Race/ethnicity: 100% white (North European descent)

Years of Completed Waves:

Years	N=	Age ranges
1930	309	Prenatal to birth
1930-1936	228	Infancy-6 yrs.[a]
1936-1948[c]	134	6-18 yrs.[b]
1965	126	35 yrs.
1975-1978	120	45 yrs.
1980-1985	100	50-55 yrs.

Comments:
a. Subjects followed through 6 years of age were known as members of the "Preschool sample."
b. Subjects followed between 7 and 18 years of age were known as members of the "Maturity sample."
c. The entire project was interrupted between 1942 and 1943, due to the absence of the research staff on war assignments. As a result all the study children missed one or more examinations during that time.

INFORMATION ON SAMPLE ATTRITION:

During the 55-year period of study, 209 of 309 Ss (67.6%) were not retrieved for further study. Attrition was due to parents losing interest in the study, being an unreliable source of information, or having difficulty getting to the clinic. The core sample consists of 100 Ss.

CONSTRUCTS MEASURED: INSTRUMENTS USED

Health and illness history: Interview, psychological examination
Mental development at 3 yrs. and older: Stanford-Binet Intelligence Scale (Forms L & M)
Mental development 3-18 mos.: Gesell Tests
Mental development 24-30 mos.: Minnesota Preschool Scale
Mental development 36 mos.-4.5 years: Merrill-Palmer Scale of Mental Tests
Personality development: Nursery school observation
Social functioning: Phrase Association tests, Interviews with subjects and mothers
Cognitive development: Standard Developmental/Intelligence Tests

REPRESENTATIVE REFERENCES:

Berkey, C. S., Reed, R. B., & Valadian, J. (1983). Longitudinal growth standards for preschool children. *Annals of Human Biology, 10*(1), 57-67.
Gardner, J., & Valadian, I. (1983). Changes over thirty years in an index of gynecological health. *Annals of Human Biology, 10*(1), 41-55.
Stuart, H. C., & Reed, R. B. (1959). Description of project. Paper No. 1. *Pediatrics, 24*(5), 875-885.
Valadian, I., & Porter, D. (1976). *Physical growth and development: From conception to maturity.* Boston: Little, Brown.

CURRENT STATUS OF THE STUDY:

a. Further waves of data collection are planned.
b. Data are in machine-readable format.
c. Data are conditionally available for secondary analysis from the study contact person.

■ The California Child Health and Development Studies, 1959

van den Berg, Bea J.; Oechsli, Frank W.; and Christianson, Roberta C.

Contact person: Bea J. van den Berg
Address: School of Public Health
                  University of California at Berkeley
                  140 Warren Hall
                  Berkeley, CA 94720
Telephone No.:   (415) 642-8130

SUBSTANTIVE TOPICS COVERED:

This study investigates the relationships of biologic, genetic, medical, and environmental factors in parents, including events in the pregnancy, labor, and delivery, to the normal and abnormal development of their offspring.

CHARACTERISTICS OF THE ORIGINAL SAMPLE:

Year the study began: 1959
Subject selection process: Subjects selected were women who applied for prenatal care at Kaiser Foundation Hospital in Oakland, California, from 1959 to 1966.
Total number of subjects at Time 1: N = 20,754 pregnancies (Cohort 1)
Ages at Time 1: 20-39 yrs. (mothers)
Sex distribution: 100% female (mothers); Approximately equal numbers of females and males (children)
Socioeconomic status: Approximately 66% middle/upper middle class, 34% working class
Race/ethnicity: 65% white, 24% African-American, 4% Asian-American, 3% Hispanic, 4% other

Years of Completed Waves:

Years	N=	Age ranges
(Cohort 1: Mothers)[a]		
1959-1960	15,865	20-39 yrs.
1965-1968	3,500	26-47 yrs.
1969-1971	3,000	30-50 yrs.
1971-1972	3,000	32-55 yrs.
1977-1979	1,700	38-61 yrs.
(Cohort 2: Children)		
1959-1967	19,044	Birth
1966-1968	18,685	1 yr.
1965-1972	17,025	5 yrs.
(Cohort 3: Children)[b]		
1965-1968	4,000	5 yrs.± 1 mo.
1969-1971	3,400	5 yrs.± 1 mo.
1971-1972	3,600	9-11 yrs.
1977-1979	2,000	15-17 yrs.

Comments:
a. Cohort was derived from a larger sample (N = 20,754 Ss) of pregnant women. Mothers (Cohort 1) were interviewed during the development examinations of their children.
b. A subcohort of children at age 5, who received developmental examinations at two time periods (1965-1968 and 1977-1979), was derived from Cohort 2, and followed to ages 15 to 17 years.

INFORMATION ON SAMPLE ATTRITION:

During the 5-year period of follow-up of Cohort 2, 2,019 of 19,044 Ss (10.6%) were not retrieved for further study. Reasons for sample attrition included death, institutionalization, and adoption. Attrition among Ss in Cohort 3 approximated 15%. Due to missing information, sample attrition over the 17-year period of study of Cohort 1 (mothers) could not be assessed.

CONSTRUCTS MEASURED: INSTRUMENTS USED

Fertility history, health history, marital history, education, occupation, family income, exact date of last menstrual period, usage and type of contraceptives, planning of pregnancy, psychological orientation to pregnancy: Interview with pregnant mother
Health history: Medical records
Anthropometrics (at 5 yrs.): CHDS Developmental Examination (vision, hearing, speech, and physical exams)
Intelligence: Peabody Picture Vocabulary Test
Cognitive ability: Raven's Progressive Matrices
Health history, lifestyle items: Interview with mother
Lifestyle and health history: Questionnaire

REPRESENTATIVE REFERENCES:

Christianson, R. E., van den Berg, B. J., Milkovich, L., & Oechsli, F. W. (1981). Incidence of congenital anomalies among white and black live births with long-term follow up. *American Journal of Public Health, 71,* 1333-1341.

van den Berg, B. J., Christianson, R. E., & Oechsli, F. W. (1988). The California Child Health and Development Studies of the School of Public Health, University of California at Berkeley. *Paediatric and Perinatal Epidemiology, 2,* 265-282.

Yerushalmy, J. (1969). The California Child Health Development Studies: Study design and some illustrative findings on congenital heart disease. In *Congenital Malformations, Proceeding of the Third International Congress Series No. 204* (pp. 299-306).

Yerushalmy, J., van den Berg, B. J., Erhardt, C. L., & Jacobziner, H. (1965). Birth weight and gestation as indices of "immaturity." *American Journal of Diseases of Children, 109,* 43-57.

CURRENT STATUS OF THE STUDY:

a. Further waves of data collection are planned.

b. Most of the data are in machine-readable format.

c. Data are available for secondary analysis from the National Technical Information Service, 5285 Port Royal Road, Springfield, VA 22161.

Critical Issues in the Development of At-Risk Infants, 1975

Wallace, Ina; and Escalona, Sibylle K.

Contact Person: Ina Wallace
Address: Albert Einstein College of Medicine
                Rose F. Kennedy Center, Room 222
                1410 Pelham Parkway South
                Bronx, NY 10461
Telephone No.: (212) 430-2471

SUBSTANTIVE TOPICS COVERED:

The study examines demographic background, family functioning, caretaking patterns, cognitive development, psychosocial development, and mother/child relations of at-risk infants and their families.

CHARACTERISTICS OF THE ORIGINAL SAMPLE:

Year the study began: 1975
Subject selection process: Infants in Jacobi Neonatal Intensive Care Unit, weighing less than 2,250 grams, or gestational age less than 37 weeks, were asked to participate in the study.
Total number of subjects at Time 1: N = 127
Ages at Time 1: 7 mos.
Sex distribution: Approximately equal numbers of females and males throughout
Socioeconomic status: 50% working class, 25% poverty class, 25% middle class
Race/ethnicity: 50% African-American, 25% Hispanic, 25% white

Years of Completed Waves:

Years	N=	Age ranges
1975-1977	127	7 mos.
1976-1977	117	15 mos.
1977-1978	102	28 mos.
1977-1979	104	34 mos.
1978-1979	110	40 mos.
1981	73	6 yrs.
1984-1985	60	9 yrs.

INFORMATION ON SAMPLE ATTRITION:

During the 9-year period of study, 67 of 127 Ss (52.8%) were not retrieved for further study. The core sample consists of 65 Ss.

CONSTRUCTS MEASURED: INSTRUMENTS USED

Neurological status of the infant: Einstein Neonatal Neurobehavioral Scale
Infant development: Bayley Scales of Infant Development
Intelligence: Stanford-Binet Intelligence Scale; Wechsler Intelligence Scale for
    Children (Revised), or Wechsler Preschool and Primary Scale of Intelligence
Sensorimotor development: Einstein Scales of Sensorimotor Development
Nonverbal communicative abilities: Gestural communication signals rating scales
Development of body image: Body image precursors rating scales
Symbol development: Matching scale of symbolic function rating scales
Impulse control: Impulse control rating scales
Achievement motivation: Achievement motivation rating
Level of aspirant: Level of aspiration experiment
Complexity level of abstraction used in building from set of toys: World Test
Reading skills: Wide Range Achievement Test
Development of visual-motor integration: Developmental test of visual-motor integration
Physical closeness between mother and child, maternal involvement, overt conflict
    between mother and child: Parental interview
Health status of the child: Pediatric and neurological examinations
Body image: Human Draw-A-Person

REPRESENTATIVE REFERENCES:

Escalona, S. K. (1984). Social and other environmental influences on the cognitive and personal-
    ity development of low birthweight infants. *American Journal of Mental Deficiency, 88,*
    508-512.
Escalona, S. K. (1987). *Critical issues in early development of premature infants.* New Haven,
    CT: Yale University Press.
Rose, S. A., & Wallace, I. F. (1985). Cross modal and intramodal transfer as predictors of mental
    development in full term and preterm infants. *Developmental Psychology, 21,* 949-962.
Rose, S. A., & Wallace, I. F. (1985). Visual recognition memory: A predictor of later cognitive
    functioning in preterms. *Child Development, 54,* 686-694.

CURRENT STATUS OF THE STUDY:

a. No further waves of data collection are planned.
b. Data are in machine-readable format.
c. The data are not yet available for secondary analysis.

■ California Children of Divorce Project, 1971

Wallerstein, Judith S.[1]

Contact Person: Judith S. Wallerstein
Address: Center for the Family in Transition
                         5725 Paradise Drive
                         Building B, Suite 300
                         Corte Madera, CA 94925
Telephone No.:   (415) 924-5750
Comments:
1. During the first 5 years of the study, Dr. Joan Kelly was co-principal investigator of the project.

SUBSTANTIVE TOPICS COVERED:

The study examines divorce-related experiences of children. Specifically, the study focuses on the following: the experiences and outcomes for children age 2 to 18 at the time of the decisive marital separation and during the 10-year aftermath; the impact of divorce on parent-child relationships during the same period; the parents' experience and outcome at the same time.

CHARACTERISTICS OF THE ORIGINAL SAMPLE:

Year the study began: 1971
Subject selection process: Subjects were selected by invitation from the community and from attorneys to participate in a study on the impact of divorce on children. Ss were drawn from a nonclinical population in a largely middle class, suburban county in Northern California. A total of 60 families consented to participate in the study.
Total number of subjects at Time 1: N = 131 children[a]
Ages at Time 1: 2.5-18 yrs.
Sex distribution: Approximately equal numbers of females and males throughout
Socioeconomic status: 72% middle/upper middle class, 28% working class
Race/ethnicity: 89% white, 8% Asian-American, and 3% African-American
Comments:
a. 120 parents were also studied.

Years of Completed Waves:

Years	N=	Age ranges
1971-1972	131	2.5-18 yrs.
1973-1974	114	4-20 yrs.
1975-1976	121	5-23 yrs.
1980-1982	114	11-29 yrs.

INFORMATION ON SAMPLE ATTRITION:

During the 10-year period of study, 17 of 131 Ss (13%) were not retrieved for further study. Two families with five children were lost to all follow-ups. Another two families, also with five children, reconciled and, although they were reinterviewed, were excluded from further analysis. Of the remaining 121 children, though not all were seen at each follow-up, significant information was available about them from parents and other family members. The core sample consists of 114 Ss and their parents.

CONSTRUCTS MEASURED: INSTRUMENTS USED

Psychological functioning; attitudes toward parents and siblings; view of conflict, divorce; relationship with parents and step-siblings; expectations and plans for future: Individual clinical interviews with child at each wave

Psychological functioning; relationship with each other and each child; relationship with parents; issues of conflict; relationship with new spouse (if remarried): Individual clinical interviews with parents at each wave

Academic and social functioning of child: Teacher reports

REPRESENTATIVE REFERENCES:

Wallerstein, J. S. (1987). Children of divorce: Report of a ten-year follow-up of early latency-age children. *American Journal of Orthopsychiatry, 75*(2), 199-211.

Wallerstein, J. (1988). *Second chances: Men, women, and children a decade after divorce.* New York: Tichnor & Fields.

Wallerstein, J. S., & Corbin, S. B. (1989). Daughters of divorce: Report from a ten-year follow-up. *American Journal of Orthopsychiatry, 59,* 593-604.

Wallerstein, J., & Kelly, J. (1980). *Surviving the breakup: How children and parents cope with divorce.* New York: Basic Books.

CURRENT STATUS OF THE STUDY:

a. No further waves of data collection are planned.

b. Most data are in machine-readable format.

c. Data are not available for secondary analysis.

■ Ypsilanti Perry Preschool Project, 1962

Weikart, David P.; and Schweinhart, Lawrence J.

Contact Person: David P. Weikart
Address: High/Scope Educational Research Foundation
                 600 North River Street
                 Ypsilanti, MI 48198-2898
Telephone No.:   (313) 485-2000

SUBSTANTIVE TOPICS COVERED:

The study examines the effectiveness of preschool and home visit intervention for African-American, low-income children at high risk for school failure. Outcomes throughout school years are examined as well as at age 19. Age 19 outcomes included high school graduation, employment, welfare dependence, and criminal activity.

CHARACTERISTICS OF THE ORIGINAL SAMPLE:

Year the study began: 1962
Subject selection process: All subjects selected were children from the Perry School attendance area in Ypsilanti, Michigan. Parents reported all low socio-economic status; child's Stanford-Binet IQ in range of 65-90 at project entry.
Total number of subjects at Time 1: N = 123
Ages at Time 1: 4 yrs.
Sex distribution: Approximately equal numbers of females and males (Experimental group); 60% male, 40% female (Control group)
Socioeconomic status: 100% poverty class
Race/ethnicity: 100% African-American

Years of Completed Waves:

Years	N=	Age ranges
(Cohort 1: Experimental Ss)		
1962-1966	58	3-7 yrs.
1967	58	4-8 yrs.
1968	58	5-9 yrs.
1969	58	6-10 yrs.
1970	58	7-11 yrs.
1971	58	8-12 yrs.
1972	58	9-13 yrs.
1973	58	10-14 yrs.
1974	58	11-15 yrs.
1978-1980	54	19 yrs.
1988-1990	49	28 yrs.

Years of Completed Waves, Continued:

Years	N=	Age ranges
(Cohort 2: Control Ss)		
1962-1966	65	3-7 yrs.
1967	65	4-8 yrs.
1968	65	5-9 yrs.
1969	65	6-10 yrs.
1970	65	7-11 yrs.
1971	65	8-12 yrs.
1972	65	9-13 yrs.
1973	65	10-14 yrs.
1974	65	11-15 yrs.
1978-1980	61	19 yrs.
1988-1990	55	28 yrs.

INFORMATION ON SAMPLE ATTRITION:

During the 28-year period of study, 19 of 123 Ss (15.4%) were not retrieved for further study: 9 of 58 Ss (15.5%) in the Experimental group; and 10 of 65 Ss (15.4%) in the Control group. The core sample consists of 104 Ss from both groups: 49 Ss from the Experimental group; and 55 Ss from the Control group.

CONSTRUCTS MEASURED: INSTRUMENTS USED

Intellectual performance: Stanford-Binet Intelligence Scale, Wechsler Intelligence Scale for Children
Nonverbal intellectual performance: Leiter International Performance Scale
Psycholinguistic abilities: Illinois Test of Psycholinguistic Abilities
Aptitude: Illinois Test of Psycholinguistic Abilities
Vocabulary, intelligence: Peabody Picture Vocabulary Test
Scholastic achievement: California Achievement Test
Scholastic abilities in everyday life: Adult APL Survey
Academic history, scholastic attainment, scholastic placement, grades, absences, disciplinary incidents: School records
Classroom conduct, scholastic motivation: Pupil Behavior Inventory
Scholastic potential, social maturity: Ypsilanti Rating Scale
Commitment to schooling, homework, school conduct: Youth Interview
High school satisfaction: Young Adult Interview
Parental roles in discipline and education, role models: Case Study Interview
Medical history: Hospital records

Socioeconomic Status

Current and past jobs: Youth Interview
Current and past jobs, unemployment, income sources, savings, debt, ownership, job satisfaction, plans: Young Adult Interview
Attitudes toward money, goal orientation: Case Study Interview

Social Responsibility

Delinquent behavior, membership, peer relations, activities, health, attitudes, life objectives: Youth Interview
Crime and delinquency, arrest, memberships, help seeking, people problems, pregnancies, family relations, activities, health, general attitudes: Young Adult Interview
Juvenile detentions, petitions, dispositions; adult arrest, prosecution, sentences: Police and court records
Welfare assistance, use of social services: State social service records
Behavior during interview: Interviewer questionnaire
Church and religion, sense of responsibility: Case Study Interview

REPRESENTATIVE REFERENCES:

Berrueta-Clement, J. R., Schweinhart, L. J., Barnett, W. S., Epstein, A. S., & Weikart, D. P. (1984). Changed lives: The effects of the Perry Preschool program on youths through age 19 (*Monographs of the High/Scope Educational Research Foundation, 8*) Ypsilanti, MI: High/Scope Press.
Schweinhart, L. J., & Weikart, D. P. (1980). Young children grow up: The effects of the Perry Preschool Program on youths through age 15. *Monographs of the High/Scope Educational Research Foundation, 7.* Ypsilanti, MI: High/Scope Press.
Schweinhart, L. J., & Weikart, D. P. (1983). The Effects of the Perry Preschool Program on youths through age 15—A summary. In *As the twig is bent . . . lasting effects of preschool programs. Consortium for longitudinal studies* Hillsdale, NJ: Lawrence Erlbaum.
Schweinhart, L. J., & Weikart, D. P. (1988). The High/Scope Perry Preschool Program. *Fourteen ounces of prevention: A casebook for practitioners.* Washington, DC: American Psychological Association.

CURRENT STATUS OF THE STUDY:

a. Further waves of data collection are planned.
b. Most of the data are in machine-readable format.
c. Data will soon be available for secondary analysis.

■ Ypsilanti Preschool Curriculum Demonstration Project, 1967

Weikart, David P.; and Schweinhart, Lawrence J.

Contact Person: David P. Weikart
Address: High/Scope Educational Research Foundation
                 600 North River Street
                 Ypsilanti, MI 48198-2898
Telephone No.:   (313) 485-2000

SUBSTANTIVE TOPICS COVERED:

The study examines three different types of preschool curricula in an intervention for disadvantaged children: a structured Language Curriculum (similar to DISTAR); a Cognitively Oriented Curriculum (later High/Scope); and a child-centered traditional nursery school curriculum.

CHARACTERISTICS OF THE ORIGINAL SAMPLE:

Year the study began: 1967
Subject selection process: Children in the Ypsilanti, Michigan, school district whose families reported very low socioeconomic status, and whose Stanford-Binet IQ at age 3 was between 65 and 85.
Total number of subjects at Time 1: N = 71
Ages at Time 1: 3 yrs.
Sex distribution: Approximately equal numbers of females and males throughout
Socioeconomic status: 100% poverty class
Race/ethnicity: 62% African-American, 38% white (combining all three cohorts)

Years of Completed Waves:

Years	N=	Age ranges
(Cohort 1: Cognitively Oriented Curriculum)		
1967-1969	24	3-5 yrs.
1970	23	4-6 yrs.
1971	23	5-7 yrs.
1972	23	6-8 yrs.
1973	23	7-9 yrs.
1974	23	8-10 yrs.
1975	23	9-11 yrs.
1978	23	12-14 yrs.
1979	18	15 yrs.
1989-1990	18	22 yrs.

Years of Completed Waves, Continued:

Years	N=	Age ranges
(Cohort 2: Behavioral Curriculum)		
1967-1969	24	3-5 yrs.
1970	23	4-6 yrs.
1971	23	5-7 yrs.
1972	23	6-8 yrs.
1973	23	7-9 yrs.
1974	23	8-10 yrs.
1975	23	9-11 yrs.
1978	23	12-14 yrs.
1979	18	15 yrs.
1989-1990	18	22 yrs.
(Cohort 3: Traditional Nursery School Curriculum)		
1967-1969	23	3-5 yrs.
1970	23	4-6 yrs.
1971	23	5-7 yrs.
1972	23	6-8 yrs.
1973	23	7-9 yrs.
1974	23	8-10 yrs.
1975	23	9-11 yrs.
1978	23	12-14 yrs.
1979	18	15 yrs.
1989-1990	18	22 yrs.

INFORMATION ON SAMPLE ATTRITION:

During the 23-year period of study, 15 of 68 Ss (22.1%) were not retrieved for further study: 6 of 24 Ss (2.5%) in Cohort 1; 6 of 24 Ss (25%) in Cohort 2; and 5 of 23 Ss (21.7%) in Cohort 3. The core sample consists of 54 Ss: 18 Ss in each cohort.

CONSTRUCTS MEASURED: INSTRUMENTS USED

Academic potential and achievement: Stanford-Binet Intelligence Scale, Peabody Picture Vocabulary Test, Illinois Test of Psycholinguistic Abilities (Experimental Edition), Arthur Adaptation of the Leiter International Performance Scale

Academic achievement: California Achievement Test (Lower and Upper Primary Forms), School records

Academic achievement (Teacher Rating): Ypsilanti Rating Scale, Academic Potential & Verbal Skill Scales

Social-emotional development: Ypsilanti Rating Scale, Social-Emotional Adjustment Factors, Pupil Behavior Inventory, Socio-Emotional Scales, Parent Questionnaire

Social-emotional development and school attitudes: Subject Questionnaire (age 15)

Social behaviors: Court and police records

Home background: Perry Demographic Questionnaire, Cognitive Home Environment Scale, Maternal Attitude Inventory

REPRESENTATIVE REFERENCES:

Schweinhart, L. J., Weikart, D. D., & Larner, M. B. (1986). Consequences of three preschool cur-
    riculum models through age 15. *Early Childhood Research Quarterly, 1*(1), 15-45.
Weikart, D. P., Epstein, A. S., Schweinhart, L. J., & Bond, J. T. (1978). The Ypsilanti Preschool
    Curriculum Demonstration Project: Preschool years and longitudinal results through fourth
    grade. *Monographs of the High/Scope Educational Research Foundation, 4.* Ypsilanti, MI:
    High/Scope Press.
Weikart, D. P., & Schweinhart, L. J. (1986). Three preschool curriculum models: Academic and
    social outcomes. *Principal, 66*(1), 62-68.
Weikart, D. P., & Schweinhart, L. J. (1987). The High/Scope Cognitively Oriented Curriculum in
    early education. In J. L. Roopnarine & J. E. Johnson (Eds.), *Approaches to early childhood
    education.* Columbus, OH: Charles E. Merrill.

CURRENT STATUS OF THE STUDY:

    a. Further waves of data collection are planned.
    b. Most of the data are in machine-readable format.
    c. Data are not currently available for secondary analysis.

■ Minnesota Transracial Adoption Study, 1973

Weinberg, Richard A.; and Scarr, Sandra

Contact Person: Richard A. Weinberg
Address: Institute of Child Development
               University of Minnesota
               51 East River Road
               Minneapolis, MN 55455
Telephone No.: (612) 624-3575

SUBSTANTIVE TOPICS COVERED:

    The study examines the cognitive and psychosocial consequences of transracial
adoption and genetic and environmental sources of individual variation in intellectual functioning.

CHARACTERISTICS OF THE ORIGINAL SAMPLE:

Year the study began: 1973
Subject selection process: Participating families were recruited through the *News-
    letter of the Open Door Society* and by letters from the State Department of
    Public Welfare Adoption Unit to families with African-American adopted
    children, 4 years of age and older, who were adopted throughout the state of
    Minnesota, through Lutheran Social Service and Children's Home Society. Of

the families known to be eligible for participation in the study, 74% did participate.

Total number of subjects at Time 1: N = 521

Ages at Time 1: 4-16 yrs.

Sex distribution: Approximately equal numbers of females and males throughout

Socioeconomic status: 100% middle class

Race/ethnicity: 25% African-American, 71% white, 4% Asian-American

Years of Completed Waves:

Years	N=	Age ranges
(Cohort 1: African-American/Interracial Adopted Children)		
1973-1975	130	4-12 yrs.
1986-1989	105	17-28 yrs.
(Cohort 2: White Adopted Children)		
1973-1975	25	4-12 yrs.
1986-1989	18	17-28 yrs.
(Cohort 3: Asian/Indian Adopted Children)		
1973-1975	21	4-12 yrs.
1986-1989	14	17-28 yrs.
(Cohort 4: Children Reared with Biological Parent)		
1973-1975	143	4-16 yrs.
1986-1989	118	17-30 yrs.
(Cohort 5: Adults)		
1973-1975	202	26-59 yrs.
1986-1989	171	39-73 yrs.

INFORMATION ON SAMPLE ATTRITION:

During the 16-year period of study, 95 of 521 Ss (18.2%), across five cohorts, were not retrieved for further study: 25 of 130 Ss (19.2%) in Cohort 1; 7 of 25 Ss (28%) in Cohort 2; 7 of 21 Ss (33.3%) in Cohort 3; 25 of 143 Ss (17.5%) in Cohort 4; and 31 of 202 Ss (15.3%) in Cohort 5. The core sample consists of 426 Ss across five cohorts: 105 Ss (Cohort 1); 18 Ss (Cohort 2); 14 Ss (Cohort 3); 118 Ss (Cohort 4); and 171 Ss (Cohort 5).

CONSTRUCTS MEASURED: INSTRUMENTS USED

Intellectual functioning: Raven's Progressive Matrices, Stanford-Binet Intelligence Test, Wechsler Intelligence Scale for Children, Wechsler Adult Intelligence Scale as age appropriate, school aptitude and achievement tests

Psychosocial and emotional adjustment: Junior Eysenck Personality Inventory, Eysenck Personality Inventory (parents), Rotter Locus of Control (father)

Child-rearing expectations: Parental attitude research instrument completed by mother

Home atmosphere and family lifestyle: Family index
Quality of family relationships, consequences to family of transracial adoption:
  Parental interview

REPRESENTATIVE REFERENCES:

Scarr, S., Scarf, E., & Weinberg, R. A. (1980). Perceived and actual similarities in biological and adoptive families: Does perceived similarity bias genetic inferences? *Behavior Genetics, 10*(5), 445-458.

Scarr, S., Weber, P. L., Weinberg, R. A. (1981). Personality resemblance among adolescents and their parents in biologically related and adoptive families. *Journal of Personality and Social Psychology, 40*(5), 885-898.

Scarr, S., & Weinberg, R. (1976). IQ test performance of black children adopted by white families. *American Psychologist, 31,* 726-739.

Scarr, S., & Weinberg, R. (1983). The Minnesota adoption studies: Genetic differences and malleability. *Child Development, 54,* 260-267.

CURRENT STATUS OF THE STUDY:

  a. No further waves of data collection are planned.
  b. Some data are in machine-readable format.
  c. The data are available for secondary analysis through the study contact person.

■ The Stony Brook High-Risk Project, 1971

Weintraub, Sheldon

Contact person: Sheldon Weintraub
Address: Department of Psychology
                 State University of New York at Stony Brook
                 Stony Brook, NY 11794
Telephone No.:   (516) 444-2990

SUBSTANTIVE TOPICS COVERED:

  The purpose of this study is to identify precursor patterns, environmental stressors, and protective factors that are differentially predictive of psychopathology.

CHARACTERISTICS OF THE ORIGINAL SAMPLE:

Year the study began: 1971
Subject selection process: Subjects selected were children of all psychiatric admissions at four local inpatient mental health facilities.
Total number of subjects at Time 1: N = 504 (children)

Ages at Time 1: 7-15 yrs.
Sex distribution: Approximately equal numbers of females and males throughout
Socioeconomic status: Predominantly lower middle class
Race/ethnicity: 87.3% white, 7.5% African-American, 3.2% Hispanic and Native
   American

Years of Completed Waves:

Years	N=	Age ranges
(Cohort 1: Children of Schizophrenic Parents)		
1971	80	7-15 yrs.
1974	*	10-17 yrs.
1974-1982[a]	65	18 yrs.
1982-and beyond[b]	44	21 yrs. and older
(Cohort 2: Children of Unipolar Depressed Parents)		
1971	154	7-15 yrs.
1974	*	10-17 yrs.
1974-1982	121	18 yrs.
1982-and beyond[b]	48	21 yrs. and older
(Cohort 3: Children of Bipolar Depressed Parents)		
1971	134	7-15 yrs.
1974	*	10-17 yrs.
1974-1982	112	18 yrs.
1982-and beyond[b]	54	21 yrs. and older
(Cohort 4: Children of Normal Parents)		
1971	136	7-15 yrs.
1974	*	10-17 yrs.
1974-1982	109	18 yrs.
1982-and beyond[b]	65	21 yrs. and older

Comments:
a. Data not available.
b. Follow-up was discontinued in the middle of phase IV due to the lack of funding.

INFORMATION ON SAMPLE ATTRITION:

During the childhood phases, 15% of the risk families and 10% of the control families dropped out. In young adulthood, attrition consisted of 18.7% for Cohort 1; 20.8% for Cohort 2; 16.4% for Cohort 3; and 19.8% for Cohort 4. In terms of sample attrition bias, the most disorganized families, and those families with the most severely ill patient-parents, were most highly represented among those who dropped out during the initial and childhood phases. During the young adult phase, those young adults who came from the most disorganized families, and who looked the most vulnerable on the childhood measures, were over-represented among those who dropped out.

CONSTRUCTS MEASURED: INSTRUMENTS USED

Spouse psychological adjustment and psychopathology: Current and Past Psychopathology Scale

Diagnostic assessment: Mini-Mult version of the Minnesota Multiphasic Personality Inventory

Assessment of spouse and home environment: Mate Adjustment Form

Marital adjustment: Marital Adjustment Test

Family functioning: Family Evaluation Form, Semistructured Interview

Child Report of Parental Behavior Inventory: Parental characteristics

Child evaluation of family environment and of parents: Environmental Q-Sort, Minnesota-Briggs History Record

Peer evaluation: Pupil Evaluation Inventory

Subject self-evaluation: Assessment Scales for Sociometric Evaluation of Secondary School Students

Parental evaluation of child behavior characteristics, teacher ratings of subject: Devereux Child Behavior Rating Scales

Background information, life history: Interview with patient's spouse

Mental functioning: Hospital Case History

Child's behavior: School Rating Behavior Scale, Hahnemann High School Behavior Scale

Referential thinking, distractibility, maintenance of attention, cognitive slippage: Laboratory battery

REPRESENTATIVE REFERENCES:

Richters, J. E., & Weintraub, S. (1990). Beyond diathesis: Toward an understanding of the high-risk environment. In J. Rolf, A. Masten, D. Cicchetti, K. Nuechterlein, & S. Weintraub (Eds.), *Risk and protective factors in the development of psychopathology*. New York: Cambridge University Press.

Weintraub, S. (1987). Risk factors in schizophrenia: The Stony Brook High-Risk Project. *Schizophrenia Bulletin, 13*(3), 439-450.

Weintraub, S., & Neale, J. M. (1984). The Stony Brook High-Risk Project. In N. F. Watt, E. J. Anthony, L. C. Wynne, & J. E. Rolf (Eds.), *Children at risk for schizophrenia: A longitudinal perspective* (pp. 243-263). New York: Cambridge University Press.

Weintraub, S., Winters, K. C., & Neale, J. M. (1985). Competence and vulnerability in children with an affectively disordered parent. In M. Rutter, C. E. Izard, & P. B. Read (Eds.), *Depression in young people* (pp. 205-220). New York: Guilford Press.

CURRENT STATUS OF THE STUDY:

a. Further waves of data collection are planned.

b. Most of the data are in machine-readable format.

c. Data are available through the Henry A. Murray Research Center, Radcliffe College, 10 Garden Street, Cambridge, MA 02138.

■ Child Development in Alternative Family Styles, 1973

Weisner, Thomas; and Eiduson, Bernice (deceased)

Contact Person: Thomas Weisner
Address: Department of Psychiatry and Biobehavioral Sciences
                 Department of Anthropology
                 University of California at Los Angeles
                 760 Westwood Plaza
                 Los Angeles, CA 90024-1759
Telephone No.:   (213) 825-6216

SUBSTANTIVE TOPICS COVERED:

The study examines the differences in growth patterns and developmental outcomes associated with different lifestyles emerging from counterculture families; identifies critical family variables affecting development in certain areas such as family relationships and interactions, environment, child-rearing attitudes and practices; contrasts family milieux and socialization patterns of traditional two-parent nuclear family rearing; assesses cognitive, social and emotional development of children in relation to different family ideologies and family environments.

CHARACTERISTICS OF THE ORIGINAL SAMPLE:

Year the study began: 1973

Subject selection process: Subjects were selected by an "informal network" of sources. Selected families were from four lifestyles: single mother, communes/living groups, social contract couples, and two-parent nuclear families. A total of 209 families, approximately 50 families per family lifestyle, were followed. The traditional families were selected by random choice from the American Medical Association directory of obstetricians.

Total number of subjects at Time 1: N = 417

Ages at Time 1: Prenatal (Cohort 1: children); 18-35 yrs. (Cohort 2: mothers)

Sex distribution: Approximately equal numbers of females and males throughout

Socioeconomic status: 60% middle/upper middle class, 30% working class, 10% poverty class

Race/ethnicity: 100% white

Years of Completed Waves:

Years	N=	Age ranges
(Cohort 1: Children)		
1973	209	Prenatal
1973	209	Birth
1973-1974	209	6 mos.
1974	209	8 mos.

Years of Completed Waves, Continued:

Years	N=	Age ranges
1974	205	1 yr.
1974-1975	205	1 yr., 6 mos.
1975	205	2 yrs.
1975-1976	205	2 yrs., 9 mos.
1976	205	3 yrs.
1977	205	4 yrs., 6 mos.
1978	205	5 yrs.
1979	205	6 yrs.
1980	205	7 yrs.
1981	205	8 yrs.
1987	203	11-12 yrs.
(Cohort 2: Mothers and Some Fathers)		
1973-1974	208	18-35 yrs.
1974-1975	208	19-36 yrs.
1976-1977	208	21-38 yrs.
1978-1979	208	23-40 yrs.
1979-1980	204	24-41 yrs.
1985-1986	202	30-47 yrs.

INFORMATION ON SAMPLE ATTRITION:

During the 17-year period of the study, 11 of 417 Ss (2.6%) from both cohorts were not retrieved for further study: 7 of 209 Ss (3.3%) for Cohort 1; 4 of 208 (1.9%) for Cohort 2. The core sample consists of 406 Ss.

CONSTRUCTS MEASURED: INSTRUMENTS USED

Birth

Neonatal status: Newborn Neurological Examination (pediatrician)
Obstetrical complications at birth (mother): Obstetrical Complications Scale (OCS)

6 Months

Level of responsiveness, alertness, affect, and initiation of activity of child: Home
observation

8 Months

Mental development, motor development, general emotional tone, task orientation,
extroversion, activity level, audiovisual awareness, motor coordination:
Bayley Scales of Infant Development (MDI, PDI, Infant Behavior Record)

One Year

Attachment to mother, separation anxiety, use of transitional objects, and exploratory behavior: Strange Situation Procedure (Ainsworth)

Mental development, motor development, general emotional tone, task orientation, extroversion, activity level, audiovisual awareness, motor coordination: Bayley Scales of Infant Development (MDI, PDI, Infant Behavior Record)

Health status of child: Physical examination (pediatrician)

18 Months

General development, motor skills; personal, social, and expressive language; conceptual comprehension: Minnesota Child Development Inventory (Ireton MCDI) (mother's rating)

Personality factors (difficult, adjusted, active, warm, outgoing, fearful, goal directed): Adjective Check List (mother's rating) (18 months, 2 years, 3 years, 5 years, 6 years)

3 Years

Attachment to mother, separation anxiety, use of transitorial objects, and explanatory behavior: Strange Situation Test (Ainsworth)

Intelligence, verbal ability, and cognitive differentiation: Stanford-Binet Intelligence Scale

Motor coordination, audiovisual awareness, activity level, task orientation, extroversion: Bayley Infant Behavior Record

Receptive language development: Peabody Picture Vocabulary Test (PPVT)

Goal-directedness and persistence: Drawer Pull (Van Leisout)

Coping skills and frustration tolerance: Room Barrier Test (Jacklin)

Language development: Articulation Test, Preschool Language Scale (Zimmerman)

Ego resiliency and suggestibility: Competing Sets (Block and Block)

Creativity in play, use of fantasy, global personological evaluation: World Test (Block)

General development, motor skills; personal, social, and expressive language; conceptual comprehension: Minnesota Child Development Inventory (Ireton MCDI) (Mother's Rating)

Social development: Vineland Social Maturity Scale (Mother's Rating)

3 Years, 9 Months

General development, motor skills; personal, social, and expressive language; conceptual comprehension: Minnesota Child Development Inventory (Ireton MCDI) (Mother's Rating)

4 Years, 6 Months

Compliance behavior at home, family interaction patterns: Home observation

6 Years

Intelligence: Revised Wechsler Intelligence Scale for Children (WISC-R) (Verbal Scale, Performance Scale, and Full Scale) (Short Form)

Level of aspiration, and frustration/tolerance levels: Unsolvable Puzzle Barrier (Stipek)

Extent of delay of gratification: Delayed Gift (Block and Block)

Level of moral development, superego differentiation: Moral Judgment Test, Concepts of Good/Bad (Block and Block)

Perceptual motor skills: Perceptual Visual Motor Test (Haworth)

Attitude toward family, spontaneity in fantasy, kinds of anxiety, coping mechanisms: Children's Apperception Test (CAT)

Level of reading recognition: Peabody Individual Achievement Test (PIAT)

Field independence, suggestibility, and ego resiliency: Children's Embedded Figures Test (CEFT) (Witkin)

Convergent-divergent thinking, imagination, and creativity: Torrance Test of Creativity

Child's identification with family: Family Relations Test—Two Houses (Szyrynski)

Sex role awareness and sex role orientation: Sex Role Learning Index (SRLI) (Edelbrock and Sugawara)

Sex role orientation, body image and self-esteem: Draw-A-Person (Harris)

Play behaviors in an unstructured play situation: Play Session (Independent ratings, Consulting Psychologist)

Involvement, attentiveness, persistence, curiosity, composedness, compliance, comfortableness with adults, responsiveness, talkativeness, willingness to come and stay, and independence: Behavior Ratings

Perceptual acuity, imagination, reality testing ability, kind of and freedom of imagination: Rorschach Ink Blot Test

Level of moral development, attitude toward home and parents; interest, friendships: Child Interview (Damon)

Global evaluation of child's performance: Consulting Psychologist ratings

Personal adjustment: Minnesota Multiphasic Personality Inventory (MMPI) (Adults)

Ability level, spatial, verbal reasoning, and numerical reasoning: Government Aptitude Test Battery (GAT-B) (Adults)

7, 8, and 12 Years

School contacts (grades 1, 2, and 6): Teacher Ratings

Academic behavior, social competence, emotional competence: Lambert Pupil Behavior Rating Scale

Personality factors (extroversion, introversion, distractibility, independence, dependence, considerateness, hostility, verbal ability, and task orientation): Schaeffer Child School Behavior Inventory

School achievement: Reading level, math level, school achievement, overall academic level

Academic record, health attendance: Xerox of school records

SRA, Metropolitan, Stanford Achievement Test: Achievement test results

Strengths, problems, physical school appearance: Teacher's description of child's performance

What teacher thinks is interesting or significant about child and his/her family: Teacher paragraph (interesting facts about child at third contact)

REPRESENTATIVE REFERENCES:

Eiduson, B. T. (1983). Conflict and stress in nontraditional families: Impact on children. *American Journal of Orthopsychiatry, 53*(3), 426-435.

Eiduson, B., Kornfein, M., Zimmerman, I. L., & Weisner, T. S. (1982). Comparative socialization practices in alternative family settings. In M. Lamb (Ed.), *Nontraditional families* (pp. 315-345). New York: Plenum.

Weisner, T. S., & Wilson-Mitchell, J. (in press). Nontraditional family lifestyles and sex typing in six year olds. *Child Development.*

CURRENT STATUS OF THE STUDY:

a. Further waves of data collection are planned.

b. Most of the data are in machine-readable format.

c. The data will be available for secondary analysis from the study contact person, and through the Henry A. Murray Research Center, Radcliffe College, 10 Garden Street, Cambridge, MA 02138.

■ Harvard Bereavement Study Project, 1966

Weiss, Robert S.; and Parkes, C. Murray

Contact Person: Robert S. Weiss
Address: Work and Family Research Unit
               University of Massachusetts at Boston
               Downtown Center
               Boston, MA 02125
Telephone No.: (617) 287-7275

SUBSTANTIVE TOPICS COVERED:

This study explores how bereavement affects the emotional and social lives of those who have lost a spouse, and examines the course of recovery from bereavement and the social or psychological factors that facilitate or impede that recovery.

CHARACTERISTICS OF THE ORIGINAL SAMPLE:

Year the study began: 1966

Subject selection process: Subjects were widows and widowers, under the age of 45 and living in Boston, whose spouses had died of natural causes (not homicide or suicide) in 1965 and 1966.

Total number of subjects at Time 1: N = 68

Ages at Time 1: Mean age = 36 yrs.

Sex distribution: 70.6% female, 29.4% male

Socioeconomic status: 47% middle/upper middle class, 39% working class, 15% poverty class

Race/ethnicity: 75% white, 25% Hispanic or African-American

Years of Completed Waves:[a]

Years	N=	Age ranges
1965-1966 (3 wks.)	68	36 yrs.
1965-1966 (8 wks.)	68	36 yrs.
1966-1967	68	37 yrs.
1966-1967	55	37 yrs.
1968-1969	51	38 yrs.

Comments:

a. The study was originally planned for only one year, since it was thought that recovery from bereavement would require no longer than one year.

INFORMATION ON SAMPLE ATTRITION:

During the 4-year period of study, 17 of 68 Ss (25%) were not retrieved for further study. The core sample consists of 51 Ss. Reasons for attrition included the following: Ss had moved or could not be located, death, and refusal to participate in follow-up interviews.

CONSTRUCTS MEASURED: INSTRUMENTS USED

Reaction to trauma, coping patterns, role adjustments, recovery process: Open-ended interview

Physical health: Health questionnaire (A comparison sample of nonbereaved subjects also responded to this questionnaire.)

REPRESENTATIVE REFERENCES:

Glick, I. O., Weiss, R. S., & Parkes, C. M. (1974). *The first year of bereavement.* New York: John Wiley.

Parkes, C. M. (1975). Determinants of outcome following bereavement. *Omega, 6*(4), 303-323.

Parkes, C. M., & Brown, R. (1972). Health after bereavement: A controlled study of young Boston widows and widowers. *Psychosomatic Medicine, 34*(5), 449-461.

Parkes, C. M., & Weiss, R. S. (1983). *Recovery from bereavement.* New York: Basic Books.

CURRENT STATUS OF THE STUDY:

a. No further waves of data collection are planned.

b. The data are not in machine-readable format.

c. Data are available for secondary analysis through the Henry A. Murray Research Center, Radcliffe College, 10 Garden Street, Cambridge, MA 02138.

■ The Kauai Longitudinal Study, 1955

Werner, Emmy

Contact Person:　Emmy Werner
Address:　　　　Department of Applied Behavioral Sciences
　　　　　　　　University of California at Davis
　　　　　　　　Davis, CA 95616
Telephone No.:　(916) 752-3621

SUBSTANTIVE TOPICS COVERED:

The study examines the magnitude of perinatal causalities and the cumulative effect of perinatal stress, poverty, and a disordered caretaking environment on the development of children from birth to age 18; developmental disabilities, with concern for prevention and early intervention; mental health problems and the consistency of these problems in young adulthood, relating these problems to biological and temperamental variables, vulnerability, caretaker-child interactions, and cultural differences in socialization; the source of resilience against the previously described problems.

CHARACTERISTICS OF THE ORIGINAL SAMPLE:

Year the study began: 1955

Subject selection process: Mothers for the study were chosen from the Kauai pregnancy and child study, investigating outcomes of all births in an entire Hawaiian community during the year 1955.

Total number of subjects at Time 1: N= 688[a]

Ages at Time 1: Prenatal and perinatal

Sex distribution: Equal numbers of females and males throughout

Socioeconomic status: 45% middle/upper middle class, 55% poverty class

Race/ethnicity: 51.6% Asian-American, 22.9% Pacific Islander, 16.3% biracial, and 9.2% white

Comments:

a. 18 infants died at birth, reducing the population from 688 to 670.

Years of Completed Waves:

Years	N=	Age ranges
1954-1955	670	4 mos. prenatal to perinatal
1955-1956	670	1 yr.
1956-1957	670	2 yrs.
1966-1967	598	10 yrs.
1972-1973	574	18 yrs.
1980-1981	57[a]	25 yrs.
1985-1988	505	30-32 yrs.

Comments:
a. Of the 57 Ss from this subsample tested at this time point, 28 were teenage mothers (now 25 years of age) and 29 were offspring of psychotic parents at age 25 (males 60.0%, females 40.0%).

INFORMATION ON SAMPLE ATTRITION:

During the 33-year period of study, 193 of 698 subjects (27.7%) were not retrieved for further study. The core sample consists of 505 Ss.

CONSTRUCTS MEASURED: INSTRUMENTS USED

Demographic Characteristics

Age of parents: Birth records
Educational level of parents: School records
Parental mental health problems: Study files and mental health register, State of Hawaii
Socioeconomic status birth, age 2 and age 10: Parental occupation, plantation pay scale
Number of persons in household by age 10, adults besides parents by age 10, number of children by age 10: Home interview by social workers and public health workers

At Birth

Evaluation by pediatricians on basis of recorded events during prenatal and neonatal periods, labor and delivery: Pre-perinatal stress score

At 1 Year

Stressful life events: Social service records and postpartum interview
Mother's coping skills: Adjective check list (one-year home interview by public health nurse)
Mothers' perception of infant's temperamental characteristics: Mother's assessment during one-year home visit

At 20 Months

Family stability: Demographic information
Social development: Vineland Social Maturity Scale (SQ)
Examiner's assessment of toddler's behavior patterns, and psychological status
Behavior patterns, examiner's assessment of quality of parent-child interaction: Developmental examinations by psychologists (Adjective checklist)
Physical status of child: Pediatrician ratings
Intellectual stimulation: Family environment assessment based on interview information
Stressful life events between birth and age 2: Interview with primary caretaker; social service records
Material opportunities: Demographic information (inferred)
Emotional support available to the child: Family stability based on demographic data

At 2-10 Years

Medical problems and acquired physical handicaps: Public health, doctors', and hospital records
Readiness and achievement in school: School records of test results (K-Grade 5)
Behavior problems (K-Grade 5): School records, mental health service records, parent checklist
Social service records; 10-year home interview: Stressful life events
Educational stimulation provided by the home, emotional support in the home: Ratings by clinical psychologists
Family environment: Demographic information (rated by clinical psychologists) and interviews by social and health care workers

At 10 Years

Intelligence: Primary Mental Abilities Tests (PMA) and factor scores, Cattell Infant Intelligence Scale (Cattell IQ)
Neuro/Psychological assessment: Bender-Gestalt Error scores
Classroom behavior: Teacher checklist
Needs assessment, long-term remedial education, special class placement, long-term mental health care, and medical care: Panel consisting of pediatrician, psychologist, and public health nurse (including diagnostic exams)

At 10-18 Years

Repeated or serious delinquency: Public records
Teenage pregnancy or abortion: Hospital records
School achievement: Cooperative School and College Ability Tests (SCAT), Sequential Tests of Educational Progress (STEP), Standardized tests from school records (grades 8-10, 12)

Stressful life events; information on health, education, and work experience: Biographical questionnaire, social service records, and postpartum records

At 18 Years

Personality: California Psychological Inventory (CPI) dimensions, individual interviews
Locus of control: Nowicki Locus of Control Test

At 18-24 Years

Mental health problems: Mental health register (1972-1979), mental health service records

At 30-32 Years

Individual's perception of stressful events in childhood, adolescence, and adulthood: Life Event Checklist
Internal/External Locus of Control: Rotter's Locus of Control Scale
Dimensions of Temperament: EAS (Excitability, Activity Level, and Sociability) Temperament Survey for Adults
Individuals' perception of major stressors and major sources of support in their adult lives: Semistructured interview and closed-ended questionnaire
Future plans: Data waves also include intergenerational data, and in the future will include the 1955 subject cohort, their parents, and their own children.

REPRESENTATIVE REFERENCES:

Werner, E. E. (1989). Children of the garden island. *Scientific American, 260*(4), 106-111.
Werner, E. E. (1989). High risk children in young adulthood: A longitudinal study from birth to 32 years. *American Journal of Orthopsychiatry, 59*(1), 72-81.
Werner, E., & Smith, R. (1977). *Kauai's children come of age.* Honolulu: University of Hawaii Press.
Werner, E., & Smith, R. (1982). *Vulnerable, but invincible: A longitudinal study of resilient children and youth.* New York: McGraw-Hill.

CURRENT STATUS OF THE STUDY:

   a. Further waves of data collection are planned.
   b. The data are in machine-readable format.
   c. The data are available for secondary analysis through the study contact person.

■ Child Stress and Coping Project, 1982

Wertlieb, Donald L.

Contact Person: Donald L. Wertlieb
Address: Department of Child Study
                Tufts University
                105 College Avenue
                Medford, MA 02155
Telephone No.: (617) 381-3355

SUBSTANTIVE TOPICS COVERED:

The study examines the relations among stress, illness, and coping and health variables for school-age children and their families, with a focus on the moderating influences of social support, cognitive, temperamental, and social demographic factors.

CHARACTERISTICS OF THE ORIGINAL SAMPLE:

Year the study began: 1982
Subject selection process: Subjects participating in the study were selected by a strati-
    fied random selection procedure from a Health Plan population. Three fourths of
    the children form a "normative" sample drawn from intact families without men-
    tal health problems, and one fourth of the sample are a "high stress" sample,
    drawn from families undergoing a higher level of stressful experiences associated
    with a marital separation within the 4-year period prior to study entry.
Total number of subjects at Time 1: N = 222
Ages at Time 1: 6-10 yrs.
Sex distribution: Approximately equal numbers of females and males throughout
Socioeconomic status: 73% middle/upper middle class, 17% poverty class, 8%
    working class, and 2% college students
Race/ethnicity: 92% white, 8% African-American

Years of Completed Waves:

Years	N=	Age ranges
(Cohort 1: Normative)		
1982-1983	130	6-7 yrs.
1983-1984	126	7-8 yrs.
1984-1985	123[a]	9-10 yrs.
(Cohort 2: High Stress)		
1982-1983	92	9-10 yrs.
1983-1984	89	10-11 yrs.
1984-1985	87[a]	11-12 yrs.

Comments
a. Estimated sample size.

INFORMATION ON SAMPLE ATTRITION:

During the 3-year period of study, 12 of the original 222 (5.4%) subjects were not available for follow-up. The core sample consists of 210 Ss.

CONSTRUCTS MEASURED: INSTRUMENTS USED

Perception of experienced stress and coping: Stress and Coping Inventory (Wertlieb)
Occurrences of major life events: Life Events Scale (Coddington; Harrison)
Self-report of experienced "hassles": The Hassles Scale (Kanner et al.)
Self-report coping strategies: Ways of Coping Checklist (Folkman & Lazarus)
Children's perception of competence: Perceived Competence Scale for Children (PCS) (Harter)
Type A/B in children: Hunter-Wolf Type A/B Scale (Hunter & Supitt)
Locus of control: Nowicki-Strickland Locus of Control Scale for Children (LCS)
Perceived control: Multidimensional Measure of Children's Perceptions of Control (MPC) (Connell)
Perceived health locus of control: Children's Health Locus of Control (Parcel & Mayer)
Cognitive style: Fruit Distraction Test & Leveling and Sharpening House Test (Santostefano)
Intelligence: Revised Wechsler Intelligence Scale for Children (WISC-R), Block Design & Vocabulary Subtest
Social support: Social Network Index (Berkman & Syme)
Social competence and behavioral symptoms: Child Behavior Checklist (Achenbach & Edelbrock)
Family demographics and resources: FPI and Family Inventory of Resources for Management (FIRM) (McCubbin et al.)
Harmony/disharmony in relationship: Marital Separation/Marital Relationship Protocols
Family coping: Family Coping Orientation for Problem Experiences (F-COPE) (McCubbin, et al.)
Temperament: Dimensions of Temperament Survey-Revised (DOTS-R) (Lerner, et al.), The Middle Childhood Temperament Questionnaire (MCTQ)
Symptoms: Pediatric Symptom Checklist (Jellinek, et al.)

REPRESENTATIVE REFERENCES:

Weigel, C., Wertlieb, D., & Feldstein, M. (1989). Perceptions of control, competence and contingency as influences on the stress-behavior symptom relationship. *Journal of Personality and Social Psychology, 56,* 456-464.

Wertlieb, D., Weigel, C., & Feldstein, M. (1987). Stress, social support and behavior symptoms in middle childhood. *Journal of Clinical Child Psychology, 16,* 204-211.

Wertlieb, D., Weigel, C., & Feldstein, M. (1988). Impact of stress and temperament on children's medical utilization. *Journal of Pediatric Psychology, 13,* 409-421.

Wertlieb, D., Weigel, C., & Feldstein, M. (1989). Stressful experiences, temperament and social support: Impact on children's behavior symptoms. *Journal of Applied Developmental Psychology, 10,* 487-503.

CURRENT STATUS OF THE STUDY:

a. No further waves of data collection are planned.

b. Most data are in machine-readable format.

c. Data are available for secondary analysis from the study contact person.

■ Sierra Project: Longitudinal Study of Character Development in College Students, 1975

Whiteley, John; and Loxley, Janet C.

Contact Person: John Whiteley
Address: Professor of Social Ecology
University of California at Irvine
Program in Social Ecology
Irvine, CA 92717
Telephone No.: (714) 856-6281

SUBSTANTIVE TOPICS COVERED:

The study reviews the longitudinal growth of moral reasoning and ego development in the transition from late adolescence to young adulthood; impact of a curriculum designed to raise the level of character development in college students; relationship of college experience and moral reasoning in college to moral reasoning in young adulthood, and the relationship between moral reasoning and moral action.

CHARACTERISTICS OF THE ORIGINAL SAMPLE:

Year the study began: 1975

Subject selection process: Freshmen who entered the University of California at Irvine in the fall of 1975

Total number of subjects at Time 1: N = 48

Ages at Time 1: 17-18 yrs.

Sex distribution: Approximately equal numbers of females and males throughout

Socioeconomic status: Information is unavailable.

Race/ethnicity: 25% African-American, 25% white, 25% Hispanic, 25% Asian-American

Years of Completed Waves:

Years	N=	Age ranges
Class of 1979:		
Cohort 1: Sierra Hall Residents (Experimental Group)		
1975-1976	48	17-18 yrs.
1976-1977	34	18-19 yrs.
1977-1978	12	19-20 yrs.
1978-1979	6	20-21 yrs.
Cohort 2: Control Group I (Lago Hall Residents)		
1975-1976	51	17-18 yrs.
1976-1977	12	18-19 yrs.
1977-1978	0	19-20 yrs.
1978-1979	0	20-21 yrs.
Cohort 3: Control Group II (Random Control)		
1975-1976	22	17-18 yrs.
Class of 1980:		
Cohort 4: Sierra Hall Residents (Experimental Group)		
1976-1977	47	17-18 yrs.
1977-1978	27	18-19 yrs.
1978-1979	28	19-20 yrs.
1979-1980	30	20-21 yrs.
Cohort 5: Control Group I (Lago Hall Residents)		
1976-1977	43	17-18 yrs.
1977-1978	15	18-19 yrs.
1978-1979	13	19-20 yrs.
1979-1980	12	20-21 yrs.
Cohort 6: Control Group II (Random Control)		
1976-1977	46	17-18 yrs.
1977-1978	46	18-19 yrs.
1978-1979	46	19-20 yrs.
1979-1980	27	20-21 yrs.
Class of 1981:		
Cohort 7: Sierra Hall Residents (Experimental Group)		
1977-1978	43	17-18 yrs.
1978-1979	25	18-19 yrs.
1979-1980	28	19-20 yrs.
1980-1981	28	20-21 yrs.
Cohort 8: Control Group I (Lago Hall Residents)		
1977-1978	42	17-18 yrs.
1978-1979	17	18-19 yrs.
1979-1980	15	19-20 yrs.
1980-1981	22	20-21 yrs.
Cohort 9: Control Group II (Random Control)		
1977-1978	32	17-18 yrs.
1978-1979	63	18-19 yrs.
1979-1980	23	19-20 yrs.
1980-1981	19	20-21 yrs.
Class of 1982:		
Cohort 10: Sierra Hall Residents (Experimental Group)		
1978-1979	46	17-18 yrs.
1979-1980	31	18-19 yrs.

Years of Completed Waves, Continued:

Years	N=	Age ranges
1980-1981	32	19-20 yrs.
1981-1982	21	20-21 yrs.
Cohort 11: Control Group I (Lago Hall Residents)		
1978-1979	34	17-18 yrs.
1979-1980	20	18-19 yrs.
1980-1981	26	19-20 yrs.
1981-1982	16	20-21 yrs.
Cohort 12: Control Group II (Random Control)		
1978-1979	33	17-18 yrs.
1979-1980	26	18-19 yrs.
1980-1981	22	19-20 yrs.
1981-1982	18	20-21 yrs.

INFORMATION ON SAMPLE ATTRITION:

During the 7-year period of study, 266 of 465 Ss (57.2%) across 11 cohorts were not retrieved for further study. Sample attrition ranged from 34.9% (Cohort 7) to 100% (Cohort 2). Reasons for sample attrition included Ss who dropped out of the study by refusing to be retested. The core sample consists of 221 Ss across 12 cohorts.

CONSTRUCTS MEASURED: INSTRUMENTS USED

Moral reasoning: Moral Judgment Interview (Kohlberg), Defining Issues Test (Rest)

Ego development: Washington University Sentence Completion Test (Loevinger)

Locus of control: Rotter Internal-External Locus of Control Scale

Psychological sense of community: Environmental Assessment Inventory, Keniston Alienation Scale

Self-esteem: Janis and Field Personality Questionnaire

Attitude toward people: Environmental Assessment Inventory ("People in General" subscale)

Sex Role Inventory: Bem Sex Role Inventory

Participant information: Background questionnaire

Student experience of college: College Experience Questionnaire

REPRESENTATIVE REFERENCES:

Loxley, J. C., & Whiteley, J. M. (1986). *Character development in college students: Vol. II. The curriculum and longitudinal results.* Schenectady, NY: Character Research Press.

Whiteley, J. M. (1980). Evaluation of character development in an undergraduate residential community. In L. Kuhmerker, M. Mentkowski, & V. L. Erickson (Eds.), *Evaluating moral development.* Schenectady, NY: Character Research Press.

Whiteley, J. M. (1982). *Character development in college students: Vol I. The freshman year.* Schenectady, NY: Character Research Press.

Whiteley, J. M., & Yokata, N. (1988). *Character development in the freshman year and our four years of undergraduate study.* Research Monograph I, Center for the Study of the Freshman Year Experience, University of South Carolina.

CURRENT STATUS OF THE STUDY:

a. Further waves of data collection are planned.

b. Most of the data are in machine-readable format.

c. Data are available for secondary analysis from the study contact person.

■ Child Custody Research Project, 1980

Wolman, Richard; and Taylor, Keith

Contact Person: Richard Wolman/Keith Taylor
Address: 59 Church Street
                 Cambridge, MA 02138
Telephone No.:   (617) 492-4619

SUBSTANTIVE TOPICS COVERED:

The Child Custody Research Project examines the psychological aspects of child custody contests. The aim is to illuminate the psychological issues intrinsic to child custody litigation.

CHARACTERISTICS OF THE ORIGINAL SAMPLE:

Year the study began: 1980

Subject selection process: Each participating family was selected from among cases filed to the Probate Court of Middlesex County, Massachusetts. Families were recruited as close as possible to the time of marital separation, with an outside limit of 6 months.

Total number of subjects at Time 1: N = 43 divorced families[1]

Ages at Time 1: Infancy-18 yrs. (children), 34 yrs. mean (parents)

Sex distribution: Approximately equal numbers of females and males throughout

Socioeconomic status: 50% middle/upper middle class, 40% working class, 10% poverty class

Race/ethnicity: 100% white

Comments:

1. Twenty-seven families involved in a custody dispute and 16 families settling issues of custody out of court.

Years of Completed Waves:

Years	N=	Age ranges
(Cohort 1: Parents)		
1980-1981[a]	85	34 yrs. (mean)
1981-1982[b]	85	35 yrs.
(Cohort 2: Children)		
1980-1981	95	Infancy-18 yrs.
1981-1982[b]	95	Infancy-19 yrs.

Comments:
a. After the initial interview and testing, at 3-month intervals during the first year, parents were contacted by telephone for follow-up interviews. At the 2-year point, child and adult subjects were reinterviewed, and baseline measures were replicated.
b. In addition to the assessment of the parents and children, parents' attorneys and children's pediatricians, teachers, day-care providers, and therapists also were administered questionnaires.

INFORMATION ON SAMPLE ATTRITION:

During the 2-year period of study, all (100%) 180 Ss (43 families) were retrieved for further study. The core sample consists of 180 Ss (95 children and 85 parents).

CONSTRUCTS MEASURED: INSTRUMENTS USED

Subjective report of custody experience: Interview
Self-esteem: Coopersmith Self-Esteem Inventory
Locus of control: Nowicki Strickland Locus of Control Scale for Children
Trust: Imber Trust Scale (Imber)
Anxiety-Separation: Separation Anxiety Test (Hansburg)
Fears, phobias, general anxiety: Croake Hinkle Fear Schedule (Checklist of children's fears)
Parent-child relationship: Swanson Parent-Child Relationship Questionnaire
Life Stress Events: Holmes & Rhae Social Readjustment Rating Scale (Holmes & Rhae)
Ego strength: Ego Strength Scale of the Minnesota Multiphasic Personality Inventory (Barron)
Behavior of child: Missouri Child Behavior Checklist (Sines et al.)
Child's perception of divorce/custody: Child Custody Research Project-developed Parent Perception, questionnaire
Relationship between client and attorney: Client-Attorney Relationship Questionnaire
Child's perception of family functioning: Family Concept Test (Van der Veen)
Role differentiation in parents vis-a-vis child rearing and perception: Experimental Test of interspousal role differentiation
Academic behavior/performance: Teacher Rating Questionnaire (Wyman & Wright)

REPRESENTATIVE REFERENCES:

Wolman, R., & Taylor, K. (1982). Child custody disputes: Psychological aspects and implications for policy change. Presented at *Divorce: From problem to opportunity,* symposium conducted before the Society for the Psychological Study of Social Issues, at the annual meeting of the American Psychological Association, Washington, D. C.

Wolman, R., & Taylor, K. (1990). *Effects of custody dispute on children.* Presentation to the American Psychological Association Annual Meeting, Boston, Massachusetts.

Wolman, R., Taylor, K., Sander, F., McGovern, S., and Weiss, R. (1980). *Child custody: Psychology on trial.* Presented at the annual meeting of the American Psychological Association, Montreal.

CURRENT STATUS OF THE STUDY:

a. Further waves of data collection are planned.
b. Most of the data are in machine-readable format.
c. Data are available for secondary analysis through the study contact person.

■ University of Rochester Child and Family Study, 1972

Wynne, Lyman; and Cole, Robert

Contact Person: Lyman Wynne
Address: Department of Psychiatry
                University of Rochester Medical Center
                300 Crittenden Boulevard
                Rochester, NY 14642
Telephone No.: (716) 275-5889

SUBSTANTIVE TOPICS COVERED:

The study examines children in relation to their families, regarding differences in parental mental disorder and psychiatric assessment; family communication and relationship patterns; and child's psychological functioning and school competence. These variables are studied in relation to one another to obtain predictive outcomes. The study emphasizes family interactions.

CHARACTERISTICS OF THE ORIGINAL SAMPLE:

Year the study began: 1972
Subject selection process: Families were selected by the following criteria: family intact and all members living together, one parent hospitalized for functional psychiatric disorders, and one son age 4, 7, or 10 years. Selection of parents was based on hospital records. The homogeneity of the sample was emphasized.

Total number of subjects at Time 1: N = 278
Ages at Time 1: 4-10 yrs.
Sex distribution: 100% male (child cohorts); predominantly female (parent cohorts)
Socioeconomic status: 50% middle class, 50% working class (approximately)
Race/ethnicity: 100% white

Years of Completed Waves:

Years	N=	Age ranges
(Cohort 1A: 4-Year-Olds)		
1972-1975	38	4 yrs.
1976-1980	26	7 yrs.
(Cohort 1B: Parents of 4-Year-Olds)		
1972-1975	28	24-50 yrs.
1976	26	27-50 yrs.
(Cohort 2A: 7-Year-Olds)		
1972-1975	45	7 yrs.
1976	38	10 yrs.
(Cohort 2B: Parents of 7-Year-Olds)		
1972-1975	45	mid-20s-50s
1976	38	mid-20s-50s
(Cohort 3A: 10-Year-Olds)		
1972-1975	61	10 yrs.
1976	44	13 yrs.
(Cohort 3B: Parents of 10-Year-Olds)		
1972-1975	61	early 30s-early 60s
1976	44	

INFORMATION ON SAMPLE ATTRITION:

During the 3-year period of study, 62 of 278 Ss (22.3%), across six cohorts, were not retrieved for further study. The core sample consists of 216 Ss across all six cohorts. Attrition within each cohort ranged from 7.1% (Cohort 1B) to 31.6% (Cohort 1A).

CONSTRUCTS MEASURED: INSTRUMENTS USED

Diagnostic typologies: Structured interviews (modified PSE), semi-structured interviews

Clinical assessment of individual parental functioning (severity and chronicity), psychosis; schizophrenic, paranoid schizophrenic, and paranoid symptom dimensions; affectivity and emotional expressivity dimensions, work and social functioning: Global Assessment Scale, dichotomized ratings of 59 clinical variables from videotaped interviews

Thought disorder and developmental level: Rorschach Ink Blot Test

Field dependence and independence: Rod and Frame Test

Intellectual functioning: Wechsler Adult Intelligence Scale

Psychophysical reactions: Pendulum eye tracking

Personality functioning: Minnesota Multiphasic Personality Inventory

Latency of deviance of associations: Goldstein Word Associations Test

Affective and cognitive functions: Gottschalk 5-minute speech sample

Historical assessment (premorbid adjustment and general historical information): Ratings of parents; medical, psychomotor, and developmental history of each parent

Communicative, cognitive, and attentional variables: deviant/healthy communications; acknowledgement code; who-to-whom patterns; focus on speech codes; agreement/disagreement codes; laughter codes; interruption/simultaneous speech codes; family clean-up procedure: Videotaped Family Interaction Task

Family consensus: Individual parental Rorschach Ink Blot Test; individual parental Thematic Apperception Test; spouse consensus Rorschach Ink Blot Test; family Rorschach Ink Blot Test; family plan-something-together task

Interpersonal warmth: Family Free Play

Positive/negative family relationship: Consensus procedures

Anger and other affective states: Individual Rorschach Ink Blot Test

Affective attributions: Thematic Apperception Test

Object relations schema: Self-rating Scale

Balance, activity, and hierarchy in family free play: Index of parent-parent-child triad observations

Couple Rorschach Ink Blot Test: Spouse Consensus

Referential communication: Referential Communication Task

Extra-familial context, supports provided by extended family, social class, ethnic and religious affiliation, community and neighborhood social network, and accessibility of helping agencies: Semistructured Interview

Historical variables, family history, medical illness, and pedigree data: Chart reviews, structured and semistructured interviews

Stages of family life cycle at times of parental episodes of illness, family rally versus disturbance in response to impact of parental illness: Structured Interview (social history)

Perceptions of child in school: Peer and teacher ratings

Perceptions of child by parent: Rochester Adaptive Behavior Interview (RABI): global ratings and quantification of item ratings

Perceptions of child by health professionals: Obstetrical, neurological, psychophysiological information: for example, cortical evoked responses, pendulum eye tracking, and autonomic functioning

Intelligence: Wechsler Intelligence Scale for Children

Projective, cognitive, and achievement factors: Rorschach Ink Blot Test, Thematic Apperception Test, Human Figure Drawing, Wechsler Reading Achievement Test, Bender Tests

Censure-praise assessment: Galvanic Skin Response

Attentional measures: Auditory and visual scanning and sensory integration

Clinical psychiatric assessment: Diagnostic typologies, global competence evaluations, Q-Sort evaluation

REPRESENTATIVE REFERENCES:

Baldwin, A. L., Cole, R. E., & Baldwin, C. P. (1982). Parental pathology, family interaction, and the competence of the child in school. *Monographs of the Society for Research in Child Development, 47*(6).

Stierlin, H., & Wynne, L. C., & Wirshing, M. (Eds.). (1983). *Psychosocial intervention in schizophrenia: An international view.* New York/Berlin: Springer-Verlag.

Wynne, L. C., & Cole, R. E. (1983). The Rochester Risk Research Program: A new look at parental diagnoses and family relationships. In H. Stierlin, L. C. Wynne, & M. Wirsching (Eds.), *Psychosocial intervention in schizophrenia: An international view* (pp. 25-48). New York/Berlin: Springer-Verlag.

Wynne, L. C., Cole, R. E., & Perkins, D. (1987). University of Rochester Child and Family Study: Risk research in progress. *Schizophrenia Bulletin, 13*(3), 463-476.

CURRENT STATUS OF THE STUDY:

a. Further waves of data collection are planned.

b. The data are in machine-readable format.

c. The data are conditionally available for secondary analysis.

Z

National Survey of Children, 1976

Zill, Nicholas; Peterson, James; and Furstenberg, Frank F., Jr.

Contact Person: Nicholas Zill
Address: Child Trends, Inc.
                 2100 M Street, N.W., Suite 610
                 Washington, DC 20037
Telephone No.:   (202) 223-6288

SUBSTANTIVE TOPICS COVERED:

The study examines the quality of life of U.S. children with regard to physical, social, and psychological well-being; academic achievement, and attitudes; and parents' quality of life with regard to marital histories, well-being, attitudes, and aspirations for children. Follow-up focused on the effects of marital disruption and changing family structure on children's well-being.

CHARACTERISTICS OF THE ORIGINAL SAMPLE:

Year the study began: 1976-1977
Subject selection process: Subjects were selected by a multistage stratified probability sampling of households, in the continental United States, containing at least one child age 7-11 years. (Up to two children in a household could be interviewed.)
Total number of subjects at Time 1: N = 2,301
Ages at Time 1: 7-11 yrs.
Sex distribution: Approximately equal numbers of females and males throughout
Socioeconomic status: Information was not available.
Race/ethnicity: 76.2% white, 21.7% African-American, 1.7% Hispanic, and 0.4% Asian-American

Years of Completed Waves:

Years	N=	Age ranges
1976-1977	2,301	7-11 yrs.
1981[a]	1,423	11-16 yrs.
1987	1,140[b]	17-22 yrs.

Comments:
a. Of children in families that had experienced a mental disruption at the time of the 1976-1977 survey, whose parents had previously reported a high-conflict of marriage, a randomly selected subsample participated in the follow-up study.
b. A subsample of 900 parents was also followed-up in 1987.

538

INFORMATION ON SAMPLE ATTRITION:

A subsample of subjects from "high-conflict" families was followed up between 1981 and 1987, during which time 283 of 1,423 Ss (19.9%) were not retrieved for further study. The core sample consists of 1,140 Ss.

CONSTRUCTS MEASURED: INSTRUMENTS USED

Quality of children's life, child health, well-being, academic achievements, attitudes, peer relations, and school behaviors: Parent-child questionnaire, personal interview with parent about child

Quality of parent's life, marital histories, well-being, attitudes, and aspirations for children, family history and demographics: Parent background questionnaire (personal interview)

Contact with absent parent; how child felt about absent parent; relationship with parent with whom the child lives; and self-perception: Child questionnaire (personal interview with child)

Pupil academic achievement; relationship with teacher; pupil's class standing; peer relations, ability to work independently; teacher's educational background: Teacher questionnaire (self-administered)

REPRESENTATIVE REFERENCES:

Furstenberg, F. F. Jr., Nord, C. W., Peterson, J. L., & Zill, N. (1983). The life course of children of divorce: Marital disruption and parental contact. *American Sociological Review, 48*(5), 656-668.

Moore, K., Nord, C., Peterson, J. (1989). Nonvoluntary sexual activity among adolescents. *Family Planning Perspectives, 21*(3), 110-114.

Peterson, J. L., & Zill, N. (1986). Marital disruption, parent-child relationships and behavior problems in children. *Journal of Marriage and the Family, 48*(2), 295-307.

Zill, N., & Peterson, J. L. (1982). Learning to do things without help. In L. Laosa & I. Siegel (Eds.), *Families as learning environments for children.* New York: Plenum.

CURRENT STATUS OF THE STUDY:

a. No further waves of data collection are planned.
b. The data are in machine-readable format.
c. The data are available for secondary analysis through the study contact person.

■ Socializing Attention: Transmitting Cultural Knowledge at Home and at School, 1988

Zukow, Patricia Goldring

Contact Person: Patricia Goldring Zukow
Address: Department of Psychology
University of California at Los Angeles
Los Angeles, CA 90024-1563
Telephone No.: (213) 206-3534

SUBSTANTIVE TOPICS COVERED:

This study examines how caregiver input facilitates the emergence of language by the use of gesture and attention-directing to differentiate the relation between words and world. In addition, the study compares and contrasts white and Hispanic samples, to pinpoint potential sources of communicative mismatch between home and school that may affect competence at school.

CHARACTERISTICS OF THE ORIGINAL SAMPLE:

Year the study began: 1988
Subject selection process: Ss were selected from birth announcements in local newspaper; through neighborhood school for Hispanic sample.
Total number of subjects at Time 1: N = 6 (caregiver-child pairs)
Ages at Time 1: 6 mos.
Sex distribution: Equal numbers of females and males throughout
Socioeconomic status: 100% middle/upper middle class (Cohort 1); 100% poverty class (Cohort 2)
Race/ethnicity: 100% white (Cohort 1); 100% Hispanic (Cohort 2)

Years of Completed Waves:

Years	N=	Age ranges
(Cohort 1: White Ss)		
1988	6	6 mos.
1988	6	7 mos.
1988	6	9 mos.
1988	6	10 mos.
1988	6	11 mos.
1988	6	1 yr.
1988	6	13 mos.
1988	6	14 mos.
1988	6	15 mos.
1988	6	16 mos.
1988	6	17 mos.

Years of Completed Waves, Continued:

Years	N=	Age ranges
1989	6	18 mos.
1989	6	19 mos.
1989	6	20 mos.
1989	6	21 mos.
1989	6	22 mos.
1989	5	23 mos.
1989	5	2 yrs.
1989	5	25 mos.
1989	5	26 mos.
1989	5	27 mos.
1989	5	28 mos.
1989	5	29 mos.
1990	5	30 mos.
(Cohort 2: Hispanic Ss)[a]		
1990	6	6 mos.

Comments:
a. Data collection for Cohort 2 is in process.

INFORMATION ON SAMPLE ATTRITION:

During the 2-year period of study for Cohort 1, 1 of 6 Ss (16.7%) was not re-trieved for further study. The core sample consists of 5 Ss. Attrition was due to one family moving out of state.

CONSTRUCTS MEASURED: INSTRUMENTS USED

Cognitive development: Bayley Scales of Infant Development
Grammatical development: Grammatical Development Questionnaire (Bates)
Early language development: Early Language Inventory (Bates)
Early lexicon: Word Production Checklist (Reznick & Goldsmith)
Caregiver beliefs regarding child development and child-rearing: Zukow Folk The-ory of Child-rearing and Child Development Interview
Mother-infant interaction: Videotape (20 minutes every month)
Solitary play: Videotape (10 minutes every month)
Semantic functions, early lexicon: Child language diary (Zukow, Reilly, & Green-field)
Lexicon development: Field notes (Zukow)

REPRESENTATIVE REFERENCES:

Manuscripts are in process.

CURRENT STATUS OF THE STUDY:

a. No further waves of data collection are planned at this time.
b. Most of the data are in machine-readable format.
c. Data will eventually be available for secondary analysis from the study contact person.

List of Data Sets by Author

Achenbach, Thomas M.; and Howell, Catherine T.: Vermont Infant Studies Project, 1980

Achenbach, Thomas M.; Conners, C. Keith; Howell, Catherine T.; McConaughy, Stephanie H.; and Quay, Herbert C.: The National Survey of Children and Youth, 1986

Ainsworth, Mary: Baltimore Longitudinal Study of Attachment, 1963

Alwin, Duane F.; Cohen, Ronald L.; and Newcomb, Theodore (deceased): Bennington Studies of Persistence and Change in Attitudes and Values, 1935

Anderson, John E. (deceased); Harris, Dale B.; and Deno, Evelyn: Minnesota Child to Adult Study, 1925

Angrist, Shirley S.; and Almquist, Elizabeth: Role Outlook Survey, 1964

Anthony, E. James; and Worland, Julien: St. Louis Risk Research Project, 1967

Astin, A. W.: The Cooperative Institutional Research Program (CIRP), 1966

Atchley, Robert: Impact of Retirement on Adjustment to Aging, 1975

Azuma, Hiroshi; and Hess, Robert D. (retired): Family Influences on School Readiness and Achievement in Japan and the United States, 1973

Bachman, Jerald G.: Youth in Transition, 1966

Bailey, Susan; Burrell, Barbara; and Ware, Norma: Concentration Choice Study, 1978

Barnett, Rosalind; Baruch, Grace (deceased); and Marshall, Nancy L.: Longitudinal Study of the Occupational Stress and Health of Women Licensed Practical Nurses and Licensed Social Workers, 1985

Bates, Elizabeth; and Bretherton, Inge: Symbolic Development, 1978

Baumrind, Diana: Family Socialization and Developmental Competence Project, 1968

Bell, Richard Q.; Ryder, Robert G.; and Halverson, Charles F., Jr.: Bethesda Longitudinal Study of Early Child and Family Development, 1964

Bengtson, Vern L.; and Gatz, Margaret: Longitudinal Study of Three-Generation Families, 1971

Berger, Alan S.; and Gagnon, John H.: High School to College Transition Study, 1970

Block, Jack; and Block, Jeanne H. (deceased): A Longitudinal Study of Ego and Cognitive Development, 1968

Bossé, Raymond; Vokonas, Pantel; and Aldwin, Carolyn M.: The Veterans Administration Normative Aging Study (NAS), 1963

Britton, Joseph H.; and Britton, Jean O.: Personality Changes in Aging: A Longitudinal Study of Community Residents, 1955
Broman, Sarah: The Collaborative Perinatal Project (NCPP), 1959
Brown, Donald R.: The Inteflex Longitudinal Study of Medical Students, 1972
Brown, Donald R.; Sanford, Nevitt; and Freedman, Mervin: Vassar Longitudinal Study, 1954
Brown, Roger; Bellugi, Ursula; and Fraser, Colin: A First Language, 1962
Brunswick, Ann F.: The Harlem Longitudinal Study of Black Youth, 1968
Busse, Ewald W.; Siegler, Ilene C.; George, Linda; Palmore, Erdman; Maddox, George L.; and Nowlin, John B.: Duke Adaptation Study (Duke Second Longitudinal Study), 1968
Butler, Edgar W.; and Schuster, Tonya L.: Riverside Community Research Project, 1963
Castelli, William P.; and Feinleib, Manning: Framingham Heart Study, 1949
Chester, Nia L.: Coping with Early Parenthood, 1979
Cicchetti, Dante; and Rizley, Ross: Harvard Child Maltreatment Project, 1979
Clarke-Stewart, Alison: Chicago Study of Child Care and Development, 1976
Clausen, John A.; Jones, Harold E. (deceased); Jones, Mary C. (deceased); and Stolz, Herbert: Oakland Growth Study (O), 1931
Cohen, Donald J.; and Dibble, Eleanor D.: Personality Development in Monozygotic Twins: A Longitudinal Study, 1967
Cohen, Sarale E.; Sigman, Marian; Beckwith, Leila; and Parmelee, Arthur H.: Early Identification of Later Developmental Problems, 1971
Coie, John D.; and Dodge, Kenneth A.: Longitudinal Study of Social Status in Elementary School Children, 1975
Colby, Anne; Kohlberg, Lawrence (deceased); Gibbs, John; and Lieberman, Marcus: Longitudinal Study of Moral Development, 1955
Connolly, James J.; and Kelly, E. Lowell (deceased): Kelly Longitudinal Study, 1935
Crandall, Virginia C.; and Roche, Alexander F.: Fels Longitudinal Study of Human Growth and Development, 1929
Cutler, Stephen J.: Oberlin Longitudinal Survey, 1970
Davis, James A.; Spaeth, Joe L.; and Greeley, Andrew M.: Career Plans and Experiences of June 1961 College Graduates, 1961
DeFries, John C.; Plomin, Robert; and Fulkes, David W.: Colorado Adoption Project, 1976
Dornbusch, Sanford M.; and Leiderman, P. Herbert: Families, Peers and Schools, 1987
Earls, Felton; and Garrison, William: Epidemiologic Study of Behavior Problems in Children, 1977
Earls, Felton; Robins, Lee; and Stiffman, Arlene: Adolescent Health Care Evaluation Study, 1984
Eder, Donna: Early Adolescent Peer Culture and Peer Relations, 1984
Egeland, Byron; and Sroufe, Alan: Mother-Child Research Project, 1975
Eichorn, Dorothy H. (retired); Bayley, Nancy (retired); Wolff, Lotte V. (deceased): Berkeley Growth Study (B), 1928

Eisenberg, Nancy: Longitudinal Study of Prosocial Development, 1977

Elias, Marjorie: Infant Care Project, 1981

Entwisle, Doris; and Alexander, Karl: The Beginning School Study, 1982

Entwisle, Doris R.; and Hayduk, Leslie A.: Early Schooling, 1971

Epstein, Joyce: Longitudinal Study of School and Family Effects, 1973

Erlenmeyer-Kimling, L.: The New York High-Risk Project, 1971

Fanshel, David: Indian Adoption Project, 1960

Fanshel, David: Columbia University Longitudinal Study: Children in Foster Care, 1966

Fiske, Marjorie L.; Thurnher, Majda; and Chiriboga, David: The Longitudinal Study of Transitions in Four Stages of Life, 1969

Fozard, James L.; and Andres, Reuben: Baltimore Longitudinal Study of Aging (BLSA), 1958

Furstenberg, Frank F., Jr.; and Brooks-Gunn, Jeanne: The Baltimore Study: Adolescent Parenthood and the Transmission of Social Disadvantage, 1966

Furstenberg, Frank F., Jr.; and Spanier, Graham B.: The Central Pennsylvania Study, 1977

Gardner, Howard; and Wolf, Dennie: Early Symbolization Project, 1974

Ginzberg, Eli; and Yohalem, Alice: Lifestyles of Educated Women, 1961

Glueck, Sheldon (deceased); and Glueck, Eleanor (deceased): The Massachusetts Reformatory Study, 1911

Glueck, Sheldon (deceased); and Glueck, Eleanor (deceased): The Women's Reformatory Study, 1920

Goldstein, Michael J.: The UCLA High-Risk Project, 1964

Goudy, Willis J.; Keith, Patricia M.; and Powers, Edward A.: Iowa Older-Workers Panel Study, 1964

Granick, Samuel; Birren, James E.; and Kleban, Morton H.: National Institute of Mental Health Study, 1957

Gray, Susan; and Klaus, Rupert: The Early Training Project, 1961

Green, Bonnie L.; Grace, Mary C.; Lindy, Jacob D.; and Gleser, Goldine C.: Longitudinal Study of the Psychosocial Effects of Disaster: Buffalo Creek Survivors in the Second Decade, 1973

Greenberg, Mark T.; and Crnic, Keith: Mother-Infant Project, 1980

Grossman, Frances K.: Pregnancy and Parenthood Project, 1975

Gurin, Gerald: Michigan Student Study: A Study of Students in a Multiversity, 1962

Hall, Vernon; and Kaye, Daniel: Early Patterns of Cognitive Development, 1973

Harding, Courtenay M.; Brooks, George W.; Ashikaga, Takamaru; Strauss, John S.; and Breier, Alan: The Vermont Longitudinal Research Project, 1955

Hastorf, Albert H.; Horowitz, Leonard; Holahan, Carol K.; Sears, Robert R. (deceased); Sears, Pauline; Cronbach, Lee; and Terman, Lewis: Terman Life Cycle Study of Children with High Ability, 1921

Hauser, Stuart T.; Powers, Sally; Jacobson, Alan; and Noam, Gil G.: Adolescence and Family Development Project, 1978

Heath, Douglas H.: The Study of Adult Development, 1960s

Helson, Ravenna: Mills Longitudinal Study, 1958

Herrenkohl, Roy C.; and Herrenkohl, Ellen C.: A Longitudinal Study of the Conse-
quences of Child Abuse, 1975
Hertzig, Margaret E.: Longitudinal Study of Temperament in Low Birthweight of
Infants, 1963
Hetherington, E. Mavis; and Clingempeel, Glen: Longitudinal Study of Adaptation
to Remarriage in Stepfamilies, 1980
Hetherington, E. Mavis; Cox, Martha; and Cox, Roger: Virginia Longitudinal
Study of Divorce, 1971
Higgins, Millicent W.; Ostrander, Leon D., Jr.; Monto, Arnold S.; Garn, Stanley
M.; Harburg, Ernest; House, James S.; Metzner, Helen L.; and Sing, Charles
F.: The Tecumseh, Michigan, Community Health Study, 1957
Holtzman, Wayne; and Diaz-Guerrero, R.: Austin-Mexico City Project, 1962
Howard, Ann; and Bray, Douglas W.: The AT&T Longitudinal Studies of Manag-
ers: Management Progress Study (MPS), 1956
Howard, Ann; and Bray, Douglas W.: The AT&T Longitudinal Studies of Manag-
ers: Management Continuity Study (MCS), 1977
Huesmann, L. Rowell; and Eron, Leonard D.: Development of Aggressive Behav-
ior, 1960
Huessy, Hans R.: Prospective Study of 500 Second Graders, 1965
Huffine, Carol; Honzik, Marjorie; and Macfarlane, Jean W. (deceased): Guidance
Study (G), 1928
Huston, Ted; McHale, Susan; and Crouter, Ann: Longitudinal Study of Family Re-
lationships, 1981
Irelan, Lola M.: Retirement History Study (RHS), 1969
Jacklin, Carol Nagy; and Maccoby, Eleanor: Stanford Longitudinal Study, 1973
Jarvik, Lissy F.: Longitudinal Study of Aging Human Twins, 1947
Jenkins, Shirley; and Norman, Elaine: Columbia University Longitudinal Study:
Family Welfare Research Program—Mothers View Foster Care, 1966
Jennings, M. Kent: Youth-Parent Socialization Panel Study, 1965
Jessor, Richard; and Jessor, Lee: The Socialization of Problem Behavior in Youth,
1969
Johnson, Dale L.: Houston Parent-Child Development Center Project, 1970
Johnston, Lloyd D.; Bachman, Jerald G.; and O'Malley, Patrick: Monitoring the
Future: A Continuing Study of Lifestyles and Values of Youth, 1976
Jordan, Thomas E.: St. Louis Baby Study, 1966
Juster, F. Thomas; Hill, Martha; and Stafford, Frank: Time Allocation Study, 1975
Kandel, Denise: Intergenerational Transmission of Deviance, 1971
Kaplan, George: Alameda County Human Population Laboratory Study, 1965
Kellam, Sheppard; Ensminger, Margaret; and Branch, Jeannette: The Woodlawn
Mental Health Longitudinal Community Epidemiological Project, 1963
Keogh, Barbara; and Bernheimer, Lucinda: Project REACH Longitudinal Study,
1977
Klag, Michael J.: The Precursors Study, 1947
Kovacs, Maria: Childhood Depression: Nosologic Developmental Aspects, 1978
Kraus, Philip E.: Longitudinal Study of Children from Kindergarten into the Adult
Years, 1953

Kuhn, Deanna: Patterns of Concrete Operational Development, 1971

Labouvie, Erich; and Pandina, Robert: Rutgers Health and Human Development Project, 1979

Langner, Thomas S.: The Family Research Project, 1966

Laosa, Luis M.: Early Environmental Experience Study, 1978

Leiderman, P. H.; and Wald, M. S.: The Impact of Home Placement Versus Foster Care, 1978

Leon, Gloria; Murray, David; and Keys, Ancel: Cardiovascular Disease Project at the University of Minnesota, 1947

Lewis, Michael: Longitudinal Study of Cognitive, Social and Affective Development, 1974

Lipsitt, Lewis P.; Buka, Stephen L., and Tsuang, Ming T.: The Collaborative Perinatal Project: Providence Site, 1959

Loney, Jan; Paternite, Carl E.; and Langhorne, John E., Jr.: The Iowa HABIT Project, 1967

Lytton, Hugh; Watts, Denise; and Dunn, Bruce E.: Longitudinal Study of the Socialization and Development of Twin Boys, 1970

Maddox, George L.; Busse, Ewald W.; Siegler, Ilene C.; George, Linda; Palmore, Erdman; and Nowlin, John B.: Duke Longitudinal Study of Aging (Duke First Longitudinal Study), 1955

Malatesta, Carol Zander: Emotional Socialization and Expressive Development in Preterm and Full-Term Infants, 1981

Marini, Margaret Mooney; Temme, Lloyd; and Coleman, James: Transition from Adolescence to Adulthood: Follow-Up Study, 1973

Markman, Howard J.; and Stanley, Scott: The Prediction and Prevention of Marital and Family Distress, 1980

Matheny, Adam P., Jr.; and Wilson, Ronald (deceased): Louisville Twin Study, 1959

Mawardi, Betty Hosmer: Longitudinal Study of Male Medical Students and Alumni, 1935

Mawardi, Betty Hosmer: Longitudinal Study of Male and Female Medical Students and Alumni, 1956

McCammon, Robert; and Tennes, Katherine: Denver Study of Human Development, 1927

McCord, Joan: Cambridge-Somerville Youth Study, 1936

McCune, Lorraine: The Development of Representational Play and Language, 1979

Miller, Louise (deceased); Dyer, Jean; Bizell, Rondell; and Sullivan, Sara: Longitudinal Study of Preschool Programs, 1968

Minde, Klaus K.: Continuities and Discontinuities in the Development of 64 Very Small Premature Infants to 4 Years of Age, 1980

Mitchell, Robert E.: Repatriated Prisoner of War Program, 1974

Mitchell, Robert E.; Graybiel, Ashton; Harlan, William R., Jr.; and Oberman, Albert: Pensacola Study of Naval Aviators, 1940

Morgan, James N.; Duncan, Gregory J.; and Hill, Martha: Panel Study of Income Dynamics (PSID), 1968

Mortimer, Jeylan T.: The Michigan Student Study: Male Follow-Up, 1962

Murray, Henry A. (deceased): Multiform Assessments of Personality Development Among Gifted College Men, 1941

Must, Aviva; Bajema, Carl J.; Johnston, Francis; and Scott, Eugenie C.: Third Harvard Growth Study, 1922

Neimark, Edith D.: Longitudinal Study of the Development of Formal Operations, 1967

Nelson, Katherine: Structure and Strategy in Learning to Talk, 1970

Nesselroade, John; and Baltes, Paul B.: Adolescent Personality Development and Historical Change, 1970

Newcomb, Michael D.; and Bentler, Peter M.: UCLA Study of Adolescent Growth, 1976

Noam, Gil G.: Trajectories of Health and Illness: A Longitudinal Follow-up Study of Child Psychiatric Patients, 1984

Olsen, Randall: National Longitudinal Survey of Youth Labor Market Experience (NLSY), 1979

Olsen, Randall; Parnes, Herbert; Borus, Michael; and Wolpin, Kenneth: National Longitudinal Surveys of Labor Market Experience (NLS), 1965

Olson, David; and Torrance, Nancy: Oral Language Competency and the Acquisition of Literacy Skills, 1979

Otto, Luther B.: Career Development Study, 1966

Patterson, Gerald R.; Reid, John B.; and Dishion, Thomas J.: Understanding and Prediction of Delinquent Child Behavior, 1984

Petersen, Anne C.: Developmental Study of Adolescent Mental Health, 1978

Powers, Edward A.; and Bultena, Gordon L.: Life After 70 in Iowa, 1960

Quinn, Robert P.; Mangione, Thomas W.; and Seashore, Stanley E.: Quality of Employment Survey: Panel Study, 1973

Radin, Norma; Williams, Edith; and Oyserman, Daphna: The Children of Primary Caregiving Fathers: An 11-Year Follow-Up, 1977

Radke-Yarrow, Marian: A Study of Child Rearing and Child Development in Normal Families and Families with Affective Disorders, 1980

Ramey, Craig T.: Carolina Abecedarian Project: Early Adolescent Follow-Up for High Risk Infants, 1972

Ramey, Craig T.: Project CARE: Carolina Approach to Responsive Education, 1977

Reinherz, Helen: Adolescent Research Project, 1976

Rest, James R.: Moral Judgment Development and Life Experience, 1972

Riccobono, John A.; Levinson, Jay R.; and Burkheimer, Graham J.: The National Longitudinal Study of the High School Class of Nineteen Seventy-Two, 1972

Rierdan, Jill E.; and Koff, Elissa: Biopsychosocial Development of Early Adolescent Girls: A Short-Term Longitudinal Study, 1982

Rierdan, Jill E.; and Koff, Elissa: Biopsychosocial Development of Early Adolescent Girls: A Long-Term Longitudinal Study, 1984

Robins, Lee; and O'Neal, Patricia: Deviant Children Grown Up, 1954

Ross, Gail; Lipper, Evelyn; and Auld, Peter A. M.: Longitudinal Follow-Up of Very Low Birthweight Preterm Infants: Neurologic, Cognitive, and Behavioral Outcome, 1978

Rubin, Kenneth H.; and Hymel, Shelley: The Waterloo Longitudinal Project, 1980

Sameroff, Arnold J.; Seifer, Ronald; Zax, Melvin; and Barocas, Ralph: Rochester Longitudinal Study, 1970

Sander, Louis: Boston University Longitudinal Study of Personality Development, 1954

Satz, Paul; Fletcher, Jack; and Morris, Robin: The Florida Longitudinal Project, 1970

Savin-Williams, Ritch C.: The Ecology of Adolescent Self-Esteem, 1978

Scarr, Sandra; and McCartney, Kathleen: An Evaluation of the Verbal Interaction Project in Bermuda, 1978

Schaie, K. Warner: Seattle Longitudinal Study, 1956

Schofield, Janet: Peer Processes in a Newly Desegregated Middle School, 1975

Sears, Robert (deceased); Maccoby, Eleanor E.; and Levin, Henry: Patterns of Child Rearing, 1951

Sewell, William H.; and Hauser, Robert M.: Wisconsin Longitudinal Study of Social and Psychological Factors in Aspiration and Achievements, 1957

Shapiro, Deborah: Columbia University Longitudinal Study: Child Welfare Research Program—Nature of Agency Services, 1966

Shipman, Virginia: The Educational Testing Service Head Start Longitudinal Study (HSLS), 1968

Shireman, Joan F.; and Johnson, Penny R.: The Family Life Project: A Longitudinal Adoption Study, 1970

Sigel, Irving E.; and Cataldo, Christine Z. (deceased): Educating the Young Thinker Program: A Distancing Model, 1970

Simmons, Roberta; and Blyth, Dale: Transition into Adolescence: A Longitudinal Study, 1974

Singer, Dorothy G.; and Singer, Jerome L.: Longitudinal Study of Television, Imagination and Aggression, 1977

Singer, Jerome L.; Singer, Dorothy G.; Desmond, Roger; Hirsch, Bennett; and Nicol, Anne: Longitudinal Study of Family Mediation and Children's Cognition, Aggression, and Comprehension of Television, 1982

Slaughter-Defoe, Diana T.: Early Intervention and Its Effects on Maternal and Child Development, 1973

Speizer, Frank; Willet, Walter; and Colditz, Graham: Nurses' Health Study, (NHSI), 1976

Spencer, Margaret: Personal and Social Adjustment of Minority Status Children, 1978

Spiegelman, Robert G.: The Seattle and Denver Income Maintenance Experiment (SIME/DIME), 1970

Spivack, George: Longitudinal Study of Early Classroom Behaviors and Later Misconduct, 1968

Steel, Lauri; and Wise, Laurie: Project Talent, 1960

Stein, Ruth E. K.; and Jessop, Dorothy Jones: Pediatric Ambulatory Care Treatment Study, 1977

Stewart, Abigail: Longitudinal Study of the Life Patterns of College-Educated Women, 1960

Stewart, Abigail: Experience-Induced Affective Development in Children and Adults, 1976

Strauss, John S.; Carpenter, William; and Bartko, John: International Pilot Study of Schizophrenia: Washington, D.C., Site, 1966

Strauss, John S.; Hisham, Hafez; Lieberman, Paul; Rakfeldt, Jack; and Harding, Courtenay M.: Yale Longitudinal Study, 1978

Streib, Gordon F.: The Cornell Study of Occupational Retirement, 1952

Streissguth, Ann P.; Martin, Donald C.; Martin, Joan C.; Barr, Helen; and Sampson, Paul D.: Seattle Longitudinal Prospective Study on Alcohol and Pregnancy, 1974

Tangri, Sandra S.: Longitudinal Study of Career Development in College-Educated Women, 1967

Thoman, Evelyn B.: Mother-Infant Interaction in Normal and High Risk Infants, 1973

Thomas, Alexander; Chess, Stella; Lerner, Jacqueline; and Lerner, Richard: New York Longitudinal Study, 1956

Thornton, Arland: Study of American Families, 1961

Torrance, E. Paul: Longitudinal Study of Creative Behavior, 1959

Vaillant, George E.: The Grant Study of Adult Development, 1938

Vaillant, George; Glueck, Sheldon (deceased); Glueck, Eleanor (deceased): Crime Causation Study: Unraveling Juvenile Delinquency, 1940

Valadian, Isabelle; Gardner, Jane; Dwyer, Joanna; and Stuart, Harold (deceased): The Stuart Study, 1930

van den Berg, Bea J.; Oechsli, Frank W.; and Christianson, Roberta C.: The California Child Health and Development Studies, 1959

Wallace, Ina;and Escalona, Sibylle K.: Critical Issues in the Development of At-Risk Infants, 1975

Wallerstein, Judith S.: California Children of Divorce Project, 1971

Weikart, David P.; and Schweinhart, Lawrence J.: Ypsilanti Perry Preschool Project, 1962

Weikart, David P.; and Schweinhart, Lawrence J.: Ypsilanti Preschool Curriculum Demonstration Project, 1967

Weinberg, Richard A.; and Scarr, Sandra: Minnesota Transracial Adoption Study, 1973

Weintraub, Sheldon: The Stony Brook High-Risk Project, 1971

Weisner, Thomas; and Eiduson, Bernice (deceased): Child Development in Alternative Family Styles, 1973

Weiss, Robert S.; and Parkes, C. Murray: Harvard Bereavement Study Project, 1966

Werner, Emmy: The Kauai Longitudinal Study, 1955

Wertlieb, Donald L.: Child Stress and Coping Project, 1982

Whiteley, John; and Loxley, Janet C.: Sierra Project: Longitudinal Study of Character Development in College Students, 1975

Wolman, Richard; and Taylor, Keith: Child Custody Research Project, 1980

Wynne, Lyman; and Cole, Robert: University of Rochester Child and Family Study, 1972

Zill, Nicholas; Peterson, James; and Furstenberg, Frank F., Jr.: National Survey of Children, 1976

Zukow, Patricia Goldring: Socializing Attention: Transmitting Cultural Knowledge at Home and at School, 1988

List of Data Sets by Title

Adolescence and Family Development Project, 1978: Stuart T. Hauser, Sally Powers, Alan Jacobson, and Gil G. Noam

Adolescent Health Care Evaluation Study, 1984: Felton Earls, Lee Robins, and Arlene Stiffman

Adolescent Personality Development and Historical Change, 1970: John Nesselroade and Paul B. Baltes

Adolescent Research Project, 1976: Helen Reinherz

Alameda County Human Population Laboratory Study, 1965: George Kaplan

AT&T Longitudinal Studies of Managers: Management Continuity Study (MCS), 1977: Ann Howard and Douglas W. Bray

AT&T Longitudinal Studies of Managers: Management Progress Study (MPS), 1956: Ann Howard and Douglas W. Bray

Austin-Mexico City Project, 1962: Wayne Holtzman and R. Diaz-Guerrero

Baltimore Longitudinal Study of Attachment, 1963: Mary Ainsworth

Baltimore Longitudinal Study of Aging (BLSA), 1958: James L. Fozard and Reuben Andres

Baltimore Study: Adolescent Parenthood and the Transmission of Social Disadvantage, 1966: Frank F. Furstenberg, Jr., and Jeanne Brooks-Gunn

Beginning School Study, 1982: Doris Entwisle and Karl Alexander

Bennington Studies of Persistence and Change in Attitudes and Values, 1935: Duane F. Alwin, Ronald L. Cohen, and Theodore Newcomb (deceased)

Berkeley Growth Study (B), 1928: Dorothy H. Eichorn (retired), Nancy Bayley (retired), and Lotte V. Wolff (deceased)

Bethesda Longitudinal Study of Early Child and Family Development, 1964: Richard Q. Bell, Robert G. Ryder, and Charles F. Halverson, Jr.

Biopsychosocial Development of Early Adolescent Girts: A Long-Term Longitudinal Study, 1984: Jill E. Rierdan and Elissa Koff

Biopsychosocial Development of Early Adolescent Girls: A Short-Term Longitudinal Study, 1982: Jill E. Rierdan and Elissa Koff

Boston University Longitudinal Study of Personality Development, 1954: Louis Sander

California Child Health and Development Studies, 1959: Bea J. van den Berg, Frank W. Oechsli, and Roberta C. Christianson

California Children of Divorce Project, 1971: Judith S. Wallerstein

Cambridge-Somerville Youth Study, 1936: Joan McCord

Cardiovascular Disease Project at the University of Minnesota, 1947: Gloria Leon, David Murray, and Ancel Keys

Career Development Study, 1966: Luther B. Otto

Career Plans and Experiences of June 1961 College Graduates, 1961: James A. Davis, Joe L. Spaeth, and Andrew M. Greeley

Carolina Abecedarian Project: Early Adolescent Follow-Up for High Risk Infants 1972: Craig T. Ramey

Central Pennsylvania Study, 1977: Frank F. Furstenberg, Jr., and Graham B. Spanier

Chicago Study of Child Care and Development, 1976: Alison Clarke-Stewart

Child Custody Research Project, 1980: Richard Wolman and Keith Taylor

Child Development in Alternative Family Styles, 1973: Thomas Weisner and Bernice Eiduson (deceased)

Child Stress and Coping Project, 1982: Donald L. Wertlieb

Childhood Depression: Nosologic Developmental Aspects, 1978: Maria Kovacs

Children of Primary Caregiving Fathers: An 11-Year Follow-Up, 1977: Norma Radin, Edith Williams, and Daphna Oyserman

Collaborative Perinatal Project (NCPP), 1959: Sarah Broman

Collaborative Perinatal Project: Providence Site, 1959: Lewis P. Lipsitt, Stephen L. Buka, and Ming T. Tsuang

Colorado Adoption Project, 1976: John C. DeFries, Robert Plomin, and David W. Fulkes

Columbia University Longitudinal Study: Children in Foster Care, 1966: David Fanshel

Columbia University Longitudinal Study: Child Welfare Research Program—Nature of Agency Services, 1966: Deborah Shapiro

Columbia University Longitudinal Study: Family Welfare Research Program—Mothers View Foster Care, 1966: Shirley Jenkins and Elaine Norman

Concentration Choice Study, 1978: Susan Bailey, Barbara Burrell, and Norma Ware

Continuities and Discontinuities in the Development of 64 Very Small Premature Infants to 4 Years of Age, 1980: Klaus K. Minde

Cooperative Institutional Research Program (CIRP), 1966: A. W. Astin

Coping with Early Parenthood, 1979: Nia L. Chester

Cornell Study of Occupational Retirement, 1952: Gordon F. Streib

Crime Causation Study: Unraveling Juvenile Delinquency, 1940: George Vaillant, Sheldon Glueck (deceased), and Eleanor Glueck (deceased)

Critical Issues in the Development of At-Risk Infants, 1975: Ina Wallace and Sibylle K. Escalona

Denver Study of Human Development, 1927: Robert McCammon and Katherine Tennes

Development of Aggressive Behavior, 1960: L. Rowell Huesmann and Leonard D. Eron

Development of Representational Play and Language, 1979: Lorraine McCune

Developmental Study of Adolescent Mental Health, 1978: Anne C. Petersen

Deviant Children Grown Up, 1954: Lee Robins and Patricia O'Neal

Duke Adaptation Study (Duke Second Longitudinal Study), 1968: Ewald W. Busse, Ilene C. Siegler, Linda George, Erdman Palmore, George L. Maddox, and John B. Nowlin

Duke Longitudinal Study of Aging (Duke First Longitudinal Study), 1955: George L. Maddox, Ewald W. Busse, Ilene C. Siegler, Linda George, Erdman Palmore, and John B. Nowlin

Early Adolescent Peer Culture and Peer Relations, 1984: Donna Eder

Early Environmental Experience Study, 1978: Luis M. Laosa

Early Identification of Later Developmental Problems, 1971: Sarale E. Cohen, Marian Sigman, Leila Beckwith, and Arthur H. Parmalee

Early Intervention and Its Effects on Maternal and Child Development, 1973: Diana T. Slaughter-Defoe

Early Patterns of Cognitive Development, 1973: Vernon Hall and Daniel Kaye

Early Schooling, 1971: Doris R. Entwisle and Leslie A. Hayduk

Early Symbolization Project, 1974: Howard Gardner and Dennie Wolf

Early Training Project, 1961: Susan Gray and Rupert Klaus

Ecology of Adolescent Self-Esteem, 1978: Ritch C. Savin-Williams

Educating the Young Thinker Program: A Distancing Model, 1970: Irving E. Sigel and Christine Z. Cataldo (deceased)

Educational Testing Service Head Start Longitudinal Study (HSLS), 1968: Virginia Shipman

Emotional Socialization and Expressive Development in Preterm and Full-Term Infants, 1981: Carol Zander Malatesta

Epidemiologic Study of Behavior Problems in Children, 1977: Felton Earls and William Garrison

Evaluation of the Verbal Interaction Project in Bermuda, 1978: Sandra Scarr and Kathleen McCartney

Experience-Induced Affective Development in Children and Adults, 1976: Abigail Stewart

Families, Peers and Schools, 1987: Sanford M. Dornbusch and P. Herbert Leiderman

Family Influences on School Readiness and Achievement in Japan and the United States 1973: Hiroshi Azuma and Robert D. Hess (retired)

Family Life Project: A Longitudinal Adoption Study, 1970: Joan F. Shireman and Penny R. Johnson

Family Research Project, 1966: Thomas S. Langner

Family Socialization and Developmental Competence Project, 1968: Diana Baumrind

Fels Longitudinal Study of Human Growth and Development, 1929: Virginia C. Crandall and Alexander F. Roche

First Language, 1962: Roger Brown, Ursula Bellugi, and Colin Fraser

Florida Longitudinal Project, 1970: Paul Satz, Jack Fletcher, and Robin Morris

Framingham Heart Study, 1949: William P. Castelli and Manning Feinleib

Grant Study of Adult Development, 1938: George E. Vaillant

Guidance Study (G), 1928: Carol Huffine, Marjorie Honzik, and Jean W. Macfarlane (deceased)

Harlem Longitudinal Study of Black Youth, 1968: Ann F. Brunswick
Harvard Bereavement Study Project, 1966: Robert S. Weiss and C. Murray Parkes
Harvard Child Maltreatment Project, 1979: Dante Cicchetti and Ross Rizley
High School to College Transition Study, 1970: Alan S. Berger and John H. Gagnon
Houston Parent-Child Development Center Project, 1970: Dale L. Johnson
Impact of Home Placement Versus Foster Care, 1978: P. H. Leiderman and M. S. Wald
Impact of Retirement on Adjustment to Aging, 1975: Robert Atchley
Indian Adoption Project, 1960: David Fanshel
Infant Care Project, 1981: Marjorie Elias
Inteflex Longitudinal Study of Medical Students, 1972: Donald R. Brown
Intergenerational Transmission of Deviance, 1971: Denise Kandel
International Pilot Study of Schizophrenia: Washington, D.C., Site, 1966: John S. Strauss, William Carpenter, and John Bartko
Iowa HABIT Project, 1967: Jan Loney, Carl E. Paternite, and John E. Langhorne, Jr.
Iowa Older-Workers Panel Study, 1964: Willis J. Goudy, Patricia M. Keith, and Edward A. Powers
Kauai Longitudinal Study, 1955: Emmy Werner
Kelly Longitudinal Study, 1935: James J. Connolly and E. Lowell Kelly (deceased)
Lifestyles of Educated Women, 1961: Eli Ginzberg and Alice Yohalem
Life After 70 in Iowa, 1960: Edward A. Powers and Gordon L. Bultena
Longitudinal Follow-Up of Very Low Birthweight Preterm Infants: Neurologic, Cognitive, and Behavioral Outcome, 1978: Gail Ross, Evelyn Lipper, and Peter A. M. Auld
Longitudinal Study of Adaptation to Remarriage in Stepfamilies, 1980: E. Mavis Hetherington and Glen Clingempeel
Longitudinal Study of Aging Human Twins 1947: Lissy F. Jarvik
Longitudinal Study of Career Development in College-Educated Women, 1967: Sandra S. Tangri
Longitudinal Study of Children from Kindergarten into the Adult Years, 1953: Philip E. Kraus
Longitudinal Study of Cognitive, Social and Affective Development, 1974: Michael Lewis
Longitudinal Study of Creative Behavior, 1959: E. Paul Torrance
Longitudinal Study of Early Classroom Behaviors and Later Misconduct, 1968: George Spivack
Longitudinal Study of Ego and Cognitive Development, 1968: Jack Block and Jeanne H. Block (deceased)
Longitudinal Study of Family Mediation and Children's Cognition, Aggression, and Comprehension of Television, 1982: Jerome L. Singer, Dorothy G. Singer, Roger Desmond, Bennett Hirsch, and Anne Nicol
Longitudinal Study of Family Relationships, 1981: Ted Huston, Susan McHale, and Ann Crouter
Longitudinal Study of Male Medical Students and Alumni, 1935: Betty Hosmer Mawardi

Longitudinal Study of Male and Female Medical Students and Alumni, 1956: Betty Hosmer Mawardi
Longitudinal Study of Moral Development, 1955: Anne Colby, Lawrence Kohlberg (deceased), John Gibbs, and Marcus Lieberman
Longitudinal Study of Preschool Programs, 1968: Louise Miller (deceased), Jean Dyer, Rondell Bizell, and Sara Sullivan
Longitudinal Study of Prosocial Development, 1977: Nancy Eisenberg
Longitudinal Study of School and Family Effects, 1973: Joyce Epstein
Longitudinal Study of Social Status in Elementary School Children, 1975: John D. Coie and Kenneth A. Dodge
Longitudinal Study of Television, Imagination and Aggression, 1977: Dorothy G. Singer and Jerome L. Singer
Longitudinal Study of Temperament in Low Birthweight of Infants, 1963: Margaret E. Hertzig
Longitudinal Study of the Consequences of Child Abuse, 1975: Roy C. Herrenkohl and Ellen C. Herrenkohl
Longitudinal Study of the Development of Formal Operations, 1967: Edith D. Neimark
Longitudinal Study of the Life Patterns of College-Educated Women, 1960: Abigail Stewart
Longitudinal Study of the Occupational Stress and Health of Women Licensed Practical Nurses and Licensed Social Workers, 1985: Rosalind Barnett, Grace Baruch (deceased), and Nancy L. Marshall
Longitudinal Study of the Psychosocial Effects of Disaster: Buffalo Creek Survivors in the Second Decade, 1973: Bonnie L. Green, Mary C. Grace, Jacob D. Lindy, and Goldine C. Gleser
Longitudinal Study of the Socialization and Development of Twin Boys, 1970: Hugh Lytton, Denise Watts, and Bruce E. Dunn
Longitudinal Study of Three-Generation Families, 1971: Vern L. Bengtson and Margaret Gatz
Longitudinal Study of Transitions in Four Stages of Life, 1969: Marjorie L. Fiske, Majda Thurnher, and David Chiriboga
Louisville Twin Study, 1959: Adam P. Matheny, Jr., and Ronald Wilson (deceased)
Massachusetts Reformatory Study, 1911: Sheldon Glueck (deceased) and Eleanor Glueck (deceased)
Michigan Student Study: Male Follow-Up, 1962: Jeylan T. Mortimer
Michigan Student Study: A Study of Students in a Multiversity, 1962: Gerald Gurin
Mills Longitudinal Study, 1958: Ravenna Helson
Minnesota Child to Adult Study, 1925: John E. Anderson (deceased), Dale B. Harris, and Evelyn Deno
Minnesota Transracial Adoption Study, 1973: Richard A. Weinberg and Sandra Scarr
Monitoring the Future: A Continuing Study of Lifestyles and Values of Youth, 1976: Lloyd D. Johnston, Jerald G. Bachman, and Patrick O'Malley
Moral Judgment Development and Life Experience, 1972: James R. Rest

Prediction and Prevention of Marital and Family Distress, 1980: Howard J. Markman and Scott Stanley

Pregnancy and Parenthood Project, 1975: Frances K. Grossman

Project CARE: Carolina Approach to Responsive Education, 1977: Craig T. Ramey

Project REACH Longitudinal Study, 1977: Barbara Keogh and Lucinda Bernheimer

Project Talent, 1960: Lauri Steel and Laurie Wise

Prospective Study of 500 Second Graders, 1965: Hans R. Huessy

Quality of Employment Survey: Panel Study, 1973: Robert P. Quinn, Thomas W. Mangione, and Stanley E. Seashore

Repatriated Prisoner of War Program, 1974: Robert E. Mitchell

Retirement History Study (RHS), 1969: Lola M. Irelan

Riverside Community Research Project, 1963: Edgar W. Butler and Tonya L. Schuster

Rochester Longitudinal Study, 1970: Arnold J. Sameroff, Ronald Seifer, Melvin Zax, and Ralph Barocas

Role Outlook Survey, 1964: Shirley S. Angrist and Elizabeth Almquist

Rutgers Health and Human Development Project, 1979: Erich Labouvie and Robert Pandina

Seattle and Denver Income Maintenance Experiment (SIME/DIME), 1970: Robert G. Spiegelman

Seattle Longitudinal Prospective Study on Alcohol and Pregnancy, 1974: Ann P. Streissguth, Donald C. Martin, Joan C. Martin, Helen Barr, and Paul D. Sampson

Seattle Longitudinal Study, 1956: K. Warner Schaie

Sierra Project: Longitudinal Study of Character Development in College Students, 1975: John Whiteley and Janet C. Loxley

Socialization of Problem Behavior in Youth, 1969: Richard Jessor and Lee Jessor

Socializing Attention: Transmitting Cultural Knowledge at Home and at School, 1988: Patricia Goldring Zukow

St. Louis Baby Study, 1966: Thomas E. Jordan

St. Louis Risk Research Project, 1967: James E. Anthony and Julien Worland

Stanford Longitudinal Study, 1973: Carol Nagy Jacklin and Eleanor Maccoby

Stony Brook High-Risk Project, 1971: Sheldon Weintraub

Structure and Strategy in Learning to Talk, 1970: Katherine Nelson

Stuart Study, 1930: Isabelle Valadian, Jane Gardner, Joanna Dwyer, and Harold Stuart (deceased)

Study of Adult Development, 1960s: Douglas H. Heath

Study of American Families, 1961: Arland Thornton

Study of Child Rearing and Child Development in Normal Families and Families with Affective Disorders, 1980: Marian Radke-Yarrow

Symbolic Development, 1978: Elizabeth Bates and Inge Bretherton

Terman Life Cycle Study of Children with High Ability, 1921: Albert H. Hastorf, Leonard Horowitz, Carol K. Holahan, Robert R. Sears (deceased), Pauline Sears, Lee Cronbach, and Lewis Terman

Tecumseh, Michigan, Community Health Study, 1957: Millicent W. Higgins, Leon D. Ostrander, Jr., Arnold S. Monto, Stanley M. Garn, Ernest Harburg, James S. House, Helen L. Metzner, and Charles F. Sing

Third Harvard Growth Study, 1922: Aviva Must, Carl J. Bajema, Francis Johnston, and Eugenie C. Scott

Time Allocation Study, 1975: Thomas F. Juster, Martha Hill, and Frank Stafford

Trajectories of Health and Illness: A Longitudinal Follow-Up Study of Child Psychiatric Patients, 1984: Gil G. Noam

Transition from Adolescence to Adulthood: Follow-Up Study, 1973: Margaret Mooney Marini, Lloyd Temme, and James Coleman

Transition into Adolescence: A Longitudinal Study, 1974: Roberta Simmons and Dale Blyth

UCLA High-Risk Project, 1964: Michael J. Goldstein

UCLA Study of Adolescent Growth, 1976: Michael D. Newcomb and Peter M. Bentler

Understanding and Prediction of Delinquent Child Behavior, 1984: Gerald R. Patterson, John B. Reid, and Thomas J. Dishion

University of Rochester Child and Family Study, 1972: Lyman Wynne and Robert Cole

Vassar Longitudinal Study, 1954: Donald R. Brown, Nevitt Sanford, and Mervin Freedman

Vermont Infant Studies Project, 1980: Thomas M. Achenbach and Catherine T. Howell

Vermont Longitudinal Research Project, 1955: Courtenay M. Harding, George W. Brooks, Takamaru Ashikaga, John S. Strauss, and Alan Breier

Veterans Administration Normative Aging Study (NAS), 1963: Raymond Bossé, Pantel Vokonas, and Carolyn M. Aldwin

Virginia Longitudinal Study of Divorce, 1971: E. Mavis Hetherington, Martha Cox, and Roger Cox

Waterloo Longitudinal Project, 1980: Kenneth H. Rubin and Shelley Hymel

Wisconsin Longitudinal Study of Social and Psychological Factors in Aspiration and Achievements, 1957: William H. Sewell and Robert M. Hauser

Women's Reformatory Study, 1920: Sheldon Glueck (deceased) and Eleanor Glueck (deceased)

Woodlawn Mental Health Longitudinal Community Epidemiological Project, 1963: Sheppard Kellam, Margaret Ensminger, and Jeannette Branch

Yale Longitudinal Study, 1978: John S. Strauss, Hafez Hisham, Paul Lieberman, Jack Rakfeldt, and Courtenay M. Harding

Youth in Transition, 1966: Jerald G. Bachman

Youth-Parent Socialization Panel Study, 1965: M. Kent Jennings

Ypsilanti Perry Preschool Project, 1962: David P. Weikart and Lawrence J. Schweinhart

Ypsilanti Preschool Curriculum Demonstration Project, 1967: David P. Weikart and Lawrence J. Schweinhart

Author Index

Subject Index

About the Authors

Erin Phelps received her Ed.D., with a specialization in human development and research methodology, from the Harvard Graduate School of Education, in 1981. As a Senior Research Associate at the Henry A. Murray Research Center of Radcliffe College, she is currently doing research on the nature of the effects of peer collaboration on mathematics and science learning in middle childhood and on some of the factors that contribute to young women's reluctance to pursue careers in mathematics and science fields.

Kristen L. Savola received an M.A., with a concentration in psychology, from the Harvard Graduate School of Education. As a Senior Research Assistant at the Henry A. Murray Research Center of Radcliffe College, she has been engaged in a NIMH-funded project to develop a national archive of longitudinal mental health data. In fall 1991 she will be enrolling in the MD program at Stanford University School of Medicine, where she will pursue her interest in women's health care.

Copeland H. Young is currently a Senior Research Assistant at the Henry A. Murray Research Center of Radcliffe College. He received a B.A. in Psychology from Harvard University. His central interests include developmental psychopathology and cognitive-developmental research, and he has assisted in several longitudinal and evaluative research projects involving inpatient adolescents and adults at McLean Hospital, Belmont, Massachusetts.